A C

CHRISTIAN POLITICS.

READER,

THINK not by the title of this part, that I am doing the same work which I lately revoked in my "Political Aphorisms;" though I concluded that book to be *quasi non scriptum*, I told you I recanted not the doctrine of it, which is for the empire of God, and the interest of government, order, and honesty in the world. This is no place to give you the reasons of my revocation, besides that it offended my superiors, and exercised the tongues of some in places, where other matters would be more profitable: pass by all that concerneth our particular states and times, and you may know by that what principles of policy I judge divine. And experience teacheth me, that it is best for men of my profession, to meddle with no more, but to leave it to the Contzeu's, the Arnisæus's, and other Jesuits, to promote their cause by voluminous politics. The pope's false-named church is a kingdom, and his ministers may write of politics more congruously, and (it seems) with less offence, than we. Saith the "Geographia Nubiensis" aptly, "There is a certain king dwelling at Rome called the pope," &c. when he goeth to describe him. Nothing well suits with our function, but the pure doctrine of salvation; let statesmen and lawyers mind the rest.

Two things I must apologize for in this part. 1. That it is maimed by defect of those directions to princes, nobles, parliament men, and other magistrates, on whose duty the happiness of kingdoms, churches, and the world dependeth. To which I answer, That those must teach them whom they will hear; while my reason and experience forbid me, as an unacceptable person, to speak to them without a special invitation, I can bear the censures of strangers, who knew not them or me. I am not so proud as to expect that men so much above me, should stoop to read any directions of mine; much less to think me fit to teach them. Every one may reprove a poor servant, or a beggar (it is part of their privilege). But great men must not be so much as admonished by any but themselves, and such as they will hear. At least nothing is a duty which a man hath reason to think is like to do much more harm than good. And my own judgment is much against pragmatical, presumptuous preachers, who are over-forward to meddle with their governors, or their affairs, and think that God sendeth them to reprove persons and things that are strange to them, and above them; and vent their distastes upon uncertain reports, or without a call.

2. And I expect both to be blamed and misunderstood, for what I here say in the confutation of Master Richard Hooker's "Political Principles," and my own citation of Bishop Bilson, and such others. But they must observe, 1. That it is not all in Master Hooker's first and eighth book, which I gainsay; but the principle of the people's being the fountain of authority, or that kings receive their office itself from them, with the consequents hereof. How far the people have, in any countries, the power of electing the persons, families, or forms of government, or how far nature giveth them propriety, and the consequents of this, I meddle not with at all. 2. Nor do I choose Master Hooker out of any envy to his name and honour, but I confess I do it, to let men know truly whose principles these are. And if any (causelessly) question, whether the eighth (imperfect) book be in those passages his own, let them remember that the sum of all that I confute, is in his first book, which is old, and highly honoured, by——you know whom. And I will do him the honour, and myself the dishonour, to confess, that I think the far greater number of casuists and authors of politics, papists, and protestants, are on his side, and fewest on mine: but truth is truth.

On the subjects' duty I am larger, because, if they will not hear, at least I may boldly and freely instruct them.

If in the latter part there be any useful cases of conscience left out, it is because I could not remember them. Farewell.

CHAPTER I.

GENERAL RULES FOR AN UPRIGHT CONVERSATION.

SOLOMON saith, Prov. x. 9, "He that walketh uprightly walketh surely." And perfection and uprightness are the characters of Job, Job i. 1, 8; ii. 3. And in the

Scripture to be upright or righteous, and to walk uprightly, and to do righteously, are the titles of those that are acceptable to God. And by uprightness is meant not only sincerity as opposed to hypocrisy; but also rectitude of heart and life, as opposed to crookedness or sin; and this as it is found in various degrees: of which we use to call the lowest degree that is saving by the name of sincerity, and the highest by the name of perfection.

Concerning uprightness of life, I shall, I. Briefly tell you some of those blessings that should make us all in love with it, and, II. Give you some necessary rules of practice.

1. Uprightness of heart and life is a certain fruit of the Spirit of grace, and consequently a mark of our union with Christ, and a proof of our acceptableness with God. "My defence is of God, who saveth the [738]upright in heart," Psal. vii. 10. "For the righteous Lord loveth righteousness, and his countenance doth behold the upright," Psal. xi. 7. It is a title that God himself assumeth; "Good and upright is the Lord," Psal. xxv. 8. "To show that the Lord is upright, he is my Rock, and no unrighteousness is in him," Psal. xcii. 15. And God calleth himself the Maker, the Director, the Protector, and the Lover of the upright. "God made man upright," Eccl. vii. 29. "The Lord knoweth the way of the righteous," Psal. i. 6. "What man is he that feareth the Lord? him will he teach in the way that he shall choose," Psal. xxv. 12. "He layeth up sound wisdom for the righteous; he is a buckler to them that walk uprightly," Prov. ii. 7.

2. The upright are the pillars of human society, that keep up truth and justice in the world: without whom it would be but a company of liars, deceivers, robbers, and enemies, that live in constant rapine and hostility. There were no trust to be put in one another, further than self-interest did oblige men. "Lord, who shall abide in thy tabernacle? Who shall dwell in thy holy hill? He that walketh uprightly, and worketh righteousness, and speaketh the truth in his heart," Psal. xv. 1, 2. Therefore the wicked, and the enemies of peace, and destroyers of societies, are still described as enemies to the upright. "For lo, the wicked bend their bow, they make ready their arrow upon the string, that they may privily shoot at the upright in heart. If the foundations be destroyed, what can the righteous do?" Psal. xi. 2, 3. "The just and upright man is laughed to scorn," Job xii. 4. "The wicked have drawn out the sword to slay such as be of upright conversation," Psal. xxxvii. 14. And indeed it is for the upright's sake that societies are preserved by God, as Sodom might have been for ten Lots. At least they are under the protection of omnipotency themselves. "He that walketh righteously and speaketh uprightly, he that despiseth the gain of oppression, that shaketh his hand from holding of bribes, that stoppeth his ear from hearing of blood, that shutteth his eyes from seeing evil; he shall dwell on high, his place of defence shall be the munitions of rocks: bread shall be given him; his waters shall be sure. Thine eyes shall see the king in his beauty: they shall behold the land that is very far off," Isa. xxxiii. 15, 16. "The upright shall have good things in possession," Prov. xxviii. 10. "The house of the wicked shall be overthrown; but the tabernacle of the upright shall flourish," Prov. xiv. 11.

3. Uprightness affordeth peace of conscience, and quietness and holy security to the soul. This was Paul's rejoicing, the testimony of his conscience, that "in simplicity and godly sincerity he had had his conversation in the world, and not in fleshly wisdom," 2 Cor. i. 12. And this was David's comfort: "For I have kept the ways of the Lord, and have not wickedly departed from my God; for all his judgments were before me, and as for his statutes, I did not depart from them. I was also upright before him, and have kept myself from mine iniquity. Therefore hath the Lord recompensed me according to my righteousness;—with the merciful thou wilt show thyself merciful, and with the upright thou wilt show thyself upright," 2 Sam. xxii. 22-24. Yea, peace is too little; exceeding joy is the portion, and most beseeming condition of the upright. "Be glad in the Lord, and rejoice, ye righteous, and shout for joy, all ye that are upright in heart," Psal. xxxii. 11. "Rejoice in the Lord, O ye righteous, for

2

praise is comely for the upright," Psal. xxxiii. 1. "The righteous shall be glad in the Lord, and trust in him, and all the upright in heart shall glory," Psal. lxiv. 10. "Light is sown for the righteous, and gladness for the upright in heart," Psal. xcvii. 11. The Spirit that sanctifieth them, will comfort them.

4. As the upright, so their upright life and duties are specially delightful and acceptable to God, Prov. xv. 8. The prayer of the upright is his delight, Psal. xv. 2. Therefore God blesseth their duties to them, and they are comforted and strengthened by experience of success. "The way of the Lord is strength to the upright, but destruction shall be to the workers of iniquity," Prov. x. 29. "Do not my words do good to him that walketh uprightly," Micah ii. 7.

5. No carnal policies, no worldly might, no help of friends, nor any other human means, doth put a man in so safe a state, as uprightness of heart and life. To walk uprightly, is to walk surely, because such walk with God, and in his way, and under his favour, and his promise; and if God be not sufficient security for us, there is none. "Surely the righteous shall give thanks unto thy name; the upright shall dwell in thy presence," Psal. cxl. 13. "The integrity of the upright shall guide them, but the perverseness of transgressors shall destroy them. The righteousness of the upright shall deliver them, but transgressors shall be taken in their own naughtiness," Prov. xi. 3, 6.

6. Lastly, the failings and weaknesses of the upright are pardoned, and therefore they shall certainly be saved, Rom. vii. 24, 25; viii. 1. The upright may say in all their weaknesses as Solomon; "I know also, my God, that thou triest the heart, and hast pleasure in uprightness; as for me, in the uprightness of my heart, I have willingly offered all these things," 1 Chron. xxix. 17. "God will do good to them that are good, and to them that are upright in their hearts," Psal. cxxv. 4. The upright love him, Cant. i. 4, and are loved by him. "No good thing will he withhold from them," Psal. lxxxiv. 11. The way to right comforting the mind of man, is to show to him his uprightness, Job xxxiii. 23. "And whoso walketh uprightly shall be saved," Prov. xxviii. 18. "For the high way of the upright is to depart from evil; and he that keepeth his way, preserveth his soul," Prov. xvi. 17. I conclude with Psal. xxxvii. 37, "Mark the upright man, and behold the just, for the end of that man is peace."

II. The true rules of an upright life are these that follow.

1. He that will walk uprightly must be absolutely devoted and subjected unto God: he must have a God, and the true God, and but one God; not notionally only, but in sincerity and reality: he must have a God whose word shall be an absolute law to him; a God that shall command himself, his time, his estate, and all that he hath, or that he can do; a God whose will must be his will, and may do with him what he please; and who is more to him than all the world; whose love will satisfy him as better than life, and whose approbation is his sufficient encouragement and reward.[1]

2. His hope must be set upon heaven as the only felicity of his soul: he must look for his reward and the end of all his labours and patience in another world; and not with the hypocrite, dream of a felicity that is made up first of worldly things, and then of heaven, when he can keep the world no longer. He that cannot, that doth not in heart, quit [739]all the world for a heavenly treasure, and venture his all upon the promise of better things hereafter, and forsaking all, take Christ and everlasting happiness for his portion, cannot be upright in heart or life.[2]

3. He must have an infallible teacher (which is only Christ) and the encouragement of pardoning grace when he faileth, that he sink not by despair; and therefore he must live by faith on a Mediator. And he must have the fixed principle of a nature renewed by the Spirit of Christ.[3]

4. He that will walk uprightly, must have a certain, just, infallible rule; and must hold to that, and must try all by it; and this is only the word of God. The teachings of men must be valued as helps to understand this word; and the judgments of our teachers, and those that are wiser than ourselves, must be of great authority with us in

subordination to the Scripture. But neither the learned, nor the godly, nor the great, must be our rule in co-ordination with the word of God.[4]

5. He that will walk uprightly, must have both a solid and a large understanding, to know things truly as they are, and to see all particulars which must be taken notice of, in all the cases which he must determine, and all the actions which his integrity is concerned in.[5] 1. There is no walking uprightly in the dark. Zeal will cause you to go apace; but not at all to go right, if judgment guide it not. Erroneous zeal will make you to do evil with double violence, and with blasphemous fathering your sins on God, and with impenitence and justification of your sin. This made Paul mad in persecuting the church. Prov. xv. 21, "Folly is joy to him that is destitute of wisdom; but a man of understanding walketh uprightly." No man can do that well which he understandeth not well. Therefore you must study and take unwearied pains for knowledge; wisdom never grew up with idleness, though the conceit of wisdom doth no where more prosper. This age hath told us to what dangerous precipices men will be carried by an ignorant zeal. 2. And the understanding must be large, or it cannot be solid; when many particulars are concerned in an action, the overlooking of some may spoil the work. Narrow-minded men are turned as the weathercock, with the wind of the times, or of every temptation; and they seldom avoid one sin, but by falling into another. It is prudence that must manage an upright life: and prudence seeth all that must be seen, and putteth every circumstance into the balance; for want of which, much mischief may be done, while you seem to be doing the greatest good.[6] "The prudent man looketh well to his going," Prov. xiv. 15. "See therefore that ye walk circumspectly, (at a hair's breadth,) not as fools, but as wise."

6. But because you will object, that, alas, few even of the upright, have wits so strong as to be fit for this, I add, that he that will walk uprightly, must in the great essential parts of religion have this foresaid knowledge of his own, and in the rest at least he must have the conduct of the wise. And therefore, 1. He must be wise in the great matters of his salvation, though he be weak in other things. 2. And he must labour to be truly acquainted who are indeed wise men, that are meet to be his guides: and he must have recourse to such in cases of conscience, as a sick man to his physician. It is a great mercy to be so far wise, as to know a wise man from a fool, and a counsellor from a deceiver.[7]

7. He that will walk uprightly must be the master of his passion; not stupid, but calm and sober. Though some passion is needful to excite the understanding to its duty, yet that which is inordinate doth powerfully deceive the mind. Men are very apt to be confident of what they passionately apprehend; and passionate judgments are frequently mistaken, and ever to be suspected; it being exceeding difficult to entertain any passion which shall not in some measure pervert our reason; which is one great reason why the most confident are ordinarily the most erroneous and blind. Be sure therefore whenever you are injured, or passion any way engaged, to set a double guard upon your judgments.[8]

8. He that will walk uprightly, must not only difference between simple good and evil, but between a greater good and a less; for most sin in the world consisteth in preferring a lesser good before a greater. He must still keep the balance in his hand, and compare good with good; otherwise he will make himself a religion of sin, and prefer sacrifice before mercy; and will hinder the gospel and men's salvation for a ceremony, and violate the bonds of love and faithfulness for every opinion which he calleth truth; and will tithe mint and cummin, while he neglecteth the great things of the law. When a lesser good is preferred before a greater, it is a sin, and the common way of sinning. It is not then a duty when it is inconsistent with a greater good.[9]

9. He must ever have a conjunct respect to the command and the end: the good of some actions is but little discernible any where, but in the command; and others are evidently good because of the good they tend to. We must neither do evil and break a law, that good may come by it; nor yet pretend obedience to do mischief, as if God

4

had made his laws for destruction of the church or men's souls, and not for edification.[10]

10. He must keep in union with the universal church, and prefer its interest before the interest of any party whatsoever, and do nothing that tendeth to its hurt.[11]

11. He must love his neighbour as himself, and do as he would be done by, and love his enemies and forgive wrongs; and bear their defamations as his own.[12]

12. He must be impartial, and not lose his judgment and charity in the opinion or interest of a party or sect: nor think all right that is held or done by those that he best liketh; nor all wrong that is held or done by those that are his adversaries. But judge of the words and deeds of those that are against him, as if they had been said or done by those of his own side: else he will live in slandering, backbiting, and gross unrighteousness.[13]

[740]13. He must be deliberate in judging of things and persons; not rash or hasty in believing reports or receiving opinions; not judging of truths by the first appearance, but search into the naked evidence: nor judging of persons by prejudice, fame, and common talk.[14]

14. He must be willing to receive and obey the truth at the dearest rate, especially of laborious study, and a self-denying life; not taking all to be truth that costeth men dear, nor yet thinking that truth indeed can be over-prized.[15]

15. He must be humble and self-suspicious, and come to Christ's school as a little child; and not have a proud overvaluing of himself and his own understanding. The proud and selfish are blind and cross, and have usually some opinions or interests of their own, that lie cross to duty, and to other men's good.[16]

16. He must have an eye to posterity, and not only to the present time or age; and to other nations, and not only to the country where he liveth. Many things seem necessary for some present strait or work that we would do (which in the next age may be of mischievous effects); especially in ecclesiastical and political professions, covenants and impositions, we must look further than our present needs. And many things seem necessary for a local, narrow interest, which those at a distance will otherwise esteem.[17]

17. He that will walk uprightly must be able to bear the displeasure of all the world, when the interest of truth requireth it; yea, to be rejected of learned and good men themselves; and account man's favour no better than it is; not to despise it as it is a means to any good, but to be quite above it as to his own interest. Not that uprightness doth use to make a man despised by the upright; but that it may bring him under their censure in some particulars, which are not commonly received or understood to be of God.[18]

18. He must make it a great part of the work of his life to kill all those carnal desires, which the sensual make it their work and felicity to please; that appetite, sense and lust, and self-will may not be the constant perverters of his life; as a fool in a dropsy studieth to please his thirst, and a wise man to cure it.[19]

19. He must live a life of constant and skilful watchfulness, apprehending himself in continual danger; and knowing his particular corruptions, temptations, and remedies. He must have a tender conscience, and keep as far as possible from temptation, and take heed of unnecessary approaches or delightful thoughts of sin. Oh what strong resolutions, what sound knowledge, have the near-baits of sensuality (meat, drink, lust, and pleasures) overcome! Never think yourselves safe among near-temptations, and opportunities of sinning.[20]

20. Live as those that are going to the grave; die daily, and look on this world as if you did look on it out of the world to which you go. Let faith as constantly behold the world unseen, as your eye seeth this. Death and eternity make men wise: we easily confess and repent of many things when we come to die, which no counsels or sermons could make us penitently confess before. Death will answer a thousand objections and temptations, and prove many vanities to be sin, which you thought the

preacher did not prove: dying men are not drawn to drunkenness, filthiness, or time-wasting sports; nor flattered into folly by sensual baits; nor do they then fear the face or threats of persecutors. As it is from another world that we must fetch the motives, so also the defensative of an upright life. And oh happy are they that faithfully practise these rules of uprightness![21]

Though it be my judgment that much more of the doctrine of politics or civil government belongeth to theology,[22] than those men understand, who make kings and laws to be mere human creatures, yet to deliver my reader from the fear lest I should meddle with matters that belong not to my calling, and my book from that reproach, I shall overpass all these points, which else I should have treated of, as useful to practise in governing and obeying. 1. Of man as sociable, and of communities and societies, and the reason of them, of their original, and the obligation on the members. 2. Of a city, and of civility. 3. Of a republic in general. (1.) Of its institution, (2.) Of its constitution, and of its parts. (3.) Of its species. (4.) Of the difference between it, 1. And a community in general. 2. A family. 3. A village. 4. A city. 5. A church. 6. An accidental meeting. (5.) Of its administrations. (6.) Of the relation between God's government and man's, and God's law and man's, and of their difference; and between man's judging and God's judging. Nay, I will not only gratify you, by passing over this and much more in the theory, but also as to the practical part, I shall pass over, 1. The directions for supreme governors. 2. And for inferior magistrates towards God, and their superiors, and the people. 3. And the determination of the question, How far magistrates have to do in matters of religion? Whether they be christian or heathen? 4. How far they should grant or not grant liberty of conscience, (as it is called,) viz. of judging, professing, and practising in matters of religion; with other such matters belonging to government: and all the controversies about titles and supremacy, conservations, forfeitures, decays, dangers, remedies, and restorations, which belong either to politicians, lawyers, or divines; all these I pretermit, save only that I shall venture to leave a few brief memorandums with civil governors (instead of directions) for securing the interest of Christ, and the church, and men's salvation; yet assuring the reader that I omit none of this out of any contempt of the matter, or of magistracy, or as if I thought them not worthy of all our prayers and assistance, or thought their office of small concernment to the welfare of the world and of the church; but for those reasons, which all may know that know me and the government under which we live, and which I must not tell to others.

[1] Psal. lxxiii. 25; lxiii. 3; 1 Cor. iv. 3, 4; Phil. iii. 8, 9, 18, 19; Psal. iv. 7, 8; Luke xii. 4; Matt. vi. 1-3.

[2] Luke xiv. 26, 27, 33, 34; xviii. 22; Matt. vi. 19, 20; 1 John ii. 15; Phil. iii. 18, 21.

[3] John xii. 16; xv. 1, &c.; iii. 5, 6; Rom. viii. 8, 9.

[4] 2 Tim. iii. 15; Isa. viii. 20; 1 Thess. v. 12; Isa. xxxiii. 21; Jam. iv. 12; Heb. viii. 10, 16; Neh. ix. 13, 14; Psal. xix. 7; cxix. 1-3.

[5] Prov. i. 5; x. 23; xvii. 27; iii. 4; Psal. cxi. 10; Eph. i. 10; Acts xxvi. 18; Col. i. 9; ii. 2; 2 Tim. ii. 7; 1 Cor. xiv. 5, 20.

[6] Luke xxiv. 45; Matt. xv. 16; Eph. v. 17; 1 Tim. i. 7; Prov. viii. 5; John xii. 40; 2 Pet. ii. 12; Rom. iii. 11; Matt. xiii. 19, 23; Isa. lii. 13; Hos. xiv. 9; Prov. xiv. 15, 18; xviii. 15; xxii. 3; viii. 12; Eph. v. 15; Psal. ci. 2.

[7] Psal. cxix. 98; Prov. i. 6-8; xii. 15, 18; xiii. 1, 14, 20; xv. 2, 7, 12, 31; xxii. 17; xxv. 12; Eccl. xii. 11; Dan. xii. 3, 10; Matt. xxiv. 45; Psal. xxxvii 30; Eccl. ii. 13; Isa. xxxiii. 6; Matt. xii. 42; Luke i. 17; xxi. 15; Acts vi. 3; 2 Pet. iii. 15; Mal. ii. 6, 7; 1 Thess. v. 12, 13; Heb. xiii. 7, 17; Tit. i. 9, 13; ii. 1, 8; 2 Tim. iv. 3.

[8] Prov. xiv. 29; Col. iii. 8.

[9] Matt. ix. 13; xii. 7; Psal. xl. 6; li. 16; 1 Sam. xv. 22.

[10] 2 Cor. x. 8; xiii. 10; Rom. xv. 2; xiv. 9; 1 Cor. xiv. 26; 2 Cor. xii. 19; Rom. iii. 8.

[11] Eph. iv. 12, &c.; 1 Cor. xii.

[12] Matt. xxii. 39; v. 43, 44; vii. 12.

[13] Jam. iii. 15-18; Gal. ii. 13, 14; Deut. xxv. 16; 1 Cor. vi. 9.

[14] Matt. vii. 1, 2; John vii. 24; Rom. xiv. 10, 13; 1 Pet. i. 17.

[15] Luke xiv. 26, 33; xii. 4; Prov. xxiii. 23.

[16] Matt. xviii. 3; Prov. xxvi. 12, 16; xxviii. xx; 1 Cor. iii. 18; Prov. iii. 7.

[17] Judg. viii. 27; 1 Cor. vii. 35; 1 Kings xiv. 16; xv. 26; Deut. xxix. 22; Exod. xii. 26; Josh. iv. 6, 22; xxii. 24, 25.

[18] 1 Cor. iv. 3, 4; John v. 44; Luke xiv. 26; Gal. ii. 13, 14; Acts xi. 2, 3.

[19] Col. iii. 4, 5; Rom. vi. 1, &c.; xiii. 12, 13; viii. 13.

[20] Matt. xxiv. 42; xxv. 13; Mark xiii. 37; 1 Thess. v. 6; 1 Pet. iv. 7; 1 Cor. xvi. 15; Matt. vi. 13; xxvi. 41.

[21] Eccl. vii. 2-6; 2 Cor. iv. 16; v. 1, 7, 8; Luke xii. 17-20; xvi. 20, &c.; Matt. xxv. 3-8; Acts vii. 56, 60.

[22] Among the Jews it was all one to be a lawyer and a divine; but not to be a lawyer and a priest.

[741]

CHAPTER II.

MEMORANDUMS TO CIVIL RULERS FOR THE INTEREST OF CHRIST, THE CHURCH, AND MEN'S SALVATION.

Mem. I. Remember that your power is from God, and therefore for God, and not against God, Rom. xiii. 2-4. You are his ministers, and can have no power except it be given you from above, John xix. 11. Remember therefore that as constables are your officers and subjects, so you are the officers and subjects of God and the Redeemer; and are infinitely more below him than the lowest subject is below you; and that you owe him more obedience than can be due to you; and therefore should study his laws, (in nature and Scripture,) and make them your daily meditation and delight, Josh. i. 3-5; Psal. i. 2, 3; Deut. xvii. 18-20. And remember how strict a judgment you must undergo when you must give account of your stewardship, and the greater your dignities and mercies have been, if they are abused by ungodliness, the greater will be your punishment, Luke xvi. 2; xii. 48.[23]

Mem. II. Remember therefore and watch most carefully that you never own or espouse any interest which is adverse to the will or interest of Christ; and that you never fall out with his interest or his ordinances; and that no temptation ever persuade you that the interest of Christ, and the gospel, and the church, is an enemy to you, or against your real interest; and that you keep not up suspicions against them: but see that you devote yourselves and your power wholly to his will and service, and make all your interest stand in a pure subservience to him, as it stands in a real dependence on him.[24]

Mem. III. Remember that, under God, your end is the public good; therefore desire nothing to yourselves, nor do any thing to others, which is really against your end.

Mem. IV. Remember therefore that all your laws are to be but subservient to the laws of God, to promote the obedience of them with your subjects, and never to be either contrary to them, nor co-ordinate, or independent on them; but as the by-laws of corporations are in respect to the laws and will of the sovereign power, which have all their life and power therefrom.

Mem. V. Let none persuade you that you are such terrestrial animals that have nothing to do with the heavenly concernments of your subjects; for if once men think that the end of your office is only the bodily prosperity of the people, and the end of the ministry is the good of their souls, it will tempt them to prefer a minister before you, as they prefer their souls before their bodies; and they that are taught to contemn these earthly things, will be ready to think they must contemn your office; seeing no means, as such, can be better than the end. There is no such thing as a temporal

7

happiness to any people, but what tendeth to the happiness of their souls; and must be thereby measured, and thence be estimated. Though ministers are more immediately employed about the soul, yet your office is ultimately for the happiness of souls, as well as theirs; though bodily things (rewards or punishments) are the means, by which you may promote it; which ministers, as such, may not meddle with. Therefore you are *custodes utriusque tabulæ*, and must bend the force of all your government to the saving of the people's souls. And as to the objection from heathen governors, distinguish between the office, and an aptitude to exercise it: the office consisteth, 1. In an obligation to do the duty; 2. And in authority to do it. Both these a heathen ruler hath (else the omission were a duty, and not a sin). But it is the aptitude to do the duty of his place which a heathen wanteth; and he wanteth it culpably; and therefore the omission is his sin; even as it is the sin of an insufficient minister that he doth not preach. For the question is of the like nature, and will have the like solution: Whether an ignorant minister be bound to preach, who is unable or heretical? It is aptitude that he wanteth, and neither authority nor obligation, if he be really a minister; but he is obliged in this order, first to get abilities, and then to preach: so is it in the present case.[25]

Mem. VI. Encourage and strengthen a learned, holy, self-denying, serious, laborious ministry; as knowing, that the same Lord hath commissioned them in the institution of their office, who instituted yours; and that it is such men that are suited to the work, for which their office was appointed; and that souls are precious; and those that are the guides and physicians of souls, can never be too well furnished, nor too diligent. And the church hath no where prospered on earth, but in the prosperity of the abilities, holiness, and diligence of their pastors: God hath always built by such, and the devil hath pulled down by pulling down such.

Mem. VII. Remember that the people that are seriously religious, that love, and worship, and obey the Lord, with all their heart, are the best of your subjects, and the honour of your dominions: see therefore that serious godliness be every where encouraged, and that the profane and ignorant rabble be never encouraged in their enmity and opposition to it: and that true fanaticism, hypocrisy, and schism, be so prudently discountenanced and suppressed, that none may have encouragement to set themselves against godliness, under the slander or pretension of such names. If christianity be better than heathenism, those christians then are they that must be countenanced, who go further in holiness, and charity, and justice, than heathens do, rather than those that go no further (besides opinions and formalities) than a Cato, a Plato, or Socrates have done. If all religion were a deceit, it were fit to be banished, and atheism professed, and men confess themselves to be but brutes. But if there be a God, there must be a religion; and if we must be religious, we must sure be so in seriousness, and not in hypocrisy and jest. It being no such small, contemptible matter, to be turned into dissembling compliment.[26]

[742]*Mem.* VIII. Endeavour the unity and concord of all the churches and christians that are under your government, and that upon the terms which all Christ's churches have sometime been united in; that is, In the Holy Scriptures implicitly, as the general rule; in the ancient creeds explicitly, as the sum of our *credenda*; and in the Lord's prayer, as the summary of our *expetenda*; and in the decalogue, as the summary of our *agenda*; supposing, that we live in peaceable obedience to our governors, whose laws must rule us not only in things civil, but in the ordering of those circumstances of worship and discipline, which God hath left to their determination.

Mem. IX. Let all things in God's worship be done to edification, decently, and in order, and the body honour God, as well as the soul; but yet see that the ornaments or garments of religion be never used against the substance; but that holiness, unity, charity, and peace, have alway the precedency.

Mem. X. Let the fear of sinning against God be cherished in all, and let there be a tenderness for such as are over-scrupulous and fearful in some smaller things: and let not things be ordered so, as shall most tend to the advantage of debauched consciences, that dare say or do any thing for their carnal ends. For they are truest to their governors, that are truest to their God; and when it is the wrath of God and hell that a man is afraid of, it is pity he should be too eagerly spurred on. The unconscionable sort will be true to their governors, no longer than it serves their interest; therefore conscientiousness should be encouraged.[27]

Mem. XI. If the clergy, or most religious people, offend, let their punishment be such as falleth only on themselves, and reacheth not Christ, nor the gospel, nor the church. Punish not Christ for his servants' failings, nor the gospel for them that sin against it; nor the souls of the people, for their pastors' faults; but see that the interest of Christ and men's souls be still secured.[28]

Mem. XII. If the dissensions of lawyers or statesmen make factions in the commonwealth, let not the fault be laid on religion, though some divines fall into either faction. When the difference is not in divinity, but in law cases, blame not religion for that, which it hath no hand in: and watch against Satan, who alway laboureth to make civil factions or differences tend to the dishonour of religion, and the detriment of the church and gospel.

Mem. XIII. Take those that are covetous, ambitious, or selfish, and seek for preferment, to be the unfittest to be consulted with in the matters of religion, and the unfittest to be trusted with the charge of souls. And let the humble, mortified, self-denying men, be taken as fitter pastors for the churches.

Mem. XIV. Side not with any faction of contentious pastors, to the oppression of the rest, when the difference is in tolerable things; but rather drive them on to unity, upon condescending and forbearing terms: for there will else be no end; but the faction which you side with, will break into more factions, and the church will receive damage by the loss of the oppressed party, and by the division much more. What lamentable work the contentions of the bishops have made in the churches, in all ages, since the primitive times, all history doth too openly declare. And how much a holy, prudent, peaceable magistrate can do, to keep peace among them, more than will be done if their own impetuosity be left unrestrained, it is easy to observe; especially if he keep the sword in his own hand, and trust it not in the hands of churchmen, especially of one faction to the oppression of the rest.[29]

Mem. XV. Believe not the accusations that are brought against the faithful ministers of Christ, till they are proved; and judge not them, or any of his servants, upon the reports of adversaries, till they have spoken for themselves; for the common corruption of depraved nature, doth engage all the ungodly in such an enmity against holiness, that there is little truth or righteousness to be expected from wicked and malicious lips, for any holy cause or person. And if such persons find but entertainment and encouragement, their malice will abound, and [743]their calumnies will be impudent; which is the sense of Prov. xxix. 12, "If a ruler hearken to lies, all his servants are wicked." The example of Saul and Doeg is but such as would be ordinary, if rulers would but hearken to such calumniators.[30]

Mem. XVI. When the case is doubtful about using punishments and severities against the scrupulous in the matters of religion, remember your general directions, and see what influence they must have into such particulars; as, That the very work and end of your office is, that under your government the people may live quietly and peaceably in godliness and honesty, 1 Tim. ii. 2. And that rulers are not a terror to good works, but to evil; and for the praise of them that do good; and ministers of God to us for good; and revengers to execute wrath upon them that do evil, Rom. xiii. 3, 4. And remember the danger of persecution, as described Matt, xviii. 6, 10, 14; 1 Thess. ii. 15, 16; 2 Chron. xxxvi. 14-17. And that he that doubteth of things indifferent is damned if he do them, because he doth them not of faith, Rom. xiv. 23. And remember whom and what it is that God himself forgiveth and forbeareth. And always difference the infirmities of serious conscionable christians, from the wickedness of unconscionable and ungodly men. Yet not extenuating the wickedness of any, because of his hypocritical profession of religion.[31]

Mem. XVII. Remember that you must be examples of holiness to the people; and shun all those sins which you would have them shun, and be eminent in all those virtues which you would commend unto them.[32] This is not only necessary to the happiness of those under you, but also for the saving of yourselves. As Paul saith to Timothy, "Take heed unto thyself, and unto the doctrine, continue in them;[33] for in doing this, thou shalt both save thyself, and them that hear thee," 1 Tim. iv. 16. So may I say to rulers, Take heed to yourselves, and unto government, and continue herein; for in doing this, you will save yourselves, and those you govern. They that are good are likest to do good; but the wicked will do wickedly, Dan. xii. 10.

The chief means for rulers to become thus holy and exemplary is, 1. To hearken to the doctrine and counsel of the word of the Lord, and to meditate in it day and night, Josh. i. 3, 4; Deut. xvii. 18-20. And to have faithful, holy, and self-denying teachers, 2 Chron. xx. 20. 2. To beware of the company and counsels of the wicked. "Take away the wicked from before the king, and his throne shall be established in righteousness," Prov. xxv. 4, 5. 3. To watch most carefully against the special temptations of their great places, especially against sensuality and pride, and preferring their own honour, and interest, and will, before the honour, and interest, and will, of Jesus Christ. "Woe to thee, O land, when thy king is a child, and thy princes eat in the morning! Blessed art thou, O land, when thy king is the son of nobles, and thy princes eat in due season, for strength, and not for drunkenness!" Eccl. x. 16, 17. "It is an abomination to kings to commit wickedness; for the throne is established by righteousness," Prov. xvi. 12. 4. To remember always the end of holiness. How sure a way it is to glory hereafter, and to leave a sweet and glorious name and memorial upon earth; when wickedness is the certain way to shame on earth, and misery for ever![34]

Mem. XVIII. Rulers should not be contented to do good at home, and to be the joy and blessing of their own subjects; but also set their hearts to the promoting of faith, and holiness, and concord, throughout the churches of the world; and to improve their interests in princes and states, by amicable correspondencies and treaties to these ends; that they may be blessings to the utmost extent of their capacities. As Constantine interceded with the Persian king, to forbear the persecuting of christians in his dominion,[35] &c. But I shall presume to speak no further to my superiors; in the golden age these memorandums will be practised.

I will only annex Erasmus's image of a good prince, and of a bad, recited by Alstedius Encyclop. lib. xxiii. Polit. c. 3. p. 173, 174.

The Image of a Good Prince, out of Erasmus.

"If you will draw the picture of a good prince, delineate some celestial wight, liker to God than to a man; absolute in all perfections of virtue; given for the good of all; yea, sent from heaven for the relief of mortal men's affairs; which being (*oculatissimum*) most discerning, looketh to all! To whom nothing is more regarded, nothing more sweet, than the commonwealth; who hath more than a fatherly affection unto all. To whom every one's life is dearer than his own; who night and day is doing and endeavouring nothing else, but that it may be very well with all; who hath rewards in readiness for all that are good; and pardon for the bad, if so be they will betake them to a better course; that so freely desireth to deserve well of his subjects, that if it be needful, he will not stick to preserve their safety by his own peril; that taketh his country's commodity to be his own gain; that always watcheth, that others may sleep quietly; that leaveth himself no quiet vacancy, that his country may live in quiet vacancy, or peace; that afflicteth himself with successive cares, that his subjects may enjoy tranquillity. To conclude, on whose virtue it is, that the public happiness doth depend."

The Image of a Bad Prince. Ibid.

"If you would set forth a bad prince to the eye, you must paint some savage, horrid beast, made up of such monstrosities as a dragon, a wolf, a lion, a viper, a bear, &c. every way armed, with six hundred eyes; every way toothed; every way terrible; with hooked talons; of an insatiable paunch; fed with men's bowels; drunk with man's blood; that [744]watcheth to prey upon the lives and fortunes of all the people; troublesome to all, but specially to the good; a fatal evil to the world; which all curse and hate, who wish well to the commonwealth; which can neither be endured, because of his cruelty, nor yet taken away without the great calamity of the world, because wickedness is armed with guards and riches."

[23] Finis ad quem rex principaliter intendere debet in seipso et in subditis, est æterna beatitudo, quæ in visione Dei consistit. Et quia ista visio est perfectissimum bonum maxime movere debet regem et quemecunque dominum, ut hunc finem subditi consequantur. Lib. de Regim. Principum Thomæ adscript. Grot. de Imper. Sum. Pot. p. 9. Even Aristotle could say, Polit. vii. c. 1, 2. et eadem fine, that each man's active and contemplative life, is the end of government, and not only the public peace; and that is the best life which conduceth most to our consideration of God, and that is the worst, which calleth us off from considering and worshipping him. Vide Grot. de Imper. sum. Pot. p. 10. Quam multa injuste fieri possunt, quæ nemo possit reprehendere. Cicero de fin. Read Plutarch's Precepts of Policy, and that old men should be rulers.

[24] Read often Psal. ii. and ci.

[25] Read Bilson of Subject. p. 129. to the end of the second part, specially p. 140-142. The laws of Charles the Great. And Grotius de Imperio Sum. Pot. circa Sacra. c. 1. et per totum.

[26] Jul. Capitolin. saith of the Antonines, That they would not be saluted by filthy persons. And Lampridus of Alexander Severus, that, Nisi honestos et bonæ famæ homines ad salutationem non admisit. Jussitque ut nemo ingrediatur, nisi qui se innocentem novit: per præconem edixit, ut nemo salutaret principem qui se furem esse nosset, ne aliquando detectus capitali supplicio subderetur. Read Sebastian. Foxius de Regno Regisque institutione. Even Cræsus, Dionysius, and Julian were liberal to philosophers, and ambitious of their converse. Vera civitatis fœlicitas est, ut Dei sit amans et amata Deo; illum sibi regem, se illius populum agnoscat. August. de Civit. Dei, 1. v. c. 14.

[27] Aug. Ep. Bonifac. Omnes reges qui populo Dei non prohibuerunt nec everterunt quæ contra Dei præcepta fuerunt instituta, culpantur. Qui prohibuerunt et everterunt, super aliorum merita, laudantur.

[28] When Hunnerichus the Arian Vandal king, was resolved to banish, imprison, and otherwise persecute the orthodox bishops and pastors, he first trieth them by threatenings and divers cruelties, and after appointeth a public disputation; where his bishops and officers, having no better pretence, cruelly beat the people and pastors, and then falsely tell the king, That by tumult and clamour they avoided disputing. And at last he calleth together all the pastors that were met for the disputation, and, to insnare them, putteth an oath upon them, That after the king's death, they would take his son for their king; and that they would send no letters beyond sea. This oath divided the orthodox among themselves. For one part of the bishops and pastors said, If we refuse a lawful oath, our people will say that we forsake them, and the dissolution of the churches will be imputed to us. The other part perceiving the snare, were fain to pretend Christ's command, "Swear not at all." The king having separated them, and the officers took all their names, sendeth them all to prison. To those that took the oath, they said, Because that contrary to the command of the gospel, you would swear, you shall see your cities and churches no more, but be sent into the country to till the ground; but so that you presume not to sing psalms, or pray, or carry a book, or baptize, or ordain, or absolve. To those that refused the oath, they said, Because you desired not the reign of the king's son, and therefore refused the oath; you shall be banished to the isle of Corsica, to cut wood for the ships. Victor. Utic. p. (mihi) 456, 457. Generalis Jesuitarum ex nimio absoluti imperii amore, delaturas in scrinia sua admittit, iisque credit, non audito eo qui accusatur: quod injustitiæ genus ab ethnicis ipsis improbatur. Imperando non bonis regibus se facit similem, qui senatum magni fecerunt; sed tyrannos mavult imitari, e. g. Tarquinium

11

superbum, qui ante omnia conatus est debilitare senatus numerum et authoritatem, ut omnia suo libitu facere posset; similiter generalis cum assistentibus suis odit synodos generales, omniaque experitur, ne tales instituantur conventus, quibus rerum gestarum reddere rationem necesse habeat.—Generalis Jesuiticus in eligendis officialibus non curat quod sit cujusque talentum aut dotes eminentiores, sed quam bene secum aut cum provinciali suo conformetur. Quæ causa est cur homines viles et abjecti animi officiis præponantur, qui a superioribus duci se sinant ut nervis alienis mobile lignum. Mariana de Reform. Jesuit. cap. 13, 15, 16, 18. In Arcan. Jesuit. p. 131, 132. Recit. in Apolog. Giraldi. Nulla est latronum societas in qua justicia non plus loci habeat, quam in societate nostra, &c.—ubi non modo scientia et ignorantia in æquo sunt, sed etiam scientia impedimento est, quo minus quis consequatur præmia humano ac divino jure debita. Marian. Aphor. 84. c. 12, &c. 14. 89. Aphor. 87, &c. The rest is worth the reading, as a warning from a Jesuit to the governors of state and church. Aphor. 80. c. 11. Superiores societatis nostræ sunt homines indigni, qui officiis præsint, cum generalis metuat ac sublatos velit, quorum eminentes sunt virtutes. Boni quam mali ei suspectiores sunt. This, and abundance more, saith Mariana, a Jesuit of ninety-six years of age, learned in Hebrew, Chaldee, Syriac, Greek, and Latin, of his own society.

[29] Lamprid. numbers it with Alexander Mam. Severus's good works. Judæis privilegia reservavit; christianos esse passus est. Nam illo tempore crudelius Arianorum episcopi, presbyteri, clerici, quam rex et Vandali sæviebant. Id. p. 468.

[30] Justitiæ munus primum est, ut ne cui quis noceat nisi lacessitus injuria. Cicero. Prov. xxii. 7; xxviii. 16; Psal. cxix. 23; Prov. xxv. 2. Leg. Epist. M. Ciceronis ad fratrem.

[31] Quis mihi imponat necessitatem vel credendi quod nolim, vel quod velim non credendi. Lactant. lib. 5. c. 13.

[32] Laert. in Solon, reciteth one of his sayings, Populi rector prius se quam populum recte instituere debet: si principes et majores secundum leges vixerint, unaquæque civitas optime rege peterit, p. 31.

[33] Or spend thy time in them. Dr. Hammond.

[34] Luke xviii. 22, 24; Deut. xvii. 20; Prov. xxix. 14; xxii. 29; xvi. 13; xxxi. 3, 4; 2 Chron. xxxii. 25; xx. 16; Ezek. xxviii. 2, 5, 17; Luke xii. 19, 20; xvi. 19, 20, 25. It is a sad observation of Acosta, lib. v. c. 9. p. 474. Ac reipsa ceutoque usu observatum est, eas Indorum nationes plures ac graviores superstitionis diabolicæ species teuuisse, in quibus regum ac reipublicæ maxime potentia et peritia excelluit. Contra qui tenuiorem fortunam minusque reipublicæ accommodata sortiti sunt, in his multo idololatria parcior est: usque adeo ut nonnullas Indorum gentes omni idolorum religione vacare, quidam pro certo confirment. Ex bonæ fidei scriptoribus super alias innumeras, hæc præcipua capitur utilitas; quod non alia res æque vel bonorum regum animos ad res cum laude gerendas accendit, vel tyrannorum cupiditates cohibet, ac refrænat, dum utrique cernunt horum literis suam vitam omnem, mox in totius orbis, imo sæculorum omnium theatrum producendam. Et quicquid in abdito nunc vel patrant, vel adscito fuco prætexunt, vel metu dissimulari cogunt, verius quam ignorari, paulo post clarissimam in lucem sub oculis omnium traducendum: quam jam metu pariter ac spe libera posteritas, nec ullo corrupta studio, magno consensu recte factis applaudet, parique libertate his diversa explodet, exibilabitque. Erasm. Præfat. in Sueton.

[35] Euseb. in vita Const.

CHAPTER III.

DIRECTIONS FOR SUBJECTS CONCERNING THEIR DUTY TO THEIR RULERS.

BEING now to speak of the duties which I must practise, and to those of my own rank, I shall do it with some more freedom, confidence, and expectation of regard and practice.

Direct. I. Though I shall pass by most of the theory, and especially of the controversial points in politics, and not presume to play the lawyer's part; yet I must advise you to understand so much of the cause, and nature, and end of government, as is necessary to direct you in your obedience, and to preserve you from all temptations to rebellion. Especially take heed of those mistakes which confound sovereignty and subjection, and which delude the people with a conceit, that they are the original of power, and may intrust it as they please; and call their rulers to account, and take the forfeiture, and recall their trust, &c. It is not to flatter kings, but to give God his due, that I shall caution you against these mistakes of popularity. And first, I shall briefly lay down the truth, and then answer some few of the chief objections.

Prop. I. That there be government *in genere*, and obedience thereto, is determined even in nature, by the God of nature, in making man a sociable creature, and each man insufficient for himself, and in making republics necessary to the welfare and safety of individuals, and government necessary to these republics.[36] This therefore is not left to the people's wills; though some odd cases may be imagined, in which some individual persons may live out of a commonwealth, and not be obliged to live under civil government; yet that exception doth but confirm the general rule: even as all men ordinarily are bound to live in communion with some particular church, and know their own pastor, though yet some few may be excepted, as some ambassadors, travellers, seamen, soldiers, banished men, &c. So here, the obligation to live under government, lieth upon the generality of the world, though some few may be excepted.

Prop. II. Rulers therefore are God's officers, placed under him in his kingdom, as he is the universal, absolute Sovereign of the world; and they receive their power from God, who is the only original of power. Not only their strength from his strength, but their authority or governing power, (which is *jus regendi*,) from his supreme authority; as mayors and bailiffs in corporations receive their power from the king. Rom. xiii. 1-3, "There is no power, but of God; the powers that be, are ordained of God."

Prop. III. This governing power in genere, is not an empty name, but in the very institution containeth in it those things materially which are absolutely necessary to the end of government.

Prop. IV. Yet God hath left that which is commonly called, the specification of government; and some lower parts of the matter, and manner of exercise, undetermined; as also the individual persons or families that shall rule. In these three therefore it is that communities interpose. 1. Whether the sovereignty shall be in one, or two, or ten, or how many, and how divided for their exercise, God hath not determined. 2. Nor hath he determined of every particular, whether the power shall extend to this, or that, or the other thing, or not? Nor whether it shall be exercised thus or thus, by standing courts, or temporary judges, &c. 3. Nor hath he named the person or family that shall rule.[37]

Prop. V. Though these in the constitution are determined of by explicit or implicit contract or consent, between the ruler and the community, yet by none of these three can the people be truly and properly said to give the ruler his power of government. Not by the first or last; for both those do but determine who shall be the recipient of that power; whether one or more, and who individually. Not the second, for that is but a limiting, or bounding, or regulating the governing power, that it be not exercised to their hurt; the bounding and regulating of their power, is not the giving them power. The people having the strength, cannot be ruled against their concordant wills: and therefore, if they contract with their governors, that they will be ruled thus and thus, or not at all, this is not to give them power. Yet propriety they have, and there they may be givers. So that this bounding, or regulating, and choosing the form, and persons, and giving of their propriety, is all that they have to do. And the choosing of the family or person, is not at all a giving the power. They are but sine quibus non to that; they do but open the door to let in the governor; they do but name the family or man, to whom God, and not they, shall give the power.

As, when God hath already determined what authority the husband shall have over the wife, the wife by choosing him to be her husband, giveth him not his power, but only chooseth the man, to whom God giveth it by his standing law: though about the disposing of her estate, she may limit him by precontracts; but if she contract against his government, it is a contradiction and null. Nor if he abuse his power, doth it at all fall into her hands.

If the king by charter give power to a corporation to choose their mayor, or other officer, they do but nominate the persons that shall receive it, but it is the king's charter, and not they, that give him the power.

If a soldier voluntarily list himself under the king's general, or other commanders, he doth but choose the man that shall command him, but it is the king's commission that giveth him the power to command those that voluntarily so list themselves. And if the authority be abused or forfeited, it is not into the soldiers' hands, but into the king's.

Prop. VI. The constituting consent or contract of ancestors obligeth all their posterity, if they will have any of the protection or other benefit of government, to stand to the constitution; else governments [745]should be so unsettled and mutable, as to be uncapable of their proper end.

Prop. VII. God hath neither in nature or Scripture, estated this power of government, in whole or in part, upon the people of a mere community, (much less on subjects,) whether noble or ignoble, learned or unlearned, the part of the community, or the whole body, real or representative.[38] The people as such, have not this power, either to use or to give; but the absolute Sovereign of all the world, doth communicate the sovereign power in every kingdom, or other sort of commonwealth, from himself immediately; I say, immediately: not without the mediation of an instrument signifying his will; for the law of nature and Scripture are his instrument, and the charter of authority; nor yet so immediately, as without any kind of medium; for the consent and nomination of the community before expressed, may be *conditio sine qua non*, so far as aforesaid; but it is so immediately from God, as that there is no immediate recipient, to receive the power first from God, and convey it to the sovereign.

Prop. VIII. The natural power of individual persons over themselves, is *tota specie*different from this political or civil power. And it is not the individual's resignation of this natural power of self-disposal, unto one or more, which is the efficient cause of sovereignty or civil power.[39]

Prop. IX. If you take the word law properly, for the expression of a ruler's will obliging the governed, or making their duty; and not improperly, for mere contracts between the sovereign and the people; then it is clear in the definition itself, that neither subjects, nor the community, as such, have any legislative power. Neither nature nor Scripture hath given the people a power of making laws, either by themselves, or with the sovereign; either the sole power, or a part of it. But the very nature of government requireth, that the whole legislative power, that is, the power of making governing laws, belong to the *summa majestas*, or sovereign alone. (Unless when the *summa potestas* is in many hands, you compare the partakers among themselves, and call one party the sovereign, as having more of the sovereignty than the rest.) For those that are no governors at all, cannot perform the chief act of government, which is the making of governing laws; but the people are no governors at all, either as a community, or as subjects; so that you may easily perceive, that all the arguments for a natural democracy, are built upon false suppositions; and wherever the people have any part in the sovereignty, it is by the after constitution, and not by nature; and that kings receive not their power from the people's gift, (who never had it themselves to use or give,) but from God alone.

Prop. X. Though God have not made a universal determination for any one sort of government, against the rest, (whether monarchy, aristocracy, or democracy,)

14

because that is best for one people, which may be worse for others, yet ordinarily monarchy is accounted better than aristocracy, and aristocracy better than democracy. So much briefly of the original of power.

Object. I. But, saith worthy Mr. Richard Hooker, Eccl. Polit. lib. i. sect. 10. p. 21,[40] "That which we spake of the power of government, must here be applied to the power of making laws, whereby to govern; which power, God hath over all, and by the natural law, whereto he hath made all subject, the lawful power of making laws to command whole politic societies of men, belongeth so properly to the same entire societies, that for any prince or potentate of what kind soever upon earth, to exercise the same of himself, and not either by express commission immediately and personally received from God, or else by authority derived at first from their consent, upon whose persons they impose laws, it is no better than mere tyranny. Laws they are not therefore, which public approbation hath not made so."

Answ. Because the authority of this famous divine is with his party so great, I shall adventure to say something, lest his words do the more harm; but not by confident opposition, but humble proposal and submission of my judgment to superiors and wiser men, as being conscious of my own inferiority and infirmity. I take all this to be an assertion no where by him proved (and by me elsewhere disproved fully). Laws are the effects and signs of the ruler's will; and instruments of government. Legislation is the first part of government; and if the whole body are naturally governors, the *pars imperans* and *pars subdita* are confounded. If the most absolute monarch can make no laws, then disobeying them were no fault. It is enough that their power be derived from God immediately, though the persons be chosen by men. Their authority is not derived from the people's consent, but from God, by their consent, as a bare condition *sine qua non*. What if a community say all to their elected king, "We take not ourselves to have any governing power to give or use, but we only choose you or your family to that office which God hath instituted, who in that institution giveth you the power upon our choice;" can any man prove, that such a king hath no power, but is a tyrant; because the people disclaim the giving of the power; when indeed they do their duty? Remember that in all this we speak not of the government of this or that particular kingdom, but of kingdoms and other commonwealths indefinitely.[41]

Object. II. But, saith he, lib. viii. p. 192, "Unto me it seemeth almost out of doubt and controversy, that every independent multitude before any certain form of regimen established, hath under God supreme authority, full dominion over itself,"—

Answ. If by dominion were meant propriety, every individual hath it; but for governing power, it seemeth as clear to me, that your independent multitude hath no civil power of government at all; but only a power to choose them governors; while they have no governors, they have no governing power, for that maketh a governor.

Object. III. Ibid. "A man who is lord of himself, may be made another's servant," &c.

Answ. 1. He may hire out himself to labour for another; because he hath so far the power of himself, and his labour is his own, which he may sell for wages; but in a family, that the master be the governor to see God's laws obeyed by his servants, is of divine appointment, and this governing power [746]the servant giveth not to his master, but only maketh himself the object of it. 2. The power that nature giveth a man over himself, is *tota specie* distinct from civil government; (as Dr. Hammond hath well showed against I. G.) An individual person hath not that power of his own life as the king hath. He may not put himself to death, for that which the king may put him to death for. 3. If this were true, that every individual, by self-resignation, might give a king his power over him; yet *a posse ad esse non valet consequentia;* and that it is not so is proved, in that God the universal Sovereign hath prevented them, by determining himself, of his own officers, and giving them their power in the same charter by which he enableth the people to choose them. Therefore it is no better reasoning than to say, If all the persons in London subjected themselves to the lord mayor, he would thereby receive his power from them, when the king hath prevented that already, by giving him the power himself in his charter; and leaving only the choice of the person to them; and that under the direction of the rules which he hath given them.[42]

Object. IV. But saith he, lib. viii. p. 193, "In kingdoms of this quality, (as this we live in,) the highest governor hath indeed universal dominion, but with dependency upon that whole entire body over the several parts whereof he hath dominion; so that it standeth for an axiom in this case, The king is *major singulis, universis minor.*"

Answ. If you had included himself, it is certain that he cannot be greater than the whole, because he cannot be greater than himself. But seeing you speak of the whole in contradistinction from him, I answer, that indeed *in genere causæ finalis,* the sovereign is *universis minor,* that is, the whole kingdom is naturally more worth than one, and their felicity a greater good; or else the *bonum publicum,* or *salus populi,* could not be the end of government; but this is nothing to our case; for we are speaking of governing power as a means to this end; and so *in genere causæ efficientis,* the sovereign (yea, and his lowest officer) hath more authority or *jus regendi* than all the people as such (for they all as such have none at all); even as the church is of more worth than the pastor, and yet the pastor alone hath more authority to administer the sacraments, and to govern the people, than all the flock hath; for they have none either to use or give, (whatever some say to the contrary,) but only choose him to whom God will give it.[43]

Object. V. Saith the reverend author, lib. viii. p. 194, "Neither can any man with reason think, but that the first institution of kings, (a sufficient consideration wherefore their power should always depend on that from which it did always flow,) by original influence of power from the body into the king, is the cause of kings' dependency in power upon the body: by dependency we mean subordination and subjection."

Answ. 1. But if their institution *in genere* was of God, and that give them their power, and it never flowed from the body at all, then all your superstructure falleth with your ground-work. 2. And here you seem plainly to confound all kingdoms by turning the *pars imperans* into the *pars subdita,* and *vice versa;* if the king be subject, how are they his subjects? I will not infer what this will lead them to do, when they are taught that kings are in subordination and subjection to them. Sad experience hath showed us what this very principle would effect.

Object. VI. Ibid.[44] "A manifest token of which dependency may be this; as there is no more certain argument, that lands are held under any as lords, than if we see that such lands in defect of heirs fall unto them by escheat; in like manner it doth follow rightly that seeing dominion when there is none to inherit it, returneth unto the body, therefore they which before were inheritors of it, did hold it in dependence on the body; so that by comparing the body with the head as touching power, it seemeth always to reside in both; fundamentally and radically in one, in the other derivatively; in one the habit, in the other the act of power."

Answ. Power no more falleth to the multitude by escheat, than the power of the pastor falls to the church, or the power of the physician to the hospital, or the power of the schoolmaster to the scholars; that is, not at all. When all the heirs are dead, they are an ungoverned community, that have power to choose a governor, but no power to govern, neither (as you distinguish it) in habit nor in act, originally nor derivatively. As it is with a corporation when the mayor is dead, the power falleth not to the people.

Therefore there is no good ground given for your following question, "May a body politic then at all times withdraw in whole or in part the influence of dominion which passeth from it, if inconveniences do grow thereby?" Though you answer this question soberly yourself, it is easy to see how the multitude may be tempted to answer it on your grounds, especially if they think your inconvenience turn into a necessity; and what use they will make of your next words, "It must be presumed that supreme governors will not in such cases oppose themselves, and be stiff in detaining that, the use whereof is with public detriment." A strange presumption.

Object. VII. "The axioms of our regal government are these, *Lex facit regem*; the king's grant of any favour made contrary to law is void; *Rex nihil potest nisi quod jure potest.*"

Answ. If *lex* be taken improperly for the constituting contract between prince and people, and if your *facit* have respect only to the species and person, and not the substance of the power itself, then I contradict you not. But if *lex* be taken properly for *authoritativa constitutio debiti*, or the signification of the sovereign's will to oblige the subject, then *lex non facit regem, sed rex legem.*[45]

Object. VIII. Lib. viii. p. 210, "When all which the wisdom of all sorts can do is done for the devising of laws in the church, it is the general consent of all that giveth them the form and vigour of laws; without which they could be no more to us than the counsels of physicians to the sick. Well might they seem as wholesome admonitions and instructions, but laws could they never be, without consent of the whole church to be guided by them, whereunto both nature and the practice of the church of God set down in Scripture, is found every way so fully consonant, that God himself would not impose, [747]no not his own laws upon his people, by the hand of Moses, without their free and open consent."

Answ. 1. Wisdom doth but prepare laws, and governing power enacteth them, and giveth them their form; but the whole body hath no such governing power, therefore they give them not their form.[46] 2. The people's consent to God's laws gave them not their form or authority; this opinion I have elsewhere confuted, against a more erroneous author. Their consent to God's laws was required indeed, as naturally necessary to their obedience, but not as necessary to the being or obligation of the law. Can you think that it had been no sin in them to have disobeyed God's laws, unless they had first consented to them? Then all the world might escape sin and damnation, by denying consent to the laws of God. 3. This doctrine will teach men that we have no church laws;[47] for the whole church never signified their consent. Millions of the poorer sort have no voices in choosing parliament men or convocations; and this will teach the minor dissenting part, to think themselves disobliged for want of consenting; and will give every dissenting part or person a negative voice to all church laws. 4. A single bishop hath a governing power over his particular church, and they are bound to obey him, Heb. xiii. 7, 17. And if the governing power of one pastor be not suspended for want of the consent of any or all the people, then much less the governing power of king and parliament.

Object. IX. Lib. viii. p. 220. "It is a thing even undoubtedly natural, that all free and independent societies should themselves make their own laws; and that this power should belong to the whole, not to any certain part of a politic body———."

Answ. This is oft affirmed, but no proof at all of it; in many nations the representatives of the whole body have the legislative power, or part of it. But that is from the special constitution of that particular commonwealth, and not from nature, nor common to all nations. All that naturally belongeth to the people as such, was but to choose their law-makers, and secure their liberties, and not to make laws themselves, by themselves, or mere representers.

Object. X. Lib. viii. p. 221. "For of this thing no man doubteth, namely, that in all societies, companies, and corporations, what severally each shall be bound unto, it must be with all their assents ratified. Against all equity it were, that a man should suffer detriment at the hands of men, for not observing that which he never did, either by himself or by others, mediately agree to———."

Answ. I am one that more than doubt of that which you say no man doubteth of. Do you not so much as except God's laws, and all those that only do enforce them, or drive men to obey them? As men are obliged to obey God, whether they consent or not; so are they to obey the laws of their sovereigns, though they never consented to them, no nor to their sovereignty, as long as they are members of that commonwealth,

17

to the government whereof the sovereign is lawfully called, millions of dissenters may be bound to obey, till they quit the society.

Object. XI. Lib. viii. p. 221. "If magistrates be heads of the church, they are of necessity christians."

Answ. That can never be proved. A constitutive head indeed must be a christian, and more, even a pastor to a particular church, and Christ to the universal. This headship our kings disclaim; but a head of the church, that is, over the church, or a coercive governor of it, the king would be if he were no christian. As one that is no physician may be head over all the physicians in his kingdom; or though he be no philosopher, or artist, he may be head over all the philosophers and artists; and in all their causes have the supreme coercive power; so would the king over all protestants if he were no protestant, and over all christians if he were no christian. But you think, that he that is no member of the church cannot be the head of it. I answer, not a constitutive, essential head as the pastor is; but he may be the head over it, and have all the coercive power over it. What if the king be not a member of many corporations in his kingdom? Yet as he is head of the kingdom, he is head of, or over them, as they are parts of it.

Object. XII. Lib. viii. p. 218, 223, 224. "What power the king hath, he hath it by law: the bounds and limits of it are known; the entire community giveth order," &c. p. 223. "As for them that exercise power altogether against order, although the kind of power which they have may be of God, yet is their exercise thereof against God, and therefore not of God, otherwise than by permission, as all injustice is." p. 224. "Usurpers of power, whereby we do not mean them that by violence have aspired unto places of highest authority, but them that use more authority than they did ever receive in form and manner before mentioned. Such usurpers thereof as in the exercise of their power, do more than they have been authorized to do, cannot in conscience bind any man to obedience."

Answ. It is true that no man can exercise more power than he hath: the power that we speak of being ἐξουσία, *jus regendi*, it is impossible to use more authority than they have; though they may command beyond and without authority. And it is true, that where a man hath no authority or right to command, he cannot directly bind obedience. But yet a ruler may exercise more power than man ever gave him, and oblige men to obedience thereby. God giveth them power to govern for his glory, according to his laws, and to promote obedience to those laws of God (in nature and Scripture) by subordinate laws of their own. And all this the sovereign may do, if the people, at the choice of him or his family, should only say, We take you for our sovereign ruler: for then he may do all that true reason or Scripture make the work of a sovereign ruler, even govern the people by all such just means as tend to the public good and their everlasting happiness: and yet that people that should do no more but choose persons or families to govern them, and set them no bounds, do give no power to those they choose, but determine of the persons that shall have power from God. Yet it is granted you, that if the person or family chosen, contract with them to govern only with such and such limitations, they have bound themselves by their own contract; and thus both specifications of government and degrees of power come in by men. But always distinguish, 1. Between the people's giving away their propriety, (in [748]their goods, labours, &c. which they may do,) and giving authority, or governing power (which they have not to give). 2. Between their naming the persons that shall receive it from the universal King, and giving it themselves. 3. Between bounding and limiting power, and giving power. 4. And between a sovereign's binding himself by contract, and being bound by the authority of others.[48] If they be limited by contracts, which are commonly called the constitutive or fundamental laws, it is their own consent and contract that effectively obligeth and limiteth them; of which indeed the people's will may be the occasion, when they resolve that they will be governed on no other terms: but if the contract limit them not, but they be chosen simply to be the *summæ potestates*, without naming any particular powers either by concession or restraint, then as to ruling they are absolute as to men, and limited only by God, from whose highest power they can never be exempt, who in nature and Scripture restraineth them from all that is impious and unjust, against his laws and honour, or against the public happiness and safety. And here also remember, that if any shall imagine that God restraineth a magistrate when it is not so, and that the commands of their governors are contrary to the word of God, when it is no such matter, their error will not justify their disobedience.

Though I have answered these passages of this reverend author, it is not to draw any to undervalue his learned writings, but to set right the reader in the principles of his obedience, on which the practice doth so much depend.

And I confess, that other authors of politics say as much as Mr. Hooker saith, both papists and protestants; but not all, nor I think the soundest: I will instance now in Alstedius only, (an excellent person, but in this mistaken,) who saith, Encyclop. lib. xxiii. Polit. cap. 3. p. 178. *Populus universus dignior et potior est tum magistratu tum ephoris.— Hinc recte docent Doct. Politici, populum obtinere regnum et jura majestatis proprietate et dominio: principem et ephoros usu et administratione*(whereas the people have not the *regnum vel jura majestatis* any way at all).*—Si administratores officium suum facere nolint, si impia, et iniqua mandent, si contra dilectionem Dei et proximi agant, populus propriæ salutis curam arripiet, imperium male utentibus abrogabit, et in locum eorum alios substituet.—Porro ephori validiora ipso rege imperia obtinent: principem enim constituunt et deponunt; id quod amplissimum est præeminentiæ argumentum. Atque hæc prærogative mutuis pactis stabilitur.—Interim princeps summam potestatem obtinere dicitur, quatenus ephori administrationem imperii, et cumulum potestatis ipsi committunt. Denique optimatum universorum potestas non est infinita et absoluta, sed certis veluti rhetris et clathris definita, utpote non ad propriam libidinem, sed ad utilitatem et salutem populi alligata. Hinc illorum munia sunt regem designare, constituere, inaugurare, constitutum consiliis et auxiliis juvare; sine consensu et approbatione principis, quamdiu ille suum officium facit, nihil in reipublicæ negotiis suscipere: nonnunquam conventum inscio principe agere, necessitate reipublicæ exigente.—Populum contra omnis generis turbatores et violatores defendere.—*I suppose Mr. Hooker's principles and Alstedius's were much the same. I will not venture to recite the conclusion, cap. 12. p. 199. R. 5. de resistendo Tyranno.

Many other authors go the same way, and say that people have the *majestas realis*(both papists, and protestants, and heathens). But I suppose that what I have said against Hooker will serve to show the weakness of their grounds: though it is none of my purpose to contradict either Hooker or any other, so far as they open the odiousness of the sin of tyranny, (which at this day keepeth out the gospel from the far greatest part of the world, and is the greatest enemy to the kingdom of Christ,) nor yet as they plead for the just liberties of the people; but I am not for their authority.

Direct. II. Begin with an absolute, universal, resolved obedience to God, your Creator and Redeemer, who is your sovereign King, and will be your final, righteous Judge. As he that is no loyal subject to the king, can never well obey his officers; so he that subjecteth not his soul to the original power of his Creator, can never well obey the derivative power of earthly governors.

Object. But, you may say, experience teacheth us, that many ungodly people are obedient to their superiors as well as others. I answer, materially they are, but not formally, and from a right principle, and to right ends: as a rebel against the king, may obey a justice of peace for his own ends, as long as he will let him alone, or take his part; but not formally, as he is the king's officer; so ungodly men may flatter princes and magistrates for their own ends, or on some low and by-account, but not sincerely as the officers of God. He is not like to be truly obedient to man, that is so foolish, dishonest, and impious, as to rebel against his Maker; nor to obey that authority which he first denieth, in its original and first efficient cause. Whatever Satan and his servants may say, and however some hypocrites may contradict in their practices the religion which they profess, yet nothing is more certain, than that the most serious, godly christians, are the best subjects upon earth; as their principles themselves will easily demonstrate.

19

Direct. III. Having begun with God, obey your governors as the officers of God, with an obedience ultimately divine.[49] All things must be done in holiness by the holy. That is, God must be discerned, obeyed, and intended in all; and therefore in magistrates in a special manner. In two respects magistrates are obeyed, or rather flattered, by the ungodly; first, as they are men that are able to do them corporal good or hurt: as a horse, or dog, or other brute will follow you for his belly, and loveth to be where he fareth best. Secondly, as the head of his party, and encourager of him in his evil way, when he meets with rulers that will be so bad. Wicked men love wicked magistrates for being the servants of Satan; but faithful men must honour and obey a magistrate, as an officer of God; even a magistrate as a magistrate, and not only as holy, is an officer of the Lord of all. Therefore the fifth commandment is as the hinge of the two tables; many of the ancients thought that it was the last commandment of the first table, and the moderns think it is the first commandment of the last table; for it commandeth our duty to the noblest sort of men; but not merely as men, but as the officers of [749]God. They debase magistrates that look at them merely as those that master other men, as the strongest beast doth by the weaker: nothing will make you sincere and constant in your honouring and obeying them, but taking them as the officers of God, and remembering by whose commission they rule, and whose work they do; that "they are the ministers of God to us for good," Rom. xiii. 1-5. If you do not this, 1. You wrong God, whose servants they are; for he that despiseth, despiseth not man but God. 2. You wrong the magistrate, as much as you should do an ambassador, if you took him to be the messenger of some Jack Straw, or some fellow that signifieth no more than his personal worth importeth. 3. And you wrong yourselves; for while you neglect the interest and authority of God in your rulers, you forfeit the acceptance, protection, and reward of God. Subjects as well as servants must learn that great lesson, Col. iii. 23-25, "Whatsoever ye do, do it heartily as to the Lord, and not unto men: knowing that of the Lord ye shall receive the reward of the inheritance, for ye serve the Lord Christ: but he that doth wrong shall receive for the wrong, which he hath done; and there is no respect of persons." So Eph. vi. 5-8. Magistrates are as truly God's officers as preachers: and therefore as he that heareth preachers heareth him, so he that obeyeth rulers obeyeth him: the exceptions are but the like in both cases: it is not every thing that we must receive from preachers; nor every thing that we must do at the command of rulers; but both in their proper place and work, must be regarded as the officers of God; and not as men that have no higher authority than their own to bear them out.

Direct. IV. Let no vices of the person cause you to forget the dignity of his office, The authority of a sinful ruler is of God, and must accordingly be obeyed: of this read Bishop Bilson at large in his excellent treatise of Christian Subjection; against the papists that excommunicate and depose princes whom they account heretics, or favourers of them. Those sins which will damn a man's soul, and deprive him of heaven, will not deprive him of his kingdom, nor disoblige the subjects from their obedience. An infidel, or an ungodly christian, (that is, a hypocrite,) is capable of being a prince, as well as being a parent, husband, master; and the apostle hath taught all, as well as servants, their duty to such. 1 Pet. ii. 18-21, "Servants, be subject to your masters with all fear; and not only to the good and gentle, but also to the froward; for this is thankworthy, if a man for conscience toward God, endure grief, suffering wrongfully. For what glory is it if when you are buffeted for your faults, you take it patiently? but if when ye do well and suffer for it ye take it patiently, this is acceptable with God; for even hereunto were ye called." Though it be a rare mercy to have godly rulers, and a great judgment to have ungodly ones, it is such as must be borne.[50]

Direct. V. Do not either divulge or aggravate the vices of your governors to their dishonour; for their honour is necessary to the public good. If they have not care of their own honour, yet their subjects must have a care of it. If once they be dishonoured, they will the more easily be contemned, hated, and disobeyed. Therefore the dishonouring of the rulers tendeth to the dissolution of the government, and ruin of the commonwealth. Only in two cases did the ancient christians aggravate the wickedness of their governors. 1. In case they were such cruel monsters as Nero, who lived to the misery of mankind. 2. In case they were not only open enemies of the church of Christ, but their honour stood in competition with the honour of christianity, piety, and honesty, as in Julian's case; I confess against Nero and Julian both living and dead, (and many like them,) the tongues and pens of wise and sober persons have been very free; but the fifth commandment is not to be forgotten, "Honour thy father and mother;" and 1 Pet. ii. 17, "Fear God, honour the king;"[51]though you must not call evil good, yet you may conceal and hide evil: Ham was cursed for opening his father's nakedness. Though you must flatter none in their sins, nor hinder their repentance, but further it by all righteous means, yet must you speak honourably of your rulers, and endeavour to breed an honourable esteem of them in the people's minds; and not as some, that think they do well, if they can secretly make their rulers seem odious, by opening and aggravating their faults.

Direct. VI. Subdue your passions, that no injuries which you may suffer by them, may disturb your reason, and make you dishonour them by way of revenge. If you may not revenge yourselves on private men, much less on magistrates; and the tongue may be an unjust revenger, as well as the hand. Passion will provoke you to be telling all men, Thus and thus I was used, and to persuade you that it is no sin to tell the truth of what you suffered: but remember, that the public good, and the honour of God's officers, are of greater value, than the righting of a particular person that is injured. Many a discontented person hath set kingdoms on fire, by divulging the faults of governors for the righting of themselves.

Object. But shall cruel and unrighteous or persecuting men do mischief, and not hear of it, nor be humbled for it?

Answ. 1. Preachers of the gospel, and others that have opportunity, may privately tell them of it, to bring them to repentance, (if they will endure it,) without dishonouring them by making it public. 2. Historians will tell posterity of it, to their perpetual infamy (if repentance and well-doing recover not their honour).[52]Flatterers abuse the living, but truth will dishonour their wickedness when they are dead: for it is God's own decree, "That the memory of the just is blessed, but the name of the wicked shall rot," Prov. x. 7. 3. And God himself will fully be avenged upon the impenitent for ever, having told you, "That it were better for him that offendeth one of his little ones, that a millstone were hanged about his neck, and he were drowned in the depth of the sea."[53] And is not all this enough, without the revenge of your passionate tongues? To speak evil of dignities, and despise dominion, and bring railing accusations, are the sins of the old licentious heretics. Christ left us his example, not to revile the meanest, when we are reviled, 1 Pet. ii. 23. If you believe, that God will justify the innocent, and avenge them speedily, Luke xviii. 7, 8, what need you be so forward to justify and avenge yourselves?

Object. If God will have their names to rot, and spoken evil of when they are dead, why may I not do it while they are alive?

Answ. There is a great deal of difference between [750]a true historian and a self-avenger in the reason of the thing, and in the effects: to dishonour bad rulers while they live, doth tend to excite the people to rebellion, and to disable them to govern; but for truth to be spoken of them when they are dead, doth only lay an odium upon the sin, and is a warning to others, that they follow them not in evil: and this no wicked prince was ever so great and powerful as to prevent; for it is a part of God's resolved judgment. Yet must historians so open the faults of the person, as not to bring the office into contempt, but preserve the reverence due to the authority and place of governors.[54]

Direct. VII. By all means overcome a selfish mind, and get such a holy and a public spirit, as more regardeth God's honour, and the public interest, than your own. It is selfishness that is the great rebel and enemy of God, and of the king, and of our neighbour. A selfish, private spirit careth not what the commonwealth suffereth, if he

21

himself may be a gainer by it. To revenge himself, or to rise up to some higher place, or increase his riches, he will betray and ruin his king, his country, and his nearest friends. A selfish, ambitious, covetous man, is faithful to no man, longer than he serveth his ends; nor is he any further to be trusted, than his own interest will allow. Self-denial, and a public spirit, are necessary to every faithful subject.

Direct. VIII. Wish not evil to your governors in your secret thoughts; but if any such thought would enter into your hearts, reject it with abhorrence. Eccles. x. 20, "Curse not the king, no, not in thy thoughts; and curse not the rich in thy bedchamber; for a bird of the air shall carry the voice, and that which hath wings shall tell the matter." A feverish, misguided zeal for religion, and a passionate discontent for personal injuries, do make many greatly guilty in this point; they would be much pleased, if God would show some grievous judgment upon persecutors; and take no warning by Christ's rebukes of James and John, but secretly are wishing for fire from heaven, not knowing what manner of spirit they are of. They cherish such thoughts as are pleasing to them, though they dare not utter them in words. And he that dare wish hurt, is in danger of being drawn by temptation to do hurt.

Object. But may we not pray for the cutting off of persecutors? And may we not give God thanks for it, if he do it himself, without any sinful means of ours?

Answ. 1. Every ruler that casteth down one sect or party of christians, and setteth up another, (perhaps as true to the interest of christianity as they,) is not to be prayed against, and his destruction wished by the suffering party. 2. If he be a persecutor of christianity and piety itself, as heathens and infidels are, yet if his government do more good than his persecution doth harm, you may not so much as wish his downfall. 3. If he were a Nero, or a Julian, you must pray first for his conversion; and if that may not be, then next for his restraint, and never for his destruction, but on supposition that neither of the former may be attained (which you cannot say). 4. You must pray for the deliverance of the persecuted church, and leave the way and means to God, and not prescribe to him. Hurtful desires and prayers are seldom of God. 5. You may freelier rejoice afterwards, than desire it before: because when a Julian is cut off, you know that God's righteous will is accomplished; when before you knew not that it was his will: yet after, it is the deliverance of the church, and not the hurt of a persecutor as such, that you must give thanks for: be very suspicious here, lest partiality and passion blind you.[55]

Direct. IX. Learn how to suffer; and know what use God can make of your sufferings, and think not better of prosperity, and worse of suffering, than you have cause.[56] It is a carnal, unbelieving heart, that maketh so great a matter of poverty, imprisonment, banishment, or death, as if they were undone, if they suffer for Christ, or be sent to heaven before the time; as if kingdoms must be disturbed to save you from suffering: this better beseems an infidel or a worldling, that takes his earthly prosperity for his portion, and thinks he hath no other to win or lose. Do you not know what the church hath gained by suffering? how pure it hath been when the fire of persecution hath refined it? and how prosperity hath been the very thing that hath polluted it, and shattered it all to pieces; by letting in all the ungodly world into the visible communion of the saints, and by setting the bishops on contending for superiority, and overtopping emperors and kings? Many thousands that would be excellent persons in adversity, cannot bear a high or prosperous state, but their brains are turned, and pride and contention maketh them the scorn of the adversaries that observe them.

Direct. X. Trust God, and live by faith; and then you will find no need of rebellious or any sinful means. Do you believe, that both the hearts and lives of kings, and all their affairs, are in the hands of God? If not, you are atheists. If you do, then do you not think that God is fitter than you to dispose of them? He that believeth, will not make haste. Deliverance from persecutions must be prayed and waited for, and not snatched by violence, as a hungry dog will snatch the meat out of his master's hands, and bite his fingers. Do you believe, "That all shall work together for good to them that love God?" Rom. viii. 28. And do you believe, that the godly are more than conquerors; when they are killed all day, and counted as sheep unto the slaughter? ver. 32-35. And do you believe, that it is cause of exceeding joy, when for the sake of righteousness you are hated and persecuted, and all manner of evil is falsely spoken of you? Matt. v. 10-12. If you do not, you believe not Christ; if you do, will you strive by sinful means against your own good, and happiness, and joy? Will you desire to conquer, when you may be more than conquerors? Certainly, the use of sinful means doth come from secret unbelief and diffidence. Learn to trust God, and you will easily be subject to your governors.

Direct XI. Look not for too great matters in the world: take it but for that wilderness which is the way to the promised land of rest. And then you [751]will not count it strange to meet with hard usage and sufferings from almost all. "Beloved, think it not strange concerning the fiery trial, which is to try you, as if some strange thing happened to you; but rejoice in that ye are partakers of the sufferings of Christ," 1 Pet. iv. 12, 13. Are you content with God and heaven for your portion? If not, how are you christians? if you are, you have small temptation to rebel or use unlawful means for earthly privileges.[57] Paul saith, he "took pleasure in persecutions," 2 Cor. xii. 10. Learn you to do so, and you will easily bear them.

Direct. XII. Abhor the popular spirit of envy, which maketh the poor, for the most part, think odiously of the rich and their superiors; because they have that which they had rather have themselves. I have long observed it, that the poor labouring people are very apt to speak of the rich, as sober men speak of drunkards; as if their very estates, and dignity, and greatness, were a vice.[58] And it is very much to flatter their own conscience, and delude themselves with ungrounded hopes of heaven. When they have not the spirit of regeneration and holiness, to witness their title to eternal life, they think their poverty will serve the turn; and they will ordinarily say, that they hope God will not punish them in another world, because they have had their part in this: but they will easily believe, that almost all rich and great men go to hell; and when they read Luke xvi. of the rich man and Lazarus, they think they are the Lazaruses, and read it as if God would save men merely for being poor, and damn men for being great and rich; when yet they would themselves be as rich and great, if they knew how to attain it. They think that they are the maintainers of the commonwealth, and the rich are the caterpillars of it, that live upon their labours, like drones in the hive, or mice and vermin that eat the honey, which the poor labouring bees have long been gathering. For they are unacquainted with the labours and cares of their governors, and sensible only of their own. This envious spirit exceedingly disposeth the poor to discontents, and tumults, and rebellions; but it is not of God, James iii. 15-17.

Direct. XIII. Keep not company with envious murmurers at government; for their words fret like a canker, and their sin is of an infecting kind. What a multitude were drawn into the rebellion of Korah, who, no doubt, were provoked by the leader's discontented words.[59] It seemeth they were for popularity. "Ye take too much upon you, seeing all the congregation are holy, every one of them, and the Lord is among them: wherefore then lift you up yourselves above the congregation of the Lord?—Is it a small thing that thou hast brought us up out of a land that floweth with milk and honey, to kill us in the wilderness; except thou make thyself altogether a prince over us?—Wilt thou put out the eyes of these men?" Numb. xvi. 3, 13, 14. What confidence, and what fair pretences are here! so probable and plausible to the people, that it is no wonder that multitudes were carried to rebellion by it! Though God disowned them by a dreadful judgment, and showed whom he had chosen to be the governors of his people.

Direct. XIV. Keep humble, and take heed of pride. The humble are ready to obey and yield, and not only to be subject to magistrates, but to all men, even voluntarily to be subject to them that cannot constrain them. "Be all of you subject one to another," 1 Pet. v. 5. It is no hard matter for a twig to bow, and for a humble soul to yield and obey another, in any thing that is lawful. But the proud take subjection for vassalage, and obedience for slavery, and say, Who is lord over us? our tongues are our own: what lord shall control us? Will we be made slaves to such and such?[60] "Only from pride cometh contention," Prov. xiii. 10. By causing impatience, it causeth disobedience and sedition.

Direct. XV. Meddle not uncalled with the matters of superiors, and take not upon you to censure their actions, whom you have neither ability, fitness, or authority to censure. How commonly will every tradesman and labourer at his work, be censuring the counsels and government of the king; and speaking of things, which they never had means sufficiently to understand! Unless you had been upon the place, and heard all the debates and consultations, and understood all the circumstances and reasons of the business, how can you imagine that at so great a distance you are competent judges? Fear God, and judge not that you be not judged.[61] If busy-bodies and meddlers with other men's matters, among equals, are condemned, 2 Thess. iii. 11; 1 Tim. v. 13; 1 Pet. iv. 15; much more when they meddle, and that censoriously, with the matters of their governors. If you would please God, know and keep your places, as soldiers in an army, which is their comely order and their strength.

Direct. XVI. Consider the great temptations of the rich and great; and pity them that stand in so dangerous a station, instead of murmuring at them, or envying their greatness. You little know what you should be yourselves, if you were in their places, and the world, and the flesh, had so great a stroke at you, as they have at them. He that can swim in calmer water, may be carried down a violent stream. It is harder for that bird to fly, that hath many pound weights tied to keep her down, than that which hath but a straw to carry to her nest. It is harder mounting heaven-wards with lordships and kingdoms, than with your less impediments. Why do you not pity them that stand on the top of barren mountains, in the stroke of every storm and wind, when you dwell in the quiet, fruitful vales? Do you envy them that must go to heaven, as a camel through a needle's eye, if ever they come there? And are you discontented, that you are not in their condition? Will you rebel and fight to make your salvation as difficult as theirs? Are you so unthankful to God for your safer station, that you murmur at it, and long to be in the more dangerous place?

Direct. XVII. Pray constantly and heartily for the spiritual and corporal welfare of your governors. And you have reason to believe, that God who hath commanded you to put up such prayers, will not suffer them to be wholly lost, but will answer them some way to the benefit of them that perform the duty, 1 Tim. ii. 1-3. And the very performance of it will do us much good of itself; for it will keep the heart well disposed to our governors, and keep out all sinful desires of their hurt; or control them and cast them out, if they come in: prayer is the exercise of love and good desires; and exercise increaseth and confirmeth habits. If any ill wishes against your governors should steal into your minds, the next time you pray for them, conscience will accuse [752]you of hypocrisy, and either the sinful desires will corrupt or end your prayers, or else your prayers will cast out those ill desires. Certainly the faithful, fervent prayers of the righteous, do prevail much with God: and things would go better than they do in the world, if we prayed for rulers as heartily as we ought.

Object. For all the prayers of the church, five parts of six of the world are yet idolaters, heathens, infidels, and Mahometans; and for all the prayers of the reformed churches, most of the christian part of the world are drowned in popery, or gross ignorance and superstition, and the poor Greek churches have Mahometan or tyrannical governors, and carnal, proud, usurping prelates domineer over the Roman church; and there are but three protestant kings on the whole earth! And among the Israelites themselves, who have priests and prophets to pray for their princes, a good king was so rare, that when you have named five or six over Judah, (and never a one after the division over Israel,) you scarce know where to find the rest. What good then do your prayers for kings and magistrates?

Answ. 1. As I said before, they keep the hearts of subjects in an obedient, holy frame. 2. Were it not for prayers, those few good ones would be fewer, or worse than they are; and the bad ones might be worse, or at least do more hurt to the church than they now do. 3. It is not to be expected, that all should be granted in kind that believers pray for; for then not only kings, but all the world should be converted and saved; for we should pray for every one. But God who knoweth best how to distribute his mercies, and to honour himself, and refine his church by the malice and persecution of his enemies, will make his people's prayers a means of that measure of good which he will do for rulers, and by them in the world; and that is enough to encourage us to pray. 4. And indeed, if when proud, ungodly worldlings have sold their souls by wicked means, to climb up into places of power, and command, and domineer over others, the prayers of the faithful should presently convert and save them all, because they are governors; this would seem to charge God with respect of persons, and defect of justice, and would drown the world in wickedness, treasons, bloodshed, and confusion, by encouraging men by flatteries, or treacheries, or murders, to usurp such places, in which they may both gratify their lusts, and after save their souls, while the godly are obliged to pray them into heaven. It is no such hearing of prayers for governors which God hath promised. 5. And yet, I must observe, that most christians are so cold and formal in their prayers for the rulers of the world, and of the church, that we have great reason to impute the unhappiness of governors very much to their neglect; almost all men are taken up so much with their own concernments, that they put off the public concernments of the world, and of the church and state, with a few customary, heartless words; and understand not the meaning of the three first petitions of the Lord's prayer, and the reason of their precedency, or put them not up with that feeling as they do the other three. If we could once observe, that the generality of christians were more earnest and importunate with God, for the hallowing of his name through all the world, and the coming of his kingdom, and the obeying of his will in earth, as it is in heaven, and the conversion of the kings and kingdoms of the world, than for any of their personal concernments, I should take it for a better prognostic of the happiness of kings and kingdoms, than any that hath yet appeared in our days. And those that are taken up with the expectations of Christ's visible reign on earth, would find it a more lawful and comfortable way, to promote his government thus by his own appointed officers, than to rebel against kings, and seek to pull them down, on pretence of setting up him that hath appointed them, whose kingdom (personally) is not of this world.[62]

Direct. XVIII. When you are tempted to dishonourable thoughts of your governors, look over the face of all the earth, and compare your case with the nations of the world; and then your murmurings may be turned into thankfulness for so great a mercy. What cause hath God to difference us from other nations, and give us any more than an equal proportion of mercy with the rest of the world? Have we deserved to have a christian king, when five parts of the world have rulers that are heathens and Mahometans? Have we deserved to have a protestant king, when all the world hath but two more? How happy were the world, if it were so with all nations, as it is with us! Remember how unthankfulness forfeiteth our happiness.

Direct. XIX. Consider as well the benefits which you receive by governors, as the sufferings which you undergo; and especially consider of the common benefits, and value them above your own. He that knoweth what man is, and what the world is, and what the temptations of great men are, and what he himself deserveth, and what need the best have of affliction, and what good they may get by the right improvement of it, will never wonder nor grudge to have his earthly mercies mixed with crosses, and to find some salt or sourness in the sauce of his pleasant dishes. For the most luscious is not of best concoction. And he that will more observe his few afflictions, than his many benefits, hath much more selfish tenderness of the flesh, than ingenuous thankfulness to his Benefactor. It is for your good that rulers are the ministers of God, Rom. xiii. 3-5. Perhaps you will think it strange, that I say to you (what I have oft said) that I think there are not very many rulers, no, not tyrants and persecutors, so bad, but that the godly that live under them, do receive from their government more good than hurt; and (though it must be confessed, that better governors would do better, yet) almost the worst are better than none. And none are more beholden to God for magistrates, than the godly are, however none suffer so much by them in most places of the world.[63] My reason is, 1. Because the multitude of the needy, and the dissolute prodigals, if they were all ungoverned, would tear out the throats of the more wealthy and industrious; and as robbers use men in their houses, and on the highway, so would such persons use all about them, and turn all into a constant war. And hereby all honest industry would be [753]overthrown, while the fruit of men's labours were all at the mercy of every one that is stronger than the owner; and a robber can take away all in a night, which you have been labouring for many years, or may set all on fire over your heads; and more persons would be killed in these wars by those that sought their goods, than tyrants and persecutors use to kill (unless they be of the most cruel sort of all). 2. And it is plain, that in most countries, the universal enmity of corrupted nature to serious godliness would inflame the rabble, if they were but ungoverned, to commit more murders and cruelties upon the godly, than most of the persecutors in the world have committed. Yet I deny not, in most places there are a sober sort of men of the middle rank that will hear reason, and are more equal to religion than the highest or the lowest usually are. But suppose these sober men were the more numerous, yet is the vulgar rabble the more violent, and if rulers restrained them not, would leave few of the faithful alive on earth. As many volumes as are written of the martyrs, who have suffered by persecutors, I think they saved the lives of many more than they murdered. Though this is no thanks to them, it is a mercy to others. As many as Queen Mary martyred, they had been far more if she had but turned the rabble loose upon them and never meddled with them by authority. I do not think Nero or Dioclesian martyred near so many, as the people turned loose upon them would have done. Much more was Julian a protector of the church from the popular rage, though, in comparison of a Constantine or a Theodosius, he was a plague. If you will but consider thus the benefits of your common protection, your thankfulness for rulers would overcome your murmurings. In some places, and at some times, perhaps the people would favour the gospel, and flock after Christ, if rulers hindered them not; but that would not be the ordinary case, and their unconstancy is so great, that what they built up one day in their zeal, the next day they would pull down in fury.

Direct. XX. Think not that any change of the form of government, would cure that which is caused by the people's sin, or the common pravity of human nature. Some think they can contrive such forms of government, as that rulers shall be able to do no hurt: but either they will disable them to do good, or else their engine is but glass, and will fail or break when it comes to execution. Men that are themselves so bad and unhumbled, as not to know how bad they are, and how bad mankind is, are still laying the blame upon the form of government when any thing is amiss, and think by a change to find a cure. As if when an army is infected with the plague, or composed of cowards, the change of the general, or form of government, would prove a cure. But if a monarch be faulty, in an aristocracy you will but have many faulty governors for one; and in a democracy a multitude of tyrants.[64]

Direct. XXI. Set yourselves much more to study your duty to your governors, than the duty of your governors to you; as knowing, that both your temporal and eternal happiness depend much more upon yourselves, than upon them.[65] God doth not call you to study other men's duties so much as your own. If your rulers sin, you shall not answer for it; but if you sin yourselves, you shall. If you should live under the Turk, that would oppress and persecute you, your souls shall speed never the worse for this; it is not you, but he that should be damned for it. If you say, But it is we that should be oppressed by it; I answer, 1. How small are temporal things to a true believer, in comparison of eternal things! Have not you a greater hurt to fear, than the killing of your bodies by men? Luke xii. 4. 2. And even for this life, do you not believe that your lives and liberties are in the power of God, and that he can relieve you from the oppression of all the world, by less than a word, even by his will? If you believe not this, you are atheists; if you do, you must needs perceive that it concerneth you more to care for your duty to your governors, than for theirs to you; and not so much to regard what you receive, as what you do; nor how you are used by others, as how you behave yourselves to them. Be much more afraid lest you should be guilty of murmuring, dishonouring, disobeying, flattering, not praying for your governors, than lest you suffer any thing unjustly from them. 1 Pet. iv. 13-17, "Let none of you suffer as a murderer, or as a thief, or as an evil-doer, or as a busybody in other men's matters; yet if any man suffer as a christian, let him not be ashamed, but let him glorify God on this behalf.—If ye be reproached for the name of Christ, ye are happy." Live so, that all your adversaries may be forced to say, as it was said of Daniel, "We shall not find any occasion against this Daniel, except we find it against him concerning the law of his God," Dan. vi. 5. Let none be able justly to punish you as drunkards, or thieves, or slanderers, or fornicators, or perjured, or deceivers, or rebellious, or seditious; and then never fear any suffering for the sake of Christ or righteousness. Yea, though you suffer as Christ himself did, under a false accusation of disloyalty, fear not the suffering nor the infamy, as long as you are free from the guilt. See that all be well at home, and that you be not faulty against God or your governors, and then you may boldly commit yourselves to God, 1 Pet. ii. 23, 24.

Direct. XXII. The more religious any are, the more obedient should they be in all things lawful. Excel others in loyalty, as well as in piety. Religion is so far from being a just pretence of rebellion, that it is the only effectual bond of sincere subjection and obedience.

Direct. XXIII. Therefore believe not them that would exempt the clergy from subjection to the civil powers. As none should know the law of God so well as they, so none should be more obedient to kings and states, when the law of God so evidently commandeth it. Of this read "Bilson of Christian Subjection" (who besides many others, saith enough of this). The arguments of the papists from the supposed incapacity of princes, would exempt physicians, and others arts and sciences, from under their government, as well as the clergy.

Direct. XXIV. Abase not magistrates so far, as to think their office and power extend not to matters of religion and the worship of God. Were they only for the low and contemptible matters of this world, their office would be contemptible and low. To help you out in this, I shall answer some of the commonest doubts.

Quest. I. Is the civil magistrate judge in controversies of faith or worship?

Who shall be judge in points of faith and worship?

[754]*Answ.* It hath many a time grieved me to hear so easy a question frequently propounded, and pitifully answered, by such as the public good required to have had more understanding in such things. In a word, judgment is public or private. The private judgment, which is nothing but a rational discerning of truth and duty, in order to our own choice and practice, belongeth to every rational person. The public judgment is ever in order to execution. Now the execution is of two sorts, 1. By the sword. 2. By God's word applied to the case and person. One is upon the body or estate; the other is upon the conscience of the person, or of the church, to bring him to repentance, or to bind him to avoid communion with the church, and the church to avoid communion with him.[66] And thus public judgment is civil or ecclesiastical; coercive and violent in the execution; or only upon consenters and volunteers. In the first, the magistrate is the only judge, and the pastors in the second. About faith or worship, if the question be, Who shall be protected as orthodox, and who shall be punished by the sword as heretical, idolatrous, or irreligious? here the magistrate is the only judge. If the question be, Who shall be admitted to church communion as orthodox, or ejected and excommunicated as heretical or profane? here the pastors are the proper judges. This is the truth, and this is enough to end all the voluminous

wranglings upon the question, Who shall be judge? and to answer the cavils of the papists against the power of princes in matters of religion. It is pity that such gross and silly sophisms, in a case that a child may answer, should debase christian princes, and take away their chief power, and give it to a proud and wrangling clergy, to persecute and divide the church with.[67]

Of the oath of supremacy.

Quest. II. May our oath of supremacy be lawfully taken, wherein the king is pronounced supreme governor in all causes ecclesiastical as well as civil?

Answ. There is no reason of scruple to him that understandeth, 1. That the title causes ecclesiastical is taken from the ancient usurpation of the pope and his prelates, who brought much of the magistrate's work into their courts, under the name of causes ecclesiastical. 2. That our canons, and many declarations of our princes, have expounded it fully, by disclaiming all proper pastoral power. 3. That by governor is meant only one that governeth coercively, or by sword; so that it is no more than to swear That in all causes ecclesiastical, so far as coercive government is required, it belongeth not to pope or prelates under him; but to the king and his officers or courts alone: or, That the king is chief in governing by the sword in causes ecclesiastical as well as civil. So that if you put spiritual instead of ecclesiastical, the word is taken materially, and not formally; not that the king is chief in the spiritual government, by the keys of excommunication and absolution, but that he is chief in the coercive government about spiritual matters, as before explained.[68]

Quest. III. Is not this to confound the church and state, and to give the pastor's power to the magistrate?

Answ. Not at all; it is but to say that there may be need of the use both of the word and sword against the same persons, for the same offence; and the magistrate only must use one, and the pastors the other. An heretical preacher may be silenced by the king upon pain of banishment, and silenced by the church upon pain of excommunication. And what confusion is there in this?

Quest. IV. But hath not the king power in cases of church discipline, and excommunication itself?

Answ. There is a magistrate's discipline, and a pastoral discipline. Discipline by the sword, is the magistrate's work; discipline by the word is the pastor's work. And there is a coercive excommunication, and a pastoral excommunication. To command upon pain of corporal punishment, that a heretic or impenitent, wicked man shall forbear the sacred ordinances and privileges, a magistrate may do; but to command it only upon divine and spiritual penalties, belongeth to the pastors of the church. The magistrate hath power over their very pastoral work, though he have not power in it, so as to do it himself. Suppose but all the physicians of the nation to be of divine institution, with their colleges and hospitals, and in the similitude you will see all the difficulties resolved, and the next question fully answered.[69]

Quest. V. Seeing the king, and the pastors of the church, may command and judge to several ends in the same cause, suppose they should differ, which of them should the church obey?

Answ. Distinguish here, 1. Between a right judgment and a wrong. 2. Between the matter in question; which is either, 1. Proper in its primary state to the magistrate. 2. Or proper primarily to the pastor. 3. Or common to both (though in several sorts of judgment). And so I answer the question thus.

1. If it be a matter wherein God himself hath first determined, and his officers do but judge in subordination to his law, and declare his will, then we must obey him that speaketh according to the word of God, if we can truly discern it; and not him that we know goeth contrary to God.[70] As if the magistrate should forbid communion with Arians or heretics, and the pastors command us to hold communion with them as no heretics; here the magistrate is to be obeyed (because God is to be obeyed) before the pastors, though it be in a matter of faith and worship. If you say, Thus you make all the people judges; I answer you, And so you must make them such

private judges, to discern their own duty, and so must every man; or else you must rule them as beasts or madmen, and prove that there is no heaven or hell for any in the world but kings and pastors; or, at least, that the people shall be saved or damned for nothing, but obeying or not obeying their governors; and if you could prove that, you are never the nearer reconciling the contradictory commands of those governors.

2. But if the matter be not fore-determined by God, but left to man; then, 1. If it be the magistrate's proper work, we must obey the magistrate only. 2. If it be about the pastor's proper work, the pastor is to be obeyed; though the magistrate [755]gainsay it, so be it he proceed according to the general rules of his instructions, and the matter be of weight. As if the magistrate and the pastors of the church do command different translations or expositions of the Bible to be used, or one forbiddeth and another commandeth the same individual person to be baptized, or receive the sacrament of the Lord's supper, or to be esteemed a member of the church; if the people know not which of them judgeth right, it seemeth to me they should first obey their pastors, because it is only in matters intimately pertaining to their office. I speak only of formal obedience, and that of the people only, for, materially, prudence may require us rather to do as the magistrate commandeth, *quod, non quia*, to avoid a greater evil. And it is always supposed that we patiently bear the magistrate's penalties, when we obey not his commands. 3. But in points common to them both, the case is more difficult. But here you must further distinguish, first, between points equally common, and points unequally common; secondly, between determinations of good, or bad, or indifferent consequence as to the main end and interest of God and souls. 1. In points equally common to both, the magistrate is to be obeyed against the pastors; because he is more properly a commanding governor, and they are but the guides or governors of volunteers; and because, in such cases, the pastors themselves should obey the magistrate; and therefore the people should first obey him.[71] 2. Much more in points unequally common, which the magistrate is more concerned in than the pastors, the magistrate is undoubtedly to be first obeyed. Of both, there might instances be given about the circumstantials or adjuncts of God's worship. As the place of public worship, the situation, form, bells, fonts, pulpits, seats, precedency in seats, tables, cups, and other utensils; church bounds by parishes, church ornaments, gestures, habits, some councils, and their order, with other such like; in all which, *cæteris paribus*, for my part I would rather obey the laws of the king, than the canons of the bishops, if they should disagree. 3. But in cases common to both, in which the pastor's office is more nearly and fully concerned than the magistrate's, the case is more difficult: as at what hour the church shall assemble; what part of Scripture shall be read; what text the minister shall preach on; how long prayer, or sermon, or other church exercises shall be; what prayers the minister shall use; in what method he shall preach; and what doctrine he shall deliver, and the people hear; with many such like. These do most nearly belong to the pastoral office, to judge of as well as to execute; but yet in some cases the magistrate may interpose his authority. And herein, 1. If the one party do determine clearly to the necessary preservation of religion, and the other to the ruin of it, the disparity of consequents maketh a great disparity in the case; for here God himself hath predetermined, who commandeth that "all be done to edification." As for instance, if a christian magistrate ordain, that no assembly shall consist of above forty or a hundred persons, when there are so many preachers and places of meeting, that it is no detriment to men's souls; and especially, when the danger of infection, or other evil, warranteth it, then I would obey that command of the magistrate, though the pastors of the church were against it, and commanded fuller meetings. But if a Julian should command the same thing, on purpose to wear out the christian religion, and when it tendeth to the ruin of men's souls, (as when preachers are so few, that either more must meet together, or most must be untaught, and excluded from God's worship,) here I would rather obey the pastors that command the contrary, because they do but deliver the command of God, who determineth consequently of the

necessary means, when he determineth of the end. But if the consequents of the magistrate's and the pastor's commands should be equally indifferent, and neither of them discernibly good or bad, the difficulty then would be at the highest, and such as I shall not here presume to determine.[72]

No doubt but the king is the supreme governor over all the schools, and physicians, and hospitals in the land, that is, he is the supreme in the civil coercive government: he is supreme magistrate over divines, physicians, and schoolmasters; but not the supreme divine, physician, or schoolmaster. When there is any work for the office of the magistrate, that is, for the sword, among any of them, it belongeth only to him, and not at all to them: but when there is any work for the divine, the physician, the schoolmaster, or if you will, for the shoemaker, the tailor, the watchmaker, this belongeth not to the king to do, or give particular commands for: but yet it is all to be done under his government; and on special causes he may make laws to force them all to do their several works aright, and to restrain them from abuses. As (to clear the case in hand) the king is informed that physicians take too great fees of their patients, that some through ignorance, and some through covetousness, give ill compounded medicines and pernicious drugs: no doubt but the king, by the advice of understanding men, may forbid the use of such drugs as are found pernicious to his subjects, and may regulate not only the fees, but the compositions and attendances of physicians. But if he should command, that a man in a fever, or dropsy, or consumption, shall have no medicine, but this or that, and so oft, and in such or such a dose, and with such or such a diet; and the physicians, whom my reason bindeth me to trust, (and perhaps my own experience also,) do tell me that all these things are bad for me, and different tempers and accidents require different remedies, and that I am like to die, or hazard my health, if I obey not them contrary to the king's commands, here I should rather obey my physicians: partly, because else I should sin against God, who commandeth me the preservation of my life; and partly, because this matter more belongeth to the physician, than to the magistrate. Mr. Richard Hooker, Eccles. Polit. lib. viii. p. 223, 224, giveth you the reason more fully.[73]

Direct. XXV. Give not the magistrate's power to any other; whether to the people, on pretence of [756]their *majestatis realis,* (as they call it,) or the pope, or prelates, or pastors of the church, upon pretence of authority from Christ, or of the distinction of ecclesiastical government and civil. The people's pretensions to natural authority, or real majesty, or collation of power, I have confuted before, and more elsewhere. The pope's, prelate's, and pastor's power of the sword in causes ecclesiastical, is disproved so fully by Bishop Bilson *ubi supra,* and many more, that it is needless to say much more of it.[74] All protestants, so far as I know, are agreed that no bishop or pastor hath any power of the sword, that is, of coercion, or force upon men's bodies, liberties, or estates, except as magistrates derived from their sovereign. Their spiritual power is only upon consenters, in the use of God's word upon the conscience, either generally in preaching, or with personal application in discipline. No courts or commands can compel any to appear or submit, nor lay the mulct of a penny upon any, but by their own consent, or the magistrate's authority. But this the papists will few of them confess: for if once the sword were taken from them, the world would quickly see that their church had the hearts of few of those multitudes, whom by fire and sword they forced to seem their members; or at least, that, when the windows were opened, the light would quickly deliver poor souls from the servitude of those men of darkness. For then few would fear the unrighteous excommunication of mere usurpers.[75] It is a manifold usurpation by which their kingdom is upheld. (For a kingdom it is rather to be called than a church.) 1. They usurp the power of the keys or ecclesiastical government over all the world, and make themselves pastors of those churches, which they have nothing to do to govern. Their excommunications of princes or people, in other lands or churches that never took them for their pastors, is a usurpation the more odious, by how much the power usurped is more holy, and the performance in so large a parish as the whole world, is naturally impossible to the

Roman usurper. 2. Under the name of ecclesiastical jurisdiction, they usurp the magistrate's coercive power in such causes as they call ecclesiastical. 3. Yea, and they claim an immunity to their clergy from the civil government, as if they were no subjects of the king, or the king had not power to punish his offending subjects. 4. *In ordine ad spiritualia*, they claim yet more of the magistrate's power. 5. And one part of them give the pope directly in temporals a power over kings and kingdoms. 6. Their most eminent divines do ordinarily maintain, that the pope may excommunicate kings and interdict kingdoms, and that an excommunicated king is no king, and may be killed. It is an article of their religion, determined of in one of their approved general councils, (Later. sub. Innoc. III. can. 3,) That if temporal lords will not exterminate heretics from their lands, (such as the Albigenses, that denied transubstantiation, mentioned can. 2,) the pope may give their dominions to others, and absolve their vassals from their fealty. And when some of late would have so far salved their honour, as to invalidate the authority of that council, they will not endure it, but have strenuously vindicated it; and indeed whatever it be to us, with them it is already enrolled among the approved general councils. Between the Erastians, who would have no government but by magistrates, and papists, who give the magistrate's power to the pope and his prelates, the truth is in the middle; that the pastors have a nunciative and directive power from Christ, and a discipline to exercise by the word alone, or volunteers; much like the power of a philosopher in his school, or a physician in his hospital, supposing them to be by divine right.

Direct. XXVI. Refuse not to swear allegiance to your lawful sovereign. Though oaths are fearful, and not to be taken without weighty cause, yet are they not to be refused when the cause is weighty, as here it is. Must the sovereign be sworn to do his office for you, and must he undertake so hard and perilous a charge for you, which he is no way able to go through, if his subjects be not faithful to him? And shall those subjects refuse to promise and swear fidelity? This is against all reason and equity.

Direct. XXVII. Think not that either the pope, or any power in the world, can dispense with this your oath, or absolve you from the bond of it, or save you from the punishment due from God, to the perjured and perfidious. Of this see what I have written before against perjury.

Direct. XXVIII. Do nothing that tendeth to bring the sacred bonds of oaths into an irreligious contempt, or to make men take the horrid crime of perjury to be a little sin. Sovereigns have no sufficient security of the fidelity of their subjects, or of their lives, or kingdoms; if once oaths and covenants be made light of, and men can play fast and loose with the bonds of God, which lie upon them. He is virtually a traitor to princes and states, who would bring perjury and perfidiousness into credit, and teacheth men to violate oaths and vows. For there is no keeping up human societies and governments, where there is no trust to be put in one another. And there is no trust to be put in that man, that maketh no conscience of an oath or vow.[76]

Direct. XXIX. Be ready to your power to defend your governors, against all treasons, conspiracies, and rebellions.[77] For this is a great part of the duty of your relation. The wisdom and goodness necessary to government, is much personal in the governors themselves; but the strength (without which laws cannot be executed, nor the people preserved) is in the people, and the prince's interest in them; therefore if you withdraw your help in time of need, you desert and betray your rulers, whom you should defend. If you say, it is they that are your protectors. I answer, true; but by yourselves. They protect you by wisdom, council, and authority, and you must protect them by obedience and strength. Would you have them protect you rather by mercenaries or foreigners? If not, you must be willing to do your parts, and not think it enough in treasons, [757]invasions, or rebellions, to sit still and save yourselves, and let him that can lay hold on the crown, possess it. What prince would be the governor of a people, that he knew would forsake him in his need?

Direct. XXX. Murmur not at the payment of those necessary tributes, by which the common safety must be preserved, and the due honour of your governors kept up.

Sordid covetousness hath been the ruin of many a commonwealth. When every one is shifting for himself, and saving his own, and murmuring at the charge by which their safety must be defended, as if kings could fight for them, without men and money; this selfishness is the most pernicious enemy to government, and to the common good. Tribute and honour must be paid to whom it doth belong. Rom. xiii. 6, 7, "For they are God's ministers, attending continually on this very thing." And none of your goods or cabins will be saved, if by your covetousness the ship should perish.

Direct. XXXI. Resist not, where you cannot actually obey: and let no appearance of probable good that might come to yourselves, or the church, by any unlawful means, (as treason, sedition, or rebellion,) ever tempt you to it. For evil must not be done that good may come by it: and all evil means are but palliate and deceitful cures, that seem to help a little while, but will leave the malady more perilous at last, than it was before. As it is possible, that lying or perjury might be used to the seeming service of a governor at the time, which yet would prepare for his after danger, by teaching men perfidiousness; even so rebellions and treasons may seem at present to be very conducible to the ends of a people or party that think themselves oppressed; but in the end it will leave them much worse than it found them.[78]

Object. But if we must let rulers destroy us at their pleasure, the gospel will be rooted out of the earth: when they know that we hold it unlawful to resist them, they will be imboldened to destroy us, and sport themselves in our blood; as the papists did by the poor Albigenses, &c.

Answ. All this did signify something if there were no God, that can easilier restrain and destroy them at his pleasure, than they can destroy or injure you. But if there be a God, and all the world is in his hand, and with a word he can speak them all into dust; and if this God be engaged to protect you, and hath told you, that the very hairs of your head are numbered, and more regardeth his honour, and gospel, and church, than you do, and accounteth his servants as the apple of his eye, and hath promised to hear them and avenge them speedily, and forbid them to avenge themselves; then it is but atheistical distrust of God, to save yourselves by sinful means, as if God either could not or would not do it: thus he that saveth his life shall lose it. Do you believe that you are in the hands of Christ, and that men cannot touch you but by his permission; and that he will turn all your sufferings to your exceeding benefit? And yet will you venture on sin and hell to escape such sufferings from men? Wolves, and bears, and lions, that fight most for themselves, are hated and destroyed by all; so that there are but few of them in the land. But though a hundred sheep will run before a little dog, the master of them taketh care for their preservation. And little children that cannot go out of the way from a horse or cart, every one is afraid of hurting. If christians behaved themselves with that eminent love, and lowliness, and meekness, and patience, and harmlessness, as their Lord hath taught them and required, perhaps the very cruelty and malice of their enemies would abate and relent; and "when a man's ways please God, he would make his enemies to be at peace with him;"[79] but if not, their fury would but hasten us to our joy and glory. Yet note, that I speak all this only against rebellion, and unlawful arms and acts.

Direct. XXXII. Obey inferior magistrates according to the authority derived to them from the supreme, but never against the supreme, from whom it is derived. The same reasons which oblige you to obey the personal commands of the king, do bind you also to obey the lowest constable, or other officer: for they are necessary instruments of the sovereign power, and if you obey not them, the obedience of the sovereign signifieth almost nothing. But no man is bound to obey them beyond the measure of their authority; much less against those that give them their authority.

Direct. XXXIII. No human power is at all to be obeyed against God: for they have no power, but what they receive from God; and all that is from him, is for him. He giveth no power against himself; he is the first efficient, the chief dirigent, and ultimate final cause of all.[80] It is no act of authority, but resistance of his authority, which contradicteth his law, and is against him. All human laws are subservient to his laws, and not co-ordinate, much less superior. Therefore they are *ipso facto* null, or have no obligation, which are against him: yet is not the office itself null, when it is in some things thus abused; nor the magistrate's power null, as to other things. No man must commit the least sin against God, to please the greatest prince on earth, or to avoid the greatest corporal suffering.[81] "Fear not them that can kill the body, and after that have no more that they can do; but fear him, who is able to destroy both body and soul in hell: yea, I say unto you, fear him," Luke xii. 4. "Whether we ought to obey God rather than men, judge ye," Acts v. 29. "Not fearing the wrath of the king: for he endured, as seeing him that is invisible.—Others were tortured, not accepting deliverance," &c. Heb. xi. 27, 35. "Be it known unto thee, O king, that we will not serve thy gods, nor worship the golden image," &c. Dan. iii. 18.

Object. If we are not obliged to obey, we are not obliged to suffer; for the law obligeth primarily to obedience, and only secondarily *ad pœnam*, for want of obedience. Therefore where there is no primary obligation to obedience, there is no secondary obligation to punishment.

Answ. The word obligation, being metaphorical, must in controversy be explained by its proper terms. The law doth first *constituere debitum obedientiæ, et propter inobedientiam debitum pœnæ.* Here then you must distinguish, 1. Between obligation *in foro conscientiæ*, and *in foro humano*. 2. Between an obligation *ad pœnam* by that law of man, and an obligation *ad patiendum* by another divine law. And so the answer is this: first, If the higher powers, e. g. [758]forbid the apostles to preach upon pain of death or scourging, the dueness both of the obedience and the penalty, is really null, in point of conscience; however *in foro humano* they are both due; that is, so falsely reputed in that court: therefore the apostles are bound to preach notwithstanding the prohibition, and so far as God alloweth they may resist the penalty, that is, by flying: for properly there is neither *debitum obedientiæ nec pœnæ*. Secondly, But then God himself obligeth them not to "resist the higher powers," Rom. xiii. 1-3, and "in their patience to possess their souls." So that from this command of God, there is a true obligation *ad patiendum*, to patient suffering and non-resistance, though from the law of man against their preaching, there was no true obligation *aut ad obedientiam, aut ad pœnam.* This is the true resolution of this sophism.

Direct. XXXIV. It is one of the most needful duties to governors, for those that have a call and opportunity, (as their pastors,) to tell them wisely and submissively of those sins which are the greatest enemies to their souls; and not the smallest enemies to their government, and the public peace.[82] All christians will confess, that sin is the only forfeiture of God's protection, and the cause of his displeasure, and consequently the only danger to the soul, and the greatest enemy to the land. And that the sins of rulers, whether personal, or in their government, have a far more dangerous influence upon the public state, than the sins of other men. Yea, the very sins which upon true repentance may be pardoned as to the everlasting punishment, may yet be unpardoned as to the public ruin of a state: as the sad instance of Manasseh showeth. 2 Kings xxiii. 26, "Notwithstanding the Lord turned not from the fierceness of his great wrath, wherewith his anger was kindled against Judah, because of all the provocations that Manasseh had provoked him withal." Chap. xxiv. 3, 4, "Surely at the commandment of the Lord came this upon Judah, to remove them out of his sight for the sins of Manasseh according to all that he did; and also for the innocent blood that he shed, (for he filled Jerusalem with innocent blood,) which the Lord would not pardon." And yet this was after Josiah had reformed. So Solomon's sin did cause the rending of the ten tribes from his son's kingdom: yea, the bearing with the high places, was a provoking sin in kings, that otherwise were upright. Therefore sin being the fire in the thatch, the quenching of it must needs be an act of duty and fidelity to governors; and those that tempt them to it, or soothe and flatter them in it, are the greatest enemies they have. But yet it is not every man that must reprove a governor, but those that have a call and opportunity; nor must it be done by them imperiously, or reproachfully, or publicly to their dishonour, but privately, humbly, and with love, honour, reverence, and submissiveness.

Object. But great men have great spirits, and are impatient of reproof, and I am not bound to that which will do no good, but ruin me.

Answ. 1. It is an abuse of your superiors, to censure them to be so proud and brutish, as not to consider that they are the subjects of God, and have souls to save or lose, as well as others: will you judge so hardly of them before trial, as if they were far worse and foolisher than the poor, and take this abuse of them to be an excuse for your other sin? No doubt there are good rulers in the world, that will say to Christ's ministers, as the Prince Elector Palatine did to Pitiscus, charging him to tell him plainly of his faults, when he chose him to be the Pastor Aulicus.[83]

2. How know you beforehand what success your words will have? Hath the word of God well managed no power? yea, to make even bad men good? Can you love your rulers, and yet give up their souls in despair, and all for fear of suffering by them?

3. What if you do suffer in the doing of your duty? Have you not learned to serve God upon such terms as those? Or do you think it will prove it to be no duty, because it will bring suffering on you? These reasons savour not of faith.

Direct. XXXV. Think not that it is unlawful to obey in every thing which is unlawfully commanded. It may in many cases be the subject's duty, to obey the magistrate who sinfully commandeth him. For all the magistrate's sins in commanding, do not enter into the matter or substance of the thing commanded: if a prince command me to do the greatest duty, in an ill design, to some selfish end, it is his sin so to command; but yet that command must be obeyed (to better ends). Nay, the matter of the command may be sinful in the commander, and not in the obeyer. If I be commanded without any just reason to hunt a feather, it is his sin that causelessly commandeth me so to lose my time; and yet it may be my sin to disobey it, while the thing is lawful; else servants and children must prove all to be needful, as well as lawful, which is commanded them before they must obey. Or the command may at the same time be evil by accident, and the obedience good by accident, and *per se.* Very good accidents, consequence, or effects, may belong to our obedience, when the accidents of the command itself are evil. I could give you abundance of instances of these things.

Direct. XXXVI. Yet is not all to be obeyed that is evil but by accident, nor all to be disobeyed that is so: but the accidents must be compared; and if the obedience will do more good than harm, we must obey; if it will evidently do more harm than good, we must not do it. Most of the sins in the world are evil by accident only, and not in the simple act denuded of its accidents, circumstances, or consequents. You may not sell poison to him that you know would poison himself with it, though to sell poison of itself be lawful. Though it be lawful simply to lend a sword, yet not to a traitor that you know would kill the king with it, no nor to one that would kill his father, his neighbour, or himself. A command would not excuse such an act from sin.[84] He was slain by David, that killed Saul at his own command, and if [759]he had but lent him his sword to do it, it had been his sin. Yet some evil accidents may be weighed down by greater evils, which would evidently follow upon the not doing of the thing commanded.

Direct. XXXVII. In the question, whether human laws bind conscience, the doubt is not of that nature, as to have necessary influence upon your practice. For all agree, that they bind the subject to obedience, and that God's law bindeth us to obey them. And if God's law bind us to obey man's law, and so to disobey them be materially a sin against God's law, this is as much as is needful to resolve you in respect of practice: no doubt, man's law hath no primitive obliging power at all, but a derivative from God, and under him; and what is it to bind the conscience (an improper speech) but to bind the person to judge it his duty, (*conscire,*) and so to do it. And no doubt but he is bound to judge it his duty, that that is immediately by human

34

law, and remotely by divine law, and so the contrary to be a sin proximately against man, and ultimately against God. This is plain, and the rest is but logomachy.

Direct. XXXVIII. The question is much harder, whether the violation of every human penal law be a sin against God, though a man submit to the penalty. (And the desert of every sin is death.) Master Richard Hooker's last book unhappily ended, before he gave us the full reason of his judgment in this case, these being the last words: "Howbeit, too rigorous it were, that the breach of every human law should be a deadly sin: a mean there is between those extremities, if so be we can find it out—."[85] Amesius hath diligently discussed it, and many others. The reason for the affirmative is, because God bindeth us to obey all the lawful commands of our governors; and suffering the penalty, is not obeying; the penalty being not the primary intention of the lawgiver, but the duty; and the penalty only to enforce the duty: and though the suffering of it satisfy man, it satisfieth not God, whose law we break by disobeying. Those that are for the negative, say, That God binding us but to obey the magistrate, and his law binding but *aut ad obedientiam, aut ad pœnam*, I fulfil his will, if I either do or suffer: if I obey not, I please him by satisfying for my disobedience. And it is none of his will, that my choosing the penalty should be my sin or damnation. To this it is replied, That the law bindeth *ad pœnam*, but on supposition of disobedience; and that disobedience is forbidden of God: and the penalty satisfieth not God, though it satisfy man. The other rejoins, That it satisfieth God, in that it satisfieth man; because God's law is but to give force to man's, according to the nature of it. If this hold, then no disobedience at all is a sin in him that suffereth the penalty. In so hard a case, because more distinction is necessary to the explication, than most readers are willing to be troubled with, I shall now give you but this brief decision.[86] There are some penalties which fulfil the magistrate's own will as much as obedience, which indeed have more of the nature of a commutation, than of penalty: (as he that watcheth not or mendeth not the highways, shall pay so much to hire another to do it: he that shooteth not so oft in a year, shall pay so much: he that eateth flesh in Lent, shall pay so much to the poor: he that repaireth not his hedges, shall pay so much:) and so in most amercements, and divers penal laws; in which we have reason to judge, that the penalty satisfieth the lawgiver fully, and that he leaveth it to our choice. In these cases I think we need not afflict ourselves with the conscience or fear of sinning against God. But there are other penal laws, in which the penalty is not desired for itself, and is supposed to be but an imperfect satisfaction to the lawgiver's will, and that he doth not freely leave us to our choice, but had rather we obeyed than suffered; only he imposeth no greater a penalty, either because there is no greater in his power, or some inconvenience prohibiteth; in this case I should fear my disobedience were a sin, though I suffered the penalty. (Still supposing it an act that he had power to command me.)

Direct. XXXIX. Take heed of the pernicious design of those atheistical politicians, that would make the world believe, that all that is excellent among men, is at enmity with monarchy, yea, and government itself; and take heed on the other side, that the most excellent things be not turned against it by abuse.

Here I have two dangers to advertise you to beware: the first is of some Machiavelian, pernicious principles, and the second of some erroneous, unchristian practices.

For the first, there are two sorts of atheistical politicians guilty of them. The first sort are some atheistical flatterers, that to engage monarchs against all that is good, would make them believe that all that is good is against them and their interest. By which means, while their design is to steal the help of princes, to cast out all that is good from the world, they are most pernicious underminers of monarchy itself. For what readier way to set all the world against it, than to make them believe that it standeth at enmity to all that is good. These secret enemies would set up a leviathan to be the butt of common enmity and opposition.

35

The other sort are the professed enemies of monarchy, who in their zeal for popular government, do bring in all that is excellent, as if it were adverse to monarchy. 1. They would (both) set it at enmity with politicians. 2. With lawyers. 3. With history. 4. With learning. 5. With divines. 6. With all christian religion. 7. And with humanity itself.

Object. I. The painters of the leviathan scorn all politics, as ignorant of the power of monarchs, except the atheistical inventions of their own brains. And the adversaries of monarchy say, The reading of politics will satisfy men against monarchy; for in them you ordinarily find that the *majestas realis* is in the people, and the *majestas personalis* in the prince; that the prince receiveth all his power from the people, to whom it is first given, and to whom it may be forfeited and escheat: with much more of the like, as is to be seen in politicians of all religions.

Answ. 1. It is not all politics that go upon those principles: and one mistake in writers is no disgrace to the true doctrine of politics, which may be vindicated from such mistakes. 2. As almost all authors of politics take monarchy for a lawful species of government, so most or very many (especially of the moderns) do take it to be the most excellent sort of unmixed government. Therefore they are no enemies to it.

Object. II. For lawyers, they say, That, 1. Civilians set up reason so high, that they dangerously measure the power of monarchs by it; insomuch, that the most famous pair of zealous and learned defenders of monarchy, Barclay and Grotius, do assign many cases, in which it is lawful to resist princes by arms, and more than so.[87] 2. And the common lawyers, they say, are all for the law, and ready to say as Hooker,*Lex facit regem*; and what power the king hath, he hath it by law, The bounds are known, p. 218. He is *singulis major, et universis minor, &c.*

[760]*Answ.* 1. Sure the Roman civil laws were not against monarchy, when monarchs made so many of them. And what power reason truly hath, it hath from God, whom none can over-top; and that which reason is abused unjustly to defend, may be well contradicted by reason indeed. 2. And what power the laws of the land have, they have by the king's consent and act: and it is strange impudence to pretend, that his own laws are against him. If any misinterpret them, he may be confuted.

Object. III. For historians, say they, Be but well-versed in ancient history, Greek and Roman, and you shall find them speak so ill of monarchy, and so much for popularity, and liberty, and magnifying so much the defenders of the people's liberty against monarchs, that it will secretly steal the dislike of monarchy, and the love of popular liberty into your minds.[88]

Answ. It must be considered in what times and places the ancient Greek and Roman historians did live.[89] They that lived where popular government was in force and credit, wrote according to the time and government which they lived under; yet do they extol the virtues and heroic acts of monarchs, and often speak of the vulgar giddiness and unconstancy. And for my part, I think he that readeth in them those popular tumults, irrationalities, furies, unconstancies, cruelties, which even in Rome and Athens they committed, and all historians record, will rather find his heart much alienated from such democratical confusions. And the historians of other times and places do write as much for monarchy, as they did for democracy.

Object. IV. Some of them revile at Aristotle and all universities, and say, That while multitudes must be tasters and pretenders to the learning which they never can thoroughly attain, they read many dangerous books, and receive false notions; and these half-witted men are the disturbers of all societies. Do you not see, say they, that the two strongest kingdoms in the world, are kept up by keeping the subjects ignorant. The Greek and Latin empires were ruined by the contention of men that did pretend to learning. The Turk keepeth all in quiet by suppressing it: and the pope confineth it almost all to his instruments in government, and keepeth the common people in ignorance; which keepeth them from matter of quarrel and disobedience.[90]

Answ. I hope you will not say, that Rome or Athens of old did take this course. And we will not deny, but men of knowledge are more subject to debates, and questionings, and quarrels about right and wrong, than men of utter ignorance are. Beasts fall not out about crowns or kingdoms, as men do. Dogs and swine will not scramble for gold, as men will do, if you cast it among them: and it is easier to keep swine or sheep, than men; and yet it is not better to be swine or sheep, than men; nor to be governors of beasts, than men. Dead men are quieter than the living, and blind men will submit to be led more easily than those that see; and yet it is not better to be a king of brutes, or blind men, or dead men, than of the living that have their sight. A king of men that have many disagreements, is better than a king of beasts that all agree. And yet true knowledge tendeth to concord, and to the surest and constantest obedience.

Object. V. But their chief calumniations are against divines. They say, That divines make a trade of religion; and under pretence of divine laws, and conscience, and ecclesiastical discipline, they subjugate both prince and people to their will, and set up courts which they call ecclesiastical, and keep the people in dependence on their dictates, and teach them to disobey upon pretence that God is against the matter of their obedience; and also by contending for their opinions, or for superiority and domination over one another, they fill kingdoms with quarrels, and break them into sects and factions, and are the chief disturbers of the public peace.[91]

Answ. We cannot deny that carnal, ignorant, worldly, proud, unholy pastors, have been and are the great calamity of the churches: but that is no more disgrace to their office, or to divinity, than it is to philosophy or reason, that philosophers have been ignorant, erroneous, divided, and contentious; nor than it is to government, that kings and other rulers have been imperfect, bad, contentious, and filled the world with wars and bloodshed. Nay, I rather think that this is a proof of the excellency of divinity: as the reason of the aforesaid imperfections and faultiness of philosophers and rulers, is because that philosophy and government are things so excellent, that the corrupt, imperfect nature of man, will not reach so high, as to qualify any man to manage them, otherwise than with great defectiveness; so also divinity, and the pastoral office, are things so excellent and sublime, that the nature of lapsed man will not reach to a capacity of being perfect in them. So that the faultiness of the nature of man, compared with the excellency of the things to be known and practised by divines, is the cause of all these faults that they complain of; and nature's vitiosity, if any thing, must be blamed. Certainly, the pastoral office hath men as free from ignorance, worldliness, pride, and unquietness, as any calling in the world. To charge the faults of nature upon that profession, which only discovereth, but never caused them, yea, which would heal them, if they are to be healed on earth, judge whether this dealing be not foolish and injurious, and what will be the consequents if such unreasonable persons may be heard. And therefore, though leviathan and his spawn, among all that is good, bring down divines, and the zealots for democracy have gloried of their new forms of commonwealths, as inconsistent with a clergy, their glory is their shame to all but infidels. Let them help us to take down and cure the ignorance, pride, carnality, worldliness, and contentiousness of the clergy, and we will be thankful to them; but to quarrel with the best of men for the common pravity of nature, and to reproach the most excellent science and function, because depraved nature cannot attain or manage them in perfection, this is but to play the professed enemies of mankind.

Object. VI. These atheists or infidels also do spit their venom against christianity and godliness itself, and would make princes believe, that the principles of it are contrary to their interest, and to government and peace: and they fetch their cavils, 1. From the Scripture's contemptuous expressions of worldly wealth and greatness. 2. From its prohibition of revenge and maintaining our own right. 3. From the [761]setting it above all human laws; and by its authority and obscurity, filling the minds of men with scrupulosity. 4. From the divisions which religion occasioneth in the world: and, 5. From the testimonies of the several sects against each other. I shall answer them particularly, though but briefly.

Object. I. Say the infidel politicians, How can subjects have honourable thoughts of their superiors, when they believe that to be the word of God, which speaketh so contemptuously of them?[92] As Luke vi. 24, "Woe to you that are rich! for ye have received your consolation." Jam. v. 1-3, "Go to now, ye rich men, weep and howl for your miseries that shall come upon you." Ver. 5, 6, "Ye have lived in pleasure on earth, and been wanton—Ye have condemned and killed the just."—Luke xii. 21. Chap. xvi. the parable of the rich man and Lazarus, is spoken to make men think of the rich as miserable, damned creatures. Ezek. xxi. 25, "Thou profane, wicked prince of Israel." Prov. xxv. 5, "Take away the wicked from before the king." Prov. xxix. 12, "If a ruler hearken to lies, all his servants are wicked:" the contempt of greatness is made a part of the christian religion.

Answ. 1. As if there were no difference between the contempt of riches and worldly prosperity, and the contempt of government. He is blind that cannot see that riches and authority are not the same: yea, that the overvaluing of riches is the cause of seditions, and the disturbance of governments, when the contempt of them removeth the chief impediments of obedience and peace. 2. And may not governors be sufficiently honoured, unless they be exempted from the government of God? and unless their sin must go for virtue? and unless their duty, and their account, and the danger of their souls, be treacherously concealed from them? God will not flatter dust and ashes; great and small are alike to him. He is no respecter of persons: when you can save the greatest from death and judgment, then they may be excepted from all those duties which are needful to their preparation. 3. And is it not strange, that God should teach men to contemn the power which he himself ordaineth? and which is his own? Hath he set officers over us, for the work of government, and doth he teach us to despise them? There is no show of any such thing in Scripture: there are no principles in the world that highlier advance and honour magistracy, than the christian principles, unless you will make gods of them, as the Roman senate did of the Antonines, and other emperors.

Object. II. How can there be any government, when men must believe that they must not resist evil, but give place to wrath, and turn the other cheek to him that smiteth them, and give their coat to him that taketh away their cloak, and lend, asking for nothing again? Is not this to let thieves and violent, rapacious men rule all, and have their will, and go unpunished? What use is there then for courts or judges? And when Christ commandeth his disciples, that though the kings of the nations rule over them, and exercise authority, and are called benefactors, yet with them it shall not be so.[93]

Answ. These were the old cavils of Celsus, Porphyry, and Julian; but very impudent. As though love and patience were against peace and government. Christ commandeth nothing in all these words, but that we love our neighbour as ourselves, and love his soul above our wealth, and that we do as we would be done by, and use not private revenge, and take not up the magistrate's work: and is this doctrine against government? It is not magistrates, but ministers and private christians, whom he commandeth not to resist evil, and not to exercise lordship, as the civil rulers do. When it will do more hurt to the soul of another, than the benefit amounteth to, we must not seek our own right by law, nor must private men revenge themselves. All law-suits, and contentions, and hurting of others, which are inconsistent with loving them as ourselves, are forbidden in the gospel. And when was government ever disturbed by such principles and practices as these? Nay, when was it disturbed but for want of these? When was there any sedition, rebellion, or unlawful wars, but through self-love, and love of earthly things, and want of love to one another? How easily might princes rule men, that are thus ruled by love and patience!

Object. III. Christianity teacheth men to obey the Scriptures before their governors, and to obey no law that is contrary to the Bible; and when the Bible is so large, and hath so many passages hard to be understood, and easily perverted, some of these will be always interpreted against the laws of men; and then they are taught to fear no man against God, and to endure any pains or death, and to be unmoved by all the penalties which should enforce obedience; and to rejoice in this as a blessed martyrdom, to the face of kings; and those that punish them, are reproached as persecutors, and threatened with damnation, and made the vilest men on earth, and represented odious to all.[94]

Answ. The sum of all this objection is, That there is a God. For if that be not denied, no man can deny that he is the Universal Governor of the world; and that he hath his proper laws and judgment, and rewards and punishments, or that magistrates are his ministers, and have no power but from him; and consequently, that the commands, and threats, and promises of God, are a thousand-fold more to be regarded, than those of men.[95] He is a beast, and not a man, that feareth not God more than man, and that feareth not hell more than bodily sufferings: and for the Scriptures, 1. Are they any harder to be understood than the law of nature itself? Surely the characters of the will of God *in natura rerum,* are much more obscure than in the Scriptures. Hath God sent so great a messenger from heaven, to open to mankind the mysteries of his kingdom, and tell them what is in the other world, and bring life and immortality to light, and yet shall his revelation be accused as more obscure than nature itself is? If an angel had been sent from heaven to any of these infidels [762]by name, to tell them but the same that Scripture telleth us, sure they would not have reproached his message with such accusations. 2. And are not the laws of the land about smaller matters, more voluminous and difficult? And shall that be made a reproach to government? And for misinterpretation, it is the fault of human nature, that is ignorant and rash, and not of the Scriptures. Will you tell God, that you will not obey him, unless he will make his laws so, as no man can misinterpret them? When or where were there ever such laws? God will be God, and Judge of the world, whether you will or not; and he will not be an underling to men, nor set their laws above his own, to avoid your accusations. If there be another life of joy or misery, it is necessary that there be laws according to which those rewards and punishments are to be adjudged. And if rulers oppose those who are appointed to promote obedience to them, they must do it at their perils; for God will render to all according to their works.

Object. IV. Doth not experience tell the world, that christianity every where causeth divisions, and sets the world together by the ears? What a multitude of sects are there among us at this day; and every one thinketh that his salvation lieth upon his opinion! And how can princes govern men of so contrary minds, when the pleasing of one party is the losing of the rest? We have long seen that church divisions shake the safety of the state. If it were not that few that are called christians are such indeed, and serious in the religion which themselves profess, there were no quietness to be expected; for those that are most serious, are so full of scruples, and have consciences still objecting something or other against their obedience, and are so obstinate in their way, as thinking it is for their salvation, that all ages and nations have been fain to govern them by force as beasts, which they have called persecution.[96]

Answ. 1. There is no doctrine in the world so much for love, and peace, and concord as the doctrine of Christ is. What doth it so much urge and frequently inculcate? What doth it contain but love and peace from end to end? Love is the sum and end of the gospel, and the fulfilling of the law. To love God above all, and our neighbours as ourselves, and to do as we would be done by, is the epitome of the doctrine of Christ and his apostles. 2. And therefore christianity is only the occasion, and not the cause of the divisions of the earth. It is men's blindness and passions and carnal interests rebelling against the laws of God, which is the make-bate of the world, and filleth it with strife. The wisdom from above is first pure, then peaceable, gentle, easy to be entreated, full of mercy and good fruits; it blesseth the peace-makers and the meek. But it is the rebellious wisdom from beneath, that is earthly, sensual, and devilish, which causeth envy and strife, and thereby confusion and every evil work, James iii. 15-17; Matt. v. 6-8. So that the true, genuine christian is the best subject and peaceablest man on earth. But seriousness is not enough to make a christian; a man may be passionately serious in an error; understanding must lead and seriousness follow. To be zealous in error is not to be zealous in christianity; for the error is contrary to christian verity. 3. As I said before, it is a testimony of the excellency of religion that it thus occasioneth contention. Dogs and swine do not contend for crowns and kingdoms, nor for sumptuous houses or apparel; nor do infants trouble the world or themselves with metaphysical, or logical, or mathematical disputes; idiots do not molest the world with controversies, nor fall thereby into sects and parties. Nor yet do wise and learned persons contend about chaff, or dust, or trifles. But as excellent things are matter of search, so are they matter of controversy, to the most excellent wits. The hypocritical christians that you speak of, who make God and their salvation give place to the unjust commands of men, are indeed no christians, as not taking Christ for their sovereign Lord; and it is not in any true honour of magistracy that they are so ductile, and will do any thing, but it is for themselves, and their carnal interest; and when that interest requireth it, they will betray their governors, as infidels will do. If you can reduce all the world to be infants, or idiots, or brutes, yea, or infidels, they will then trouble the state with no contentions for religion or matters of salvation. But if the governed must be brutified, what will the governors be? 4. All true christians are agreed in the substance of their religion; there is no division among them about the necessary points of faith or duty. Their agreement is far greater than their disagreement; which is but about some smaller matters, where differences are tolerable; therefore they may all be governed without any such violence as you mention. If the common articles of faith, and precepts of christian duty, be maintained, then that is upheld which all agree in; and rulers will not find it needful to oppress every party or opinion save one, among them that hold the common truths. Wise and sober christians lay not men's salvation upon every such controversy; nor do they hold or manage them unpeaceably to the wrong of church or state, nor with the violation of charity, peace, or justice. 5. Is there any of the sciences which afford not matter of controversy? If the laws of the land did yield no matter of controversy, lawyers and judges would have less of that work than now they have. And was there not greater diversity of opinions and worship among the heathens than ever was among christians? What a multitude of sects of philosophers and religions had they! And what a multitude of gods had they to worship! And the number of them still increased as oft as the senate pleased to make a god of the better sort of their emperors when they were dead. Indeed one emperor, (of the religion of some of these objectors,) Heliogabalus, bestirred himself with all his power to have reduced all religion to unity, that is, he would have all the worship brought to his god to whom he had been priest: saith Lampridius in his life, *Dicebat Judæorum et Samaritanorum religiones et christianam devotionem, illuc transferendam, &c.* And therefore he robbed, and maimed, and destroyed the other gods, *id agens ne quis Romæ Deus nisi Heliogabalus coleretur.* But as the effect of his monstrous, abominable filthiness of life was to be thrust into a [763]privy, killed, and dragged about the streets, and drowned in the Tiber; so the effect of his desired unity, was to bring that one god or temple into contempt, whereto he would confine all worship. The differences among christians are nothing in comparison of the differences among heathens.[97] The truth is, religion is such an illustrious, noble thing, that dissensions about it, like spots in the moon, are much more noted by the world, than about any lower, common matters. Men may raise controversies in philosophy, physic, astronomy, chronology, and yet it maketh no such noise, nor causeth much offence or hatred in the world; but the devil and corrupted nature have such an enmity against religion, that they are glad to pick any quarrel against it, and blame it for the imperfections of all that learn it, and should practise it. As if grammar should be accused for every error or fault that the boys are guilty of in learning it; or the law were to be accused for all the differences of lawyers, or contentions of the people; or physic were to be accused for all the differences or errors of physicians; or meat and drink were culpable because of men's excesses and diseases. There is no doctrine or practice in the world, by which true unity and concord can be maintained, but by seriousness in the true religion. And when all contention cometh for want of religion, it is impudence to blame religion for it, which is the only cure. If rulers will protect all that agree in that which is justly to be called the christian religion, both for doctrine and practice; and about their small and tolerable differences, will use no other violence but only to compel them to live in peace, and to suppress the seditious, and those that abuse and injure government or one another; they will find that christianity tendeth not to divisions, nor to the hinderance or disturbance of government or peace. It is passion, and pride, and selfishness that doth this, and not religion; therefore let these and not religion be restrained. But if they will resolve to suffer none to live in peace, but those that in every punctilio are all of one opinion, they must have but one subject that is sincere in his religion, (for no two will be in every thing of the same apprehension, no more than of the same complexion,) and all the rest must be worldly hypocrites, that while they are heartily true to no religion, will profess themselves of any religion which will serve their present turns; and these nominal christians will be ready to betray their rulers, or do any mischief which their carnal interest requireth.[98]

Object. V. What witness need we more than their own accusations of one another?[99] For the papists, how many volumes have the protestants written against them as enemies to all civil government; alleging even the decrees of their general councils, as Later. sub Innoc. III. Can. 3. And for the protestants, they are as deeply charged by the papists, as you may see in the "Image of both Churches," and "Philanax Anglicus," and abundance more. For Calvin and the presbyterians and puritans, let the prelates tell you how peaceable they are. And the papists and puritans say that the prelatists are of the same mind, and only for their own ends pretend to greater loyalty than others. There are no two among them more famous for defending government, than Hooker and Bilson. And what Hooker saith for popular power, his first and eighth books abundantly testify: and even Bishop Bilson himself defendeth the French and German protestant wars; and you may judge of his loyal doctrine by these words, p. 520, "Of Christian Subjection:" "If a prince should go about to subject his kingdom to a foreign realm, or change the form of the commonwealth from impery to tyranny, or neglect the laws established by common consent of prince and people, to execute his own pleasure; in these and other cases which might be named, if the nobles and commons join together to defend their ancient and accustomed liberty, regimen, and laws, they may not well be counted rebels."[100]

Answ. 1. If it be clear that christianity as to its principles, is more for love, and concord, and subjection, than any other rational doctrine in the world, then if any sect of christians shall indeed be found to contradict these principles, so far they contradict christianity: and will you blame religion because men contradict it? or blame Christ's doctrine because men disobey it? Indeed every sect that hath something of its own to make a sect, besides christian religion, which maketh men mere christians, may easily be guilty of such error as will corrupt the christian religion. And as a sect, they have a divided interest which may tempt them to dividing principles; but none more condemn such divisions than Christ. 2. And indeed, though a christian as such is a credible witness; yet a sect or faction as such, doth use to possess men with such an envious, calumniating disposition, that they are little to be believed when they accuse each other! This factious zeal is not from above, but is earthly, sensual, and devilish; and therefore where this is, no wonder if there be strife, and false accusing, and confusion, and every evil work. But as these are no competent witnesses, so whether or no they are favoured by Christ, you may judge if you will read but those three chapters, Matt. v. Rom. xii. James iii. I may say here as Bishop Bilson in the place which is accused, p. 521. "IT IS EASY FOR A RUNNING AND RANGING HEAD TO SIT AT HOME IN HIS CHAMBER AND CALL MEN REBELS, HIMSELF BEING THE RANKEST." 3. For the papists I can justify them from your accusation, [764]so far as they are christians; but as they are papists let him justify them that can. Indeed usurpation of government is the very essence of popery; for

41

which all other christians blame them; and therefore there is small reason that christianity should be accused for them. 4. And for the protestants, both episcopal and disciplinarians, the sober and moderate of them speak of one another in no such language as you pretend. For the episcopal, I know of none but railing papists, that accuse them universally of any doctrines of rebellion: and for the practices of some particular men, it is not to be alleged against their doctrine. Do you think that Queen Elizabeth, to whom Bishop Bilson's book was dedicated, or King Charles, to whom Mr. Hooker's book was dedicated, took either of them to be teachers of rebellion? It is not every different opinion in politics that proveth men to be against subjection. He that can read such a book as Bilson's for "Christian Subjection against Antichristian Rebellion," and yet deny him to be a teacher of subjection, hath a very hard forehead. For the controversies, I shall say no more of them here, but what I have said before to Mr. Hooker. And as for Calvin and the disciplinarians, or puritans, as they are called, they subscribe all the confessions for magistracy, and take the same oaths of allegiance and supremacy, as others do; and they plead and write for them: so that for my part I know not of any difference in their doctrine. Hear what Bishop Andrews saith, (who was no rebel,) in his "Tortura Torti," p. 379, 380. *Calvinus autem ut papam regem; ita regem papam non probavit; neque nos quod in papa detestamur, in rege approbamus; at et ille nobiscum, et nos cum illo sentimus, easdem esse in ecclesia christiana regis Jacobi partes, quæ Josiæ fuerunt in Judaica; nec nos ultra quicquam fieri ambimus—*: that is, "But Calvin neither liked a pope-king, nor a king-pope; nor do we approve of that in the king, which we detest in the pope. But he with us, and we with him, do judge, that King James hath as much to do in the christian church, as Josias had in the Jewish church; and we go not about to get any more." And after, *Sub primatus nomine, papatum novum rex non invehit in ecclesiam; sic enim statuit, ut non Aaroni pontifici, ita nec Jeroboamo regi, jus ullum esse conflatum a se vitulum populo proponendi, ut adoret, (id est,) non vel fidei novos articulos, vel cultus divini novas formulas procudendi:* that is, "The king doth not bring into the church a new papacy, under the name of primacy; for thus he judgeth, (or determineth,) that neither Aaron the priest, nor Jeroboam the king, had any right to propose the calf which they had made, to the people to be adored; that is, neither to hammer (or make) new articles of faith, or new forms of divine worship." And p. 379, 380. *Quos vero puritanos appellat, si regium primatum detestantur, detestandi ipsi. Profitentur enim, subscribunt, jurant indies; sed et illi quod faciunt ingenue faciunt, et societatem in hoc Torti, ipsumque adeo Tortum, tanquam mendacem hominem, (et alibi de aliis, et hic de se,) ac sycophantem egregium detestantur.* that is, "And for those he calleth puritans, if they detest the king's supremacy, they are to be detested; for they daily profess, subscribe, and swear to it; and what they do, they do ingenuously; and they detest the society of Tortus in this, and Tortus himself, as a lying man, (elsewhere of others, and here of themselves,) and an egregious sycophant." By these testimonies judge what protestants think of one another in point of loyalty.

5. And why are not all the other christians taken into your enumeration? the Armenians, Abassins, and all the Greek churches? whom the papists so frequently reproach as flatterers or servile, because they still gave so much to their emperors. Have you any pretence for your accusation as against them? Unless perhaps from the tumults which Alexandria in its greatness was much addicted to, which is nothing to the doctrine of christianity, nor to the practice of all the rest.

Christianity is most for loyalty and subjection.

Having answered these cavils of the late atheistical or infidel politicians, I shall next show, though briefly, yet by plentiful evidence, that christianity and true godliness is the greatest strength of government, and bond of subjection, and means of peace, that ever was revealed to the world: which will appear in all these evidences following.

1. Christianity teacheth men to take the higher powers as ordained of God, and to obey them as God's ministers or officers, having an authority derived immediately from God; so that it advanceth the magistrate as God's officer, as much higher than infidels advance him, (who fetch his power no higher than force or choice,) as a

servant of God is above a servant of men; which is more than a man is above a dog.[101]

2. Christianity telleth us that our obedience to magistrates is God's own command, and so that we must obey him by obeying them. And as obedience to a constable is more procured by the king's laws than by his own commands, so obedience to a king is far more effectually procured by God's laws than by his own. If God be more above a king, than a king is above a worm, the command of God must be a more powerful obligation upon every understanding person, than the king's. And what greater advantage can a king have in governing, than to have subjects whose consciences do feel themselves bound by God himself, to obey the king and all his officers.

Object. But this is still with exception, if it be not in things forbidden of God; and the subjects are made judges whether it be so or no.

Answ. And woe to that man that grudgeth that God must be obeyed before him; and would be himself a god to be obeyed in things which God is against! The subjects are made no public judges, but private discerners of their duties; and so you make them yourselves: or else they must not judge whether the king or a usurper were to be obeyed; or whether the word of a king or of a constable, if they be contradictory, is to be preferred. To judge what we must choose or refuse is proper to a rational creature: even brutes themselves will do something like it by instinct of nature, and will not do all things according to your will. You would have us obey a justice of peace no further than our loyalty to the king will give leave: and therefore there is greater reason that we should obey the higher powers no further than our loyalty to God will give leave.[102] But if men pretend God's commands for any thing which he commandeth not, magistrates bear not the sword in vain, and subjects are commanded by God not to resist. If they punish them rightfully, God will bear the rulers out in it; if they punish them wrongfully or persecute them for well doing, God will severely punish them, who so wronged his subjects, [765]and abused the authority which he committed to their trust.

3. The christian religion bindeth subjects to obedience upon sorer penalties than magistrates can inflict; even upon pain of God's displeasure, and everlasting damnation, Rom. xiii. 2, 3. And how great a help this is to government it is so easy to discern, that the simpler sort of atheists do persuade themselves, that kings devised religion to keep people in obedience with the fears of hell. Take away the fears of the life to come, and the punishment of God in hell upon the wicked, and the world will be turned into worse than a den of serpents and wild beasts; adulteries, and murders, and poisoning kings, and all abomination, will be freely committed, which wit or power can think to cover or bear out! Who will trust that man that believeth not that God doth judge and punish?

4. The christian religion doth encourage obedience and peace with the promise of the reward of endless happiness (*cæteris paribus*); heaven is more than any prince can give. If that will not move men, there is no greater thing to move them. Atheism and infidelity have no such motives.

5. Christianity teacheth subjects to obey not only good rulers but bad ones, even heathens themselves, and not to resist when we cannot obey. Whereas among heathens, princes ruled no longer than they pleased the soldiers or the people; so that Lampridius marvelled that Heliogabalus was no sooner butchered, but suffered to reign three years: *Mirum fortasse cuipiam videatur Constantine venerabilis, quod hæc clades quam retuli loco principum fuerit; et quidem prope triennio, ita ut nemo inventus fuerit qui istum a gubernaculis Romanæ majestatis abduceret, cum Neroni, Vitellio, Caligulæ cæterisque hujusmodi nunquam tyrannicida defuerit.*[103]

6. Christianity and godliness do not only restrain the outward acts, but rule the very hearts, and lay a charge upon the thoughts, which the power of princes cannot reach. It forbiddeth to curse the king in our bedchamber, or to have a thought or desire of evil against him; it quencheth the first sparks of disloyalty and disorder; and

the rule of the outward man followeth the ordering of the heart; and therefore atheism, which leaveth the heart free and open to all desires and designs of rebellion, doth kindle that fire in the minds of men, which government cannot quench; it corrupteth the fountain; it breaketh the spring that should set all a going; it poisoneth the heart of commonwealths.[104]

7. Christianity and godliness teach men patience, that it may not seem strange to them to bear the cross, and suffer injuries from high and low; and therefore that impatience which is the beginning of all rebellion being repressed, it stayeth the distemper from going any further.

8. Christianity teacheth men self-denial as a great part of their religion;[105] and when selfishness is mortified, there is nothing left to be a principle of rebellion against God or our superiors. Selfishness is the very predominant principle of the ungodly; it is only for themselves that they obey when they do obey; no wonder therefore if the author of Leviathan allow men to do any thing when the saving of themselves requireth it. And so many selfish persons as there be in a kingdom, so many several interests are first sought, which for the most part stand cross to the interests of others: the godly have all one common centre; they unite in God, and therefore may be kept in concord; for God's will is a thing that may be fulfilled by all as well as one; but the selfish and ungodly are every one his own centre, and have no common centre to unite in, their interests being ordinarily cross and inconsistent.

9. Christianity teacheth men by most effectual arguments, to set light by the riches and honours of the world, and not to strive for superiority; but to mind higher things, and lay up our treasure in a better world, and to condescend to men of low degree. It forbiddeth men to exalt themselves lest they be brought low; and commandeth them to humble themselves that God may exalt them; and he that knoweth not that pride and covetousness are the great disquieters of the world, and the cause of contentions, and the ruin of states, knoweth nothing of these matters. Therefore if it were but by the great urging of humility and heavenly-mindedness, and the strict condemning of ambition and earthly-mindedness, christianity and godliness must needs be the greatest preservers of government, and of order, peace, and quietness in the world.[106]

10. Christianity teacheth men to live in the love of God and man. It maketh love the very heart, and life, and sum, and end of all other duties of religion. Faith itself is but the bellows to kindle in us the sacred flames of love. Love is the end of the gospel, and the fulfilling of the law. To love all saints with a special love, even with a pure heart and fervently, and to love all men heartily with a common love; to love our neighbour as ourselves; and to love our very enemies; this is the life which Christ requireth, upon the penalty of damnation; and if love thus prevail, what should disturb the government, peace, or order of the world?

11. Christianity teacheth men to be exact in justice, distributive and commutative; and to do to others as we would they should do to us: and where this is followed kings and states will have little to molest them, when *gens sine justitia est sine remige navis in unda.*

12. Christianity teacheth men to do good to all men as far as we are able, and to abound in good works, as that for which we are redeemed and new made; and if men will set themselves wholly to do good, and be hurtful and injurious to none, how easy will it be to govern such!

13. Christianity teacheth men to forbear and to forgive, as ever they will be forgiven of God, and the strong to bear the infirmities of the weak, and not to please themselves, but one another to their edification; not to be censorious, harsh, or cruel, nor to place the kingdom of God in meats, and drinks, and days, but in righteousness, peace, and joy in the Holy Ghost; to bear one another's burdens, and to restore them with the spirit of meekness that are overtaken in a fault, and to be peaceable, gentle, easy to be entreated, full of mercy and good fruits, without partiality and hypocrisy,

and to speak evil of no man; and where this is obeyed, how quietly and easily may princes govern![107]

14. Christianity setteth before us the perfectest pattern of all this humility, meekness, contempt of worldly wealth and greatness, self-denial and obedience, that ever was given in the world. The eternal Son of God incarnate, would condescend to earth and flesh, and would obey his superiors after the flesh, in the repute of the world; and would pay [766]tribute, and never be drawn to any contempt of the governors of the world, though he suffered death under the false accusation of it. He that is a christian, endeavoureth to imitate his Lord: and can the imitation of Christ, or of his peaceable apostles, be injurious to governors? Could the world but lay by their serpentine enmity against the holy doctrine and practice of christianity, and not take themselves engaged to persecute it, nor dash themselves in pieces on the stone which they should build upon, nor by striving against it provoke it to fall on them and grind them to powder, they never need to complain of disturbances by christianity or godliness.[108]

15. Christianity and true godliness containeth, not only all those precepts that tend to peace and order in the world, but also strength, and willingness, and holy dispositions for the practising of such precepts. Other teachers can speak but to the ears, but Christ doth write his laws upon the heart; so that he maketh them such as he commandeth them to be: only this is the remnant of our unhappiness, that while he is performing the cure on us, we retain a remnant of our old diseases, and so his work is yet imperfect: and as sin in strength is it that setteth on fire the course of nature, so the relics of it will make some disturbance in the world, according to its degree; but nothing is more sure than that the godliest christian is the most orderly and loyal subject, and the best member (according to his parts and power) in the commonwealth; and that sin is the cause, and holiness the cure of all the disorders and calamities of the world.

16. Lastly, Consult with experience itself, and you will find, that all this which I have spoken, hath been ordinarily verified.[109] What heathenism tendeth to, you may see even in the Roman government (for there you will confess it was at the best). To read of the tumults, the cruelties, the popular unconstancy, faction, and injustice; how rudely the soldiers made their emperors, and how easily and barbarously they murdered them, and how few of them from the days of Christ till Constantine did die the common death of all men, and escape the hands of those that were their subjects; I think this will satisfy you, whither men's enmity to christianity tendeth: and then to observe how suddenly the case was altered, as soon as the emperors and subjects became christian (till in the declining of the Greek empire, some officers and courtiers who aspired to the crown did murder the emperors): and further to observe, that the rebellious doctrines and practices against governors, have been all introduced by factions and heresies, which forsook christianity so far before they incurred such guilt; and that it is either papal usurpation (which is in its nature an enemy to princes) that hath deposed and trampled upon emperors and kings, or else some mad enthusiastics that overrun religion and their wits, that at Munster, (and in England some lately,) by the advantage of their prosperity, have dared to do violence against sovereignty; but the more any men were christians and truly godly, the more they detested all such things; all this will tell you that the most serious and religious christians, are the best members of the civil societies upon earth.

II. Having done with the first part of my last direction, I shall say but this little of the second; let christians see that they be christians indeed, and abuse not that which is most excellent to be a cloak to that which is most vile. 1. In reading politics, swallow not all that every author writeth in conformity to the polity that he liveth under. What perverse things shall you read in the popish politics (Contzen, and abundance such)! What usurpation on principalities, and cruelties to christians, under the pretence of defending the church, and suppressing heresies!

2. Take heed in reading history that you suffer not the spirit of your author to infect you with any of that partiality which he expresseth to the cause which he espouseth. Consider in what times and places all your authors lived, and read them accordingly with the just allowance. The name of liberty was so precious, and the name of a king so odious to the Romans, Athenians, &c., that it is no wonder if their historians be unfriendly unto kings.

3. Abuse not learning itself to lift you up with self-conceitedness against governors! Learned men may be ignorant of polity; or at least unexperienced, and almost as unfit to judge, as of matters of war or navigation.

4. Take heed of giving the magistrate's power to the clergy, and setting up secular, coercive power under the name of the power of the keys: and it had been happy for the church if God had persuaded magistrates in all ages to have kept the sword in their own hands, and not have put it into the clergy's hands, to fulfil their wills by:[110] for, 1. By this means the clergy had escaped the odium of usurpation and domineering, by which atheistical politicians would make religion odious to magistrates for their sakes. 2. And by this means greater unity had been preserved in the church, while one faction is not armed with the sword to tread down the rest: for if divines contend only by dint of argument, when they have talked themselves and others aweary they will have done; but when they go to it with dint of sword, it so ill becometh them, that it seldom doth good, but the party often that trusteth least to their reason, must destroy the other, and make their cause good by iron arguments. 3. And then the Romish clergy had not been armed against princes to the terrible concussions of the christian world, which histories at large relate, if princes had not first lent them the sword which they turned against them. 4. And then church discipline would have been better understood, and have been more effectual; which is corrupted and turned to another thing, and so cast out, when the sword is used instead of the keys, under pretence of making it effectual: none but consenters are capable of church communion: no man can be a christian, or godly, or saved [767]against his will; and therefore consenters and volunteers only are capable of church discipline: as a sword will not make a sermon effectual, no more will it make discipline effectual: which is but the management of God's word to work upon the conscience. So far as men are to be driven by the sword to the use of means, or restrained from offering injury to religion, the magistrate himself is fittest to do it. It is noted by historians as the dishonour of Cyril of Alexandria, (though a famous bishop,) that he was the first bishop that like a magistrate used the sword there, and used violence against heretics and dissenters.

5. Above all, abuse not the name of religion for the resistance of your lawful governors: religion must be defended and propagated by no irreligious means. It is easy before you are aware, to catch the fever of such a passionate zeal as James and John had, when they would have had fire from heaven to consume the refusers and resisters of the gospel: and then you will think that any thing almost is lawful, which doth but seem necessary to the prosperity of religion. But no means but those of God's allowance do use to prosper, or bring home that which men expect: they may seem to do wonders for awhile, but they come to nothing in the latter end, and spoil the work, and leave all worse than it was before.

Direct. XL. Take heed of mistaking the nature of that liberty of the people, which is truly valuable and desirable, and of contending for an undesirable liberty in its stead.[111] It is desirable to have liberty to do good, and to possess our own, and enjoy God's mercies, and live in peace: but it is not desirable to have liberty to sin, and abuse one another, and hinder the gospel, and contemn our governors. Some mistake liberty for government itself; and think it is the people's liberty to be governors: and some mistake liberty for an exemption from government, and think they are most free, when they are most ungoverned, and may do what they list: but this is a misery, and not a mercy, and therefore was never purchased for us by Christ. Many desire servitude and calamity under the name of liberty: *optima est reipublicæ forma,* saith

46

Seneca, *ubi nulla libertas deest, nisi licentia pereundi.* As Mr. R. Hooker saith, lib. viii. p. 195, "I am not of opinion, that simply in kings the most, but the best limited, power is best, both for them and the people: the most limited is that which may deal in fewest things: the best, that which in dealing is tied to the soundest, perfectest, and most indifferent rule, which rule is the law: I mean not only the law of nature and of God, but the national law consonant thereunto: happier that people whose law is their king in the greatest things, than that whose king is himself their law."

Yet no doubt but the lawgivers are as such, above the law as an authoritative instrument of government, but under it as a man is under the obligation of his own consent and word: it ruleth subjects in the former sense; it bindeth the *summam potestatem* in the latter.

Direct. XLI. When you have done all that you can in just obedience, look for your reward from God alone. Let it satisfy you that he knoweth and approveth your sincerity. You make it a holy work if you do it to please God; and you will be fixed and constant, if you take heaven for your reward (which is enough, and will not fail you); but you make it but a selfish, carnal work, if you do it only to please your governors, or get preferment, or escape some hurt which they may do you, and are subject only in flattery, or for fear of wrath, and not for conscience sake. And such obedience is uncertain and unconstant; for when you fail of your hopes, or think rulers deal unjustly or unthankfully with you, your subjection will be turned into passionate desires of revenge. Remember still the example of your Saviour, who suffered death as an enemy to Cæsar, when he had never failed of his duty so much as in one thought or word. And are you better than your Lord and Master? If God be all to you, and you have laid up all your hopes in heaven, it is then but little of your concernment (further than God is concerned in it) whether rulers do use you well or ill, and whether they interpret your actions rightly, or what they take you for, or how they call you; but it is your concernment that God account you loyal, and will judge you so, and justify you from men's accusations of disloyalty, and reward you with more than man can give you. Nothing is well done, especially of so high a nature as this, which is not done for God and heaven, and which the crown of glory is not the motive to.

I have purposely been the larger on this subject, because the times in which we live require it, both for the settling of some, and for the confuting the false accusations of others, who would persuade the world that our doctrine is not what it is; when through the sinful practices of some, the way of truth is evil spoken of, 2 Pet. ii. 2.

Tit. 2. A fuller resolution of the cases, 1. Whether the laws of men do bind the conscience? 2. Especially smaller and penal laws?

The word conscience signifieth either, 1. In general according to the notation of the word, The knowledge of our own matters; *conscire*; the knowledge of ourselves, our duties, our faults, our fears, our hopes, our diseases, &c. 2. Or more limitedly and narrowly, The knowledge of ourselves and our own matters in relation to God's law and judgment; *Judicium hominis de seipso prout subjicitur judicio Dei*, as Amesius defineth it.

2. Conscience is taken, 1. Sometimes for the act of self-knowing. 2. Sometimes for the habit. 3. Sometimes for the faculty, that is, for the intellect itself, as it is a faculty of self-knowing. In all these senses it is taken properly. 4. And sometimes it is used (by custom) improperly, for the person himself, that doth *conscire*; or for his will (another faculty).

3. The conscience may be said to be bound, 1. Subjectively, as the *subjectum quod*, or the faculty obliged. 2. Or objectively, as *conscire*, the act of conscience, is the thing *ad quod*, to which we are obliged.

And upon those necessary distinctions I thus answer to the first question.

Prop. 1. The act or the habit of conscience is not capable of being the subject obliged; no more than any other act or duty: the act or duty is not bound, but the man to the act or duty.

2. The faculty or judgment is not capable of being the object, or *materia ad quam*, the thing to which we are bound. A man is not bound to be a man, or to have an intellect, but is made such.

3. The faculty of conscience (that is, the intellect) is not capable of being the immediate or nearest *subjectum quod*, or subject obliged. The reason is, Because the intellect of itself is not a free-working faculty, but acteth necessarily per *modum naturæ* further than it is under the empire of the will; and therefore intellectual and moral habits are by all men distinguished.

4. All legal or moral obligation falleth directly upon the will only: and so upon the person as a [768]voluntary agent; so that it is proper to say, The will is bound, and The person is bound.

5. Improperly and remotely it may be said, The intellect (or faculty of conscience) is bound, or the tongue, or hand, or foot is bound; as the man is bound to use them.

6. Though it be not proper to say, That the conscience is bound, it is proper to say, That the man is bound to the act and habit of conscience, or to the exercise of the faculty.

7. The common meaning of the phrase, that we are bound in conscience, or that conscience is bound, is that we are bound to a thing by God, or by a divine obligation, and that it is a sin against God to violate it; so that divines use here to take the word conscience in the narrower theological sense, as respect to God's law and judgment doth enter the definition of it.

8. Taking conscience in this narrower sense, to ask, Whether man's law as man's do bind us in conscience, is all one as to ask, Whether man be God.[112]

9. And taking conscience in the large or general sense, to ask, Whether man's laws bind us in conscience subjectively, is to ask, Whether they bind the understanding to know our duty to man? And the tenor of them will show that, while they bind us to an outward act, or from an outward act, it is the man that they bind to or from that act, and that is, as he is a rational, voluntary agent; so that a human obligation is laid upon the man, on the will, and on the intellect, by human laws.

10. And human laws, while they bind us to or from an outward act, do thereby bind us as rational free agents, knowingly to choose or refuse those acts; nor can a law which is a moral instrument any otherwise bind the hand, foot, or tongue, but by first binding us to choose or refuse it knowingly, that is, conscientiously, so that a human bond is certainly laid on the mind, soul, or conscience, taken in the larger sense.

11. Taking conscience in the stricter sense, as including essentially a relation to God's obligation, the full sense of the question plainly is but this, Whether it be a sin against God to break the laws of man? And thus plain men might easily understand it. And to this it must be answered, That it is in two respects a sin against God to break such laws or commands as rulers are authorized by God to make; 1. Because God commandeth us to obey our rulers: therefore he that (so) obeyeth them not, sinneth against a law of God. God obligeth us in general to obey them in all things which they are authorized by him to command; but their law determineth of the particular matter; therefore God obligeth us (in conscience of his law) to obey them in that particular. 2. Because by making them his officers, by his commission he hath given them a certain beam of authority, which is divine as derived from God; therefore they can command us by a power derived from God: therefore to disobey is to sin against a power derived from God. And thus the general case is very plain and easy, How man sinneth against God in disobeying the laws of man, and consequently how (in a tolerable sense of that phrase) it may be said, that man's laws do or do not bind the conscience, (or rather, bind us in point of conscience,) or by a divine obligation. Man is not God; and therefore, as man, of himself can lay no divine obligation on us. But man being God's officer, 1. His own law layeth on us an obligation derivatively divine (for it is no law which hath no obligation, and it is no authoritative obligation which is not derived from God). 2. And God's own law bindeth us to obey man's laws.

Quest. II. But is it a sin to break every penal law of man?

Answ. 1. You must remember that man's law is essentially the signification of man's will; and therefore obligeth no further than it truly signifieth the ruler's will.

2. That it is the act of a power derived from God; and therefore no further bindeth, than it is the exercise of such a power.

3. That it is given, 1. Finally for God's glory and pleasure, and for the common good (comprehending the honour of the ruler and the welfare of the society ruled). And therefore obligeth not when it is, (1.) Against God. (2.) Or against the common good. 2. And it is subordinate to God's own laws, (in nature and Scripture,) and therefore obligeth not to sin, or to the violation of God's law.[113]

4. You must note that laws are made for the government of societies as such universally; and so are fitted to the common case, for the common good. And it is not possible but that a law which prescribeth a duty which by accident is so to the most, should meet with some particular subject to whom the case is so circumstantiated as that the same act would be to him a sin: and to the same man it may be ordinarily a duty, and in an extraordinary case a sin. Thence it is that in some cases (as Lent fasts, marriages, &c.) rulers oft authorize some persons to grant dispensations in some certain cases: and hence it is said, that necessity hath no law.

Hereupon I conclude as followeth:

1. It is no sin to break a law which is no law, as being against God, or not authorized by him, (as of a usurper, &c.) See R. Hooker, Conclus. lib. viii.

2. It is no law so far as it is no signification of the true will of the ruler, whatever the words be: therefore so far it is no sin to break it.

3. The will of the ruler is to be judged of, not only by the words, but by the ends of government, and by the rules of humanity.

4. It being not possible that the ruler in his laws can foresee and name all exceptions, which may occur, it is to be supposed that it is his will that the nature of the thing shall be the notifier of his will, when it cometh to pass; and that if he were present, and this case fell out before him, which the sense and end of the law extendeth not to, he would say, This is an excepted case.

5. There is therefore a wide difference between a general law, and a personal, particular mandate; as of a parent to a child, or a master to a servant; for [769]this latter fully notifieth the will of the ruler in that very case, and to that very person. And therefore it cannot be said that here is any exception, or that it is not his will; but in a universal or general law, it is to be supposed that some particular excepted cases will fall out extraordinarily, though they cannot be named; and that in those cases, the ruler's will dispenseth with it.

6. Sometimes also the ruler doth by the mere neglect of pressing or executing his own laws, permit them to grow obsolete, and out of use; and sometimes he forbeareth the execution of them for some time, or to some sort of persons; and by so doing, doth notify that it was not his will that at such a time, and in such cases, they should oblige. I say not that all remissness of execution is such a sign; but sometimes it is: and the very word of the lawgiver may notify his dispensation or suspending will. As for instance, upon the burning of London, there were many laws (about coming to parish churches, and relief of the poor of the parish, and the like) that the people became uncapable of obeying; and it was to be supposed, that the ruler's will would have been to have excepted such cases if foreseen; and that they did dispense with them when they fell out.

7. Sometimes also the penalty of violating a law, is some such mulct or service, which the ruler intendeth as a commutation for the duty, so that he freely leaveth it to the choice of the subject which he will choose. And then it is no sin to pay the mulct, and omit the action; because it crosseth not the lawgiver's will.

8. Sometimes also the law may command this principally for some men's sake, which so little concerns others, that it should not extend to them at all, were it not lest the liberty of them should be an impediment to the obedience of others, and

49

consequently of the common good. In which case, if those persons so little concerned, do but omit the action secretly, so as to be no scandal or public hurt, it seemeth that they have the implicit consent of the rulers.

9. Sometimes particular duties are commanded with this express exception, "Unless they have just and reasonable impediment." As for coming every Lord's day to church, &c.; which seemeth to imply, that (though in cases where the public good is concerned, the person himself shall not be judge, nor at all as to the penalty, yet that) in actions of an indifferent nature in themselves, this exception is still supposed to be implied, "unless we have just and reasonable impediments," of which in private cases, as to the crime, we may judge.

10. I need not mention the common, natural exceptions: as that laws bind not to a thing when it becometh naturally impossible; or *cessante materia, rel capacitate subjecti obligati*, &c.

11. Laws may change their sense in part by the change of the lawgiver; for the law is not formally to us his law that is dead and was once our ruler, but his that is alive and is now our ruler. If Henry the Eighth make a law about the outward acts of religion, (as for coming to church, &c.) and this remain unrepealed in King Edward's, Queen Mary's, Queen Elizabeth's, King James's days, &c., even till now; as we are not to think that the lawgivers had the same sense and will, so neither that the law hath the same sense and obligation; for if the general words be capable of several senses, we must not take it as binding to us in the sense it was made in, but in the sense of our present lawgivers or rulers, because it is their law.

12. Therefore if a law had a special reason for it at the first making, (as the law for using bows and arrows,) that reason ceasing, we are to suppose the will of the lawgiver to remit the obligation, if he urge not the execution, and renew not the law.

13. By these plain principles many particular difficulties may be easily resolved, which cannot be foreseen and named, e. g. the law against relieving a beggar bindeth not, when he is like to die if he be not relieved; or in such a case as after the burning of London, when there was no parish to bring him to. A law that is but for the ordering of men's charity, (to soul or body, by preaching or alms,) will not disoblige me from the duties of charity themselves, in cases where Scripture or nature proveth them to be imposed by God. A law for fasting will not bind me, when it would be destructive to my body; even on God's sabbaths duties of mercy were to be preferred to rest and sacrifices.

14. If God's own laws must be thus expounded, that When two duties come together, and both cannot be done, the lesser ceaseth at that time to be a duty, and the greater is to be preferred, man's laws must also be necessarily so expounded: and the rather, because man's laws may be contradictory, when God's never are so, rightly understood.

15. Where the subject is to obey, so far he must discern which of the laws inconsistent is to be preferred; but in the magistratical execution, the magistrate or judge must determine.

E. g. One law commandeth that all the needy poor be kept on the parish where they were born or last lived. Another law saith, that nonconformable ministers of the gospel, who take not the Oxford oath, shall not come within five miles of city or corporation, (though they were born there,) or any place where they have been preachers. In case of necessity what shall they do? *Answ.* Whither they shall go for relief, they must discern as well as they can; but whither they shall be carried or sent, the magistrate or constable must discern and judge.

Also whether he shall go with a constable that by one law bringeth him to a place, which by the other law he is forbid on pain of six months' imprisonment in the common gaol to come to? *Answ.* If he be not voluntary in it, it is not his fault: and if one bring him thither by force, and another imprison him for being there, he must patiently suffer it.

50

16. But out of such excepted cases, the laws of our rulers (as the commands of parents) do bind us as is afore explained; and it is a sin against God to violate them.

17. Yea, when the reason of the law reacheth not our particular case and person, yet when we have reason to judge, that it is the ruler's will that all be bound for the sake of some, and the common order and good will be hindered by our exemption, we must obey to our corporal detriment, to avoid the public detriment, and to promote the public good.

[36] Nihil Deo qui omnem mundum hunc regit, acceptius, quam concilia cœcusque nominum quæ civitates appellantur. Cicero.

[37] Grotius de Imper. Sum. Potest. c. i. p. 7, 8. Sunt qui objiciant reges quædam imperare non posse, nisi consensus ordinum accesserit: sed hi non vident quibus in locis id juris est, ibi summum imperium non esse penes reges, sed aut penes ordines, aut certe penes id corpus, quod rex et juncti constituunt, ut Bodinus, Suarezius, Victoria, aliique, aliunde demonstrarunt: certum summum imperium totum, et aliquid imperare non posse, ideo tantum quod alter vetet aut intercedat, plane sunt ἀσύστατα.

[38] So foolish and bad is the multitude too often, that it made Aristippus hold it as probable, that a wise man should not endanger himself for his country, because wisdom is not to be cast away for the commodity of fools. Laert. in Aristip. But a wise man must be wise for others, and not only for himself.

[39] It was one of the Roman laws of the twelve tables, Vendendi filium patri potestas esto. But this law rather giveth the father that power, than declareth it to be naturally in him. Nature alloweth him no other selling of him, than what is for his child's own good.

[40] So p. 23. The same error of the original of power hath Acosta, 1. ii. c. 2. p. 208. with many other Jesuits and papists.

[41] Bishop Andrews in Tortur. Tort. p. 385. Actuos homo non distinguit inter formam, atque authoritatem regiminis; forma de hominibus esse potest: de cœlo semper est authoritas. An rex sit supra leges, Vid. Seb. Fox. lib. ii. de Instit. Reg.

[42] Dion Cass. saith, that when Euphates the philosopher would kill himself, Veniam dederat ei Adrianus citra ignominiam et infamiam, ut cicutam tum propter senectutem, tum etiam propter gravem morbum, bibere possit. In vita Adrian.

[43] Against the people's being the givers of power, by conjoining all their own in one, in church or state, see Mr. D. Cawdry's Review of Mr. Hooker's Survey, p. 154, &c.

[44] So lib. viii. p. 211, 218, 220.

[45] Lib. viii. p. 195. Trita in scholis, neminem sibi imperare posse; neminem sibi legem posse dicere, a qua mutata voluntate nequeat recedere: summum ejus esse imperium qui ordinario jure derogare valeat. Et quibus evincitur jus summæ potestatis non limitari per legem positivum. Hinc et Augustinus dixit imperatorem non esse subjectum legibus suis.—Grotius de Imp. p. 149, 150.

[46] Hanc video sapientissimorum fuisse sententiam. Legem nec hominum ingeniis excogitatam, nec scitum aliquod esse populorum; sed æternum quiddam, quod universum mundum regeret, imperandi prohibendique sapientia. Cicero de Leg.

[47] How considerable a part of England is London! Yet in this convocation, which hath made the new changes in the liturgy and book of ordination, London had not one clerk of their choosing: for being to choose but two, they chose only Mr. Calamy and myself; who were neither of us accepted, or ever there. Now if your opinion be true; Quær. 1. Whether you make not this convocation's decrees to be but counsels to us? 2. Or at least whether the city of London, or the London ministers, be not made free from detriment, as not consenters? You will free them and me, especially from detriment for our not conforming to this convocation's acts as such; upon reasons which I do not own myself, as generally by you laid down.

[48] Potestas maritalis est a Deo: applicatio ejus potestatis ad certam personam ex consensu venit quo tamen ipsum jus non datur. Nam si ex consensu daretur, posset

consensu etiam dissolvi matrimonium, aut conveniri ne maritus fœminæ imperaret. Quod minime verum est. Imperatoria potestas non est penes electores: ergo nec ab ipsis datur; sed ab ipsis tamen certæ personæ applicatur. Jus vitæ et necis non est penes cives antequam in rempublicam coeant. Privatus enim jus vindictæ non habet: ab iisdem tamen applicatur ad cœtum aut personam aliquam. Grotius de Imperio, p. 270.

[49] Greg. Nazianzen cited by Bilson of Subjection, p. 361. Thou reignest together with Christ;-rulest with him; thy sword is from him; thou art the image of God.

[50] Victor. Utic. saith of Victorianus proconsul of Carthage, that even to an Arian persecuting, usurping tyrant, Pro rebus sibi commissis semper fidelissimus habebatur; and the like of Sebastian and others, p. 460.

[51] Mark vii. 10; x. 19.

[52] Lamprid. saith of Alex. Severus that, Amavis literatos homines, vehementer eos etiam reformidans, nequid de se asperum scriberent. Universal. Histor. p. 132. Tiberius bellua luto et sanguine macerata; sui tegendi peritissimus artifex; totus tamen posteritatis oculis patuit, Deo hypocrisim detractione larvæ; plectente.

[53] Matt. xviii. 6; Mark ix. 42; Luke xvii. 2; Jude 7-9.

[54] Sext. Aurel. Victor, de Calig. De quo nescio an decuerit memoriæ prodi, nisi forte quia juvat de principibus nosse omnia, ut improbi saltem famæ metu talia declinent.

[55] They are dangerous passages which Petrarch hath, though a good, learned, and moderate man. Dial. 49. Non tot passim essent domini nec tam late furerent, nisi populi insanirent et cuique civium pro se charior foret res privata quam publica; voluptas quam gloria, pecunia quam libertas, vita quam virtus—Et statim—Et sane si vel unum patria civem bonum habeat, malum dominum diutius non habebit. The meaning is too plain; abundance of the most learned writers have such passages which must be read with caution; though I would draw none to the other extreme. Petrarch's 68 Dial. and 85 Dial. de bono domino, is as smart as the former; but yet speaketh not all that contra reges, which he doth contra dominos. However he says that, Inter regem et tyrannum non discernunt Graii, &c.——So Sir Thomas More in his Poems: Regibus e multis regnum bene qui reget unum: vix tamen unus erit, si tamen unus erit. And that of Senec. Trag. ult. Tantum ut noceat, cupit esse potens.——

[56] Bias interrogatus, quidnam esset difficile? Ferre, inquit, fortiter mutationem rerum in deterius. Laert. p. 55.

[57] Phil. iii. 7, 8, 11, 12.

[58] Univers. Hist. p. 140. Dicas imperatorem orbis Epictetum, Neronem mancipium: irrisum esse summo fastigio, cum servaret dignus, imperaret indignus; nullumque esse malum, quin aliqua boni gutta cordiatus.

[59] Numb. xvi.

[60] Psal. xii. 6, 7; Prov. xvi. 18; xix. 13.

[61] Matt. vii. 1-3.

[62] Object. Si id juris orbis obtineat status religionis erit instabilis; mutato regis animo religio mutabitur. Resp. Unicum hic solatium in Divina est providentia; omnium animos Deus in potestate sua habet; sed speciali quodam modo cor regis in manu Domini. Deus et per bonos et per malos reges opus suum operatur. Interdum tranquillitas, interdum tempestas ecclesiæ utilior. Nempe si pius est qui impetat, si diligens lector sacræ Scripturæ, si assiduus in precibus, si Ecclesiæ Catholicæ reverens, si peritos attente audiens, multum per ilium proficit veritas. Sin distorto est et corrupto judicio, pejus id ipsi cedit quam ecclesiæ. Nam ipsum grave manet judicium regis ecclesiæ, qui ecclesiam inultam non sinet. Grotius de Imper. p. 210. John xviii. 36.

[63] Dicunt Stoici, sapientes non modo liberos esse verum et reges: cum sit regnum imperium nemini obnoxium, quod de sapientibus solis asseritur. Statuere enim oportere principem de bonis et malis; hæc autem malorum scire neminem. Similiter ad

magistratus, et judicia et oratoriam solos illos idoneos, neminemque malorum. Laert. in Zenone.

[64]   Eam rempublicam optimam dicunt Stoici, quæ sit mixta ex regno et populari dominatu, optimorumque potentia. Laert. in Zenone.

[65]   Bad people make bad governors: in most places the people are so wilful and tenacious of their sinful customs, that the best rulers are not able to reform them. Yea many a ruler hath cast off his government, being wearied with mutinous and obstinate people. Plato would not meddle with government in Athens. Quia plebs altis institutis et moribus assueverat. Laert. in Platone. And many other philosophers that were fittest for government, refused it on the same account, through the disobedience of the people.

[66]   Of these things see my propositions of the difference of the magistrate's and pastor's power to Dr. Lud. Moul.

[67]   The Rex sacrorum among the Romans, was debarred from exercising any magistracy. Plut. Rom. Quest. 63.

[68]   See Bilson of Subject. p. 238, 256. Princes only be governors in things and causes ecclesiastical; that is, with the sword. But if you infer, ergo, Bishops be no governors in those things, meaning, no dispensers, guiders, nor directors of those things, your conclusion is larger, &c. So p. 256.

[69]   It was somewhat far that Carolus Magnus went to be actual guide of all in his chapel in reading even in all their stops, as it is at large declared by Abbas Usperg. Chron. pag. 181.

[70]   Bishop Bilson, pag. 313. We grant they must rather hazard their lives, than baptize princes which believe not, or distribute the Lord's mysteries to them that repent not, but give wilful and open signification of impiety, &c. Beda Hist. Eccles. lib. ii. c. 5, telleth us, that Melitus bishop of London, (with Justus,) was banished by the heirs of king Sabereth, because he would not give them the sacrament of the Lord's supper, which they would needs have before they were baptized.

[71]   Bishop Andrews in Tort. Tort. p. 383. Cohibeat Regem Diaconus, si cum indignus sit, idque palam constet, accedat tamen ad sacramentum: cohibeat et medicus si ad noxium quid vel insalubre manum admoveat: cohibeat et equiso inter equitandum adigat equum per locum præruptum, vel solebrosum, cui subsit periculum: etiamne medico? etiamne equisoni suo subjectus rex? Sed de majori potestate loquitur; sed ea, ad rem noxiam procul arcendam. Qua in re charitatis semper potestas est maxima. Here you see what church government is, and how kings are under it, and how not, in Bishop Andrews' sense.

[72]   Bilson, p. 399, saith, The election of bishops in those days belonged to the people, and not the prince, and though Valens by plain force placed Lucius there, yet might the people lawfully reject him as no bishop, and cleave to Peter their pastor.

[73]   Too many particular laws about little matters breed contention. Alex. Severus would have distinguished all orders of men by their apparel: sed hoc Ulpiano, et Paulo displicuit; dicentibus plurimum rixarum fore, si faciles essent homines ad injurias. And the emperor yielded to them. Lamprid. in Alex. Severus. Lipsius, ubi leges multæ, ibi lites multæ et vita moresque pravi. Non multæ leges bonos mores faciunt, sed paucæ fideliter servatæ.

[74]   N. B. Quæ habet Andrews Tort. Tort. p. 310. Quando et apud vos dictio juris exterior, clavis proprie non sit: eamque vos multis sæpe mandatis, qui liacorum in sorte sunt, exortes sane sacri ordinis universi.

[75]   Lege Epist. Caroli Calvi ad Papam inter Hinc mari Rhemensis Epistolas Cont. Papæ Usurpationes. Isidor. Hispal. sent. iii. cap. 51. Cognoscant principes seculi, Deo debere se rationem reddere propter ecclesiam quam a Christo tuendam suspiciunt. Nam sive augeatur pax et disciplina ecclesiæ per fideles principes, sive solvatur, ille ab eis rationem exigit, qui eorum potestati suam ecclesiam credidit. Leo Epist. ad Leonem Imp. Debes incunctantur advertere, regiam potestatem, tibi non solum ad mundi regimen, sed maxime ad ecclesiæ præsidium esse collatam. See the

judgment of Jo. Parisiensis, Franciscus Victoria, and Widdrington in Grot. de Imper. pag. 23. Lege Lud. Molinæi Discourse of the Powers of the Cardinal Chigi.

[76] Perjurii pœna divina exitium, humana dedecus. Cicero. Agesilaus sent thanks to his enemies for their perjury, as making then no question of their overthrow. Perjuri numinis contemptores. Plutarch. Theodosius execrabatur cum legisset superbiam dominantium, præcipue perfidos et ingratos. Paul. Diaconus, 1. 2.

[77] See the instance of loyalty in Mascelzer against his own brother Gildo (a rebel). Paul. Diacon. lib. iii. initio.

[78] Bilson of Subject, p. 236. Princes have no right to call or confirm preachers, but to receive such as be sent of God, and give them liberty for their preaching, and security for their persons: and if princes refuse so to do, God's labourers must go forward with that which is commanded them from heaven; not by disturbing princes from their thrones, nor invading their realms, as your holy father doth, and defendeth he may do; but by mildly submitting themselves to the powers on earth, and meekly suffering for the defence of the truth, what they shall inflict. So he.

[79] Prov. xvi. 7.

[80] Rom. xiii. 1-4; xi. 36.

[81] Si aliquid; jusserit proconsul, aliud jubeat imperator, nunquid dubitatur, illo contempto, illi esse serviendum? Ergo si aliud imperator, aliud jubeat Deus, quid judicatur? Major potestas Deus: da veniam O imperator. August, de Verb. Domin. Matth. Serm. 6.

[82] Vetus est verumque dictum, Miser est imperator cui vera reticentur. Grotius de Imp. p. 245. Principi consule non dulciora, sed optima; is one of Solon's sentences in Laert. de Solon. Therefore it is a horrid villany of the Jesuits, which is expressed in Secret. Instruct. in Arcanis Jesuit. p. 5-8, 11. To indulge great men and princes in those opinions and sins which please them, and to be on that side that their liberty requireth to keep their favour to the society. So Maffæinus, 1. iii. c. 11. in vita ipsius Loyolæ. Alexander Severus so greatly hated flatterers, that Lampridius saith, Siquis caput flexisset aut blandius aliquid dixisset, uti adulator, vel abjiciebatur, si loci ejus qualitas pateretur; vel ridebatur ingeuti cachinno, si ejus dignitas graviori subjacere non posset injuriæ Venit ad Attilam post victoriam Marullus poeta ejus temporis egregius, compositumque in adulationem carmen recitavit: in quo ubi Attila per interpretem cognovit se Deum et Divina stirpe ortum vanissime prædicari, aspernatus sacrilegæ adulationis impudentiam, cum autore carmen exuri jusserat. A qua severitate subinde temperavit, ne scriptores cæteri a laudibus ipsius celebrandis terrerentur. Callimach. Exp. in Attila, p. 353.

[83] Melch. Adam. in vit. Barth. Pitisci.

[84] It was one of the Roman laws of the twelve tables, Justa imperia sunto, iisque cives modeste ac sine recusatione parento.

[85] Eccl. Polit. lib. viii. p. 224.

[86] On second thoughts this case is fullier opened afterward.

[87] Leg. quæ de Grotio post, p. 731.

[88] So Hollingshed maketh parliaments so mighty as to take down the greatest kings, &c.

[89] As Aug. Traj. the Antonines, &c. It is confessed that most historians write much for liberty against tyranny. But the heathens do it much more than the christians.

[90] Langius saith, that in his own hearing, Jodocus Præses Senat. Mechlin. Magna contentione tuebatur, neminem posse vel unius legis intelligentiam consequi, qui quicquam sciret in bonis literis, et addebat, vix esse tres in orbe qui leges Cæsareas intelligerent.

[91] Read Bishop Andrews Tort. Tort., Bishop Bilson of Christian Subjection, Robert Abbot, Jewel, Field, &c., who will fully show that true church power is no way injurious to kings. De regum authoritate, quod ex jure divino non sit Tortus probat:

asseri enim scriptorum sententia communi: at nec omnium, nec optimorum. Andr. Tort. Tort. p. 384.

[92]   Just such occasions as papists bring against the reformers, did the heathens bring against the christians, as you may see in Eunapius in Ædesio. At egregii illi viri et bellicosi confusis perturbatisque rebus omnibus debellasse Deos incruentis quidem, sed ab avaritiæ crimine non puris manibus gloriabantur, sacrilegium et impietatis crimen laudi sibi assumentes, idem postea in sacra loca invexerunt Monachos, sic dictos homines quidem specie, sed vitam turpem porcorum more exigentes, qui in popatulo infinita et infanda scelere committebant, quibus tamen pietatis pars videbatur, sacri loci reverentiam proculcari. O partiality!

[93]   Rom. xii. 17, 19, 20; Luke vi. 28-30; Matt. v. 39-41; Luke xx. 25, 26.

[94]   Le Blanc in his Travels, p. 88, saith of some heathen kings, They are all jealous of our religion, holding, that the christians adore one God, great above the rest, that will not suffer any others; and that he sets a greater esteem and value upon innocent, poor, and simple people, than upon the rich, kings and princes; and that princes had need to preserve to themselves the affections and esteem of their subjects, to reign with greater ease.

[95]   So Bishop Bilson of Subject, p. 243. Princes be supreme; not in respect that all things be subject to their wills, which were plain tyranny, not christian authority: but that all persons within their realms are bound to obey their laws, or abide their pains. So p. 242.

[96]   The differences are oft among the lawyers which set the commonwealth on fire, and then they are charged on divines, e. g. Grotius de Imper. p. 55. Si arma in eos reges sumpta sunt in quos totum populi jus translatum erat, ac qui proinde non precario sed proprio jure imperabant, laudari salva pietate non possunt, quemcunque tandem prætextum aut eventum habuerint. Sin alicubi reges tales fuere qui pactis, sive positivis legibus, et senatus alicujus aut ordinum decretis astringerentur, in hos ut summum imperium non obtinent, arma ex optimatum tanquam superiorum sententia, sumi, justis de causis potuerint. Multi enim reges, etiam qui sanguinis jure succedunt, reges sunt nomine magis quam imperio—Sed fallit imperitos quod illam quotidianam et maxime in oculos incurrentem rerum administrationem, quæ sæpe in optimatum statu penes unum est, ab interiore reipublicæ constitutione non satis discernunt. Quod de regibus dixi, idem multo magis de iis acceptum volo, qui et re et nomine non reges sed principes fuere, h. e. non summi, sed primi. p. 54.

[97]   Jactavit caput inter præcisos phanaticos et genitalia sibi devinxit, &c. Lamprid.

[98]   Eunapius saith of his master Chrysanthius, that when Julian had made him, Primarium pontificem totius illius ditionis, in munere tamen suo non morose ac superbe se gessit; junioribus urgendo haud gravis (sicut plerique omnes in unum consentientes, callide ferventerque faciundum censebant); neque christianis molestus admodum: quippe tanta erat morum in eo lenitas atque simplicitas, ut per Lydiam propemodum ignorata fuerit sacrorum in pristinum restitutio. Eo factum est, ut cum priora aliter cecidissent, nihil innovatum neque mutatio insignis accepta videretur, sed præter expectationem cuncta placide sapirentur. Moderation in a heathen was his benefit.

[99]   Vestra doctrina est, nisi princeps vobis ex animo sit, quantumvis legitimus hæres sit, regno excludi, alium eligi posse. Posse dixi? immo oportere. Hæc Clementina vestra fuit. Bishop Andrews of the Papists, Tort. Tort. p. 327.

[100]   So p. 381, 382. "If others do but stand on their guard to keep their lives and families from the bloody rage of their enemies, seeking to put whole towns and provinces of them to the sword, against all law and reason, and to disturb the kingdoms in the minority of the right governors: or if they defend their ancient and christian liberties, covenanted and agreed on by those princes, to whom they first submitted themselves, and ever since confirmed and allowed by the kings that have succeeded: if in either of these two cases the godly require their right, and offer no

wrong, impugn not their princes, but only save their own lives, you cry, Rebellious heretics, rebellious Calvinists, fury, frenzy, mutiny; and I know not what. You may pursue, depose, and murder princes, when the bishop of Rome biddeth you, and that without breach of duty, law, or conscience, to God or man, as you vaunt, though neither life nor limbs of yours be touched. We may not so much as beseech princes that we may be used like subjects, not like slaves; like men, not like beasts, that we may be convented by laws before judges, not murdered in corners by inquisitors. We may not so much as hide our heads, nor pull our necks out of the greedy jaws of that Romish wolf, but the foam of your unclean mouth is ready to call us by all the names you can devise." So far Bilson.

[101]   Rom. xv. 1-4.

[102]   Bishop Bilson ubi sup. p. 259. As bishops ought to discern which is truth before they teach; so must the people discern who teacheth right before they believe. Pag. 261, 262. Princes as well as others must yield obedience to bishops speaking the word of God; but if bishops pass their commission, and speak beside the word of God, what they list, both prince and people may despise them. See him further, p. 259-262, proving that all have a *judicium discretionis.*

[103]   Cicero saith, that every good man was in his heart, or as much as in him lay, one that killed Cæsar.

[104]   1 Pet. iv. 12.

[105]   Luke xiv. 9, 33.

[106]   Ungebantur reges non per dominum, sed qui cæteris crudeliores existerent, et paulo post ab unctoribus non pro veri examinatione, trucidabantar, aliis electis trucioribus. Gildas de exc. Brit.

[107]   Rom. xiv.; xv. 1; Gal. vi. 1-4; James iii. 15-17; Tit. iii. 2.

[108]   Luke xx. 18; Matt. xxi. 42, 44; Acts iv. 11; 1 Pet. ii. 7, 8; Zech. xii. 3.

[109]   Read the lives of all the philosophers, orators, and famous men of Greece or Rome, and try whether the christians or they were more for monarchy. Arcesilaus regum neminem magnopere coluit: quamobrem legatione ad Antigonum fungens pro patria, nihil obtinuit. Hesich. in Arces. It is one of Thales's sayings in Laert. Quid difficile? Regem vidisse tyrannum senem. Chrysippus videtur aspernator regum modice fuisse. Quod cum tam multa scripserit (libros 705.) nulli unquam regi quicquam adscripserit. Seneca saith (Traged. de Here. fur.) periolously, Victima haud ulla amplior potest, magisque opima mactari Jovi, Quam rex iniquus. Cicero pro Milon. Non se obstrinxit scelere siquis tyrannum occidat, quamvis familiarem. Et 5. Tusc. Nulla nobis cum tyrannis societas est, neque est contra naturam spoliare eum quem honestum est necare. Plura habet similia.

[110]   See Bilson of Subject, p. 525, 526. Proving from Chrysostom, Hilary, Origen, that pastors may use no force or terror, but only persuasion, to recover their wandering sheep. Bilson, ibid. p. 541. Parliaments have been kept by the king and his barons, the clergy wholly excluded, and yet their acts and statutes good: and when the bishops were present, their voices from the Conquest to this day were never negative. By God's law you have nothing to do with making laws for kingdoms and commonwealths: you may teach, you may not command: persuasion is your part, compulsion is the prince's, &c. Thus Bishop Bilson. So p. 358.

[111]   1 Pet. ii. 16; Gal. v. 13; 2 Pet. ii. 19; Gal. iv. 26; 2 Cor. iii. 17.

[112]   Having spoken of this controversy, in my "Life of Faith," as an easy thing, in which I thought we were really agreed, while we seemed to differ, which I called a pitiful case, some brethren (who say nothing against the truth of what I said) are offended at me as speaking too confidently, and calling that so easy which Bishop Sanderson and so many others did make a greater matter of; I retract the words, if they be unsuitable either to the matter or the readers: but as to the matter and the truth of the words, I desire the reader but to consider how easy a case Mr. P. maketh of it, Eccl. Pol. and how heinous a matter he maketh of our supposed dissent: and if after all this it shall appear, that the nonconformists do not at all differ from Hooker,

Bilson, and the generality of the conformists in this point, let him that is willing to be represented as odious and intolerable to rulers and to mankind, for that in which we do not differ, proceed to backbite me for saying that it is a pitiful case; and pretending that we are agreed.

[113] It is not Mr. Humphrey alone that hath written that laws bind not in conscience to obedience which are against the public good. The greatest casuists say the same, excepting the case of scandal: he that would see this in them may choose but these two special authors, Bapt. Fragos. de Regimine Reipublicæ, and Greg. Sayrus in his Clavis Regia, and in them he shall find enough more cited. Though I think some further cautions would make it more satisfactory.

CHAPTER IV.

DIRECTIONS TO LAWYERS ABOUT THEIR DUTY TO GOD.

GENTLEMEN, you need not meet these directions with the usual censures or suspicions, that divines are busying themselves with the matters of your calling, which belong not to them, and which they do not understand; you shall see that I will as much forbear such matters as you can well desire. If your calling be not to be sanctified by serving God in it, [770]and regulating it by his law, it is then neither honourable nor desirable. But if it be, permit me very briefly so far to direct you.[114]

Direct. I. Take the whole frame of polity together, and study each part in its proper place, and know it in its due relation to the rest; that is, understand first the doctrine of polity and laws *in genere*, and next the universal polity and laws of God *in specie*; and then study human polity and laws, as they stand in their due subordination to the polity and laws of God, as the by-laws of corporations do to the general laws of the land.

He that understandeth not what polity and law is *in genere*, is unlike to understand what divine or human polity or law is *in specie*; he that knoweth not what government is, and what a community, and what a politic society is, will hardly know what a commonwealth or church is: and he that knoweth not what a commonwealth is *in genere*, what is its end, and what its constitutive parts, and what the efficient causes, and what a law, and judgment, and execution is, will study but unhappily the constitution or laws of the kingdom which he liveth in.

And he that understandeth not the divine *dominium et imperium*, as founded in creation, (and refounded in redemption,) and man's subjection to his absolute Lord, and the universal laws which he hath given in nature and Scripture to the world, can never have any true understanding of the polity or laws of any kingdom in particular; no more than he can well understand the true state of a corporation, or the power of a mayor, or justice, or constable, who knoweth nothing of the state of the kingdom, or of the king, or of his laws. What ridiculous discourses would such a man make of his local polity or laws! He knoweth nothing worth the knowing, who knoweth not that all kings and states have no power but what is derived from God, and subservient to him; and are all his officers, much more below him, than their justices and officers are to them; and that their laws are of no force against the laws of God, whether of natural or supernatural revelation. And therefore it is most easy to see, that he that will be a good lawyer must first be a divine; and that the atheists that deride or slight divinity, do but play the fools in all their independent broken studies. A man may be a good divine that is no lawyer, but he can be no good lawyer that understandeth not theology. Therefore let the government and laws of God have the first and chiefest place in your studies, and in all your observation and regard.

1. Because it is the ground of human government, and the fountain of man's power and laws.

2. Because the divine polity is also the end of human policy; man's laws being ultimately to promote our obedience to the laws of God, and the honour of his government.

3. Because God's laws are the measure and bound of human laws; against which no man can have power.

4. Because God's rewards and punishments are incomparably more regardable than man's; eternal joy or misery being so much more considerable than temporal peace or suffering; therefore though it be a dishonour to lawyers to be ignorant of languages, history, and other needful parts of learning, yet it is much more their dishonour to be ignorant of the universal government and laws of God.[115]

Direct. II. Be sure that you make not the getting of money to be your principal end in the exercise of your function; but the promoting of justice, for the righting of the just, and the public good; and therein the pleasing of the most righteous God.[116] For your work can be to you no better than your end. A base end doth debase your work. I deny not, but your competent gain and maintenance may be your lower end, but the promoting of justice must be your higher end, and sought before it. The question is not, Whether you seek to live by your calling; for so may the best; nor yet, Whether you intend the promoting of justice; for so may the worst (in some degree). But the question is, Which of these you prefer? and which you first and principally intend? He that looketh chiefly at his worldly gain, must take that gain instead of God's reward, and look for no more than he chiefly intended; for that is formally no good work, which is not intended chiefly to please God, and God doth not reward the servants of the world; nor can any man rationally imagine, that he should reward a man with happiness hereafter, for seeking after riches here. And if you say that you look for no reward but riches, you must look for a punishment worse than poverty; for the neglecting of God and your ultimate end, is a sin that deserveth the privation of all which you neglect; and leaveth not your actions in a state of innocent indifferency.

Direct. III. Be not counsellors or advocates against God, that is, against justice, truth, or innocency. A bad cause would have no patrons, if there were no bad or ignorant lawyers. It is a dear-bought fee, which is got by sinning; especially by such a wilful, aggravated sin, as the deliberate pleading for iniquity, or opposing of the truth.[117] Judas's gain and Ahithophel's counsel will be too hot at last for conscience, and sooner drive them to hang themselves in the review, than afford them any true content: as St. James saith to them that he calleth to weep and howl for their approaching misery, "Your riches are corrupted, and your garments moth-eaten, your gold and silver is cankered, and the rust of them shall be a witness against you, and shall eat your flesh as it were fire: ye have heaped treasure together for the last days." Whatever you say or do against truth, and innocency, and justice, you do it against God himself. And is it not a sad case that among professed christians, there is no cause so bad but can find an advocate for a fee? I speak not against just counsel to a man that hath a bad cause (to tell him it is bad, and persuade him to disown it); nor do I speak against you for pleading against excessive penalties or damages; for so far your cause is good, though the main cause of your client was bad; but he that speaketh or counselleth another for the defence of sin, or the wronging of the innocent, or the defrauding another of his right, and will open his mouth to the injury of the just, for a [771]little money, or for a friend, must try whether that money or friend will save him from the vengeance of the universal Judge (unless faith and true repentance, which will cause confession and restitution, do prevent it).

The Romans called them thieves, that by fraud, or plea, or judgment got unlawful gain, and deprived others of their right.

Lampridius saith of Alexander Severus, *Tanti eum stomachi fuisse in eos judices qui furtorum fama laborassent, etiamsi damnati non essent, ut si eos casu aliquo videret, commotione animi stomachi choleram evomeret, toto vultu inardescente, ita ut nihil posset loqui.* And afterwards, *Severissimus judex contra fures, appellans eosdem quotidianorum scelerum reos, et solos hostes inimicosque reipublicæ.* Adding this instance, *Eum notarium, qui falsum causæ brevem in consilio imperatorio retulisset, incisis digitorum nervis, ita ut nunquam posset scribere, deportavit.* And that he caused Turinus one of his courtiers to be tied in the market-place to a

58

stake, and choked to death with smoke, for taking men's money on pretence of furthering their suits with the emperor; *Præcone dicente, Fumo punitur, qui vendidit fumum.* He strictly prohibited buying of offices, saying, *Necesse est ut qui emit, vendat: Ego vere nin patiar mercatores potestatum: quos si patiar, damnare non possum.* The frowns or favour of man, or the love of money, will prove at last a poor defence against his justice whom by injustice you offend.[118]

The poet could say,

Justum	et	tenacem	propositi	virum,
Non	civium	ardor	prava	jubentium
Non		vultus	instantis	tyranni,

Mente quatit solida:——Horat.

But if men would first be just, it would not be so hard to bring them to do justly; saith Plautus,

| Justa | autem | ab | injustis | petere | insipientia | est: |

Quippe illi iniqui jus ignorant neque tenent.

Direct. IV. Make the cause of the innocent as it were your own; and suffer it not to miscarry through your slothfulness and neglect.[119] He is a lover of money more than justice, that will sweat in the cause of the rich that pay him well, and will slubber over and starve the cause of the poor, because he getteth little by them. Whatever your place obligeth you to do, let it be done diligently and with your might; both in your getting abilities, and in using them. Scævola was wont to say, (ut lib. Pandect. 42. tit. refer.) *Jus civile vigilantibus scriptum est, non dormientibus.* Saith Austin,*Ignorantia judicis plerumque est calamitas innocentis.* And as you look every labourer that you hire should be laborious in your work, and your physician should be diligent in his employment for your health; so is it as just that you be diligent for them whose cause you undertake, and where God who is the lover of justice doth require it.

Direct. V. Be acquainted with the temptations which most endanger you in your place, and go continually armed against them with the true remedies, and with christian faith, and watchfulness, and resolution. You will keep your innocency, and consequently your God, if you see to it that you love nothing better than that which you should keep. No man will chaffer away his commodity for any thing which he judgeth to be worse and less useful to him. Know well how little friends or wealth will do you in comparison of God, and you will not hear them when they speak against God, Luke xiv. 26; xvii. 33. When one of his friends was importunate with P. Rutilius to do him an unjust courtesy, and angrily said, "What use have I of thy friendship, if thou wilt not grant my request?" He answered him, "And what use have I of thy friendship, if for thy sake I must be urged to do unjustly?" It is a grave saying of Plutarch, *Pulchrum quidem est justitia regnum adipisci: pulchrum etiam justitiam anteponere: nam virtus alterum ita illustrem reddidit, ut regno dignus judicaretur; alterum ita magnum ut id contemneret.* Plut. in Lycurg. et Numa. But especially remember who hath said, "What shall it profit a man to win all the world, and lose his soul?" And that temptations surprise you not, be deliberate and take time, and be not too hasty in owning or opposing a cause or person, till you are well informed; as Seneca saith of anger, so say I here, *Dandum semper est tempus: veritatem enim dies aperit. Potest pœna dilata exigi; cum non potest exacta revocari.* It is more than a shame to say, I was mistaken, when you have done another man wrong by your temerity.[120]

[114] Legum mihi placet autoritas; sed earum usus hominum nequitia depravatur: itaque piguit perdiscere, quo inhoneste uti nollem, et honeste vix possem, etsi vellem. Petrarch. in vita sua.

[115] Male se rectum putat, qui regulam summæ rectitudinis ignorat. Ambros. de Offic.

[116] It was an ill time when Petr. Bless. said, "Officium officialium est hodie jura confundere, lites suscitare, transactiones rescindere, dilationes innectere, supprimere veritatem, fovere mendacium, quæstum sequi, æquitatem vendere, inhiare actionibus, versutias concinnare."

[117] Bias fertur in causis orandis summus atque vehementissimus fuisse, bonam tamen in partem dicendi vim exercere solitum. Laert. p. 53. Justum est homines justitiam diligere; non autem justitiam propter homines postponere. Gregor. Reg. Justitia non novit patrem, vel matrem; veritatem novit; personam non novit; Deum imitatur.—Cassian. Plutarch saith, that Callicratidas being offered a great sum of money (of which he had great need to pay his seamen) if he would do an unjust act, refused: to whom saith Cleander his counsellor, "Ego profecto hæc accepissem, si fuissem Callicratidas." He answered, "Ego accepissem, si fuissem Cleander."

[118] Facile est justitiam homini justissimo.

[119] Vix potest negligere, qui novit æquitatem: nec facile erroris vitio fordescit, quem doctrina purgaverit. Cassiodor.

[120] Chilon in Laert. p. 43. (mihi) saith, Sibi non esse conscium in tota vita ingratitudinis: una tamen re se modice moveri, quod cum semel inter amicos illi judicandum esset, neque contra jus agere aliquid vellet, persuaserit amico judicium a se provocaret, ut si nimirum utrumque et legem et amicum servaret. This was his injustice of which he repented.

CHAPTER V.

THE DUTY OF PHYSICIANS.

NEITHER is it my purpose to give any occasion to the learned men of this honourable profession, to say that I intermeddle in the mysteries of their art. I shall only tell them, and that very briefly, what God and conscience will expect from them.

Direct. I. Be sure that the saving of men's lives and health, be first and chiefly in your intention, before any gain or honour of your own. I know you may lawfully have respect both to your maintenance and honour; but in a second place only, as a far less good than the lives of men. If money be your ultimate end, you debase your profession, which, as exercised by you, can be no more to your honour or comfort than your own intention carrieth it. It is more the end than the means that ennobleth or debaseth men; if gain be the thing which you chiefly seek, the matter is not very great (to you) whether you seek it by medicining men or beasts, or by lower means than either of them. To others indeed it may be a very great benefit, whose lives you have been a means to save; but to yourselves it will be no greater than your intention maketh it. If the honouring and pleasing God, and the public good, and the saving of men's lives, be really first and highest in your desires, then it is God that you serve in your profession; otherwise you do but serve yourselves. And take heed lest you here deceive yourselves, by thinking that the good of others is your end, and dearer to you than your gain, because your reason telleth you it is better and ought to be preferred: for God and the public good are not every man's end, that can speak highly of them, and say they should be so. If most of the world do practically prefer their carnal prosperity even before their souls, while they speak [772]of the world as disgracefully as others, and call it vanity; how much more easily may you deceive yourselves, in preferring your gain before men's lives, while your tongue can speak contemptuously of gain!

Direct. II. Be ready to help the poor as well as the rich; differencing them no further than the public good requireth you to do. Let not the health or lives of men be neglected, because they have no money to give you: many poor people perish for want of means, because they are discouraged from going to physicians, through the emptiness of their purses; in such a case you must not only help them gratis, but also appoint the cheapest medicines for them.

Direct. III. Adventure not unnecessarily on things beyond your skill, but in difficult cases persuade your patients to use the help of abler physicians, if there be any to be had, though it be against your own commodity. So far should you be from envying the greater esteem and practice of abler men, and from all unworthy aspersions or detraction, that you should do your best to persuade all your patients to seek their counsels, whenever the danger of their lives or health requireth it. For their lives are of greater value than your gain. So abstruse and conjectural is the business of your profession, that it requireth very high accomplishments to be a physician indeed. If there concur not, 1. A natural strength of reason and sagacity; 2. And a great deal of study, reading, and acquaintance with the way of excellent men; 3. And considerable experience of your own, to ripen all this; you have cause to be very fearful and cautelous in your practice, lest you sacrifice men's lives to your ignorance and temerity. And one man that hath all these accomplishments in a high degree, may do more good than a hundred smatterers: and when you are conscious of a defect in any of these, should not reason and conscience command you to persuade the sick to seek out to those that are abler than yourselves? Should men's lives be hazarded, that you may get by it a little sordid gain? It is so great a doubt whether the ignorant, unexperienced sort of physicians, do cure or hurt more, that it hath brought the vulgar in many countries into a contempt of physicians.[121]

Direct. IV. Depend on God for your direction and success. Earnestly crave his help and blessing in all your undertakings. Without this all your labour is in vain. How easy is it for you to overlook some one thing among a multitude that must be seen, about the causes and cure of diseases; unless God shall open it to you, and give you a clear discerning, and a universal observation! And when twenty considerable things are noted, a man's life may be lost, for want of your discerning one point more. What need have you of the help of God, to bring the fittest remedies to your memory! and much more to bless them when they are administered! as the experience of your daily practice may inform you (where atheism hath not made men fools).

Direct. V. Let your continual observation of the fragility of the flesh, and of man's mortality, make you more spiritual than other men, and more industrious in preparing for the life to come, and greater contemners of the vanities of this world. He that is so frequently among the sick, and a spectator of the dead and dying, is utterly unexcusable if he be himself unprepared for his sickness or for death. If the heart be not made better, when you almost dwell in the house of mourning, it is a bad and deplorate heart indeed. It is strange that physicians should be so much suspected of atheism as commonly they are; and *religio medici* should be a word that signifieth irreligiousness: sure this conceit was taken up in some more irreligious age or country; for I have oft been very thankful to God, in observing the contrary, even how many excellent, pious physicians there have been in most countries where the purity of religion hath appeared, and how much they promoted the work of reformation; (such as Crato, Platerus, Erastus, and abundance more that I might name;) and in this land and age, I must needs bear witness, that I have known as many physicians religious proportionally as of any one profession, except the preachers of the gospel. But as no men are more desperately wicked, than those that are wicked after pious education, and under the most powerful means of their reformation; so it is very like that those physicians that are not truly good are very bad; because they are bad against so much light, and so many warnings; and from some of these it is like this censorious proverb came. And indeed man's nature is so apt to be affected with things that are unusual, and to lose all sense of things that are grown common, that no men have more need to watch their hearts, and be afraid of being hardened, than those that are continually under the most quickening helps and warnings. For it is very easy to grow customary and senseless under them; and then the danger is, that there are no better means remaining, to quicken such a stupid, hardened heart. Whereas those that enjoy such helps but seldom, are not so apt to lose the sense and benefit of them. The sight of a sick or dying man, doth usually much awaken those that have such sights but seldom; but who are more hardened than soldiers and seamen, that live continually as among the dead? When they have twice or thrice seen the field covered with men's carcasses, they usually grow more obdurate than any others. And this is it that physicians are in danger of, and should most carefully avoid. But certainly an atheistical or ungodly physician, is unexcusably blind. To say, as some do, that they study nature so much, that they are carried away from God; is as if you should say, they study the work so much, that they forget the workman; or, they look so much on the book, that they overlook the sense; or, that they study medicine so much, that they forget both the patient and his health. To look into nature and not see God, is as to see the creatures, and not the light by which we see them; or to see the trees and houses, and not to see the earth that beareth them. For God is the creating, conserving, dirigent, final Cause of all. Of Him, and through Him, and to Him, are all things; He is all in all. And if they know not that they are the subjects of this God, and have immortal souls, they are ill proficients in the study of nature, that know no better the nature of man. To boast of their acquisitions in other sciences, while they know not what a man is, or what they are themselves, is little to the honour of their understandings. You that live still as in the sight of death, should live as in the sight of another world, and excel others in spiritual wisdom, and holiness, and sobriety, as your advantages by these quickening helps excel.

Direct. VI. Exercise your compassion and charity to men's souls, as well as to their bodies; and speak to your patients such words as tend to prepare them [773]for their change. You have excellent opportunities, if you have hearts to take them. If ever men will hear, it is when they are sick; and if ever they will be humbled and serious, it is when the approach of death constraineth them. They will hear that counsel now with patience, which they would have despised in their health. A few serious words about the danger of an unregenerate state, and the necessity of holiness, and the use of a Saviour, and the everlasting state of souls, for aught you know, may be blest to their conversion and salvation. And it is much more comfortable for you to save a soul, than cure the body. Think not to excuse yourselves by saying, It is the pastor's duty; for though it be theirs *ex officio*, it is yours also *ex charitate*. Charity bindeth every man, as he hath opportunity, to do good to all; and especially the greatest good. And God giveth you opportunity, by casting them in your way; the priest and Levite that passed by the wounded man, were more to be blamed for not relieving him, than those that never went that way, and therefore saw him not, Luke x. 32. And many a man will send for the physician, that will not send for the pastor: and many a one will hear a physician that will despise the pastor. As they reverence their landlords, because they hold their estates from them, so do they the physician, because they think they can do much to save their lives. And alas, in too many places the pastors either mind not such work, or are insufficient for it; or else stand at odds and distance from the people; so that there is but too much need of your charitable help. Remember therefore, that he that "converteth a sinner from the error of his way, shall save a soul from death, and shall hide a multitude of sins," James v. 20. Remember that you are to speak to one that is going into another world, and must be saved now or never! And that all that ever must be done for his salvation must be presently done, or it will be too late. Pity human nature, and harden not your hearts against a man in his extreme necessity. O speak a few serious words for his conversion (if he be one that needs them) before his soul be past your help, in the world from which there is no return.

[121] As overvaluing men's own understandings in religion, is the ruin of souls and churches; so overvaluing men's raw, unexperienced apprehensions in physic costeth multitudes their lives. I know not whether a few able, judicious, experienced physicians cure more or the rest kill more.

CHAPTER VI.

DIRECTIONS TO SCHOOLMASTERS ABOUT THEIR DUTY FOR THEIR CHILDREN'S SOULS.

PASSING by all your grammatical employment, I shall only leave you these brief directions, for the higher and more noble exercises of your profession.

Direct. I. Determine first rightly of your end; and then let it be continually in your eye, and let all your endeavours be directed in order to the attainment of it. If your end be chiefly your own commodity or reputation, the means will be distorted accordingly, and your labours perverted, and your calling corrupted, and embased, (to yourselves,) by your perverse intentions. See therefore, 1. That your ultimate end be the pleasing and glorifying of God. 2. And this by promoting the public good, by fitting youth for public service. And, 3. Forming their minds to the love and service of their Maker. 4. And furthering their salvation, and their welfare in the world. These noble designs will lift up your minds, to an industrious and cheerful performance of your duties! He that seeketh great and heavenly things, will do it with great resolution and alacrity; when any drowsy, creeping pace, and deceitful, superficial labours, will satisfy him that hath poor and selfish ends. As God will not accept your labours as any service of his, if your ends be wrong, so he useth not to give so large a blessing to such men's labours as to others.

Direct. II. Understand the excellency of your calling, and what fair opportunities you have to promote those noble ends; and also how great a charge you undertake; that so you may be kept from sloth and superficialness, and may be quickened to a diligent discharge of your undertaken trust. 1. You have not a charge of sheep or oxen, but of rational creatures. 2. You have not the care of their bodies, but of their minds; you are not to teach them a trade to live by only in the world, but to inform their minds with the knowledge of their Maker, and to cultivate their wits, and advance their reason, and fit them for the most man-like conversations. 3. You have them not (as pastors) when they are hardened in sin by prejudice and long custom; but you have the tenderest twigs to bow, and the most tractable age to tame; you have paper to write on (not wholly white, but that) which hath the fewest blots and lines to be expunged. 4. You have them not as volunteers, but as obliged to obey you, and under the correction of the rod; which with tender age is a great advantage. 5. You have them not only for your auditors in a general lecture, (as preachers have them at a sermon,) but in your nearest converse, where you may teach them as particularly as you please, and examine their profiting, and call them daily to account. 6. You have them not once a week, (as preachers have them,) but all the week long, from day to day, and from morning until night. 7. You have them at that age, which doth believe their teachers, and take all upon trust, before they are grown up to self-conceitedness, and to contradict and quarrel with their teachers (as with their pastors they very ordinarily do). All these are great advantages to your ends.

Direct. III. Labour to take pleasure in your work, and make it as a recreation, and take heed of a weary or diverted mind. 1. To this end consider often what is said above; think on the excellency of your ends, and of the worth of souls, and of the greatness of your advantages. 2. Take all your scholars as committed to your charge by Jesus Christ; as if he had said to you, Take these whom I have so dearly bought, and train them up for my church and service.[122] 3. Remember what good one scholar may do, when he cometh to be ripe for the service of the church or commonwealth! How many souls some of them may be a means to save! Or if they be but fitted for a private life, what blessings may they be to their families and neighbours! And remember what a joyful thing it will be, to see them in heaven with Christ for ever! How cheerfully should such excellent things be sought! If you take pleasure in your work, it will not only be an ease and happiness to yourselves, but greatly further your diligence and success. But when men have a base esteem of their employment, and look at children as so many swine or sheep, or have some higher matters in their eye, and make their schools but the way to some preferment, or more desired life, then usually they do their work deceitfully, and any thing will serve the turn, because they are weary of it, and because their hearts are somewhere else.

Direct. IV. Seeing it is divinity that teacheth [774]them the beginning and the end of all their other studies, let it never be omitted or slightly slubbered over, and thrust into a corner; but give it the precedency, and teach it them with greater care and diligence, than any other part of learning; especially teach them the catechism and the holy Scriptures. If you think that this is no part of your work, few wise men will

63

choose such teachers for their children. If you say as some sectaries, that children should not be taught to speak holy words, till they are more capable to understand the sense, because it is hypocrisy, or taking the name of God in vain; I have answered this before, and showed that words being the signs, must be learned in order to the understanding of the sense, or thing that is signified; and that this is not to use such words in vain, how holy soever, but to the proper end for which they are appointed. Both in divine and human learning, the memories of children must first be furnished in order to the furnishing of their understandings afterwards. And this is a chief point of the master's skill, that time be not lost, nor labour frustrated. For the memories of children are as capacious as men's of riper age; and therefore they should be stored early, with that which will be useful to them afterwards: but till they come to some maturity of age, their judgments are not ripe for information about any high or difficult points. Therefore teach them betimes the words of catechisms and some chapters of the Bible; and teach them the meaning by degrees as they are capable. And make them perceive that you take this for the best of all their learning.

Direct. V. Besides the forms of catechism, which you teach them, speak often to them some serious words, about their souls, and the life to come, in such a plain, familiar manner, as tendeth most to the awakening of their consciences, and making them perceive how greatly what you say concerneth them. A little such familiar serious discourse, in an interlocutory way, may go to their hearts, and never be forgotten; when mere forms alone are lifeless and unprofitable. Abundance of good might be done on children, if parents and schoolmasters did well perform their parts in this.

Direct. VI. Take strict account of their spending the Lord's day! how they hear, and what they remember; and how they spend the rest of the day. For the right spending of that day, is of great importance to their souls! And a custom of play and idleness on that day, doth usually debauch them, and prepare them for much worse. Though they are from under your eye on the Lord's day, yet if on Monday they be called to account, it will leave an awe upon them in your absence.

Direct. VII. Pray with them, and for them. If God give not the increase by the dews of heaven, and shine not on your labours, your planting and watering will be all in vain. Therefore prayer is as suitable a means as teaching, to do them good; and they must go together. He that hath a heart to pray earnestly for his scholars, shall certainly have himself most comfort in his labours; and it is likely that he shall do most good to them.

Direct. VIII. Watch over them, by one another, when they are behind your backs, at their sports or converse with each other. For it is abundance of wickedness that children use to learn and practise, which never cometh to their masters' ears; especially in some great and public schools. They that came thither to learn sobriety and piety of their masters, do oftentimes learn profaneness, and ribaldry, and cursing, and swearing, and scorning, deriding, and reviling one another, of their ungracious school-fellows. And those lessons are so easily learnt, that there are few children but are infected with some such debauchery, though their parents and masters watch against it; and perhaps it never cometh to their knowledge. So also for gaming and robbing orchards, and fighting with one another, and reading play-books and romances, and lying, and abundance other vices which must be carefully watched against.

Direct. IX. Correct them more sharply for sins against God, than for their dulness and failing at their books. Though negligence in their learning is not to be indulged, yet smart should teach them especially to take heed of sinning; that they may understand that sin is the greatest evil.

Direct. X. Especially curb or cashier the leaders of impiety and rebellion, who corrupt the rest. There are few great schools but have some that are notoriously debauched; that glory in their wickedness; that in filthy talking, and fighting, and cursing, and reviling words, are the infecters of the rest. And usually they are some of the bigger sort, that are the greatest fighters, and master the rest, and by domineering over them, and abusing them, force them both to follow them in their sin and to conceal it. The correcting of such, or expelling them if incorrigible, is of great necessity to preserve the rest; for if they are suffered the rest will be secretly infected and undone, before the master is aware. This causeth many that have a care of their children's souls, to be very fearful of sending them to great and public schools, and rather choose private schools that are freer from that danger; it being almost of as great concernment to children, what their companions be, as what their master is.

[122] Many of the greatest divines have given God great thanks for their schoolmasters, and left their names on record with honour, as Calvin did by Corderius, Beza by Melchior Volmarius, &c.

CHAPTER VII.

DIRECTIONS FOR SOLDIERS, ABOUT THEIR DUTY IN POINT OF CONSCIENCE.

THOUGH it is likely that few soldiers will read what I shall write for them, yet for the sake of those few that will, I will do as John Baptist did, and give them some few necessary directions, and not omit them as some do, as if they were a hopeless sort of men.

Direct. I. Be careful to make your peace with God, and live in a continual readiness to die. This being the great duty of every rational man, you cannot deny it to be especially yours, whose calling setteth you so frequently in the face of death. Though some garrison soldiers are so seldom, if ever, put to fight, that they live more securely than most other men, yet a soldier, as such, being by his place engaged to fight, I must fit my directions to the ordinary condition and expectation of men in that employment. It is a most irrational and worse than beastly negligence, for any man to live carelessly in an unpreparedness for death, considering how certain it is, and how uncertain the time, and how unconceivably great is the change which it inferreth: but for a soldier to be unready to die, who hath such special reason to expect it, and who listeth himself into a state which is so near it, this is to live and fight like beasts, and to be soldiers before you understand what it is to be a christian or a man. First, therefore, make sure that your souls are regenerate and reconciled unto God by Christ; and that when you die, you have a part in heaven; and that you are not yet in the state of sin and nature: an unrenewed unsanctified soul is sure to go to hell, by [775]what death or in what cause soever he dieth. If such a man be a soldier, he must be a coward or a madman; if he will run upon death, when he knoweth not whither it will send him, yea, when hell is certainly the next step, he is worse than mad: but if he know and consider the terribleness of such a change, it must needs make him tremble when he thinks of dying. He can be no good soldier that dare not die; and who can expect that he should dare to die, who must be damned when he dieth? Reason may command a man to venture upon death; but no reason will allow him to venture upon hell. I never knew but two sorts of valiant soldiers: the one was boys, and brutish, ignorant sots, who had no sense of the concernments of their souls; and the other (who only were truly valiant) were those that had made such preparations for eternity, as, at least, persuaded them that it should go well with them when they died. And many a debauched soldier I have known, whose conscience hath made them cowards, and shift or run away when they should venture upon death, because they knew they were unready to die, and were more afraid of hell than of the enemy. He that is fit to be a martyr, is the fittest man to be a soldier: he that is regenerate, and hath laid up his treasure and his hopes in heaven, and so hath overcome the fears of death, may be bold as a lion, and ready for any thing, and fearless in the greatest perils. For what should he fear, who hath escaped hell, and God's displeasure, and hath conquered the king of terrors? But fear is the duty and most rational temper of a guilty soul; and the more fearless such are, the more foolish and more miserable.

Direct. II. Be sure you have a warrantable cause and call. In a bad cause it is a dreadful thing to conquer, or to be conquered. If you conquer, you are a murderer of all that you kill; if you are conquered and die in the prosecution of your sin, I need not tell you what you may expect. I know we are here upon a difficulty which must be tenderly handled: if we make the sovereign power to be the absolute and only judge, whether the soldier's cause and call be good; then it would follow, that it is the duty of all the christian subjects of the Turk, to fight against Christianity as such, and to destroy all christians when the Turk commandeth it; and that all the subjects of other lands are bound to invade this or other such christian kingdoms, and destroy their kings, whenever their popish or malicious princes or states shall command them; which being intolerable consequences, prove the antecedent to be intolerable. And yet on the other side, if subjects must be the judges of their cause and call, the prince shall not be served, nor the common good secured, till the interest of the subjects will allow them to discern the goodness of the cause. Between these two intolerable consequents, it is hard to meet with a just discovery of the mean. Most run into one of the extremes, which they take to be the less, and think that there is no other avoiding of the other. The grand errors in this, and a hundred like cases, come from not distinguishing aright the case *de esse*, from the case *de apparere*, or *cognoscere*, and not first determining the former, as it ought, before the latter be determined. Either the cause which subjects are commanded to fight in, is really lawful to them, or it is not. (Say not here importunely, Who shall judge? For we are now but upon the question *de esse*.) If it be not lawful in itself, but be mere robbery or murder, then come to the case of evidence; either this evil is to the subject discernible by just means, or not: if it be, I am not able for my part to justify him from the sin, if he do it, no more than to have justified the three witnesses, Dan. iii. if they had bowed down to the golden calf, or Dan. vi. if he had forborne prayer, or the apostles, if they had forborne preaching, or the soldiers for apprehending and crucifying Christ, when their superiors commanded them. For God is first to be obeyed and feared. But if the evil of the cause be such, as the subject cannot by just and ordinary means discern, then must he come next to examine his call; and a volunteer unnecessarily he may not be in a doubtful cause: it is so heinous a sin to murder men, that no man should unnecessarily venture upon that which may prove to be murder for aught he knoweth. But if you ask what call may make such a doubtful action necessary, I answer, It must be such as warranteth it, either from the end of the action, or from the authority of the commander, or both. And from the end of the action, the case may be made clear, That if a king should do wrong to a foreign enemy, and should have the worse cause, yet if the revenge which that enemy seeketh would be the destruction of the king and country, or religion, it is lawful and a duty to fight in the defence of them. And if the king should be the assailant, or beginner, that which is an offensive war in him (for which he himself must answer) may be but a defensive war in the commanded subjects, and they be innocent: even on the highway, if I see a stranger provoke another by giving him the first blow, yet I may be bound to save his life from the fury of the avenging party. But whether, or how far, the bare command of a sovereign may warrant the subjects to venture in a doubtful cause, (supposing the thing lawful in itself, though they are doubtful,) requireth so much to be said to it, which civil governors may possibly think me too bold to meddle with, that I think it safest to pass it by; only saying, that there are some cases in which the ruler is the only competent judge, and the doubts of the subject are so unreasonable, that they will not excuse the sin of his disobedience; and also, that the degree of the doubt is oft very considerable in the case. But suppose the cause of the war be really lawful in itself, and yet the subject is in doubt of it, yea, or thinketh otherwise; then is he in the case, as other erroneous consciences are, that is, entangled in a necessity of sinning, till he be undeceived, in case his rulers command his service. But which would be the greater sin, to do it or not, the ends and circumstances may do much to determine; but doubtless in true necessity to save the king and state, subjects may be compelled to fight in a just cause, notwithstanding that they mistake it for unjust; and if the subject have a private discerning judgment, so far as he is a voluntary agent, yet the sovereign hath a public determining judgment, when a neglecter is to be forced to his duty. Even as a man that thinketh it unlawful to maintain his wife and children, may be compelled lawfully to do it.

So that it is apparent, that sometimes the sovereign's cause may be good, and yet an erroneous conscience may make the soldiers' cause bad, if they are volunteers, who run unnecessarily upon that which they take for robbery and murder; and yet that the higher powers may force even such mistakers to defend their country, and their governors, in a case of true necessity. And it is manifest that sometimes the cause of the ruler may be bad, and yet the cause of the soldier good; and that sometimes the cause may be bad and sinful to them both, and sometimes good and lawful unto both.

Direct. III. When you are doubtful whether your cause and call be good, it is (ordinarily) safest to sit still, and not to venture in so dangerous a case, without [776]great deliberation and sufficient evidence to satisfy your consciences. Neander might well say of Solon's law, which punished them that took not one part or other in a civil war or sedition, *Admirabilis autem illa atque plane incredibilis, quæ honoribus abdicat eum, qui orta seditione nullam factionem secutus sit.*[123] No doubt, he is a culpable neuter that will not defend his governors and his country, when he hath a call; but it is so dreadful a thing to be guilty of the blood and calamities of an unjust war, that a wise man will rather be abused as a neuter, than run himself into the danger of such a case.

Direct. IV. When necessity forceth you to go forth in a just war, do it with such humiliation and unwillingness as beseemeth one that is a patient, a spectator, and an actor, in one of the sorest of God's temporal judgments. Go not to kill men, as if you went to a cock-fight, or a bear-baiting. Make not a sport of a common calamity; be not insensible of the displeasure of God, expressed in so great a judgment. What a sad condition is it to yourselves, to be employed in destroying others! If they be good, how sad a thought is it, that you must kill them! If they are wicked, how sad is it that by killing them you cut off all their hopes of mercy, and send them suddenly to hell! How sad an employment is it, to spoil and undo the poor inhabitants where you come! to cast them into terrors, to deprive them of that which they have long been labouring for! to prepare for famine, and be like a consuming pestilence where you come! Were it but to see such desolations, it should melt you into compassion; much more to be the executioners yourselves. How unsuitable a work is it to the grace of love! Though I doubt not but it is a service which the love of God, our country, and our rulers, may sometimes justify and command, yet (as to the rulers and masters of the business) it must be a very clear and great necessity that can warrant a war. And, as to the soldiers, they must needs go with great regret, to kill men by thousands, whom they love as themselves. He that loveth his neighbour as himself, and blesseth, and doth good to his persecuting enemy, will take it heavily to be employed in killing him, even when necessity maketh it his duty. But the greatest calamity of war is the perniciousness of it to men's souls. Armies are commonly that to the soul, as a city infected with the plague is to the body; the very nurseries and academies of pride, and cruelty, and drunkenness, and whoredom, and robbery, and licentiousness; and the bane of piety, and common civility, and humanity. Not that every soldier cometh to this pass; the hottest pestilence killeth not all; but oh how hard is it to keep up a life of faith and godliness in an army! The greatness of their business, and of their fears and cares, doth so wholly take up their minds and talk, that there is scarce any room found for the matters of their souls, though unspeakably greater. They have seldom leisure to hear a sermon, and less to pray. The Lord's day is usually taken up in matters that concern their lives, and therefore can pretend necessity; so that it must be a very resolute, confirmed, vigilant person, that is not alienated from God. And then it is a course of life, which giveth great opportunity to the tempter, and advantage to temptations, both to errors in judgment, and viciousness of heart and life; he that never tried it can hardly conceive how difficult it is to keep up piety and innocency in an army. If you will suppose that there is no difference in the cause, or the ends and accidents, I take it to be much more desirable to serve God in a prison, than in an army; and that the condition of a prisoner hath far less in it to tempt the foolish, or to afflict the wise, than a military. (Excepting those whose life in garrisons and lingering wars, doth little differ from a state of peace.) I am not simply against the lawfulness of war; (nor as I conceive, Erasmus himself, though he saw the sinfulness of that sort of men; and use to speak truly of the horrid wickedness and misery of them that thirst for blood, or rush on wars without necessity;) but it must be a very extraordinary army, that is not constituted of wolves and tigers, and is not unto common honesty and piety the same that a stews or whorehouse is to chastity. And oh how much sweeter is the work of an honest physician that saveth men's lives, than of a soldier, whose virtue is shown in destroying them! or a carpenter's, or mason's, that adorneth cities with comely buildings, than a soldier's that consumeth them by fire![124]

Direct. V. Be sure first that your cause be better than your lives, and then resolve to venture your lives for them. It is the hazarding of your lives, which in your calling you undertake; and therefore be not unprepared for it; but reckon upon the worst, and be ready to undergo whatever you undertake. A soldier's life is unfit for one that dare not die. A coward is one of the most pernicious murderers; he verifieth Christ's saying in another sense, "he that saveth his life shall lose it." While men stand to it, it is usually but few that die; because they quickly daunt the enemy, and keep him on the defensive part; but when once they rout, and run away, they are slain on heaps, and fall like leaves in a windy autumn. Every coward that pursueth them is imboldened by their fear, and dare run them through, or shoot them behind, that durst not so near have looked them in the face; and maketh it his sport to kill a fugitive, or one that layeth down his weapons, that would fly himself from a daring presence. Your cowardly fear betrayeth the cause of your king and country; it betrayeth the lives of your fellow-soldiers, while the running of a few affrighted dastards, lets in ruin upon all the rest; and it casteth away your own lives, which you think to save. If you will be soldiers, resolve to conquer or to die. It is not so much skill or strength that conquereth, as boldness. It is fear that loseth the day, and fearlessness that winneth it. The army that standeth to it, getteth the victory, though they fight never so weakly; for if you will not run the enemy will. And if the lives of a few be lost by courage, it usually saveth the lives of many (though wisdom still is needful in the conduct). And if the cause be not worth your lives, you should not meddle with it.

Direct. VI. Resolve upon an absolute obedience to your commanders, in all things consistent with your obedience to God, and the sovereign power. Disobedience is no where more intolerable than in an army; where it is often unfit for a soldier to know the reason of his commands; and where self-conceitedness and wilfulness are inconsistent with [777]their common safety, and the lives of many may pay for the disobedience of a few. If you cannot obey, undertake not to be soldiers.

Direct. VII. Especially detest all murmurings, mutinies, sidings, and rebellions. For these are to an army like violent fevers to the body, or like a fire in a city, and would make an army the greatest plague to their king and country. How many emperors, kings, and commanders have lost their dignities and lives, by the fury of mutinous, enraged soldiers! And how many kingdoms and other commonwealths have been thus overthrown, and betrayed into the enemy's hands! And how many thousands and millions of soldiers have thereby lost their lives! In your discontents and murmuring passions, you may quickly set the house on fire over your heads, and when you feel your misery repent too late. Passion may begin that which fruitless penitence must end. The leaders of mutinies may easily have many fair pretences to inflame an army into discontents: they may aggravate many seeming injuries; they may represent their commanders as odious and unworthy, by putting an ill appearance on their actions: but in the end it will appear, that it was their own advancement which they secretly aimed at, and the destruction of the present government, or the soldiers' ruin, which is like to be the effect. A mutinous army is likest hell of any thing I know among God's creatures, and next hell, there is scarce a worse place for their commanders to be in.

Direct. VIII. Use not your power or liberty to the robbing, or oppressing, or injury of any. Though military thieves and oppressors may escape the gallows more than others, they shall come as soon to hell as any. If you plunder, and spoil, and tyrannize over the poor people, under pretence of supplying your own wants, there is a God in heaven that will hear their cries, and will avenge them speedily, though you seem to go scot-free for a time. You may take a pride in domineering over others, and making yourselves lords by violence of other men's estates, and when you see none that will question you for it, you may take that which you have most mind to. But the poor and oppressed have a just Defender, who hath a severer punishment for you than the sword or gallows! And though he take you not in the very fact, and his sentence is not presently executed, yet be certain of it, that your day is coming.

Direct. IX. Take heed lest custom, and the frequency of God's judgments, do harden your hearts into a reprobate stupidity. Many a man that formerly by the sight of a corpse, or the groanings of the sick, was awakened to serious thoughts of his latter end, when he cometh into an army, and hath often seen the dead lie scattered on the earth, and hath often escaped death himself, groweth utterly senseless, and taketh blockishness to be valour, and custom maketh such warnings to be of no effect. You can scarce name a more strange and lamentable proof of the maddening and hardening nature of sin! that men should be most senseless, when they are in the greatest danger! and least fear God, when they are among his dreadful judgments! and least hear his voice, when his calls are loudest! and live as if they should not die, when they look death so often in the face, and see so many dead before them! That they should be most regardless of their endless life, when they are nearest it; and sense itself hath such notable advantage to tell them of all this! What a monstrous kind of sottish stupidity is this! Think whither the soul is gone, when you see the carcass on the earth; and think where your own must be for ever.

Direct. X. Take heed of falling into drunkenness and sensuality, though temptations and liberty be never so great. It is too common with soldiers, because they are oft put to thirst and wants, to think they may lawfully pour it in, when they come at it, without moderation or restraint: even as many poor men take a gluttonous meal for no sin, because they have so many days of hunger; so is it with such soldiers in their drink: till drunkenness first have wounded their consciences, and afterwards grow common, till it have debauched and seared them; and then they have drowned religion and reason, and are turned sottish, miserable brutes.

Direct. XI. If necessity deprive you of the benefits of God's public or stated worship, see that you labour to repair that loss, by double diligence in those spiritual duties, which yet you have opportunity for. If you must march or watch on the Lord's days, redeem your other time the more. If you cannot hear sermons, be not without some profitable book, and often read it; and let your meditations be holy, and your discourses edifying. For these you have opportunities, if you have hearts.

Direct. XII. Take heed that command or successes do not puff you up and make you overvalue yourselves, and incline you to rebel against your governors. What lamentable effects hath England lately seen of this! A silly, half-witted soldier, if he be but made a captain, doth carry it as if he were wiser than the preachers, or the judge! as if his dignity had added to his wit! When victories have laid the power at men's feet, and they think now that none is able to control them, how few are they that abuse not such success to their undoing, and are not conquered by the pride of their own hearts, when they have conquered others! How ordinarily do they mis-expound the providence of God, and think he hath put the government into their hands, because they have the strength; and from the histories of former successful rebels, and the fairness of their opportunity, encourage themselves to rebel, and think they do but what is their duty! How easily do they justify themselves in those unlawful deeds, which impartial by-standers see the evil of! And how easily do they quiet their consciences, when they have but power enough to raise up flatterers, and to stop the mouth of wholesome reprehension! How lamentably doth prosperity make them drunk, and sudden advancement overturn their brains! And their greatness, together with their pride and fury, preserveth them from the accesses of wisdom, and of sober men, that so their malady may have no remedy: and there, like a drunken man, they rave awhile, and speak big words, and lay about them, and glory in the honour of a pestilence, that they can kill men; and we must not speak to them, till their heads are settled, and they come to themselves, and that is not usually till the hand of God have laid them lower than it found them, and then perhaps they will again hear reason; unless pride hath left their souls as desperate as at last it doth their bodies or estates. The experience of this age may stand on record, as a teacher to future generations, what power there is in great successes, to conquer both reason, religion, righteousness, professions, vows, and all obligations to God and man, by puffing up the heart with pride, and thereby making the understanding drunken.

[123] Neander in Chron. p. 104.

[124] And though I ignore not that it is a much more fashionable and celebrated practice in young gentlemen to kill men, than to cure them; and that mistaken mortals think it to be the noblest exercise of virtue, to destroy the noblest workmanship of nature, (and indeed in some few cases, the requisiteness and danger of destructive valour, may make its actions become a virtuous patriot,) yet when I consider the character given of our great Master and Exemplar, that he went about doing good, and healing all manner of sicknesses—I cannot but think such an employment worthy of the very noblest of his disciples. Mr. Boyle's Experiment. Philos. p. 303, 304.

[778]

CHAPTER VIII.

DIRECTONS AGAINST MURDER.
Tit. 1. Advice against Murder.

THOUGH murder be a sin which human nature and interest do so powerfully rise up against, that one would think besides the laws of nature, and the fear of temporal punishment, there should need no other argument against it; and though it be a sin which is not frequently committed, except by soldiers; yet because man's corrupted heart is liable to it, and because one sin of such a heinous nature may be more mischievous than many small infirmities, I shall not wholly pass by this sin, which falls in order here before me. I shall give men no other advice against it, than only to open to them, 1. The causes; 2. The greatness; and 3. The consequents of the sin.

I. The causes of murder, are either the nearest, or the more radical and remote. The opening of the nearest sort of causes, will be but to tell you, how many ways of murdering the world is used to! And when you know the cause the contrary to it is the prevention. Avoid these causes, and you avoid the sin.

1. The greatest cause of the cruellest murders is unlawful wars. All that a man killeth in an unlawful war, he murdereth; and all that the army killeth, he that setteth them at work by command or counsel, is guilty of himself. And therefore, how dreadful a thing is an unrighteous war! And how much have men need to look about them, and try every other lawful way, and suffer long, before they venture upon war! It is the skill and glory of a soldier, when he can kill more than other men. He studieth it; he maketh it the matter of his greatest care, and valour, and endeavour; he goeth through very great difficulties to accomplish it; this is not like a sudden or involuntary act. Thieves and robbers kill single persons; but soldiers murder thousands at a time: and because there is none at present to judge them for it, they wash their hands as if they were innocent, and sleep as quietly as if the avenger of blood would never come.

Oh what devils are those counsellors and incendiaries to princes and states, who stir them up to unlawful wars!

2. Another cause and way of murder, is by the pride and tyranny of men in power; when they do it easily, because they can do it; when their will and interest is their rule, and their passion seemeth a sufficient warrant for their injustice. It is not only Neros, Tiberiuses, Domitians, &c. that are guilty of this crying crime; but oh! what man that careth for his soul, had not rather be tormented a thousand years, than have the blood-guiltiness of a famous, applauded Alexander, or Cæsar, or Tamerlane, to answer for! So dangerous a thing is it to have power to do mischief, that Uriah may fall by a David's guilt, and Crispus may be killed by his father Constantine. Oh what abundance of horrid murders do the histories of almost all empires and kingdoms of the world afford us! The maps of the affairs of Greeks and Romans, of Tartarians, Turks, Russians, Germans, of heathens and infidels, of papists and too many protestants, are drawn out with too many purple lines, and their histories written in letters of blood. What write the christians of the infidels, the orthodox of the Arians, (Romans, or Goths, or Vandals,) or the most impartial historians of the mock-catholics of Rome, but "blood, blood, blood." How proudly and loftily doth a tyrant look, when he telleth the oppressed innocent that displeaseth him, "Sirrah, I will make you know my power! Take him, imprison him, rack him, hang him!" Or as Pilate to Christ, John xix. 10, "Knowest thou not that I have power to crucify thee, and have power to release thee?" "I will make you know that your life is in my hand: heat the furnace seven times hotter," Dan. iii. Alas, poor worm! hast thou power to kill? So hath a toad, or adder, or mad dog, or pestilence, when God permitteth it. Hast thou power to kill? But hast thou power also to keep thyself alive? and to keep thy corpse from rottenness and dust? and to keep thy soul from paying for it in hell? or to keep thy conscience from worrying thee for it to all eternity? With how trembling a heart and ghastly look wilt thou at last hear of this, which now thou gloriest in! The bones and dust of the oppressed innocents, will be as great and honourable as thine; and their souls perhaps in rest and joy, when thine is tormented by infernal furies. When thou art in Nebuchadnezzar's glory, what a mercy were it to thee, if thou mightest be turned out among the beasts, to prevent thy being turned out among the devils! If killing and destroying be the glory of thy greatness, the devils are more honourable than thou; and as thou agreest with them in thy work and glory, so shalt thou in the reward.

3. Another most heinous cause of murder is, a malignant enmity against the godly, and a persecuting, destructive zeal. What a multitude of innocents hath this consumed! And what innumerable companies of holy souls are still crying for vengeance on these persecutors! The enmity began immediately upon the fall, between the woman's and the serpent's seed. It showed itself presently in the two first men that were born into the world. A malignant envy against the accepted sacrifice of Abel, was able to make his brother to be his murderer. And it is usual with the devil, to cast some bone of carnal interest also between them, to heighten the malignant enmity. Wicked men are all covetous, voluptuous, and proud; and the doctrine and practice of the godly, doth contradict them and condemn them: and they usually espouse some wicked interest, or engage themselves in some service of the devil, which the servants of Christ are bound in their several places and callings to resist. And then not only this resistance, though it be but by the humblest words or actions, yea, the very conceit that they are not for their interest and way, doth instigate the befooled world to persecution. And thus an Ishmael and an Isaac, an Esau and a Jacob, a Saul and a David, cannot live together in peace; Gal. iv. 29, "But as then he that was born after the flesh, persecuted him that was born after the Spirit, even so it is now." Saul's interest maketh him think it just to persecute David; and religiously he blesseth those that furthered him; 1 Sam. xxiii. 21, "Blessed be ye of the Lord, for ye have compassion on me." He justifieth himself in murdering the priests, because he thought that they helped David against him; and Doeg seemeth but a dutiful subject, in

executing his bloody command, 1 Sam. xxii. And Shimei thought he might boldly curse him, 2 Sam. xvi. 7, 8. And he could scarce have charged him with more odious sin, than to be "A bloody man, and a man of Belial." If the prophet speak against Jeroboam's political religion, he will say, "Lay hold on him," 1 Kings xiii. 4. Even Asa will be raging wrathful, and imprison the prophet that reprehendeth his sin, 2 Chron. xvi. 10. Ahab will feed Micaiah in a prison with the bread and water of affliction, if he contradict him, 1 Kings xxii. 27. And even Jerusalem killed the prophets, and stoned them which were sent to gather them under the gracious wing of Christ, Matt. xxiii. 37. "Which [779]of the prophets did they not persecute?" Acts vii. 52. And if you consider but what streams of blood since the death of Christ and his apostles, have been shed for the sake of Christ and righteousness, it will make you wonder, that so much cruelty can consist with humanity, and men and devils should be so like. The same man, as Paul, as soon as he ceaseth to shed the blood of others, must look in the same way to lose his own. How many thousands were murdered by heathen Rome in the ten persecutions! and how many by the Arian emperors and kings! and how many by more orthodox princes in their particular distastes! And yet how far hath the pretended vicar of Christ outdone them all! How many hundred thousands of the Albigenses, Waldenses, and Bohemians, hath the papal rage consumed! Two hundred thousand the Irish murdered in a little space, to outgo the thirty or forty thousand which the French massacre made an end of! The sacrifices offered by their fury in the flames, in the Marian persecution here in England, were nothing to what one day hath done in other parts. What volumes can contain the particular histories of them? What a shambles was their inquisition in the Low Countries! And what is the employment of it still? So that a doubting man would be inclined to think, that papal Rome is the murderous Babylon, that doth but consider, "How drunken she is with the blood of the saints, and the martyrs of Jesus; and that the blood of saints will be found in her, in her day of trial," Rev. xvii. 6; xviii. 24. If we should look over all the rest of the world, and reckon up the torments and murders of the innocent, (in Japan, and most parts of the world, wherever Christianity came,) it may increase your wonder, that devils and men are still so like. Yea, though there be as loud a testimony in human nature against this bloodiness, as almost any sin whatsoever; and though the names of persecutors always stink to following generations, how proudly soever they carried it for a time; and though one would think a persecutor should need no cure but his own pride, that his name may not be left as Pilate's in the creed, to be odious in the mouths of the ages that come after him; yet for all this, so deep is the enmity, so potent is the devil, so blinding a thing is sin, and interest, and passion, that still one generation of persecutors doth succeed the others; and they kill the present saints, while they honour the dead ones, and build them monuments, and say, "If we had lived in the days of our fathers, we would not have been partakers with them in the prophets' blood." Read well Matt. xxiii. 29, to the end. What a sea of righteous blood hath malignity and persecuting zeal drawn out!

4. Another cause of murder is, rash and unrighteous judgment; when judges are ignorant, or partial, or perverted by passion, or prejudice, or respect of persons: but though many an innocent hath suffered this way, I hope among christians, this is one of the rarest causes.

5. Another way of murder is by oppression and uncharitableness; when the poor are kept destitute of necessaries to preserve their lives: though few of them die directly of famine, yet thousands of them die of those sicknesses which they contract by unwholesome food. And all those are guilty of their death, either that cause it by oppression, or that relieve them not when they are able and obliged to it, James v. 1-5.

6. Another way and cause of murder is, by thieves and robbers, that do it to possess themselves of that which is another man's: when riotousness or idleness hath consumed what they had themselves, and sloth and pride will not suffer them to labour, nor sensuality suffer them to endure want, then they will have it by right or wrong, whatever it cost them. God's laws or man's, the gallows or hell, shall not deter

them; but have it they will, though they rob and murder, and are hanged and damned for it. Alas! how dear a purchase do they make! How much easier are their greatest wants, than the wrath of God, and the pains of hell!

7. Another cause of murder is, guilt and shame. When wicked people have done some great disgraceful sin, which will utterly shame them or undo them if it be known, they are tempted to murder them that know it, to conceal the crime and save themselves. Thus many a whoremonger hath murdered her that he hath committed fornication with; and many a whore hath murdered her child (before the birth or after) to prevent the shame. But how madly do they forget the day, when both the one and the other will be brought to light! And the righteous Judge will make them know, that all their wicked shifts will be their confusion, because there is no hiding them from him.

8. Another cause is, furious anger, which mastereth reason, and for the present makes them mad; and drunkenness, which doth the same. Many a one hath killed another in his fury or his drink; so dangerous is it to suffer reason to lose its power, and to use ourselves to a Bedlam course! And so necessary is it, to get a sober, meek, and quiet spirit, and mortify and master these turbulent and beastly vices.

9. Another cause of murder is, malice and revenge. When men's own wrongs or sufferings are so great a matter to them, and they have so little learned to bear them, that they hate that man that is the cause of them, and boil with a revengeful desire of his ruin. And this sin hath in it so much of the devil, that those that are once addicted to it, are almost wholly at his command. He maketh witches of some, and murderers of others, and wretches of all! who set themselves in the place of God, and will do justice as they call it for themselves, as if God were not just enough to do it. And so sweet is revenge to their furious nature, (as the damning of men is to the devil,) that revenged they will be, though they lose their souls by it; and the impotency and baseness of their spirits is such, that they say, Flesh and blood is unable to bear it.

10. Another cause of murder is, a wicked impatience with near relations, and a hatred of those that should be most dearly loved. Thus many men and women have murdered their wives and husbands, when either adulterous lust hath given up their hearts to another, or a cross, impatient, discontented mind, hath made them seem intolerable burdens to each other; and then the devil that destroyed their love and brought them thus far, will be their teacher in the rest, and show them how to ease themselves, till he hath led them to the gallows, and to hell. How necessary is it to keep in the way of duty, and abhor and suppress the beginnings of sin!

11. And sometimes covetousness hath caused murder, when one man desireth another man's estate. Thus Ahab came by Naboth's vineyards to his cost. And many a one desireth the death of another, whose estate must fall to him at the other's death. Thus many a child in heart is guilty of the murder of his parents, though he actually commit it not; yea, a secret gladness when they are dead, doth show the guilt of some such desires while they were living; and the very abatement of such moderate mourning, as natural affection should procure, (because the estate is thereby come to them as the heirs,) doth show that such are far from innocent. Many a Judas for covetousness hath betrayed another; many [780]a false witness for covetousness hath sold another's life; many a thief for covetousness hath taken away another's life, to get his money; and many a covetous landlord hath longed for his tenant's death, and been glad to hear of it; and many a covetous soldier hath made a trade of killing men for money. So true is it, "That the love of money is the root of all evil;" and therefore is one cause of this.

12. And ambition is too common a cause of murder, among the great ones of the world. How many have despatched others out of the world, because they stood in the way of their advancement! For a long time together it was the ordinary way of rising, and dying, to the Roman and Greek emperors; for one to procure the murder of the emperor, that he might usurp his seat, and then to be so murdered by another himself; and every soldier that looked for preferment by the change, was ready to be

an instrument in the fact. And thus hath even the Roman seat of his mock-holiness, for a long time and oft received its successors, by the poison or other murdering of the possessors of the desired place. And alas, how many thousands hath that see devoured to defend its universal empire, under the name of the spiritual headship of the church! How many unlawful wars have they raised or cherished, even against christian emperors and kings! How many thousands have been massacred! how many assassinated, as Henry the Third, and Henry the Fourth, of France! besides those that fires and inquisitions have consumed: and all these have been the flames of pride. Yea, when their fellow-sectaries in Munster, and in England, (the anabaptists and seekers,) have catched some of their proud disease, it hath worked in the same way of blood and cruelty.

But besides these twelve great sins, which are the nearest cause of murder, there are many more which are yet greater, and deeper in nature, which are the roots of all; especially these:

1. The first cause is, the want of true belief of the word of God, and the judgment and punishment to come, and the want of the knowledge of God himself: atheism and infidelity.

2. Hence cometh the want of the true fear of God, and subjection to his holy laws.

3. The predominance of selfishness in all the unsanctified, is the radical inclination to murder, and all the injustice that is committed.

4. And the want of charity, or loving our neighbour as ourselves, doth bring men near to the execution, and leaveth little inward restraint.

By all this you may see how this sin must be prevented. (And let not any man think it a needless work. Thousands have been guilty of murder that once thought themselves as far from it as you.) 1. The soul must be possessed with the knowledge of God, and the true belief of his word and judgment. 2. Hereby it must be possessed of the fear of God, and subjection to him. 3. And the love of God must mortify the power of selfishness. 4. And also must possess us with a true love to our neighbours, yea, and enemies for his sake. 5. And the twelve forementioned causes of murder will be thus destroyed at the root.

II. And some further help it will be to understand the greatness of this sin. Consider therefore, 1. It is an unlawful destroying, not only a creature of God, but one of his noblest creatures upon earth! even one that beareth (at least, the natural) image of God. Gen. ix. 5, 6, "And surely, your blood of your lives will I require; at the hand of every beast will I require it; and at the hand of man; at the hand of every man's brother will I require the life of man. Whoso sheddeth man's blood, by man shall his blood be shed; for in the image of God made he man." Yea, God will not only have the beast slain that killeth a man, but also forbiddeth there the eating of blood, verse 4, that man might not be accustomed to cruelty.

2. It is the opening a door to confusion, and all calamity in the world; for if one man may kill another without the sentence of the magistrate, another may kill him; and the world will be like mastiffs or mad dogs, turned all loose on one another, kill that kill can.

3. If it be a wicked man that is killed, it is the sending of a soul to hell, and cutting off his time of repentance, and his hopes. If it be a godly man, it is a depriving of the world of the blessing of a profitable member, and all that are about him of the benefits of his goodness, and God of the service, which he was here to have performed. These are enough to infer the dreadful consequents to the murderer, which are such as these.

III. 1. It is a sin which bringeth so great a guilt, that if it be repented of, and pardoned, yet conscience very hardly doth ever attain to peace and quietness in this world; and if it be unpardoned, it is enough to make a man his own executioner and tormentor.

2. It is a sin that seldom escapeth vengeance in this life: if the law of the land take not away their lives, as God appointeth, Gen. ix. 6, God useth to follow them with his extraordinary plagues, and causeth their sin to find them out; so that the bloodthirsty man doth seldom live out half his days. The treatises purposely written on this subject, and the experience of all ages, do give us very wonderful narratives of God's judgments, in the detecting of murderers and bringing them to punishment. They go about awhile like Cain, with a terrified conscience, afraid of every one they see, till seasonable vengeance give them their reward, or rather send them to the place where they must receive it.

3. For it is eternal torment, under the wrath of God, which is the final punishment which they must expect (if very great repentance, and the blood of Christ, do not prevent it). There are few I think that by shame and terror of conscience, are not brought to such a repentance for it, as Cain and Judas had, or as a man that hath brought calamity on himself; and therefore wish they had never done it, because of their own unhappiness thereby (except those persecutors or murderers that are hardened by error, pride, or power); but this will not prevent the vengeance of God in their damnation: it must be a deep repentance proceeding from the love of God and man, and the hatred of sin, and sense of God's displeasure for it, which is only found in sanctified souls! And alas, how few murderers ever have the grace to manifest any such renovation and repentance!

Tit. 2. Advice against Self-murder.

Though self-murder be a sin which nature hath as strongly inclined man against, as any sin in the world that I remember, and therefore I shall say but little of it; yet experience telleth us, that it is a sin that some persons are in danger of, and therefore I shall not pass it by.

The prevention of it lieth in the avoiding of these following causes of it.

Direct. I. The commonest cause is prevailing melancholy, which is near to madness; therefore to prevent this sad disease, or to cure it if contracted, and to watch them in the mean time, is the chief prevention of this sin. Though there be much more hope of the salvation of such, as want the use of their understandings, because so far it may be called [781]involuntary, yet it is a very dreadful case, especially so far as reason remaineth in any power. But it is not more natural for a man in a fever to thirst and rave, than for melancholy, at the height, to incline men to make away themselves. For the disease will let them feel nothing but misery and despair, and say nothing, but, I am forsaken, miserable, and undone! And not only maketh them weary of their lives, (even while they are afraid to die,) but the devil hath some great advantage by it, to urge them to do it; so that if they pass over a bridge, he urgeth them to leap into the water; if they see a knife, they are presently urged to kill themselves with it; and feel, as if it were, something within them importunately provoking them, and saying, Do it, do it now; and giving them no rest. Insomuch, that many of them contrive it, and cast about secretly how they may accomplish it.

Though the cure of these poor people belong as much to others' care as to their own, yet so far as they yet can use their reason, they must be warned, 1. To abhor all these suggestions, and give them not room a moment in their minds.

And, 2. To avoid all occasions of the sin, and not to be near a knife, a river, or any instrument which the devil would have them use in the execution.

And, 3. To open their case to others, and tell them all, that they may help to their preservation.

4. And especially to be willing to use the means, both physic, and satisfying counsel, which tend to cure their disease. And if there be any rooted cause in the mind that was antecedent to the melancholy, it must be carefully looked to in the cure.

Direct. II. Take heed of worldly trouble and discontent; for this also is a common cause. Either it suddenly casteth men into melancholy, or without it of itself overturneth their reason, so far as to make them violently despatch themselves; especially, if it fall out in a mind where there is a mixture of these two causes: 1.

Unmortified love to any creature. 2. And an impotent and passionate mind; their discontent doth cause such unquietness, that they will furiously go to hell for ease. Mortify therefore first your worldly lusts, and set not too much by any earthly thing: if you did not foolishly overvalue yourselves, or your credit, or your wealth or friends, there would be nothing to feed your discontent: make no greater a matter of the world than it deserveth, and you will make no such great matter of your sufferings.

And, 2. Mortify your turbulent passions, and give not way to Bedlam fury to overcome your reason. Go to Christ, to beg and learn to be meek and lowly in spirit, and then your troubled minds will have rest, Matt. xi. 28, 29. Passionate women, and such other feeble-spirited persons, that are easily troubled and hardly quieted and pleased, have great cause to bend their greatest endeavours to the curing of this impotent temper of mind, and procuring from God such strengthening grace, as may restore their reason to its power.

Direct. III. And sometimes sudden passion itself, without any longer discontent, hath caused men to make away themselves. Mortify therefore and watch over such distracting passions.

Direct. IV. Take heed of running into the guilt of any heinous sin. For though you may feel no hurt from it at the present, when conscience is awakened, it is so disquieting a thing, that it maketh many a one hang himself. Some grievous sins are so tormenting to the conscience, that they give many no rest, till they have brought them to Judas's or Ahithophel's end. Especially take heed of sinning against conscience, and of yielding to that for fear of men, which God and conscience charge you to forbear. For the case of many a hundred as well as Spira, may tell you into what calamity this may cast you. If man be the master of your religion, you have no religion; for what is religion, but the subjection of the soul to God, especially in the matters of his worship; and if God be subjected to man, he is taken for no-god. When you worship a god that is inferior to a man, then you must subject your religion to the will of that man. Keep God and conscience at peace with you, if you love yourselves, though thereby you lose your peace with the world.

Direct. V. Keep up a believing foresight of the state which death will send you to. And then if you have the use of reason, hell at least will hold your hands, and make you afraid of venturing upon death. What repentance are you like to have, when you die in the very act of sin? and when an unmortified lust or love of the world, doth hurry you to the halter by sinful discontent? and what hope of pardon without repentance? How exceeding likely therefore is it, that whenever you put yourselves out of your present pain and trouble you send your souls to endless torments! And will it ease you to pass from poverty or crosses into hell? Or will you damn your souls, because another wrongeth you? Oh the madness of a sinner! Who will you think hath wronged you most, when you feel hell-fire? Are you weary of your lives, and will you go to hell for ease? Alas, how quickly would you be glad to be here again, in a painfuller condition than that which you were so weary of! yea, and to endure it a thousand years! Suppose you saw hell before your eyes, would you leap into it? Is not time of repentance a mercy to be valued? Yea, a little reprieve from endless misery is better than nothing. What need you make haste to come to hell? Will it not be soon enough, if you stay thence as long as you can? And why will you throw away your hopes, and put yourselves past all possibility of recovery, before God put you so himself?

Direct. VI. Understand the wonders of mercy revealed, and bestowed on mankind in Jesus Christ; and understand the tenor of the covenant of grace. The ignorance of this is it that keepeth a bitter taste upon your spirits; and maketh you cry out, Forsaken and undone; when such miracles of mercy are wrought for your salvation. And the ignorance of this is it that maketh you foolishly cry out, There is no hope; the day of grace is past; it is too late; God will never show me mercy! When his word assureth all that will believe it, that "whoever confesseth and forsaketh his sins, shall have mercy," Prov. xxviii. 13. "And if we confess our sins, he is faithful and just to forgive," 1 John i. 9. "And that whoever will, may freely drink of the waters of life," Rev. xxii. 17. "And that whoever believeth in him, shall not perish, but have everlasting life," John iii. 16. I have no other hope of my salvation, but that gospel which promiseth pardon and salvation unto all, that at any time repent and turn to God by faith in Christ: and I dare lay my salvation on the truth of this, that Christ never rejected any sinner, how great soever, that at any time in this life was truly willing to come to him, and to God by him. "He that cometh unto me I will in no wise cast out," John vi. 37. But the malicious devil would fain make God seem odious to the soul, and representeth love itself as our enemy, that we might not love him! Despair is such a part of hell, that if he could bring us to it, he would think he had us half in hell already: and then he would urge us to despatch ourselves, that we might be there indeed, and our despair might be uncurable. How blind is he that seeth not the devil in all this!

[782]

CHAPTER IX.

DIRECTIONS FOR THE FORGIVING OF ENEMIES, AND THOSE THAT INJURE US; AGAINST WRATH, AND MALICE, AND REVENGE, AND PERSECUTION.

IT is not only actual murder which is forbidden in the sixth commandment, but also all inordinate wrath, and malice, and desires of revenge, and injuring the person of our neighbour or our enemy: for so the Prophet and Judge of the church hath himself expounded it, Matt. v. 21, 22. Anger hath a hurting inclination, and malice is a fixed anger, and revenge is the fruit of both or either of them. He that will be free from injurious actions, must subdue the wrath and malice which is their cause. Heart murders and injuries must be carefully rooted up; "For out of the heart proceed all evil thoughts and murders," &c. Matt. xv. 19. This is the fire of hell on which an evil tongue is set, Jam. iii. 6. And this must be quenched if you would be innocent.

Direct. I. See God in your neighbour, and love him for that of God which is upon him. If he be holy, he hath the moral image of God. If he be unholy, he hath his natural image as he is a man. He is not only God's creature, but his reasonable creature, and the lord of his inferior works: and art thou a child of God, and yet canst not see him, and love him in his works? Without God he is nothing, whom thou art so much offended with: and though there be somewhat in him which is not of God, which may deserve thy hatred, yet that is not his substance or person: hate not, or wrong not that which is of God. It would raise in you such a reverence, as would assuage your wrath, if you could but see God in him that you are displeased with.

Direct. II. To this end observe more the good which is in your neighbour, than the evil. Malice overlooketh all that is good and amiable, and can see nothing but that which is bad and detestable: it hearkeneth more to them that dispraise and open the faults of others, than to those that praise them and declare their virtues: nor that good and evil must be confounded; but the good as well as the evil must be acknowledged. We have more use ourselves for the observation of their virtues than of their faults; and it is more our duty: and were it never so little good that is in them, the right observing of it, at least would much diminish your dislike.

Direct. III. Learn but to love your neighbour as yourself, and this will make it easy to you both to forbear him and forgive him. With yourself you are not apt to be so angry. Against yourself you bear no malice, nor desire no revenge that shall do you hurt. As you are angry with yourself penitently for the faults you have committed, but not so as to desire your own destruction, or final hurt; but with such a displeasure as tendeth to your recovery; so also must you do by others.

Direct. IV. To this end be sure to mortify your selfishness. For it is the inordinate respect that men have to themselves, which maketh them aggravate the faults of all that are against them, or offend them. Be humble and self-denying, and you will think yourselves so mean and inconsiderable, that no fault can be very great, nor deserve much displeasure, merely as it is against you. A proud, self-esteeming man is easily provoked, and hardly reconciled without great submission; because he thinketh so highly of himself, that he thinketh heinously of all that is said or done against him; and he is so over-dear to himself, that he is impatient with his adversary.

Direct. V. Be not your own judge in cases of settled malice or revenge; but let some impartial, sober by-stander be the judge. For a selfish, passionate, distempered mind, is very unlike to judge aright. And most men have so much of these diseases, that they are very unfit to be judges in their own case. Ask first some wise, impartial man, whether it be best for thee to be malicious and revengeful against such a one that thou thinkest hath greatly wronged thee, or rather to love him and forgive him.

Direct. VI. Take time to deliberate upon the matter, and do nothing rashly in the heat of passion against another. Wrath and malice will vanish, if you bring the matter into the light, and use but those effectual considerations which will show their sinfulness and shame; I shall therefore next here set down some such considerations, as are most powerful to suppress them.

Consid. I. Remember first, That whoever hath offended you, hath offended God by greater injuries, and if God forgive him the greater, why should not you forgive the less? The same fault which he did against you, is a greater crime as against God than as against you. And many a hundred more hath he committed. It is a small matter to displease such a worm as man, in comparison of the displeasing of Almighty God; and should not his children imitate their heavenly Father? Doth he remit the pains of hell, and cannot you forbear your passionate revenge? Let me ask you, whether you desire that God should forgive him his sins or not? (both that and all the rest which he hath committed:) if you say, no, you are devilish and inhuman, who would not have God forgive a sinner; if you say, yea, you condemn, yea, and contradict yourselves, while you say you would have God forgive him, and yet yourselves will not forgive him. (I speak not of necessary correction, but revenge.)

Consid. II. Consider also that you have much more yourselves to be forgiven by God, or you are undone for ever. There is no comparison between other men's offences against you, and your offences against God, either for the number of them, or the greatness, or the desert. Dost thou owe to God ten thousand talents, and wilt thou lay hold on thy brother for a hundred pence? See then thy doom, Matt. xviii. 34; the tormentors shall exact thy debt to God. Doth it beseem that man to aggravate or revenge his little injuries, who deserveth damnation, and forfeiteth his soul every day and hour? and hath no hope of his own salvation, but by the free forgiveness of all his sins?

Consid. III. Either thou art thyself a member of Christ or not. If not, thou art yet under the guilt of all the sins that ever thou didst commit. And doth it beseem that man to be severe and revengeful against others, that must forever be damned for his own transgressions, if a speedy conversion do not prevent it? Sure you have somewhat else to think on, than of your petty injuries from men! But if thou be indeed a member of Christ, thy sins are all pardoned by the price of thy Redeemer's blood! And canst thou feel the sweetness of so great a mercy, and not feel a strong obligation on thee to forgive thy brother? Must Christ be a sacrifice for thy offences? and must thy brother, who offended thee, be sacrificed to thy wrath?

Consid. IV. Thou art not forgiven of God, if thou dost not forgive. For, 1. If ever the love of God and the blood of Christ had come in power upon thy heart, they would undoubtedly have caused thee to forgive thy brother. 2. Yea, God hath made thy [783]forgiving others to be a condition, without which he will not finally or plenarily forgive thee. Thou hast no warrant to pray or hope for pardon upon any lower terms; but "Forgive us our trespasses, as we forgive them that trespass against us; for if ye forgive not men their trespasses, neither will your Father forgive your trespasses," Matt. vi. 14, 15. Likewise, saith Christ, "shall my heavenly Father do also unto you, (even deliver you to the tormentors,) if from your hearts ye forgive not every one his brother their trespasses," Matt. xviii. 35. "For he shall have judgment without mercy that hath showed no mercy, and mercy rejoiceth against judgment," James ii. 13.

Consid. V. Remember also that you have need of forgiveness from others, as well as they have need of it from you. Have you wronged none? Have you provoked none? Have you not passions which must be pardoned? and a nature which must be borne with? Can so corrupt a creature as man is, be no annoyance to those he liveth with? Sure all the sins which burden yourself, and displease the Lord, must needs be some trouble to all about you: and he that needeth pardon, is obliged the more to pardon others.

Consid. VI. Nay, it is the unhappiness of all mankind, that their corruptions will in some measure be injurious to all that they have to do with; and it is impossible for such distempered sinners to live together, and not by their mistakes, or selfishness, or passions, to exercise the patience and forbearance of each other. Therefore you must either be malicious and revengeful against all mankind, or else against none on such accounts as are common to all.

Consid. VII. Observe also how easily you can forgive yourselves, though you do a thousand-fold more against yourselves, than ever any enemy did. It is not their wrongs or offences against you that you are in any danger of being damned for; you shall not suffer for their sins, but for your own. In the day of judgment, it is not your sufferings from others, but your own offences against God, that will be charged upon you: and if ever you be undone, it will be by these. Men or devils can never do that against you, which by every sin you do against yourselves. No robber, no oppressor, no persecutor, no deceiver, can ever hurt you so much as you hurt yourselves. And yet how gently do you take it at your own hands! How easily do you pardon it to yourselves! How lovingly do you think of yourselves! So far are you from malice or revenge against yourselves, that you can scarce endure to hear plainly of your sins! but are more inclined to bear malice against those that do reprove you. Judge whether this be equal dealing, and loving your neighbours as yourselves?

Consid. VIII. Consider how great a crime it is, for a worm to usurp the authority of God, and censure him for not doing justice, and to presume to anticipate his judgment, and take the sword as it were out of his hands, as all do that will be their own avengers. It is the magistrate, and not you, that beareth the sword of public justice; and what he doth not, God will do in his time and way. "Dearly beloved, avenge not yourselves, but rather give place unto wrath; for it is written, Vengeance is mine, I will repay, saith the Lord. Therefore if thine enemy hunger, feed him; if he thirst, give him drink; for in so doing thou shalt heap coals of fire on his head. Be not overcome of evil, (that is, the evil that is done against you,) but overcome evil with good," Rom. xii. 19-21. He that becometh a revenger for himself, doth by his actions as it were say to God, Thou art unjust, and dost not do me justice, and therefore I will do it for myself. And shall such an impatient, blaspheming atheist go unpunished?

Consid. IX. Consider how much fitter God is than you, to execute revenge and justice on your enemies. He hath the highest authority, and you have none: he is impartial and most just, and you are unrighteous and perverted by selfishness and partiality. He is eternal and omniscient, and seeth to the end, and what will be the consequent; and therefore knoweth the fittest season and degree; but you are short-sighted creatures, that see no further than the present day, and know not what will be to-morrow, and therefore may be ignorant of a hundred things, which would stop you and change your counsel if you had foreseen them. He is most wise and good, and knoweth what is fit for every person, and how to do good with as little hurt as may be in the doing of it; but you are ignorant of yourselves, and blinded by interest and passion, and are so bad yourselves, that you are inclined to do hurt to others. At least, for aught you know, you may miscarry in your passion, and come off with guilt and a wounded conscience; but you may be sure that God will not miscarry, but will do all in perfect wisdom, and righteousness, and truth.

79

Consid. X. Do you not understand that your passion, malice, and revenge, 1. Do hurt yourselves much more than they can hurt another, and, 2. Much more than any other can hurt you? Would you be revenged on another; and will you therefore hurt yourselves? The stone of reproach which you cast at him, doth fly back into your face, and wound yourselves. Do you feel that the fire of passion and malice are like a scorching fever, which overthrow your health and quietness, and fill you full of restlessness and pain? And will you do this against yourselves, because another hath abused you? Did not he that offended you do enough against you? If you would have more, why are you offended with him? If you would not have more, why do you inflict it on yourselves? If you love disquietness, why do you complain of him that doth disquiet you? If you do not, why do you disquiet yourselves? and that much more than he can do? He that wrongeth you toucheth but your estates, or bodies, or names; it may be it is but by a blast of wind, the words of his mouth; and will you therefore wound yourselves at the very heart? God hath locked up your heart from others; none can touch that but yourselves. Their words, their wrongs cannot reach your hearts, unless you open them the door, yea, unless it be your own doing. Will you take the dagger which pierced but your skin, and pierce your own hearts with it, because another so much wronged you? If you do, blame no one for it so much as yourselves; blame them for touching your estates or names, but blame yourselves for all that is at your hearts. And if you might desire another's hurt, it is folly to hurt yourselves much more, and to do a greater mischief to yourselves, that so you may do a less to him. If you rail at him, or slander or defame him, you touch but his reputation; if you trouble him at law, you touch but his estate; if you beat him, it reacheth but to his flesh; but the passion and guilt is a fire in your own hearts; and the wrath of God which you procure, doth fall upon your souls for ever! I have heard but of a few that have said openly, I am contented to be damned, so I may but be avenged; but many thousands speak it by their deeds. And oh how just is their damnation, who will run into hell that they may hurt another! Even as I have heard of some passionate wives and [784]children, who have hanged themselves, or cut their throats, to be revenged on their husbands or parents by grieving them.

Consid. XI. Remember that malice and hurtfulness are the special sins and image of the devil. All sin is from him as the tempter; but some sins are so eminently his own, that they may be called the nature and image of the devil; and those are principally, rebellion against God, malignity or enmity to good, pride or self-exaltation, lying and calumny, and malice, hurtfulness, and murder; these are above the sins of mere sensuality or carnality, and most properly denominate men (in whom they prevail) the serpent's seed. I speak but as Christ himself hath spoken, John viii. 44, to those that were esteemed the wisest and most (ceremoniously) religious of those times: "Ye are of your father the devil, and the lusts of your father ye will do. He was a murderer from the beginning, and abode not in the truth, because there is no truth in him. When he speaketh a lie, he speaketh of his own: for he is a liar, and the father of it." And what pity is it that a man that should bear the image of God, should be transformed as it were into an incarnate devil, by being like to Satan, and bearing his image!

Consid. XII. The person that you are angry with, is either a child of God, or of the devil, and one that must live either in heaven or hell. If he be a child of God, will not his Father's interest and image reconcile you to him? Will you hate and hurt a member of Christ? If you have any hope of being saved yourselves, are you not ashamed to think of meeting him in heaven, whom you hated and persecuted here on earth? If there were any shame and grief in heaven, it would overwhelm you there with shame and grief, to meet those in the union of those blessed joys, whom you hated and abused. Believe unfeignedly that you must dwell with them for ever in the dearest intimacy of eternal love, and you cannot possibly rage against them, nor play the devils against those, with whom you must live in unity before God. But if they be wicked men, and such as must be damned, (as malice will make you easily believe,) are they not miserable enough already, in being the slaves of sin and Satan? And will they not be miserable time enough and long enough in hell? Do you thirst to have them tormented before the time? O cruel men! O devilish malice! Would you wish them more punishment than hell-fire? Can you not patiently endure to see a poor sinner have a little prosperity and ease, who must lie in everlasting flames? But the truth is, malicious men are ordinarily atheists, and never think of another world; and therefore desire to be the avengers of themselves, because they believe not that there is any God to do it, or any future judgment and execution to be expected.

Consid. XIII. And remember how near both he and you are to death and judgment, when God will judge righteously betwixt you both. There are few so cruelly malicious, but if they both lay dying they would abate their malice and be easily reconciled, as remembering that their dust and bones will lie in quietness together, and malice is a miserable case to appear in before the Lord. Why then do you cherish your vice, by putting away the day of death from your remembrance? Do you not know that you are dying? Are a few more days so great a matter with you, that you will therefore do that because you have a few more days to live, which else you durst not do or think of? O hearken to the dreadful trumpet of God, which is summoning you all to come away; and methinks this should sound a retreat to the malicious, from persecuting those with whom they are going to be judged. God will shortly make the third, if you will needs be quarrelling! Unless it be mastiff dogs or fighting cocks, there are scarce any creatures but will give over fighting, if man or beast do come upon them that would destroy or hurt them both.

Consid. XIV. Wrathful and hurtful creatures are commonly hated and pursued by all; and loving, gentle, harmless, profitable creatures, are commonly beloved. And will you make yourselves like wild beasts or vermin, that all men naturally hate and seek to destroy? If a wolf, or a fox, or an adder do but appear, every man is ready to seek the death of him, as a hurtful creature, and an enemy to mankind; but harmless creatures no one meddleth with (unless for their own benefit and use): so if you will be malicious, hurtful serpents, that hiss, and sting, and trouble others, you will be the common hatred of the world, and it will be thought a meritorious work to mischief you; whereas if you will be loving, kind, and profitable, it will be taken to be men's interest to love you, and desire your good.

Consid. XV. Observe how you unfit yourselves for all holy duties, and communion with God, while you cherish wrath and malice in your hearts. Do you find yourselves fit for meditation, conference, or prayer while you are in wrath? I know you cannot: it both undisposeth you to the duty, and the guilt affrighteth you, and telleth you that you are unfit to come near to God. As a fever taketh away a man's appetite to his meat, and his disposition to labour, so doth wrath and malice destroy both your disposition to holy duties, and your pleasure in them. And conscience will tell you that it is so terrible to draw near God in such a case, that you will be readier (were it possible) to hide yourselves as Adam and Eve, or fly as Cain, as not enduring the presence of God. And therefore the Common-prayer book, above all other sins, enableth the pastor to keep away the malicious from the sacrament of communion; and conscience maketh many that have little conscience in any thing else, that they dare not come to that sacrament, while wrath and malice are in their breasts: and Christ himself saith, "If thou bring thy gift unto the altar, and there rememberest that thy brother hath aught against thee; leave there thy gift before the altar, and go thy way, first be reconciled to thy brother, and then come and offer thy gift. Agree with thine adversary quickly while thou art in the way with him, lest at any time the adversary deliver thee to the judge, and the judge deliver thee to the officer, and thou be cast into prison," &c. Matt. v. 23-25.

Consid. XVI. And your sin is aggravated, in that you hinder the good of those that you are offended with, and also provoke them to add sin to sin, and to be as furious and uncharitable as yourselves. If your neighbour be not faulty, why are you so displeased with him? If he be, why will you make him worse? Will you bring him to amendment by hatred or cruelty? Do you think one vice will cure another? Or is any man like to hearken to the counsel of an enemy? or to love the words of one that hateth him? Is malice and fierceness an attractive thing? Or rather is it not the way to drive men further from their duty, and into sin, by driving them from you who pretend to reform them by such unlikely, contrary means as these? And as you do your worst to harden them in their faults, and to make them hate whatever you would persuade them to; so at present you seek to kindle in their breasts the same fire of malice or passion which is kindled in yourselves. As love is the most effectual way to cause love; so passion is the most effectual [785]cause of passion, and malice is the most effectual cause of malice, and hurting another is the powerfullest means to provoke him to hurt you again if he be able; and weak things are ofttimes able to do hurt, when injuries boil up their passions to the height, or make them desperate. If your sinful provocations fill him also with rage, and make him curse, or swear, or rail, or plot revenge, or do you a mischief, you are guilty of this sin, and have a hand in the damnation of his soul, as much as in you lieth.

Consid. XVII. Consider how much fitter means there are at hand to right yourself, and attain any ends that are good, than by passion, malice, or revenge. If your end be nothing but to do mischief, and make another miserable, you are to the world as mad dogs, and wolves, and serpents to the country; and they that know you, will be as glad when the world is rid of you, as when an adder or a toad is killed. But if your end be only to right yourselves, and to reclaim your enemy, or reform your brother, fury and revenge is not the way. God hath appointed governors to do justice in commonwealths and families, and to those you may repair, and not take upon you to revenge yourselves. And God himself is the most righteous Governor of all the world, and to him you may confidently refer the case, when magistrates and rulers fail you; and his judgment will be soon enough and severe enough. And if you would rather have your neighbour reclaimed than destroyed, it is love and gentleness that is the way, with peaceable convictions, and such reasonings as show that you desire his good. Overcome him with kindness, if you would melt him into repentance, and heap coals of fire on his head. If thy enemy hunger, feed him; if he thirst, give him drink: this is overcoming evil with good (and not by beastly fury to overcome him); but when you are drawn to sinful passion and revenge, you are overcome of evil, Rom. xii. 19-21. If you would do good, it must be by good, and not by evil.

Consid. XVIII. Remember also how little you are concerned in the words or actions of other men towards you, in comparison of your carriage to yourselves and them. You have greater matters to mind, than your little sufferings by them; even the preserving of your innocency and your peace with God. It is your own actions, and not theirs, that you must answer for. You shall not be condemned for suffering wrong, but for doing wrong you may. All their injuries against you make you not the less esteemed of God, and therefore diminish not your felicity: it is themselves that they mortally wound, even to damnation, if they impenitently oppress another: keep yourselves and you keep your salvation, whatever others do against you.

Consid. XIX. Remember that injuries are your trials and temptations; God trieth you by them, and Satan tempteth you by them. God trieth your love, and patience, and obedience; that you may be perfect as your heavenly Father is perfect, and may be indeed his children, while you "love your enemies, and bless them that curse you, and do good to them that hate you, and pray for them that despitefully use you and persecute you," Matt. v. 44, 45; and being tried you may receive the crown of life, James i. 3, 4, 12. And Satan on the other side is at work, to try whether he can draw you by injuries to impatiency, and to hatred, malice, revenge, or cruelty, and so damn your souls by the hurting of your bodies. And when you foreknow his design, will you let him overcome? Hear every provoking word that is given you, and every injury that is done unto you, as if a messenger from Satan were sent to buffet you, or to speak that provoking language in his name; and as if he said to you, I come from the devil to call thee all that is naught and to abuse thee, and to try whether I can thus provoke thee to passion, malice, railing, or revenge, to sin against God and damn thy soul. If you knew one came to you from the devil on this errand, tell me how you would entertain him. And do you not know that this is indeed the case? "Fear none of those things which thou shalt suffer: behold, the devil shall cast some of you into prison that ye may be tried, and ye shall have tribulation ten days; be thou faithful to the death and I will give thee a crown of life," Rev. ii. 10. As trying imprisonments, so all other trying injuries are from the devil by God's permission, whoever be his instruments; and will you be overcome by him when you foreknow the end of his attempts?

Consid. XX. Lastly, set before you the example of our Lord Jesus Christ: see whether he was addicted to wrath and malice, hurtfulness or revenge. If you will not imitate him, you are none of his disciples; nor will he be your Saviour. A serious view of the holy pattern of love, and meekness, and patience, and forgiveness, which is set before us in the life of Christ, is a most powerful remedy against malice and revenge; and will cure it, if any thing will cure it. Phil. ii. 5-7, "Let this mind be in you, which was also in Christ Jesus, who being in the form of God,—yet made himself of no reputation, and took upon him the form of a servant." 1 Pet. iv. 1, "Forasmuch then as Christ hath suffered in the flesh, arm yourselves likewise with the same mind." 1 Pet. ii. 19-25, "For this is thankworthy, if a man for conscience toward God, endure grief, suffering wrongfully; for what glory is it if when ye be buffeted for your faults, ye shall take it patiently: but if when ye do well and suffer for it, ye take it patiently, this is acceptable with God. For even hereunto were ye called; because Christ also suffered for us, leaving us an ensample that ye should follow in his steps; who did no sin, neither was guile found in his mouth; who when he was reviled, reviled not again; when he suffered, he threatened not, but committed it to him that judgeth righteously." Think not to live and reign with Christ, if you will not follow, and suffer with him. It is impudent presumption, and not faith, to look to be like the saints in glory, while you are like the devil in malice and cruelty.

CHAPTER X.

CASES RESOLVED ABOUT FORGIVING INJURIES AND DEBTS, AND ABOUT SELF-DEFENCE, AND SEEKING RIGHT BY LAW OR OTHERWISE.

THE cases about forgiving, and revenging, are many, and some of them difficult: I shall resolve those of ordinary use in our practice, and pass by the rest.

Quest. I. Is a man bound to forgive all injuries and damages that are done him? If not, what injuries be they which every man is obliged to forgive?

Answ. To both these questions I briefly answer, 1. We must distinguish between a crime or sin against God, and the common good; and an injury or damage to ourselves. 2. And between public justice and private revenge. 3. And between those damages which fall upon myself only, and those that by me redound to others, (as wife or children, &c.) 4. And between the remitting of a punishment, and the remitting of reparations of my loss. 5. And [786]between the various punishments to be remitted. He that will confound any of these shall sooner deceive himself and others, than resolve the doubts.

Prop. I. It frequently falleth out, that it is not in our power to remit the penalty of a crime; no, not the temporal penalty. For this is a wrong to God the universal Governor, and God only can forgive it, and man no further than God hath commissioned him. Murder, whoredom, drunkenness, swearing, &c. as they are sins against God, the magistrate is bound to punish, and private men to endeavour it by the magistrate. And if it may be said, that the sovereign ruler of a nation hath power to forgive such crimes, the meaning is no more than this: 1. That as to the species of these sins, if he do forgive the temporal punishment which in his office he should have inflicted, yet no human power can question him for it, because he hath none on earth above him; but yet God will question him, and show him that he had no power to dispense with his laws, nor disoblige himself from his duty. 2. And that in some cases an individual crime may be forgiven by the magistrate as to the temporal punishment, even where the ends of the law and government require it; but this must not be ordinary.

Prop. II. It is not always in the power of the magistrate to remit the temporal punishment of heinous crimes, against the common good. Because it is ordinarily necessary to the common good that they be punished; and his power is for the common good, and not against it. The enemies of the public peace must by punishment be restrained.

Prop. III. Much less is it in the power of a private man to remit a penalty to be inflicted by a magistrate. And what I say of magistrates, holdeth of parents, and other governors, *cæteris paribus*, according to the proportion of their authority.

Prop. IV. I may by just means exact satisfaction for damages to myself, in my reputation or estate, when the ends of christianity, even the honour of God, and the public good, and the benefit of men's souls, require it; that is, when I only vindicate these by lawful means, as they are the talents which God hath committed to me for his service, and for which he will call me to account. It may fall out that the vindicating of a minister's or other christian's name from a slander, may become very needful for the interest and honour of religion, and for the good of many souls. And if I have an estate which I resolve to use for God, and a thief or a deceiver take it from me, who will do no good with it but hurt, I may be bound to vindicate it; that I may be enabled to do good, and may give God a comfortable account of my stewardship; besides the suppressing of thievery and deceit, as they are against the common good.

Prop. V. When my estate is not entirely my own, but wife or child or any other is a sharer in it, it is not wholly in my power to remit any debt or damage out of it, but I must have the consent of them that are joint-owners; unless I be intrusted for them.

Prop. VI. If I be primarily obliged to maintain wife and children, or any others, with my estate, I am bound on their behalf to use all just means to vindicate it from any that shall injuriously invade it; otherwise I am guilty of their sufferings whom I should maintain; I may no more suffer a thief than a dog to go away with my children's meat.

Prop. VII. And as I must vindicate my estate for others to whom I am intrusted to administer it by God, so must I for myself also, so far as God would have me use it myself. For he that hath charged me to provide for my family, requireth also that I famish not myself; and he hath required me to love my neighbour but as myself; and therefore as I am bound to vindicate and help my neighbour if a thief or oppressor would rob him, (according to my place and power,) so must I do also for myself. In all these seven cases I am not obliged to forgive.

But on the other side, in all these cases following, I am bound to forgive and let go my right.

Prop. I. As the church may declare to penitent sinners, the remission of the eternal punishment, so may it remit the temporal punishment of excommunication, to the penitent; yea, this they are obliged by Christ to do, ministerially, as under him.

Prop. II. When the repentance and satisfaction of the sinner is like to conduce more to the public good, and the honour of God, and other ends of government, than his punishment would do, a private man may not be obliged to prosecute him before the magistrate, and the magistrate hath power to forgive him as to the penalty which it belongeth to him to inflict. (Though this may not extend to the remitting of crimes ordinarily and frequently, nor to the remitting of some sort of heinous crimes at all; because this cannot attain the ends of government as aforesaid.)

Prop. III. All personal wrongs, so far as they are merely against myself, and disable me not from my duty to God and my neighbour, I may and must forgive: for my own interest is put more in my own power; and here it is that I am commanded to forgive. If you say that I am bound to preserve my own life and soul as much as another's; I answer, it is true, I am bound to preserve my own and another's ultimately for the service and glory of God; and God's interest in me I cannot remit or give away.

As there is no obligation to duty but what is originally from God, so there is none but what is ultimately for God, even to please and glorify him.

Object. But if this be all, I shall forgive no wrongs; for there is none which doth not some way hinder me in my duty. *Answ.* Yes, there may be many to your body, your estate, and name, which yet may be no disablement or hinderance to you, except you make it so yourself: as if you receive a box on the ear, or be slandered or reviled where none heareth it but yourself, or such as will make no evil use of it, or if a little be diminished injuriously out of a superfluous estate, or so as to be employed as well as you would have done. 2. But I further answer this objection in the next propositions.

Prop. IV. If my patient suffering a personal injury, which somewhat hindereth me from my duty, be like to be as great a service to God, or to do more good, than by that duty I should do, I ought to pass by and forgive that injury; because then God's interest obligeth me not to vindicate my right.

Prop. V. If when I am injured, and thereby disabled from doing some good which I should else have done, I am not able by seeking reparation or the punishment of the person, to recover my capacity, and promote the service of God, I am bound to pass by and remit that injury. (I speak not of the criminal part, but the injury as such; for a man may be bound to bring a thief to punishment, on the account of God's honour, and the common good, though else he might forgive the injury to himself.)

Prop. VI. If it be probable that he that defraudeth me of my estate, will do more good with it than I should have done, I am not bound to vindicate it from him for my own interest (though as he is criminal, and the crime is hurtful, as an ill example, to the common good, so I may be bound to it). Nay, were it not for the said criminal respect, I am bound rather to let him take it, than to vindicate it by any |787|such means as would break charity, and do more hurt than good.

Prop. VII. If I am absolutely trusted with the person or estate of another, I may so far forgive the wrongs done to that other, upon sufficient reasons, as well as against myself.

Prop. VIII. A private man may not usurp the magistrate's power, or do any act which is proper to his office, nor yet may he break his laws, for the avenging of himself; he may use no other means than the law of God and his sovereign do allow him. Therefore he may not rail, or revile, or slander, or rob, or strike, or hurt any, (unless in case of defence, as afterward,) nor take any other prohibited course.

Prop. IX. No rigour or severity must be used to right myself, where gentler means may probably do it; but the most harmless way must first be tried.

Prop. X. In general, all wrongs, and debts, and damages, must be forgiven, when the hurt is like to be greater, which will come by our righting ourselves, than that which by forbearance we shall sustain; and all must be forgiven where God's law or man's forbiddeth us not to forgive. Therefore a man that will here know his duty, must conduct his actions by very great prudence (which if he have not himself, he must make use of a guide or counsellor): and he must be able to compare the evil which he suffereth with the evil which will in probability follow his vindication, and to discern which of them is the greater; or else he can never know how far and when he may and must forgive. And herein he must observe,

1. That hurt that cometh to a man's soul is greater than the hurt that befalleth the body; and therefore if my suing a man at law be like to hurt his soul by uncharitableness, or to hurt my own, or the souls of others, by scandal or disturbances, I must rather suffer any mere bodily injuries, than use that means; but if yet greater hurt to souls would follow that bodily suffering of mine, the case is then altered the other way. So if by forgiving debts or wrongs, I be liker to do more good to the soul of him whom I forgive, or others, than the recovery of my own, or the righting of myself, is like any way to equal, I am obliged to forgive that debt or wrong.

2. The good or hurt which cometh to a community or to many, is (*cæteris paribus*) to be more regarded than that which cometh to myself or any one alone. Because many are of more worth than one; and because God's honour (*cæteris paribus*)

is more concerned in the good of many than of one. Therefore I must not seek my own right to the hurt of many, either of their souls or bodies, unless some greater good require it.

3. The good or hurt of public persons, magistrates, or pastors, is (*cæterisc paribus*) of more regard than the good or hurt of single men: therefore (*cæteris paribus*) I must not right myself to the dishonour or hurt of governors; (no, though I were none of their charge or subjects;) because the public good is more concerned in their honour or welfare than in mine. The same may be said of persons by their gifts and interests more eminently serviceable to God and the common good than I am.

4. The good or hurt of a near relation, of a dear friend, of a worthy person, is more to be regarded by me, *cæteris paribus*, than the good or hurt of a vile, unworthy person, or a stranger. And therefore the Israelites might not take usury of a poor brother, which yet they might do of an alien of another land! The laws of nature and friendship may more oblige me to one than to another, though they were supposed equal in themselves. Therefore I am not bound to remit a debt or wrong to a thief, or deceiver, or a vile person, when a nearer or worthier person would be equally damnified by his benefit. And thus far, (if without any partial self-love a man can justly estimate himself,) he may not only as he is nearest himself, but also for his real worth, prefer his own commodity before the commodity of a more unworthy and unserviceable person.

5. Another man's necessities are more regardable than our own superfluities; as his life is more regardable than our corporal delights. Therefore it is a great sin for any man to reduce another to extremity, and deprive him of necessaries for his life, merely to vindicate his own right in superfluities, for the satisfaction of his concupiscence and sensual desires. If a poor man steal to save his own or his children's lives, and the rich man vindicate his own, merely to live in greater fulness or gallantry in the world, he sinneth both the sin of sensuality and uncharitableness (but how far for the common good he is bound to prosecute the thief as criminal, is a case which depends on other circumstances). And this is the most common case, in which the forgiving of debts and damages is required in Scripture, viz. When the other is poor and we are rich, and his necessities require it as an act of charity (and also the former case, when the hurt by our vindication is like to be greater than our benefit will countervail).

Quest. II. What is the meaning of those words of Christ, Matt. v. 38-42, "Ye have heard that it hath been said, An eye for an eye, and a tooth for a tooth: but I say unto you, that ye resist not evil; but whosoever shall smite thee on thy right cheek, turn to him the other also; and if any man will sue thee at the law, and take away thy coat, let him have thy cloak also; and whosoever shall compel thee to go a mile, go with him two: give to him that asketh thee; and from him that would borrow of thee turn thou not away?"

Answ. The meaning of the text is this: as if he had said, Because you have heard that magistrates are required to do justice exactly between man and man, and to take an eye for an eye, &c. therefore you may perhaps believe those teachers who would persuade you that for any man to exact this satisfaction, is no fault: but I tell you that duties of charity must be performed, as well as justice must be done; and though it must be the magistrate's duty to do you this justice, it is not your duty always to require it, but charity may make the contrary to be your duty. Therefore I say unto you, overvalue not the concernments of your flesh, nor the trifles of this world; but if a man abuse you, or wrong you in these trifles, make no great matter of it, and be not presently inflamed to revenge, and to right yourselves; but exercise your patience and your charity to him that wrongeth you, and by an habituated stedfastness herein, be ready to receive another injury with equal patience, yea many such, rather than to fly to an unnecessary vindication of your right. For what if he give you another stroke? Or what if he also take your cloak? Or what if he compel you to go another mile for him? Let him do it; let him take it; how small is your hurt! What inconsiderable things are these! Your resistance and vindication of your right may violate charity and peace, and inflame his passion, and kindle your own, and hurt both your souls, and draw you into other sins, and cost you dearer than your right was worth: whereas your patience, and yieldingness, and submission, and readiness to serve another, and to let go your own for peace and charity, may shame him or melt him, and prevent contention, and keep your own and the public [788]peace, and may show the excellency of your holy religion, and win men's souls to the love of it, that they may be saved. Therefore instead of exacting or vindicating your utmost right, set light by your corporal sufferings and wrongs, and study and labour with all your power to excel in charity, and to do good to all, and to stoop to any service to another, and humble yourselves, and exercise patience, and give and lend according to your abilities, and pretend not justice against the great duties of charity and patience. So that here is forbidden both violent and legal revenge for our corporal abuses, when the law of charity or patience is against it: but this disobligeth not magistrates to do justice, or men to seek it, in any of the cases mentioned in the seven first propositions.

Quest. III. Am I bound to forgive another, if he ask me not forgiveness? The reason of the question is, because Christ saith, Luke xvii. 3, 4, "If thy brother trespass against thee, rebuke him: and if he repent, forgive him; and if he trespass against thee seven times in a day, and seven times in a day turn again to thee, saying, I repent, thou shalt forgive him."

Answ. In the resolving of this, while some have barely affirmed, and others denied, for want of distinguishing, they have said worse than nothing. It is necessary that we distinguish,

1. Between the forgiving of an enemy, and of a stranger, and of a neighbour, and of a brother, as such.

2. Between the several penalties to be remitted (as well as revenges to be forborne). And so briefly the case must be thus resolved.

Prop. I. An enemy, a stranger, and a neighbour, as such, must be forgiven (in the cases before asserted) though they ask not forgiveness, nor say, I repent: for,

1. Many other scriptures absolutely require it.

2. And forgiving them as such, is but the continuing them in our common charity, as men, or neighbours; that is, our not endeavouring to ruin them, or do them any hurt, and our hearty desiring and endeavouring their good, according to their capacities or ours; and thus far we must forgive them.

Prop. II. A brother also must be thus far forgiven, though he say not, I repent; that is, we must love him as a man, and wish and endeavour his good to our power.

Prop. III. A brother as a brother, is not to be so forgiven, as to be restored to our estimation and affection, and usage of him as a brother, either in spiritual account, or intimate special love and familiarity, as long as he is impenitent in his gross offences; and that is, till he turn again and say, I repent. A natural brother is still to be loved as a natural brother. For that kind of love dependeth not on his honesty or repentance. But,

1. A brother in a religious sense,

2. Or a bosom, familiar friend, are both unfit for to be received in these capacities, till they are penitent for gross offences; therefore the church is not to pardon the impenitent, in point of communion, nor particular christians to pardon them in their esteem and carriage; nor am I bound to take an unfit person to be my bosom friend to know my secrets: therefore if either of these offend, I must not forgive them, that is, by forgiveness continue them in the respect and usage of this brotherhood, till they repent; and this (first especially) is the brother mentioned in the text.

Quest. IV. Is it lawful to sue a brother at law? The reason of the question is, from the words of the apostle Paul, 1 Cor. vi. 7, "There is utterly a fault among you, because ye go to law one with another. Why do ye not rather take wrong? why do ye not rather suffer yourselves to be defrauded?"

Answ. 1. Distinguish betwixt going to law before heathens, or other enemies to the christian religion, and before christian magistrates.

2. Between going to law in malice for revenge, and going merely to seek my right, or to seek the suppression and reformation of sin.

3. Between going to law when you are bound to forgive, and when you are not.

4. And between going to law in haste and needlessly, and going to law as the last remedy, in case of necessity, when other means fail.

5. And between going to law when the hurt is like to be greater than the benefit, and going to law when it is likely to do good. There is a great deal of difference between these cases.

Prop. I. Christians must rather suffer wrong, than go to law before the enemies of religion, when it is like to harden them, and to bring christianity into contempt.

Prop. II. It is not lawful to make law and justice the means of private unlawful revenge; nor to vent our malice, nor to oppress the innocent.

Prop. III. Whenever I am bound to forgive the trespass, wrong, or debt, then it is unlawful to seek my own at law. For that is not forgiving.

Prop. IV. There are many other remedies which must first be tried (ordinarily) before we go to law. As,

1. To rebuke our neighbour for his wrong, and privately to desire necessary reparations.

2. To take two or three to admonish him; or to refer the matter to arbitrators (or in some cases to a lot). And if any make law their first remedy needlessly, while the other means should first be used, it is a sin.

Prop. V. It is not lawful to go to law-suits, when prudence may discern that the hurt which may come by it, will be greater than the benefit; (either by hardening the person, or disturbing ourselves, or scandalizing others against religion, or drawing any to ways of unpeaceableness and revenge, &c.) The foreseen consequences may overrule the case.

But on the other side, *Prop.* I. It is lawful to make use of christian judicatories, so it be done in a lawful manner; yea, and in some cases, of the judicatories of infidels.

Prop. II. The suppressing of sin, and the defending of the innocent, and righting of the wronged, being the duty of governors, it is lawful to seek these benefits at their hands.

Prop. III. In cases where I am not obliged to forgive, (as I have showed before some such there be,) I may justly make use of governors as the ordinance of God.

Prop. IV. The order and season is when I have tried other means in vain; when persuasion or arbitration will do no good, or cannot be used with hope of success.

Prop. V. And the great condition to prove it lawful is, when it is not like to do more hurt than good, either directly of itself, or by men's abuse; when religion, or the soul of any man, or any one's body, or estate, or name, is not like to lose more than my gain, or any other benefits, will compensate; when all these concur, it is lawful to go to law.

Quest. V. Is it lawful to defend my person, life, or estate against a thief, or murderer, or unjust invader, by force of arms?

Answ. You must distinguish, 1. Between such defence as the law of the land alloweth, and such as it forbiddeth.

[789]2. Between necessary and unnecessary actions of defence.

Prop. I. There is no doubt but it is both lawful and a duty to defend ourselves by such convenient means as are likely to attain their end, and are not contrary to any law, of God or man. We must defend our neighbour if he be assaulted or oppressed, and we must love our neighbour as ourselves.

Prop. II. This self-defence by force, is then lawful, when it is necessary, and other more gentle means have been uneffectual, or have no place (supposing still that the means be such as the law of God or man forbiddeth not).

Prop. III. And it is necessary to the lawfulness of it, that the means be such as in its nature is like to be successful, or like to do more good than harm.

But on the other side, *Prop.* I. We may not defend ourselves by any such force as either the laws of God or our rulers, thereto authorized by him, shall forbid. For,

1. The laws are made by such as have more power over our lives, than we have over them ourselves.

2. And they are made for the good of the commonwealth; which is to be preferred before the good or life of any single person. And whatever selfish infidels say, both nature and grace do teach us to lay down our lives, for the welfare of the church or state, and to prefer a multitude before ourselves. Therefore it is better to be robbed, oppressed, or killed, than to break the peace of the commonwealth.

Prop. II. Therefore a private man may not raise an army to defend his life against his prince, or lawful governor. Perhaps he might hold his hands if personally he went about to murder him, without the violation of the public peace; but he cannot raise a war without it.

Prop. III. We may not do that by blood or violence, which might be done by persuasion, or by any lawful, gentle means: violence must be used, even in defence, but in case of true necessity.

Prop. IV. When self-defence is like to have consequents so ill, as the saving of ourselves cannot countervail, it is then unlawful *finis gratia*, and not to be attempted.

Prop. V. Therefore if self-defence be unlikely to prevail, our strength being inconsiderable, and when the enemy is but like to be the more exasperated by it, and our sufferings like to be the greater; nature and reason teach us to submit, and use the more effectual (lawful) means.

Quest. VI. Is it lawful to take away another's life, in the defending of my purse or estate?

Answ. 1. You must again distinguish between such defence as the law of the land alloweth, and such as it forbiddeth.

2. Between what is necessary, and what is unnecessary.

3. Between a life less worth than the prize which he contendeth for, and a life more worth than it, or than mine own.

4. Between the simple defence of my purse, and the defence of it and my life together.

5. Between what I do with purpose and desire, and what I do unwillingly through the assailant's temerity or violence.

6. And between what I do in mere defence, and what I do to bring a thief or robber unto legal punishment. And so I answer,

Prop. I. You may not defend your purse, or your estate, by such actions, as the law of the land forbiddeth; (unless it go against the law of God;) because it is to be supposed, that it is better a man's estate or purse be lost, than law and public order violated.

Prop. II. You may not (against an ordinary thief or robber) defend your purse with the probable hazard of his life, if a few good words, or other safe and gentle means, which you have opportunity to use, be like to serve turn without such violence.

Prop. III. If it might be supposed that a prince, or other person of great use and service to the commonwealth, should in a frolic, or otherwise, assault your person for your estate or purse, it is not lawful to take away his life by a defensive violence, if you know it to be he; because (though in some countries the law might allow it you, yet) *finis gratia* it is unlawful; because his life is more necessary to the common good than yours.

Prop. IV. If a pilfering thief would steal your purse, without any violence which hazardeth your life, (ordinarily,) you may not take away his life in the defending of it. Because it is the work of the magistrate to punish him by public justice, and your defence requireth it not.

Prop. V. All this is chiefly meant, of the voluntary, designed taking away of his life; and not of any lawful action, which doth it accidentally against your will.

On the other side, *Prop.* I. If the law of the land allow you to take away a man's life in the defending of your purse, it removeth the scruple, if the weight of the matter also do allow it: because it supposeth, that the law taketh the offender to be worthy of death, and maketh you in that case the executioner of it. And if, indeed, the crime be such as deserveth death, you may be the executioner when the law alloweth it.

Prop. II. And this is more clear, when the robber for your money doth assault your life, or is like for aught you see to do it.

Prop. III. And when gentler means will not serve the turn, but violence is the only remedy which is left you, which is like to avail for your defence.

Prop. IV. And when the person is a vile offender, who is rather a plague and burden to the commonwealth than any necessary member of it.

Prop. V. If you desire not, and design not his death, but he rush upon it himself in his fury, while you lawfully defend your own, the case is yet less questionable.

Prop. VI. If a thief have taken your purse, though you may not take away his life after to recover it, (because it is of less value,) nor yet in revenge (because that belongeth not to private men); yet if the law require or allow you to pursue him to bring him to a judicial trial, if you kill him while he resisteth, it is not your sin; because you are but suppressing sin in your place, according to the allowance of the law.

Quest. VII. May I kill or wound another in the defence or vindication of my honour, or good name?

Answ. No: not by private assault or violence; but if the crime be so great, that the law of the land doth punish it with death, if that law be just, you may in some cases seek to bring the offender to public justice; but that is rare, and otherwise you may not do it. For,

1. It belongeth only to the magistrate, and not to you, to be the avenger.

2. And killing a man can be no meet defence against calumny or slander; for if you will kill a man for prevention, you kill the innocent; if you kill him afterwards, it is no defence, but an unprofitable revenge, which vindicateth not your honour, but dishonoureth you more. Your patience is your honour, and your bloody revenge doth show you to be so like the devil, the destroyer, that it is your greatest shame.

3. It is odious pride which maketh men overvalue [790]their reputation among men, and think that a man's life is a just compensation to them for their dishonour! Such bloody sacrifices are fit to appease only the bloodthirsty spirit! But what is it that pride will not do and justify?

CHAPTER XI.

SPECIAL DIRECTIONS TO ESCAPE THE GUILT OF PERSECUTING. DETERMINING ALSO THE CASE ABOUT LIBERTY IN MATTERS OF RELIGION.

THOUGH this be a subject which the guilty cannot endure to hear of, yet the misery of persecutors, the blood, and groans, and ruins of the church, and the lamentable divisions of professed christians, do all command me not to pass it by in silence; but to tell them the truth, "whether they will hear, or whether they will forbear;" though they were such as Ezek. iii. 7-9, 11.

Direct. I. If you would escape this dreadful guilt, understand well what persecution is. Else you may either run into it ignorantly, or oppose a duty as if it were persecution.

The verb *persequor* is often taken in a good sense, for no more than *continuato motu vel ad extremum sequor*; and sometimes for the blameless prosecution of a delinquent; but we take it here as the English word persecute is most commonly taken, for *inimico affectu insequor*, a malicious or injurious hurting or persecuting another, and that for the sake of religion or righteousness. For it is not common injuries which we here intend to speak of. Three things then go to make up persecution. 1. That it be the hurting of another, in his body, liberty, relations, estate, or reputation. 2. That it be done injuriously, to one who deserveth it not, in the particular which is the cause. 3. That it be for the cause of religion or of righteousness, that is, for the truth of God which we hold or utter; or for the worship of God which we perform; or for obedience to the will of God revealed in his laws. This is the cause on the sufferer's part, whatever is intended by the persecutor.

There are divers sorts of persecutions. As to the principles of the persecutors: 1. There is a persecution which is openly professed to be for the cause of religion; as heathens and Mahometans persecute christians as christians. And there is a hypocritical persecution when the pretended cause is some odious crime, but the real cause is men's religion, or obedience to God. This is the common persecution, which nominal christians exercise on serious christians, or on one another. They will not say that they persecute them because they are godly or serious christians, but that is the true cause; for if they will but set them above God, and obey them against God, they will abate their persecution. Many of the heathens thus persecuted the christians too, under the name of ungodly, and evil-doers; but the true cause was, because they obeyed not their commands in the worshipping of their idol gods. So do the papists persecute and murder men, not as professors of the truth, (which is the true cause,) but under the name of heretics and schismatics, or rebels against the pope, or whatever their malice pleaseth to accuse them of. And profane, nominal christians seldom persecute the serious and sincere directly by that name, but under some nickname which they set upon them, or under the name of hypocrites, or self-conceited, or factious persons, or such like. And if they live in a place, and age, where there are many civil wars or differences, they are sure to fetch some odious name or accusation thence: which side soever it be that they are on, or if they meddle not on any side, they are sure by every party whom they please not, to hear religion loaded with such reproaches as the times will allow them to vent against it. Even the papists who take this course with protestants, it seems by Acosta are so used themselves, not by the heathens, but by one another, yea, by the multitude, yea, by their priests. For so saith he, speaking of the parish priests among the Indians, having reproved their dicing, carding, hunting, idleness. Lib. iv. cap. 15. p. 404, 405. *Itaque is cui pastoralis Indorum cura committitur, non solum contra diaboli machinas et naturæ incentiva pugnare debet; sed jam etiam confirmatæ hominum consuetudini et tempore et turba præpotenti sese objicere; et ad excipienda invidorum ac malevolorum tela forte pectus opponere; qui siquid a profano suo instituto abhorrentem viderint; proditorem, hypocritam, hostem clamant*: that is, He therefore to whom the pastoral care of the Indians is committed, must not only fight against the engines of the devil, and the incentives of nature; but also now must object or set himself against the confirmed custom of men, which is grown very powerful both by time, and by the multitude; and must valiantly oppose his breast, to receive the darts of the envious and malevolent, who if they see any thing contrary to their profane fashion (or breeding) cry out, A traitor, a hypocrite, an enemy. It seems then that this is a common course.

2. Persecution is either done in ignorance or knowledge. The commonest persecution is that which is done in ignorance and error; when men think a good cause to be bad, or a bad cause to be good, and so persecute truth while they take it to be falsehood, or good while they take it to be evil, or *obtrude by violence their errors for truths*, and their evils as good and necessary things. Thus Peter testifieth of the Jews, who killed the Prince of life; Acts iii. 13, 14, 17, "I know that through ignorance you did it, as did also your rulers." And Paul; 1 Cor. ii. 8, "Which none of the princes of this world knew; for had they known it, they would not have crucified the Lord of glory." And Christ himself saith, John xvi. 3, "These things will they do unto you, because they have not known the Father, nor me." And Paul saith of himself, Acts xxvi. 9, "I thought verily with myself, that I ought to do many things contrary to the name of Jesus of Nazareth, which thing I also did," &c. And, 1 Tim. i. 13, "that it was

ignorantly in unbelief, that he was a blasphemer, a persecutor, and injurious." And on the other side, some persecute truth and goodness while they know it to be so. Not because it is truth or goodness, but because it is against their carnal, worldly interest and inclination. As the conscience of a worldling, a drunkard, a whoremonger, beareth witness against his sin while he goeth on in it; so ofttimes doth the conscience of the persecutor; and he hath secret convictions, that those whom he persecuteth are better and happier than himself.

3. As to the cause, sometimes persecution is for Christianity and godliness in the gross, or for some great essential point; and sometimes it is only for some particular truth or duty, and that perhaps of a lower nature, so small or so dark, that it is become a great controversy, whether it be truth or error, duty or sin. In some respects it is more comfortable to the persecuted, and more heinous in the persecutor, that the suffering be for the greatest things. For this leaveth no doubt in the mind, whether our cause be good or not; and this showeth that the [791]persecutor's mind is most alien from God and truth; but in some other respect, it is an aggravation of the sin of the persecutor, and of the comfort of the persecuted, when it is for smaller truths and duties. For it is a sign of great uncharitableness and cruelty, when men can find in their hearts to persecute others for little things; and it is a sign of a heart that is true to God, and very sincere, when we will rather suffer any thing from man, than renounce the smallest truth of God, or commit the smallest sin against him, or omit the smallest duty, when it is a duty.

4. Sometimes persecution is directly for religion; that is, for matters of professed faith or worship: and sometimes it is for a civil or a common cause; yet still it is for our obedience to God, (or else it is not the persecution which we speak of,) though the matter of it be some common or civil thing: as if I were persecuted merely for giving to the poor, or helping the sick, or for being loyal to my prince, and to the laws, or for doing my duty to my parents, or because I will not bear false witness, or tell a lie, or subscribe a falsehood, or any such like; this is truly persecution, whatever the matter of it be, as long as it is truly for obeying God that we undergo the suffering.

I omit many other less considerable distributions: and also those afflictions which are but improperly called persecutions (as when a man is punished for a fault in a greater measure than it deserveth. This is injustice but not persecution, unless it be his religion and obedience to God, which is the secret cause of it).

Direct. II. Understand well the greatness of the sin of persecution, that you may be kept in a due fear of being tempted to it. Here therefore I shall show you how great a sin it is.

1. Persecution is a fighting against God: so it is called Acts v. 39. And to fight against God, is odious malignity, and desperate folly. 1. It is venomous malignity, for a creature to fight against his Creator, and a sinner against his Redeemer who would save him; and for so blind a worm to rise up against the wisdom of the all-knowing God! and for so vile a sinner to oppose the Fountain of love and goodness! 2. And what folly can be greater, than for a mole to reproach the sun for darkness? or a lump of earth to take up arms against the Almighty, terrible God? Art thou able to make good thy cause against him? or to stand before him when he is offended, and chargeth thee with sin? Hear a Pharisee; "And now I say unto you, refrain from these men, and let them alone; for if this counsel or this work be of men, it will come to nought: but if it be of God, ye cannot overthrow it; lest haply ye be found even to fight against God," Acts v. 38, 39. Or hear Christ himself; "I am Jesus, whom thou persecutest; it is hard for thee to kick against the pricks," Acts ix. 4, 5; with bare feet or hands to beat the thorns! How unmeet a match is man for God! He needeth not so much as a word to take away thy soul, and crush thee to the lowest hell. His will alone can lay thee under thy deserved pains. Canst thou conquer the Almighty God? Wilt thou assault the power which was never overcome, or storm Jehovah's throne or kingdom? First try to take down the sun, and moon, and stars from the firmament, and to stop the course of the rivers, or of the sea; and to rebuke the winds, and turn night into day,

and winter into summer, and decrepid age into vigorous youth. Attempt not greater matters till thou hast performed these; it is a greater matter than any of these, to conquer God, whose cause thou fightest against. Hear him again; Isa. xlv. 9, "Woe unto him that striveth with his Maker! let the potsherd strive with the potsherds of the earth. Shall the clay say to him that fashioneth it, What makest thou? or thy work, He hath no hands?" And Isaiah xlv. 2. "Who would set the briers and thorns against me in battle? I would go through them, I would burn them together," Isa. xxvii. 4. Woe to the man that is not content to go to fight with men, but chooseth the most dreadful God to be his enemy! It had been better for thee, that all the world had been against thee.

2. Persecution opposeth the gracious design of our Redeemer, and hindereth his gospel, and work of mercy to the world, and endeavoureth the ruin of his kingdom upon earth. Christ came to save men, and persecutors raise up their power against him, as if they envied salvation to the world. And if God have made the work of man's redemption the most wonderful of all his works which ever he revealed to the sons of men, you may easily conceive what thanks he will give them that resist him in so high and glorious a design. If you could pull the stars out of the firmament, or hinder the motions of the heavens, or deny the rain to the thirsty earth, you might look for as good a reward for this, as for opposing the merciful Redeemer of the world, in the blessed work of man's salvation.

3. Persecution is a resisting or fighting against the Holy Ghost. Saith Stephen to the Jews, "Ye stiffnecked and uncircumcised in heart and ears; ye do always resist the Holy Ghost: as your fathers did, so do ye," Acts vii. 51. If you silence the ministers who are the means by which the Spirit worketh, in the illuminating and sanctifying of souls, Acts xxvi. 17, 18; or if you afflict men for those holy duties, which the Spirit of God hath taught them to perform, or would force men from that which the Spirit of Christ is sent to draw them to; this is to raise war against that Spirit, into whose name you were yourselves baptized.

4. Persecution endeavoureth the damnation of men's souls, either by depriving them of the preaching of the gospel which should save them, or by forcing them upon that sin for which God will condemn them. Yea, the banishing or silencing of one faithful preacher, may conduce to the damnation of many hundreds! If it be said, that others who are set up in their stead may save men's souls as well as they, I answer, 1. God seldom, if ever, did qualify supernumeraries for the work of the ministry! Many a nation hath had too few, but I never read of any nation that had too many, who were well qualified for that great and difficult work, no, not from the days of Christ till now! So that if they are all fit men, there are none of them to be spared; but all are too few, if they conjoin their greatest skill and diligence. Christ biddeth us pray the Lord of the harvest, to send forth more labourers into his harvest; but never biddeth us pray to send out fewer, or to call any in that were but tolerably fitted for the work. 2. Many persecutors banish all preachers of the gospel, and set up no other to do the service which they were called to. And it is rarely seen, that any who can find in their hearts to cast out any faithful ministers of Christ, have hearts to set up better, or any that are competent, in their stead; but it is ordinarily seen, that when the judgment is so far depraved, as to approve of the casting out of worthy men; it is also so far depraved as to think an ignorant, unskilful, heartless, or scandalous sort of ministers, to be as fit to save men's souls as they. And how many poor congregations in the eastern and western churches (nay, how many thousands) have ignorant, ungodly, sensual pastors, who are such unsavoury salt, as to be unfit for the land, or for the [792]dunghill! whilst men are extinguishing the clearest lights, or thrusting them into obscurity, Matt. v. 13-15; Luke xiv. 35. 3. And there may be something of suitableness between a pastor and the flock, which may give him advantage to be more profitable to their souls, than another man of equal parts. 4. And, though God can work by the weakest means, yet ordinarily we see that his work upon men's souls is so far moral, as that he usually prospereth men according to the fitness of their labours to the work! And some men

have far more success than others. He that should expel a dozen or twenty of the ablest physicians out of London, and say, There are enough left in their steads, who may save men's lives as well as they, might, notwithstanding that assertion, be found guilty of the blood of no small numbers. And as men have sometimes an aversion to one sort of food, (as good as any to another man,) and as this distemper is not laudable; and yet he that would force them to eat nothing else but that which they so abhor, were liker to kill them than to cure them; so is it with the souls of many. And there are few who have any spiritual discerning and relish, but have some special sense of what is helpful or hurtful to their souls, in sermons, books, and conference, which a stander-by is not so fit to judge of as themselves. So that it is clear, that persecution driveth men towards their damnation! And, oh how sad a case it is, to have the damnation of one soul to answer for! (Which is worse than the murdering of many bodies.) Much more to be guilty of the perdition of a multitude!

5. Persecution is injustice, and oppression of the innocent! And what a multitude of terrible threatenings against this sin, are found throughout the holy Scriptures! Doth a man deserve to be cruelly used, for being faithful to his God, and for preferring him before man? and for being afraid to sin against him? or for doing that which God commandeth him, and that upon pain of greater sufferings than man can inflict upon him? Is it not his Saviour that hath said, "Fear not them that can kill the body, and after that have no more that they can do; but fear him who after he hath killed, hath power to cast into hell: yea, I say unto you, fear him." Though christianity was once called, "A sect which every where was spoken against," Acts xxviii. 22; and Paul was accused as a pestilent fellow, and a mover of sedition among the people, Acts xxiv. 5; and Christ was crucified as a usurper of the crown; yet innocency shall be innocency still, in spite of malice and lying accusations; because God will be the final Judge, and will bring all secret things to light, and will justify those whom injustice hath condemned, and will not call them as slandering tongues have called them. Yea, the consciences of the persecutors are often forced to say, as they did of Daniel, Dan. vi. 5, "We shall not find any occasion against this Daniel, except we find it against him concerning the law of his God." And therefore the net which they were fain to lay for him, was a law against his religion, or prayers to God; for a law against treason, sedition, swearing, drunkenness, fornication, &c. would have done them no service! And yet they would fain have aspersed him there, ver. 4. Jer. xxii. 13, "Woe to him that buildeth his house by unrighteousness!" &c. Isa. xxxiii. 1, "Woe to thee that spoilest, and thou wast not spoiled!" Isa. v. 20, "Woe to them that call evil good, and good evil!" Jer. ii. 34, "In thy skirts is found the blood of the souls of the poor innocents." Prov. vi. 16, 17, "Hands that shed innocent blood, the Lord doth hate," &c.

6. Persecution maketh men likest unto devils, and maketh them his most notable servants in the world.[125] Many wicked men may neglect that duty which they are convinced they should do. But to hate it, and malice men that do it, and seek their ruin; this, if any thing, is work more beseeming a devil than a man. These are the commanders in the armies of the devil, against the cause and kingdom of the Lord! John viii. 42, 44. And accordingly shall they speed.

7. Persecution is an inhuman, disingenuous sin, and showeth an extinction of the light of nature. A good-natured man, if he had no grace at all, would abhor to be cruel, and to oppress his brethren; and that merely because they are true to their consciences, and obey their God, while they do no hurt to any others. If they had deserved execution, an ingenuous nature would not be forward to be their executioner; much more when they deserve encouragement and imitation: it is no honour to be numbered with bloodthirsty men.

8. It is a sin that hath so little of commodity, honour, or pleasure to invite men to it, that maketh it utterly without excuse, and showeth, that the serpentine nature is the cause, Gen. iii. 15. What get men by shedding the blood of innocents, or silencing the faithful preachers of the gospel? What sweetness could they find in cruelty, if a malicious nature made it not sweet?

9. It is a sin which men have as terrible warnings against from God, as any sin in the world, that I can remember. 1. In God's threatenings. 2. In sad examples, and judgments in this life, even on posterity. 3. And in the infamy that followeth the names of persecutors, when they are dead.

1. How terrible are those words of Christ, Matt. xviii. 6, "But whoso shall offend one of these little ones that believe in me, it were better for him that a millstone were hanged about his neck, and that he were drowned in the depth of the sea." How terrible is that character which Paul giveth of the Jews; 1 Thess. ii. 15, 16, "Who both killed the Lord Jesus, and their own prophets, and have persecuted us: and they please not God, and are contrary to all men; forbidding us to speak to the gentiles that they might be saved, to fill up their sins alway; for the wrath is come upon them to the uttermost." Such terrors against persecutors are so common through the Scriptures, that it would be tedious to recite them.

2. And for examples, the captivity first, and afterwards the casting off of the Jews, may serve instead of many. 2 Chron. xxxvi. 16, "But they mocked the messengers of God, and despised his words, and misused his prophets, until the wrath of the Lord arose against his people, till there was no remedy." And of the casting off, see Matt. xxiii. 37, 38, "O Jerusalem, Jerusalem, thou that killest the prophets, and stonest them that are sent unto thee, how oft would I have gathered thy children together, as a hen gathereth her chickens under her wings, and ye would not! Behold, your house is left unto you desolate----." And ver. 34-36, "Behold, I send unto you prophets, and wise men, and scribes; and some of them ye shall kill and crucify, and some of them shall ye scourge in your synagogues, and persecute them from city to city: that upon you may come all the righteous blood shed upon the earth, from the blood of righteous Abel unto the blood of [793]Zacharias son of Barachias, whom ye slew between the temple and the altar. Verily I say unto you, All these things shall come on this generation." To give you the particular examples of God's judgments against persecutors, and their posterity after them, would be a voluminous work; you may find them in the holy Scriptures, and the church's Martyrologies.

3. And by a marvellous providence, God doth so overrule the tongue of fame, and the pens of historians, and the thoughts of men, that commonly the names of persecutors stink when they are dead; yea, though they were never so much honoured and flattered while they were alive! What odious names are the names of Pharaoh, Ahab, Pilate, Herod, Nero, Domitian, Dioclesian, &c.! What a name hath the French massacre left on Charles the Ninth! and the English persecution on Queen Mary! And so of others throughout the world. Yea, what a blot leaveth it on Asa, Amaziah, or any that do but hurt a prophet of the Lord! The eleventh chapter of the Hebrews, and all the Martyrologies that are written to preserve the name of the witnesses of Christ, are all the records of the impiety and the perpetual shame of those by whom they suffered. Even learning, and wisdom, and common virtue, have got that estimation in the nature of man, that he that persecuteth but a Seneca, a Cicero, a Demosthenes, or a Socrates, hath irrecoverably wounded his reputation to posterity, and left his name to the hatred of all succeeding ages. Prov. x. 7, "The memory of the just is blessed, but the name of the wicked shall rot."

4. The persecution of godliness as such in ministers or private christians, is one of the most visible undoubted marks of one that is yet unsanctified, and in a state of sin and condemnation; for it showeth most clearly the predominancy of the serpentine nature in the persecutor. Though Asa in a peevish fit may imprison the prophet, and those christians that are engaged in a sect or party, may in a sinful zeal be injurious to those of the contrary party; and yet there may remain some roots of uprightness within; yet he that shall set himself to hinder the gospel, and the serious practice of godliness in the world, and to that end hinder or persecute the preachers, and professors, and practisers of it, hath the plainest mark of a child of the devil, and the most visible brand of the wrath of God upon his soul, of any sort of men on earth. If there might be any hope of grace in him, that at present doth but neglect or disobey

the gospel, and doth not himself live a godly life, (as indeed there is not,) yet there can be no possibility that he should have grace at that present, who hateth and opposeth it; and that he should be justified by the gospel who persecuteth it; and that he should be a godly man, who setteth himself against the godly, and seeketh to destroy them.

10. And it is a far more heinous sin in a professed christian, than in an infidel or heathen. For these do according to the darkness of their education, and the interest of their party, and the principles of their own profession. But for a professed christian to persecute christianity, and one that professeth to believe the gospel, to persecute the preachers and serious practisers of the doctrine of the gospel; this is so near that sin which is commonly said to be the unpardonable sin against the Holy Ghost, that it is not easy to perceive a difference; and if I did consent to that description of the unpardonable sin, I should have little hope of the conversion of any one of these. But, however, they make up such a mixture of hypocrisy, and impiety, and cruelty, as showeth them to exceed all ordinary sinners, in malignity and misery. They are a self-condemned sort of men; out of their own mouths will God condemn them. They profess themselves to believe in God, and yet they persecute those that serve him: they dare not speak against the preaching and practising of the doctrine of godliness, directly, and in plain expressions; and yet they persecute them, and cannot endure them! They fight against the interest and law of God the Father, Son, and Holy Ghost, when they have in baptism vowed themselves unto his service. Of all men on earth, these men will have least to say for their sin, or against their condemnation.

11. Lastly, Remember that Christ taketh all that is done by persecutors against his servants for his cause, to be done as to himself, and will accordingly in judgment charge it on them. So speaketh he to Saul, Acts ix. 5, 6, "Saul, Saul, why persecutest thou me?—I am Jesus, whom thou persecutest." And Matt. xxv. 41-46, even to them that did not feed, and clothe, and visit, and relieve them, he saith, "Verily, I say unto you, inasmuch as ye did it not to one of the least of these, ye did it not to me." What then will he say to them that impoverished and imprisoned them? Remember, that it is Christ reputatively, whom thou dost hate, deride, and persecute.

Direct. III. If you would escape the guilt of persecution, the cause and interest of Christ in the world must be truly understood. He that knoweth not that holiness is Christ's end, and Scripture is his word and law, and that the preachers of the gospel are his messengers, and that preaching is his appointed means, and that sanctified believers are his members, and the whole number of them are his mystical body; and all that profess to be such, are his visible body, or kingdom in the world; and that sin is the thing which he came to destroy, and the devil, the world, and the flesh, are the enemies which he causeth us to conquer; I say, he that knoweth not this, doth not know what christianity or godliness is, and therefore may easily persecute it in his ignorance. If you know not, or believe not, that serious godliness in heart and life, and serious preaching and discipline to promote it, are Christ's great cause and interest in the world, you may fight against him in the dark, whilst ignorantly you call yourselves his followers. If the devil can but make you think that ignorance is as good as knowledge, and pharisaical formality, and hypocritical shows, are as good as spiritual worship, and rational service of God; and that seeming and lip-service is as good as seriousness in religion; and that the strict and serious obeying of God, and living as we profess, according to the principles of our religion, is but hypocrisy, pride, or faction (that is, that all are hypocrites who will not be hypocrites, but seriously religious): I say, if Satan can bring you once to such erroneous, malignant thoughts as these, no wonder if he make you persecutors. O value the great blessing of a sound understanding! for if error blind you, (either impious error, or factious error,) there is no wickedness so great, but you may promote it, and nothing so good and holy, but you may persecute it, and think all the while that you are doing well. John xvi. 2, "They shall put you out of the synagogues; yea, the time cometh, that whosoever killeth you, will think that he doth God service." What prophet so great, or saint so holy, that did not suffer by such hands? Yea, Christ himself was persecuted as a sinner, that never sinned.

Direct. IV. And (if you would escape the guilt of persecution) the cause and interest of Christ must be highest in your esteem, and preferred before all [794]worldly, carnal interests of our own. Otherwise the devil will be still persuading you, that your own interest requireth you to suppress the interest of Christ; for the truth is, the gospel of Christ is quite against the interest of carnality and concupiscence; it doth condemn ambition, covetousness, and lust; it forbiddeth those sins on pain of damnation, which the proud, and covetous, and sensual love, and will not part with; and therefore it is no more wonder to have a proud man, or a covetous man, or a lustful, voluptuous man to be a persecutor, than for a dog to fly in his face who takes his bone from him. If you love your pride, and lust, and pleasures, better than the gospel, and a holy life, no marvel if you be persecutors; for these will not well agree together: and though sometimes the providence of God may so contrive things, that an ambitious hypocrite may think that his worldly interest requireth him to seem religious, and promote the preaching and practice of godliness; this is but seldom, and usually not long. For he cannot choose but quickly find that Christ is no patron of his sin, and that holiness is contrary to his worldly lusts. Therefore if you cannot value the cause of godliness above your lusts and carnal interests, I cannot tell you how to avoid the guilt of persecution, nor the wrath and vengeance of Almighty God.

Direct. V. Yea, though you do prefer Christ's interest in the main, you must carefully take heed of stepping into any forbidden way, and espousing any interest of your own or others, which is contrary to the laws or interest of Christ. Otherwise in the defence or prosecution of your cause, you will be carried into a seeming necessity of persecuting before you are aware. This hath been the ruin of multitudes of great ones in the world. When Ahab had set himself in a way of sin, the prophet must reprove him; and then he hateth and persecuteth the prophet, because he prophesied not good of him, but evil.[126] When Jeroboam thought that his interest required him to set up calves at Dan and Bethel, and to make priests for them of the basest of the people, the prophet must speak against his sin; and then he stretcheth out his hand against him, and saith, "Lay hold on him." If Asa sin, and the prophet tell him of it, his rage may proceed to imprison his reprover.[127] If Amaziah sin with the idolaters, the prophet must reprove him, and he will silence him, or smite him. And silenced he is, and what must follow? 2 Chron. xv. 16, "The king said to him, Art thou made of the king's counsel? Forbear: why shouldst thou be smitten? (This seemeth to be gentle dealing.) Then the prophet forbore and said, I know that God hath determined to destroy thee, because thou hast done this, and hast not hearkened to my counsel." If Pilate do but hear, "If thou let this man go, thou art not Cæsar's friend,"[128] he thinketh it is his interest to crucify Christ: as Herod thought it his interest to kill him, and therefore to kill so many other infants, when he heard of the birth of a king of the Jews. Because of an Herodias and the honour of his word, Herod will not stick to behead John the Baptist; and another Herod will kill James with the sword, and imprison Peter, because he seeth that it pleaseth the Jews.[129] Instances of this desperate sin are innumerable. There is no way so common, by which Satan hath engaged the rulers of the world against the kingdom of Jesus Christ, and against the preachers of his gospel, and the people that obey him, than by persuading them as Haman did Ahasuerus, Esther iii. 8, 9, "There is a certain people scattered abroad, and dispersed among the people in all the provinces of thy kingdom, and their laws are diverse from all people, neither keep they the king's laws: therefore it is not for the king's profit to suffer them; if it please the king, let it be written that they may be destroyed." When once the devil hath got men, by error or sensuality, to espouse an interest that Christ is against, he hath half done his work: for then he knoweth, that Christ or his servants will never bend to the wills of sinners, nor be reconciled to their wicked ways, nor take part with them in a sinful cause. And then it is easy for Satan to persuade such men, that these precise preachers and people are their enemies, and are against their interest and honour, and that they are a turbulent, seditious sort of people, unfit to be governed (because they will not be false to God, nor take part with the devil, nor be friends to sin). When once Nebuchadnezzar hath set up his golden image, he thinks he is obliged in honour to persecute them that will not bow down, as refractory persons that obey not the king. When Jeroboam is once engaged to set up his calves, he is presently engaged against those that are against them; and that is against God, and all his servants. Therefore as rulers love their souls, let them take heed what cause and interest they espouse.

Direct. VI. To love your neighbours as yourselves, and do as you would be done by, is the infallible means to avoid the guilt of persecution. "For charity suffereth long, and is kind, it envieth not, it is not easily provoked, it thinketh no evil, rejoiceth not in iniquity, but rejoiceth in the truth; it beareth all things, believeth all things, hopeth all things, endureth all things," 1 Cor. xiii. 4-7. "Love worketh no ill to his neighbour; therefore love is the fulfilling of the law," Rom. xiii. 10. And if it fulfil the law, it wrongeth no man. When did you see a man persecute himself? imprison, banish, defame, slander, revile, or put to death himself (if he were well in his wits)? Never fear persecution from a man that "loveth his neighbour as himself, and doth as he would be done by," and is not selfish and uncharitable.

Direct. VII. Pride also must be subdued, if you would not be persecutors. For a proud man cannot endure to have his word disobeyed, though it contradict the word of God: nor can he endure to be reproved by the preachers of the gospel; but will do as Herod with John the Baptist, or as Asa, or Amaziah, by the prophets! Till the soul be humble, it will not bear the sharp remedies which our Saviour hath prescribed, but will persecute him that would administer them.

Direct. VIII. Passion must be subdued, and the mind kept calm, if you would avoid the guilt of persecution. Asa was in a rage when he imprisoned the prophet (a fit work for a raging man). And Nebuchadnezzar was in a rage and fury when he commanded the punishment of the three witnesses, Dan. iii. 13. "The wrath of man worketh not the will of God," Jam. i. 20. The nature of wrathfulness tendeth to hurting those you are angry with. And wrath is impatient, and unjust, and will not hear what men can say, but rashly passeth unrighteous sentence. And it blindeth reason, so that it cannot see the truth.

Direct. IX. And hearkening to malicious backbiters and slanderers, and favouring the enemies of godliness in their calumnies, will engage men in persecution ere they are aware. For when the wicked are in the favour and at the ear of rulers, [795]they have opportunity to vent those false reports, which they never want a will to vent! And any thing may be said of men behind their backs, with an appearance of truth, when there is none to contradict it. If Haman may be heard, the Jews shall be destroyed, as not being for the king's profit, nor obedient to his laws. If Sanballat and Tobiah may be heard, the building of the walls of Jerusalem shall signify no better than an intended rebellion. They are true words, though to some ungrateful, which are spoken by the Holy Ghost, Prov. xxix. 12, "If a ruler hearken to lies, all his servants are wicked" (for they will soon accommodate themselves to so vicious a humour). Prov. xxv. 4, 5, "Take away the dross from the silver, and there shall come forth a vessel for the finer. Take away the wicked from before the king, and his throne shall be established in righteousness." If the devil might be believed, Job was one that served God for gain, and might have been made to curse him to his face. And if his servants may be believed, there is nothing so vile which the best men are not guilty of.

Direct. X. Take heed of engaging yourselves in a sect or faction. For when once you depart from catholic charity, there groweth up instead of it, a partial respect to the interest of that sect to which you join; and you will think that whatsoever doth promote that sect, doth promote christianity; and whatever is against that sect, is against the church or cause of God. A narrow, sectarian, separating mind, will make all the truths of God give place to the opinions of his party; and will measure the prosperity of the gospel in the world, by the prosperity of his party, as if he had forgot that there are any more men on the face of the earth, or thought God regarded none but them. He will not stick to persecute all the rest of the church of Christ, if the interest of his sect require it. When once men incorporate themselves into a party, it possesseth them with another spirit, even with a strange uncharitableness, injustice, cruelty, and partiality! What hath the christian world suffered by one sect's persecuting another, and faction rising up in fury to maintain its own interest, as if it had been to maintain the being of all religion! The bloodthirsty papists, whose inquisition, massacres, and manifold murders, have filled the earth with the blood of innocents, is a sufficient testimony of this. And still here among us they seem as thirsty of blood as ever, and tell us to our faces, that they would soon make an end of us, if we were in their power: as if the two hundred thousand lately murdered in so short a time in Ireland, had rather irritated than quenched their thirst. And all faction naturally tendeth to persecution. Own not therefore any dividing opinions or names; maintain the unity of the body of Christ (not of the body of the pope). Let christian and catholic, be all your titles, as to your religion. "Mark those that cause divisions and offences, and avoid them," Rom. xvi. 17.

Direct. XI. To this end, overvalue not any private or singular opinions of your own or others. For if once spiritual pride and ignorance of your own weakness, hath made you espouse some particular opinion as peculiarly your own; you will dote on the brats of your own brains, and will think your conceits to be far more illuminating and necessary than indeed they are; as if men's sincerity lay in the embracing of them, and their salvation on the receiving of them! And then you will make a party for your opinion, and will think all that are against it deserve to be cast out, as enemies to reformation, or to the truth of God, or to the church. And perhaps twenty years after, experience may bring you to your wits, and make you see either the falsehood or the smallness of all those points which you made so great a matter of; and then what comfort will you have in your persecutions?

Direct. XII. Obey not the solicitations of selfish, passionate disputers. Bishops and divines falling out among themselves, and then drawing princes to own their quarrels, when they find their arguments will not serve, hath been the distraction, division, and ruin of the christian world. And he that falleth in with one of the parties, to bear out that by the ruin of the other, is lost himself in their contentions. Would rulers let wrangling bishops and disputers alone, and never lend them their swords to end their differences, unless the substance of religion be endangered, they would be weary of quarrelling, and would chide themselves friends, and no such tragical consequents would follow, as do when the sword interposeth to suppress the discountenanced party, and to end their syllogisms and wranglings in blood.

Direct. XIII. Take heed lest an uncharitable, hurting spirit do prevail, under the name of holy zeal. As it did with James and John, when they would have fire from heaven to have revenged the contempt of their ministry: to whom Christ saith, "Ye know not what manner of spirit ye are of," Luke ix. 55. The difference between a christian zeal, and an envious, contentious, censorious, hurtful zeal, is excellently described by the apostle James, chap. iii. throughout. "Where envying and strife is, there is confusion, and every evil work. The wisdom from above is first pure, then peaceable, gentle, easy to be entreated, full of mercy and good works, without partiality and hypocrisy."

Direct. XIV. The catholic church, and particular churches, and our communion with each, must be distinguished; and a man must not be cast out of our catholic communion, because by some tolerable difference he is uncapable of communion with some particular church. If a man be impenitent in any heresy or sin, which is contrary to the common nature of christianity or godliness, and so unfit for catholic communion, he is to be cast out of christian communion: but if some particular church do impose any unnecessary doctrine or practice, and he dare not approve it, or join in it (be it right or wrong); yea, or if he withdraw himself from one church, through the badness of the minister, or through any falling out between them, and join to another that hath a minister more suitable to his case; these are not crimes to be punished with ejection from catholic communion. He that is not fit for communion with some one particular church, may be fit for communion with many others, that give him no such occasion of difference or distaste. Without catholic principles persecution will not be avoided.

Direct. XV. Let church union and communion be laid upon none but catholic terms, which are possible and fit for all to be agreed in.[130] Common reason will tell any impartial man, that there can be no more effectual engine to divide the churches, and raise contentions and persecutions, than to make laws for church communion, requiring such conditions as it is certain the members cannot consent to. If any man knew that my opinion is against the doctrine of transubstantiation, or of the Dominican's predetermination, and he would make a law, that no man shall have communion with that church who subscribeth not to these, he unavoidably excludeth me (unless I be such a beast, as to believe nothing soundly, and therefore to say any thing). [796]If ever the churches agree, and christians be reconciled, it must be by leaving out all dividing impositions, and requiring nothing as necessary to communion, which all may not rationally be expected to consent in. Now these catholic principles of communion must be such as these.

1. Such points of faith only as constitute christianity, and which every upright christian holdeth; and therefore only such as are contained in our baptismal covenant or profession, which maketh us christians; and not those other which only some stronger christians believe or understand; because the weak are not to be cast out of the family of Christ.

2. Such points as the primitive churches did agree in, and not innovations, which they never practised or agreed in; for they are our pattern, and were better than we; and no more can be necessary to our concord and communion, than was to theirs.[131]

3. Such points as all the church hath some time or other at least agreed in; for what reason can we have to think that the churches should now agree in that, which they never hitherto agreed in.

4. Such points as all the true christians in the world are now agreed in; for otherwise we shall exclude some true christians from our christian communion.

5. No points of worship, much less of modes and circumstances, which are not necessary, and more necessary to the church's good, than is the communion of all those persons, who by dissenting are like to be separated or cast out, and whose omission would not do more hurt, than this separation and division is like to do.

6. Especially no such things must be made necessary to communion, as the most conscientious are ordinarily fearful of and averse to, and may be forborne without any great detriment to godliness.

Object. But, it will be said, that catholic communion indeed requireth no more than you say; but particular churches may require more of their members, for that may be necessary or fit for a member of this particular church, which is not so to all.

Answ. Catholic communion is that which all christians and churches have with one another, and the terms of it are such as all christians may agree in. Catholic communion is principally existent and exercised in particular churches (as there is no existent christianity or faith, which existeth not in individual christians). Therefore if one particular church may so narrow the door of its communion, then another and another, and every one may do so; if not by the same particular impositions, yet by some other of the like nature; for what power one church hath herein, others have; and then catholic communion will be scarce found existent externally in the world: but a mere catholic christian would be denied communion in every particular church he cometh to. And how do you hold catholic communion, when you will admit no mere catholic christian as such to your communion, but only such as supererogate according to your private church terms?

2. But grant that every church may impose more upon its members, it must be only that which is necessary to those common things which all agree in; and then the necessity will be discernible to all sober-minded persons, and will prevent divisions; as it is necessary that he that will communicate with our churches, do join with them in the same translation of Scripture, and version of the Psalms, and under the same pastor, as the rest of the church doth: for here the church cannot use variety of pastors, translations, versions, &c. to fit the variety of men's humours; there is an evident necessity, that if they will be one society, they must agree in the same, in each of these. Therefore when the church hath united in one, if any man refuse that one person or way which the church is necessarily united in, he refuseth communion with that church, and the church doth not excommunicate him! But if that church agree on things hurtful or unnecessary, as necessary to its communion, it must bear the blame of the separations itself!

3. And grant yet that some churches cannot admit such scrupulous persons to her communion as dare not join in every punctilio, circumstance, or mode; it doth not follow that those persons must therefore be excommunicated, or forbidden to worship God among themselves, without that which they scruple; or to join in or with a congregation which imposeth no such things upon them. Persecution will unavoidably come in, upon such domineering, narrow terms as those. The man is a christian still, though he scruple one of our modes or ceremonies, and is capable of catholic communion. And if private and little inconveniences shall be thought a sufficient cause, to forbid all such the public worshipping of God, on pretence that in one nation there must not be variety of modes, this is a dividing principle, and not catholic, and plungeth men into the guilt of persecution. It was not so in the churches of the Roman empire. In the days of Basil, his church and that at Neocæsarea differed; and ordinarily, several bishops used several forms of prayer and worship, in their several churches, without offence. And further,

Direct. XVI. Different faults must have different penalties; and excommunication or forbidding men all public worship of God, must not be the penalty of every dissent. Is there no smaller penalty sufficient, if a doubtful subscription or ceremony be scrupled, than to silence ministers therefore from preaching the gospel, or excommunicating men, and forbidding them to worship God at all except they can do this? This is the highest ecclesiastical penalty that can be laid on men for the greatest heresy or crime. Doubtless there are lesser punishments that may suffice for lesser faults.

Direct. XVII. Every friend of Christ and the church, must choose such penalties for ministers and private christians, who offend, as are least to the hinderance of the gospel, or hurtful to the people's souls. Therefore silencing ministers is not a fit penalty for every fault which they commit! The providence of God (as I said before) hath furnished the world with so few that are fit for that high and sacred work, that no man can pretend that they are supernumeraries, or unnecessary, and that others may be substituted to the church's profit: for the number is so small, that all are much too few; and so many as are silenced, so many churches (either the same or others) must be unsupplied or ill supplied. And God working ordinarily by means, we may conclude, that silencing of such preachers, doth as plainly tend to men's damnation, as the prohibiting of physicians doth to their death, and more. And it is not the part of a friend, either of God or men, to endeavour the damnation of one soul, much less of multitudes, because a minister hath displeased him. If one man must pay for another man's sins, let it be a pecuniary mulct, or the loss of a member, rather than the loss of his soul. It is more merciful every time a minister offendeth, to cut off a hand or an arm of some of his flock, than to say to him, Teach them no more the way to salvation, that so they may be damned. If a father offend, and his children must needs pay for all his faults, it is better [797]to beat the children, or maim them, than forbid him to feed them, when there is none else to do it, and so to famish them. What reason is there that men's souls should be untaught, because a minister hath offended?

I know still, those men that care not for their own souls, and therefore care as little for others, will say, What if the people have but a reader, or a weak, ignorant, lifeless preacher? doth it therefore follow that the people must be damned? I answer, No: no more than it followeth that the city that hath none but women physicians must die of their sicknesses, or that they that live only upon grass or roots must famish. Nature may do more to overcome a disease without a physician in one than in another. Some perhaps are converted already, and have the law written in their hearts, and are taught of God, and can make shift to live without a teacher; but for the rest, whose diseases need a skilful, diligent physician, whose ignorance and impenitence extremely need a skilful, diligent, lively teacher, he that depriveth them of such, doth take the probable course to damn them! And it is the same course which the devil himself would take; and he partly knoweth what tendeth to men's damnation! He that knoweth what a case the heathen, infidel, Mahometan world is in for want of teachers; and what a case the Greek church, the Muscovites, the Abassines, Syrians, Armenians, papists, and most of the christians of the world are in, for want of able, skilful, godly pastors, will lay his hand on his mouth, and meddle with such reasonings as these no more.

Object. But by this device you will have the clergy lawless, or, as the papists, exempt them from the magistrate's punishments, for fear of depriving the people of instruction.

Answ. No such matter: it is the contrary that I am advising; I would have them punished more severely than other men, as their sins are more aggravated than other men's. Yea, and I would have them silenced when it is meet, and that is in two cases: viz. If they commit such capital crimes, as God and man would have punished with death, it is fit they die (and then they are silenced): for in this case it is supposed that their lives (by their impunity) are like to do more hurt than good. 2. If their heresy, insufficiency, scandal, or any fault whatever, do make them more hurtful than profitable to the church, it is fit they be cast out. If their ministry be not like to do more good than their faults to do harm, let them be silenced! But if it be otherwise, then let them be punished in their bodies or purses, rather than the people's souls should suffer. The laws have variety of penalties for other men! Will none of those suffice for ministers?

But alas! what talk I of their faults? Search all church history, and observe whether in all ages ministers have not been silenced rather for their duties than their faults; or, for not subscribing to some unnecessary opinion or imposition of a prevailing party; or about some wrangling controversies which church disturbers set afoot! There is many a poor minister would work in Bridewell, or be tied to shovel the streets all the rest of the week, if he might but have liberty to preach the gospel! And would not such a penalty be sufficient for a dissent in some unnecessary point? As it is not every fault that a magistrate is deposed for by the sovereign, but such as make him unfit for the place, so is it also with the ministers.

Direct. XVIII. Malignity and profaneness must not be gratified or encouraged. It must be considered, how "the carnal mind is enmity against God; for it is not subject to his law, nor can be;" and that enmity is put between the woman's and the serpent's seed;[132] and that the whole business of the world is but the prosecution of the war between the armies of Christ and Satan; and that malignity inclineth the ungodly world to slander and reproach the servants of the Lord; and they are glad of any opportunity to make them odious, or to exasperate magistrates against them; and that their silencing and fall is the joy of the ungodly. And if there be any civil differences or sidings, the ungodly rabble will take that side, be it right or wrong, which they think will do most to the downfal of the godly, whom they hate. Therefore besides the merits of the particular cause, a ruler that regardeth the interest of the gospel, and men's salvation, must have some care that the course which he taketh against godly ministers and people, when they displease him, be such as doth not strengthen the hands of evil-doers, nor harden them, increase them, or make them glad. I do not say, that a ruler must be against whatever the ungodly part is for; or that he must be for

102

that which the major part of godly men are for (I know this is a deceitful rule). But yet that which pleaseth the malignant rabble, and displeaseth or hurteth the generality of godly men, is so seldom pleasing to God, that it is much to be suspected.

Direct. XIX. The substance of faith, and the practice of godliness, must be valued above all opinions, and parties, and worldly interests; and godly men accounted, as they are, (*cæteris paribus,*) the best members both of church and state. If rulers once knew the difference between a saint and a sensualist, "a vile person would be contemned in their eyes, and they would honour them that fear the Lord," Psal. xv. 4. And if they honoured them as God commandeth them, they would not persecute them; and if the promoting of practical godliness were their design, there were little danger of their oppressing those that must be the instruments of propagating it, if ever it prosper in the world.

Direct. XX. To this end, remember the near and dear relation which every true believer standeth in to God the Father, Son, and Holy Ghost. They are called by God, "His peculiar treasure,—his jewels,—his children,—the members of Christ,—the temples of the Holy Ghost;—God dwelleth in them by love, and Christ by faith, and the Spirit by all his sanctifying gifts."[133] If this were well believed, men would more reverence them on God's account, than causelessly to persecute them. "He that toucheth you, toucheth the apple of my eye," Zech. ii. 8.

Direct. XXI. Look not so much on men's infirmities, as to overlook or make light of all that is good in them. But look as much at the good as at the evil; and then you will see reason for lenity, as well as for severity; and for love and tenderness, rather than for hatred and persecution; and you will discern that those may be serviceable to the church, in whom blinded malice can see nothing worthy of honour or respect.

Direct. XXII. Estimate and use all lesser matters, as means to spiritual worship and practical holiness. If there be any thing of worth in controversies, and ceremonies, and such other matters of inferior rank, it is as they are a means to the power of godliness, which is their end. And if once they be no otherwise esteemed, they will not be made use of against the interest of godliness, to the silencing of the preachers, and persecuting the professors of it.

Direct. XXIII. Remember that the understanding is not free (save only participative, as it is subject [798]to the will). It acteth of itself *per modum naturæ*, and is necessitated by its object (further than as it is under the power of the will). A man cannot hold what opinion he would himself, nor be against what he would not have to be true; much less can he believe as another man commandeth him. My understanding is not at my own command; I cannot be of every man's belief that is uppermost. Evidence, and not force, is the natural means to compel the mind; even as goodness, and not force, is the natural means to win men's love. It is as wise a thing to say, Love me, or I will kill thee; as to say, Believe me, or I will kill thee.

Direct. XXIV. Consider that it is essential to religion, to be above the authority of man (unless as they subserve the authority of God). He that worshippeth a God that is subject to any man, must subject his religion to that man. (But this is no religion, because it is no God whom he worshippeth.) But if the God whom I serve be above all men, my religion or service of him must needs be also above the will of men.

Direct. XXV. Consider that an obedient disposition towards God's law, and a tender conscience which feareth in the smallest matter to offend him, is a substantial part of holiness, and of great necessity to salvation. It is part of the excellency of the soul, and therefore to be greatly encouraged by governors. To drive this out of the world, is to drive out godliness, and make men rebels against their Maker. And nothing is more certain, than that the violent imposing of unnecessary, disputable things in the worship of God, doth unavoidably tend either to debauch the conscience, and drive men from their obedience to God, or to destroy them, or undo them in the world: for it is not possible, that all conscionable persons should discern the lawfulness of all such disputable things.

103

Direct. XXVI. Remember that such violence in doubtful matters, is the way to set up the most debauched atheists, and consequently to undo church and commonwealth. For whatever oaths or subscriptions you require, he that believeth not that there is a God or a devil, a heaven or a hell, will yield to all, and make no more of perjury or a lie, than to eat a bit of bread! If you cast out all ministers that will not swear or subscribe this or that form about things doubtful, you will cast out never an atheist or debauched infidel by it. All that have no conscience, will be kept in; and all that are true to God and their conscience, if they think it is sin which you require of them, will be cast out. And whither this tendeth, you may easily foresee.

Direct. XXVII. Remember that if by force you do prevail with a man to go against his conscience, you do but make him dissemble and lie. And if hypocrites be not hateful to you, why do you cry out so much against hypocrites (where you cannot prove your accusation)? But if they be so hateful, why do you so eagerly make men hypocrites? Whatever their tongues may say, you can scarce believe yourselves, that prisons or fire will change men's judgments in matters of faith and duty to God.

Direct. XXVIII. Consider not only whether the thing which you impose be sin in itself, but also what it is to him that thinketh it a sin. His own doubting conscience may make that a sin to him, which is no sin to another. "And he that doubteth, (whether such or such a meat be lawful,) is condemned if he eat, because he eateth not of faith: for whatsoever is not of faith is sin," Rom. xiv. 23. And is it like to be damnation to him that doth it against his conscience? And will you drive on any man towards damnation? "Destroy not him with thy meat for whom Christ died," Rom. xiv. 15; 1 Cor. viii. 11.

If it be objected, That then there will be no government, if every man must be left to his own conscience. I answer, That the Holy Ghost did not fear such objectors, when he laid down this doctrine here expressed. 1. It is easy to distinguish between things necessary and things unnecessary. 2. And between great penalties and small. And first, It followeth not that a man must be left to his own conscience in every thing, because he must be so in some things. In things necessary, as it is a sin to do them doubtingly, so it may be a greater sin to leave them undone; (as for a man to maintain his family, or defend his king, or hear the word of God, &c.) He that can say, My conscience is against it, must not be excused from a necessary duty: and he that can say, My conscience bids me do it, must not be excused in a sin. But yet the apostle knew what he said, when he (that was a greater church governor than you) determined the case of mutual forbearance, as in Rom. xiv. and xv. and 1 Cor. viii. Secondly, And he is not wholly left to himself, who is punished with a small penalty for a small offence: for if a man must be still punished more, as long as he obeyeth God and his conscience, before men, an honest man must not be suffered to live. For he will certainly do it to the death.

Direct. XXIX. Remember the wonderful variety of men's apprehensions, which must be supposed in all laws! Men's faces are scarce more various and unlike, than their understandings are: for besides that nature hath diversified intellects as well as faces, the diversity and unlikeness is much increased by variety of educations, company, representations, accidents, cogitations, and many other causes. It is wiser to make laws, that all men shall take the same physic, or eat only the same meat, or that all shoes shall be of a size, and all clothes of the same bigness, upon supposition that all men's health, or appetite, or feet, or bodies, are alike; than to make laws that all men shall agree (or say that they agree) in every opinion, circumstance, or ceremony, in matters of religion.

Direct. XXX. Remember especially, that most christians are ignorant, and of weak understandings, and not able to make use of all the distinctions and subtleties which are needful, to bring them over to your mind in doubtful and unnecessary things. Therefore the laws which will be the means of peace, must suppose this weakness and ignorance of most subjects! And how convenient it is, to say to a poor, ignorant christian, Know this, or profess this or that, which the ablest, godly pastors themselves are not agreed in, or else thou shalt be imprisoned or banished, I leave to equal men to judge.

Direct. XXXI. Human infirmities must be supposed in the best and strongest christians. All have their errors and their faults; divines themselves as well as others. Therefore either some errors and faults must be accounted tolerable, or else no two persons must tolerate one another in the world, but kill on till the strongest only shall survive. "Brethren, if a man be overtaken in a fault, ye which are spiritual, restore such a one in the spirit of meekness, considering thyself, lest thou also be tempted. Bear ye one another's burdens, and so fulfil the law of Christ," Gal. vi. 1, 2. And if the strong must be borne with themselves, "then they that are strong ought to bear the infirmities of the weak, and not to please themselves; but every one to please his neighbour for his good to edification; for even Christ pleased not himself," &c. Rom. xv. 1-3. "And him that is [799]weak in the faith we must receive; but not to doubtful disputations," Rom. xiv. 1.

Direct. XXXII. The pastors must not be impatient under the abuses which they receive from weak or distempered brethren. We must excel others in patience, and meekness, and forbearance, as much as we do in knowledge, and in other graces. If the nurse or mother will take every word or action of the child, as if it were the injury of an enemy, there will be no preservation of the family in peace! If children cry, or fight, or chide, or make any foul or troublesome work, the mother will not therefore turn them out of doors, or use them like strangers, but remember that it is her place and duty to bear with that weakness which she cannot cure. The proud impatience of the pastors hath frequently brought them into the guilt of persecution, to the alienating of the people's hearts, and the distraction and division of the churches: when poor, distempered persons are offended with them, and it may be revile them, and call them seducers, or antichristian, or superstitious, or what their pride and passion shall suggest: or if some weak ones raise up some erroneous opinions, alas! many pastors have no more wit, or grace, or pity, than presently to be rough with them, and revile them again, and seek to right themselves by ways of force, and club down every error and contention; when they should overcome them by evidence of truth, and by meekness, patience, and love. (Though there be place also for severity, with turbulent, implacable, impenitent heretics.)

Direct. XXXIII. Time of learning and overcoming their mistakes, must be allowed to those that are misinformed. We must not turn those of the lower forms out of Christ's school, because they learn not as much as those of the higher forms in a few weeks or years. The Holy Ghost teacheth those who for the time might have been teachers of others, and yet had need to be taught the first principles, Heb. v. 11, 12. He doth not turn them out of the church for their non-proficiency. And where there is ignorance there will be error.

Direct. XXXIV. Some inconveniences must be expected and tolerated, and no perfect order or concord expected here on earth. It is not good reasoning to say, If we suffer these men, they will cause this or that disorder or inconvenience: but you must also consider whither you must drive it, if you suffer them not; and what will be the consequents. He that will follow his conscience to a prison, will likely follow it to death. And if nothing but death, or prison, or banishment can restrain them from what they take to be their duty, it must be considered how many must be so used; and whether (if they were truly faulty) they deserve so much: and if they do, yet whether the evils of the toleration or of the punishment are like to be the greater. Peace and concord will never be perfect, till knowledge and holiness be perfect.

Direct. XXXV. You may go farther in restraining than in constraining; in forbidding men to preach against approved doctrines or practices of the church, than in forcing them to preach for them, or to subscribe or speak their approbation or assent: if they be not points or practices of great necessity, a man may be fit for the ministry and church communion, who meddleth not with them, but preacheth the wholesome truths of the gospel, and lets them alone. And, because no duty is at all times a duty, a sober man's judgment will allow him to be silent at many an error, when he dare not subscribe to or approve the least. But if here any proud and cruel pastors shall come in with their lesser, selfish incommodities, and say, if they do not approve of what we say and do, they will secretly foment a faction against us; I should answer them, that as good men will foment no faction, so if such proud, impatient, turbulent men, will endure none that subscribe not to all their opinions, or differ from them in a circumstance or a ceremony, they shall raise a greater faction (if they will call it so) against themselves, and make the people look on them as tyrants and not as pastors; and they shall see in the end, when they have bought their wit by dear experience, that they have but torn the church in pieces, by preventing divisions by carnal means, and that they have lost themselves, by being over-zealous for themselves; and that doctrine and love are the instruments of a wise shepherd, that loveth the flock, and understands his work.

Direct. XXXVI. Distinguish between the making of new laws or articles of belief, and the punishing of men for the laws already made. And think not that we must have new laws or canons, every time the old ones are broken; or that any law can be made which can keep itself from being broken. Perverseness in this error hath brought the church to the misery which it endureth. God hath made a universal law sufficient for the universal church, in matters of faith and holy practice; leaving it to men to determine of necessary circumstances which were unfit for a universal law: and if the sufficiency of God's law were acknowledged in men's practices, the churches would have had more peace: but when particular countries have their particular volumes of articles, confessions, liturgies, and I know not what else to be subscribed to, and none must preach that will not say, or write, or swear, That he believeth all this to be true and good, and nothing in it to be against the word of God, this engine racks the limbs of the churches all to pieces. And then what is the pretence for this epidemical calamity? Why no better than this, Every heretic will subscribe to the Scriptures, and take it in his own sense. And what followeth? Must we needs therefore have new laws which heretics will not subscribe to, or which they cannot break? It is the commendation of God's law, as fit to be the means of unity, that all are so easily agreed to it in terms, and therefore would agree in the sense if they understood it. But they will not do so by the laws of men: all or many heretics in the primitive times, would profess assent to the church's creed; no doubt in a corrupt and private sense; but the churches therefore did not make new creeds; till about three hundred years after Christ, they began to put in some particular words to obviate heretics, which Hilary complained of as the cause of all their divisions! And what if heretics will subscribe to all you bid them, and take it in their own corrupted sense? Must you therefore be still making new laws and articles, till you meet with some which they cannot misunderstand, or dare not thus abuse? What if men will misinterpret and break the laws of the land? Must they be made new till none can mis-expound or violate them? Sure there is a wiser way than this: God's word containeth in sufficient expressions, all that is necessary to be subscribed to: require none therefore to subscribe to any more (in matters of faith or holy practice); but if you think any articles need a special interpretation, let the church give her sense of those articles; and if any man preach against that sense, and corrupt the word of God which he hath subscribed, let his fault be proved, and let him be admonished and censured as it deserves: censured, I say, not for not subscribing more than Scripture, but for corrupting the Scriptures to which he hath subscribed, or breaking God's laws which he promised to observe.

[800]*Direct.* XXXVII. The good of men, and not their ruin, must be intended in all the discipline of the church: or the good of the church, when we have but little hope of theirs. If this were done, it would easily be perceived, that persecution is an unlikely means to do good by.

Direct. XXXVIII. Neither unlimited liberty in matters of religion must be allowed, nor unnecessary force and rigour used, but tolerable differences and parties must be tolerated, and intolerable ones by the wisest means suppressed. And to this end, by the counsel of the most prudent, peaceable divines, the tolerable and the intolerable must be statedly distinguished! And those that are only tolerated must be under a law for their toleration, prescribing them their terms of good behaviour; and those that are approved, must moreover have the countenance and maintenance of the magistrate: and if this were done, 1. The advantage of the said encouragement from governors, 2. With the regulation of the toleration, and the magistrates' careful government of the tolerated, would prevent both persecution, and most of the divisions and calamities of the church. Thus did the ancient christian emperors and bishops: (and was their experience nothing?) The Novatians (as good and orthodox men) were allowed their own churches and bishops even in Constantinople, at the emperor's nose. Especially if it be made the work of some justices, 1. To judge of persons to be tolerated, and grant them patents, 2. And to overrule them and punish them when they deserve it: no other way would avoid so many inconveniences.

Direct. XXXIX. The things intolerable are these two: 1. (Not the believing, but) the preaching and propagating of principles contrary to the essentials of godliness or christianity, or government, justice, charity, or peace. 2. The turbulent, unpeaceable management of those opinions which in themselves are tolerable. If any would preach against the articles of the creed, the petitions of the Lord's prayer, or any of the ten commandments, he is not to be suffered; and if any that are orthodox do in their separated meetings, make it their business to revile at others, and destroy men's charity, or to stir men up to rebellion or sedition, or contempt of magistracy; none of this should be endured.

As for those libertines that under the name of liberty of conscience do plead for a liberty of such vicious practices, and in order thereto would prove that the magistrate hath nothing to do in matters of religion, I have preached and wrote so much against them, whilst that error reigned, and I find it so unseasonable now the constitution of things looks another way, that I will not weary myself and the reader with so unnecessary a task as to confute them. Only I shall say, that Rom. xiii. telleth us that rulers are a terror to them that do evil; and that heretics and turbulent firebrands do evil; therefore rulers should be a terror to them; and that if all things are to be done to the glory of God, and his interest is to be set highest in the world, then magistrates and government are for the same end; and if no action which we do, is of so base a nature, as ultimately to be terminated in the concernments of the flesh, much less is government so vile a thing, when rulers are in Scripture called gods, as being the officers of God.

Direct. XL. Remember death, and live together as men that are near dying, and must live together in another world. The foolish expectation of prosperity and long life, is it which setteth men together by the ears. When Ridley and Hooper were both in prison, and preparing for the flames, their contentions were soon ended, and Ridley repented of his persecuting way. If the persecutors and persecuted were shut up together in one house that hath the plague, in the time of this lamentable contagion, it is two to one but they would be reconciled. When men see that they are going into another world, it takes off the edge of their bitterness and violence; and the apprehensions of the righteous judgment of God, doth awe them into a patience and forbearance with each other. Can you persecute that man on earth, with whom you look to dwell in heaven? (But to restrain a man from damning souls, by heresy or turbulency, or any such course, my conscience would not forbid it me if I were dying.)

Direct. XLI. Let the proud themselves, who will regard no higher motives, remember how fame and history will represent them to posterity when they are dead. There is no man that desireth his name should stink and be odious to future generations: there is nothing that an ambitious man desireth more, than a great surviving name. And will you knowingly and wilfully then expose it to perpetual contempt and hatred? Read over what history you please, and find out the name of one persecutor if you can, that is not now a word of ignomiy, and doth not rot, as

God hath threatened! If you say, that it is only in the esteem of such as I, or the persecuted party; neither your opinion shall be judge nor mine; but the opinion and language of historians, and of the wisest men, who are the masters of fame. Certainly that report of holy Scripture and history which hath prevailed, will still prevail; and while there are wise, and good, and merciful men in the world, the names and manners of the foolish, and wicked, and cruel will be odious, as they continue at this day.

I have wrote these directions to discharge my duty, for those that are willing to escape the guilt of so desperate a sin; but not with any expectation at all, that it should do much good with any considerable number of persecutors; for they will not read such things as these; and God seldom giveth professed christians over to this sin, till they have very grievously blinded their minds, and hardened their hearts, and by malignity and obstinacy are prepared for his sorest judgments; and I know that whoever will live godly in Christ Jesus (it is not said, "who professeth to believe in Christ Jesus," but, "to live godly") shall suffer persecution, and that the cross must still be the passage to the crown.[134]

[125] Dæmones ex hominibus fieri quidam opinati sunt, perpetua criminum licentia, &c. Quod ut forte tolerabiliter dictum sit, malarum voluntatem similitudo efficit, qua homo malus atque in malis obstinatus pene dæmonem æquat. Petrarch. de Injusto Domin.

[126] 1 Kings xxii. 8, 27; xiii. 2, 4.
[127] 2 Chron. xvi. 10.
[128] John xix. 12.
[129] Matt. ii. 16-18; xiv. 6-9; Mark vi. 19, 21, 22; Acts i. 2-4.
[130] See my "Treatise of a True Catholic, and Catholic Church."
[131] See Vincent. Lirinens.
[132] Rom. viii. 7, 8; Gen. iii. 15.
[133] Exod. xix. 5; 1 Pet. ii. 9; Tit. ii. 14; 2 Cor. vi. 16-18; Mal. iii. 17, 18; Eph. iii. 17; 1 Cor. iii. 16; 2 Tim. i. 14; 1 John iv. 15, 16.
[134] 2 Tim. iii. 11, 12; Matt. v. 11, 12; Luke xiv. 26, 33.

CHAPTER XII.

DIRECTIONS AGAINST SCANDAL AS GIVEN.

SCANDAL being a murdering of souls, is a violation of the general law of charity, and of the sixth commandment in particular. In handling this subject, I shall, 1. Show you what is true scandal given to another. 2. What things go under the name of scandal, which are not it, but are falsely so named. 3. What are the particular ways and sorts of scandal. 4. The greatness of this sin. 5. Directions to avoid it.

Scandal what it is.

I. I shall not need to stand upon the etymology of the word scandal; whether it come from σκάζω, claudico, as Erasmus thought, or from σκάμβον, curvum, &c. Martinius, Stephanus, Lyserus, &c. have sufficiently done it, [801]whither I refer you. As for the sense of the word, it is past doubt, that the ordinary use of it in Scripture is for a stumblingblock for a man to fall upon, or a trap to insnare a man; and in the Old Testament it is often used for a stumbling-stone, on which a man may fall into any corporal calamity, or a snare to hurt or ruin a man in the world; (as Exod. x. 7; 1 Sam. xviii. 21; xxv. 31; Psal. cxix. 165; Ezek. vii. 19, Sept.) But in the New Testament, (which speaketh more of spiritual hurts,) it is taken for a stumblingblock or temptation, by which a man is in danger of falling into sin, or spiritual loss, or ruin, or dislike of godliness, or any way to be turned from God, or hindered in a religious, holy way; (and if sometimes it be taken for grieving or troubling, it is as it hereby thus hindereth or insnareth;) so that to scandalize, is sometimes taken for the doing of a blameless action, from which another unjustly taketh occasion to fall, or sin, or be perverted: but when it signifieth a sin, (as we take it in this place,) then to scandalize is, by something unlawful of itself, or at least unnecessary, which may occasion the spiritual hurt or ruin of another. 1. The matter is either something that is simply sinful, (and then it is a double sin,) or something indifferent or unnecessary, and then it is simply the sin of scandal. 2. It must be that which may occasion another's fall, I say, occasion; for no man can forcibly cause another man to sin, but only occasion it, or tempt him to it, as a moral cause.

What is not scandal, that is by many so called.

II. By this you may see, 1. That to scandalize, is not merely to displease or grieve another; for many a man is displeased, through his folly and vice, by that which tendeth to his good; and many a man is tempted (that is, scandalized) by that which pleaseth him; when Christ saith, "If thy right eye or hand offend (or scandalize) thee, pluck it out, or cut it off," &c. Matt. v. he doth not, by offending, mean displeasing, or grieving; for by so offending it may profit us; but he plainly meaneth, If it draw thee to sin; or else he had never added, "That it is better to enter maimed into life, than having two eyes or hands to be cast into hell!" That is, in a word, Thy damnation is a greater hurt than the loss of hand or eye, and therefore if there were no other way to avoid it, this would be a very cheap way. So *pedem offendere in lapidem*, is to stumble upon a stone. The most censorious and humorous sort of men, have got a notion, that whatever offendeth or displeaseth them is scandalous! And they think that no man must do any thing which grieveth or displeaseth them, lest he be guilty of scandal; and by this trick whoever can purchase impatience and peevishness enough, to be always displeased with the actions of others, shall rule the world. But the truth is, the ordinary way of scandalizing these men is by pleasing them.

I will give you one instance of scandal in Scripture, which may help this sort of people better to understand it, Gal. ii. 10-16. Peter there giveth true scandal to the Jews and gentiles; he walked not uprightly according to the truth of the gospel, but laid a stumblingblock before the Jews and gentiles; and this was not by displeasing the Jews, but by pleasing them. The Jews thought it a sin to eat with the gentiles, and to have communion with uncircumcised men. Peter knew the contrary, but for fear of them of the circumcision, lest they should be offended at him as a sinner, he "withdrew and separated himself." This scandal tended to harden the Jews in their sinful separation, and to seduce the gentiles into a conceit of the necessity of circumcision; and Barnabas was carried away with the dissimulation. Here you may see, that if any think it a sin in us to have communion in such or such congregations, with such persons, in such worship, which God alloweth us not to separate from, it is a sin of scandal in us to separate to avoid these men's offence. We scandalize them and others, even by pleasing them, and by avoiding that which they falsely called scandalous. And if we would not scandalize them, we must do that which is just, and not by our practice hide the sound doctrine, which is contrary to their separating error.

2. And it is as apparent that to scandalize another, is not (as is vulgarly imagined by the ignorant) to do that which is commonly reputed sinful, or which hath the appearance of a sin, or which will make a man evil thought of or spoken of by others; yet commonly when men say, This is a scandalous action, they mean, it is an action which is reproachful or of evil report as a sin. And therefore in our English speech it is common to say of one that slandereth another, that he raised a scandal of him. But this is not the meaning of the word in Scripture: materially indeed scandal may consist in any such thing which may be a stumblingblock to another; but formally it is the tempting of another, or occasioning his fall, or ruin, or hurt, which is the nature of scandalizing. And this is done more seldom by committing open, disgraceful sins, and doing that which will make the doer evil spoken of; for by that means others are the more assisted against the temptation of imitating him; but scandal is most commonly found in those actions, which are under least reproach among men, or which have the most plausible appearance of good in them, when they are evil! For these are apter to deceive and overthrow another.

3. And it is also apparent, that it is no sinful scandalizing to do a duty or necessary action, which I have not power to forbear, though I know that another will

be offended, or fall by it into sin. If God have made it my duty, even at this time, I must not disobey him, and omit my duty, because another will make it an occasion of his sin. It must be either a sinful or an indifferent action that is scandal, or something that is in my power to do or to forbear; yet this must be added, that affirmatives binding not *ad semper*, to all times, and no duty being a duty at every moment, it may oft fall out, that that which else would have been my duty at this time, may become at this time no duty but a sin, by the evil consequents which I may foresee, as if another man will make it an occasion of his fall. So that this may oblige me to defer a duty to a fitter time and place. For all such duties as have the nature of a means, are never duties when they cross the interest of their chief ends, and make against that which they are used to effect. And therefore here christian prudence, foreseeing consequents, and weighing the good and evil together, is necessary to him that will know a duty from a sin, and a scandal from no scandal.

The sorts of scandalizing.

III. The several ways of scandalizing are these following: 1. Scandal is either intended or not intended, either that which is done maliciously of set purpose, or that which is done through negligence, carelessness, or contempt. Some men do purposely contrive the fall or ruin of another; and this is a devilish aggravation of the sin: and some do hurt to others while they intend it not; yet this is far from excusing them from sin; for it is voluntary as an omission of the will, though not as its positive choice: that is called voluntary which the will is chargeable with, or culpable of; and it is chargeable with its [802]omissions, and sluggish neglects of the duty which it should do. Those that are careless of the consequent of their actions, and contemn the souls of other men, and will go their own way, come of it what will, and say, Let other men look to themselves, are the commonest sort of scandalizers; and are as culpable as a servant that would leave hot water or fire when the children are like to fall into it; or that would leave straw or gunpowder near the fire, or would leave open the doors, though not of purpose to let in the thieves.

2. Scandal is that which tendeth to another's fall, either directly or indirectly, immediately or remotely. The former may easily be foreseen; but the latter requireth a large foreseeing, comparing understanding; yet this kind of scandal also must be avoided; and wise men that would not undo men's souls while they think no harm, must look far before them, and foresee what is like to be the consequent of their actions at the greatest distance and at many removes.

3. Scandals also are aptitudinal or actual: many things are apt to tempt and occasion the ruin of another, which yet never attain so bad an end, because God disappointeth them; but that is no thanks to them that give the scandal.

4. Scandal also as to the means of it, is of several sorts. 1. By doctrine. 2. By persuasion. 3. By alluring promises. 4. By threats. 5. By violence. 6. By gifts. 7. By example. 8. By omission of duties, and by silence: by all these ways you may scandalize.

1. False doctrine is directly scandalous; for it seduceth the judgment, which then misguideth the will, which then misruleth the rest of the faculties. False doctrine, if it be in weighty, practical points, is the pernicious plague of souls and nations.

2. Also the solicitations of seducers and of tempting people are scandalous, and tend to the ruin of souls; when people have no reason to draw a man to sin, they weary him out by tedious importunity. And many a one yields to the earnestness, or importunity, or tediousness of a persuasion, who could easily resist it if it came only with pretence of reason.

3. Alluring promises of some gain or pleasure that shall come by sin, is another scandal which doth cause the fall of many. The course that Satan tried with Christ, "All this will I give thee," was but the same which he found most successful with sinners in the world. This is a bait which sinners will themselves hunt after, if it be not offered them. Judas will go to the Pharisees with a "What will ye give me, and I will deliver him unto you?" Peter saith of the scandalous heretics of his time, "They allure

through the lust of the flesh, through much wantonness, those that were clean escaped from them who live in error; while they promise them liberty, they themselves are the servants of corruption," 2 Pet. ii. 18, 19.

4. Threatenings also and scorns are scandals, which frighten unbelieving souls into sin. Thus Rabshakeh thought to prevail with Hezekiah. Thus Nebuchadnezzar Dan. iii. thought to have drawn those three worthies to idolatry. Thus the Pharisees thought to have frightened the apostles from preaching any more in the name of Christ, Acts iv. 17, 21. Thus Saul thought to have perverted the disciples, by breathing out threatenings against them, Acts ix. 1.

5. And what words will not do, the ungodly think to do by force; and it enrageth them, that any should resist their wills, and that their force is patiently endured. What cruel torments, what various sorts of heavy sufferings, have the devil and his instruments devised, to be stumblingblocks to the weak, to affright them into sin!

6. Gifts also have blinded the eyes of some who seemed wise: "As oppression maketh a wise man mad, so a gift destroyeth the heart," Eccles. vii. 7. What scandals have preferments proved to the world, and how many have they ruined! Few are able to esteem the reproach of Christ to be greater riches than the treasures of the world.

7. And evil examples are the commonest sort of scandals:[135] not as they offend, or grieve, or are apparently sinful; but as they seem good, and therefore are temptations to the weak to imitate them. So apt are men to imitation, especially in evil, that they will do what they see another do, without examining whether it be justifiable or not. Especially if it be the example either of great men, or of learned men, or of men reputed eminently godly, or of a multitude, any of these the people are apt to imitate: this therefore is the common way of scandal. When people do that which is evil as if it were good, and thereby draw the ignorant to think it good, and so imitate them. Or else when they do that which is lawful itself, in such a manner as tendeth to deceive another, and draw him to that which is indeed unlawful; or to hinder him in any thing that is good.

8. Lastly, Even silence and omissions also may be scandalous, and draw another into error and sin. If by silence you seem to consent to false doctrine, or to wicked works, when you have opportunity to control them, hereby you draw others to consent also to the sin: or if you omit those public or private duties, which others may be witnesses of, you tempt them to the like omission, and to think they are no duties, but indifferent things: for in evil they will easily rest in your judgment, and say that you are wiser than they; but they are not so ductile and flexible to good.

5. Scandals also are distinguishable by the effects; which are such as these:

1. Some scandals do tempt men to actual infidelity, and to deny or doubt of the truth of the gospel.

2. Some scandals would draw men but into some particular error, and from some particular truth, while he holds the rest.

3. Some scandals draw men to dislike and distaste the way of godliness; and some to dislike the servants of God.

4. Some scandals tend to confound men, and bring them to utter uncertainties in religion.

5. Some tend to terrify men from the way of godliness.

6. Some only stop them for a time, and discourage or hinder them in their way.

7. Some tend to draw them to some particular sin.

8. And some to draw them from some particular duty.

9. And some tend to break and weaken their spirits, by grief or perplexity of mind.

10. And as the word is taken in the Old Testament, the snares that malicious men lay to entrap others in their lives, or liberties, or estates, or names, are called scandals. And all these ways a man may sinfully scandalize another.

And that you may see that the scandal forbidden in the New Testament, is always of this nature, let us take notice of the particular texts where the word is used. And first, to scandalize is used actively in these following texts: in Matt. v. before cited, and in the other evangelists citing the same words, the sense is clear; that the offending of a hand or eye, is not displeasing, nor seeking of ill report; but hindering our salvation by drawing us to sin. So in Matt. xviii. 8; and Mark ix. 42, 43, where the sense [803]is the same. In Matt. xvii. 27, "Lest we should offend them," &c. is not only, lest we displease them, but lest we give them occasion to dislike religion, or think hardly of the gospel, and so lay a stumblingblock to the danger of their souls. So Matt. xviii. 6, and Mark ix. "Whoso shall offend one of these little ones that believe in me," &c. that is, not who shall displease them, but whoso by threats, persecutions, cruelties, or any other means, shall go about to turn them from the faith of Christ, or stop them in their way to heaven, or hinder them in a holy life: though these two texts seem nearest to the denied sense, yet that is not indeed their meaning. So in John vi. 6, "Doth this offend you?" that is, doth this seem incredible to you, or hard to be believed, or digested? Doth it stop your faith, and make you distaste my doctrine? So 1 Cor. viii. 13, "If meat scandalize my brother;" our translators have turned it, "If meat make my brother to offend." So it was not displeasing him only, but tempting him to sin, which is the scandalizing here reproved.

View also the places where the word scandal is used. Matt. xiii. 41, Πάντα τὰ σκάνδαλα, All scandals, translated, "All things that offend," doth not signify All that is displeasing; but all temptations to sin, and hinderances or stumblingblocks that would have stopped men in the ways to heaven. So in Matt. xvi. 23, (a text as like as any to be near the denied sense; yet indeed,) "Thou art a scandal to me," (translated an offence,) doth not only signify, Thou displeasest me, but, Thou goest about to hinder me in my undertaken office, from suffering for the redemption of the world; it was an aptitudinal scandal, though not effectual. So Matt. xvii. 7, "It must be that scandals come," (translated offences,) that is, that there be many stumblingblocks set before men in their way to heaven. So Luke xvii. 1, to the same sense. And Rom. ix. 33, "I lay in Zion a stumbling-stone, and a rock of scandal," (translated offence,) that is, such as will not only be displeasing, but an occasion of utter ruin to the unbelieving, persecuting Jews; according to that of Simeon, Luke ii. 34, "This child is set for the fall and rising again of many in Israel." Rom. xi. 9, "Let their table be made a snare, a trap, and a stumblingblock." The Greek word εἰς σκάνδαλον doth not signify a displeasure only, but an occasion of ruin. So Rom. xiv. 13, expoundeth itself, "That no man put a stumblingblock or an occasion to fall into his brother's way." The Greek word is, or a scandal. This is the just exposition of the word in its ordinary use in the New Testament.[136] So Rom. xvi. 17, "Mark them which cause divisions and scandals," (translated offences,) that is, which lay stumblingblocks in the way of christians, and would trouble them in it, or turn them from it. So 1 Cor. i. 23, "To the Jews a stumblingblock," that is, a scandal, (as the Greek word is,) as before expounded. So Gal. v. 11, "The scandal of the cross," translated the offence, doth signify not the bare reproach, but the reproach as it is the trial and stumblingblock of the world, that maketh believing difficult. So 1 John ii. 10, "There is no scandal in him," translated, no occasion of stumbling. These are all the places that I remember where the word is used.

The passive verb σκανδαλίζομαι, to be scandalized, is often used. As Matt. xi. 6, "Blessed is he that is not scandalized," (translated, offended in me,)[137] that is, who is not distasted with my person and doctrine through carnal prejudices; and so kept in unbelief: there were many things in the person, life, and doctrine of Christ, which were unsuitable to carnal reason and expectation. These men thought them to be hard and strange, and could not digest them, and so were hindered by them from believing: and this was being offended in Christ. So in Matt. xiii. 57, and Mark vi. 3, "They were offended in, or at him;" that is, took a dislike or distaste to him for his words. And Matt. xiii. 21, "When persecution ariseth, by and by they are offended;"[138] that is, they stumble and fall away: and Matt. xv. 12, "The Pharisees were offended," (or scandalized,[139]) that is, so offended as to be more in dislike of Christ. And Matt. xxiv. 10, "Then shall many be offended," (or scandalized,) that is, shall draw back and fall away from Christ. And Matt. xxvi. 31, 33; Mark xiv. 27, 29, "All ye shall be offended because of me," &c. "Though all men shall be offended (or scandalized) yet will I never be scandalized;" that is, brought to doubt of Christ, or to forsake him, or deny him, or be hindered from owning their relation to him. So John xvi. 1, "These things have I spoken that ye should not be offended;" that is, that when the time cometh, the unexpected trouble may not so surprise you, as to turn you from the faith, or stagger you in your obedience or hope. Rom. xiv. 21, doth exactly expound it; "It is good neither to eat flesh, or drink wine, or any thing whereby thy brother stumbleth, or is scandalized, (or offended,) or made weak:" it is a making weak. So 2 Cor. xi. 29, "Who is offended;" that is, stumbled, or hindered, or ready to apostatize. So much for the nature and sorts of scandal.

IV. You are next to observe the aggravations of this sin. Which briefly are such as these:

1. Scandal is a murdering of souls; it is a hindering of men's salvation, and an enticing or driving them towards hell. And therefore in some respect worse than murder, as the soul is better than the body.

2. Scandal is a fighting against Jesus Christ, in his work of man's salvation. "He came to seek and to save that which was lost;" and the scandalizer seeketh to lose and destroy that which Christ would seek and save.

3. Scandal robbeth God of the hearts and service of his creatures; for it is a raising in them a distaste of his people, and word, and ways, and of himself: and a turning from him the hearts of those that should adhere unto him.

4. Scandal is a serving of the devil, in his proper work of enmity to Christ, and perdition of souls; scandalizers do his work in the world, and propagate his cause and kingdom.

V. The means of avoiding the guilt of scandal, are as followeth.

Direct. I. Mistake not (with the vulgar) the nature of scandal, as if it lay in that offending men, which is nothing but grieving or displeasing them; or in making yourselves to be of evil report; but remember that scandal is that offending men, which tempteth them into sin from God and godliness, and maketh them stumble and fall, or occasioneth them to think evil of a holy life. It is a pitiful thing to hear religious persons plead for the sin of man-pleasing, under the name of avoiding scandal; yea, to hear them set up a usurped dominion over the lives of other men, and all by the advantage of the word scandal misunderstood. So that all men must avoid whatever a censorious person will call scandalous, when he meaneth nothing else himself by scandal, than a thing that is of evil report, with such as he. Yea, pride itself is often pleaded for by this [804]misunderstanding of scandal; and men are taught to overvalue their reputations, and to strain their consciences to keep up their esteem, and all under pretence of avoiding scandal; and in the mean time they are really scandalous, even in that action by which they think they are avoiding it. I need no other instance, than the case of unwarrantable separation. Some will hold communion with none but the rebaptized; some think an imposed liturgy is enough to prove communion with such a church unlawful (at least in the use of it); and almost every sect do make their differences a reason for their separating from other churches. And if any one would hold communion with those that they separate from, they presently say, That it is scandalous to do so, and to join in any worship which they think unlawful: and by scandal they mean no more, but that it is among them of evil report, and is offensive or displeasing to them. Whereas indeed the argument from scandal should move men to use such communion, which erroneous, uncharitable, dividing men do hold unlawful. For else by avoiding that communion I shall lay a stumblingblock in the way of the weak; I shall tempt him to think that a duty is a sin, and weaken his charity, and draw him into a sinful separation, or the neglect of some ordinances of God, or opportunities of getting good. And it is this temptation which is indeed the scandal. This is before proved in the instance of Peter, Gal. ii. who scandalized or hardened the Jews, by yielding to a sinful separation from the gentiles, and fearing the censoriousness of the Jews, whom he sought to please; and the offending of whom he was avoiding, when he really offended them, that is, was a scandal, or temptation to them.

Direct. II. He that will escape the guilt of scandal, must be no contemner of the souls of others, but must be truly charitable, and have a tender love to souls. That which a man highly valueth, and dearly loveth, he will be careful to preserve, and loth to hurt. Such a man will easily part with his own rights, or submit to losses, injuries, or disgrace, to preserve his neighbour's soul from sin. Whereas a despiser of souls will insist upon his own power, and right, and honour, and will entrap and damn a hundred souls, rather than he will abate a word, or a ceremony, which he thinks his interest requireth him to exact. Tell him that it will insnare men's souls in sin, and he is ready to say as the Pharisees to Judas, "What is that to us? See thou to that." A dog hath as much pity on a hare, or a hawk on a partridge, as a carnal, worldly, ambitious Diotrephes, or an Elymas, hath of souls. Tell him that it will occasion men to sin, to wound their consciences, to offend their God, it moveth him no more than to tell him of the smallest incommodity to himself: he will do more to save a horse or a dog of his own, than to save another's soul from sin. To lay snares in their way, or to deprive them of the preaching of the gospel, or other means of their salvation, is a thing which they may be induced to, by the smallest interest of their own; yea, though it be but a point of seeming honour. And therefore when carnal, worldly men do become the disposers of matters of religion, it is easy to see what measure and usage men must expect; yea, though they assume the office and name of pastors, who should have the most tender, fatherly care of the souls of all the flocks, yet will their carnal inclinations and interests engage them in the work of wolves, to entrap, or famish, or destroy Christ's sheep.

Direct. III. Also you must be persons who value your own souls, and are diligently exercised in saving them from temptations; or else you are very like to be scandalizers and tempters of the souls of others. And therefore when such a man is made a church governor as is unacquainted with the renewing work of grace, and with the inward government of Christ in the soul, what devilish work is he like to make among the sheep of Christ, under the name of government! What corrupting of the doctrine, worship, or discipline of Christ! What inventions of his own to insnare men's consciences! and driving them on, by armed force, to do that which, at least to them, is sin, and which can never countervail the loss, either of their souls, or of the church, by such disturbances! How merciless will he be, when a poor member of Christ shall beg of him but to have pity on his soul! and tell him, I cannot do this, or swear this, or subscribe this, without the guilt of a deliberate sin; and I cannot sin without displeasing God, and hindering my salvation. He that dare wilfully sin himself, and make it his deliberate choice, and dare play away his own salvation, at the poorest game that the devil will invite him to, and will sell his own soul at the basest price, even for a little pelf, or pleasure, or high titles, for so short a time, certainly this man is unlike to be very tender of the souls of others, or to stick at scandalizing and insnaring them, or to care any more to murder souls, than a butcher doth to kill a hog: Judas's heart will make them sell their Lord, or his flock, at Judas's price; and prepare themselves for Judas's reward. And hence it is, that the carnal seed, even within the church, hath ordinarily persecuted the spiritual seed. For saith Paul, "As he that was born after the flesh persecuted him that was born after the Spirit, even so it is now," Gal. iv. 29.

Direct. IV. To be well acquainted with the methods of Satan, and the way of particular temptations, is a great help against your scandalizing others. He that seeth the devil as the principal in each temptation, and knoweth in what manner he engageth his instruments to carry on his work, and whither all this tendeth at the last, will scarce be willing to serve such a master in so bad a work. Remember that scandalizers and tempters of others, and hinderers of men's salvation, are the servants of the devil, and are executing his malice, for the damnation of their brethren's souls. And what reward can they expect for such a work from such a master? The devil useth them but as men do ferrets, whose mouths are sealed, because they must not partake of the prey; but only bring it to their master's hand. Live in a constant watchful resistance of temptations yourselves, and you will have no mind to the drudgery of tempting others.

Direct. V. Set not yourselves upon any worldly, ambitious design. For the love of the riches and honours of the world, will not only engage you in a course of sinning, but also make it seem your interest, to make others as bad and miserable as yourselves, and to drive them on to serve your interests by their sin.

Direct. VI. Take heed lest a fleshly inclination do draw you to the love of fleshly pleasures. And that your minds be not set upon the pleasing of your fancies, sense, or appetite; either in meat, or drink, or clothes, or dwellings, or recreations, or any such delights: if once the love of these grow strong, it will conquer your reason, and seduce it into libertinism, and make you think that a voluptuous, flesh-pleasing life, (so it be not by gross disgraced sins,) is but the lawful use of the creature, which Christ hath purchased not only for our necessity, but for our delight; and that the contrary opinion is but the too much rigour of such as understand not their christian liberty.

[805]*Direct.* VII. Be not rashly and ignorantly zealous in soliciting and importuning others to your private opinions, before you are certain that they are of God. Oh what abundance of zeal and labour hath many a man laid out, to make others of his mind, in the points of antinomianism, anabaptism, separation, popery, &c. thinking that the saving of their souls had lain upon it; and at last they find, that as they erred themselves, so all their labour was but to scandalize the weak, and lay a stumblingblock in their way to heaven!

Direct. VIII. Never persuade any man (much less compel him) to any thing unnecessary, which he taketh to be a sin (whatever you take it for yourselves). For if he judge it a sin, it is a sin to him. No man can innocently do that which he thinketh is forbidden him of God. And shall a thing unnecessary be preferred before the saving of a soul? yea, before the souls of thousands, as by many merciless men it is? Indeed, if there be an antecedent necessity, (as well as a lawfulness in the thing,) and such a necessity as is not in your power to take away, then the doing it will be his sin, and the not doing it his greater sin; and the greater sin is greatliest to be avoided (but by convenient means).

Direct. IX. Remember the charge which you have of the souls of one another. Though you be not magistrates or pastors; (for their care of souls is so unquestionable and so great, that scandal in them is like parents murdering their own children;) yet no private man must say as Cain, "Am I my brother's keeper?" Every man is bound to do his best for the saving of his neighbour; much more to forbear infecting, seducing, scandalizing, and destroying him.

Direct. X. Keep up a special tenderness of the weak. So doth God himself, and so must we. "He gathereth the lambs with his arms," &c. Isa. xl. 11. If his infants cry he doth not therefore knock out their brains, or turn them out of doors. Nor doth he say, they are not his children, for every ignorance or peevish passion which they are guilty of. Christ doth not turn men out of his school, because they want knowledge. For why then will he have little children come? And what do they come for, but to learn? He doth not hate his new-born babes, but feedeth and nurseth them with a special tenderness; and he hath commanded and communicated the like tenderness to his ministers; who must not be weak with the weak, and froward with the froward, but in meekness and patience must bear with the weak, and endure their bitterest censures and requitals. "For the servant of the Lord must not strive, but be gentle to all men, apt to teach, patient, in meekness instructing those that oppose themselves," &c. 2 Tim. ii. 24, 25. And if they are long learning before they come to the knowledge of the truth, they are not therefore to be cast off. He that can read Rom. xiv. and xv.;

1 Cor. xii. 12; viii.; Gal. vi.; and yet can be so merciless and cruel, as to cast men out of the ministry or church, or to ruin them, for tolerable weakness, which God hath so earnestly charged us to bear with in our brethren, either he doth not understand what he readeth, or not believe it, or hath somewhat else which he more regardeth at his heart, than the authority or love of God.

Direct. XI. Do not censure every man to be wilful or obstinate, who is not of your opinion, when he hath heard your reasons, how clear soever they may seem to you. Alas! how many things are there besides wilful obstinacy, to hinder one man from being as wise as another! If a few times repeating over the reasons of an opinion, is enough to implant it in all the hearers, why do your children go so long to school, and after that to the universities? And why are you so long preaching to all your parishioners? Sure you preach not novelties to them as long as you live! And yet thirty or forty years' painful preaching, even of the same fundamentals of religion, shall leave many ignorant of them in the best of parishes in the land. There must be a right and ripe disposition in the hearers, or else the clearest reasoning may be uneffectual. A disused or unfurnished mind, that hath not received all the truths which are presupposed to those which you deliver, or hath not digested them into a clear understanding, may long hear the truest reasons, and never apprehend their weight. There is need of more ado than a bare unfolding of the truth, to make a man receive it in its proper evidence. Perhaps he hath been long prepossessed with contrary opinions, which are not easily rooted out. Or if he be but confident of the truth of some one opinion, which is inconsistent with yours, no wonder if he cannot receive that which is contrary to what he so verily believeth to be the truth. There is a marvellous variety of men's apprehensions, of the same opinions or reasons, as they are variously represented to men, and variously pondered, and as the natural capacity of men is various, and as the whole course of their lives, their education, company, and conversation, have variously formed their minds. It is like the setting together all the parts of a watch when it is in pieces; if any one part of many be misplaced, it may necessitate the misplacing of those that follow, without any wilful obstinacy in him that doth it. If in the whole frame of sacred truth, there be but some one misunderstood, it may bring in other mistakes, and keep out many truths, even from an honest, willing mind. And who is there that can say, he is free from error? Have not you perceived in yourselves, that the truths which you heard a hundred times over, to little purpose, when you were children, were received more convincingly and satisfyingly when you were men? And that you have found a delightful clearness in some points on a sudden, which before you either resisted, or held with little observation or regard? And yet it is common with the scandalizers of souls, to cry out against all that conform not to their opinions and will, as soon as they have heard their reasons, that they are stubborn, and refractory, and wilful, and factious, and so turn from arguments to clubs; as if they had never known themselves or others, nor how weak and dark the understandings of almost all men are. But they shall have judgment without mercy, who show no mercy. And when their own errors shall all be opened to them by the Lord, they will be loth they should all be imputed to their wilful obstinacy. And perhaps these very censorious men, may prove themselves to have been on the wrong side; for pride and uncharitableness are usually erroneous.

Direct. XII. Engage not yourselves in an evil cause. For if you do, it will engage you to draw in others; you will expect your friends should take your part, and think as you think, and say as you say; though it be never so much against truth or righteousness.

Direct. XIII. Speak not rashly against any cause or persons before you are acquainted with them; or have well considered what you say. Especially take heed how you believe what a man of any sect in religion doth speak or write against his adversaries of a contrary sect. If experience had not proved it in our days, beyond contradiction, it would seem incredible how little men are to be believed in this case,[140] and how the false reports will run among the [806]people of the sect, against those whom the interest of their opinion and party engageth them to misrepresent![141]Think not that you are excusable for receiving or venting an ill report, because you can say, He was an honest man that spoke it; for many that are otherwise honest, do make it a part of their honesty to be dishonest in this. They think they are not zealous enough for those opinions which they call their religion, unless they are easy in believing and speaking evil of those that are the adversaries of it. When it may be upon a just trial, all proveth false; and then all the words which you ignorantly utter against the truth, or those that follow it, are scandals or stumblingblocks to the hearers, to turn them from it, and make them hate it.[142] I am not speaking against a just credulity; there must be human belief, or else there can be no human converse; but ever suspect partiality in a party. For the interest of their religion is a more powerful charm to the consciences of evil speakers, than personal interest or bribes would be. How many legends tell us this, how easily some men counted godly, have been prevailed with to lie for God!

Direct. XIV. Take heed of mocking at a religious life; yea, or of breaking any jests or scorns at the weaknesses of any in religious exercises, which may possibly reflect upon the exercises themselves. Many a thousand souls have been kept from a holy life, by the scorns of the vulgar, that speak of it as a matter of derision or sport. Reading the Scriptures, and holy conference, and prayer, and instructing our families, and the holy observation of the Lord's day, and church discipline, are commonly the derision of ungodly persons, who can scorn that which they can neither confute nor learn; and weak people are greatly moved by such senseless means. A mock or jeer doth more with them than an argument; they cannot endure to be made a laughing-stock. Thus was the name of the crucified God the derision of the heathens, and the scandal of the world, both Jews and gentiles. And there is scarce a greater scandal or stumblingblock at this day, which keepeth multitudes from heaven, than when the devil can make it either a matter of danger or of shame to be a christian, or to live a holy, mortified life. Persecution and derision are the great successful scandals of the world. And therefore seeing men are so apt to be turned off from Christ and godliness, never speak unreverently or disrespectfully of them. It is a profane and scandalous course of some, that if a preacher have but an unhandsome tone or gesture they make a jest of it, and say, He whined, or he spoke through the nose, or some such scorn they cast upon him; which the hearers quickly apply to all others, and turn to a scorn of preaching, or prayer, or religion itself: or if men differ from each other in opinion in matters of religion, they are presently inclined to deride them for something in their worshipping of God! And while they deride a man as an anabaptist, as an independent, as a presbyterian, as prelatical, they little know what a malignant tincture it may leave upon the hearer's mind, and teach carnal persons to make a jest of all alike.

Direct. XV. Impute not the faults of men to Christ, and blame not religion for the faults of them that sin against it. This is the malignant trick of Satan, and his blinded instruments: if a hypocrite miscarry, or if a man that in all things else hath walked uprightly, be overthrown by a temptation in some odious sin, they presently cry out, These are your professors! your religious people! that are so precise, and pure, and strict! Try them, and they will appear as bad as others! If a Noah be once drunk, or a Lot be overthrown thereby, or a David commit adultery and murder, or a Peter deny his master, or a Judas betray him, they presently cry out, They are all alike! and turn it to the scorn of godliness itself. Unworthy beasts! As if Christ's laws were therefore to be scorned, because men break them! and obedience to God were bad, because some are disobedient! Hath Christ forbidden the sins which you blame, or hath he not? If he have not, blame them not, for they are no sins; if he have, commend the justness and holiness of his laws. Either the offenders you blame, did well or ill. If they did well, why do you blame them? If they did ill, why do you not commend religion, and the Scripture which condemneth them? Either it is best for all men to live in such sins as those which these lapsed persons or hypocrites committed, or it is not. If it be, why are you offended with them for that which you allow? If it be not, why do you soothe up the wicked in their sins, and excuse an ungodly life, because of the falls of such as seem religious? There is no common ingenuity in this, but malicious spite against God and holiness (of which more in the next chapter).

Direct. XVI. Make not use of civil quarrels to lay an odium upon religion. It is ordinary with ungodly, malicious men, to labour to turn the displeasure of rulers against men of integrity; and if there be any broils or civil wars, to snatch any pretence, how false soever, to call them traitors and enemies to government. If it be but because they are against a usurper, or because some fanatic persons (whom they oppose) have behaved themselves rebelliously or disobediently; a holy life (which is the greatest friend to loyalty) must be blamed for all. And all is but to gratify the devil in driving poor souls from God and holiness.

Direct. XVII. When you think it your duty to speak of the faults of men that profess a godly life, lay the blame only on the person, but speak as much and more in commendations of godliness itself; and commend that which is good in them, while you discommend that which is evil. Is their praying bad? Is their instructing their families, and sanctifying the Lord's day, bad? Is their fearing sin, and obeying God, bad? If not, why do you not say as much to commend them for these, or at least to commend these in themselves, as you do to discommend them for their faults? Why do you not fear lest the hearers should be drawn to dislike a godly life by your disgracing persons accounted godly? and therefore warn them to think never the worse of godliness for this? You that give the poison, should in reason give an antidote, if it be not your design to poison souls. Is it really your design by speaking against men accounted godly, to draw the hearers to the hatred of godliness, or is it not? If it be, you are incarnate devils: if it be not, why do you endeavour it, by making odious the persons, under the name of professors and godly men? And why do you not speak more to draw people to a godly life? and to imitate them in that which is good, while they disclaim them in that which is evil?

Direct. XVIII. Be especially tender of the reputations of those, that the souls of men have most dependence on: as the preachers of the gospel, and the eminentest men for knowledge and religiousness.[143] Not that I desire that sin should be the better thought of for being theirs, or that evil should [807]be called good in any; but experience hath told the world since God and the devil had their several ways and servants upon earth, that it hath been the devil's most usual successful course, to wound religion through the sides of the religious, and to blame the persons, when he would turn men from the way! For he knoweth that religious persons have their faults, and in them his malice may find somewhat to fasten on; but religion hath no fault, and malice itself is seldom so impudent, as to speak directly against a holy, heavenly life. But the way is to make those disgraceful and odious, who are noted to lead such a life; and then secretly to infer, If those that seem godly be no better, you need not be godly, you are as well as you are. This religion is but a fantasy; a needless, if not a troublesome, hurtful thing. Seeing therefore that the devil hath no blow at religion, so fair as by striking at the persons of the preachers and professors of it, every friend of Christ must be acquainted with his design, and must not serve him in it, but counter-work him, and preserve the reputation even of the persons of the religious: not so much in charity to them, but for the people's souls, and the honour of Christ.

Direct. XIX. Let all that preach and profess the gospel, and a godly life, be sure that they live according to their profession; that the name of God be not evil spoken of among the wicked through their misdoings, Rom. ii. It was the aggravation of David's sin which God would not quite forgive, that he made the enemies of the Lord blaspheme, 2 Sam. xii. 14. "Servants must count their masters worthy of all honour, that the name of God and his doctrine be not blasphemed," 1 Tim. vi. 1. The duties of good women are particularly named by the apostle, Tit. ii. 3-5, with this motive to the practice of them, "That the word of God be not blasphemed." Obedience to government is commanded with this motive, 1 Pet. ii. 15, "For so is the will of God, that with well-doing you may put to silence the ignorance of foolish men." And ver. 11, 12, "Dearly beloved, I beseech you, as strangers and pilgrims, abstain from fleshly lusts which war against the soul: having your conversation honest among the gentiles, that whereas they speak against you as evil-doers, they may by your works which they shall behold, glorify God in the day of visitation." And it was the aggravation of the heretics' sin, that "many shall follow their pernicious ways, by reason of whom the way of truth shall be evil spoken of," 2 Pet. ii. 2. Oh then, how carefully should ministers and all that are godly walk! The blind world cannot read the gospel in itself, but only as it is exemplified by the lives of men: they judge not of the actions of men by the law, but of the law of God by men's actions! Therefore the saving or damning of men's souls, doth lie much upon the lives of the professors of religion; because their liking or disliking a holy life doth depend upon them. Saith Paul of young women, "I will that—they give no occasion to the adversary to speak reproachfully; for some are already turned aside after Satan," 1 Tim. v. 14, 15. Hence it is, that even the appearance of evil is so carefully to be avoided, by all that fear God, lest others be drawn by it to speak evil of godliness. Every scandal (truly so called) is a stab to the soul of him that is scandalized, and a reproachful blot to the christian cause. I may say of the faults of christians, as Plutarch doth of the faults of princes, A wart or blemish in the face is more conspicuous and disgraceful than in other parts.

Direct. XX. Let no pretence of the evil of hypocrisy make you so contented with your secret innocency, as to neglect the edification and satisfaction of your neighbours. When it is only your own interest that is concerned in the business, then it is no matter whether any man be acquainted with any good that you do; and it is a very small matter how they judge, or what they say of you; the approbation of God alone is enough. No matter who condemneth you, if he justify you. But when the vindication of your innocency, or the manifestation of your virtue, is necessary to the good of your neighbours' souls, or to the honour of your sacred profession, the neglect of it is not sincerity, but cruelty.

[135] Heb. xi. 26.

[136] So Rev. ii. 14. Balaam did βαλλεῖν σκάνδαλον, lay a scandal, or stumblingblock before the Israelites; that is, a temptation to sin.

[137] Luke vii. 23.

[138] Mark vi. 3.

[139] Mark iv. 17.

[140] Psal. cxix. 69.

[141] Vix equidem credar. Sed cum sint præmia falsi Nulla; ratam debet testis habere fidem. Ovid.

[142] Rom. iii. 7, 8; James iii. 14; Job xiii. 7, 8.

[143] Ita comparatum est ut virtutem non suspiciamus, neque ejus imitandæ studio corripimur nisi eum in quo ea conspicitur, summo honore et amore prosequamur. Plutar. in Cat. Utic.

CHAPTER XIII.

DIRECTIONS AGAINST SCANDAL TAKEN, OR AN APTNESS TO RECEIVE HURT, BY THE WORDS OR DEEDS OF OTHERS.

It was not only an admonition, but a prophecy of Christ, when he said, "Woe to the world because of offences! It must be that offences come." And, "Blessed is he that is not offended or scandalized in me." He foreknew that the errors and misdoings of some, would be the snare and ruin of many others; and that, when "damnable heresies arise, many will follow their pernicious ways, by reason of whom the way of truth shall be evil spoken of," 2 Pet. i. 2. Like men in the dark, where if one catch a fall, he that comes next him falls upon him.

There are four sorts of persons that use to be scandalized or hurt by the sins of others.

1. Malignant enemies of Christ and godliness, who are partly hardened in their malice, and partly rejoiced at the dishonour of religion, and insult over those that give the offence, or take occasion by it to blaspheme or persecute.

2. Some that are more equal, and hopeful, and in greater possibility of conversion, who are stopped by it in their desires, and purposes, and attempts of a godly life.

3. Unsound professors, or hypocrites, who are turned by scandals from the way of godliness, which they seemed to walk in.

4. Weak christians, who are troubled and hindered in their way of piety, or else drawn into some particular error or sin, though they fall not off.

So that the effects of scandal may be reduced to these two: I. The perverting of men's judgments, to dislike religion, and think hardly either of the doctrine or practice of Christianity. II. The imboldening of men to commit particular sins, or to omit particular duties; or at least the troubling and hindering them in the performance: against which, I shall first give you distinctly some meditative directions, and then some practical directions against them both together.

I. *Direct.* I. Consider what an evident sign it is of a very blind or malicious soul, to be so apt to pick quarrels with God and godliness, because of the sins of other men.

Love thinketh not ill of those we love: ill will and malice are still ready to impute whatever is amiss to those whom they hate. Enmity is contentious and slanderous; and will make a crime of virtue itself, and from any topic fetch matter of reproach. There is no witness seemeth incredible to it, who speaketh any thing that is evil of those they hate. An argument *a baculo ad verbera* is sufficient. Thus did the heathens by the primitive christians; [808]and will you do thus by God? Will you terrify your own consciences, when they shall awake, and find such an ugly serpent in your bosom, as malice and enmity against your Maker and Redeemer? It is the nature of the devil, even his principal sin. And will you not only wear his livery, but bear his image, to prove that he is your father? and by community of natures, to prove that you must also have a communion with him in condemnation and punishment? And doth not so visible a mark of devilism upon your souls, affright you, and make you ready to run away from yourselves? Nothing but devilish malice can charge that upon God or godliness, which is done by sinners against his laws. Would you use a friend thus? If a murder were done, or a slander raised of you, or your house were fired, or your goods stolen, would you suspect your friend of it? or any one that you honoured, loved, or thought well of? You would not certainly, but rather your enemy, or some lewd and dissolute persons that were most likely to be guilty. You are blinded by malice, if you see not how evident a proof of your devilish malice this is, to be ready, when men that profess religion do any thing amiss, to think the worse of godliness or religion for it! The cause of this suspicion is lodged in your own hearts.

Direct. II. Remember that this was the first temptation, by which the devil overthrew mankind, to persuade them to think ill of God, as if he had been false to his word, and had envied them their felicity. "Ye shall not surely die: for God doth know that in the day ye eat thereof, then your eyes shall be opened, and ye shall be as gods, knowing good and evil," Gen. iii. 4, 5. And will you not be warned by the calamity of all the world, to take heed of thinking ill of God, and of his word, and of believing the devil's reports against him?

Direct. III. Consider that to think ill of God, is to think him to be a devil; and to think ill of godliness, is to take it to be wickedness: and can man be guilty of a more devilish crime? Nay, is it not worse than the devil that tempteth you to it can commit. To be God is to be good, even the infinite, eternal, perfect good, in whom is no evil, nor none can be. To be a devil, is to be evil, even the chief that do evil, and would draw others so to do. It is not an ugly shape in which a painter doth represent the devil, which showeth us his ugliness indeed: an enemy of godliness is liker to him than that picture: it is his sinfulness against God, which is his true deformity. Therefore to suspect God to be evil, is to suspect him to be the devil, so horrid a blasphemy doth this sin partake of. And if godliness be bad, then he that is the author and end of it cannot be good.

Direct. IV. Consider what horrible blindness it is to impute men's faults to God, who is the greatest adversary to sin in all the world, and who will most severely punish it, and to godliness, which is perfectly its contrary. There is no angel in heaven so little to be suspected to be the friend of sin as God. Creatures are mutable in themselves; angels have the innocent imperfection of creatures; saints on earth have a culpable imperfection through the remainder of sin. If you had only suspected these, you might have had some pretence for it; but to quarrel with God or godliness, is madder than to think that light is the cause of darkness.

Direct. V. And think what extremity of injury and injustice this is to God, to blame him or his laws for those sins of men which are committed against him and his laws. Who is it that sin is committed against but God? Is it not he that made the laws, which it is the transgression of? Are not those laws, think you, strict enough against it? Is it not their strictness which such as you dislike? Were they laws that would give you leave to be worldly, sensual, and proud, you would never quarrel with them; and yet you charge men's sins on these laws, because they are so strict against them. Do you impute sin to God, because he will judge men for it to hell-fire, and cast them for ever out of his glorious presence into misery? O cursed impudence! How righteous is God in condemning such malicious souls! Tell us if you can, would you have had God to have forbidden sin more strictly? or condemned it more severely? or punished it more terribly? If you would, you pray for greater vengeance than hell upon yourselves! Woe to you, when he executeth but so much as he hath already threatened! Shall the crime of rebels be imputed to the king, against whom they rebel? If a thief shall rob you, or a servant deceive you, or a son despise you, is he just that will so much increase your injury, as to lay the blame of all upon yourselves? You will say, It is not God that we are offended with. But if it be at a holy life, it is at God; for what is godliness, but the loving, and serving, and obeying God? If you say, that it is not godliness neither; why then do you distaste or speak against a godly life on this occasion? If you say, It is these hypocrites only that we dislike: what do you dislike them for? Is it for their virtue or their vices? If it be for their sins, why then do you not speak and do more against sin, in yourselves and others? We will concur with you to the utmost in opposing sin wherever it be found. If it be their hypocrisy that you blame, persuade yourselves and other men to be sincerely godly. How would you have hypocrisy avoided? By an open profession to serve the devil? or by sincerity in serving God? If the latter, why then do you think evil of the most serious obedience to God? Alas! all christian countries are too full of hypocrites. Every one that is baptized, and professeth Christianity, is a saint or a hypocrite! All drunken, covetous, ambitious, sensual, unclean christians, are hypocrites, and not christians indeed. And these hypocrites can quietly live a worldly, fleshly life, and never lament their own hypocrisy, nor their perfidious violating their baptismal vow. But if one that seemeth diligent for his soul, prove a hypocrite, or fall into any scandalous sin, here they presently make an outcry; not to call the man from his sin, but to make a godly, diligent life seem odious to all, by telling men, These are your godly men. It is godliness that they quarrel with, while they pretend only to find fault with sin. Why else do not you find fault with the same sin equally in all? or, at least, persuade men by such examples to be less sinful, and more watchful, and not to be less religious and more loose? Tell me truly of any one that is more against sin than God, or any thing more contrary to it than godliness and true religion, or any men that do more against it than the most religious, and then I will join with you in preferring those. Till then, remember how you condemn yourselves, when you condemn them that are better than yourselves.

Direct. VI. Think what a foolish, audacious thing it is to set yourselves against your God and Judge. Will you accuse him of evil, because men do evil? Are you fit to judge him? Are guilty worms either wise or just enough for such an attempt, or strong enough to bear it out? What do you but set your faces against heaven, and profess rebellion against God, when you blame his laws and government, and think the obeying and serving him to be evil?

Direct. VII. Consider what cruelty it is to yourselves, to turn the faults of others to your ruin, [809]which should be your warning to avoid the like. If another man sin, will you not only do so too, but be the more averse to repentance and reformation? Will you cut your throat, because another cut his finger, or did so before you? Why should you do yourselves such mischief?

Direct. VIII. Remember that this was the design of the devil in tempting religious people to sin, not only to destroy them, but to undo you and others by their falls. If he can make you think the worse of religion, he hath his design and will; he hath killed many at a blow. Yea, perhaps the sinner may repent, and be forgiven, when you that are driven from repentance and godliness by the scandal, may be damned. And will you so far gratify the devil, in the wilful destruction of yourselves? Sin is contagious; and this is your catching of the infection, if it prevail to drive you further from God. And thus this plague devoureth multitudes.

Direct. IX. He that will think ill of godliness for men's sins, shall never want occasion of such offence, nor such temptations to fly from God. If you are so foolish or malignant, as to pick quarrels with God and godliness for men's faults, (which nothing but God and godliness can reform,) you may set up your standard of defiance against heaven, and see what you will get by it in the end. For God will not remove all occasion of your scandal. There ever have been and will be hypocrites in the church on earth. Noah's ark had a Ham; Abraham's family had an Ishmael, and Isaac's an Esau, and David's an Absalom, and Christ's a Judas. The falls of good men are cited in Scripture, to admonish you to take heed. Noah, Lot, David, Joseph's brethren, &c. have left a mark behind them where they fell, that you may take a safer way. If you will make all such the occasion of your malignity, you turn your medicine into your poison, and choose hell because some others choose it, or because some stumbled in the way to heaven.

And for those who are imboldened in sin, because they see their superiors or religious men commit it, or read that David, Noah, Peter, &c. fell, let them consider,

Direct. I. That it is rule, and not example, that you must chiefly live by. Do the laws of God by which you must be judged, allow of sin? If they do, then fear it not.

Direct. II. Is not the example of Christ much better than a sinner's? If you will follow examples, follow the best, even that which was given you purposely to imitate. The greatest and most learned man is fallible, and the most religious is not wholly free from sin: sincerity writeth after a perfect copy, though it cannot reach it.

Direct. III. Consider that sin is not the better, but the worse, for being committed by a religious, a great, or a learned man. Their place, their knowledge, and profession aggravateth it. And shall that imbolden you which God most hateth?

Direct. IV. And consider that when he that falleth by a surprise, doth rise again by repentance, and is pardoned, those that are hereby imboldened to sin deliberately and impenitently, shall be condemned. You may sin with David or Peter when you will, but you cannot rise with them by true repentance, without that grace which you wilfully resist and forfeit.

Direct. V. Lastly, Consider that the best men, and the greatest, are the most dangerous tempters, when they mislead us. A David was a stronger temptation to Bathsheba, than another man could have been. A Peter might sooner mislead Barnabas, and others, into a sinful dissimulation and separation, than another could have done. Therefore do not think that where your danger is greatest, your venturousness should be most.

Practical Directions against Offence and Hurt by others.

Direct. I. Lay well your foundation, and understand the nature and reasons of religion; and then you will be so far from disliking it for the errors and falls of others, that it will be written upon your minds, as with a beam of the sun, That there can be no reason against obeying God, and against the careful securing of our salvation. This will be the first and undoubted principle, which nothing in the world can make you question. Whatever scandals, persecutions, or sufferings may attend a holy life, you will still be past doubt that there is no other way; no other eligible, no other tolerable, no other rational, or that will lead to happiness. Whatever falls out in the world, if the most great, or learned, or religious fall away, it will not make you question, Whether a man be a living creature, nor whether the sun be light, nor whether two and two be four. No more should it make you question, Whether God be better than the creature, heaven than earth, or a life of holiness than a life of sin. You will say as Peter, "Lord, whither should we go? thou hast the words of eternal life," John vi. 68. Whatever scandals are given, or whatever befall the church, or if all the disciples of Christ forsake him, this remaineth as sure as that the earth is under us, that there is no other way than holiness, for a wise man once to take into his thoughts.

Direct. II. Get once a sincere love to God and a holy life, and then no scandals will make you jealous of it, nor think of looking any other way. It is want of true and hearty love, that maketh you so easily taken off.

Direct. III. To this end, know religion by experience; and this will put you past all doubt of his goodness. He that never tasted sugar, may be persuaded by argument that it is not sweet, or may think it bitter when he seeth another spit it out; and he that knoweth godliness but by looking on, or hearsay, may thus be drawn to think it bad; but so will not he that hath truly tried it: I mean not only to try what it is to hear, and read, and pray; but what it is to be humble, holy, and heavenly, both in heart and life.

Direct. IV. When you see any man sin, be sure you do that duty which it calls you to. Every fall that you see of others doth call you to see the odiousness of sin (as you will do when you see a drunkard spewing, or a thief at the whipping-post). And it calleth you to search for and lament the root of such sin in yourselves, and to set your watch more strictly upon such a warning; and it calls you to compassionate the sinner, and if you have hope and opportunity to endeavour his recovery. If you will consciously do this duty which is your own, you will be the less in danger of hurt by scandal. It is duty that must help to prevent infection.

Direct. V. Be watchful among all men, high and low, learned or unlearned, good and bad. Venture not blindly upon the singular opinion of any men whatsoever; nor into any new unproved way. Remember that all men are a temptation to others; and therefore be armed and watch against such temptation. Know well what it is, that is the peculiar temptation, which the quality of those that you have to do with, layeth before you. Spend no day or hour in any company, good or bad, without a wise and careful vigilancy.

Direct. VI. Be as little as you can in scandalous [810]and tempting company. Presume not to touch pitch, and promise yourselves to escape defilement. Especially fly from two sorts of scandals. First, The discourses and societies of heretical or schismatical men, who speak perverse things to draw away disciples after them, Acts xx. 30. Those that presume to run into such snares, and think their own understanding and stability are sufficient to preserve them, do show by their pride that they are near a fall, 1 Cor. x. Secondly, The company of sensual persons, at stage-plays, gaming, inordinate plays, and wanton dalliance. For this is to bring your tinder and gunpowder to the fire; and the less you fear it, the greater is your danger.

Direct. VII. Look more at the good that is in others, than at their faults and falls. The fly that will fall on none but the galled, ulcerous place, doth feed accordingly. Is a professor of religion covetous, drunk, or other ways scandalous? Remember that it is his covetousness or drunkenness that is bad. Reprove that, and fly from it, and spare not; but religion is good; let that therefore be commended and imitated. Leave the carrion to dogs and crows to feast upon; but do you choose out the things that are commendable, and mind, and mention, and imitate those.

Direct. VIII. Lastly, Think and speak as much against the sin and danger of taking scandal, as against the sin and danger of giving it. When others cry out, These are your religious people, do you cry out as much against their malignity and madness, who will dislike or reproach religion for men's sins; which is to blame the law-makers or laws, because they are broken; or to fall out with health, because many that once were in health fall sick; or to find fault with eating, because some are lean; or with clothing, because some are cold. Open to yourselves and others, what a wicked and perilous thing this is, to fall out with godliness, because some are ungodly that seem godly. Many cry out against scandal, that never think what a heinous sin it is to be scandalized, or to suffer men's sins to be a scandal to you; and to be the worse, because that others are so bad. No one must differ from them in an opinion, or a fashion of apparel, or in a mode or form of worship, but some are presently scandalized; not knowing that it is a greater sin in them to be scandalized, than in the other by such means (supposing them to be faulty) to give them the occasion. Do you know what it is to be scandalized or offended in the Scripture sense? It is not merely to be displeased, or to dislike another's actions (as is before said); but it is to be drawn into some sin, or hindered from some duty, or stopped in the course of religion, or to think the worse of truth, or duty, or a godly life, because of other men's words or actions: and do you think him a good christian, and a faithful or constant friend to godliness, who is so easily brought to quarrel with it? or is so easily turned from it, or hindered in it? Some peevish, childish persons are like sick stomachs, that no meat can please; you cannot dress it so curiously, but they complain that it is naught, or this aileth it, or that aileth it, when the fault is in themselves; or like children, or sick persons, that can scarce be touched but they are hurt: do you think that this sickliness or curiosity in religion is a credit to you? This is not the tenderness of conscience which God requireth, to be easily hurt by other men's differences or faults. As it is the shame of many ladies and gentlewomen, to be so curious and troublesomely neat, that no servant knoweth how to please them; so is it in religion a sign of your childish folly, and worse, to be guilty of such proud curiosity, that none can please you who are not exactly of your mind and way. All men must follow your humours in gestures, fashions, opinions, formalities, and modes, or else you are troubled, and offended, and scandalized; as if all the world were made to please and humour you! or you were wise enough, and great and good enough, to be the rule of all about you! Desire and spare not, that yourselves and all men should please God as exactly as is possible. But if the want of that exactness in doubtful things, or a difference in things disputable and doubtful among true christians, do thereupon abate or hinder your love or estimation of your brethren, or communion with them, or any other christian duty, or tempt you into censoriousness or contempt of your brethren, or to schism, persecution, or any other sin; it is you that are the great offenders, and you that are like to be the sufferers; and have cause to lament that sinful aptness to be thus scandalized.

CHAPTER XIV.

DIRECTIONS AGAINST SOUL MURDER, AND PARTAKING OF OTHER MEN'S SINS.

THE special directions given part iii. chap. xxii. to parents and masters, will in this case be of great use to all others; but because it is here seasonable to speak of it further, under the sixth commandment, and the matter is of the greatest consequence, I shall, 1. Tell you how men are guilty of soul murder. 2. And then give you some general directions for the furthering of men's salvation. 3. And next give you some special directions for christian exhortation and reproofs.

First, Men are guilty of soul murder by all these ways. 1. By preaching false soul-murdering doctrine. Such as denieth any necessary point of faith, or holy living; such as is opposite to a holy life, or to any particular necessary duty; such as maketh sin to be no sin; which calls good evil, and evil good; which putteth darkness for light, and light for darkness.

2. By false application of true doctrine, indirectly reflecting upon and disgracing that holiness of life, which in terms they preach for; by prevarication undermining that

cause which their office is appointed to promote; as they do, who purposely so describe any vice, that the hearers may be drawn to think that strict and godly practices are either that sin itself, or but a cloak to hide it.

3. By bringing the persons of the most religious into hatred, by such false applications, reflections, or secret insinuations, or open calumnies; making men believe that they are all but hypocrites, or schismatics, or seditious, or fanatical, self-conceited persons! Which is usually done either by impudent slanders raised against some particular men, and so reflected on the rest; or by the advantage of factions, controversies, or civil wars; or by the falls of any professors, or the crimes of hypocrites; whereupon they would make the world believe that they are all alike; as if Christ's family were to be judged of by Peter's fall or Judas's falsehood. And the odious representation of godly men doth greatly prevail to keep others from godliness, and is one of the devil's most successful means, for the damnation of multitudes of souls.

4. The disgrace of the persons of the preachers of the gospel, doth greatly further men's damnation. For when the people think their teachers to be hypocrites, [811]covetous, proud, and secretly as bad as others, they are very like to think accordingly of their doctrine, and that all strict religion is but hypocrisy, or at least to refuse their help and counsels. Even Plutarch noted, that "It so comes to pass that we entertain not virtue, nor are rapt into a desire of imitating it, unless we highly honour and love the person in whom it is discerned." And if they see or think the preacher himself to be of a loose, and careless, and licentious life, they will think that the like is very excusable in themselves; and that his doctrine is but a form of speech, which his office bindeth him to say; but is no more to be regarded by them than by himself.

Two ways is men's damnation thus promoted. 1. By the ill lives of hypocritical, ungodly preachers, who actually bring their own persons into disgrace, and thereby also the persons of others, and consequently their sacred work and function. 2. By wicked preachers and people, who through a malignant hatred of those that are abler and better than themselves, and an envy of their reputation, do labour to make the most zealous and faithful preachers of the gospel, to be thought the most hypocritical, or erroneous, or factious and schismatical.

5. The neglect of ministerial duties is a common cause of sin, and of men's damnation. When they that take the charge of souls, are either unable or unwilling to do their office; when they teach them too seldom, or too unskilfully, in an unsuitable manner; not choosing that doctrine which they most need, or not opening it plainly and methodically in a fitness to their capacities, or not applying it with necessary seriousness and urgency to the hearers' state. When men preach to the ungodly who are near to damnation, in a formal pace, like a schoolboy saying his lesson, or in a drowsy, reading tone, as if they came to preach them all asleep, or were afraid of wakening them. When they speak of sin, and misery, and Christ, of heaven and hell, as if by the manner they came to contradict the matter, and to persuade men that there are no such things.

The same mischief followeth the neglect of private, personal inspection. When ministers think that they have done all, when they have said a sermon, and never make conscience of labouring personally to convince the ungodly, and reclaim offenders, and draw sinners to God, and confirm the weak. And the omission (much more the perversion and abuse) of sacred discipline, hath the like effects. When the keys of the church are used to shut out the good, or not used when they ought, to rebuke or shut out the impenitent wicked ones; nor to difference between the precious and the vile; it hardeneth multitudes in their ungodliness, and persuadeth them that they are really of the same family of Christ as the godly are, and have their sins forgiven, because they are partakers of the same holy sacraments. (Not knowing the difference between the church mystical and visible, nor between the judgment of ministers and of Christ himself.)

6. Parents' neglect of instructing children, and other parts of holy education, is one of the greatest causes of the perdition of mankind, in all the world: but of this elsewhere.

7. Magistrates' persecution or opposition to religion, or discountenancing those that preach it, or most seriously practise it, tendeth to deceive some, who over-reverence the judgment of superiors, and to affright others from the obedience of God.

8. Yea, the negligence of magistrates, masters, and other superiors, omitting the due rebuke of sinners, and due correction of the offenders, and the due encouragement of the good, is a great cause of the wickedness and damnation of the world.

9. But above all, when they make laws for sin, or for the contempt, or dishonour, or suppression of religion, or the serious practice of it; this buildeth up Satan's kingdom most effectually, and turneth God's ordinance against himself: thousands under infidel and ungodly princes, are conducted by obedience to damnation; and their rulers damn them as honourably as the physician killed his patients, who boasted that he did it *secundum artem*, according to the rules of art.

10. The vulgar example of the multitude of the ungodly, is a great cause of men's impiety and damnation. They must be well resolved for God and holiness, who will not yield to the major vote, nor be carried down the common stream, nor run with the rabble to excess of riot. When christianity is a sect which is every where spoken against, it proveth so narrow a way, that few have a mind to walk in it. Men think that they are at least excusable, for not being wiser and better than the multitude. Singularity in honour, or riches, or strength, or health, is accounted no crime; but singularity in godliness, is, at least, thought unnecessary. What! will you be wiser than all the town, or, than such and such superiors? is thought a good reprehension of godliness, where it is rare; even by them who hereby conclude their superiors, or all the town, to be wiser than God.

11. Also the vulgar's scorning and deriding godliness, is a common cause of murdering souls: because the devil knoweth, that there cannot one word of solid reason be brought against the reason of God, and so against a holy life; he therefore teacheth men to use such weapons as they have. A dog hath teeth, and an adder hath a sting, though they have not the weapons of a man. A fool can laugh, and jeer, and rail; and there is no great wit or learning necessary, to smile, or grin, or call a man a puritan, or precisian, or heretic, or schismatic, or any name which the malice of the age shall newly coin. Mr. Robert Bolton largely showeth how much the malignity of his age did vent itself against godliness, by the reproachful use of the word, puritan. When reason can be bribed to take the devil's part, (either natural or literate reason,) he will hire it at any rate; but when it cannot, he will make use of such as he can get. Barking or hissing may serve turn, where talking and disputing cannot be procured. Drum and trumpets in an army, serve the turn instead of oratory, to animate cowards, and drown the noise of dying men's complaints and groans. Thousands have been mocked out of their religion and salvation at once, and jeered into hell, who now know whether a scorn, or the fire of hell, be the greater suffering. As tyrants think that the greatest, and ablest, and wisest men, must either be drawn over to their party or destroyed; so the tyrant of hell, who ruleth in the children of disobedience, doth think that if reason, learning, and wit, cannot be hired to dispute for him against God, they are to be suppressed, silenced, and disgraced; which the noise of rude clamours and foolish jeers is fit enough to perform.

12. Also idle, senseless prating against religion as a needless thing, doth serve turn to deceive the simple; ignorant people, who converse with no wiser men, are ordinarily taken with the silly cavils of a drunken sot, who hath but a little more volubility or looseness of tongue than his companions. It would make one's head and heart ache, to hear with what reverend nonsense one of them will talk against the

doctrines or practices of godliness, and [812]how submissively the tractable herd receiveth and consenteth to his documents!

13. Also it tendeth much to the helping of Satan, and murdering of souls, to keep up the reputation of the most ungodly, and to keep down the reputation of the good. The devil knoweth that sin itself is such a thing, as few men can love barefaced, or commend; and that goodness or holiness is such a thing, as few men can hate, or at least condemn, in its proper name and colours. Therefore he seeketh to make the reputation of the persons serve to promote or hinder the cause which he is for or against. He that is ashamed to say of drunkenness or whoredom, that they are good and honest practices, dare yet say of drunkards and whoremongers, They are very honest men; and by their reputation take off some of the odiousness of the sin, and reconcile the hearers to it. And he that cannot for shame say of the forbearing of sin, and living a holy life, in heavenly contemplation, prayer, and obedience, that these are hypocrisy, schism, or sedition, covetousness, deceit, and pride; yet dare say of the person who practiseth them, that he is as covetous, deceitful, proud, hypocritical, schismatical, or seditious, as any others who make no profession of religion. And the devil knoweth, that though good doctrine hath no mixture of evil, nor Christ himself any blemish or spot, yet the best persons are so faulty or defectible, that an ill report of them is less incredible, there being too much matter to raise a suspicion on. And through their sides, it is easiest to wound the doctrine or holiness which they profess.

14. Also persuading sinners to do evil, and dissuading them from a godly life, is another way of murdering souls. The devil's temptations are most by instruments; he hath his preachers as well as Christ; and it were well if they did not overgo us in earnestness, frequency, and constancy. Where is there a poor soul that is moved by God to turn and live, but the devil hath some at hand to drive them from it? by persuading them that it is needless, and that all is well with them, and telling them some dismal stories of a holy life.

15. Another way of soul murder, is by laying baits of deceit and sin before the sinner: as men destroy rats and mice by baits, and sweetened poison; or catch fishes or birds by covering their death with something which they most love; so doth the devil and his instruments destroy souls: the baits of a pleasant cup, or pleasant company, or pleasant meats, or pleasant sports, or plays, or games; a feast, a tavern, an alehouse, a whore, a stage-play, a romance, a pair of cards or dice, can do the deed. If he can possibly, he will prove it a thing lawful; if he cannot, he will prove it a venial sin; if that cannot be, he will drown consideration, and stop the mouth of reason and conscience, and cry, Drive on. Some have yet higher baits than these, lordships and lands, dominion and honour, to choke their souls.

16. Also an honest name for sin, and a dishonest name for duty to God, doth serve the turn for many men's perdition. To call drunkenness, good fellowship, or, to take a cup; and gluttony, good housekeeping; and voluptuousness, recreation or pastime; and pride, the maintaining of their honour; and worldliness, good husbandry; and prodigality, liberality; and lust and whoredom, love, and having a mistress; and oppression, the seeking of their due; and perfidious dissimulation, courtship; and jeering, wittiness. These, and more such, are traps for souls. And of the same use is the calling of duties by names of vice, which tend to make them odious or contemptible.

17. Also the flattering of sinners, and praising them in their sin, is a soul-murdering encouragement to them in ill-doing; and great sinners seldom want such enemies.

18. An obedient readiness to all that wicked superiors command, is an encouragement to them to proceed in mischief. If parents or masters command their inferiors to spend the Lord's day in dancing, or other unlawful exercises; or bid them steal, or lie, or forbid them to worship God; those that obey them, do harden them in their sin. As Daniel and the three witnesses had done the king, if they had obeyed him.[144]

19. Also when those that have power to hinder sin, and further godliness, do not do it. When they either give men leave to sin, or forbear their duty when they should restrain it. He that stands by, and seeth his neighbour robbed or murdered, and doth not what he can to save him, is guilty of the sin, and the sufferer's hurt.

20. Silence, when we are obliged to reprove a sinner, or to instruct the ignorant, or exhort the obstinate, or any way speak for men's salvation, is injurious to their souls, and maketh us partakers of their sin. Soul murder may be done by bare omissions.

21. Opposing magistrates, ministers, or any others, in the discharge of their duty for godliness, or against sin, is an act of hostility against God, and men's salvation.

22. An unnecessary occasioning of sin, or doing that needlessly, which we may foresee that by accident another will destroy himself by, is to be guilty of his sin and destruction; as he is that would sell poison to him, that he might foresee would kill himself with it; or lend fire to his neighbour, who he knoweth will burn his house with it. But of this before, in the chapter of scandal.

23. They that are guilty of schisms or church divisions, are murderers of souls; by depriving them of that means (the concord and harmony of believers) which God hath appointed for men's conviction and salvation;[145] and by setting up before them the greatest scandal, to bring religion into contempt, and debilitate the godly.

24. Those also that mourn not for the sins of the times, and confess them not to God, and pray not against them, and pray not for the sinners when they ought, are thus guilty.[146]

25. And so are they that secretly rejoice in sin, or consent to it, or approve it when it is done; which if they manifest, it is pernicious to others also.

26. Lastly, A coldness or indifferency in the doing of our duty against sin, without just zeal, and pity to the sinner, and reverence to the truth, is a way of guilt, and hurteth others. To reprove sin, as Eli did his sons; or to speak against it lightly as between jest and earnest, is the way to make the sinner think that it is a small or jesting matter. To persuade men to conversion or a godly life, without a melting love and pity to their souls, and without the reverence of God, and seriousness of mind, which the nature and weight of the thing requireth, is the way to harden them in their sin and misery. All these ways may a man be guilty, first, of the sin, and secondly, the perdition of another.

But here (on the negative part) take notice of these things following.

How we are not guilty of other men's sin or ruin.

1. That properly no man doth partake of the same formal, numerical sin, which is another's; *noxa caput* [813]*sequitur.* The sin is individuated and informed by the individual will of the offender. It is not possible that another man's sin should be properly and formally mine, unless I were individually and formally that same man, and not another. If two men set their hands to the same evil deed, they are distinct causes and subjects of the distinct formal guilt; though con-causes, and partial causes of the effect: so that it is only by multiplication that we make the sin or guilt of another to become the matter of sin to us, the form resulting from ourselves.

2. All men that are guilty of the sin and damnation of other men, are not equally guilty; not only as some are pardoned upon repentance, and some remain impenitent and unpardoned; but as some contribute wilfully to the mischief, and with delight, and in a greater measure; and some only in a small degree, by an oversight, or small omission, or weak performance of a duty, by mere infirmity or surprise.

3. All that do not hinder sin, or reprove it, are not guilty of it; no more than all that do not punish it; but those only that have power and opportunity, and so are called by God to do it.

4. If another man will sin, and destroy his soul, by the occasion of my necessary duty, I must not cease my duty to prevent such men's sin or hurt; else one or other will by their perverseness, excuse me from almost all the duty which I should do. I must

not cease praying, hearing, sacraments, nor withdraw from church communion, because another will turn it to his sin; else Satan should use the sin of others to frustrate all God's worship. Yet I must add, that many things cease to be a duty, when another will be so hurt by them.

5. I am not guilty of all men's sins, which are committed in my presence; no, though I know beforehand that they will sin. For my calling or duty may lead me into the presence of those, that I may foreknow will sin. Wicked men sin in all that they do, and yet it followeth not, that I must have nothing to do with them. Many a failing which is his sin, may a minister or church be guilty of, even in that public worship of God, which yet I am bound to be present at.

But of all these somewhat is said before, chap. xii.

[144] Dan. iii., vi.

[145] John xvii. 21, 25.

[146] Ezek. ix. 4; Zeph. iii. 17, 18.

CHAPTER XV.

GENERAL DIRECTIONS FOR THE FURTHERING OF THE SALVATION OF OTHERS.

THE great means which we must use for the salvation of our neighbours are,

Direct. I. Sound doctrine: let those who are their instructors, inculcate the wholesome principles of godliness; which are, self-denial, mortification, the love of God and man, the hopes of heaven, universal, absolute obedience to God; and all this by faith in Jesus Christ, according to the holy Scriptures. Instead of novelties, or vain janglings, and perverse disputings, teach them these principles here briefly named, over and over a hundred times; open these plainly, till they are well understood. There are the necessary, saving things; this is the doctrine which is according to godliness, which will make sound christians, of sound judgments, sound hearts, sound conversations, and sound consciences! God sanctifieth his chosen ones by these truths.

Direct. II. Therefore do your best to help others to the benefit of able and faithful pastors and instructors. A fruitful soil is not better for your seed, nor a good pasture for your horse or cattle, nor wholesome diet for yourselves, than such instructors are for your neighbours' souls. If you love them, you should be more desirous to help them to good teachers, or plant them under a sound and powerful ministry, than to procure them any worldly benefits. One time or other the word may prevail with them. It is hopeful to be still in mercy's way.

Direct. III. The concord of their teachers among themselves, is a great help to the saving of the flock. "That they all may be one, as thou Father art in me, and I in thee, that they also may be one in us; that the world may believe that thou hast sent me," John xvii. 21, 25. Concord much furthereth reverence and belief; and consequently men's salvation (so it be a holy concord).

Direct. IV. The concord also of godly, private christians hath the same effect. When the ignorant see here a sect and there a sect, and hear them condemning one another, it teacheth them to contemn them all, and think contemptibly of piety itself; but concord layeth an awe upon them.

Direct. V. The blameless, humble, loving, heavenly lives of christians, is a powerful means of winning souls. Preach therefore every one of you, by such a conversation to all your neighbours, whom you desire to save.

Direct. VI. Keep those whom you would save in a humble, patient, learning posture; and keep them from proud wranglings, and running after novelties and sects. The humble learner takes root downward, and silently groweth up to wisdom; but if once they grow self-conceited, they turn to wranglings, and place their religion in espoused, singular opinions, and in being on this or that side or church; and fall into divided congregations, where the business is to build up souls by destroying charity, and teaching sectaries to overvalue themselves, and despise dissenters; till at last they run themselves out of breath, and perhaps fall out with all true religion.

Direct. VII. Do what you can to place them in good families, and when they are to be married, to join them to such as are fit to be their helpers. In families and relations of that sort, people are so near together, and in such constant converse, that it will be very much of the help or hinderance of their salvation.

Direct. VIII. Keep them also as much as is possible in good company, and out of bad, seducing company; especially those that are to be their familiars. The world's experience telleth us what power company hath, to make men better or worse: and what a great advantage it is to work any thing on men's minds, to have interest in them, and intimacy with them; especially with those that are yet to receive their deepest impressions.

Direct. IX. Keep them from the most dangerous baits, opportunities, and temptations to sensuality. Withdraw the tinder and gunpowder from the fire. There is no curing a drunkard ordinarily in an alehouse or tavern, nor a fornicator while he is near the objects of his lust, nor a glutton at a full, enticing table. Set them at a farther distance from the danger, if you would have them safe. *Nemo diu tutus periculo proximus.* Senec.

Direct. X. Take the advantage of their personal afflictions, or any other notable warnings that are near them. Keep them oft in the house of mourning, where death may be as in their sight; and keep them out of the house of foolish mirth. The time of sickness is an awakening time, and powerfully openeth [814]the ear to counsel. The sight of the dead or dying persons, the hearing of sick men's wishes and complaints, the sight of graves and dead men's bones, (if not too oft to make it customary,) doth often force the most foolish and obstinate to some man-like, profitable thoughts; when the noise of foolish mirth and sports, at rabble-meetings, stage-plays, and May-games, riotings, or immoderate, rude, or tempting plays, do kill all sober, saving motions, and undispose the mind to all that is good. Though seasonable and useful delights are lawful, yet such as are unseasonable, immoderate, insnaring, scandalous, or unprofitable, are pernicious and poison to the soul.

Direct. XI. Engage them in the reading of the holy Scriptures, and of such books of practical divinity, as do at once most plainly acquaint them with the principles of religion, and piercingly set them home upon the conscience; that judgment and affection, head and heart, may be edified at once. Such suitable books may be daily their companions; and it is a great advantage to them, that they may have a powerful sermon when they please, and read over the same things as oft as the frailty of their memories do require. Such private, innocent companions have saved many a soul.

Direct. XII. Engage them in a constant course of prayer (whether it be with a book, or form, or without, according to the parts and condition of the person). For the often approaching to God in so holy a work, will affright or shame a man from sin, and stir him up to serious thoughts of his salvation, and engage him to a godly life.

Direct. XIII. If you would have all these means effectual to men's conversion and salvation, show them all hearty love and kindness, and do them all the good you can. Men are naturally more easily sensible of the good of their bodies, than of their souls; and a kindness to the body is thankfully received, and may prepare them to receive a greater benefit. What you are unable to do for them yourselves, solicit those that are able to do; or, if you cannot do that neither, at least show your pity and good-will. Love is the most powerful preacher in the world.

Direct. XIV. Be sure that you have no fallings out or quarrels with any that you would do good upon. And to that end, usually it is the best way, to have as little to do with them in buying and selling, or any worldly matters, where mine and thine may come in competition, as possibly you can: or, if you cannot avoid it, you must be content to part with somewhat of your right, and suffer some wrongs, for fear of hurt to your neighbour's soul. Even godly persons, yea, parents and children, brethren and sisters, usually fall out about mine and thine. And when self-interest hath bred the quarrel, they usually think ill of the person who is supposed to injure them; and then they are made uncapable of receiving any spiritual good by him, and if he seem religious they are oft alienated from religion for his sake. And all unconverted persons are selfish, and usually look that you should fulfil their desires, and suit yourselves to their interest, without respect to right or wrong, or to your own sufferings! Yet such as these must be pitied and helped; and therefore it is usually best to avoid all chaffering or worldly dealings with them, lest you lose them. And when that cannot be, you must judge a little departing from your own right, to be a very cheap price to procure the good of a neighbour's soul.

Direct. XV. See that in matters of religion you neither run too far from such men in things lawful, nor yet do any thing sinful in compliance with them. By concurring with them in any sin, you will harden them, and hinder their conversion; and so you will by singular or violent opposition in things indifferent. Those persons are quite mistaken, who think that godly men must go as far from the ungodly as ever they can, in lawful things; and say, The ungodly do thus, and therefore we must do otherwise. Paul was of another mind and practice, when he circumcised Timothy, and "became all things to all men, to save some." To place religion in things indifferent, and to cry out against lawful things as sinful, or to fly from others by needless singularities, is a great cause of the hardening and perdition of multitudes, turning their hearts against religion, and making them think that it is but unnecessary scruple, and that religious persons are but self-conceited, brain-sick people, that make to themselves a duty of their superstition, and condemn all that be not as humorous as they. Lay not such stumblingblocks before any whose souls you desire to save.

CHAPTER XVI.

SPECIAL DIRECTIONS FOR CHRISTIAN CONFERENCE, EXHORTATION, AND REPROOF.

Tit. 1. Motives to Christian Conference and Exhortation.

THE right use of speech being a duty of so great importance, as I have before showed about the government of the tongue; and it being a way of communication, by which we are all obliged to exercise our love to one another, even in the greatest matter, the saving of souls; I shall first endeavour to persuade them to this duty, who make too little conscience of it; and that by these following considerations.

Motive I. Consider that it is the exercise of our humanity: reason and speech do difference us from brutes. If by being reasonable we are men, then by using reason we live as men; and the first communicative use of reason is by speech: by thinking, we exercise reason for ourselves; by speaking, we exercise it (first) for others. Therefore if our reason be given us for the highest uses to ourselves, (to know God and eternal life, and the means thereto,) then certainly our speech is also given us for the same highest uses, by way of communication unto others. Use therefore your tongues to those noble ends for which they were given you. Use them as the tongues of men, to the ends which human nature is created for.

Motive II. There is no subject so sublime and honourable for the tongue of man to be employed about, as the matters of God, and life eternal. Children will talk of childish toys, and countrymen talk of their corn and cattle, and princes and statesmen look down on these with contemptuous smiles, as much below them: but crowns and kingdoms are incomparably more below the business of a holy soul! The higher subjects philosophers treat of, the more honourable (if well done) are their discourses. But none is so high as God and glory.

Motive III. It is the most profitable subject to the hearers. A discourse of riches, at the most, can but direct them how to grow rich; a discourse of honours usually puffeth up the minds of the ambitious: and if it could advance the auditors to |815]honour, the fruit would be a vanity little to be desired. But a discourse of God, and heaven, and holiness, doth tend to change the hearers' minds into the nature of the things discoursed of: it hath been the means of converting and sanctifying many a thousand souls. As learned discourses tend to make men learned in the things discoursed of, so holy discourses tend to make men holy. For as natural generation begetteth not gold or kingdoms, but a man; so speech is not made to communicate to others (directly) the wealth, or health, or honours, or any extrinsical things which the speaker hath; but to communicate those mental excellencies which he is possessed of. Prov. xvi. 21, 22, "The sweetness of the lips increaseth learning. Understanding is a well-spring of life to him that hath it." Prov. x. 13, 21, "In the lips of him that hath understanding, wisdom is found.—The lips of the righteous feed many." Prov. xv. 7, "The lips of the wise disperse knowledge; but the heart of the foolish doth not so." Prov. xx. 15, "There is gold, and a multitude of rubies; but the lips of knowledge are a precious jewel." Prov. x. 20, "The tongue of the just is as choice silver; the heart of the wicked is little worth."

Motive IV. Holy discourse is also most profitable to the speaker himself. Grace increaseth by the exercise. Even in instructing others and opening truth, we are ofttimes more powerfully led up to further truth ourselves, than by solitary studies. For speech doth awaken the intellectual faculty, and keepeth on the thoughts in order, and one truth oft inferreth others, to a thus excited and prepared mind. And the tongue hath a power of moving on our hearts; when we blow the fire to warm another, both the exercise and the fire warm ourselves: it kindleth the flames of holy love in us, to declare the praise of God to others; it increaseth a hatred of sin in us, to open its odiousness to others. We starve ourselves, when we starve the souls which we should cherish.

Motive V. Holy and heavenly discourse is the most delectable. I mean in its own aptitude, and to a mind that is not diseased by corruption. That which is most great, and good, and necessary, is most delectable. What should best please us, but that which is best for us? and best for others? and best in itself? The excellency of the subject maketh it delightful! And so doth the exercise of our graces upon it: and serious conference doth help down the truth into our hearts, where it is most sweet. Besides that nature and charity make it pleasant to do good to others. It can be nothing better than a subversion of the appetite by carnality and wickedness, that maketh any one think idle jests, or tales, or plays, to be more pleasant than spiritual, heavenly conference; and the talking of riches, or sports, or lusts, to be sweeter than to talk of God, and Christ, and grace, and glory. A holy mind hath a continual feast in itself in meditating on these things, and the communicating of such thoughts to others, is a more common, and so a more pleasant feast.

Motive VI. Our faithfulness to God obligeth us to speak his praise, and to promote his truth, and plead his cause against iniquity. Hath he given us tongues to magnify his name, and set before us the admirable frame of all the world, to declare his glory in? And shall we be backward to so sweet and great a work? How precious and useful is all his holy word! What light, and life, and comfort may it cause! And shall we bury it in silence? What company can we come into almost, where either the barefaced committing of sin, or the defending of it, or the opposition of truth or godliness, or the frigidity of men's hearts towards God, and supine neglect of holy things, do not call to us, if we are the servants of God, to take his part; and if we are the children of light, to bear our testimony against the darkness of the world; and if we love God, and truth, and the souls of men, to show it by our prudent, seasonable speech? Is he true to God, and to his cause, that will not open his mouth to speak for him?

Motive VII. And how precious a thing is an immortal soul, and therefore not to be neglected! Did Christ think souls to be worth his mediation, by such strange condescension, even to a shameful death? Did he think them worth his coming into flesh to be their teacher? And will you not think them worth the speaking to?

Motive VIII. See also the greatness of your sin, in the negligence of unfaithful ministers. It is easy to see the odiousness of their sin, who preach not the gospel, or do no more than by an hour's dry and dead discourse, shift off the serious work which they should do, and think they may be excused from all personal oversight and helping of the people's souls all the week after. And why should you not perceive that a dumb, private christian is also to be condemned, as well as a dumb minister? Is not profitable conference your duty, as well as profitable preaching is his? How many persons condemn themselves, while they speak against unfaithful pastors! being themselves as unfaithful to families and neighbours, as the other are to the flock!

Motive IX. And consider how the cheapness of the means, doth aggravate the sin of your neglect, and show much unmercifulness to souls. Words cost you little; indeed alone, without the company of good works, they are too cheap for God to accept of. But if a hypocrite may bring so cheap a sacrifice, who is rejected, what doth he deserve that thinketh it too dear? What will that man do for God, or for his neighbour's soul, who will not open his mouth to speak for them? He seemeth to have less love than that man in hell, Luke xvi. who would so fain have had a messenger sent from another world, to have warned his brethren, and saved them from that place of torment.

Motive X. Your fruitful conference is a needful help to the ministerial work. When the preacher hath publicly delivered the word of God to the assembly, if you would so far second him, as in your daily converse to set it home on the hearts of those that you have opportunity to discourse with, how great an assistance would it be to his success! Though he must teach them publicly, and from house to house, Acts xx. 20, yet is it not possible for him to be so frequent and familiar in daily conference with all the ignorant of the place, as those that are still with them may be. You are many, and he is but one, and can be but in one place at once. Your business bringeth you into their company, when he cannot be there. O happy is that minister who hath such a people, who will daily preach over the matter of his public sermons in their private conference with one another! Many hands make quick work. This would most effectually prevail against the powers of darkness, and cast out Satan from multitudes of miserable souls.

Motive XI. Yea, when ministers are wanting, through scarcity, persecution, or unfaithfulness and negligence, the people's holy, profitable conference would do much towards the supplying of that want. There have few places and ages of the world been so happy, but that learned, able, faithful pastors have been so few, that we had need to pray to the Lord of the harvest to send forth more. And it is nothing unusual to have those few silenced or hindered from the preaching of the gospel, by the factions or the [816]malignity of the world! And it is yet more common to have ignorant or ungodly persons in that office, who betray the people's souls by their usurpation, impiety, or slothfulness. But if in all such wants, the people that fear God would do their part in private conference, it would be an excellent supply. Ministers may be silenced from public preaching, when you cannot be silenced from profitable discourse.

Motive XII. It is a duty that hath many great advantages for success. 1. You may choose your season; if one time be not fit, you may take another. 2. You may choose the person, whom you find to have the greatest necessity or capacity, and where your labour is likeliest to take. 3. You may choose your subject, and speak of that which you find most suitable. There is no restraint nor imposition upon you, to hinder your liberty in this. 4. You may choose your arguments by which you would enforce it. 5. Interlocutory conference keepeth your auditors attentive, and carrieth them on along with you as you go. And it maketh the application much more easy, by their nearness and the familiarity of the discourse; when sermons are usually heard but as an insignificant sound, or words of course. 6. You may at your pleasure go back and repeat those things which the hearer doth not understand, or doth forget; which a preacher in the pulpit cannot do without the censure of the more curious auditors. 7.

You may perceive by the answers of them whom you speak to, what particulars you need most to insist on, and what objections you should most carefully resolve; and when you have satisfied them, and may proceed. All which it is hard for a minister to do in public preaching; and is it not a great sin to neglect such an advantageous duty?

Motive XIII. And it should somewhat encourage you to it, that it is an unquestionable duty, when many other are brought into controversy. Ministers preach under the regulation of human laws and canons, and it is a great controversy with many, whether they shall preach, when they are silenced or forbidden by their superiors; but whether you may speak for God and for men's salvation in your familiar conference, no man questioneth, nor doth any law forbid it.

Motive XIV. Hath not the fruitful conference of others, in the days of your ignorance, done good to you? Have you not been instructed, convinced, persuaded, and comforted by it? What had become of you, if all men had let you alone, and passed you by, and left you to yourselves? And doth not justice require that you do good to others, as others have done to you, in the use of such a tried means?

Motive XV. Consider how forward the devil's servants are to plead his cause! How readily and fiercely will an ignorant, drunken sot pour out his reproaches and scorns against religion! and speak evil of the things which he never understood! How zealously will a papist, or heretic, or schismatic, promote the interest of his sect, and labour to proselyte others to his party! And shall we be less zealous and serviceable for Christ, than the devil's servants are for him? and do less to save souls, than they will do to damn them?

Motive XVI. Nay, in the time of your sin and ignorance, if you have not spoken against religion, nor taught others to curse, or swear, or speak in ribald, filthy language, yet, at least, you have spent many an hour in idle, fruitless talk? And doth not this now oblige you to show your repentance by more fruitful conference? Will you since your conversion speak as unprofitably as you did before?

Motive XVII. Holy conference will prevent the guilt of foolish, idle talk. Men will not be long silent, but will talk of somewhat, and if they have not profitable things to talk of, they will prate of vanity. All the foolish chat, and frothy jests, and scurrilous ribaldry, and envious backbiting, which taketh up men's time, and poisoneth the hearers, is caused by their want of edifying discourse, which should keep it out. The rankest wits and tongues will have most weeds, if they be not cultivated and taught to bear a better crop.

Motive XVIII. Your tongues will be instrumental to public good or public hurt. When filthy, vain, and impious language is grown common, it will bring down common plagues and judgments! And if you cross not the custom, you seem to be consenters, and harden men in their sin. But holy conference may, at least, show that some partake not of the evil, and may free them from the plague, if they prevail not with others so far as to prevent it. "Then they that feared the Lord spake often one to another: and the Lord hearkened, and heard it, and a book of remembrance was written before him for them that feared the Lord, and thought upon his name. And they shall be mine, saith the Lord of hosts, in that day when I make up my jewels; and I will spare them, as a man spareth his own son that serveth him," Mal. iii. 16, 17.

Motive XIX. Consider what great necessity there is every where of fruitful, edifying speech. 1. In the multitude of the ignorant; and the greatness of their ignorance. 2. The numbers of the sensual and obstinate. 3. The power of blindness, and of every sin: what root it hath taken in the most of men. 4. The multitude of baits which are every where before them. 5. The subtilty of Satan and his instruments in tempting. 6. The weakness and unconstancy of man, that hath need of constant solicitation. 7. The want of holy, faithful pastors, which maketh private men's diligence the more necessary. And in such necessity to shut up our mouths, is to shut up the bowels of our compassion, when we see our brother's need; and how then doth the love of God dwell in us? 1 John iii. 17. To withhold our exhortation, is as the withholding of corn from the poor in a time of famine, which procureth a curse, Prov.

134

xi. 26. And though in this case men are insensible of their want, and take it not ill to be passed by, yet Christ that died for them will take it ill.

Motive XX. Lastly, Consider how short a time you are like to speak; and how long you must be silent. Death will quickly stop your breath, and lay you in the dark, and tell you that all your opportunities are at an end. Speak now, for you have not long to speak. Your neighbours' lives are hastening to an end, and so are yours; they are dying and must hear no more, (till they hear their doom,) and you are dying and must speak no more; and they will be lost for ever if they have not help: pity them then, and call on them to foresee the final day; warn them now, for it must be now or never: there is no instructing and admonishing them in the grave. Those sculls which you see cast up, had once tongues which should have praised their Creator and Redeemer, and have helped to save each other's souls; but now they are tongueless. It is a great grief to us that are now here silenced, that we used not our ministry more laboriously and zealously while we had time. And will it not be so with you, when death shall silence you, that you spake not for God while you had a tongue to speak?

Let all these considerations stir up all that God hath taught a holy language, to use it for their Master's service while they may, and to repent of sinful silence.

[817]

Tit. 2. Directions for Christian Conference and Edifying Speech.

Direct. I. The most necessary direction for a fruitful tongue is to get a well-furnished mind, and a holy heart, and to walk with God in holiness yourselves: for out of the abundance of the heart the mouth will speak. That which you are fullest of, is readiest to come forth. 1. Spare for no study or labour to get understanding in the things of God: it is a weariness to hear men talk foolishly of any thing, but no where so much as about divine and heavenly things. A wise christian instructed to the kingdom of God, hath a treasury in his mind, out of which he can bring forth things new and old, Matt. xiii. 52. "Go from the presence of a foolish man, when thou perceivest not in him the lips of knowledge," Prov. xiv. 7. 2. Get all that holiness in yourselves, to which you would persuade another. There is a strange communicating power in the course of nature, for every thing to produce its like. Learning and good utterance is very helpful; but it is holiness that is aptest to beget holiness in others. Words which proceed from the love of God, and a truly heavenly mind, do most powerfully tend to breed in others that love of God and heavenly-mindedness. 3. Live in the practice of that which you would draw your neighbour to practise. A man that cometh warm from holy meditation, or fervent prayer, doth bring upon his heart a fulness of matter, and an earnest desire, and a fitness to communicate that good to others, which he himself hath felt.

Direct. II. Especially see that you soundly believe yourselves what you are to speak to others. He that hath secret infidelity at his heart, and is himself unsatisfied whether there be a heaven and hell, and whether sin be so bad and holiness so necessary as the Scripture speaks, will speak but heartlessly of them to another; but if we believe these things, as if we saw them with our eyes, how heartily shall we discourse of them!

Direct. III. Keep a compassionate sense of the misery of ignorant, ungodly, impenitent souls. Think what a miserable bondage of darkness and sensuality they are in; and that it is light that must recover them: think oft how quickly they must die, and what an appearance they must make before the Lord, and how miserable they must be for ever, if now they be not convinced and sanctified! And sure this will stir up your bowels to pity them, and make you speak.

Direct. IV. Subdue foolish shame or bashfulness, and get a holy fortitude of mind. Remember what a sin it is to be ashamed of such a Master, and such a cause and work, which all would be glad to own at last; and that when the wicked are not ashamed of the service of the devil, and the basest works. And remember that threatening, "Whosoever shall be ashamed of me and of my words in this adulterous and sinful generation, of him also shall the Son of man be ashamed, when he cometh in the glory of his Father with the holy angels," Mark viii. 38.

Direct. V. Be always furnished with those particular truths which may be most useful in this service. Study to do your work (in your degree) as ministers study to do theirs; who are not contented with the habitual furniture of their minds, but they also make particular preparations for their particular work. If you are to go into the field to your labour, you will take those tools with you by which it must be done: so do when you go abroad among any that you may do good to, and be not unfurnished for edifying discourse.

Direct. VI. Speak most of the greatest things, (the folly of sin, the vanity of the world, the certainty and nearness of death and judgment, the overwhelming weight of eternity, the necessity of holiness, the work of redemption, &c.) and choose not the smaller matters of religion to spend your time upon (unless upon some special reason). Among good men that will not lose their time on vanity, the devil too oft prevaileth, to make them lose it by such religious conference, as is little to edification, that greater matters may be thereby thrust out; such as Paul calleth "Vain janglings, and doting about questions which engender strife, and not godly edifying:" as about their several opinions or parties, or comparing one preacher or person with another, or such things as tend but little to make the hearers more wise, or holy, or heavenly.

Direct. VII. Suit all your discourse to the quality of your auditors. That which is best in itself, may not be best for every hearer. You must vary both your subject and manner of discourse, 1. According to the variety of men's knowledge: the wise and the foolish must not be spoken to alike. 2. According to the variety of their moral qualities: one may be very pious, and another weak in grace, and another only teachable and tractable, and another wicked and impenitent, and another obstinate and scornful. These must not be talked to with the same manner of discourse. 3. According to the variety of particular sins which they are inclined to; which in some is pride, in some sensuality, lust, or idleness, in some covetousness, and in some an erroneous zeal against the church and cause of Christ. Every wise physician will vary his remedies, not only according to the kind of the disease, but according to its various accidents, and the complexion also of the patient.

Direct. VIII. Be sure to do most where you have most authority and obligation. He that will neglect and slight his family, relations, children, and servants, who are under him, and always with him, and yet be zealous for the conversion of strangers, doth discover much hypocrisy, and showeth, that it is something else than the love of souls, or sense of duty, which carrieth him on.

Direct. IX. Never speak of holy things, but with the greatest reverence and seriousness you can. The manner as well as the matter is needful to the effect. To talk of sin and conversion, of God and eternity, in a common, running, careless manner, as you speak of the men, and the matters of the world, is much worse than silence, and tendeth but to debauch the hearers, and bring them to a contempt of God and holiness. I remember myself, that when I was young, I had sometime the company of one ancient godly minister, who was of weaker parts than many others, but yet did profit me more than most; because he would never in prayer or conference speak of God, or the life to come, but with such marvellous seriousness and reverence, as if he had seen the majesty and glory which he talked of.

Direct. X. Take heed of inconsiderate, imprudent passages, which may mar all the rest, and give malignant auditors advantage of contempt and scorn. Many honest christians, through their ignorance, thus greatly wrong the cause they manage (I would I might not say, many ministers). Too few words is not so bad, as one such imprudent, foolish word too much.

Direct. XI. Condescend to the weak, and bear with their infirmity. If they give you foolish answers, be not angry and impatient with them; yea, or if they perversely cavil and contradict. "For the servant of the Lord must not strive, but be gentle to all men, apt to teach, patient, in meekness instructing [818]opposers, if God peradventure

136

will give them repentance to the acknowledging of the truth," 2 Tim. ii. 24, 25. He is a foolish physician that cannot bear the words of a phrenetic or delirant patient.

Direct. XII. When you are among those that can teach you, be not so forward to teach as to learn. Be not eager to vent what you have to say, but desirous to hear what your betters have to say. Questions in such a case should be most of your part: it requireth great skill and diligence to draw that out of others, which may profit you; and be not impatient if they cross your opinions, or open your ignorance. Yea, those that you can teach in other things, yet in some things may be able to add much to your knowledge.

Tit. 3. Special Directions for Reproof and Exhortation for the good of others.

This duty is so great, that Satan hindereth it with all his power, and so hard, that most men quite omit it (unless an angry reproach may go for christian exhortation): and some spoil it in the management; and some proud, censorious persons mistake the exercise of their pride and passion, for the exercise of a charitable christian duty; and seem to be more sensible of their neighbour's sin and misery, than of their own. Therefore that you miscarry not in so needful a work, I shall add these following directions.

Direct. I. Be sure first that your reproof have a right end; and then let the manner be suited to that end. If it be to convince and convert a soul, it must be done in a manner likely to prevail; if it be only to bear down the argument of a deceiver, to preserve the standers-by, to vindicate the honour of God and godliness, and to dishonour sin, and to disgrace an obstinate factor for the devil, then another course is fit. Therefore resolve first, by the quality of the cause and person, what must be your end.

Direct. II. Be sure that you reprove not that as a sin, which is no sin; either by mistaking the law or the fact. To make duties and sins of our own opinions and inventions, and then to lay out our zeal on these, and censure or reprove all that think not as hardly of such things as we; this is to make ourselves the objects of the hearers' pity; and not to exercise just pity towards others! Such reproofs deserve reproof; for they discover great ignorance, and pride, and self-conceitedness, and very much harden sinners in their way; and make them think that all reproof is but the vanity of fantastical hypocrites. In some cases with a child, or servant, or private friend, or for prevention, we may speak of faults upon hearsay or suspicion; but it must be as of things uncertain, and as a warning rather than a reproof. In ordinary reproof, you must understand the case before you speak; it is a shame to say after, I thought it had been otherwise. Such an erroneous reproof is worse than none.

Direct. III. Choose not the smallest sins to reprove, nor the smallest duties to exhort them to. For that will make them think that all your zeal is taken up with little matters, and that there is no great necessity of regarding you; and conscience will be but little moved by your speech: when greater things will greatly and more easily affect men.

Direct. IV. Stop not (with unregenerate men) in the mention of particular sins or duties; but make use of particulars to convince them of a state of sin and misery. It is easy to convince a man that he is a sinner; and when that is done, he is never the more humbled or converted: for he will tell you, that all are sinners; and therefore he hopeth to speed as well as you. But you must make him discern his sinful state, and show him the difference between a penitent sinner, and an impenitent; a converted sinner, and an unconverted; a justified, pardoned sinner, and an unjustified, unpardoned one; or else you will do him but little good.

Direct. V. Suit the manner of your reproof to the quality of the person. It is seldom that a parent, master, or superior, must be reproved by a private inferior; and when it is done, it must be done with great submission and respect. An angry, peevish person must be dealt with tenderly, as you handle thorns; but a duller, sottish person, must be more earnestly and warmly dealt with. So also a greater sin must be roughly handled, or with greater detestation, than a less.

Direct. VI. Take a fit season. Not when a man is in drink, or passion, or among others where the disgrace will vex and harden him; but in secret between him and you (if his conversion be your end).

Direct. VII. Do all in love and tender pity. If you convince not the hearer that you do it in unfeigned love, you must (usually) expect to lose your labour; because you make not advantage of his self-love, to promote your exhortations: therefore the exhorting way should be more frequent than the reproving way; for reproof disgraceth and exasperateth, when the same thing contrived into an exhortation may prevail.[147]

Direct. VIII. Therefore be as much or more in showing the good which you would draw them to, as the evil which you would turn them from. For they are never savingly converted, till they are won to the love of God and holiness; therefore the opening of the riches of the gospel, and the love of God, and the joys of heaven, must be the greatest part of your treaty with a sinner.

Direct. IX. And labour so to help him to a true understanding of the nature of religion, that he may perceive that it is not only a necessary but a pleasant thing. All love delights: it is the slander and misrepresentation of godliness by the devil, the world, and the flesh, which maketh mistaken sinners shun it. The way to convert them, and win their hearts to it, is to make them know how good and pleasant it is, and to confute those calumnies.

Direct X. Yet always insert the remembrance of death, and judgment, and hell. For the drowsy mind hath need to be awakened; and love worketh best when fear subserveth it. It is hard to procure a serious audience and consideration of things from hardened hearts, if the sight of death and hell do not help to make them serious. Danger which must be escaped, must be known and thought on. These things put weight and power into your speech.

Direct. XI. Do all as with divine authority; and therefore have ready some plain texts of Scripture for the duty and against the sin you speak of.[148] Show them where God himself hath said it.

Direct. XII. Seasonable expostulations, putting themselves to judge themselves in their answer, hath a convincing and engaging force. As when you show them Scripture, ask them, Is not this the word of God? Do you not believe that it is true? Do you think he that wrote this, knoweth not better than you or I? &c.

Direct. XIII. Put them on speedy practice, and prudently engage them to it by their promise. As if you speak to a drunkard, draw him to promise you to come no more (at least, of so long a time) into an alehouse; or not drink ale or wine but by the consent of his wife, or some sober, household [819]friend, who may watch over him. Engage the voluptuous, the unchaste, and gamester, to forsake the company which insnareth them. Engage the ungodly to read the Scripture, to frequent good company, to pray morning and night (with a book or without, as they are best able). Their promise may bring them to such a present change of practice, as may prepare for more.

Direct. XIV. If you know any near you, who are much fitter than yourselves, and liker to prevail, procure them to attempt that which you cannot do successfully.[149]At least when sinners perceive that it is not only one man's opinion, it may somewhat move them to reverence the reproof.

Direct. XV. Put some good book into their hands, which is fitted to the work which you would have done. And get them to promise you seriously to read it over, and consider it; as if it be for the conversion of a careless sinner, Mr. Whateley's, or Mr. Swinnock's "Treatise of Regeneration;" or some other treatise of repentance and conversion. If it be for one that is prejudiced against a strict religious life, Mr. Allen's "Vindication of Godliness." If it be an idle, voluptuous person, who wasteth precious time in plays or needless recreations, in gaming or an idle life, Mr. Whateley's sermon, called "The Redemption of Time." If it be a prayerless person, Dr. Preston's "Saint's Daily Exercise:" if it be a drunkard, Mr. Harris's "Drunkard's Cup:" and for many reigning, particular sins, a book called "Solomon's Prescription against the Plague:" for directions in the daily practice of godliness, "The Practice of Piety," or Mr. Thomas Gouge's "Directions," &c. Such books may speak more pertinently than you can; and be as constant food to their sober thoughts, and so may further what you have begun.

Direct. XVI. When you cannot speak, or where your speaking prevaileth not, mourn for them; and earnestly pray for their recovery.[150] A sad countenance of Nehemiah remembered Artaxerxes of his duty. A sigh or a tear for a miserable sinner, may move his heart, when exhortation will not. He hath a heart of stone, who will have no sense of his condition, when he seeth another weeping for him.

Quest. But is it always a duty to reprove or exhort a sinner? How shall I know when it is my duty, and when it is not?

Answ. It is no duty in any of these cases following. 1. In general, When you have sufficient reason to judge, that it will do more harm than good, and will not attain its proper end; for God hath not appointed us to do hurt under pretence of duty; it is no means which doth cross the end which it should attain. As prayer and preaching may be a sin, when they are like to cross their proper end; so also may reproof be.

2. Therefore it must not be used when it apparently hindereth a greater good. As we may not pray or preach when we should be quenching a fire in the town, or saving a man's life: so when reproof doth exclude some greater duty or benefit, it is unseasonable, and no duty at that time. Christ alloweth us to forbear the casting of pearls before swine, or giving that which is holy to dogs, because of these two reasons forementioned, It is no means to the contemptuous, and they will turn again and all to rend us.[151] Much more, if he be some potent enemy of the church, who will not only rend us, but the church itself, if he be so provoked: reproving him then is not our duty.

3. Particularly, When a man is in a passion or drunk usually it is no season to reprove him.

4. Nor when you are among others, who should not be witnesses of the fault, or the reproof; or whose presence will shame him, and offend him (except it be only the shaming of an incorrigible or malicious sinner which you intend).

5. Nor when you are uncertain of the fact which you would reprove, or uncertain whether it be a sin.

6. Or when you have no witness of it, (though you are privately certain,) with some that will take advantage against you as slanderers, a reproof may be omitted.

7. And when the offenders are so much your superiors, that you are like to have no better success than to be accounted arrogant; a groan or tears is then the best reproof.

8. When you are so utterly unable to manage a reproof, that imprudence or want of convincing reason, is like to make it a means of greater hurt than good.

9. When you foresee a more advantageous season, if you delay.

10. When another may be procured to do it with much more advantage, which your doing it may rather hinder.

In all these cases, that may be a sin, which at another time may be a duty.

But still remember, first, That pride, and passion, and slothfulness, is wont to pretend such reasons falsely, upon some slight conjectures, to put by a duty. Secondly, That no man must account another a dog or swine, to excuse him from this duty, without cogent evidence. And it is not every wrangling opposition, nor reproach and scorn, which will warrant us to give a man up as remediless, and speak to him no more; but only such, 1. As showeth a heart utterly obdurate, after long means. 2. Or will procure more suffering to the reprover, than good to the offender. 3. That when the thing is ordinarily a duty, the reasons of our omission must be clear and sure, before they will excuse us.[152]

Quest. Must we reprove infidels or heathens? What have we to do to judge them that are without?

Answ. Not to the ends of excommunication, because they are not capable of it,[153]which is meant 1 Cor. v. But we must reprove them, first, In common compassion to their souls. What were the apostles and other preachers sent for, but to call all men from their sins to God? Secondly, And for the defence of truth and godliness, against their words, or ill examples.

[147] 2 Thess. iii. 15; 2 Cor. ii. 4; Gal. vi. 1; 2 Tim. ii. 25; 1 Thess. v. 13.
[148] Col. iii. 16.
[149] Ezek. xxxiii. xxxiv.; Gal. vi. 1; Tit. ii. 4.
[150] Ezek. ix. 4; 2 Pet. ii. 7, 8.
[151] Prov. ix. 7, 8; Matt. vii. 6.
[152] Gen. xx. 36; Job xiii. 13; Heb. xiii. 22; 2 Pet. i. 13; 2 Tim. ii. 25, 26.
[153] Deut. xxii. 1.

CHAPTER XVII.

DIRECTIONS FOR KEEPING PEACE WITH ALL MEN.

PEACE is so amiable to nature itself, that the greatest destroyers of it do commend it; and those persons in all times and places, who are the cause that the world cannot enjoy it, will yet speak well of it, and exclaim against others as the enemies of peace; as if there were no other name but their own sufficient to make their adversaries odious. As they desire salvation, so do the ungodly desire peace; which is with a double error; one about the nature of it, and another about the conditions and other means. By [820]peace they mean, the quiet, undisturbed enjoyment of their honours, wealth, and pleasures; that they may have their lusts and will without any contradiction; and the conditions on which they would have it are, the compliance of all others with their opinions and wills, and humble submission to their domination, passions, or desires. But peace is another thing, and otherwise to be desired and sought. Peace in the mind is the delightful effect of its internal harmony, as peace in the body is nothing but its pleasant health, in the natural position, state, action, and concord of all the parts, the humours, and spirits: and peace in families, neighbourhoods, churches, kingdoms, or other societies, is the quietness and pleasure of their order and harmony; and must be attained and preserved by these following means.

Direct. I. Get your own hearts into a humble frame; and abhor all the motions of pride and self-exalting. A humble man hath no high expectations from another; and therefore is easily pleased or quieted. He can bow and yield to the pride and violence of others, as the willow to the impetuous winds. His language will be submissive; his patience great; he is content that others go before him; he is not offended that another is preferred. A low mind is pleased in a low condition. But pride is the gunpowder of the mind, the family, the church, and state; it maketh men ambitious, and setteth them on striving who shall be the greatest. A proud man's opinion must always go for truth, and his will must be a law to others, and to be slighted or crossed seemeth to him an unsufferable wrong. And he must be a man of wonderful compliance, or an excellent artificer in man-pleasing and flattery, that shall not be taken as an injurious undervaluer of him: he that overvalueth himself, will take it ill of all that do not also overvalue him. If you (forgetfully) go before him, or overlook him, or neglect a compliment, or deny him something which he expected, or speak not honourably of him, much more if you reprove him, and tell him of his faults, you have put fire to the gunpowder, you have broke his peace, and he will break yours if he can. Pride broke the peace between God and the apostate angels; but nothing unpeaceable must be in heaven; and therefore by self-exalting they descended into darkness; and Christ by self-humbling ascended unto glory. It is a matter of very great difficulty to live peaceably in any family, church, or society with any one that is very proud. They expect so much of you, that you can never answer all their expectations, but will displease them by your omissions, though you neither speak or do any thing to displease them. What is it but the lust of pride which causeth most of the wars and bloodshed throughout the world? The pride of two or three men, must cost many

140

thousands of their subjects the loss of their peace, estates, and lives. *Delirant reges, plectuntur Achivi.* What were the conquests of those emperors, Alexander, Cæsar, Tamerlane, Mahomet, &c. but the pernicious effects of their infamous pride; which like gunpowder taking fire in their breasts, did blow up so many cities and kingdoms, and call their villanies by the name of valour, and their murders and robberies by the name of war? If one man's pride do swell so big, that his own kingdom cannot contain it, the peace of as much of the world as he can conquer is taken to be but a reasonable sacrifice to this infernal vice. The lives of thousands, both subjects and neighbours, (called enemies by this malignant spirit,) must be cast away, merely to make this one man the ruler of the rest, and subdue the persons of others to his will. Who perhaps when he hath done, will say that he is no tyrant, but maketh the *bonum publicum* his end; and is kind to men against their wills; and killeth, and burneth, and depopulateth countries, for men's corporal welfare; as the papists poison, and burn, and butcher men for the saving of souls. *Cuncta ferit dum cuncta timet, desævit in omnes.* They are the *turbines*, the hurricanes or whirlwinds of the world, whose work is to overturn and ruin. *Tantum ut noceat cupit esse potens.* Whether they burn and kill by right or wrong is little of their inquiry; but how many are killed? and how many have submitted to their pride and wills? As when Q. Flavius complained that he suffered innocently, Valerius answered him, *Non sua re interesse, dummodo periret.* That was nothing to his business or concernment so he did but perish: which was plainer dealing than these glorious conquerors used, but no whit worse. He that cannot command the putrid humours out of his veins, nor the worms out of his bowels, nor will be able shortly to forbid them to crawl or feed upon his face, will now damn his soul and shed men's blood, to obtain the predomination of his will. And when he hath conquered many, he hath but made him many enemies, and may find, that in *tot populis vix una fides.* A quiet man can scarce with all his wit tell how to find a place where he may live in peace, where pride and cruelty will not pursue him, or the flames of war will not follow him and find him out; and perhaps he may be put to say as Cicero of Pompey and Cæsar, *Quem fugiam scio; quem sequar nescio.* And if they succeed by conquest, they become to their subjects almost as terrible as to their enemies. So that he that would approach them with a petition for justice, must do it as Augustus spake to a fearful petitioner, as if he did *assem dare elephanto;* or as if they dwelt in the inaccessible light, and must be served as God with fear and trembling. And those that flatter them as glorious conquerors, do but stir up the fire of their pride, to make more ruins and calamities in the earth, and do the work of a raging pestilence. As an Athenian orator said to the men of Athens, when they would have numbered Alexander with the gods, *Cavete ne dum cælum liberaliter donetis, terram et domicilia propria amittatis.* Take heed while you so liberally give him heaven, lest he take away your part of earth. And when their pride hath consumed and banished peace, what have they got by it? That which a Themistocles, after trial, would prefer a grave to, *Si una via ad solium duceret, altera ad sepulchrum.*——That which Demosthenes preferred banishment before. That which the wisest philosophers refused at Athens, The great trouble of government. *Inexpertus ambit; expertus odit.* Cyneas asked Pyrrhus when he was preparing to invade the Romans, "What shall we do when we have conquered the Romans?" He answered, "We will go next to Sicily." "And what shall we do when Sicily is conquered?" said he: Pyrrhus said, "We will go next to Africa." "And what shall we do next?" said the other: "Why then," said he, "we will be quiet, and merry, and take our ease." "And," said Cyneas, "if that be last and best, why may we not do so now?" It is for quietness and peace that such pretend to fight and break peace; but they usually die before they obtain it (as Pyrrhus did); and might better have permitted peace to stand, than pull it down to build it better. As one asked an old man at Athens, "Why they called themselves philosophers?" who answered, "Because we seek after wisdom." Saith he, "If you are but seeking it at this age, when do you think to find it?" So I may say to the proud warriors of the world, If so many men must be killed, and so many conquered in seeking [821]peace, when will it that way be found? But perhaps they think that their wisdom and goodness are so great, that the world cannot be happy unless they govern it: but what could have persuaded them to think so, but their pride? *Nihil magis ægris prodest, quam ab eo curari a quo voluerint:* saith Seneca. Patients must choose their own physicians. Men use to give them but little thanks, who drench them with such benefits, and bring them to the potion of peace so hot, that the touch of the cup must burn their lips, and who in goodness cut the throats of one part, that their government may be a blessing to the survivors. In a word, it is pride that is the great incendiary of the world, whether it be found in high or low. It will permit no kingdom, family, or church to enjoy the pleasant fruits of peace.

Direct. II. If you would be peaceable, be not covetous lovers of the world, but be contented with your daily bread. Hungry dogs have seldom so great plenty of meat, as to content them all, and keep them from falling out about it. If you over-love the world, you will never want occasions of discord: either your neighbour selleth too dear, or buyeth too cheap of you, or over-reacheth you, or gets before you, or some way or other doth you wrong; as long as he hath any thing which you desire, or doth not satisfy all your expectations. Ambitious and covetous men must have so much room, that the world is not wide enough for many of them: and yet, alas! too many of them there are: and therefore they are still together by the ears, like boys in the winter nights, when the bedclothes are too narrow to cover them; one pulleth, and another pulleth, and all complain. You must be sure that you trespass not in the smallest measure, nor encroach on the least of his commodities, that you demand not your own, nor deny him any thing that he desireth, nor get any thing which he would have himself, no nor ever give over feeding his greedy expectations, and enduring his injustice and abuse, if you will live peaceably with a worldly-minded man.

Direct. III. If you will be peaceable, love your neighbours as yourselves. Love neither imagineth, nor speaketh, nor worketh any hurt to others: it covereth infirmities; it hopeth all things; it endureth all things, 1 Cor. xiii. 7. Selfishness and want of love to others, causeth all the contentions in the world. You can bear with great faults in yourselves, and never fall out with yourselves for them; but with your neighbours you are quarrelling for those that are less! Do you fall out with another because he hath spoken dishonourably or slightly of you, or slandered you, or some way done you wrong? You have done a thousand times worse than all that against yourselves, and yet can bear too patiently with yourselves! If another speak evil of you, he doth not make you evil: it is worse to make you bad than to call you so: and this you do against yourselves. Doth your neighbour wrong you in your honour or estate? But he endangereth not your soul! he doth not forfeit your salvation! he doth not deserve damnation for you, nor make your soul displeasing to God! But all this you do against yourselves, (even more than all the devils in hell do,) and yet you are too little offended with yourselves. See here the power of blind self-love! If you loved your neighbours as yourselves, you would agree as peaceably with your neighbours almost as with yourselves. Love them more, and you will bear more with them, and provoke them less.

Direct. IV. Compose your minds to christian gentleness and meekness, and suffer not passion to make you either turbulent and unquiet to others, or impatient and troublesome to yourselves. A gentle and quiet mind hath a gentle, quiet tongue. It can bear as much wrong as another can do (according to its measure); it is not in the power of Satan; he cannot at his pleasure send his emissary, and by injuries or foul words, procure it to sin; but a passionate person is frequently provoking or provoked. A little thing maketh him injurious to others; and a little injury from others disquieteth himself. He is daily troubling others or himself, or both. Coals of fire go from his lips: it is his very desire to provoke and vex those that he is angry with: his neighbour's peace and his own are the fuel of his anger, which he consumeth in a moment. To converse with him and not provoke him, is a task for such as are eminently meek and self-denying: he is as the leaves of the asp tree, that never rest, unless the day be very calm. The smallest breath of an angry tongue, can shake him out of his tranquillity, and turn him into an ague of disquietness. The sails of the wind-mill are scarce more at the wind's command, than his heart and tongue are at the command of Satan; he can move him almost when he please. Bid but a neighbour speak some hard speeches of him, or one of his family neglect or cross him, and he is presently like the raging sea, whose waves cast up the mire and dirt. An impatient man hath no security of his own peace for an hour: any enemy or angry person can take it from him when they please. And being troubled, he is troublesome to all about him. If you do not in patience possess your souls, they will be at the mercy of every one that hath a mind to vex you. Remember then that no peace can be expected without patience; nor patience without a meek and gentle mind. Remember "the ornament of a meek and quiet spirit, is of great price in the sight of God," 1 Pet. iii. 4. And that "the wisdom from above is first pure, and then peaceable, gentle, and easy to be entreated," James iii. 17. And that the Eternal "Wisdom from above, hath bid you learn of him to be meek and lowly in spirit as ever you would find rest to your souls," Matt. xi. 28, 29. And he that loseth his own peace is likest to break the peace of others.

Direct. V. Be careful to maintain that order of government and obedience, which is appointed of God for the preservation of peace, in families, churches, and commonwealths. If you will break this vessel, peace will flow out and be quickly spilt. What peace in schools, but by the authority of the schoolmaster? or in armies, but by the authority of the general? If an unwise and ungodly governor do himself violate the foundations and boundaries of peace, and either weakly or wilfully make dividing laws, no wonder if such wounds do spend the vital blood and spirits of that society: it being more in the power of the governors than of the subject, to destroy peace or to preserve it. And if the subjects make not conscience of their duty to their superiors, the banks of peace will soon be broken down, and all will be overwhelmed in tumult and confusion. Take heed therefore of any thing that tendeth to subvert government: disobedience or rebellion seldom wanteth a fair pretence; but it more seldom answereth the agent's expectation. It usually pretendeth the weaknesses, miscarriages, or injurious dealings of superiors; but it as usually mendeth an inconvenience with a mischief. It setteth fire on the house to burn up the rats and mice that troubled it. It must be indeed a grievous malady that shall need such a mischief for its remedy. Certainly it is no means of God's appointment. Take heed therefore of any thing which would dissolve these bonds. Entertain not dishonourable thoughts of your governors, and receive not, nor utter any dishonourable words [822]against them, if they be faulty open not their shame: their honour is their interest, and the people's too; without it they will be disabled for effectual government. When subjects, or servants, or children are saucily censorious of superiors, and make themselves judges of all their actions, even those which they do not understand, and when they presume to defame them, and with petulant tongues to cast contempt upon them, the fire is begun, and the sacred bonds of peace are loosed. When superiors rule with piety, justice, and true love to their subjects, and inferiors keep their place and rank, and all conspire the public good, then peace will nourish, and not till then.

Direct. VI. Avoid all revengeful and provoking words. When the poison of asps is under men's lips, (Rom. iii. 13,) no wonder if the hearers' minds that are not sufficiently antidoted against it, fester. Death and life are in the power of the tongue, Prov. xviii. 21. When the tongue is as a sword, yea, a sharp sword, (Psal. lvii. 4,) and when it is purposely whetted, (Psal. lxiv. 3,) no marvel if it pierce and wound them that are unarmed. But "by long forbearing a prince is persuaded, and a soft tongue breaketh the bone," Prov. xxv. 15. A railer is numbered with those that a christian must not eat with, 1 Cor. v. For christianity is so much for peace, that it abhorreth all that is against it. Our Lord when he was reviled, reviled not again, and in this was our example, 1 Pet. ii. 21, 23. A scorning, railing, reproachful tongue, "is set (as James saith, iii. 6.) on fire of hell, and it setteth on fire the course of nature;" even persons, families, churches, and commonwealths. Many a ruined society may say by experience, "Behold, how great a matter a little fire kindleth," James iii. 5.

143

Direct. VII. Engage not yourselves too forwardly or eagerly in disputes, nor at any time without necessity: and when necessity calleth you, set an extraordinary watch upon your passions. Though disputing is lawful, and sometimes necessary to defend the truth, yet it is seldom the way of doing good to those whom you dispute with: it engageth men in partiality, and passionate, provoking words, before they are aware; and while they think they are only pleading for the truth, they are militating for the honour of their own understandings. They that will not stoop to hear you as learners, while you orderly open the truth in its coherent parts, will hardly ever profit by your contendings, when you engage a proud person to bend all his wit and words against you. The servant of the Lord must not strive, but be gentle to all men, apt to teach, &c. 2 Tim. ii. 24.[154]

Direct. VIII. Have as little to do with men, in matters which their commodity is concerned in, as you can. As in chaffering, or in any other thing where mine and thine is much concerned: for few men are so just as not to expect that which others account unjust; and the nearest friends have been alienated hereby.

Direct. IX. Buy peace at the price of any thing which is not better than it. Not with the loss of the favour of God, or of our innocency, or true peace of conscience, or with the loss of the gospel, or ruin of men's souls; but you must often part with your right for peace, and put up wrongs in word or deed. Money must not be thought too dear to buy it, when the loss of it will be worse than the loss of money, to yourselves or those that you contend with. If a soul be endangered by it, or societies ruined by it, it will be dear-bought money which is got or saved by such means. He is no true friend of peace, that will not have it except when it is cheap.

Direct. X. Avoid censoriousness; which is the judging of men or matters that you have no call to meddle with, and the making of matters worse than sufficient proof will warrant you. Be neither busy-bodies, meddling with other men's matters, nor peevish aggravaters of all men's faults. "Judge not, that ye be not judged; for with what measure you mete, it shall be measured to you again," Matt. vii. 1, 2. You shall be censured, if you will censure: and if Christ be a true discerner of minds, it is they that have beams in their own eyes, who are the quickest perceivers of the motes in others. Censorious persons are the great dividers of the church, and every where adversaries to peace; while they open their mouths wide against their neighbours, to make the worst of all that they say and do, and thus sow the seeds of discord amongst all.

Direct. XI. Neither talk against men behind their backs, nor patiently hearken to them that use it. Though the detecting of a dangerous enemy, or the prevention of another's hurt, may sometimes make it a duty to blame them that are absent; yet this case, which is rare, is no excuse to the backbiter's sin. If you have any thing to say against your neighbour, tell it him in a friendly manner to his face, that he may be the better for it: if you tell it only to another, to make him odious, or hearken to backbiters that defame men secretly, you show that your business is not to do good, but to diminish love and peace.

Direct. XII. Speak more of the good than of the evil which is in others. There are none so bad, as to have no good in them: why mention you not that? which is more useful to the hearer, than to hear of men's faults. But of this more afterwards.

Direct. XIII. Be not strange, but lovingly familiar with your neighbours. Backbiters and slanders, and unjust suspicions, do make men seem that to one another, which when they are acquainted, they find is nothing so: among any honest, well-meaning persons, familiarity greatly reconcileth. Though indeed there are some few so proud and fiery, and bitter enemies to honest peace, that the way to be at peace with them is to be far from them, where we may not be remembered by them: but it is not so with ordinary neighbours or friends that are fallen out, nor differing christians: it is nearness that must make them friends.

Direct. XIV. Affect not a distance and sour singularity in lawful things. Come as near them as you can, as they are men and neighbours; and take it not for your duty to run as from them, lest you run into the contrary extreme.

Direct. XV. Be not over-stiff in your own opinions, as those that can yield in nothing to another. Nor yet so facile and yielding as to betray or lose the truth. It greatly pleaseth a proud man's mind, when you seem to be convinced by him, and to change your mind upon his arguments, or to be much informed and edified by him; but when you deny this honour to his understanding, and contradict him, and stiffly maintain your opinion against him, you displease and lose him; and indeed a wise man should gladly learn of any that can teach him more; and should most easily of any man let go an error, and be most thankful to any that will increase his knowledge: and not only in errors to change our minds, but in small and indifferent things to submit by silence, beseemeth a modest, peaceable man.

Direct. XVI. Yet build not peace on the foundation of impiety, injustice, cruelty, or faction; for that will prove but the way to destroy it in the end. Traitors, and rebels, and tyrants, and persecutors, and ambitious, covetous clergymen, do all pretend [823]peace for their iniquity: but what peace with Jezebel's whoredoms! Satan's kingdom is supported by a peace in sin; which Christ came to break that he might destroy it: while this strong man armed keepeth his house, his goods are in peace, till a stronger doth bind him, overcome him, and cast him out. Deceitful, sinful means of peace, have been the grand engine of Satan and the papal clergy, by which they have banished and kept out peace so many ages from most of the christian world. *Impiis me diis ecclesiæ paci consulere,* was one of the three means which Luther foretold would cast out the gospel. Where perjury, or false doctrine, or any sin, or any unjust or inconsistent terms, are made the condition of peace, men build upon stubble and briers, which God will set fire to, and soon consume, and all that peace will come to nought.

Directions for church peace I have laid down before; to which I must refer you.

[154] 1 Tim. vi. 4-6.

CHAPTER XVIII.

DIRECTIONS AGAINST ALL THEFT AND FRAUD, OR INJURIOUS GETTING AND KEEPING THAT WHICH IS ANOTHER'S, OR DESIRING IT.

HE that would know what theft is, must know what propriety is; and it is that plenary title to a thing, by which it is called our own; it is that right to any thing as mine, by which I may justly have it, possess it, use it, and dispose of it. This dominion or propriety is either absolute (and that belongeth to none but God) or subordinate, respective, and limited (which is the only propriety that any creature can have). Which is such a right which will hold good against the claim of any fellow-creature, though not against God's. And among men there are proprietors or owners which are principal, and some who are but dependent, subordinate, and limited. The simple propriety may remain in a landlord or father, who may convey to his tenant or his child a limited, dependent propriety under him. Injuriously to deprive a man of this propriety, or of the thing in which he hath propriety, is the sin which I speak of in this chapter; which hath no one name, and therefore I express it here by many. Whether it be theft, robbery, cozenage, extortion, or any other way of depriving another injuriously of his own; these general directions are needful to avoid it.

Direct. I. "Love not the world, nor the things that are in the world," 1 John ii. 15. Cure covetousness, and you will kill the root of fraud and theft. As a drunkard would easily be cured of his drunkenness, if you could cure him of his thirst and love to drink; so an extortioner, thief, or deceiver, would easily be cured of their outward sin, if their hearts were cured of the disease of worldliness. The love of money is the root of all this evil. Value these things no more than they deserve.

Direct. II. To this end, acquaint your hearts with the greater riches of the life to come; and then you will meet with true satisfaction. The true hopes of heaven will cure your greedy desires of earth. You durst not then forfeit your part in that perpetual

145

blessedness, for the temporal supply of some bodily want: you durst not with Adam part with Paradise for a forbidden bit; nor as Esau profanely sell your birthright for a morsel. It is the unbelief and contempt of heaven, which maketh men venture it for the poor commodities of this world.

Direct. III. Be contented to stand to God's disposal; and suffer not any carking, discontented thoughts to feed upon your hearts. When you suffer your minds to run all day long upon your necessities and straits, the devil next tempteth you to think of unlawful courses to supply them. He will show you your neighbour's money, or goods, or estates, and tell you how well it would be with you if this were yours; he showed Achan the golden wedge; he told Gehazi how unreasonable it was that Naaman's money and raiment should be refused: he told Balaam of the hopes of preferment which he might have with Balak; he told Judas how to get his thirty pieces; he persuaded Ananias and Sapphira, that it was but reasonable to retain part of that which was their own. Nay, commonly it is discontents and cares which prepare poor wretches for those appearances of the devil, which draweth them to witchcraft for the supplying of their wants. If you took God for your God, you would take him for the sufficient disposer of the world, and one that is fitter to measure out your part of earthly things than you yourselves: and then you would rest in his wisdom, will, and fatherly providence; and not shift for yourselves by sinful means. Discontentedness of mind, and distrust of God, are the cause of all such frauds and injuries. Trust God, and you will have no need of these.

Direct. IV. Remember what promises God hath made for the competent supply of all your wants. Godliness hath the promise of this life and of that to come: all other things shall be added to you, if you seek first God's kingdom and the righteousness thereof, Matt. vi. 33. They that fear the Lord shall want nothing that is good, Psal. xxxvii. "All things shall work together for good to them that love God," Rom. viii. 28. "Let your conversation be without covetousness, and be content with such things as ye have; for he hath said, I will never leave thee nor forsake thee," Heb. xiii. 5. Live by faith on these sufficient promises, and you need not steal.

Direct. V. Overvalue not the accommodation and pleasure of the flesh, and live not in the sins of gluttony, drunkenness, pride, gaming, or riotous courses, which may bring you into want, and so to seek unlawful maintenance. He that is a servant to his flesh cannot endure to displease it, nor can bear the want of any thing which it needeth. But he that hath mastered and mortified his flesh, can endure its labour and hunger, yea, and death too if God will have it so. Large revenues will be too little for a fleshly-minded person; but a little will serve him that hath brought it under the power of reason. *Magna pars libertatis est bene moratus venter,* saith Seneca: a well-nurtured, fair-conditioned belly is a great part of a man's liberty, because an ill-taught and ill-conditioned belly is one of the basest slaveries in the world. As a philosopher said to Diogenes, If thou couldst flatter Dionysius, thou needest not eat herbs; but saith Diogenes, If thou couldst eat herbs, thou needest not flatter Dionysius: he took this for the harder task: so the thief and deceiver will say to the poor, If you could do as we do, you need not fare so hardly; but a contented poor man may better answer him and say, If you could fare hardly as I do, you need not deceive or steal as you do. A proud person, that cannot endure to dwell in a cottage, or to be seen in poor or patched apparel, will be easily tempted to any unlawful way of getting, to keep him from disgrace, and serve his pride. A glutton whose heaven is in his throat, must needs fare well, however he come by it: a tippler must needs have provision for his guggle, by right or by wrong. But a humble man and a temperate |824|man can spare all this, and when he looketh on all the proud man's furniture, he can bless himself as Socrates did in a fair, with, *Quam multa sunt quibus ipse non egeo!* How many things be there which I have no need of! And he can pity the sensual desires which others must needs fulfil; even as a sound man pitieth another that hath the itch, or the thirst of a sick man in a fever, that crieth out for drink. As Seneca saith, "It is vice and not nature which needeth much:" nature, and necessity, and duty are contented with a little. But he that must have the pleasure of his sin, must have provision to maintain that pleasure. Quench the fire of pride, sensuality, and lust, and you may spare the cost of fuel, Rom. xiii. 13, 14; viii. 13.

Direct. VI. Live not in idleness or sloth; but be laborious in your callings, that you may escape that need or poverty which is the temptation to this sin of theft. Idleness is a crime which is not to be tolerated in christian societies. 2 Thess. ii. 6, 8, 10, 12, "Now we command you, brethren, in the name of our Lord Jesus Christ, that ye withdraw yourselves from every brother that walketh disorderly, and not after the tradition which he received of us: for ye know how ye ought to follow us; for we behaved not ourselves disorderly among you, neither did we eat any man's bread for nought; but worked with labour and travail night and day, that we might not be chargeable to any of you; not because we have not power, but to make ourselves an ensample to you to follow us; for when we were with you, this we commanded you, that if any would not work, neither should he eat: for we hear that there are some among you that walk disorderly, working not at all, but are busy-bodies; now them that are such, we command and exhort by our Lord Jesus Christ, that with quietness they work and eat their own bread." Eph. iv. 28, "Let him that stole, steal no more, but rather let him labour, working with his hands the thing that is good, that he may have to give to him that needeth." He that stealeth to maintain his idleness, sinneth that he may sin; and by one sin getteth provision for another: you see here that you are bound not only to work to maintain yourselves, but to have to give to others in their need.

Direct. VII. Keep a tender conscience, which will do its office, and not suffer you to sin without remorse. A seared, senseless conscience will permit you to lie, and steal, and deceive, and will make no great matter of it, till God awaken it by his grace or vengeance. Hence it is that servants can deceive their masters, or take that which is not allowed them, and buyers and sellers over-reach one another, because they have not tender consciences to reprove them.

Direct. VIII. Remember always that God is present, and none of your secrets can be hid from him. What the better are you to deceive your neighbour or your master, and to hide it from their knowledge, as long as your Maker and Judge seeth all? when it is he that you most wrong, and with him that you have most to do, and he that will be the most terrible avenger! What blinded atheists are you, who dare do that in the presence of the most righteous God, which you durst not do if men beheld you!

Direct. IX. Forget not how dear all that must cost you, which you gain unlawfully. The reckoning time is yet to come. Either you will truly repent or not; if you do, it must cost you remorse and sorrow, and shameful confession, and restitution of all that you have got amiss; and is it not better to forbear to swallow that morsel, which must come up again with heartbreaking grief and shame? But if you repent not unfeignedly, it will be your damnation; it will be opened in judgment to your perpetual confusion, and you must pay dear for all your gain in hell. Never look upon the gain therefore, without the shame and damnation which must follow. If Achan had foreseen the stones, and Gehazi the leprosy, and Ahab the mortal arrow, and Jezebel the licking of her blood by dogs, and Judas the hanging or precipitation, and Ananias and Sapphira the sudden death, or any of them the after misery, it might have kept them from their pernicious gain. Usually even in this life, a curse attendeth that which is ill gotten, and bringeth fire among all the rest.

Direct. X. If you are poor, consider well of the mercy which that condition may bring you, and let it be your study how to get it sanctified to your good. If men understood and believed that God doth dispose of all for the best, and make them poor to do them good, and considered what that good is which poverty may do them, and made it their chief care to turn it thus to their gain, they would not find it so intolerable a thing, as to seek to cure it by fraud or thievery. Think what a mercy it is, that you are saved from those temptations to over-love the world, which the rich are undone by. And that you are not under those temptations to intemperance, and excess, and pride as they are: and that you have such powerful helps for the mortification of the flesh, and victory over the deceiving world. Improve your poverty, and you will escape these sins.

Direct. XI. If you are but willing to escape this sin, you may easily do it by a free confession to those whom you have wronged or are tempted to wrong. He that is not willing to forbear his sin, is guilty before God, though he do forbear it. But if you are truly willing, it is easy to abstain. Do not say, that you are willing till necessity pincheth you or you see the bait; for if you are so, you may easily prevent it at that time when you are willing. If ever you are willing indeed, take that opportunity, and if you have wronged any man, go and confess it to him (in the manner I shall afterwards direct). And this will easily prevent it; for shame will engage you, and self-preservation will engage him to take more heed of you. Or, if you have not yet wronged any, but are strongly tempted to it, if you have no other sufficient remedy, go tell him, or some other fit person, that you are tempted to steal and to deceive in such or such a manner, and desire them not to trust you. If you think the shame of such a confession too dear a price to save you from the sin, pretend no more that you are truly willing to forbear it, or that ever you did unfeignedly repent of it.

Tit. 2. Certain Cases of Conscience about Theft and Injury.

Quest. I. Is it a sin for a man to steal in absolute necessity, when it is merely to save his life?

Answ. The case is very hard. I shall, I. Tell you so much as is past controversy, and then speak to the controverted part. 1. If all other unquestionable means be not first used, it is undoubtedly a sin. If either labouring or begging will save our lives, it is unlawful to steal. Yea, or if any others may be used to intercede for us. Otherwise it is not stealing to save a man's life, but stealing to save his labour, or to gratify his pride and save his honour. 2. It is undoubtedly a sin if the saving of our lives by it, do bring a greater hurt to the commonwealth or other men, than our lives are worth. 3. And it is a sin if it deprive the owner of his life, he being a person more worthy and useful to the common good. These cases are no matter of controversy.

4. And it is agreed of, that no man may steal beforehand [825]out of a distrustful fear of want. 5. Or if he take more than is of necessity to save his life. These cases also are put as out of controversy.

But whether in an innocent, absolute necessity it be lawful to steal so much as is merely sufficient to save one's life, is a thing that casuists are not agreed on. They that think it lawful, say that the preservation of life is a natural duty, and preservation of propriety is but a subservient thing which must give place to it. So Amesius de Conscient. lib. v. cap. 50, maketh it one case of lawful taking that which is another's, *Si irrationabiliter censeatur dominus invitus: ut in eis quæ accipit aliquis ex alieno ad extremam et præsentem suam necessitatem sublevandam, cui alia ratione succurrere non potest. Hoc enim videtur esse ex jure naturali, divisione rerum antiquiore et superiore; quod jure humano quo facta est divisio rerum non potuit abrogari: Quo sensu non male dicitur, omnia fieri communia in extrema necessitate.*

On the other side, those that deny it say, that the same God that hath bid us preserve our lives, hath appointed propriety, and forbidden us to steal, without excepting a case of necessity, and therefore hath made it simply evil, which we may not do for the procurement of any good: and the saving of a man's life will not prove so great a good, as the breaking of God's law will be an evil.

For the true determining of this case, we must distinguish of persons, places, and occasions. 1. Between those whose lives are needful to the public good and safety, and those that are not of any such concernment. 2. Between those that are in an enemy's or a strange country, and those that are in their own. 3. Between those that are in a commonwealth, and those that are either in a community, or among people not embodied or conjoined. 4. Between those that take but that which the refuser was bound to give them, and those that take that which he was not bound to give them. And so I answer,

1. Whensoever the preservation of the life of the taker is not, in open probability, like to be more serviceable to the common good, than the violation of the right of propriety will be hurtful, the taking of another man's goods is sinful, though it be only to save the taker's life. For the common good is to be preferred before the good of any individual.

2. In ordinary cases, the saving of a man's life will not do so much good as his stealing will do hurt. Because the lives of ordinary persons are of no great concernment to the common good; and the violation of the laws may encourage the poor to turn thieves, to the loss of the estates and lives of others, and the overthrow of peace and order. Therefore ordinarily it is a duty, rather to die, than take another man's goods against his will, or without his consent.

3. But in case that the common good doth apparently more require the preservation of the person's life, than the preservation of propriety and the keeping of the law in that instance, it is then no sin (as I conceive): which may fall out in many instances.

As, (1.) In case the king and his army should march through a neighbour prince's country, in a necessary war against their enemies; if food be denied them in their march, they may take it rather than perish. (2.) In case the king's army in his own dominions have no pay, and must either disband or die, if they have not provision, they may rather take free quarter, in case that their obedience to the king, and the preservation of the country, forbiddeth them to disband. (3.) When it is a person of so great honour, dignity, and desert, as that his worth and serviceableness will do more than recompense the hurt: as if Alexander or Aristotle were on ship-board with a covetous ship-master, who would let them die rather than relieve them. (4.) When a child taketh meat from a cruel parent that would famish him, or a wife from such a cruel husband! Or any man taketh his own by stealth from another who unjustly detaineth it, when it is to save his life. For here is a fundamental right *ad rem*, and the heinousness of his crime that would famish another, rather than give him his own, or his due, doth take off the scandal and evil consequents of the manner of taking it. (5.) But the greatest difficulty is, in case that only the common law of humanity and charity bind another to give to one that else must die, and he that needeth may take it so secretly that it shall in likelihood never be known, and so never be scandalous, nor encourage any other to steal! May not the needy then steal to save his life? This case is so hard, that I shall not venture to determine it; but only say that he that doth so in such a case, must resolve when he hath done, to repay the owner if ever he be able (though it be but a piece of bread); or to repay him by his labour and service, if he have no other way, and be thus able; or if not so, to confess it to him that he took it from, and acknowledge himself his debtor (unless it be to one whose cruelty would abuse his confession).

Quest. II. If another be bound to relieve me and do not, may I not take it, though it be not for the immediate saving of my life?

Answ. If he be bound only by God's law to relieve you, you must complain to God, and stay till he do you right, and not break his law and order, by righting yourself, in case you are not in the necessity aforesaid. If he be bound also by the law of man to relieve you, you may complain to the rulers, and seek your right by their assistance; but not by stealth.

Quest. III. If another borrow or possess my goods or money, and refuse to pay me, and I cannot have law and justice against him, or am not rich enough to sue him, may I not take them if I have an opportunity?

Answ. If he turn your enemy in a time of war, or live under another prince, with whom you are at war, or where your prince alloweth you to take it; there it seemeth undoubtedly lawful to take your own by that law of arms, which then is uppermost. But when the law that you are under forbiddeth you, the case is harder. But it is certain that propriety is in communities, and is in order of nature antecedent to human government in republics; and the preservation of it is one of the ends of government.

Therefore I conceive that in case you could take your own so secretly, or in such a manner as might no way hinder the ends of government as to others, by encouraging thievery or unjust violence, it is not unlawful before God, the end of the law being the chief part of the law; but when you cannot take your own without either encouraging theft or violence in others, or weakening the power of the laws and government by your disobedience, (which is the ordinary case,) it is unlawful: because the preservation of order and of the honour of the government and laws, and the suppression of theft and violence, is much more necessary than the righting of yourself, and recovering your own.

Quest. IV. If another take by theft or force from me, may I not take my own again from him, by force or secretly, when I have no other way?

Answ. Not when you do more hurt to the commonwealth by breaking law and order, than your own benefit can recompense; for you must rather suffer than the commonwealth should suffer; but you may when no such evils follow it.

[826]*Quest.* V. If I be in no necessity myself, may I not take from rich men to give to the poor who are in extreme necessity?

Answ. The answer to the first case may suffice for this; in such cases wherein a poor man may not take it for himself, you may not take it for him. But in such cases as he may take it for himself, and no one else is fit to do it, he himself being unable, you may do it (when no accidental consequents forbid you).

Quest. VI. If he have so much as that he will not miss it, and I be in great want, though not like to die of famine, may I not take a little to supply my want?

Answ. No: because God hath appointed the means of just propriety; and what is not gotten by those means, is none of yours by his approbation. He is the giver of riches; and he intendeth not to give to all alike: if he give more to others he will require more of them. And if he give less to you, it is the measure which he seeth to be meetest for you; and the condition in which your obedience and patience must be tried; and he will not take it well, if you will alter your measure by forbidden means, and be carvers for yourselves, or level others.

Quest. VII. There are certain measures which humanity obligeth a man to grant to those in want, and therefore men take without asking: as to pluck an apple from a tree, or as Christ's disciples, to rub the ears of corn to eat; if a Nabal deny me such a thing, may I not take it?

Answ. If the laws of the land allow it you, you may; because men's propriety is subjected to the law for the common good. But if the law forbid it you, you may not; except when it is necessary to save your life, upon the terms expressed under the first question.

Quest. VIII. May not a wife, or child, or servant take more than a cruel husband, or parent, or master doth allow? suppose it be better meat or drink?

Answ. How far the wife hath a true propriety herself, and therefore may take it, dependeth on the contract and the laws of the land; which I shall not now meddle with. But for children and servants, they may take no more than the most cruel and unrighteous parents or masters do allow them; except to save their lives upon the conditions in the first case: but the servant may seek relief of the magistrate; and he may leave such an unrighteous master: and the child must bear it patiently as the cross by which it pleaseth God to try him; unless that the government of the parent be so bad, as to tend to his undoing; and then I think he may leave his parents for a better condition (except it be when their own necessity obligeth him to stay and suffer for their help and benefit). For it is true that a child oweth as much to his parents as he can perform, by way of gratitude, for their good: but it is true also, that a parent hath no full and absolute propriety in his child, as men have in their cattle, but is made by nature their guardian for their benefit; and therefore when parents would undo their children's souls or bodies, the children may forsake them, as being forsaken by them; further than as they are obliged in gratitude to help them, as is aforesaid.

Quest. IX. If a man do deserve to lose somewhat which he hath by way of punishment, may I not take it from him?

Answ. Not unless the law either make you a magistrate or officer to do it, or allow and permit it at the least; because it is not to you that the forfeiture is made: or if it be, you must execute the law according to the law, and not against it; for else you will offend in punishing offences.

Quest. X. But what if I fully resolve, when I take a thing in my necessity, to repay the owner, or make him satisfaction if ever I be able?

Answ. That is some extenuation of the sin, but no justification of the fact; which is otherwise unjustifiable, because it is still without his consent.

Quest. XI. What if I know not whether the owner would consent or not?

Answ. In a case where common custom and humanity alloweth you to take it for granted that he would not deny it you, (as to pluck an ear of corn, or gather an herb for medicine in his field,) you need not scruple it; unless you conjecture that he is a Nabal and would deny you. But otherwise if you doubt of his consent, you must ask it, and not presume of it without just cause.

Quest. XII. What if I take a thing from a friend but in a way of jest, intending to restore it?

Answ. If you have just grounds to think that your friend would consent if he knew it, you will not be blamable: but if otherwise, either you take it for your own benefit and use, or you take it only to make sport by; the former is theft, for all your jest; the latter is but an unlawful way of jesting.

Quest. XIII. What if I take it from him, but to save him from hurting his body with it: as if I steal poison from one that intended to kill himself by it; or take a sword from a drunken man that would hurt himself; or a knife from a melancholy man? Or what if it be to save another; as to take a madman's sword from him who would kill such as are in his way, or any angry man's that will kill another?

Answ. This is your duty according to the sixth commandment, which bindeth you to preserve your neighbour's life; so be it these conditions be observed: 1. That you keep not his sword for your benefit and advantage, nor claim a property in it; but give it his friends, or deliver it to the magistrate. 2. That you do nothing without the magistrate, in which you may safely stay for his authority and help: but if two be fighting, or thieves be robbing or murdering a man, or another's life be in present danger, you must help them without staying for the magistrate's authority. 3. That you make not this a pretence for the usurping of authority, or for resisting or deposing your lawful prince, or magistrate, or parent, or master, or of exercising your own will and passions against your superiors; pretending that you take away their swords to save themselves or others from their rage, when it is indeed but to hinder justice.

Quest. XIV. May I not then much more take away that by which he would destroy his own or other men's souls: as to take away cards or dice from gamesters; or heretical or seditious books, or play-books and romances; or to pull down idols which the idolators do adore, or are instruments of idolatry?

Answ. There is much difference in the cases, though the soul be more precious than the body: for, 1. Here there is supposed to be so much leisure and space as that you may have time to tell the magistrate of it, whose duty primarily it is: whereas in the other case it is supposed that so much delay would be a man's death. Therefore your duty is to acquaint the magistrate with the sin and danger, and not to anticipate him, and play the magistrate yourself. Or in the case of cards, and dice, and hurtful books, you may acquaint the persons with the sin, and persuade them to cast them away themselves. 2. Your taking away these instruments is not like to save them: for the love of the sin, and the will to do it, remain still; and the sinner will but be hardened by his indignation against your irregular course of charity. 3. Men are bound to save men's bodies whether they will or not, because it may be so done; [827]but no man can save another's soul against his will! And it is God's will that their salvation or damnation shall be more the fruit of their own wills, than of any other's. Therefore, though it is possible to devise an instance, in which it is lawful to steal a poisonous book or idol from another, (when it is done so secretly as will encourage no disobedience or disorder; nor is like to harden the sinner, but indeed to do him good, &c.) yet ordinarily all this is unlawful for private men, that have no government of others, or extraordinary interest in them.[155]

Quest. XV. May not a magistrate take the subjects' goods, when it is necessary for their own preservation?

Answ. I answered this question once heretofore in my "Political Aphorisms:" and because I repent of meddling with such subjects, and of writing that book, I will leave such cases hereafter for fitter persons to resolve.

Quest. XVI. But may I not take from another for a holy use; as to give to the church or maintain the bishops? If David took the hallowed bread in his necessity, may not hallowed persons take common bread?

Answ. If holy persons be in present danger of death, their lives may be saved as other men's on the terms mentioned in the first case. Otherwise God hath no need of theft or violence; nor must you rob the laity to clothe the clergy; but to do such evil on pretence of piety and good, is an aggravation of the sin.

[155] A wife or near friend that is under no suspicion of alienating the thing to their own commodity, nor of ill designs, may go somewhat further in such cases, than an inferior or a stranger.

CHAPTER XIX.

GENERAL DIRECTIONS AND PARTICULAR CASES OF CONSCIENCE, ABOUT CONTRACTS IN GENERAL, AND ABOUT BUYING AND SELLING, BORROWING AND LENDING, USURY, &c. IN PARTICULAR.

Tit. 1. General Directions against injurious Bargaining and Contracts.

BESIDES the last directions, chap. xviii., take these as more nearly pertinent to this case.

Direct. I. See that your hearts have the two great principles of justice deeply and habitually innaturalized or radicated in them, viz. The true love of your neighbour, and the denial of yourself; which in one precept are called, The loving of your neighbour as yourself. For then you will be freed from the inclination to injuries and fraud, and from the power of those temptations which carry men to these sins. They will be contrary to your habitual will or inclination; and you will be more studious to help your neighbour, than to get from him.

Direct. II. Yet do not content yourself with these habits, but be sure to call them up to act, whenever you have any bargaining with others; and let a faithful conscience be to you as a cryer to proclaim God's law, and say to you, Now remember love and self-denial, and do as you would be done by. If Alexander Severus so highly valued this saying, *Quod tibi fieri non vis, alteri ne feceris,* as to make it his motto, and write and engrave it on his doors and buildings (having learned it of some christians or Jews, saith Lampridius); what a crime and shame is it for Christ's own professed disciples neither to learn nor love it! Put home the question when you have any bargaining with others, How would I be dealt with myself, if my case were the same with his?

Direct. III. When the tempter draweth you to think only of your own commodity and gain, remember how much more you will lose by sin, than your gain can any way amount to. If Achan, Gehazi, Ahab, Judas, &c. had foreseen the end, and the greatness of their loss, it would have curbed their covetous desires. Believe God's word from the bottom of your heart, that you shall lose things eternal if you sinfully get things temporal, and then you will not make haste to such a bargain, to win the world and lose your souls.

Direct. IV. Understand your neighbour's case aright, and meditate on his wants and interest. You think what you want yourself; but you think not whether his wants with whom you deal, may not be as great as yours: consider what his commodity costeth him; or what the toil of the workman's labour is; what house rent he hath to pay, and what a family to maintain; and whether all this can be well done upon the rates that you desire to trade with him. And do not believe every common report of his riches, or of the price of his commodity; for fame in such cases is frequently false.

Direct. V. Regard the public good above your own commodity. It is not lawful to take up or keep up any oppressing monopoly or trade, which tendeth to enrich you by the loss of the commonwealth or of many.

Direct. VI. Therefore have a special regard to the laws of the country where you live; both as to your trade itself, and as to the price of what you sell or buy. For the law is made for the public benefit, which is to be preferred before any private man's. And when the law doth directly or indirectly set rates upon labours or commodities, ordinarily they must be observed; or else you will commit two sins at once, injury and disobedience.

Direct. VII. Also have special respect to the common estimate, and to the market price. Though it be not always to be our rule, yet ordinarily it must be a considerable part of it, and of great regard.

Direct. VIII. Let not imprudent thinking make you seem more covetous than you are. Some imprudent persons cannot tell how to make their markets without so many words, even about a penny or a trifle, that it maketh others think them covetous, when it is rather want of wit. The appearance of evil must be avoided. I know some that are ready to give a pound to a charitable use at a word, who will yet use so many words for a penny in their bargaining as maketh them deeply censured and misunderstood. If you see cause to break for a penny or a small matter, do it more handsomely in fewer words, and be gone: and do not tempt the seller to multiply words, because you do so.

Direct. IX. Have no more to do in bargaining with others, especially with censorious persons, than you needs must; for in much dealing usually there will be much misunderstanding, offence, censure, and complaint.

Direct. X. In doubtful cases, when you are uncertain what is lawful, choose that side which is safest to the peace of your consciences hereafter; though it be against your commodity, and may prove the losing of your right.

Tit. 2. Cases of Conscience about Justice in Contracts.

Quest. I. Must I always do as I would be done by? Or hath this rule any exceptions?

[828]*Answ.* The rule intendeth no more but that your just self-denial and love to others, be duly exercised in your dealings with all. And, 1. It supposeth that your own will or desires be honest and just, and that God's law be their rule. For a sinful will may not be made the rule of your own actions or of other men's. He that would have another make him drunk, may not therefore make another drunk: and he that would abuse another man's wife, may not therefore desire that another man would lust after or abuse his wife. He that would not be instructed, reproved, or reformed, may not therefore forbear the instructing or reproving others. And he that would kill himself, may not therefore kill another. But he that would have no hurt done to himself injuriously, should do none to others: and he that would have others do him good, should be as willing to do good to them.

2. It supposeth that the matter be to be varied according to your various conditions. A parent that justly desireth his child to obey him, is not bound therefore to obey his child; nor the prince to obey his subjects; nor the master to do all the work for his servants, which he would have his servants do for him. But you must deal by another as you would (regularly) have them deal by you, if you were in their case, and they in yours. And on these terms it is a rule of righteousness.

Quest. II. Is a son bound by the contract which his parents or guardians made for him in his infancy?

Answ. To some things he is bound, and to some things not. The infant is capable of being obliged by another upon four accounts: 1. As he is the parents' own (or a master's to whom he is in absolute servitude). 2. As he is to be ruled by the parents. 3. As he is a debtor to his parents for benefits received. 4. As he is an expectant, or capable of future benefits to be enjoyed upon conditions to be performed by him. 1. No parents or lord have an absolute propriety in any rational creature; but they have a propriety *secundum quid, et ad hoc:* and a parent's propriety doth in part expire or abate, as the son groweth up to the full use of reason, and so hath a greater propriety in himself. Therefore he may oblige his son only so far as his propriety extendeth, and to such acts, and to no other; for in those his will is reputatively his son's will. As if a parent sell his son to servitude, he is bound to such service as beseemeth one man to put another to. 2. As he is rector to his child, he may by contract with a third person promise that his child shall do such acts, as he hath power to command and cause him to do: as to read, to hear God's word, to labour as he is able; but this no longer than while he is under his parent's government: and so long obedience requireth him to perform their contracts, in performing their commands. 3. The child having received his being and maintenance from them, remains obliged to them as his benefactors in the debt of gratitude as long as he liveth: and that so deeply that some have questioned whether ever he can requite them (which *quoad valorem beneficii* he can do only by furthering their salvation; as many a child hath been the cause of the parent's conversion). And so far as the son is thus a debtor to his parents, he is obliged to do that which the parents by contract with a third person shall impose upon him. As if the parents could not be delivered out of captivity, but by obliging the son to pay a great sum of money, or to live in servitude for their release: though they never gave him any money, yet is he bound to pay the sum, if he can get it, or to perform the servitude; because he hath received more from them, even his being. 4. As the parents are both owners, (*secundum quid,*) and rulers, and benefactors to their child, in all three respects conjunct, they may oblige him to a third person who is willing to be his benefactor, by a conditional obligation to perform such conditions that he may possess such or such benefits: and thus a guardian or any friend who is fit to interpose for him, may oblige him. As to take a lease in his name, in which he shall be bound to pay such a rent, or do such a service, that he may receive such a commodity which is greater. Thus parents oblige their children under civil governments to the laws of the society or kingdom, that they may have the protection and benefits of subjects. In these cases the child can complain of no injury; for it is for his benefit that he is obliged: and the parent (in this respect) cannot oblige him to his hurt: for if he will quit the benefit, he may be freed when he will from his obligation, and may refuse to stand to the covenant if he dislike it. If he will give up his lease, he may be disobliged from the rent and service.

In all this you may see that no man can oblige another against God or his salvation: and therefore a parent cannot oblige a child to sin, nor to forbear hearing or reading the word of God, or praying, or any thing necessary to his salvation: nor can he oblige him to hear an heretical pastor; nor to marry an infidel or wicked wife, &c.

And here also you may perceive on what grounds it is that God hath appointed parents to oblige their children in the covenant of baptism, to be the servants of God and to live in holiness all their days.

And hence it is apparent, that no parents can oblige their children to be miserable, or to any such condition which is worse than to have no being.

Also that when parents do (as commonly they do) profess to oblige their children as benefactors for their good, the obligation is then to be interpreted accordingly: and the child is then obliged to nothing which is really his hurt.

Yea, all the propriety and government of parents, cannot authorize them to oblige the child to his hurt, but in order to some greater good, either to the parents themselves, or to the commonwealth, or others; at least that which the parents apprehend to be a greater good: but if they err through ignorance or partiality, and bind the child to a greater hurt for their lesser good, (as to pay two hundred pounds to save them from paying one hundred pounds,) whether their injury and sin do excuse the child from being obliged to any more than the proportion of the benefit required, I leave undetermined.

Quest. III. But what if the parents disagree, and one of them will oblige the child, and the other will not?

Answ. 1. If it be an act of the parents as mere proprietors for their own good, either of them may oblige him in a just degree; because they have severally a propriety. 2. If it be an act of government, (as if they oblige him to do this or that act of service at their command in his minority,) the father may oblige him against the mother's consent, because he is the chief ruler; but not the mother against the father's will, though she may without it.

Quest. IV. Is a man obliged by a contract which he made in ignorance or mistake of the matter?

Answ. I have answered this before in the case of marriage, part iii. chap. i.: I add here,

1. We must distinguish between culpable and inculpable error. 2. Between an error about the principal matter, and about some smaller accidents or circumstances. 3. Between a case where the law of the land or the common good interposeth, and where it doth not.

[829]1. If it be your own fault that you are mistaken you are not wholly freed from the obligation; but if it was your gross fault, by negligence or vice, you are not at all freed; but if it were but such a frailty as almost all men are liable to, so that none but a person of extraordinary virtue or diligence could have avoided the mistake, then equity will proportionably make you an abatement or free you from the obligation. So far as you were obliged to understand the matter, so far you are obliged by the contract; especially when another is a loser by your error.

2. An inculpable error about the circumstances, or smaller parts, will not free you from an obligation in the principal matter; but an inculpable error in the essentials will.

3. Except when the law of the land or the common good, doth otherwise overrule the case; for then you may be obliged by that accident. In divers cases the rulers may judge it necessary, that the effect of the contract shall depend upon the bare words, or writings, or actions; lest false pretences of misunderstanding should exempt deceitful persons from their obligations, and nothing should be a security to contractors. And then men's private commodity must give place to the law and to the public good.

4. Natural infirmities must be numbered with faults, though they be not moral vices, as to the contracting of an obligation, if they be in a person capable of contracting. As if you have some special defect of memory or ignorance of the matter which you are about. Another who is no way faulty by over-reaching you, must not be a loser by your weakness. For he that cometh to the market, or contracteth with another that knoweth not his infirmity, is to be supposed to understand what he doth, unless the contrary be manifest: you should not meddle with matters which you understand not; or if you do, you must be content to be a loser by your weakness.

5. Yet in such cases, another that hath gained by the bargain, may be obliged by the laws of equity and charity, to remit the gain, and not to take advantage of your weakness; but he may so far hold you to it, as to secure himself from loss; except in cases where you become the object of his charity, and not of commutative justice only.

Quest. V. Is a drunken man, or a man in a transporting passion, or a melancholy person, obliged by a contract made in such a case?

Answ. Remember still, that we are speaking only of contracts about matters of profits or worldly interest; and not of marriage or any of another nature. And the question as it concerneth a man in drunkenness or passion, is answered as the former about culpable error; and as it concerneth a melancholy man, it is to be answered as the former question, in the case of natural infirmity. But if the melancholy be so great

155

as to make him uncapable of bargaining, he is to be esteemed in the same condition as an idiot, or one in deliration or distraction.

Quest. VI. But may another hold a man to it, who in drunkenness or passion maketh an ill bargain, or giveth or playeth away his money; and repenteth when he is sober?

Answ. He may (ordinarily) take the money from the loser, or him that casteth it thus away; but he may not keep it for himself: but if the loser be poor, he should give it to his wife or children whom he robbeth by his sin: if not, he should either give it to the magistrate or overseer for the poor, or give it to the poor himself. The reason of this determination is, because the loser hath parted with his propriety, and can lay no further claim to the thing; but yet the gainer can have no right from another's crime: if it were from an injury, he might, so far as is necessary to reparations; but from a crime he cannot; for his loss is to be estimated as a mulct or penalty, and to be disposed of as such mulcts as are laid on swearers and drunkards are. Only the person by his voluntary bargain, hath made the other party instead of the magistrate, and authorized him (in ordinary cases) to dispose of the gain, for the poor or public good.

Quest. VII. Am I obliged by the words or writings which usually express a covenant, without any covenanting or self-obliging intention in me, when I speak or write them?

Answ. Either you utter or write those words with a purpose to make another believe that you intend a covenant; or at least by culpable negligence, in such a manner as he is bound so to understand you, or justified for so understanding you: or else you so use the words, as in the manner sufficiently to signify that you intend no covenant or self-obligation. In the former case you bind yourself (as above said); because another man is not to be a loser, nor you a gainer or a saver, by your own fraud or gross negligence. But in the latter case you are not bound, because an intent of self-obliging is the internal efficient of the obligation; and a signification of such an intent, is the external efficient, without which it cannot be. If you read over the words of a bond, or repeat them only in a narrative, or ludicrously; or if a scrivener write a form of obligation of himself, to a boy for a copy, or to a scholar for a precedent, these do not induce any obligation in conscience, nor make you a debtor to another. Thus also the case of the intent of the baptizer or baptized (or parent) is to be determined.

Quest. VIII. May a true man promise a robber money, for the saving of his life, or of a greater sum, or more precious commodity?

Answ. Yes, in case of necessity, when his life or estate cannot better be preserved; and so taxes may be paid to an enemy in arms, or to a plundering soldier (supposing that it do no other hurt, which is greater than the good). Any man may part with a lesser good to preserve a greater; and it is no more voluntary or imputable to our wills, than the casting of our goods into the sea to save the vessel and our lives.

Quest. IX. May I give money to a judge, or justice, or court officer, to hire him to do me justice, or to keep him from doing me wrong; or to avoid persecution?

Answ. You may not, in case your cause be bad, give any thing to procure injustice against another; no nor speak a word for it nor desire it: this I take as presupposed. You may not give money to procure justice, when the law of the land forbiddeth it, and when it will do more hurt accidentally to the others than good to you: when it will harden men in the sin of bribery, and cause them to expect the like from others. But except it be when some such accidental greater hurt doth make it evil, it is as lawful as to hire a thief not to kill me: when you cannot have your right by other means, you may part with a smaller matter for a greater.

Quest. X. But if I make such a contract, may the other lawfully take it of me?

Answ. No: for it is now supposed that it is unlawful on his part.

Quest. XI. But if under necessity of force I promise money to a robber, or a judge, or officer, am I bound to perform it when my necessity is over?

Answ. You have lost your own propriety by your [830]covenant, and therefore must not retain it; but he can acquire no right by his sin: and therefore some say that in point of justice you are not bound to give it him, but to give it to the magistrate for the poor; but yet prudence may tell you of other reasons *a fine* to give it the man himself, though justice bind you not to it; as in case that else he may be revenged and do you some greater hurt; or some greater hurt is any other way like to be the consequent; which it is lawful by money to prevent. But many think that you are bound to deliver the money to the thief or officer himself; because it is a lawful thing to do it, though he have no just title to it; and because it was your meaning, or the signification of your words in your covenant with him; and if it were not lawful to do it, it could not be lawful to promise to do it, otherwise your promise is a lie. To this, those of the other opinion say, that as a man who is discharged of his promise by him that it was made to, is not to be accounted false if he perform it not; so is it as to the thief or officer in question; because he having no right, is to you as the other that hath quit his right. And this answer indeed will prove, that it is not strict injustice not to pay the money promised; but it will not prove that it is not a lie to make such a promise with an intent of not performing it, or that it is not a lie to make it with an intent of performing it, and not to do it when you may. Though here a Jesuit will tell you that you may say the words of a promise, with an equivocation or mental reservation to a thief or persecuting magistrate (of which see more in the chapters of lying, vows, and perjury). I am therefore of opinion that your promise must be sincerely made, and according to the true intent of it you must offer the money to the thief or officer; except in case the magistrate forbid you, or some greater reason lie against it, which you foresaw not when you made the promise. But the offender is undoubtedly obliged not to take the money.

The same determination holdeth as to all contracts and promises made to such persons, who by injurious force constrained us to make them. There is on us an obligation to veracity, though none to them in point of justice, because they have no proper right; nor may they lawfully take our payment or service promised them. And in case that the public good unexpectedly cross our performance, we must not perform it: such like is the case of conquerors, and those that upon conquest become their vassals or subjects upon unrighteous terms. But still remember, that if it be not only a covenant with man, but a vow to God, which maketh him a party, the case is altered, and we remain obliged.

Quest. XII. But may I promise the thief or bribe-taker to conceal his fault? And am I obliged to the performance of such a promise?

Answ. This is a promise of omitting that which else would be a duty. It is ordinarily a duty to reveal a thief and bribe-taker that he may be punished. But affirmatives bind not *ad semper*, no act (especially external) is a duty at all times, therefore not this, of revealing an offender's fault. And if it be not always a duty, then it must be none when it is inconsistent with some greater benefit or duty; for when two goods come together, the greater is to be preferred: therefore in case that you see in just probability, that the concealment of the sinner will do more hurt to the commonwealth or the souls of men, than the saving of your life is like to do good, you may not promise to conceal him, or if you sinfully promise it, you may not perform it; but in case that your life is like to be a greater good than the not promising to conceal him, then such a promise is no fault, because the disclosing him is no duty. But to judge rightly of this is a matter of great difficulty. If it be less than life which you save by such a promise, it oft falls out that it is a lesser good than the detecting of the offence.

But it will here be said, If I promise not to conceal a robber, I must conceal him nevertheless; for when he hath killed me, I cannot reveal him: and I must conceal the bribe-taker; for till I have promised secrecy, I cannot prove him guilty. And he that promiseth to forbear a particular good action whilst he liveth, doth yet reserve his life for all other good works; whereas if he die, he will neither do that nor any other. But this case is not so easily determined: if Daniel die, he can neither pray nor do any good on earth. And if he live he may do much other good, though he never pray; and yet he might not promise to give over praying to save his life. I conceive that we must distinguish of duties essential to the outward part of christianity, or of constant, indispensable necessity; and duties which are alterable, and belong only to some persons, times, and places; also between the various consequents of omissions. And I conceive that ordinarily a man may promise for the saving of his life, that he will forbear a particular, alterable duty or relation; as to read such a commentary, to speak with such a minister, to be a magistrate or a minister, &c. in case we have not before bound ourselves never to give over our calling till death; and in case that the good which will follow our forbearance, is likely (to a judicious person) to be greater than the evil. But no man may promise to omit such a duty as God hath made necessary during life; as not to love God, or fear, or trust him; not to worship him, and call upon him, and praise him; not to do good to men's souls or bodies in the general; or not to preach or pray while I am a minister of Christ; or not at all to govern while you are a governor; for all these contradict some former and greater promises or duties. Nor may you omit the smallest duty to save your life, at such a time when your death is like to do more good, than your life would do without that one duty. Apply this to the present case.

Quest. XIII. If another man deceive me into a promise or covenant against my good, am I bound to perform it when I have discovered the deceit?

Answ. Yes, 1. In case that the law of the land, or other reasons for the public good, require it. 2. Or in case that you were faulty by negligence, heedlessness, or otherwise guilty of your own deceit, in any considerable and avoidable degree. Otherwise, in that measure that he deceived you, and in those respects, you are not obliged.

Quest. XIV. If the contracting parties do neither of them understand the other, is it a covenant? Or if it be, whose sense must carry it?

Answ. If they understand not each other in the essentials of the contract, it is no contract in point of conscience; except where the laws for the public safety do annex the obligation to bare external act. But if they understand not one another in some circumstances, and be equally culpable or innocent, they must come to a new agreement in those particulars; but if one party only be guilty of the misunderstanding, he must bear the loss, if the other insist on it.

Quest. XV. Am I bound to stand to the bargains which my friend, or trustee, or servant maketh for me, when it proveth much to my injury or loss?

Answ. Yes, 1. If they exceed not the bounds of that commission or trust which they received from you. 2. Or if they do, yet if by your former trusting and using them, or by any other sign, you have [831]given the other party sufficient cause to suppose them intrusted by you to do what they do, so that he is deceived by your fault, you are bound at least to see that he be no loser by you; though you are not bound to make him a gainer, unless you truly signified that you authorized them to make the contract. For if it be merely your friend's or servant's error, without your fault, it doth not bind you to a third person. But how far you may be bound to pardon that error to your friend or servant, is another question; and how far you are bound to save them harmless. And that must be determined by laying together all other obligations between them and you.

Quest. XVI. If I say I will give such or such a one this or that, am I bound thereby to do it?

Answ. It is one thing to express your present mind and resolution, without giving away the liberty of changing it; and it is another thing to intend the obliging of yourself to do the thing mentioned. And that obligation is either intended to man, or to God only; and that is either in point of rendition and use, or in point of veracity, or the performance of that moral duty of speaking truth. If you meant no more in saying, I will do it, or I will give it, but that this is your present will, and purpose, and resolution, yea, though it add the confident persuasion that your will shall not change; yet this no further obligeth you than you are obliged to continue in that will; and a man's confident resolutions may be lawfully changed upon sufficient cause. But if you intended to alienate the title to another, or to give him present right, or to oblige yourself for the future to him by that promise; or to oblige yourself to God to do it by way of peremptory assertion, as one that will be guilty of a lie if you perform it not; or if you dedicate the thing to God by those words as a vow; then you are obliged to do accordingly (supposing nothing else to prohibit it).

Quest. XVII. Doth an inward promise of the mind not expressed, oblige?

Answ. In a vow to God it doth; and if you intend it as an assertion obliging you in point of veracity, it doth so oblige you that you must lie. But it is no contract, nor giveth any man a title to what you tacitly thought of.

Quest. XVIII. May I promise an unlawful thing (simply so) without an intention of performing it, to save my life from a thief or persecutor?

Answ. No: because it is a lie, when the tongue agreeth not with the heart. Indeed those that think a lie is no sin when it hurteth not another, may justify this, if that would hold good; but I have before confuted it, part i. in the chapter against lying.

Quest. XIX. May any thing otherwise unlawful become a duty upon a promise to do it?

Answ. This is answered before, part i. chapter of perjury and vows: a thing unlawful will be so still, notwithstanding a vow or promise; and some so of that also which is unlawful antecedently but by accident; as e. g. It is not simply unlawful to cast away a cup of wine or a piece of silver (for it is lawful upon a sufficient cause); but it is unlawful to do it without any sufficient cause. Now suppose I should contract with another that I will do it; am I bound by such a contract? Many say no, because the matter is unlawful though but by accident; and the contract cannot make it lawful. I rather think that I am bound in such a case; but yet that my obligation doth not exclude me wholly from sin; it was a sin before I promised it (or vowed it) to cast away a farthing causelessly. And if I causelessly promised it, I sinned in that promise; but yet there may be cause for the performance: and if I have entangled myself in a necessity of sinning whether I do it or not, I must choose the lesser sin; for that is then my duty. (Though I should have chosen neither as long as I could avoid it.) In a great and hurtful sin I may be obliged rather to break my covenant than to commit it, yet it is hard to say so of every accidental evil: my reasons are, 1. Because the promise or covenant is now an accident to be put into the balance; and may weigh down a lighter accident on the other side (but I know that the great difficulty is to discern which is indeed the preponderating accident).

2. I think if a magistrate command me to do any thing which by a small accident is evil (as to spend an hour in vain, to give a penny in vain, to speak a word which, antecedently, was vain) that I must do it; and that then it is not vain because it manifesteth my obedience (otherwise obedience would be greatly straitened). Therefore my own contract may make it my duty; because I am able to oblige myself as well as a magistrate is. 3. Because covenant-breaking (and perjury) is really a greater sin than speaking a vain word; and my error doth not make it no sin, but only entangles me in a necessity of sinning which way soever I take.

Quest. XX. If a man make a contract to promote the sin of another for a reward, (as a corrupt judge or lawyer, officer or clerk, to promote injustice; or a resetter, to help a thief; or a bawd or whore, for the price of fornication,) may he take the reward, when the sin is committed (suppose it repented of)?

Answ. The offender that promised the reward, hath parted with his title to the money; therefore you may receive it of him (and ought, except he will rightly dispose of it himself); but withal to confess the sin and persuade him also to repent: but you may not take any of that money as your own (for no man can purchase true propriety by iniquity); but either give it to the party injured, (to whom you are bound to make satisfaction,) or to the magistrate or the poor, according as the case particularly requireth.

Quest. XXI. If I contract, or bargain, or promise to another, between us two, without any legal form or witness, doth it bind me to the performance?

Answ. Yes, *in foro conscientiæ*, supposing the thing lawful; but if the thing be unlawful *in foro Dei*, and such as the law of the land only would lay hold of you about, or force you to, if it had been witnessed, then the law of the land may well be avoided, by the want of legal forms and witnesses.

Quest. XXII. May I buy an office for money in a court of justice?

Answ. Some offices you may buy (where the law alloweth it, and it tendeth not to injustice); but other offices you may not: the difference the lawyers may tell you better than I, and it would be tedious to pursue instances.

Quest. XXIII. May one buy a place of magistracy or judicature for money?

Answ. Not when your own honour or commodity is your end: because the common good is the end of government; and to a faithful governor, it is a place of great labour and suffering, and requireth much self-denial and patience. Therefore they that purchase it as a place of honour, gain, or pleasure, either know not what they undertake, or have carnal ends; else they would rather purchase their liberty and avoid it. But if a king, or a judge, or other magistrate, see that a bad man (more unfit to govern) is like to be put in, if he be put by, it is lawful for him to purchase the people's deliverance at a very dear rate (even by a lawful war, which is more [832]than money, when the sovereign's power is in such danger): but the heart must be watched, that it pretend not the common good, and intend your own commodity and honour; and the probable consequents must be weighed; and the laws of the land must be consulted also; for if they absolutely prohibit the buying of a place of judicature, they must be obeyed.[156] And ill effects may make it sinful.

Quest. XXIV. May one sell a church benefice, or rectory, or orders?

Answ. If the benefice be originally of your own gift, it is at first in your power to give part or all, to take some deductions out of it or not: but if it be really given to the church, and you have but the patronage or choice of the incumbent, it is sacrilege to sell it for any commodity of your own: but whether you may take somewhat out of a greater benefice, to give to another church which is poorer, dependeth partly on the law of the land, and partly upon the probable consequents. If the law absolutely forbid it, (supposing that unlawful contracts cannot be avoided unless some lawful ones be restrained,) it must be obeyed for the common good; and if the consequent of a lawful contract be like to be the more hurtful encouragement of unlawful ones, such examples must be forborne, though the law were not against them. But to sell orders is undoubted simony; (that is, the office of the ministry, or the act of ordination;) though scribes may be paid for writing instruments.

Quest. XXV. May a man give money for orders or benefices, when they cannot otherwise be had?

Answ. This is answered in quest. xxii. 1. If the law absolutely forbid it, for the common safety, you may not. 2. If your end be chiefly your own commodity, ease, or honour, you may not. But in case you were clear from all such evils, and the case were only this, whether you might not give money to get in yourself, to keep out a heretic, a wolf, or insufficient man, who might destroy the people's souls, I see not but it might well be done.

Quest. XXVI. May I give money to officers, servants, or assistants for their furtherance?

Answ. For writings or other servile acts about the circumstantials you may; but not (directly or indirectly) to promote the simoniacal contract. What you may not give to the principal agent, you may not give his instruments or others for the same end.

Quest. XXVII. May I give or do any thing afterward by way of gratitude, to the patron, bishop, or any others, their relations or retainers?

Answ. Not when the expectation of that gratitude was a (secret or open) condition of the presentation or orders; and you believe that you should not else have received them: therefore promised gratitude is but a kind of contracting. Nor may you show gratitude by any scandalous way, which seemeth simony. Otherwise, no doubt but you may be prudently grateful for that or any other kindness.

Quest. XXVIII. May not a bishop or pastor take money for sermons, sacraments, or other offices?

Answ. Not for the things themselves; he must not sell God's word and sacraments, or any other holy thing. But they that serve at the altar may live on the altar, and the elders that rule well are worthy of double honour; and the mouth of the ox that treadeth out the corn should not be muzzled. They may receive due maintenance while they perform God's service, that they may be vacant to attend their proper work.

Quest. XXIX. May one person disoblige another of a promise made to him?

Answ. Yes, if it be no more than a promise to that person; because a man may give away his right; but if it be moreover a vow to God, or you intend to oblige yourself in point of veracity under the guilt of a lie if you do otherwise, these alter the case, and no person can herein disoblige you.

Quest. XXX. But what if the contract be bound by an oath, may another then release me?

Answ. Yes, if that oath did only tie you to perform your promise; and were no vow to God, which made him a party by dedicating any thing to him; for then the oath being but subservient to the promise, he that dischargeth you from the promise, dischargeth you also from the oath which bound you honestly to keep it.

Quest. XXXI. Am I bound by a promise when the cause or reason of it proveth a mistake?

Answ. If by the cause you mean only the extrinsical reasons which moved you to it, you may be obliged nevertheless for finding your mistake; only so far as the other was the culpable cause, (as is aforesaid,) he is bound to satisfy you; but if by the cause you mean the formal reason, which constituteth the contract, then the mistake may in some cases nullify it (of which enough before).

Quest. XXXII. What if a following accident make it more to my hurt than could be foreseen?

Answ. In some contracts it is supposed or expressed, that men do undertake to run the hazard; and then they must stand obliged. But in some contracts, it is rationally supposed that the parties intend to be free, if so great an alteration should fall out. But to give instances of both these cases would be too long a work.

Quest. XXXIII. What if something unexpectedly fall out, which maketh it injurious to a third person? I cannot sure be obliged to injure another.

Answ. If the case be the latter mentioned in the foregoing answer, you may be thus free; but if it be the former, (you being supposed to run the hazard, and secure the other party against all others,) then either you were indeed authorized to make this bargain, or not; if not, the third person may secure his right against the other; but if you were, then you must make satisfaction as you can to the third person. Yea, if you made a covenant without authority, you are obliged to save the other harmless, unless he knew your power to be doubtful, and did resolve to run the hazard.

Quest. XXXIV. What if something fall out which maketh the performance to be a sin?

Answ. You must not do it; but you must make the other satisfaction for all the loss which you were the cause of, unless he undertook to stand to the hazard of this also (explicitly or implicitly).

Quest. XXXV. Am I obliged if the other break covenant with me?

Answ. There are covenants which make relations (as between husband and wife, pastor and flock, rulers and subjects); and covenants which convey title to commodities, of which only I am here to speak. And in these there are some conditions which are essential to the covenant; if the other first break these conditions, you are disobliged. But there are other conditions which are not essential, but only necessary to some following benefit, whose non-performance will only forfeit that particular benefit; and there are conditions which are only undertaken subsequent duties, trusted on the honesty of the performer; and in these a failing doth not disoblige you. These latter are but improperly called conditions.

Quest. XXXVI. May I contract to perform a thing which I foresee is like to become impossible [833]or sinful, before the time of performance come, though it be not so at present.

Answ. With all persons you must deal truly; and with just contractors openly; but with thieves, and murderers, and persecutors, you are not always bound to deal openly. This being premised, either your covenant is absolutely, This I will do, be it lawful or not, possible or impossible; and such a covenant is sin and folly: or it is conditional, This I will do, if it continue lawful, or possible: this condition (or rather exception) is still implied where it is not expressed, unless the contrary be expressed: therefore such a covenant is lawful with a robber with whom you are not bound to deal openly; because it is but the concealing from him the event which you foresee. As e. g. you have intelligence that a ship is lost at sea, or is like to be taken by pirates, which the robber expecteth shortly to come safe into the harbour: you may promise him to deliver up yourself his prisoner, when that ship cometh home. Or you know a person to be mortally sick, and will die before the next week; you may oblige yourself to marry or serve that person two months hence; for it is implied, if he or she be then alive. But with equal contractors, this is unlawful, with whom you are obliged not only to verity but to justice; as in the following cases will be further manifested.

Tit. 3. Special Cases about Justice in Buying and Selling.

Quest. I. Am I bound to endeavour that he whom I deal with may be a gainer by the bargain as well as I?

Answ. Yes, if you be equally in want, or in the like condition; but if he be very poor, and you be rich, charity must be so mixed with justice, that you must endeavour that it be more to his commodity than yours (if he be one indeed that you owe charity to). And if you be poor, and he be rich, you may be willing to be the only gainer yourself, so be it you covet not another's, nor desire that he be wronged; for when he hath power to deal charitably, you may be willing of his charity or kindness.

Quest. II. May I desire or take more than my labour or goods are worth, if I can get it?

Answ. 1. Not by deceit, persuading another that they are worth more than they are. 2. Not by extortion, working upon men's ignorance, error, or necessity (of which more anon). 3. Not of any one that is poorer than yourself, or of any one that intendeth but an equal bargain. 4. But if you deal with the rich, who in generosity stick not at a small matter, and are willing another should be a gainer by them, and understand what they do, it is lawful to take as much as they will give you.

Quest. III. May I ask in the market more than my goods are truly worth?

Answ. In the case last mentioned you may; when you are selling to the rich, who are willing to show their generosity, and to make you gainers. But then the honest way is to say, it is worth but so much; but if you will give so much more because I need it, I will take it thankfully. Some think also where the common custom is to ask more than the worth, and people will not buy unless you come down from your first demand, that then you may lawfully ask more, because else there is no trading with such people. My judgment in this case is this, 1. That ordinarily it is better to ask no more at all but a just gain; and that the inconveniences of doing otherwise are greater than any on the other side; for he that heareth you ask unjustly may well think that you would take unjustly if you could get it, and consequently that you are unjust. 2. But this just gain lieth not always just in an indivisible quantity, or determinate price. A man that hath a family to maintain by his trade, may lawfully take a proportionable, moderate gain; though if he take less he may get something too. To be always just at a word is not convenient; for he that may lawfully get two or three shillings or more in the pound of the rich, may see cause to let a poorer person have it for less; but never ask above what it is reasonable to take. 3. And if you once peremptorily said, I will take no less, then it is not fit to go from your word. 4. And if you do meet with such fools or proud gallants, who will not deal with you unless you ask dear, it is just that when they have given you more than it is worth, you tell them so, and offer them the overplus again. And for them that expect that you abate much of your asking, it is an inconvenience to be borne, which will be ever to your advantage when you are once better known.

Quest. IV. How shall the worth of a commodity be judged of?

Answ. 1. When the law setteth a rate upon any thing (as on bread and drink with us) it must be observed. 2. If you go to the market, the market price is much to be observed. 3. If it be in an equal contract, with one that is not in want, you may estimate your goods as they cost you, or are worth to you, though it be above the common price; seeing the buyer is free to take or leave them. 4. But if that which you have to sell be extraordinarily desirable, or worth to some one person more than to you or another man, you must not make too great an advantage of his convenience or desire; but be glad that you can pleasure him, upon equal, fair, and honest terms. 5. If there be a secret worth in your commodity which the market will take no notice of, (as it is usual in a horse,) it is lawful for you to take according to that true worth if you can get it. But it is a false rule of them that think their commodity is worth as much as any one will give.

Quest. V. Is it lawful to make a thing seem better than it is, by trimming, adorning, or setting the best side outward or in sight; or to conceal the faults of what I am to sell?

Answ. It is lawful to dress, polish, adorn, or set out your commodity, to make it seem as it is indeed, but not to make it seem better than it is: except in some very few unusual cases; as if you deal with some fantastical fool, who will not buy it, nor give you the true worth, except it be so set out, and made in some respects to seem better than it is. It is lawful so far to serve their curiosity or humour, as to get the worth of your commodity. But if you do it to get more than the worth by deceiving, it is a sin. And such glossing hath so notable an appearance of deceit, that for that scandal it should be avoided.

2. And as for concealing the fault, the case is the same; you ought not to deceive your neighbour, but to do as you would be done by; and therefore must not conceal any fault which he desireth or is concerned to know. Except it be when you deal with one who maketh a far greater matter of that fault than there is cause, and would wrong you in the price if it were known: yea, and that exception will not hold neither, except in a case when you must needs sell, and they must buy it: because, 1. You may not have another man's money against his will, though it be no more than the thing is worth. 2. Because it will be scandalous when the fault is known by him that buyeth it.

Quest. VI. What if the fault was concealed from me when I bought it, or if I were deceived or over-reached by him that sold it me, and gave more than [834]the worth, may I not repair my loss by doing as I was done by?

Answ. No: no more than you may cut another's purse, because yours was cut; you must do as you would be done by, and not as you are done by. What you may do with the man that deceived you, is a harder question; but doubtless you may not wrong an honest man, because you were wronged by a knave.

Object. But it is taken for granted in the market, that every man will get as much as he can have, and that *caveat emptor* is the only security; and therefore every man trusteth to his own wit, and not to the seller's honesty, and so resolveth to run the hazard.

Answ. It is not so among christians, nor infidels who profess either truth or common honesty. If you come among a company of cut-purses, where the match is made thus, Look thou to thy purse, and I will look to mine, and he that can get most let him take it! then indeed you have no reason to trust another. But there are no tradesmen or buyers who will profess that they look not to be trusted, or say, I will lie or deceive you if I can. Among thieves and pirates such total distrust may be allowed; but among sober persons in civil societies and converse, we must in reason and charity expect some truth and honesty, and not presume them to be all liars and deceivers, that we may seem to have allowance to be such ourselves. Indeed we trust them, not absolutely as saints, but with a mixture of distrust, as fallible and faulty men: and so as to trust our own circumspection above their words, when we know not the persons to be very just. But we have no cause to make a market a place of mere deceit, where every one saith, Trust not me, and I will not trust thee; but let us all take one another for cheats and liars, and get what we can! Such censures savour not of charity, or of just intentions.

Quest. VII. What if I foresee a plenty and cheapness in a time of dearth, which the buyer foreseeth not, (as if I know that there are ships coming in with store of that commodity which will make it cheap,) am I bound to tell the buyer of it, and hinder my own gain?

Answ. There may be some instances in trading with enemies, or with rich men, that regard not such matters, or with men that are supposed to know it as well as you, in which you are not bound to tell them. But in your ordinary equal trading, when you have reason to think that the buyer knoweth it not, and would not give so dear if he knew it, you are bound to tell him; because you must love your neighbour as yourself, and do as you would be done by, and not take advantage of his ignorance.

Quest. VIII. If I foresee a dearth, may I not keep my commodity till then?

Answ. Yes, unless it be to the hurt of the commonwealth; as if your keeping it in be the cause of the dearth, and your bringing it forth would help to prevent it.

Quest. IX. May one use many words in buying and selling?

Answ. You must use no more than are true, and just, and useful: but there are more words needful with some persons who are talkative and unsatisfied than with others.

Quest. X. May I buy as cheap as I can get it, or give less than the thing is worth?

Answ. If it be worth more to you than the market price, (through your necessity,) you are not bound to give above the market price. If it be worth less to you than the market price, you are not bound to give more than it is worth to you, as suited to your use. But you must not desire nor seek to get another's goods or labour for less than it is worth in both these respects (in common estimate, and to you).

Quest. XI. May I take advantage of another's necessity to buy for less than the worth, or sell for more: as e. g. a poor man must needs have money suddenly for his goods, though he sell them but for half the worth; and I have no need of them: am I bound to give him the worth when I have no need? and when it is a great kindness to him to give him any thing in that strait? So also when I have no desire to sell my horse, and another's necessity maketh him willing to give more than he is worth, may I not take it?

Answ. To the first case: you must distinguish between an act of justice and of charity; and between your need of the thing and the worth of it to you. Though you have no need of the poor man's goods, yet if you buy them, both justice and charity require that you give him as much as they are worth to you, though not so much as they are worth in the market: yea, and that you buy them of him in his necessity; for if you give him but what they are worth to you, you are no loser by it; and you should do another good, when it is not to your own hurt or loss. By what they are worth to you, I mean so much as that you be no loser. As, if it be meat or drink, though you have no present need, perhaps you will shortly have need, and if you buy not that, you must buy as much of somewhat else. In strict justice you may be a saver, but not a gainer, by buying of the poor in their necessity. 2. But if you buy a durable commodity for less than it is worth, you should take it but as a pledge, and allow the seller liberty to redeem it if he can, that he may get more after of another. 3. And to the poor in such necessity, charity must be exercised as well as justice. Therefore if you are able to lend them money to save them the loss of underselling, you should do it. (I account that man only able who hath money which no greater service of God requireth.) And if you are not able yourself, you should endeavour to get some others to relieve him, if you can without a greater inconvenience.

And for the second case, it is answered before: you may not take more than it is worth, ever the more for another's necessity; nor in any other case than you might have done it in, if there had been no such necessity of his.

Quest. XII. May I not make advantage of another's ignorance or error in bargaining?

Answ. Not to get more than your commodity is worth, nor to get his goods for less than the worth; no, nor to get the true worth against his will, or with scandal: but if it be only to get a true worth of your own commodity when he is willing, but would be offended if his ignorance in some point were cured, you may so far make use of his ignorance to a lawful end, as is said before in the case of concealing faults.

Quest. XIII. May I strive to get before another, to get a good bargain which he desireth?

Answ. Yes, if you do it not out of a greedy mind, nor to the injury of one that is poorer than yourself: you should rather further the supply of your neighbour's greater needs; otherwise speed and industry in your calling is no fault, nor yet the crossing of a covetous man's desires: you are not bound to let every man have what he would have.

Quest. XIV. May I buy a thing out of another's hand, or hire a servant which another is about or is treating with? Or may I call a chapman from another to buy of me?

[835]*Answ.* There are some cases in which you may not do it, and some in which you may. You may not do it out of a greedy covetousness; nor to the injury of the poor: nor when the other hath gone so far in the bargain that it cannot be honestly broken; for then you injure the third person, and tempt the other to a sin: nor may you do it so as to disturb the due and civil order, which should be among moderate men in trading. And it is a great matter how the thing is accounted of by the custom of the country or market where you bargain; for where it is of ill report, and accounted as unjust, the scandal should make you avoid such a course. But yet in some cases it is lawful, and in some a needful duty. It is lawful when none of the foresaid reasons (or any such other) are against it: it is a duty when charity to the poor or oppressed doth require it. As e. g. a poor man must needs sell his land, his horse, his corn, or goods: a covetous oppressor offereth him less than it is worth. The poor man must take his offer if he can get no more: the oppressor saith that it is injustice for any one to take his bargain out of his hand, or offer money till he have done: in this case it may be a duty, to offer the poor man the worth of his commodity, and save him from the oppressor. A covetous man offereth a servant or labourer less than their service or labour is worth; and will accuse you, if you interrupt his bargain and would offer his servant more: in this case it may be your duty to help the servant to a better master. A chapman is ready to be cheated by an unconscionable tradesman, to give much more for a commodity than its worth: charity may oblige you in such a case to offer it him cheaper. In a word, if you do it for your own gain, in a greedy manner, it is a sin; but if you do it when it is not scandalous or injurious, or do it in charity for another's good, it is lawful, and sometimes a duty.

Quest. XV. May I dispraise another's commodity to draw the buyer to my own?

Answ. This case is sufficiently answered in the former: 1. You may not use any false dispraise: 2. Nor a true one out of covetousness, nor in a scandalous manner. 3. But you may help to save another from a cheater, by opening the deceit in charity to him.

Quest. XVI. What should I do in doubtful cases, where I am uncertain whether the thing be just or not?

Answ. Causeless, perplexing, melancholy scruples, which would stop a man in the course of his duty, are not to be indulged: but in rational doubts, first use your utmost diligence (as much as the nature of the cause requireth) to be resolved; and if yet you doubt, be sure to go the safer way, and to avoid sin rather than loss, and to keep your consciences in peace.

Quest. XVII. If the buyer lose the commodity between the bargain and the payment, (as if he buy your horse, and he die before payment, or presently after,) what should the seller do to his relief?

Answ. If it were by the seller's fault, or by any fault in the horse which he concealed, he is to make the buyer full satisfaction. If it were casually only, rigorous justice will allow him nothing; and therefore if it be either to a man that is rich enough to bear it without any great sense of the loss, or in a case where in common custom the seller always standeth to the loss, mere justice will make him no amends. But if it be where custom makes some abatement judged a duty, or where the person is so poor as to be pinched by the loss, that common humanity, which all good men use in bargaining, which tempereth justice with charity, will teach men to bear their part of the loss; because they must do as they would be done by.

Quest. XVIII. If the thing bought and sold prove afterward of much more worth than was by either party understood, (as in buying of ambergris and jewels it oft falleth out,) is the buyer bound to give the seller more than was bargained for?

Answ. Yes, if it were the seller's mere ignorance and insufficiency in that business which caused him so to undersell it (as if an ignorant countryman sell a jewel or ambergris, who knoweth not what it is, a moderate satisfaction should be made him). But if it were the seller's trade, in which he is to be supposed to be sufficient, and if it be taken for granted beforehand, that both buyer and seller will stand to the bargain whatever it prove, and that the seller would have abated nothing if it had proved less worse than the price, then the buyer may enjoy his gain; much more if he run any notable hazard for it, as merchants use to do.

Quest. XIX. What if the title of the thing sold prove bad, which was before unknown?

Answ. If the seller either knew it was bad, or through his notable negligence was ignorant of it, and did not acquaint the buyer with so much of the uncertainty and danger as he knew, or if it was any way his fault that the buyer was deceived, and not the buyer's fault, he is bound to make him proportionable satisfaction. As also in case that by law or bargain he be bound to warrant the title to the buyer. But not in case that it be their explicit or implicit agreement that the buyer stand to the hazard, and the seller hath done his duty to make him know what is doubtful.

Quest. XX. What if a change of powers or laws do overthrow the title, almost as soon as it is sold, (as it oft falls out about offices and lands,) who must bear the loss?

Answ. The case is near the same with that in quest. xvii. It is supposed that the seller should have lost it himself if he had kept it but a little longer; and that neither of them foresaw the change; and therefore that the seller hath all his money, rather for his good hap, than for his lands or office (which the buyer hath not). Therefore except it be to a rich man that feeleth not the loss, or one that expressly undertook to stand to all hazards, foreseeing a possibility of them, charity and humanity will teach the seller to divide the loss.

The same is the case of London now consumed by fire; where thousands of suits are like to rise between the landlords and the tenants. Where the providence of God (permitting the burning zeal of some papists) hath deprived men of the houses which they had hired or taken leases of, humanity and charity requireth the rich to bear most of the loss, and not to exact their rents or rebuilding from the poor, whatever the law saith, which could not be supposed to foresee such accidents. Love your neighbours as yourselves; do as you would be done by; and oppress not your poor brethren; and then by these three rules you will yourselves decide a multitude of such doubts and difficulties, which the uncharitable only cannot understand.

Tit. 4. Cases of Conscience about Lending and Borrowing.

Quest. I. May a poor man borrow money, who knoweth that he is unable to repay it, and hath no rational proof that he is very likely to be able hereafter?

Answ. No: unless it be when he telleth the lender truly of his case, and he is willing to run the hazard; else it is mere thievery covered with the cheat of [836]borrowing; for the borrower desireth that of another, which he would not lend him, if he expected it not again; and to take a man's money or goods against his will is robbery.

Object. But I am in great necessity.

Answ. Begging in necessity is lawful; but stealing or cheating is not, though you call it borrowing.

Object. But it is a shame to beg.

Answ. The sin of thievish borrowing is worse than shame.

Object. But none will give me if I beg.

Answ. If they will give but to save your life at the present, you must take it, though they give you not what you would have: the poorest beggar's life is better than the thief's.

Object. But I hope God may enable me to pay hereafter.

Answ. If you have no rational way to manifest the soundness of that hope to another, it is but to pretend faith and hope for thievery and deceit.

Object. God hath promised, that those that fear him shall want no good thing. And therefore I hope I may be able to repay it.

Answ. If you want not, why do you borrow? If you have enough to keep you alive by begging, God maketh good all his promises to you; yea, or if you die by famine. For he only promiseth you that which is best; which for aught you know may be beggary or death. God breaketh not promise with his servants who die in common famine, no more than with them who die in plagues or wars. Make not God the patron of sin; yea, and your faith a pretence for your distrust. If you trust God, use no sinful means; if you trust him not, this pleading of his promise is hypocrisy.

Quest. II. May a tradesman drive a trade with borrowed money, when his success, and so his repayment, is utterly an uncertain thing?

Answ. There are some trades where the gain is so exceeding probable, next to certain, as may warrant the borrowing of money to manage them, when there is no rational probability of failing in the payment. And there are some tradesmen, who have estates of their own, sufficient to repay all the money which they borrow. But otherwise, when the money is rationally hazardous, the borrower is bound in conscience to acquaint the lender fully with the hazard, that he may not have it against his will. Otherwise he liveth in constant deceit or thievery. And if he do happen to repay it, it excuseth not his sin.

Quest. III. If a borrower be utterly unable to pay, and so break while he hath something, may he not retain somewhat for his food or raiment?

Answ. No: unless it be in order to set up again in hope to repay his debts: for all that he hath being other men's, he may not take so much as bread to his mouth, out of that which is theirs, without their consent.

Quest. IV. But if a man have bound himself to his wife's friends upon marriage to settle so much upon her or her children, and this obligation was antecedent to his debts, may he not secure that to his wife or children, without any injury to his creditors?

Answ. The law of the land must much decide this controversy. If the propriety be actually before transferred to wife or children, it is theirs, and cannot be taken from them; but if it were done after by a deed of gift to defraud the creditors, then that deed of gift is invalid, till debts be paid. If it be but an obligation and no collation of propriety, the law must determine who is to be first paid; and whether the wife be supposed to run the hazard of gaining or losing with the husband: and though the laws of several countries herein differ, and some give the wife more propriety than others do, yet must they in each place be conscientiously observed, as being the rule of such propriety. But we must see that there be no fraudulent intent in the transaction.

167

Quest. V. May not a tradesman retain somewhat to set up again, if his creditors be willing to compound for a certain part of the debt?

Answ. If he truly acquaint them with his whole estate, and they voluntarily allow him part to himself, either in charity, or in hope hereafter to be satisfied, this is no unlawful course; but if he hide part from them, and make them believe that the rest is all, this is but a thievish procurement of their composition or consent.

Quest. VI. May a borrower lawfully break his day of promised payment, in case of necessity?

Answ. True necessity hath no law: that is, a man is not bound to do things naturally impossible; but if he might have foreseen that necessity, or the doubtfulness of his payment at the day, it was his sin to promise it, unless he put in some limitation, If I be able, and acquainted the lender with the uncertainty. However it be, when the time is come, he ought to go to his creditor, and tell him of his necessity, and desire further time, and endeavour to pay it as soon as he is able: and if he be not able, to make him what satisfaction he can, by his labour, or any other lawful way.

Quest. VII. May I borrow of one to pay another, to keep my day with the first?

Answ. Yes, if you deal not fraudulently with the second, but are able to pay him, or acquaint him truly with your case.

Quest. VIII. Suppose that I have no probability of paying the last creditor, may I borrow of one to pay another, and so live upon borrowing; or must I rather continue in one man's debt?

Answ. If you truly acquaint your creditors with your state, you may do as is most to your convenience. If the first creditor be able and willing rather to trust you longer, than that you should borrow of another to pay him, you may continue his debtor, till you can pay him without borrowing, but if he be either poor or unwilling to bear with you, and another that is able be willing to venture, you may better borrow of another to pay him. But if they be all equally unwilling to stand to any hazard by you, then you must rather continue in the first man's debt, because if you wrong another you will commit another sin: nay, you cannot borrow in such a case, because it is supposed that the other will not lend, when he knoweth your case. And you must not at all conceal it from him.

Object. But it may be my ruin to open my full state to another.

Answ. You must not live upon cheating and thievery to prevent your ruin: and what can it be less to get another man's money against his will, if you hide your case, which if he knew he would not lend it you.

Object. But what if I tell him plainly, that I will pay him certainly by borrowing of another, though I cannot pay him for mine own, and though I be not like to pay the last?

Answ. If you truly thus open your case to every one that you borrow of, you may take it, if they will lend it; for then you have their consent: and it is supposed, that every one is willing to run the hazard of being the last creditor.

Quest. IX. May I lend upon pledges, pawns, or mortgages for my security?

Answ. Yes, so you take not that from a poor man [837]for a pledge, which is necessary to his livelihood and maintenance: as the bed which he should lie on, the clothes which he should wear, or the tools which he should work with; and be not cruel on pretence of mercy.

Quest. X. May I take the forfeiture and keep a pledge or mortgage upon covenants?

Answ. If it be among merchants and rich men, an act of merchandise, and not of mere security for money lent, then it is another case: as if they make a bargain thus, Take this jewel or this land for your money; and it shall be yours if I pay you not at such a day: I am willing to stand to the hazard of uncertainty; if I pay you not, suppose it is for my own commodity, and not through disability. In this case it is lawful to take the forfeiture, or detain the thing. But if it be properly but a pledge to secure the money, then the final intent is but that your money may be repaid; and you may not take the advantage of breaking a day, to take that from another which is none of your own. Justice will allow you only to take so much as your money came to, and to give the overplus (if there be any) to the debtor. And mercy will require you rather to forgive the debt, than to keep a pledge which he cannot spare, but to his ruin and misery, (as his food, his raiment, his tools, his house, &c.) unless you be in as great necessity as he.

Quest. XI. May I take the bond or promise of a third person as security for my money?

Answ. Yes, in case that other be able and willing to be responsible; for you have his own consent; but great caution should be used, that you take no man that is insufficient, from whom mercy forbiddeth you to take it, in case the principal debtor fail; unless you take his suretiship but *in terrorem*, resolving not to take it of him: and also that you faithfully tell the sureties that you must require it of them in case of non-payment, and therefore try whether indeed they are truly willing to pay it: for if they be such as truly presume that you will not take it of them, or will take it ill to be sued for it, you should not take their suretiship, unless you purpose not to seek it (except in necessity).

Quest. XII. Is it lawful to lend upon usury, interest, or increase?

Answ. This controversy hath so many full treatises written on it, that I cannot expect that so few words as I must lay out upon it should satisfy the studious reader. All the disputes about the name of usury I pass by; it being, The receiving any additional gain as due for money lent, which is commonly meant by the word, and which we mean in the question. For the questions, Whether we may bargain for it, or tie the debtor to pay it? Whether we may take it after his gain as partaking in it, or before? Whether we must partake also in the loss, if the debtor be a loser? with other such like, are but subsequent to the main question, Whether any gain (called use) may be taken by the lender as his due for the money lent? My judgment is as followeth.

I. There is some such gain or usury lawful and commendable. II. There is some such gain or usury unlawful and a heinous sin. I shall first give my reasons of the first proposition.

I. If all usury be forbidden it is either by the law of nature, or by some positive law of supernatural revelation: if the latter, it is either by some law of Moses, or by some law of Christ: if the former, it is either as against the rule of piety to God, or against justice or charity to men. That which is neither a violation of the natural laws of piety, justice, or charity; nor against the supernaturally revealed laws of Moses or of Christ, is not unlawful. But there is some usury which is against none of all these; *ergo* there is some usury which is not unlawful.

I will first lay you down the instances of such usury, and then prove it. There is a parcel of land to be sold for a thousand pounds, which is worth forty pounds per annum, and hath wood on it worth a thousand pounds (some such things we have known): John N. is willing to purchase it; but he hath a poor neighbour, T. S. that hath no money, but a great desire of the bargain. J. N. loving his neighbour as himself, and desiring his wealth, lendeth him the thousand pounds upon usury for one year. T. S. buyeth the land, and selleth the wood for the same money, and repayeth it in a year, and so hath all the land for almost nothing; as if J. N. had purchased the land and freely given it him, after a year or two; the gift had been the same.

Object. Here you suppose the seller wronged by selling his land almost for nothing.

Answ. 1. That is nothing at all to the present case, but a different case by itself. 2. I can put many cases in which such a sale may be made without any wrong to the seller: as when it is done by some prince, or state, or noble and liberal person, purposely designing the enriching of the subjects, or after a war, as lately in Ireland. So that the question is, whether J. N. may not give T. S. a thousand or eight hundred pounds' worth of land, taking a year's rent first out of the land, or a year's use for the money, which cometh to the same sum.

169

Another: a rich merchant trading into the East Indies, having five thousand pounds to lay out upon his commodities in traffic, when he hath laid out four thousand five hundred pounds, lendeth in charity the other five hundred pounds to one of his servants to lay out upon a commodity, which when it cometh home will be worth two thousand pounds; and offereth him to secure the carriage with his own; requiring only the use of his money at six per cent. Here the taking of thirty pounds' use, is but the giving him one thousand four hundred and seventy pounds, and is all one with deducting so much of the gift.

Another instance: certain orphans having nothing left them but so much money as will by the allowed use of it find them bread and poor clothing; the guardian cannot lay it out in lands for them; and if he maintain them upon the stock, it will be quickly spent, and he must answer for it: a rich man that is their neighbour tradeth in iron works, (furnaces or forges,) or lead works, or other such commodities, in which he constantly getteth the double of the stock which he employeth, or at least twenty pounds or forty pounds in the hundred; the guardian dare not lend the money to any poor man, lest he break and never be able to pay it; therefore he lendeth it this rich man. And if he have it without usury, the poor orphans give the rich man freely twenty pounds or forty pounds a year, supposing their stock to be a hundred; if he take usury, the rich man doth but give the poor orphans some part of his constant gain.

Another instance: in a city or corporation where there is a rich trade of clothing or making silks, there is a stock of money given by legacy for the poor, and intrusted into the hands of the richest of the city, to trade with and give the poor the use of it: and there is another stock left to set up young beginners, who have not a stock to set up themselves; on condition that they give the third part of their gain to the poor, and at seven years' end resign the stock: the question is, Whether the poor should be without this use of their money, and let [838]the rich go away with it? or whether they may take it?

Now I prove that such usury is not forbidden by God.

1. It is not forbidden us by the law of Moses: (1.) Because Moses's law never did forbid it: for, 1. It is expressly forbidden as an act of unmercifulness; and therefore forbidden only to the poor and to brethren, Exod. xxii. 25; Lev. xxv. 36, 37. Yea, when the poor are not named, it is the poor that are meant; because in that country they did not keep up stocks for merchandise or trading, but lent usually to the needy only: at least the circumstances of the several texts show, that it is only lending to the needy, and not lending to drive on any enriching trades, which is meant where usury is forbidden.[157] 2. And it is expressly allowed to be used to strangers, Deut. xxiii. 19, 20, to whom nothing unjust or uncharitable might be done; only such a measure of charity was not required towards them as unto brethren. And there were more merchants of strangers that traded with them in foreign commodities, than of Jews that fetched them home: so that the prohibition of usury is in the law itself restrained only to their lending to the poor; but in the prophets who do but reprove the sin, it is expressed without that limitation, partly because it supposeth the meaning of the law to be known, which the prophets did but apply, and partly because there was little or no lending used among the Jews, but to the needy as an act of charity.

(2.) And if it had been forbidden in Moses's law only, it would not extend to christians now; because the law of Moses, as such, is not in force: the matter of it is much of the law of nature indeed; but as Mosaical, it was proper to the Jews and proselytes, or at least extended not to the christian gentiles; as is plain in 2 Cor. iii. 7; Gal. iii. 19, 24; v. 3; Ephes. ii. 15; 1 Tim. i. 7; Heb. vii. 12, 16, 19. Moses's law as such never bound any other nations, but the proselytes that joined themselves to the Jews (nor was all the world obliged so to be proselyted as to take up their laws): much less do they bind us that are the servants of Christ, so long after the dissolution of their commonwealth. So much of them as are part of the law of nature, or of any positive law of Christ, or of the civil law of any state, are binding as they are such natural, christian, or civil laws. But not one of them as Mosaical: though the Mosaical law is of great use to help us to understand the law of nature in many particular instances, in which it is somewhat difficult to us.

2. There is no positive law of Christ forbidding all usury: as for Luke vi. 32, 35, it is plainly nothing to the case; for he saith not, Lend, looking for no gain or increase, but looking for nothing again. And the context showeth that the meaning must be one of these two; either, q. d. Lend not only to them that will lend to you again when you are in want; but even to the poor, that you can never hope to borrow of; or else, Lend not only to them that are able to pay you, and where your stock is secured, but to the needy where your money is hazarded; and though they will pay you if they are able, yet you have little or no hope that ever they should be able to repay: lend so, as to be willing to make a gift of it in case the borrower never repay it. And there is no other text that can be pretended against it in the New Testament.

3. And that the law of nature doth not forbid all usury, will appear by examining the several parts of it. The law of nature forbiddeth but three sorts of sins: 1. Those that are against piety to God. 2. Those that are against our own welfare. 3. Those that are against our neighbour's good: and that is, 1. Against justice. 2. Against charity. There is none that falleth not under some of these heads.

1. And that usury is not naturally evil as against piety to God; 2. Or as against ourselves, and our own welfare; I need not prove, because no reason nor reasonable person doth lay any such accusation against it. Though they that think it absolutely unlawful, say that it is consequently against God, as every violation of his law is. But that is nothing to the case.

3. Therefore there is no doubt but the whole controversy is resolved into this last question, Whether all usury be against justice or charity to our neighbour? Justice obligeth me to give him his own; charity obligeth me to give him more than his own, in certain cases, as one that love him as myself. That which is not against justice, may be against charity; but that which is against charity, is not always against justice strictly taken. And that which is an act of true charity, is never against justice; because he that giveth his neighbour more than his own, doth give him his own and more. There is a usury which is against justice and charity; there is a usury which is against charity, but not against mere justice; and there is a usury which is against neither justice nor charity. If I prove it charitable it is superfluous to say more.

All the instances before given are notoriously charitable. That which is for the preservation of the lives and comforts of the poor, and of orphans, or for the enriching of my neighbour, is an act of charity; but such is some usury, past all doubt, as is before declared. Where the contrary is an act of cruelty, the usury is not against charity, but for it. For the rich to deny to the poor and orphans a part of that gain, which they make by the improvement of their own money, is oppression and cruelty; if it be cruel to let a beggar die or starve, when we should feed and clothe him of our own; much more to let the poor and orphans starve and perish rather than give them the increase of their own, or part of it at least. As for them that say, It may be as well improved otherwise, they are unexperienced men; it is a known falsehood as to the most, though some few may meet with such opportunities. At least it is nothing to them that cannot have other ways of improving it; who are very many.

Moreover, when it is not an act of charity, yet it may be not against charity in these cases: 1. When the lender is poor and the borrower rich; yea, it may be a sin to lend it freely. "He that oppresseth the poor to increase his riches, and he that gives to the rich, shall surely come to want," Prov. xxii. 16. It is a giving to the rich to lend freely that money which they improve to the increase of their riches. 2. When the lender is not obliged to that act of charity, though the borrower be poorer than himself. Which falleth out in a hundred cases; and may be comprised under this one general, When the lender is obliged to expend that same money in some other greater, better work: as at the same time while a man that is worth but twenty pounds a year, is in debt to a man that hath a thousand pounds a year, there may be a hundred or a

171

thousand poor people worth nothing, ready to perish, whom the rich is rather bound to succour, than him that hath but twenty pounds a year. And there may be works of piety (as to set up a school, or promote the preaching of the gospel) which may be as great as either. [839]And the richest that is, cannot do all the good that is to be done, nor relieve all the persons that are in want; therefore when he must leave much undone, if he would give all his substance, it is (*cæteris paribus*) a sin, to give that to a man that can make shift without it, and pass by a hundred in much deeper necessity and distress; so that he who either exerciseth charity in his usury, or doth nothing against charity and justice, certainly sinneth not by that usury. For all the scriptures which speak against usury, speak against it as a cruel or uncharitable thing.

Object. But it is sometimes necessary for a law to forbid that which otherwise would be good, when it cannot be done, without encouraging others to a greater evil; such as ordinary usury is; and then that law must be observed.

Answ. This is true *in thesi*, that such cases there are; but it is unproved and untrue in this case; for, 1. There is no such law. 2. There is no such reason or necessity of such a law. For God can as well make laws against unrighteous or uncharitable increase or usury, without forbidding that which is charitable and just, as he can make laws against unrighteous or uncharitable buying or selling without condemning that which was good and just; or as he can forbid gluttony, drunkenness, idleness, pride, without forbidding eating, drinking, apparel, or riches. He can easily tell men of whom and in what case to take use, and when not.

He that would see all other objections answered, and the case fully handled, hath many treatises on both sides extant to inform him.

II. That there is a sort of usury which is evil I know of no man that doubteth, and therefore need not stand to prove.

Quest. When is usury sinful?

Answ. As is before said, When it is against either justice or charity. 1. When it is like cheating bargaining, which under pretence of consent and a form of justice doth deceive or oppress, and get from another that which is not truly ours but his. 2. When you lend for increase where charity obligeth you to lend freely; even as it is a sin to lend expecting your own again, when charity obligeth you to give it. 3. When you uncharitably exact that which your brother is disabled utterly to pay, and use cruelty to procure it (be it the use or the principal). 4. When you allow him not such a proportion of the gain as his labour, hazard, or poverty doth require; but because the money is yours, will live at ease upon his labours. 5. When in case of his losses you rigorously exact your due without that abatement, or forgiving debts, (whether use or principal,) which humanity and charity require. In a word, when you are selfish, and do not as, according to true judgment, you may desire to be done by, if you were in his case.

Quest. But when am I bound to exercise this charity in not taking use?

Answ. As I said before, 1. Whenever you have no more urgent, and necessary, and excellent work, to lay out that money on, which you are so to receive. 2. Yea, though another work may be in itself better, (as to relieve many poorer, better men with that money,) yet when you cannot take it, without the utter undoing of the debtor, and bringing him into as bad a case, as any single person whom you would relieve, it is the safer side to leave the other unrelieved, (unless it be a person on whom the public good much dependeth,) rather than to extort your own from such a one to give another. Because that which you cannot get without a scandalous appearance of cruelty, is *quoad jus in re* not yours to give, till you can better get possession of it; and therefore God will not expect that you should give it to another.

In all this I imply that as you must prefer the lives of others in giving alms, before your own conveniences and comforts, and must not say, I cannot spare it, when your necessity may spare it, though not your pleasure; so also in taking use of those that you are bound to show charity to, the same rule and proportions must be observed in your charity.

Note also, that in all this it appeareth, that the case is but gradually different, between taking the use and taking the principal. For when the reason for remitting is the same, you are as well bound to remit the principal as the use.

But this difference there is, that many a man of low estate may afford to lend freely to a poorer man for a little time, who cannot afford to give it. And prudence may direct us to choose one man to lend freely to for a time, because of his sudden necessity, when yet another is fitter to give it to.

Quest. XIII. Is lending a duty? If so, must I lend to all that ask me, or to whom?

Answ. Lending is a duty, when we have it, and our brother's necessity requireth it, and true prudence telleth us, that we have no better way to lay it out, which is inconsistent with that. And therefore rich men ordinarily should both lend and give as prudence shall direct. But there is an imprudent and so a sinful lending: as, 1. When you will lend that which is another's, and you have no power to lend. 2. When you lend that which you must needs require again, while you might easily foresee that the borrower is not like to pay. Lend nothing but what you have either great probability will be repaid, or else which you are willing to give in case the debtor cannot or will not pay; or at least when suing for it will not have scandalous and worse effects than not lending. For it is very ordinary when you come to demand it and sue for it, to stir up the hatred of the debtor against you, and to make him your enemy, and to break his charity by your imprudent charity; in such a case, if you are obliged to relieve him, give him so much as you can spare, rather than lend him that which you cannot spare, but must sue for. In such cases, if charity go not without prudence, nor prudence without charity, you may well enough see when to lend, and how much.

Quest. XIV. Is it lawful to take upon usury in necessity, when the creditor doth unjustly or unmercifully require it?

Answ. Not in case that the consequents (by encouraging sin or otherwise) be like to do more hurt, than the money will do you good. Else, it is lawful when it is for your benefit; as it is lawful to take part of your wages for your work, or part of the worth of your commodity, when you cannot have the whole; and as it is lawful to purchase your rights of an enemy, or your life of a thief; as is aforesaid. A man may buy his own benefit of an unrighteous man.

Quest. XV. Doth not contracting for a certain sum of gain, make usury to be in that case unlawful, which might lawfully be taken of one that is free?

Answ. Yes, in case that contracting determine an uncertain case without sufficient cause: as if you agree, that whether the borrower gain or lose, and be poor or rich, I will have so much gain; that is, whether it prove merciful or unmerciful, I will have it. But then in that case, if it so prove unmerciful, it may not be taken without contracting, if freely offered. No contract may tie the debtor to that which is against justice or charity; and no contract may absolutely require that which may prove uncharitable; [840]unless there be a tacit condition or exception of such a case implied. Otherwise I see no scripture or reason, why a contract altereth the case, and may not be used to secure that increase which is neither unrighteous nor unmerciful: it may be the bond of equity, but not of iniquity. As in case of a certain gain by the borrower, a certain use may be contracted for; and in case of uncertain gain to the borrower, a conditional contract may be made. Yea, in case of merchandise, where men's poverty forbiddeth not such bargains, I see not but it is lawful to sell a greater uncertain gain, for a smaller certain gain; and so to make the contracts absolute (as Amesius Cas. Consc. on this question showeth). As all oppression and unmercifulness must be avoided, and all men must do as they would (judiciously) be done by; so it is a bad thing to corrupt religion, and fill the world with causeless scruples, by making that a sin which is no sin. Divines that live in great cities and among merchandise, are usually fitter judges in this case, than those that live more obscurely (without experience) in the country.

Tit. 5. Cases of Conscience about Lusory Contracts.

173

Quest. 1. Is it lawful to lay wagers upon the credit or confidence of one another's opinions or assertions in discourse? As e. g. I will lay you so much that I am in the right?

Answ. Yes, if these three things concur: 1. That the true end of the wager is, to be a penalty to him that shall be guilty of a rash and false assertion, and not to gratify the covetousness of the other. 2. That it be no greater a sum than can be demanded and paid, without breach of charity, or too much hurt to the loser (as above the proportion of his error). 3. That it be no other but what both parties are truly willing to stand to the loss of, if either of them lose, and that beforehand they truly seem so willing to each other.

Quest. II. Is it lawful to lay wagers upon horseraces, dogs, hawks, bear-baitings, or such games as depend upon the activity of beast or man?

Answ. Yes, upon the two last expressed conditions; and, 3. That it be not an exercise which is itself unlawful, by cruelty to beasts, or hazard to the lives of men, (as in fencing, running, wrestling, &c. it may fall out if it be not cautelously done,) or by the expense of an undue proportion of time in them, which is the common malignity of such recreations.

Quest. III. May I lawfully give money to see such sports, as bear-baitings, stage-plays, masks, shows, puppet-plays, activities of man or beast? &c.

Answ. There are many shows that are desirable and laudable, (as of strange creatures, monsters, rare engines, activities, &c.) the sight of which it is lawful to purchase, at a proportionable price; as a prospect through one of Galileo's tubes or such another, is worth much money to a studious person. But when the exercise is unlawful, (as all stage-plays are that ever I saw, or had just information of; yea, odiously evil; however it is very possible that a comedy or tragedy might with abundance of cautions be lawfully acted,) it is then (usually) unlawful to be a spectator either for money or on free cost. I say, (usually,) because it is possible that some one that is necessitated to be there, or that goeth to find out their evil to suppress them, or that is once only induced to know the truth of them, may do it innocently; but so do not they, who are present voluntarily and approvingly. 3. And if the recreation be lawful in itself, yet when vain persons go thither to feed a carnal fancy and vicious humour, which delighteth more in vanity, than they delight in piety, and when it wasteth their time and corrupteth their minds, and alienateth them from good, or hindereth duty, it is to them unlawful.

Quest. IV. Is it lawful to play at cards or dice for money, or at any lottery?[158]

Answ. The greatest doubt is, whether the games be lawful, many learned divines being for the negative, and many for the affirmative; and those that are for the affirmative lay down so many necessaries or conditions to prove them lawful, as I scarce ever yet saw meet together; but if they be proved at all lawful, the case of wagers is resolved as the next.

Quest. V. May I play at bowls, run, shoot, &c. or use such personal activities for money?

Answ. Yes, 1. If you make not the game itself bad, by any accident. 2. If your wager be laid for sport, and not for covetousness (striving who shall get another's money, and give them nothing for it). 3. And if no more be laid than is suitable to the sport, and the loser doth well and willingly pay.

Quest. VI. If the loser who said he was willing, prove angry and unwilling when it cometh to the paying, may I take it, or get it by law against his will?

Answ. No, not in ordinary cases: because you may not turn a sport to covetousness, or breach of charity; but in case that it be a sport that hath cost you any thing, you may in justice take your charges, when prudence forbids it not.

Tit. 6. Cases of Conscience about Losing and Finding.

Quest. I. If I find money or any thing lost, am I bound to seek out the owner, if he seek not after me? and how far am I bound to seek him?

Answ. You are bound to use such reasonable means, as the nature of the case requireth, that the true owner may have his own again. He that dare keep another man's money, because he findeth it, it is like would steal, if he could do it as secretly. Finding gives you no propriety, if the owner can be found: do as you would be done by, and you may satisfy your conscience. If nearer inquiry will not serve, you are bound to get it cried in the market, or proclaimed in the church, or mentioned in the Curranto's that carry weekly news, or any probable way, which putteth you not upon unreasonable cost or labour.

Quest. II. May I take any thing for the finding of it, as my due?

Answ. You may demand so much as shall pay for any labour or cost which you have been at about it, or finding out the owner. But no more as your due; though a moderate gratuity may be accepted, if he freely give it.

Quest. III. May I desire to find money or any thing else in my way? or may I be glad when I have found it?

Answ. You should first be unwilling that your neighbour should lose it, and be sorry that he hath lost it; but supposing that it be lost, you may moderately desire that you may find it rather than another; not with a covetous desire of the gain; but that you may faithfully gratify the owner in restoring it, or if he cannot be found may dispose of it as you ought. And you should be more sorry that it is lost, than glad that you find it, except for the owner.

Quest. IV. If no owner can be found, may I not take it and use it as mine own?

Answ. The laws of the land do usually regulate claims of propriety in such matters. Where the law giveth it to the lord of the manor, it is his, and you must give it him. Where it giveth it to no other, it is his that findeth it; and occupancy will give him [841]propriety. But so as it behoveth him to judge, if he be poor, that God's providence ordered it for his own supply; but if he be rich, that God sent it him but as to his steward, to give it to the poor.

Quest. V. If many be present when I find it, may I not wholly retain it to myself; or may I not conceal it from them if I can?

Answ. If the law overrule the case, it must be obeyed; but if it do not, you may, if you can, conceal it, and thereby become the only finder, and take it as your own, if the owner be not found: but if you cannot conceal it at the time of finding, they that see it with you, are partly the finders as well as you; though perhaps the largest share be due to the occupant.

Quest. VI. If I trust my neighbour or servant with money or goods, or if another trust me, who must stand to the loss if they be lost?

Answ. Here also the law of the land as regulating proprieties must be very much regarded; and especially the true meaning of the parties must be understood: if it was antecedently the expressed or implied meaning that one party in such or such a case should bear the loss, it must in strict justice be according to the true meaning of the parties. Therefore if a carrier that undertaketh to secure it, loseth it, he loseth it to himself. Or if one that it is lent to on that condition (explicit or implicit) lose it, it is to himself. But if a friend to whom you are beholden for the carriage, lose it, who undertook no more than to bestow his labour, the loss must be yours; yea, though it was his negligence or drunkenness that was the fault; for you took him and trusted him as he is. But if a servant, or one obliged to do it by hire, do without any other agreement, only undertake to serve you in it, and loseth it, the law or custom of the country is instead of a contract; for if the law or custom lay the loss on him, it is supposed that he consented to it in consenting to be your servant; if it lay it on you, it is supposed that you took your servant on such terms of hazard. But if it be left undecided by law and custom, you may make your servant pay only so much as is a proportionable penalty for his fault, but no more, as any satisfaction for your loss; except you agreed with him to repay such losses as were by his default. And when it is considered what strict justice doth require, it must also be considered what charity and mercy do require, that the poor be not oppressed.

175

Quest. I. Is it lawful to put oneself, or servants, especially young unestablished apprentices, into temptations of an infidel country, (or a popish,) for the getting of riches, as merchants do?[159]

Answ. This cannot be truly answered without distinguishing, 1. Of the countries they go from. 2. Of the places they go to. 3. Of the quality of the persons that go. 4. Of the causes of their going.

I. Some countries that they go from may be as bad as those that they go to, or in a state of war, when it is better to be absent, or in a time of persecution, or at least of greater temptation than they are like to have abroad. And some are contrarily as a paradise in comparison of those they go to, for holiness and helps to heaven, and for peace and opportunities of serviceableness to God and the public good.

II. Some countries which they may go to, may have as good helps for their souls as at home, if not by those of the religion of the nation, yet by christians that live among them, or by the company which goeth with them; or at least there may be no great temptations to change their religion, or debauch them, either through the civility and moderation of those they live among, or through their sottish ignorance and viciousness, which will rather turn men's hearts against them. But some countries have so strong temptations to corrupt men's understandings through the subtlety of seducers, and some have such allurements to debauch men, and some such cruelties to tempt them to deny the truth, that it is hard among them to retain one's innocency.

III. Some that go abroad are understanding, settled christians, able to make good use of other men's errors, and sins, and ill examples or suggestions, and perhaps to do much good on others; but some are young, and raw, and unexperienced, whose heads are unfurnished of those evidences and reasons by which they should hold fast their own profession against the cunning reasonings of an adversary, and their hearts are unfurnished of that love to truth, and that serious resolution, which is necessary to their safety, and therefore are like to be corrupted.

IV. Some are sent by their princes as agents or ambassadors on employments necessary to the public good; and some are sent by societies on business necessary to the ends of the society; and some go in case of extreme poverty and necessity, having no other way of maintenance at home; and some go in obedience to their parents and masters that command it them; and some go to avoid the miseries of a war, or the danger of a sharp persecution at home, or the greater temptations of a debauched or seducing age, or some great temptations in their families. But some go for fancy, and some for mere covetousness, without need.

By these distinctions the case may be answered by men that are judicious and impartial. As,

I. *Affirm.* 1. It is lawful for ambassadors to go among infidels, that are sent by princes and states; because the public good must be secured.

2. It is lawful for the agents of lawful societies or trading companies to go (*cæteris paribus*, the persons being capable); because trade must be promoted, which tendeth to the common good of all countries.

3. It is not only lawful, but one of the best works in the world, for fit persons to go on a design to convert the poor infidels and heathens where they go. Therefore the preachers of the gospel should not be backward to take any opportunity, as chaplains to ambassadors, or to factories, &c. to put themselves in such a way.

4. It is lawful for a son or servant (whose bonds extend to such a service) to go in obedience to a superior's command; and God's special protection may be trusted in a way of obedience.

5. It is lawful for one in debt to go, that hath probable hopes that way and no other to pay his debts. Because he is a defrauder if he detain other men's money, while a lawful way of repaying it may be taken.

176

6. It is lawful for a duly qualified person to go in case of extreme poverty, to be able to live in the world; and that poverty may be called extreme to one that was nobly born and educated, which would be no poverty to one that was bred in beggary.

7. It is lawful for a well qualified person, who desireth riches to serve God, and to do good with, to go in a way of trading, though he be in no poverty or necessity himself. Because God's blessing on a [842]lawful trade may be desired and endeavoured, and he that should do all the good he can, may use what lawful means he can to be enabled to do it. And other men's wants should be to us as our own, and therefore we may endeavour to be able to relieve them.

8. In a time of such civil war, when a man knoweth not which side to take, it may be better for some men to live abroad; yea, among infidels.

9. There is little to dissuade a man whose trade leadeth him into a country that is better than his own, or so sottish as to have small temptation, and that hath the company of faithful christians, with which he may openly worship God, and privately converse to his spiritual edification.

10. In urgent cases one may go for a time, where he can have no use of public church worship, so be it he have private means and opportunities of holy living.

11. It is lawful on less occasions to leave one's own country in a time of debauchery, when temptations at home are greater than those abroad, or in a time of such persecution as may lawfully be avoided, than at another time.

12. A settled christian may go more safely, and therefore lawfully, on smaller urgencies, than a young, raw, lustful, fanciful, unsettled novice may.

II. *Neg.* 1. It is not lawful for any one to seek riches or trade abroad or at home, principally for the love of riches, to raise himself and family to fulness, prosperity, or dignity: though all this may be desired when it is a means to God's service and honour, and the public good, and is desired principally as such a means.

2. It is not lawful to go abroad, especially into infidel or popish countries, without such a justifiable business, whose commodity will suffice to weigh down all the losses and dangers of the remove.

3. The dangers and losses of the soul are to be valued much above those of the body and estate, and cannot be weighed down by any mere corporal commodity.

4. It is less dangerous usually to go among Turks and heathens, (whose religion hath no tempting power to seduce men,) than among Socinians or papists, whose errors and sins are cunningly and learnedly promoted and defended.

5. It is not lawful for merchants or others for trade and love of wealth or money, to send poor raw, unsettled youths into such countries where their souls are like to be notably endangered, either by being deprived of such teaching and church helps which they need, or by being exposed to the dangerous temptations of the place; because their souls are of more worth than money.

6. It is not lawful therefore for master or servant to venture his own soul in such a case as this last mentioned; that is, so far as he is free, and without necessity doth it only for commodity sake.

7. We may not go where we cannot publicly worship God, without necessity, or some inducement from a greater good.

8. The more of these hinderances concur the greater is the sin: it is therefore a mere wilful casting away of their own souls, when unfurnished, unsettled youths (or others like them) shall for mere humour, fancy, or covetousness leave such a land as this, where they have both public and private helps for their salvation, and to go among papists, infidels, or heathens, where talk or ill example is like to endanger them, and no great good can be expected to countervail such a hazard, nor is there any true necessity to drive them, and where they cannot publicly worship God, no, nor openly own the truth, and where they have not so much as any private company to converse with, that is fit to further their preservation and salvation, and all this of their own accord, &c.

Quest. II. May a merchant or ambassador leave his wife, to live abroad?

Answ. 1. We must distinguish between what is necessitated, and what is voluntary. 2. Between what is done by the wife's consent, and what is done without. 3. Between a wife that can bear such absence, and one that cannot. 4. Between a short stay, and a long or continued stay.

1. The command of the king, or public necessities, may make it lawful, except in a case so rare as is not to be supposed (which therefore I shall not stand to describe). For though it be a very tender business to determine a difference between the public authority or interest, and family relations and interest, when they are contradictory and unreconcilable, yet here it seemeth to me, that the prince and public interest may dispose of a man contrary to the will and interest of his wife; yea, though it would occasion the loss, 1. Of her chastity. 2. Or her understanding. 3. Or her life: and though the conjugal bond do make man and wife to be as one flesh. For, 1. The king and public interest may oblige a man to hazard his own life, and therefore his wife's. In case of war, he may be sent to sea, or beyond sea, and so both leave his wife (as Uriah did) and venture himself. Who ever thought that no married man might go to foreign wars without his wife's consent? 2. Because as the whole is more noble than the part, so he that marrieth obligeth himself to his wife, but on supposition that he is a member of the commonwealth, to which he is still more obliged than to her.

2. A man may for the benefit of his family leave his wife for travel or merchandise, for a time, when they mutually consent upon good reason that it is like to be for their good.

3. He may not leave her either without or with her own consent, when a greater hurt is like to come by it, than the gain will countervail. I shall say no more of this, because the rest may be gathered from what is said in the cases about duties to wives, where many other such are handled.

Quest. III. Is it lawful for young gentlemen to travel in other kingdoms, as part of their education?[160]

Answ. The many distinctions which were laid down for answer of the first question, must be here supposed, and the answer will be mostly the same as to that, and therefore need not be repeated.

1. It is lawful for them to travel that are necessarily driven out of their own country, by persecution, poverty, or any other necessitating cause.

2. It is lawful to them that are commanded by their parents (unless in former excepted cases, which I will not stay to name).

3. It is the more lawful when they travel into countries as good or better than their own, where they are like to get more good than they could have done at home.

4. It is more lawful to one that is prudent and firmly settled both in religion, and in sobriety and temperance, against all temptations which he is like to meet with, than to one that is unfurnished for a due resistance of the temptations of the place to which he goeth.

5. It is more lawful to one that goeth in sober, wise, and godly company, or is sent with a wise and faithful tutor and overseer, than to leave young, unsettled persons to themselves.

[843]6. In a word, it is lawful when there is a rational probability, that they will not only get more good than hurt, (for that will not make it lawful,) but also more good than they could probably have other ways attained.

II. But the too ordinary course of young gentlemen's travels out of England now practised, I take to be but a most dangerous hazarding, if not a plain betraying them to utter undoing, and to make them afterwards the plagues of their country, and the instruments of the common calamity. For, 1. They are ordinarily sent into countries far worse and more dangerous than their own, where the temptations are stronger than they are fit to deal with; into some countries where they are tempted to sensuality, and into some where they are tempted to popery or infidelity. In some countries they learn to drink wine instead of beer; and arising from the smaller sort to the stronger, if they turn not drunkards, they contract that appetite to wine and strong drink, which shall prove (as Clemens Alexandrinus calleth gluttony and tippling) a throat-madness, and a belly-devil, and keep them in the sin of gulosity all their days. And in some countries they shall learn the art of gluttony, to pamper their guts in curious, costly, uncouth fashions, and to dress themselves in novel, fantastical garbs, and to make a business of adorning themselves, and setting themselves forth with proud and procacious fancies and affections, to be looked upon as comely persons to the eyes of others. In some countries they shall learn to waste their precious hours in stage-plays, and vain spectacles, and ceremonies, attendances, and visits, and to equalize their life with death, and to live to less use and benefit to the world than the horse that carrieth them. In most countries they shall learn either to prate against godliness, as the humour of a few melancholy fools, and be wiser than to believe God, or obey him, or be saved; or at least to grow indifferent and cold in holy affections and practices: for when they shall see papists and protestants, Lutherans and Calvinists, of contrary minds, and hear them reproaching and condemning one another, this cooleth their zeal to all religion, as seeming but a matter of uncertainty and contention. And when they also see how the wise and holy are made a scorn in one country, as bigots and Hugonots, and how the protestants are drunkards and worldlings in another country, and how few in the world have any true sense and savour of sound and practical religion, and of a truly holy and heavenly life, (as those few they are seldom so happy as to converse with,) this first accustometh them to a neglect of holiness, and then draweth their minds to a more low, indifferent opinion of it, and to think it unnecessary to salvation. For they will not believe that so few shall be saved as they find to be holy in the world; and then they grow to think it but a fancy and a troubler of the world.

And it addeth to their temptation, that they are obliged by the carnal ends which drew them out, to be in the worst and most dangerous company and places, that is, at princes' courts, and among the splendid gallantry of the world; for it is the fashions of the great ones which they must see, and of which when they come home they must be able to discourse: so that they must travel to the pest-houses of pomp, and lust, of idleness, gluttony, drunkenness, and pride, of atheism, irreligiousness, and impiety, that they may be able to glory what acquaintance they have got of the grandeur and gallantry of the suburbs of hell, that they may represent the way to damnation delectable and honourable to others, as well as to themselves.[161]

But the greatest danger is of corrupting their intellectuals, by converse with deceivers where they come; either infidels, or juggling Jesuits and friars: for when those are purposely trained up to deceive, how easy is it for them to silence raw and unfurnished novices, (yea, even when all their five senses must be captivated, in the doctrine of transubstantiation)! And when they are silenced they must yield: or at least they have deluding stories enough of the antiquity, universality, infallibility, unity of their church, with a multitude of lies of Luther, Calvin, Zuinglius, and other reformers, to turn their hearts and make them yield. But yet that they may be capable of doing them the more service, they are instructed for a time to dissemble their perversion, and to serve the Roman pride and faction in a protestant garb and name.

Especially when they come to Rome, and see its glory, and the monuments of antiquity, and are allured with their splendour and civilities, and made to believe that all the reports of their inquisitions and cruelties are false, this furthereth the fascination of unexperienced youths.

2. And usually all this while the most of them lay by all serious studies, and all constant employment, and make idleness and converse with the idle or with tempters, to be their daily work. And what a mind is like to come to, which is but one half year or twelve months accustomed to idleness, and to vain spectacles, and to a pleasing converse with idle and luxurious persons, it is easy for a man of any acquaintance with the world or with human nature to conjecture.

3. And they go forth in notable peril of their health or lives. Some fall into fevers, and die by change of air and drinks: some fall into quarrels in taverns, or about

their whores, and are murdered. Some few prove so stedfast against all the temptations of the papists, that it is thought conducible to the holy cause that they should be killed in pretence of some quarrel, or be poisoned. Some by drinking wine do contract such sickness, as makes their lives uncomfortable to the last. And the brains of many are so heated by it, that they fall mad.

4. And all this danger is principally founded in the quality of the person sent to travel; which are ordinarily empty lads, between eighteen and twenty-four years of age, which is the time of the devil's chief advantage; when naturally they are prone to those vices which prove the ruin of the most, though you take the greatest care of them that you can.[162] 1. Their lust is then in the highest and most untamed rage. 2. Their appetites to pleasing meats and drinks are then strongest. 3. Their frolicsome inclinations to sports and recreations are then greatest. 4. And ignorant and procacious pride beginneth then to stir. 5. All things that are most vile and vain, are then apt to seem excellent to them, by reason of the novelty of the matter as to them, who never saw such things before, and by reason of the false esteem of those carnal persons, to whose pomp, and consequently to whose judgment, they would be conformed. 6. And they are at that age exceedingly inclined to think all their own apprehensions to be right, and to be very confident of their own conceptions, and wise in their own eyes; because their juvenile intellect being then in the most affecting activity, it seemeth still clear and sure to them, because it so much affects themselves. 7. But above all, they are yet unfurnished of almost all that solid wisdom, and [844]settled holiness, and large experience, which is most necessary to their improvement of their travels, and to their resistance of all these temptations. Alas! how few of them are able to deal with a Jesuit, or hold fast their religion against deceivers! If the very vices, the ambition, the carnal policies and pomps, the filthiness and worldliness of the Roman clergy, did not become a preservative to men's minds against the temptations which would draw them to their way, and if the atheism, infidelity, whoredoms, and profaneness of papists did not become antidotes, how few were like to return uninfected! And because the Jesuits know that they can never take this stumblingblock out of the way, therefore too many of them have thought best to debauch those first whom they would proselyte, and reconcile them first to plays, and drunkenness, and whoredoms, that so the dislike of these may not hinder their reconciliation with the kingdom of Rome; yea, that a seeming necessity of a priest's pardon, may make it seem necessary to become their subjects.

And as unfurnished are these young travellers usually to resist the temptations to this sensuality, lust, and pomp, as those of popery; so that they are perfidiously sent into a pest-house, when they are in the greatest disposition to be infected. And if they come not home drunkards, gluttons, gamesters, idle, prodigal, proud, infidels, irreligious, or papists, it is little thanks to those perfidious parents, who thus perform their promise for them in baptism, by sending them to Satan's schools and university to be educated.

Whereas if they were but kept to their due studies, and under a holy government at home, till they were furnished with sound religious knowledge, and till they were rooted in holiness, and in love to a pious, sober life, and till they had got a settled hatred of intemperance and all sin, and till they had a map of the places, persons, and affairs of the world well imprinted on their minds by study and due information, then necessary travel would be more safe; and then they would be in a capacity to learn wisdom from other men's folly, and virtue from other men's vice, and piety from other men's impiety; which novices are rather apt to imitate.

5. And in the mean time the loss of all the helps which they should have at home, doth greatly tend to their destruction. For they oft travel into countries, where they shall have no public worship of God which is lawful, or which they understand; or if they have, it is usually cold preaching and dull praying, when they have need of the best, and all too little. And they have seldom such pious society to edify and quicken them by private converse, as they have, or might have, here at home; and

seldom come into such well ordered, religious families. And if human nature be prone to infection by temptations, and so averse to holiness, that all means is too little, and even in the best families folly and sensuality, and a distaste of godliness, often thrive; (as unsown weeds overspread the garden, where with great cost and labour only better things were sowed;) what then but sin and misery can be expected from those that by their own parents are banished from their native country (not so well as into a wilderness, but) into the pestilent, infected countries of the world.

I would ask those parents that plead for this crime and cruelty as a kindness; are you no wiser or better yourselves than the company into which you send your children? Can you teach them and educate them no better, nor give them better examples, than they are like to have abroad? Can you set them on no better work, for the improvement of their time? If not, why do you not repent of this your shame and misery, and reform yourselves? If you can, why will you then betray your children? Or if you cannot, are there no schools, no learned and pious men, no religious families and company at home, in your own land, where you might place them to better advantage, than thus to expose them to the tempter? Undoubtedly there are; and such as may be had at cheaper rates.[163]

6. And it is not the smallest part of the guilt and danger, that they are sent abroad without due oversight and conduct. They that do but get them some sober or honest servant to attend them, or some sober companion, think they have done well; whenas they had need of some divine or tutor of great learning, piety, prudence, and experience, whom they will reverence and obey, that may take the oversight of them, and be ready to answer any sophist that would seduce them. But the charge of this is thought too great for the safety of their own children, whom they themselves expose to a necessity of it.

I know that carnal minds will distaste all this, and have objections enough against it, and reasons of their own, to make it seem a duty to betray and undo their children's souls, and to break their promise made for them in baptism: "All this is but our preciseness: they must have experience and know the world, or else they will be contemptible *tenebriones* or owls! Whenever they go it will be a temptation, and such they must have at home. There is no other part of their age so fit, or that can be spared, and we must trust God with them wherever they are; and they that will be bad, will be bad in one place as well as another; and many are as bad that stay at home." And thus *quos perdere vult Jupiter hos dementat*; yea, the poor children and commonwealth must suffer for such parents' sottish folly. And well saith Solomon, "The rich man is wise in his own conceit," Prov. xxviii. 11. And because it is not reason indeed but pride, and the rich disease and carnality which is here to be confuted, I shall not honour them with a distinct, particular answer; but only tell them, If all companies be alike, send them to Bedlam or to a whorehouse. If all means be alike, let them be janizaries, and bred up where Christ is scorned: if you think they need but little helps, and little watching, it seems you never gave them more. And it is a pity you should have children, before you know what a man is, and how much nature is corrupted, and how much is needful to its recovery. And it is a pity that you dedicated them to God in baptism, before you believed Christ, and knew what you did, and engaged them to renounce the world, the flesh, and the devil, under a crucified Christ, while you purposed like hypocrites to train them in the school and service of the world, the flesh, and the devil, and in the contempt of the cross of Christ, or of a holy, mortified life. And if all ages be alike, and novices be equal to experienced persons, let the scholars rule their master, and let boys be parliament men and judges, and let them be your guides at home! And if acquaintance with courtship and the customs of the world, and the reputation of such acquaintance, be worth the hazarding of their souls, renounce God, and give up your names to Mammon, and be not such paltry hypocrites, as to profess that you believe the Scriptures, and stand to your baptismal vows, and place your hopes in a crucified Christ, and your happiness in God's favour and the life to come. And if the preaching of the gospel, and all such religious helps, be unnecessary to your unsettled children, dissemble not by going to church, as if [845]you took them to be necessary to yourselves. In a word, I say as Elias to the Israelites, "Why halt ye between two opinions? If God be God, follow him." If the world be God, and pride and sensuality and the world's applause be your felicity, follow it, and let it be your children's portion. Do you not see more wise, and learned, and holy, and serviceable persons among us, proportionably, in church and state, that were never sent for an education among the papists and profane, than of such as were?

But I will proceed to the directions which are necessary to those that must or will needs go abroad, either as merchants, factors, or as travellers.

Direct. I. Be sure that you go not without a clear warrant from God; which must be (all things laid together) a great probability, in the judgment of impartial, experienced, wise men, that you may get or do more good than you were like to have done at home. For if you go sinfully without a call or warrant, you put yourself out of God's protection, as much as in you is; that is, you forfeit it: and whatever plague befalls you, it will arm your accusing consciences to make it double.

Direct. II. Send with your children that travel, some such pious, prudent tutor or overseer as is afore described: and get them or your apprentices into as good company as possibly you can.

Direct. III. Send them as the last part of all their education, when they are settled in knowledge, sound doctrine, and godliness, and have first got such acquaintance with the state of the world, as reading, maps, and conversation and discourse can help them to: and not while they are young, and raw, and uncapable of self-defence, or of due improving what they see. And those that are thus prepared, will have no great lust or fancy to wander, and lose their time, without necessity; for they will know, that there is nothing better (considerably) to be seen abroad, than is at home; that in all countries, houses are houses, and cities are cities, and trees are trees, and beasts are beasts, and men are men, and fools are fools, and wise men are wise, and learned men are learned, and sin is sin, and virtue is virtue; and these things are but the same abroad as at home: and that a grave is every where a grave, and you are travelling towards it, which way ever you go. And happy is he that spendeth his little time so, as may do God best service, and best prepare him for the state of immortality.

Direct. IV. If experience of their youthful lust and pride, and vicious folly, or unsettled dangerous state, doth tell you plainly, that your child or apprentice is unfit for travel, venture them not upon it, either for the carnal ornaments of education, or for your worldly gain. For souls that cost the blood of Christ, are more precious than to be sold at so low a rate; and especially by those parents and masters that are doubly obliged to love them, and to guide them in the way to heaven, and must be answerable for them.

Direct. V. Choose those countries for your children to travel in, which are soundest in doctrine and of best example, and where they may get more good than hurt; and venture them not needlessly into the places and company of greatest danger; especially among the Jesuits and friars, or subtle heretics, or enemies of Christ.

Direct. VI. Study before you go, what particular temptations you are like to meet with, and study well for particular preservatives against them all: as you will not go into a place infected with the plague, without an antidote. It is no small task, to get a mind prepared for travel.

Direct. VII. Carry with you such books as are fittest for your use, both for preservation and edification: as to preserve you from popery, Drelincourt's and Mr. Pool's small Manual: for which use my "Key for Catholics," and "Safe Religion," and "Sheet against Popery" may not be useless. And Dr. Challoner's "Credo Ecclesiam Catholicam" is short and very strong. To preserve you against infidelity, "Vander Meulin," in Latin, and Grotius; and in English my "Reasons of the Christian Religion" may not be unfit. For your practice, the Bible and the "Practice of Piety," and Mr.

Scudder's "Daily Walk," and Mr. Reyner's "Directions," and Dr. Ames's "Cases of Conscience."

Direct. VIII. Get acquaintance with the most able reformed divines, in the places where you travel; and make use of their frequent converse, for your edification and defence. For it is the wisest and best men in all countries where you come, that must be profitable to you, if any.

Direct. IX. Set yourselves in a way of regular study if you are travellers, as if you were at home, and on a course of regular employment if you are tradesmen, and make not mere wandering and gazing upon novelties your trade and business; but redeem your time as laboriously as you would do in the most settled life. For time is precious, wherever you be; and it must be diligence every where that must cause your proficiency; for place and company will not do it without your labour. It is not a university that will make a sluggish person wise, nor a foreign land that will furnish a sensual sot with wisdom: *Cælum non animum mutant qui trans mare currunt.* There is more ado necessary to make you wise, or bring you to heaven, than to go long journeys, or see many people.

Direct. X. Avoid temptations: if you acquaint yourselves with the humours, and sinful opinions, and fashions of the time and places where you are, let it be but as the Lacedemonians called out their children to see a drunkard, to hate the sin; therefore see them, but taste them not, as you would do by poison or loathsome things. Once or twice seeing a folly and sin is enough. If you do it frequently, custom will abate your detestation, and do much to reconcile you to it.

Direct. XI. Set yourselves to do all the good you can to the miserable people in the places where you come. Furnish yourselves with the aforesaid books and arguments, not only to preserve yourselves, but also to convince poor infidels and papists. And pity their souls, as those that believe that there is indeed a life to come, where happiness and misery will show the difference between the godly and the wicked. Especially merchants and factors, who live constantly among the poor ignorant christians, Armenians, Greeks, papists, who will hear them; and among heathens (in Indostan and elsewhere) and Mahometans (especially the Persians, who allow a liberty of discourse). But above all, the chaplains of the several embassies and factories. Oh what an opportunity have they to sow the seeds of christianity among the heathen nations! and to make known Christ to the infidel people where they come! And how heavy a guilt will lie on them that shall neglect it! And how will the great industry of the Jesuits rise up in judgment against them and condemn them!

Direct. XII. The more you are deprived of the benefit of God's public worship, the more industrious must you be, in reading Scripture and good books, and in secret prayer and meditation, and in the improvement of any one godly friend that doth accompany you to make up your loss, and to be instead of public means. It will be a great comfort among infidels, [846]or papists, or ignorant Greeks, or profane people, to read sound, and holy, and spiritual books, and to confer with some one godly friend, and to meditate on the sweet and glorious subjects, which from earth and heaven are set before us; and to solace ourselves in the praises of God, and to pour out our suits before him.

Direct. XIII. And that your work may be well done, be sure that you have right ends; and that it be not to please a ranging fancy, nor a proud, vain mind, nor a covetous desire of being rich or high, that you go abroad; but that you do it purposely and principally to serve God abroad, and to be able to serve him the better when you come home, with your wit, and experience, and estates. If sincerely you go for this end, and not for the love of money, you may expect the greater comfort.[164]

Direct. XIV. Stay abroad no longer than your lawful ends and work do require: and when you come home, let it be seen that you have seen sin that you might hate it; and that by the observation of the errors and evils of the world, you love sound doctrine, spiritual worship, and holy, sober, and righteous living, better than you did before; and that you are the better resolved and furnished for a godly, exemplary, fruitful life.

One thing more I will warn some parents of, who send their sons to travel, to keep them from untimely marrying, lest they have part of their estate too soon: that there are other means better than this, which prudence may find out: if they would keep them low, from fulness and idleness, and bad company, (which a wise, self-denying, diligent man may do, but another cannot,) and engage them to as much study and business (conjunct) as they can well perform, and when they must needs marry, let it be done with prudent, careful choice; and learn themselves to live somewhat lower, that they may spare that which their son must have: this course would be better than that hazardous one in question.

[156] Whether the consequent be good or hurt is like to be greater, must be well considered.

[157] Exod. xx. 21, "Thou shalt neither vex a stranger, nor oppress him." Exod. xxiii. 9, "Thou shalt not oppress a stranger," &c. So that usury to a stranger was no oppression.

[158] Of recreations, see before.

[159] Leg. Steph. Vinan. Pigh. in Hercule prodigo, pag. 130-132. Cui peregrinatio dulcis est, non amat patriam: si dulcis est patria, amara est peregrinatio. August.

[160] Lege Eurycic. Pateani Orat. 9.

[161] Read Bishop Hall's "Quo Vadis" on this subject.

[162] Peregrinatio levia tædia quædam animorum et veluti nauseas tollit: non tollit morbos qui altius penetrarunt, quam ut externa ulla medicina huc pertingat. Id. ib.

[163] Congressus sapientum confert prudentiam: non montes, non maria. Erasm.

[164] Peregrinatio omnis obscura et sordida est iis quorum industria in patria potest esse illustris. Cicer.

CHAPTER XX.

DIRECTIONS AGAINST OPPRESSION.
Tit. 1. Motives and Directions against Oppression.

OPPRESSION is the injuring of inferiors, who are unable to resist, or to right themselves; when men use power to bear down right. Yet all is not oppression which is so called by the poor, or by inferiors that suffer; for they are apt to be partial in their own cause as well as others. There may be injustice in the expectations of the poor, as well as the actions of the rich. Some think they are oppressed, if they be justly punished for their crimes; and some say they are oppressed, if they have not their wills, and unjust desires, and may not be suffered to injure their superiors: and many of the poor do call all that oppression, which they suffer from any that are above them, as if it were enough to prove it an injury, because a rich man doth it: but yet oppression is a very common and a heinous sin.[165]

There are as many ways of oppressing others, as there are advantages to men of power against them. But the principal are these following.

1. The most common and heinous sort is the malignant injuries and cruelties of the ungodly against men that will not be as indifferent in the matters of God and salvation as themselves; and that will not be of their opinions in religion, and be as bold with sin, and as careless of their souls, as they. These are hated, reproached, slandered, abused, and some way or other persecuted commonly wherever they live throughout the world. But of this sort of oppression I have spoken before.

2. A second sort is the oppression of the subjects by their rulers; either by unrighteous laws, or cruel executions, or unjust impositions or exactions, laying on the people greater taxes, tributes, or servitude, than the common good requireth, and than

they are able well to bear. Thus did Pharaoh oppress the Israelites, till their groans brought down God's vengeance on him. But I purposely forbear to meddle with the sins of magistrates.

3. Soldiers also are too commonly guilty of the most inhuman, barbarous oppressions; plundering the poor countrymen, and domineering over them, and robbing them of the fruit of their hard labours, and of the bread which they should maintain their families with, and taking all that they can lay hold on as their own. But (unless it be a few that are a wonder in the world) this sort of men are so barbarous and inhuman, that they will neither read nor regard any counsel that I shall give them. (No man describeth them better than Erasmus.)

4. The oppression of servants by their masters I have said enough to before; and among us, where servants are free to change for better masters, it is not the most common sort of oppression; but rather servants are usually negligent and unfaithful, because they know that they are free (except in the case of apprentices).

5. It is too common a sort of oppression for the rich in all places to domineer too insolently over the poor, and force them to follow their wills, and to serve their interest be it right or wrong: so that it is rare to meet with a poor man that dare displease the rich, though it be in a cause where God and conscience do require it. If a rich man wrong them, they dare not seek their remedy at law, because he will tire them out by the advantage of his friends and wealth; and either carry it against them, be his cause never so unjust, or lengthen the suit till he hath undone them, and forced them to submit to his oppressing will.

6. Especially unmerciful landlords are the common and sore oppressors of the countrymen: if a few men can but get money enough to purchase all the land in a country, they think that they may do with their own as they list, and set such hard bargains of it to their tenants, that they are all but as their servants, yea, and live a more troublesome life than servants do: when they have laboured hard all the year, they can scarce scrape up enough to pay their landlord's rent; their necessities are so urgent, that they have not so much as leisure to pray morning or evening in their families, or to read the Scriptures, or any good book; nor scarce any room in their thoughts for any holy things: their minds are so distracted with necessities and cares, that even on the Lord's day, or at a time of prayer, they can hardly keep their minds intent upon the sacred work which they have in hand. If the freest minds have much ado to keep their thoughts in seriousness and order, in meditation, or in the worshipping of God; how hard must it needs be to a poor oppressed man, whose body is tired with wearisome labours, and his mind distracted with continual cares, how to pay his [847]rent, and how to have food and raiment for his family! How unfit is such a troubled, discontented person, to live in thankfulness to God, and in his joyful praises! Abundance of the voluptuous great ones of the world, do use their tenants and servants but as their beasts, as if they had been made only to labour and toil for them, and it were their chief felicity to fulfil their will, and live upon their favour.

Direct. I. The principal means to overcome this sin, is to understand the greatness of it. For the flesh persuadeth carnal men to judge of it according to their selfish interest, and not according to the interest of others, nor according to the true principles of charity and equity; and so they justify themselves in their oppression.

1. *Consid.* That oppression is a sin not only contrary to christian charity and self-denial, but even to humanity itself. We are all made of one earth, and have souls of the same kind: there is as near a kindred betwixt all mankind, as a specifical identity; as between one sheep, one dove, one angel, and another: as between several drops of the same water, and several sparks of the same fire; which have a natural tendency to union with each other. And as it is an inhuman thing for one brother to oppress another, or one member of the same body to set up a proper interest of its own, and make all the rest, how painfully soever, to serve that private interest; so it is for those men who are children of the same Creator. Much more for them who account

185

themselves members of the same Redeemer, and brethren in Christ by grace and regeneration, with those whom they oppress. Mal. ii. 10, "Have we not all one Father? Hath not one God created us? Why do we deal treacherously every man against his brother, by profaning the covenant of our fathers?" If we must not lie to one another, because we are members one of another, Eph. iv. 25; and if all the members must have the same care of one another, 1 Cor. xii. 25; surely then they must not oppress one another.

2. An oppressor is an antichrist and an antigod: he is contrary to God, who delighteth to do good, and whose bounty maintaineth all the world; who is kind to his enemies, and causeth his sun to shine and his rain to fall on the just and on the unjust: and even when he afflicteth doth it as unwillingly, delighteth not to grieve the sons of men.[166] He is contrary to Jesus Christ, who gave himself a ransom for his enemies, and made himself a curse to redeem them from the curse, and condescended in his incarnation to the nature of man, and in his passion to the cross and suffering which they deserved: and being rich and Lord of all, yet made himself poor, that we by his poverty might be made rich. He endured the cross and despised the shame, and made himself as of no reputation, accounting it his honour and joy to be the Saviour of men's souls, even of the poor and despised of the world. And these oppressors live as if they were made to afflict the just, and to rob them of God's mercies, and to make crosses for other men to bear, and to tread on their brethren as stepping-stones of their own advancement. The Holy Ghost is the Comforter of the just and faithful. And these men live as if it were their calling to deprive men of their comfort.

3. Yea, an oppressor is not only the agent of the devil, but his image: it is the devil that is the destroyer, and the devourer, who maketh it his business to undo men, and to bring them into misery and distress. He is the grand oppressor of the world: yet in this he is far short of the malignity of men-devils, 1. That he doth it not by force and violence, but by deceit, and hurteth no man till he hath procured his own consent to sin; whereas our oppressors do it by their brutish force and power. 2. And the devil destroyeth men, who are not his brethren, nor of the same kind; but these oppressors never stick at the violating of such relations.

4. Oppression is a sin that greatly serveth the devil, to the damning of men's souls, as well as to the afflicting of their bodies. And it is not a few, but millions, that are undone by it. For as I showed before, it taketh up men's mind and time so wholly, to get them a poor living in the world, that they have neither mind nor time for better things. They are so troubled about many things, that the one thing needful is laid aside. All the labours of many a worthy, able pastor, are frustrated by oppressors: to say nothing of the far greatest part of the world, where the tyranny and oppression of heathen infidels and Mahometan princes, keepeth out the gospel, and the means of life; nor yet of any other persecutors: if we exhort a servant to read the Scriptures, and call upon God, and think of his everlasting state, he telleth us that he hath no time to do it, but when his weary body must have rest. If we desire the masters of families to instruct and catechise their children and servants, and pray with them, and read the Scriptures and other good books to them, they tell us the same, that they have no time, but when they should sleep; and that on the Lord's day their tired bodies, and careful minds, are unfit to attend and ply such work: so that necessity quieteth their conscience in their ignorance and neglect of heavenly things, and maketh them think it only the work of gentlemen and rich men, who have leisure (but are further alienated from it by prosperity, than these are by their poverty): and thus oppression destroyeth religion, and the people's souls as well as their estates.

5. Oppression further endangereth both the souls of men, and the public peace, and the safety of princes, by tempting the poor multitude into discontents, sedition, and insurrections. Every man is naturally a lover of himself above other: and the poor, as well as the rich and rulers, have an interest of their own which ruleth them; and they will hardly honour, or love, or think well of them by whom they suffer. It is as natural almost for a man under oppression, to be discontented and complain, as for a man in

a fever to complain of sickness, heat, and thirst. No kingdom on earth is so holy and happy as to have all or most of the subjects such confirmed, eminent saints, as will be contented to be undone, and will love and honour those that undo them. Therefore men must be taken as they are. If "oppression maketh wise men mad," Eccles. vii. 7, much more the multitude, who are far from wisdom. Misery maketh men desperate, when they think that they cannot be much worse than they are. How many kingdoms have been thus fired (as wooden wheels will be when one part rubbeth too hard and long upon the other)! Yea, if the prince be never so good and blameless, the cruelty of the nobles and the rich men of the land, may have the same effects. And in these combustions, the peace of the kingdom, the lives and souls of the seditious, are made a sacrifice to the lusts of the oppressors.

Direct. II. Consider with fear how oppression turneth the groans and cries of the poor to the God of revenge against the oppressors. And go to that man that hath the tears and prayers of oppressed innocents, sounding the alarm to the vindictive justice, to awake for their relief. "And shall not God avenge his own elect, which cry day and night to [848]him, though he bear long with them? I tell you, that he will avenge them speedily," Luke xviii. 7, 8. "The Lord will be a refuge to the oppressed," Psal. ix. 9. "To judge the fatherless and the oppressed, that the man of the earth may no more oppress," Psal. x. 18. "The Lord executeth righteousness and judgment for all that are oppressed," Psal. ciii. 6; cxlvi. 7. Yea, God is doubly engaged to be revenged upon oppressors, and hath threatened a special execution of his judgment against them above most other sinners: partly as it is an act of mercy and relief to the oppressed; so that the matter of threatening and vengeance to the oppressor, is the matter of God's promise and favour to the sufferers: and partly as it is an act of his vindictive justice against such as so heinously break his laws. The oppressor hath indeed his time of power, and in that time the oppressed seem to be forsaken and neglected of God; as if he did not hear their cries: but when his patience hath endured the tyranny of the proud, and his wisdom hath tried the patience of the sufferers, to the determined time; how speedily and terribly then doth vengeance overtake the oppressors, and make them warnings to those that follow them! In the hour of the wicked and of the power of darkness Christ himself was oppressed and afflicted, Isa. liii. 7, and "in his humiliation his judgment was taken away," Acts viii. But how quickly did the destroying revenge overtake those bloody zealots, and how grievous is the ruin which they lie under to this day, which they thought by that same murder to have escaped! Solomon saith, Eccl. iv. 1, he "considered all the oppressions that are under the sun, and behold the tears of such as were oppressed, and they had no comforter; and on the side of the oppressors there was power, but they had no comforter." Which made him praise the dead and the unborn. But yet he that goeth with David into the sanctuary, and seeth the end of the oppressors, shall perceive them set in slippery places, and tumbling down to destruction in a moment, Psal. xxxvii.; lxxiii. The Israelites in Egypt seemed long to groan and cry in vain; but when the determinate time of their deliverance came, God saith, "I have surely seen the affliction of my people, and have heard their cry by reason of their task-masters; for I know their sorrows: and I am come down to deliver them.—Behold, the cry of the children of Israel is come up unto me, and I have also seen the oppression wherewith the Egyptians oppress them," Exod. iii. 7-9. Deut. xxvi. 5, 6, "The Egyptians evil entreated us, and laid upon us hard bondage, and when we cried to the Lord God of our fathers, the Lord heard our voice, and looked on our affliction, and our labour, and our oppression." See Psal. cvii. 39-42. So Psal. xii. 5, 6, "For the oppression of the poor, for the sighing of the needy, now will I arise, saith the Lord; I will set him in safety from him that puffeth at him (or would insnare him). Thou shalt keep them, O Lord, thou shalt preserve them from this generation for ever." "Trust not therefore in oppression," Psal. lxii. 10. For God is the avenger, and his plagues shall revenge the injuries of the oppressed.

Direct. III. Remember what an odious name oppressors commonly leave behind them upon earth. No sort of men are mentioned by posterity with greater hatred and contempt. For the interest of mankind directeth them hereunto, and may prognosticate it, as well as the justice of God. However the power of proud oppressors may make men afraid of speaking to their faces what they think, yet those that are out of their reach, will pour out the bitterness of their souls against them. And when once death hath tied their cruel hands, or any judgment of God hath cast them down, and knocked out their teeth, how freely will the distressed vent their grief! and fame will not be afraid to deliver their ugly picture to posterity, according to their desert. Methinks therefore that even pride itself should be a great help to banish oppression from the world. What an honourable name hath a Trajan, a Titus, an Antonine, an Alexander Severus! And what an odious name hath a Nero, a Caligula, a Commodus, a D'Alva, &c.! Most proud men affect to be extolled, and to have a glorious name survive them when they are dead; and yet they take the course to make their memory abominable; so much doth sin contradict and disappoint the sinner's hopes!

Direct. IV. Be not strangers to the condition or complaints of any that are your inferiors. It is the misery of many princes and nobles, that they are guarded about with such as keep all the lamentations of their subjects and tenants from their ears; or represent them only as the murmurings of unquiet, discontented men; so that superiors shall know no more of their inferiors' case than their attendants please; nor no more of the reproach that falleth upon themselves. Their case is to be pitied; but the case of their inferiors more (for it is their own wilful choice which hath imprisoned their understandings, with such informers; and it is their unexcusable negligence, which keepeth them from seeking truer information). A good landlord will be familiar with the meanest of his tenants, and will encourage them freely to open their complaints, and will labour to inform himself who is in poverty and distress, and how it cometh to pass; that when he hath heard all, he may understand whether it be his own oppression or his tenants' fault that is the cause: when proud, self-seeking men disdain such inferior converse, and if they have servants that do but tell them their tenants have a good bargain, and are murmuring, unthrifty, idle persons, they believe them without any more inquiry, and in negligent ignorance oppress the poor.

Direct. V. Mortify your own lusts and sinful curiosity, which maketh you think that you need so much, as tempteth you to get it by oppressing others. Know well how little is truly necessary! and how little nature (well-taught) is contented with! and what a privilege it is to need but little! Pride and curiosity are an insatiable gulf. Their daily trouble seemeth to them a necessary accommodation. Such abundance must be laid out on superfluous recreations, buildings, ornaments, furniture, equipage, attendants, entertainments, visitations, braveries, and a world of need-nots, (called by the names of handsomeness, cleanliness, neatness, conveniences, delights, usefulness, honour, civilities, comeliness, &c.) So much doth carnal concupiscence, pride, and curiosity thus devour, that hundreds of the poor must be oppressed to maintain it; and many a man that hath many score or hundred tenants who with all their families daily toil to get him provision for his fleshly lusts, doth find at the year's end, that all will hardly serve the turn, but this greedy devourer could find room for more; when one of his poor tenants could live and maintain all his family comfortably, if he had but so much as his landlord bestoweth upon one suit of clothes, or one proud entertainment, or one horse, or one pack of hounds. I am not persuading the highest to level their garb and expenses equal with the lowest; but mortify pride, curiosity, and gluttony, and you will find less need to oppress the poor, or to feed your concupiscence with the sweat and groans of the afflicted.

Direct. VI. Be not the sole judge of your own [849]actions in a controverted case; but if any complain of you, hear the judgment of others that are wise and impartial in the case. For it is easy to misjudge where self-interest is concerned.

188

Direct. VII. Love your poor brethren as yourselves, and delight in their welfare as if it were your own. And then you will never oppress them willingly; and if you do it ignorantly, you will quickly feel it and give over upon their just complaint; as you will quickly feel when you hurt yourselves, and need no great exhortation to forbear.

Tit. 2. Cases of Conscience about Oppression, especially of Tenants.

Quest. I. Is it lawful for a mean man, who must needs make the best of it, to purchase tenanted land of a liberal landlord, who setteth his tenants a much better pennyworth than the buyer can afford.

Answ. Distinguish, 1. Between a seller who understandeth all this, and one that doth not. 2. Between a tenant that hath by custom a half-title to his easier rent, and one that hath not. 3. Between a tenant that consenteth and one that consenteth not. 4. Between buying it when a liberal man might else have bought it, and buying it when a worse else would have bought it. 5. Between a case of scandal and of no scandal.

And so I answer, 1. If the landlord that selleth it expect that the buyer do use the tenants as well as he hath done, and sell it accordingly, it is unrighteous to do otherwise (ordinarily). 2. In many countries it is the custom not to turn out a tenant, nor to raise his rent; so that many generations have held the same land at the same rent; which though it give no legal title, is yet a half-title in common estimation. In such a case it will be scandalous, and infamous, and injurious, and therefore unlawful to purchase it with a purpose to raise the rent, and to do accordingly. 3. In case that a better landlord would buy it, who would use the tenant better than you can do, it is not (ordinarily) lawful for you to buy it. I either express or imply "ordinarily" in most of my solutions; because that there are some exceptions lie against almost all such answers, in extraordinary cases; which the greatest volume can scarce enumerate.

But if, 1. It be the seller's own doing to withdraw his liberality so far from his tenants, as to sell his land on hard rates, on supposition that the buyer will improve it. 2. And if it be a tenant that cannot either by custom or any other plea, put in a claim in point of equity to his easy-rented land. 3. And if as bad a landlord would buy it if you do not. 4. If it be not a real scandal: I say if all these four concur; 5. Or (alone) if the tenant consent freely to your purchase on these terms; then it is no injury. But the common course is, for a covetous man that hath money, never to consider what a loser the tenant is by his purchase, but to buy and improve the land at his own pleasure; which is no better than oppression.

Quest. II. May not a landlord take as much for his land as it is worth?

Answ. 1. Sometimes it is land that no man can claim an equitable title to hold upon an easier rent, and sometimes it is otherwise, as aforesaid, by custom and long possession, or other reasons. 2. Sometimes the tenant is one that you are obliged to show mercy to; and sometimes he is one that no more than commutative justice is due to. And so I answer, 1. If it be an old tenant who by custom or any other ground, can claim an equitable title to his old pennyworth, you may not enhance the rent to the full worth. 2. If it be one that you are obliged to show mercy as well as justice to, you may not take the full worth. 3. The common case in England is, that the landlords are of the nobility or gentry, and the tenants are poor men, who have nothing but what they get by their hard labour out of the land which they hold; and in this case some abatement of the full worth is but such a necessary mercy, as may be called justice. Note still, that by the full worth, I mean, so much as you could set it for to a stranger who expecteth nothing but strict justice, as men buy and sell things in a market.

But, 1. If you deal with a tenant as rich or richer than yourself, or with one that needeth not your mercy, or is no fit object of it; 2. And if it be land that no man can by custom claim equitably to hold on lower terms, and so it is no injury to another, nor just scandal, then you may lawfully raise it to the full worth. Sometimes a poor man setteth a house or land to a rich man, where the scruple hath no place.

Quest. III. May a landlord raise his rents, though he take not the full worth?

Answ. He may do it when there is just reason for it, and none against it. There is just reason for it when, 1. The land was much underset before. 2. Or when the land is proportionably improved. 3. Or when the plenty of money maketh a greater sum to be in effect no more than a lesser heretofore. 4. Or when an increase of persons, or other accident, maketh land dearer than it was. But then it must be supposed, 1. That no contract, 2. Nor custom, 3. Nor service and merit, do give the tenant any equitable right to his better pennyworth. And also that mercy prohibit not the change.

Quest. IV. How much must a landlord set his land below the full worth, that he may be no oppressor, or unmerciful to his tenants?

Answ. No one proportion can be determined of; because a great alteration may be made in respect to the tenant's ability, his merit, to the time and place, and other accidents. Some tenants are so rich, as is said, that you are not bound to any abatement. Some are so bad, that you are bound to no more than strict justice and common humanity to them. Some years (like the last, when a longer drought than any man alive had known, burnt up the grass) disableth a tenant to pay his rent; some countries are so scarce of money, that a little abatement is more than in another place; but ordinarily the common sort of tenants in England should have so much abated of the fullest worth, that they may comfortably live on it, and follow their labours with cheerfulness of mind, and liberty to serve God in their families, and to mind the matters of their salvation, and not to be necessitated to such toil, and care, and pinching want, as shall make them liker slaves than freemen, and make their lives uncomfortable to them, and make them unfit to serve God in their families, and seasonably mind eternal things.

Quest. V. What if the landlord be in debt, or have some present want of money, may he not then raise the rent of those lands that were underlet before?

Answ. If his pride pretend want where there is none, (as to give extraordinary portions with his daughters, to erect sumptuous buildings, &c.) this is no good excuse for oppression. But if he really fall into want, then all that his tenants hold as mere free gifts from his liberality, he may withdraw (as being no longer able to give). But that which they had by custom an equitable title to, or by contract also a legal title to, he may not withdraw. (And yet all this is his sin, if he brought that poverty culpably on himself; it is his sin in the cause, though, supposing that cause, the raising of his rent be lawful.) But it is not every debt in a rich man, who [850]hath other ways of paying it, which is a true necessity in this case; and if a present debt made it necessary only at that time, it is better (by fine or otherwise) make a present supply, than thereupon to lay a perpetual burden on the tenants, when the cause is ceased.

Quest. VI. What if there be abundance of honest people in far greater want than my tenants are, (yea, perhaps preachers of the gospel,) and I have no other way to relieve them unless I raise my rents; am I not bound rather to give to the best and poorest, than to others?

Answ. Yes, if it were a case that concerned mere giving; but when you must take away from one to give to another, there is more to be considered in it. Therefore in these two cases at least you may not raise your tenants' rents to relieve the best or poorest whosoever: 1. In case that he have some equitable title to your land, as upon the easier rent. 2. Or in case that the scandal of seeming injustice or cruelty, is like to do more hurt to the interest of religion and men's souls, than your relieving the poor with the addition would do good (which a prudent man by collation of probable consequents may satisfactorily discern): but if it were not only to preserve the comforts, but to save the lives of others in their present famine, nature teacheth you to take that which is truly your own, both from your tenants, and your servant, and your own mouths, to relieve men in such extreme distress; and nature will teach all men to judge it your duty, and no scandalous oppression. But when you cannot relieve the ordinary wants of the poor, without such a scandalous raising of your rents as will do more harm than your alms would do good, God doth not then call you to give such alms; but you are to be supposed to be unable.

Quest. VII. May I raise a tenant's rent, or turn him out of his house, because he is a bad man; by a kind of penalty?

Answ. A bad man hath a title to his own, as well as a good man; and therefore if he have either legal or equitable title, you may not; nor yet if the scandal of it is like to do more hurt, than the good can countervail which you intend. Otherwise you may either raise his rent, or turn him out, if he be a wicked, profligate, incorrigible person, after due admonition; yea, and you ought to do it, lest you be a cherisher of wickedness. If the parents under Moses's law were bound to accuse their own son to the judges in such a case, and say, "This our son is stubborn and rebellious; he will not obey our voice; he is a glutton and a drunkard; and all the men of the city must stone him till he die, to put away evil from among them," Deut. xxi. 18-21; then surely a wicked tenant is not so far to be spared, as to be cherished by bounty in his sin. It is the magistrate's work to punish him by governing justice; but it is your work as a prudent benefactor, to withhold your gifts of bounty from him. And I think it is one of the great sins of this age, that this is not done, it being one of the noblest means imaginable to reform the land, and make it happy: if landlords would thus punish or turn out their wicked, incorrigible tenants it would do much more than the magistrate can do. The vulgar are most effectually ruled by their interest, as we rule our dogs and horses more by the government of their bellies than by force. They will most obey those on whom they apprehend their good or hurt to have most dependence. If landlords would regard their tenants' souls, so much as to correct them thus for their wickedness, they would be the greatest benefactors and reformers of the land; but alas, who shall first reform the landlords? and when may it be hoped that many or most great men will be such?

Quest. VIII. May one take a house over another's head, (as they speak,) or take the land which he is a tenant to, before he be turned out of possession?

Answ. Not out of a greedy desire to be rich, nor coveting that which is another's; nor yet while he is any way injured by it; nor yet when the act is like to be so scandalous, as to hurt men's souls more than it will profit your body. If you come with the offer of a greater rent than he can give, or than the landlord hath just cause to require of him, to get it out of his hands by over-bidding him, this is mere covetous oppression. But in other cases it is lawful to take the house and land which another tenant hath possession of: as, 1. In case that he willingly leave it, and consent. 2. Or if he unwillingly (but justly) be put out; and another tenant must be provided against the time that he is to be dispossessed. 3. Yea, if he be unjustly put out, if he that succeeded him have no hand in it, nor by his taking the house or land do promote the injury, nor scandalously countenance injustice. For when a tenement is void, though by injury, it doth not follow, that no man may ever live in it more: but if the title be his that is turned out, then you may not take it of another; because you will possess another man's habitation. But if it should go for a standing rule, that no man may in any case take a house over another man's head, (as country people would have it,) then every man's house and land must be long untenanted, to please the will of every contentious or unjust possessor; and any one that hath no title, or will play the knave, may injure the true owner at his pleasure.

Quest. IX. May a rich man put out his tenants, to lay their tenements to his own demesnes, and so lay house to house, and land to land?

Answ. In two cases he may not: 1. In case he injure the tenant that is put out, by taking that from him which he hath right to, without his satisfaction and consent. 2. And in case it really tend to the injury of the commonwealth, by depopulation, and diminishing the strength of it. Otherwise it is lawful; and done in moderation by a pious man may be very convenient; 1. By keeping the land from beggary through the multitudes of poor families that overset it. 2. By keeping the more servants, among whom he may keep up a better order and more pious government in his own house, (making it as a church,) than can be expected in poor families; and his servants will (for soul and body) have a much better life, than if they married and had families, and small tenements of their own; but in a country that rather wanteth people, it is otherwise.

Quest. X. May one man be a tenant to divers tenements?

Answ. Yes, if it tend not, 1. To the wrong of any other; 2. Nor to depopulation, or to hinder the livelihood of others, while one man engrosseth more than is necessary or meet; for then it is unlawful.

Quest. XI. May one man have many trades or callings?

Answ. Not when he doth, in a covetous desire to grow rich, disable his poor neighbours to live by him on the same callings, seeking to engross all the gain to himself; nor yet when they are callings which are inconsistent; or when he cannot manage one aright, without the sinful neglect of the other. But otherwise it is as lawful to have two trades as one.

Quest. XII. Is it lawful for one man to keep shops in several market towns?

Answ. The same answer will serve as to the foregoing question.

[165] In omni certamine qui opulentior est, etiamsi accipit injuriam, tamen quia plus potest, facere videtur. Sallust. in Jugurth.

[166] Psa. cxlv.; Matt. v.; Lam. iii.

[851]

CHAPTER XXI.

CASES ABOUT, AND DIRECTIONS AGAINST, PRODIGALITY AND SINFUL WASTEFULNESS.

BECAUSE men's carnal interest and sensuality is predominant with the greatest part of the world, and therefore governeth them in their judgment about duty and sin, it thence cometh to pass that wastefulness and prodigality are easily believed to be faults, so far as they bring men to shame or beggary, or apparently cross their own pleasure or commodity: but in other cases, they are seldom acknowledged to be any sins at all; yea, all that are gratified by them, account them virtues, and there is scarce any sin which is so commonly commended; which must needs tend to the increase of it, and to harden men in their impenitency in it; and verily if covetousness, and selfishness or poverty, did not restrain it in more persons than true conscience doth, it were like to go for the most laudable quality, and to be judged most meritorious of present praise and future happiness. Therefore in directing you against this sin, I must first tell you what it is; and then tell you wherein the malignity of it doth consist: the first will be best done in the definition of it, and enumeration of the instances, and examination of each one of them.

Direct. I. Truly understand what necessary frugality, or parsimony, and sinful wastefulness are.

What necessary frugality is.

Necessary frugality or sparing is an act of fidelity, obedience, and gratitude, by which we use all our estates so faithfully for the chief Owner, so obediently to our chief Ruler, and so gratefully to our chief Benefactor, as that we waste it not any other way.

As we hold our estates under God, as Owner, Ruler, and Benefactor, so must we devote them to him, and use them for him in each relation: and christian parsimony cannot be defined by a mere negation of active wastefulness, because idleness itself, and not using it aright, is real wastefulness.

Wastefulness, what it is.

Wastefulness or prodigality is that sin of unfaithfulness, disobedience, and ingratitude, by which either by action or omission we mispend or waste some part of our estates to the injury of God, our absolute Lord, our Ruler, and Benefactor: that is, besides and against his interest, his command, and his pleasure and glory, and our ultimate end.

These are true definitions of the duty of frugality and the sin of wastefulness.

Inst. I. One way of sinful wastefulness is, In pampering the belly in excess, curiosity, or costliness of meat or drink, of which I have spoken, chap. viii. part i.

Quest. I. Are all men bound to fare alike? or when is it wastefulness and excess?

Answ. This question is answered in the foresaid chapter of gluttony, part iv. tit. 1. 1. Distinguish between men's several tempers, and strength, and appetites. 2. And between the restraint of want, and the restraint of God's law. And so it is thus resolved:

1. Such difference in quantity or quality as men's health or strength, and real benefit, requireth, may be made by them that have no want.

2. When want depriveth the poor of that which would be really for their health, and strength, and benefit, it is not their duty who have no such want to conform themselves to other men's afflictions; except when other reasons do require it.

3. But all men are bound to avoid real excess in matter, or manner, and curiosity, and to lay out nothing needlessly on their bellies; yea, nothing which they are called to lay out a better way. Understand this answer, and it will suffice you.

Inst. II. Another way of prodigality is by needless, costly visits, and entertainments.

Quest. II. What cost upon visits and entertainments is unlawful and prodigal?

Answ. 1. Not only all that which hath an ill original, as pride or flattery of the rich, and all that hath an ill end, as being merely to keep up a carnal, unprofitable interest and correspondency; but also all that which is excessive in degree. I know you will say, But that is the difficulty, to know when it is excessive. It is not altogether impertinent to say, when it is above the proportion of your own estate, or the ordinary use of those of your own rank, or when it plainly tendeth to cherish gluttony or excess in others: but these answers are no exact solution. I add therefore, that it is excess when any thing is that way expended, which you are called to expend another way.

Object. But this leaveth it still as difficult as before.

Answ. When in rational probability a greater good may be done by another way of expense, *consideratis considerandis*, and a greater good is by this way neglected, then you had a call to spend it otherwise, and this expense is sinful.

Object. It is a doubt whether of two goods it be a man's duty always to choose the greater.

Answ. Speaking of that good which is within his choice, it is no more doubt than whether good be the object of the will. If God be eligible as good, then the greatest good is most eligible.

Whether a man is bound to prefer the greatest good.

Object. But this is still a difficulty insuperable: how can a man in every action and expense discern which way it is that the greatest good is like to be attained? This putteth a man's conscience upon endless perplexities, and we shall never be sure that we do not sin; for when I have given to a poor man, or done some good, for aught I know there was a poorer that should have had it, or a greater good that should have been done.

Answ. 1. The contrary opinion legitimateth almost all villany, and destroyeth most good works as to ourselves or others. If a man may lawfully prefer a known lesser good before a greater, and be justified because the lesser is a real good, then he may be feeding his horse when he should be saving the life of his child or neighbour, or quenching a fire in the city, or defending the person of his king: he may deny to serve his king and country, and say, I was ploughing or sowing the while. He may prefer sacrifice before mercy; he may neglect his soul, and serve his body. He may plough on the Lord's day, and neglect all God's worship. A lesser duty is no duty, but a sin, when a greater is to be done. Therefore it is certain, that when two goods come together to our choice, the greater is to be chosen, or else we sin. 2. As you expect that your steward should proportion his expenses according to the necessity of your business, and not give more for a thing than it is worth, nor lay out your money upon smaller commodity, while he leaveth your greater business unprovided for; and as you expect that your servant who hath many things in the day to do, should have so much skill as to know which to prefer, and not to leave undone the chiefest, whilst he

193

spendeth his time upon the least: so doth God require that his servants labour to be so skilful in his service, as to be able to compare their businesses together, and to [852]know which at every season to prefer. If christianity required no wisdom and skill, it were below men's common trades and callings. 3. And yet when you have done your best here, and truly endeavour to serve God faithfully, with the best skill and diligence you have, you need not make it a matter of scrupulosity, perplexity, and vexation; for God accepteth you, and pardoneth your infirmities, and rewardeth your fidelity. And what if it do follow, that you know not but there may be some sinful omission of a better way? Is that so strange or intolerable a conclusion; as long as it is a pardoned failing, which should not hinder the comfort of your obedience? Is it strange to you that we are all imperfect? and imperfect in every good we do, even by a culpable, sinful imperfection? You never loved God in your lives without a sinful imperfection in your love; and yet nothing in you is more acceptable to him than your love. Shall we think a case of conscience ill resolved, unless we may conclude, that we are sure we have no sinful imperfection in our duty? If your servant have not perfect skill, in knowing what to prefer in buying and selling, or in his work, I think you will neither allow him therefore to neglect the greater and better, knowingly, or by careless negligence, nor yet would you have him sit down and whine, and say, I know not which to choose; but you would have him learn to be as skilful as he can, and then willingly and cheerfully do his business with the best skill, and care, and diligence he can, and this you will best accept.

So that this holdeth as the truest and exactest solution of this and many other such cases: He that spendeth that upon an entertainment of some great ones, which should relieve some poor distressed families, that are ready to perish, doth spend it sinfully. If you cannot see this in God's cause, suppose it were the king's, and you will see it: if you have but twenty pounds to spend, and your tax or subsidy cometh to so much; if you entertain some noble friend with that money, will the king be satisfied with that as an excuse? or will you not be told that the king should have first been served? Remember him then, who will one day ask, "Have you fed, or clothed, or visited me?" Matt. xxv. You are not absolute owners of any thing, but the stewards of God; and must expend it as he appointeth you. And if you let the poor lie languishing in necessities, whilst you are at great charges to entertain the rich without a necessity or greater good, you must answer it as an unfaithful servant.

And yet on the other side, it may fall out that a person of quality, by a seasonable, prudent, handsome, respectful entertainment of his equals or superiors, may do more good than by bestowing that charge upon the poor. He may save more than he expendeth, by avoiding the displeasure of men in power: he may keep up his interest, by which if he be faithful, he may do God and his country more service, than if he had given so much to the poor. And when really it is a needful means to a greater good, it is a duty; and then to omit it, and give that cost to the poor, would be a sin.

Object. But if this rule hold, a man must never do but one kind of good; when he hath found out the greatest, he must do nothing else.

Answ. He must always do the greatest good: but the same thing is not at all times the greatest good. Out of season and measure a good may be turned to an evil: praying in its season is better than ploughing; and ploughing in its season is better than praying, and will do more good; for God will more accept and bless it.

Object. Therefore it seemeth the prudentest way to divide my expenses according to the proportion of others of my quality; some to the poor, and some to necessary charges, and some to actions of due civility.

Answ. That there must be a just distribution is no question; because God hath appointed you several duties for your expenses: but the question is of the proportions of each respectively. Where God hath made many duties constantly necessary, (as to maintain your own bodies, your children, to pay tribute to the king, to help the poor, to maintain the charges of the church,) there all must be wisely proportioned. But entertainments, recreations, and other such after to be mentioned, which are not constant duties, may be sometimes good and sometimes sinful: and the measure of such expenses must be varied only by the rule already laid down, viz. according to the proportion of the effect or good which is like to follow: though the custom of others of the same rank may sometimes intimate what proportion will be suitable to that lawful end; and sometimes the inordinate custom of others will rather tell one what is to be avoided. Therefore true prudence (without a carnal bias) comparing the good effects together, which rationally are like to follow, is the only resolver of this doubt. Which having so largely showed, I shall refer you to it, in the solution of many of the following questions.

Inst. III. Another way of sinful wasting is upon unnecessary, sumptuous buildings.

Quest. III. When is it prodigality to erect sumptuous edifices?

Answ. Not when they are for the public good, either in point of use, or ornament and honour, so be it no greater good be thereby omitted. Therefore it is not churches, hospitals, burses, or common halls that I am speaking of. Nor when they are proportioned to the quality of the person, for the honour of magistracy, or for a man's necessary use. But when it is for ostentation of a man's riches, or rather of his pride, and for the gratifying of a carnal, irrational fancy; and when a man bestoweth more upon buildings, than is proportionable to his estate, and to his better expenses; and (to speak more exactly) when he bestoweth that upon his buildings, which some greater service calleth for at that time; it is then his prodigality and sin.

Quest. IV. Here once for all let us inquire, Whether it be not lawful, as in diet, so in buildings, recreation, and other such things, to be at some charge for our delight, as well as for our necessities?

Answ. The question is thus commonly stated, but not well; for it seemeth to imply, that no delights are necessary, and so putteth things in opposition which are oft coincident. Therefore I distinguish, 1. Of necessity: some things are necessary to our being, and some to our felicity, and some but to our smaller benefits. 2. Of delight: some delight is sinful; as gratifying a sinful humour or disposition: some is unnecessary or wholly useless; and some is necessary, either to our greater or our lesser good. And so the true solution is: (1.) The sinful delight of a proud, a covetous, a lustful, a voluptuous mind, is neither to be purchased or used. (2.) A delight wholly needless, that is, unprofitable, is sinful if it be purchased, but at the price of a farthing, or of a bit of bread, or of a minute's time; because that is cast away which purchaseth it. (3.) A delight which tendeth to the health of the body, and the alacrity of the mind, to fit it for our calling and the service of God, (being not placed in any forbidden thing,) may be both indulged and purchased, so it be not above its worth. (4.) So far as delight in houses, or sports, or any creature, tendeth to corrupt [853]our minds, and draw us to the love of this present world, and alienate our hearts from heaven, so far must they be resisted and mortified, or sanctified and turned a better way. (5.) In the utensils of our duty to God, usually a moderate, natural delight, is a great help to the duty, and may become a spiritual delight: as a delight in many books, in the preacher's utterance, in the melody of psalms, in my study, and its conveniences, in my walk for meditation, &c. And a delight in our food and recreations, maketh them much fitter to cherish health, and to attain their ends; so it be not corrupt, immoderate, or abused to evil ends.

Inst. IV. Another way of prodigality, is in needless, costly recreations.

Quest. V. Is all cost laid out upon recreations unlawful?

Answ. No: but, *cæteris paribus*, we should choose the cheapest, and be at no needless cost on them; nor lay out any thing on them which, *consideratis considerandis*, might be better bestowed. But of this before.

Inst. V. Another way of prodigality is in over-costly apparel.

Quest. VI. What may be accounted prodigality in the costliness of apparel?

Answ. Not that which is only for a due distinction of superiors from inferiors, or which is needful to keep up the vulgar's reverence to magistrates. But, 1. All that which is merely serviceable to pride, or vain curiosity, or amorous lust, or an affectation to be thought more comely and beautiful than others. 2. All that which hath more cost bestowed on it, than the benefit or end is worth. 3. Or which hath that cost which should be rather laid out another way upon better uses. The cheapest apparel must be chosen which is warm and comely, and fittest to the right ends. And we must come nearer those that are below our rank, than those above it.

Inst. VI. Also prodigality is much showed in the cost which is laid out for needless pomp and ostentation of greatness or curiosity, in keeping a numerous retinue, and in their gallantry, and in keeping many horses, and costly furniture, and attendance.

Quest. VII. When is a costly retinue and other pompous furniture to be accounted prodigality?

Answ. Not when they are needful to the honour of magistracy, and so to the government of the commonwealth; nor when it is made but a due means to some lawful end, which answereth the cost. But when it is either the fruits and maintenance of pride, or exceedeth the proportion of men's estates, or (especially) when it expendeth that which better and more necessary uses call for. It is a most odious and enormous crime, to waste so many hundred or thousand pounds a year in the vanities of pomp, and fruitless curiosities, and need-nots, while the public uses of the state and church are injured through want, and while thousands of poor families are racked with cares, and pinched with necessities round about us.

Inst. VII. Another way of prodigality is that which is called by many, keeping a good house, that is, in unnecessary abundance, and waste of meat and drink, and other provisions.

Quest. VIII. When may great housekeeping be accounted prodigality?

Answ. Not when it is but a convenient work of charity to feed the poor, and relieve the distressed, or entertain strangers, or to give such necessary entertainment to equals or superiors as is before described: but when the truest relief of the poor shall be omitted, (and it may be poor tenants racked and oppressed,) to keep up the fame and grandeur of their abundance, and to seem magnificent, and praised by men for great housekeepers. The whole and large estates of many of the rich and great ones of the world goeth this way, and so much is devoured by it, as starveth almost all good works.

Inst. VIII. Another act of prodigality is cards and dice, and other gaming; in which whilst men desire to get that which is another's, they lose and waste their own.

Inst. IX. Another act of prodigality is giving over-great portions with children: it being a sinful waste of our Master's stock, to lay it out otherwise than he would have us, and to serve our pride and self-interest in our children instead of him.

Quest. IX. When may our children's portions be accounted prodigality or too great?

Answ. Not when you provide for their comfortable living according to your estates, and give them that due proportion which consisteth with the discharge of other duties: but when all that men can get is thought little enough for their children; and the business of their lives is to live in fulness themselves as long as they can, and then to leave that to their posterity which they cannot keep themselves! When this gulf of self-pampering and providing the like for children, devoureth almost all that you can gather, and the poor and other needful uses are put off with some inconsiderable pittance; and when there is not a due proportion kept between your provision for your children, and the other duties which God requireth of you. Psal. xlix. 7-9, 11, 13, "Their inward thought is, that their houses shall be perpetuated, and their dwelling-places to generations: they call their lands after their own names.—This their way is their folly; yet their posterity approve their sayings." Psal. lxxiii. 12, "Behold, these are the ungodly who prosper in the world, they increase in riches." Psal. xvii. 14, "They have their portion in this life:—they are full of children, (or their children are full,) and they leave the rest of their substance to their babes." A parent that hath an heir, or other children, so wise, religious, and liberal, as that they are like to be more charitable and serviceable to good uses, than any other whom he can trust with his estate, should not only leave such children sufficient for themselves, but enable them as much as he can to do good; for they will be more faithful trustees to him than strangers. But a parent that hath but common and untrusty children, should do all the good he can himself, and what he would have done when he is dead, he must commit to them that are more trusty, and allow his children but their proper maintenance. And parents that have debauched, wicked, ungodly children, (such as God commanded them to cause to be put to death, Deut. xxi.) should allow them no more than their daily bread, if any thing at all (which is their own to dispose of).

Inst. X. Also to be careless in many small expenses or losses, because they are but little things, and let any such thing be cast away, is sinful prodigality.

Quest. X. How far is it a duty to be frugal in small matters, and the contrary a sin?

Answ. We must not overvalue any thing, great or small; nor be sparing out of covetousness; nor yet in an imprudent way, which seemeth to signify baseness and worldliness when it is not so; nor must we be too thinking in bargaining with others, when every penny which we get by it, is lost to one that needeth it more. But we must see that nothing of any use be lost through satiety, negligence, or contempt; for the smallest part is of God's gifts and talents, given us, not to cast away, but to use as he [854]would have us; and there is nothing that is good so small, but some one hath need of it, or some good use or other may be made of it. Even Christ when he had fed thousands by a miracle, yet commanded his disciples to "gather up the broken bread or fragments, that nothing be lost," John vi. 12. Which plainly showeth that it is a duty which the richest man that is is not exempted from, to be frugal, and sin in the greatest prince to be wasteful of any thing that is good; but this must not be in sordid covetousness, but in obedience to God, and to do good to others. He is commendable who giveth liberally to the poor, out of his abundance; but he is much more commendable who is a good husband for the poor, as worldlings are for themselves; and frugally getteth and saveth as much as he can, and denieth all superfluities to himself and all about him, that he may have the more to give to pious and charitable uses.

Inst. XI. Idleness also and negligence in our callings, is sinful wastefulness and prodigality; when either the pride of gentility maketh people think themselves too good to labour, or to look after the matters of their families, or slothfulness maketh them think it a life too toilsome for their flesh to bear. Prov. xviii. 9, "He that is slothful in his work, is brother to him that is a great waster:" these drones consume that which others labour for, but are no gatherers themselves.

Quest. XI. Is every one bound to labour in a calling?

Answ. This is answered before in its due place, part i. Every one that is able, rich or poor, must live in some profitable course of pains or labour.

Quest. XII. Is it a duty to desire and endeavour to get, and prosper, and grow rich by our labours; when Solomon saith, "Labour not to be rich?" Prov. xxiii. 4.

Answ. It is a sin to desire riches as worldlings and sensualists do, for the provision and maintenance of fleshly lusts and pride; but it is no sin, but a duty, to labour not only for labour sake, formally resting in the act done, but for that honest increase and provision, which is the end of our labour; and therefore to choose a gainful calling rather than another, that we may be able to do good, and relieve the poor. Eph. iv. 28, "Let him labour, working with his hands the thing that is good, that he may have to give to him that needeth."

Quest. XIII. Can one be prodigal in giving to the church?

Answ. Yes, if it be in a blind zeal to maintain a useless pomp or superstition; or if he give that which should be used or given otherwise: but this is a sin that few in these days are much in danger of.[167]

Quest. XIV. Can one be prodigal in giving to the poor?

Answ. Yes, when it is blindly done, to cherish idleness in wandering beggars; or with a conceit of meriting in point of commutative justice from God; or when that is given to the poor, which should be given to other uses (as in public tribute, maintenance of children, furtherance of the gospel, &c.): but this is a sin that few have need to be restrained from.

Quest. XV. May a rich man expend any thing upon (otherwise) lawful pomp, or conveniences, or pleasures, at such a time when there are multitudes of poor families in extremity of want? as now, when the flames which consumed London have left many thousands in distress?

Answ. Doubtless every man should spare as much for the relief of others as he can; and therefore should not only forbear all needless expenses, but those also that are needful but to such conveniences and accommodations as may be spared without a greater hurt, than is the want of such as that charge would relieve. To save the lives of people in want, we must spare any thing from ourselves, which our own lives can spare. And to relieve them in their deep poverty, we must abate much more than our superfluities. To expend any thing on pride and lust, is a double sin at such a time, when Lazarus is at our doors in want. If that Luke xvi. were well studied, (wherein it was that the rich man's sin and danger lay, in being clothed in purple and silk, and faring sumptuously every day, while Lazarus wanted,) it would make some sensualists wiser than they are.

But yet it must be confessed, that some few persons may be of so much worth and use to the commonwealth, (as kings and magistrates,) and some of so little, that the maintaining of the honour and succours of the former, may be more necessary than the saving of the lives of the latter. But take heed lest pride or cruelty teach you to misunderstand this, or abuse it for yourselves.

There are divers other ways of prodigality or sinful waste, which I pass by, because they are such as few are concerned in; and my purpose is not to say all that may be said, but all that is needful. As in needless music, physic, books, (which Seneca handsomely reproveth,) gifts to servants which need not, in mere ostentation of pride, to be well spoken of, and many the like; and in unlawful wars, which is the greatest sinful waster in all the world. And as for expenses in debauchery and gross wickedness, as whoredom, revenge, in sinful law-suits, &c. I here pretermit them.

Direct. II. Understand well the aggravations of this sin of prodigality: viz.

1. It is a wasting of that which is none of our own, and a robbing God of the use or service due to him in the improvement of his gifts. They are his, and not ours; and according to his pleasure only must be used. 2. It is a robbing the poor of that which the common Lord of the world hath appointed for them in his law; and they will have their action in heaven against the prodigal. 3. It is an inhuman vice, to waste that upon pleasures, pride, and needless things, which so many distressed persons stand in need of. 4. It is an injury to the commonwealth, which is weakened by the wasteful. And the covetous themselves (that are not oppressors) are much better members of public societies than the prodigal. 5. It feedeth a life of other vice and wickedness. It is a spending God's gift to feed those lusts which he abhorreth. 6. It usually engageth many others in trades and labours which are unprofitable, that they may serve the lusts of these sensual prodigals. 7. And in the conclusion, it prepareth a sad account for these wretches, when they must answer at the bar of God how they have used all his gifts and talents. Remember all these aggravations.

Direct. III. Carefully mortify that greedy fancy, and fleshly lusts, which is the wasting sin, and the devouring gulf. Quench the fire, and you may spare all this fuel. Cure the fever or dropsy, and you may spare both your drink and life. A greedy throat and a diseased fancy are never satisfied, till they have wasted the peace of your consciences with your estates, and brought you to the end of brutish sinners: wisdom, and duty, and real benefit, are contented with a little; but lust is insatiable; the voluptuous brute saith, I must have my cups, my lusts, my pleasure; and the effeminate, vicious fancy of those empty souls that mind no great and solid things, is still ranging after some vanity or other; [855]and like children, crying for every thing that they see another have: and the most needless, yea, burdensome things seem necessary to such; they say, I must needs have this, and I must needs have that, there is no being without it; when nothing needeth it, but a diseased mind, which much more needeth a cure by grace and true mortification. Subdue pride, and sensuality, and fancy, and you may escape prodigality.

Direct. IV. Remember the nearness of your account, and ask your consciences what way of expenses will please you best in the review. Whether at death and judgment it will be your comfort to find on your account, So much laid out on needless bravery, to set out this carcass which is now turning into dust; Item, so much upon proud entertainments of great ones; Item, so much on cards, and dice, and stage-plays; and so much on hounds and needless pleasures, &c. Or rather, so much to promote the preaching of the gospel; so much to set poor children to 'prentice, or to school; so much to relieve distressed families, &c. Let Matt. xxv. be well read, and your account well thought on.

Direct. V. Keep an account of your expenses, and peruse them before a fast or a sacrament; and ask conscience how it judgeth of them; yea, ask some holy, prudent friend, whether such proportions are allowable before God, and will be comfortable to you in the day of your extremity. If you are but willing to be cured, such means as these will not be in vain.

[167] Read Erasmus Colloqu. Peregrin. Relig. Ergo.

CHAPTER XXII.

CASES AND DIRECTIONS AGAINST INJURIOUS LAW-SUITS, WITNESSING, AND JUDGMENT.

Tit. 1. *Cases of Conscience about Law-suits and Proceedings.*

Quest. I. In what cases is it lawful to go to law with others?

Answ. 1. In case of necessary defence, when the plaintiff doth compel you to it. 2. When you are intrusted for orphans or others whom you cannot otherwise right. 3. When your children, or the church, or poor, whom you should do good to, are like to suffer, if you recover not your talent that God hath trusted you with for such uses, from the hands of unjust men; and they refuse all just arbitrations and other equal means which might avoid such suits. 4. When your own necessity constraineth you to seek your own, which you cannot get by easier means. 5. When your forbearance will do more hurt by encouraging knaves in their injustice, than it will do good. 6. Whenever your cause is just, and neither mercy, peace, nor the avoiding of scandal do forbid it: that is, when it is like to do more good than harm, it is then a lawful course.

But it is unlawful to go to law, 1. When you neglect just arbitrations, patience, and other needful means to avoid it. 2. When your cause is unjust. 3. When you oppress the poor by it. 4. When it is done in covetousness, revenge, or pride. 5. When the scandal or hurt to your brother, is like to be a greater harm than the righting of yourself is like to do good; then must you not go willingly to law.

Quest. II. May I sue a poor man for a debt or trespass?

Answ. 1. If he be so poor as that he cannot pay it, nor procure you satisfaction, the suit is vain, and tendeth but to cruelty. 2. If he have no means to pay, but that which will deprive him of food and raiment, and the necessaries of his life or comfort, you may not sue him unless it be for the supply of as great necessities of your own; or in trust for orphans, where you have no power to remit the debt; yea, and for them no cruelty must be used. 3. If your forbearance be like to make him abler by his diligence or other means, you should forbear if possible. 4. But if he be competently able, and refuse to pay through knavery and injustice, and you have better ways to use that money, if scandal forbid not, you may seek by law to recover your own from him.

Quest. III. May I sue a surety whose interest was not concerned in the case?

Answ. If his poverty make it not an act of cruelty, nor scandal prohibit it, you may; because he was willing, and declared his consent, that you should have the debt of him, if the principal pay not. To become surety, is to consent to this; and it is no injury to receive a man's money by his own consent and covenant. He knew that you had not lent it but on those terms; and you had reason to suppose, that he who would undertake to pay another man's debt, had sufficient reason for it, either in relation or counter-security. But as you must use mercy to the principal debtor in his poverty, so must you also to the surety.

Quest. IV. May I sue for the use of money, as well as for the principal?

Answ. This dependeth on the case of usury before resolved. In those cases in which it may not be taken, it may not be sued for; nor yet when the scandal of it will do more harm than the money will do good. But in other cases, it may be sued for on the terms as the rent of lands may.

Quest. V. May law-suits be used to disable or humble an insolent, wicked man?

Answ. You may not take up an ill cause against him, for any such good end; but if you have a good cause against him, which otherwise you would not have prosecuted, you may make use of it, to disable him from doing mischief, when really it is a probable means thereto; and when neither scandal nor other accidents do prohibit it.

Quest. VI. May a rich man make use of his friends and purse in a just cause, to bear down or tire out a poor man that hath a bad cause?

Answ. Not by bribery or any evil means; for his proceeding must be just as well as his cause. But if it be an obstinate knave that setteth himself to do hurt to others, it is lawful to make use of the favour of a righteous judge or magistrate against him; and it is lawful to humble him by the length and expensiveness of the suit, when that is the fittest means, and no unjust action is done in it; still supposing that scandal prohibit it not. But let no proud or cruel person think, that therefore they may by purse, and friends, and tedious law-suits oppress the innocent, to attain their own unrighteous wills.

Quest. VII. May one use such forms in law-suits as in the literal sense are gross untruths (in declarations, answers, or the like)?

Answ. The use of words is to express the mind; and common use is the interpreter of them: if they are such words as the notorious common use hath put another sense on, than the literal one, they must be taken in the sense which public use hath put upon them. And if that public sense be true or false, accordingly they may or may not be used.

Quest. VIII. May a guilty person plead not guilty, or deny the fact?

[856]*Answ.* Common use is the interpreter of words. If the common use of those words doth make their public sense a lie, it may not be done. But if the forensic common use of their denial is taken to signify no more but this, Let him that accuseth me, prove it; I am not bound to accuse myself, or, *In foro* I am not guilty till it be proved; then it is lawful to plead Not guilty, and deny the fact, except in cases wherein you are bound to an open confession, or in which the scandal will do more hurt than the denial will do good.

Quest. IX. Is a man ever bound to accuse himself, and seek justice against himself?

Answ. 1. In many cases a man is bound to punish himself; as when the law against swearing, cursing, or the like, must give the poor a certain mulct which is the penalty, he ought to give that money himself; and in cases where it is a necessary cure to himself, and in any case where the public good requireth it: as if a magistrate offend, whom none else will punish, or who is the judge in his own cause; he should so far punish himself as is necessary to the suppression of sin, and to the preserving of the honour of the laws; as I have heard of a justice that swore twenty oaths, and paid his twenty shillings for it. 2. A man may be bound in such a divine vengeance or judgment as seeketh after his particular sin, to offer himself to do a sacrifice to justice, to stop the judgment; as Jonah and Achan did. 3. A man may be bound to confess his guilt and offer himself to justice to save the innocent, who is falsely accused and condemned for his crime. 4. But in ordinary cases a man is not bound to be his own public accuser or executioner.

Quest. X. May a witness voluntarily speak that truth which he knoweth will further an unrighteous cause, and be made use of to oppress the innocent?

Answ. He may not do it as a confederate in that intention: nor may he do it when he knoweth that it will tend to such an event, (though threatened or commanded,) except when some weightier accident doth preponderate for the doing it, (as the avoiding of a greater hurt to others, than it will bring on the oppressed, &c.)

Quest. XI. May a witness conceal some part of the truth?

Answ. Not when he sweareth to deliver the whole truth; nor when a good cause is like to suffer, or a bad cause be furthered by the concealment; nor when he is under any other obligation to reveal the whole.

Quest. XII. Must a judge and jury proceed *secundum allegata et probata*, according to evidence and proof, when they know the witness to be false, and the truth to be contrary to the testimony; but are not able to evince it?

Answ. Distinguish between the negative and the positive part of the verdict or sentence: in the negative they must go according to the evidence and testimonies, unless the law of the land leave the case to their private knowledge. As for example, they must not sentence a thief or murderer to be punished upon their secret unproved knowledge: they must not adjudge either monies or lands to the true owner from another, without sufficient evidence and proof: they must forbear doing justice, because they are not called to it, nor enabled. But positively they may do no injustice upon any evidence or witness against their own knowledge of the truth: as they may not upon known false witness, give away a man's lands or money, or condemn the innocent; but must in such a case renounce the office; the judge must come off the bench, and the jury protest that they will not meddle, or give any verdict (whatever come of it); because God and the law of nature prohibit their injustice.

Object. It is the law that doth it, and not we.

Answ. It is the law and you; and the law cannot justify your agency in any unrighteous sentence. The case is plain and past dispute.

Tit. 2. Directions against Contentious Suits, False-witnessing, and Oppressive Judgment.

Direct. I. The first cure for all these sins, is to know the intrinsic evil of them. Good thoughts of sin are its life and strength. When it is well known, it will be hated; and when it is hated, it is so far cured.

I. The evil of contentious and unjust law-suits.

1. Such contentious suits do show the power of selfishness in the sinner; how much self-interest is inordinately esteemed. 2. They show the excessive love of the world; how much men overvalue the things which they contend for. 3. They show men's want of love to their neighbours; how little they regard another man's interest in comparison of their own. 4. They show how little such men care for the public good, which is maintained by the concord and love of neighbours. 5. Such contentions are powerful engines of the devil to destroy all christian love on both sides; and to stir up mutual enmity and wrath; and so to involve men in a course of sin, by further uncharitableness and injuries, both in heart, and word, and deed. 6. Poor men are hereby robbed of their necessary maintenance, and their innocent families subjected to distress. 7. Unconscionable lawyers and court officers, who live upon the people's sins, are hereby maintained, encouraged, and kept up. 8. Laws and courts of justice are perverted to do men wrong, which were made to right them. 9. And the offender declareth how little sense he hath of the authority or love of God, and how little sense of the grace of our Redeemer; and how far he is from being himself forgiven through the blood of Christ, who can no better forgive another.

II. The evil of false witness.

1. By false witness the innocent are injured; robbery and murder are committed under pretence of truth and justice. 2. The name of God is horribly abused, by the

crying sin of perjury (of which before). 3. The presence and justice of God are contemned, when sinners dare, in his sight and hearing, appeal to his tribunal, in the attesting of a lie. 4. Vengeance is begged or consented to by the sinner; who bringeth God's curse upon himself, and as it were desireth God to plague or damn him if he lie. 5. Satan the prince of malice and injustice, and the father of lies, and murders, and oppression, is hereby gratified, and eminently served. 6. God himself is openly injured, who is the Father and patron of the innocent; and the cause of every righteous person is more the cause of God than of man. 7. All government is frustrated, and laws abused, and all men's security for their reputations, or estates, or lives is overthrown, by false witnesses; and consequently human converse is made undesirable and unsafe. What good can law, or right, or innocency, or the honesty of the judge do any man, where false witnesses combine against him? What security hath the most innocent or worthy person, for his fame, or liberty, or estate, or life, if false witnesses conspire to defame him or destroy him? And then how shall men endure to converse with one another? Either the innocent must seek out a wilderness, and fly from the face of men as we do from lions and tigers, or else peace will be worse than war; for in war a man may fight for his life; but against false witnesses he hath no defence: but God is the [857]avenger of the innocent, and above most other sins, doth seldom suffer this to go unpunished, even in this present world; but often beginneth their hell on earth, to such perjured instruments of the devil.

III. The evil of unrighteous judgments.

1. An unrighteous judge doth condemn the cause of God himself; for every righteous cause is his. 2. Yea, he condemneth Christ himself in his members; for in that he doth it to one of the least of those whom he calleth brethren, he doth it to himself, Matt. xxv. It is a damnable sin, not to relieve the innocent and imprisoned in their distress, when we have power: what is it then to oppress them and unrighteously condemn? 3. It is a turning of the remedy into a double misery, and taking away the only help of oppressed innocency. What other defence hath innocency, but law and justice? And when their refuge itself doth fall upon them and oppress them, whither shall the righteous fly? 4. It subverteth laws and government, and abuseth it to destroy the ends which it is appointed for. 5. Thereby it turneth human society into a state of misery, like the depredations of hostility. 6. It is a deliberate, resolved sin, and not done in passion by surprise: it is committed in that place, and in that form, as acts of greatest deliberation should be done; as if he should say, Upon full disquisition, evidence, and deliberation, I condemn this person and his cause. 7. All this is done as in the name of God, and by his own commission, by one that pretendeth to be his officer or minister, Rom. iii. 3-6. For the judgment is the Lord's, 2 Chron. xix. 5-8, 10. And how great a wickedness is it thus to blaspheme, and to represent him as Satan, an enemy to truth and righteousness, to his servants and himself! As if he had said, God hath sent me to condemn this cause and person. If false prophets sin so heinously who belie the Lord, and say, He hath sent us to speak this, (which is untruth); the sin of false judges cannot be much less. 8. It is sin against the fullest and frequentest prohibitions of God. Read over Exod. xxiii. 1-3, &c.; Lev.; Deut. i. 16, 17; xvi. 18; Isa. i. 17, 20, 23; Deut. xxiv. 17; and xxvii. 19, "Cursed be he that perverteth the judgment of the stranger, the fatherless, and widow, and all the people shall say Amen." Ezra vii. 26; Psal. xxxiii. 5; xxxvii. 28; lxxii. 2; xciv. 15; cvi. 3, 30; Prov. xvii. 27; xix. 28; xx. 8; xxix. 4; xxxi. 5; Eccl. v. 8; Isa. v. 7; x. 2; lvi. 1, 2; lix. 14, 15; Jer. v. 1; vii. 5; ix. 24; Ezek. xviii. 8; xlv. 9; Hos. xii. 6; Amos v. 7, 15, 24; vi. 12; Mic. iii. 9; Zech. vii. 9; viii. 16; Gen. xviii. 19; Prov. xxi. 3, 7, 15. I cite not the words to avoid prolixity. Scarce any sin is so oft and vehemently condemned of God. 9. False judges cause the poor to appeal to God against them, and the cries of the afflicted shall not be forgotten, Luke xviii. 5-8. 10. They call for God's judgment upon themselves, and devolve the work into his hands: how can that man expect any other than a judgment of damnation, from the righteous God, who hath deliberately condemned Christ himself in his cause and servants, and sat in judgment to condemn the innocent? Psal. ix. 7-9, "The Lord hath

prepared his throne for judgment, and he shall judge the world in righteousness; he shall minister judgment to the people in uprightness; he will be a refuge for the oppressed." Psal. xxxvii. 6, "He will bring forth thy righteousness as the light, and thy judgment as the noon-day." Psal. lxxxix. 14, "Justice and judgment are the habitation of his throne." Psal. ciii. 6, "The Lord executeth righteousness and judgment for all that are oppressed." Psal. cxlvi. 7. In a word, the sentence of an unjust judge is passed against his own soul, and he calleth to God to condemn him righteously, who unrighteously condemned others. Of all men he cannot stand in judgment, nor abide the righteous doom of Christ.

Direct. II. When you well understand the greatness of the sin, find out and overcome the root and causes of it in yourselves; especially selfishness, covetousness, and passion. A selfish man careth not what another suffereth, so that his own ends and interest be promoted by it. A covetous man will contend and injure his neighbour whenever his own commodity requireth it. He so much loveth his money that it can prevail with him to sin against God, and cast away his own soul; much more to hurt and wrong his neighbour. A proud and passionate man is so thirsty after revenge, to make others stoop to him, that he careth not what it cost him to accomplish it. Overcome these inward vices, and you may easily forbear the outward sins.

Direct. III. Love your neighbours as yourselves: for that is the universal remedy against all injurious and uncharitable undertakings.

Direct. IV. Keep a tender conscience, which will not make light of sin. It is those that have seared their consciences by infidelity or a course of sinning, who dare venture with Judas or Gehazi for the prey, and dare oppress the poor and innocent, and feel not, nor fear, whilst they cast themselves on the revenge of God.

Direct. V. Remember the day when all these causes must be heard again, and the righteous God will set all straight, and vindicate the cause of the oppressed. Consider what a dreadful appearance that man is like to have at the bar of heaven, who hath falsely accused or condemned the just in the courts of men. What a terrible indictment, accusation, conviction, and sentence must that man expect! If the hearing of righteousness and the judgment to come made Felix tremble, surely it is infidelity or the plague of a stupified heart, which keepeth contentious persons, perverters of justice, false witnesses, and unjust judges from trembling.

Direct. VI. Remember the presence of that God who must be your final Judge. That he seeth all your pride and covetousness, and all your secret contrivances for revenge, and is privy to all your deceits and injuries. You commit them in his open sight.

Direct. VII. Meddle not with law-suits till you have offered an equal arbitration of indifferent men, or used all possible means of love to prevent them. Law-suits are not the first, but the last remedy. Try all others before you use them.

Direct. VIII. When you must needs go to law, compose your minds to unfeigned love towards him that you must contend with, and watch over your hearts with suspicion and the strictest care, lest secret disaffection get advantage by it: and go to your neighbour, and labour to possess his heart also with love, and to demulce his mind; that you may not use the courts of justice, as soldiers do their weapons, to do the worst they can against another, as an enemy; but as loving friends do use an amicable arbitration; resolving contentedly to stand to what the judge determineth, without any alienation of mind, or abatement of brotherly love.

Direct. IX. Be not too confident of the righteousness of your own cause; but ask counsel of some understanding, godly, and impartial men; and hear all that can be said, and patiently consider of the case, and do as you would have others do by you.

Direct. X. Observe what terrors of conscience use to haunt awakened sinners, especially on a deathbed, for such sins as false witnessing, and false judging, |858|and oppressing, and injuring the innocent, even above most other sins.

CHAPTER XXIII

CASES OF CONSCIENCE, AND DIRECTIONS AGAINST BACKBITING, SLANDERING, AND EVIL SPEAKING.

Tit. 1. Cases of Conscience about Backbiting and Evil-speaking.

Quest. I. May I not speak evil of that which is evil? and call every one truly as he is?

Answ. You must not speak a known falsehood of any man under pretence of charity or speaking well. But you are not to speak all the evil of every man which is true: as opening the faults of the king or your parents, though never so truly, is a sin against the fifth commandment, "Honour thy father and mother:" so if you do it without a call, you sin against your neighbour's honour, and many other ways offend.

Quest. II. Is it not sinful silence, and a consenting to or countenancing of the sins of others, to say nothing against them, as tender of their honour?

Answ. It is sinful to be silent when you have a call to speak: if you forbear to admonish the offender in love between him and you, when you have opportunity and just cause, it is sinful to be silent then. But to silence backbiting is no sin. If you must be guilty of every man's sin that you talk not against behind his back, your whole discourse must be nothing but backbiting.

Quest. III. May I not speak that which honest, religious, credible persons do report?

Answ. Not without both sufficient evidence and a sufficient call. You must not judge of the action by the person, but of the person by the action. Nor must you imitate any man in evil-doing. If a good man abuse you, are you willing that all men follow him and abuse you more?

Quest. IV. May I believe the bad report of an honest, credible person?

Answ. You must first consider whether you may hear it, or meddle with it: for if it be a case that you have nothing to do with, you may not set your judgment to it, either to believe it, or to disbelieve it. And if it be a thing that you are called to judge of, yet every honest man's word is not presently to be believed: you must first know whether it be a thing that he saw, or is certain of himself, or a thing which he only taketh upon report; and what his evidence and proof is; and whether he be not engaged by interest, passion, or any difference of opinion; or be not engaged in some contrary faction, where the interest of a party or cause is his temptation; or whether he be not used to rash reports and uncharitable speeches; and what concurrence of testimonies there is, and what is said on the other side; especially what the person accused saith in his own defence. If it be so heinous a crime in public judgment, to pass sentence before both parties are heard, and to condemn a man before he speak for himself; it cannot be justifiable in private judgment. Would you be willing yourselves that all should be believed of you, which is spoken by any honest man? And how uncertain are we of other men's honesty, that we should on that account think ill of others!

Quest. V. May I not speak evil of them that are enemies to God, to religion and godliness, and are open persecutors of it; or are enemies to the king or church?

Answ. You may on all meet occasions speak evil of the sin; and of the persons when you have a just call; but not at your own pleasure.

Quest. VI. What if it be one whose honour and credit countenanceth an ill cause, and his dishonour would disable him to do hurt?

Answ. You may not belie the devil, nor wrong the worst man that is, though under pretence of doing good; God needeth not malice, nor calumnies, nor injustice to his glory: it is an ill cause that cannot be maintained without such means as these. And when the matter is true, you must have a call to speak it, and you must speak it justly, without unrighteous aggravations, or hiding the better part, which should make the case and person better understood. There is a time and due manner, in which that man's crimes and just dishonour may be published, whose false reputation injureth the truth. But yet I must say, that a great deal of villany and slander is committed upon this plausible pretence; and that there is scarce a more common cloak for the most inhuman lies and calumnies.

Quest. VII. May I not lawfully make a true narration of such matters of fact, as are criminal and dishonourable to offenders? Else no man may write a true history to posterity of men's crimes.

Answ. When you have a just call to do it, you may; but not at your own pleasure. Historians may take much more liberty to speak the truth of the dead, than you may of the living: though no untruth must be spoken of either: yet the honour of princes and magistrates while they are alive is needful to their government, and therefore must be maintained, ofttimes by the concealment of their faults: and so proportionably the honour of other men is needful to a life of love, and peace, and just society; but when they are dead, they are not subjects capable of a right to any such honour as must be maintained by such silencing of the truth, to the injury of posterity: and posterity hath usually a right to historical truth, that good examples may draw them to imitation, and bad examples may warn them to take heed of sin. God will have the name of the wicked to rot; and the faults of a Noah, Lot, David, Solomon, Peter, &c. shall be recorded. Yet nothing unprofitable to posterity may be recorded of the dead, though it be true; nor the faults of men unnecessarily divulged; much less may the dead be slandered or abused.

Quest. VIII. What if it be one that hath been oft admonished in vain? May not the faults of such a one be mentioned behind his back?

Answ. I confess such a one (the case being proved, and he being notoriously impenitent) hath made a much greater forfeiture of his honour than other men; and no man can save that man's honour who will cast it away himself. But yet it is not every one that committeth a sin after admonition, who is here to be understood; but such as are impenitent in some mortal or ruling sin: for some may sin oft in a small and controverted point, for want of ability to discern the truth; and some may live in daily infirmities, (as the best men do,) which they condemn themselves for, and desire to be delivered from. And even the most impenitent man's sins must not be meddled with by every one at his pleasure, but only when you have just cause.

Quest. IX. What if it be one whom I cannot speak to face to face?

Answ. You must let him alone, till you have just cause to speak of him.

[859]*Quest.* X. When hath a man a just cause and call to open another's faults?

Answ. Negatively: 1. Not to fill up the time with other idle chat, or table talk. 2. Not to second any man, how good soever, who backbiteth others; no, though he pretend to do it to make the sin more odious, or to exercise godly sorrow for other men's sin. 3. Not whenever interest, passion, faction, or company seemeth to require it. But, affirmatively, 1. When we may speak it to his face in love and privacy, in due manner and circumstances, as is most hopeful to conduce to his amendment. 2. When, after due admonition, we take two or three, and after that tell the church (in a case that requireth it). 3. When we have a sufficient cause to accuse him to the magistrate. 4. When the magistrate or the pastors of the church, reprove or punish him. 5. When it is necessary to the preservation of another: as if I see my friend in danger of marrying with a wicked person, or taking a false servant, or trading and bargaining with one that is like to over-reach him, or going among cheaters, or going to hear or converse with a dangerous heretic or seducer; I must open the faults of those that they are in danger of, so far as their safety and my charity require. 6. When it is any treason or conspiracy against the king or commonwealth; where my concealment may be an injury to the king, or damage or danger to the kingdom. 7. When the person himself doth, by his self-justification, force me to it. 8. When his reputation is so built upon the injury of others, and slanders of the just, that the justifying of him is the condemning of the innocent, we may then indirectly condemn him, by vindicating the just; as if it be in a case of contention between two, if we cannot justify the right without dishonour to the injurious, there is no remedy but he must bear his blame. 9. When a man's notorious wickedness hath set him up as a spectacle of warning and lamentation, so that his crimes cannot be hid, and he hath forfeited his reputation, we must give others warning by his fall: as an excommunicate person, or malefactor at the gallows, &c. 10. When we have just occasion to make a bare narrative of some public matters of fact; as of the sentence of a judge, or punishment of offenders, &c. 11. When the crime is so heinous, as that all good persons are obliged to join to make it odious, as Phinehas was to execute judgment. As in cases of open rebellion, treason, blasphemy, atheism, idolatry, murders, perjury, cruelty; such as the French massacre, the Irish far greater massacre, the murdering of kings, the powder-plot, the burning of London, &c. Crimes notorious should not go about in the mouths or ears of men, but with just detestation. 12. When any person's false reputation is a seducement to men's souls, and made by himself or others the instruments of God's dishonour, and the injury of church or state, or others, though we may do no unjust thing to blast his reputation, we may tell the truth so far as justice, or mercy, or piety requireth it.

Quest. XI. What if I hear daubers applauding wicked men, and speaking well of them, and extenuating their crimes, and praising them for evil doing?

Answ. You must on all just occasions speak evil of sin; but when that is enough, you need not meddle with the sinner; no, not though other men applaud him, and you know it be false; for you are not bound to contradict every falsehood which you hear. But if in any of the twelve forementioned cases you have a call to do it, (as for the preservation of the hearers from a snare thereby; as if men commend a traitor or a wicked man to draw another to like his way,) in such cases you may contradict the false report.

Quest. XII. Are we bound to reprove every backbiter, in this age when honest people are grown to make little conscience of it, but think it their duty to divulge men's faults?

Answ. Most of all, that you may stop the stream of this common sin, ordinarily whenever we can do it without doing greater hurt, we should rebuke the tongue that reporteth evil of other men causelessly behind their backs; for our silence is their encouragement in sin.

Tit. 2. Directions against Backbiting, Slandering, and Evil Speaking.

Direct. I. Maintain the life of brotherly love. Love your neighbour as yourself.

Direct. II. Watch narrowly lest interest or passion should prevail upon you. For where these prevail, the tongue is set on fire of hell, and will set on fire the course of nature, James ii. Selfishness and passion will not only prompt you to speak evil, but also to justify it, and think you do well; yea, and to be angry with those that will not hearken to you and believe you.

Direct. III. Especially involve not yourselves in any faction, religious or secular. I do not mean that you should not imitate the best, and hold most intimate communion with them; but that you abhor unlawful divisions and sidings; and when error, or uncharitableness, or carnal interest hath broken the church into pieces where you live, and one is of Paul, and another of Apollos, and another of Cephas, one of this party, and another of that, take heed of espousing the interest of any party, as it stands cross to the interest of the whole. It would have been hardly credible, if sad experience had not proved it, how commonly and heinously almost every sect of christians do sin in this point against each other! and how far the interest of their sect, which they account the interest of Christ, will prevail with multitudes even of zealous people, to belie, calumniate, backbite, and reproach those that are against their opinion and their party! yea, how easily will they proceed beyond reproaches, to bloody persecutions! He that thinketh he doth God service by killing Christ or his disciples, will think that he doth him service by calling him a deceiver, and one that hath a devil, a blasphemer, and an enemy to Cæsar, and calling his disciples pestilent fellows and movers of sedition among the people, and accounting them as the filth and offscouring of the world. That zeal which murdered and destroyed many hundred thousand of the Waldenses and Albigenses, and thirty thousand or forty thousand in one French massacre, and two hundred thousand in one Irish massacre, and which kindled the Maryan bonfires in England, made the powder mine, and burnt the city of London, and keepeth up the Inquisition, I say, that zeal will certainly think it a service to the church, (that is, their sect,) to write the most odious lies and slanders of Luther, Zuinglius, Calvin, Beza, and any such excellent servants of the Lord. So full of horrid, impudent lies are the writings of (not one but) many sects against those that were their chief opposers, that I still admonish all posterity, to see good evidence for it, before they believe the hard sayings of any factious historian or divine, against those that are against his party. It is only men of eminent conscience, and candour, and veracity, and impartiality, who are to be believed in their bad report of others, except where notoriety or very good evidence doth command belief above their own authority and veracity. A siding factious zeal, which is hotter for [860]any sect or party, than for the common christianity and catholic church, is always a railing, a lying, and a slandering zeal, and is notably described, James iii. as "earthly, sensual, and devilish," causing "envy, strife, and confusion, and every evil work."

Direct. IV. Observe well the commonness of this sin of backbiting, that it may make you the more afraid of falling into that which so few do escape. I will not say, among high and low, rich and poor, court and country, how common is this sin; but among men professing the greatest zeal and strictness in religion, how few make conscience of it! Mark in all companies that you come into, how common it is to take liberty to say what they think of all men; yea, to report what they hear, though they dare not say that they believe it! And how commonly the relating of other men's faults, and telling what this man or that man is, or did, or said, is part of the chat to waste the hour in! And if it be but true, they think they sin not: nay, nor if they did but hear that it is true. For my part I must profess, that my conscience having brought me to a custom of rebuking such backbiters, I am ordinarily censured for it, either as one that loveth contradiction, or one that defendeth sin and wickedness, by taking part with wicked men; all because I would stop the course of this common vice of evil speaking and backbiting where men have no call. And I must thankfully profess, that among all other sins in the world, the sins of selfishness, pride, and backbiting, I have been most brought to hate and fear, by the observation of the commonness of them, even in persons seeming godly: nothing hath fixed an apprehension of their odiousness so deeply in me, nor engaged my heart against them above all other sins so much, as this lamentable experience of their prevalence in the world, among the more religious, and not only in the profane.

Direct. V. Take not the honesty of the person, as a sufficient cause to hear or believe a bad report of others. It is lamentable to hear how far men, otherwise honest, do too often here offend. Suspect evil speakers, and be not over-credulous of them. Charity thinketh not evil, nor easily and hastily believeth it. Liars are more used to evil speaking, than men of truth and credit are. It is no wrong to the best, that you believe him not when he backbiteth without good evidence.

Direct. VI. Rebuke backbiters, and encourage them not by hearkening to their tales. Prov. xxv. 23, "The north wind driveth away rain, so doth an angry countenance a backbiting tongue." It may be they think themselves religious persons, and will take it for an injury to be driven away with an angry countenance: but God himself, who loveth his servants better than we, is more offended at their sin; and that which offendeth him, must offend us. We must not hurt their souls, and displease God, by drawing upon us the guilt of their sins, for fear of displeasing them. Tell them how God doth hate backbiting, and advise them if they know any hurt by others, to go to them privately, and tell them of it in a way that tendeth to their repentance.

Direct. VII. Use to make mention of the good which is in others; (except it be unseasonable, and will seem to be a promoting of their sin): God's gifts in every man deserve commendations; and we have allowance to mention men's virtues oftener than to mention their vices. Indeed when a bad man is praised in order to the disparagement of the good, or to honour some wicked cause or action against truth

207

and godliness, we must not concur in such malicious praises; but otherwise we must commend that which is truly commendable in all. And this custom will have a double benefit against backbiting: it will use your own tongues to a contrary course, and it will rebuke the evil tongues of others, and be an example to them of more charitable language.

Direct. VIII. Understand yourselves, and speak often to others, of the sinfulness of evil-speaking and backbiting. Show them the scriptures which condemn it, and the intrinsical malignity which is in it: as here followeth.

Direct. IX. Make conscience of just reproof and exhorting sinners to their faces. Go tell them of it privately and lovingly, and it will have better effects, and bring you more comfort, and cure the sin of backbiting.

Tit. 3. The Evil of Backbiting and Evil-speaking.

1. It is forbidden of God among the heinous, damning sins, and made the character of a notorious wicked person, and the avoiding of it is made the mark of such as are accepted of God and shall be saved: Rom. i. 29, 30, it is made the mark of a reprobate mind, and joined with murder, and hating God, viz. "full of envy, debate, deceit, malignity, whisperers, backbiters." Psal. xv. 2, 3, "Lord, who shall abide in thy tabernacle? who shall dwell in thy holy hill? He that backbiteth not with his tongue, nor doeth evil to his neighbour, nor taketh up a reproach against his neighbour." And when Paul describeth those whom he must sharply rebuke and censure, he just describeth the factious sort of christians of our times. 2 Cor. xii. 20, "For I fear lest when I come, I shall not find you such as I would, and that I shall be found unto you such as ye would not: lest there be debates, envyings, wraths, strifes, backbitings, whisperings, swellings, tumults." Eph. iv. 31, "Let all bitterness, and wrath, and anger, and clamour, and evil-speaking be put away from you, with all malice, and be kind one to another, and tender-hearted—."

2. It is a sin which gratifieth Satan, and serveth his malice against our neighbour. He is malicious against all, and speaking evil, and doing hurt, are the works which are suitable to his malignity! And should a christian make his tongue the instrument of the accuser of the brethren, to do his work against each other?

3. It signifieth want of christian love. For love speaketh not evil, nor openeth men's faults without a cause, but covereth infirmities; much less will it lie and slander others, and carry about uncertain reports against them. It is not to do as you would be done by: and how essential love is to true christianity, Christ himself hath often told us.

4. It is a sin which directly serveth to destroy the hearers' love, and consequently to destroy their souls. If the backbiter understood himself, he would confess that it is his very end to cause you to hate (or abate your love to) him whom he speaketh evil of. He that speaketh good of a man, representeth him amiable; for amiableness and goodness are all one. And he that speaketh evil of a man representeth him hateful or unlovely; for hatefulness, unloveliness, and evil are all one. And as it is not the natural way of winning love, to entreat and beg it, and say, I pray you love this person, or that thing; but to open the goodness of the thing or person, which will command love: so is it not the natural way to stir up hatred, by entreating men to hate this man or that; but to tell how bad they are, which will command hatred in them that do believe it. Therefore to speak evil of another, is more than to say to the hearers, I pray you hate this man, or abate your love to him. And that the killing of love is the killing or destroying of men's souls, the apostle John doth frequently declare.

[861]5. And it tendeth also to destroy the love, and consequently the soul of him that you speak evil of. For when it cometh to his hearing, (as one way or other it may do,) what evil you have reported of him behind his back, it tendeth to make him hate you, and so to make him worse.

6. It is a great make-bate and peace-breaker wherever it is practised. It tendeth to set people together by the ears. When it is told that such a one spake evil of you in

such a place, there are then heart-burnings, and rehearsals, and sidings, and such ensuing malice as the devil intended by this design.

7. They that use to speak evil of others behind their backs, it is ten to one will speak falsehoods of them when they do not know it. Fame is too ordinarily a liar, and they shall be liars who will be its messengers. How know you whether the thing that you report is true? Is it only because a credible person spake it? But how did that person know it to be true? Might he not take it upon trust as well as you? And might he not take a person to be credible that is not? And how commonly doth faction, or interest, or passion, or credulity, make that person incredible in one thing, who is credible in others, where he hath no such temptation! If you know it not to be true, or have not sufficient evidence to prove it, you are guilty of lying and slandering interpretatively, though it should prove true; because it might have been a lie for aught you knew.

8. It is gross injustice to talk of a man's faults, before you have heard him speak for himself. I know it is usual with such to say, O we have heard it from such as we are certain will not lie. But he is a foolish and unrighteous judge, that will be peremptory upon hearing one party only speak, and knoweth not how ordinary it is for a man when he speaketh for himself, to blow away the most confident and plausible accusations, and make the case appear to be quite another thing. You know not what another man hath to say till you have heard him.

9. Backbiting teacheth others to backbite. Your example inviteth them to do the like: and sins which are common, are easily swallowed, and hardly repented of: men think that the commonness justifieth or extenuateth the fault.

10. It encourageth ungodly men to the odious sin of backbiting and slandering the most religious, righteous person. It is ordinary with the devil's family to make Christ's faithfullest servants their table talk, and the objects of their reproach and scorn, and the song of drunkards? What abundance of lies go current among such malignant persons, against the most innocent, which would all be ashamed, if they had first admitted them to speak for themselves. And such slanders and lies are the devil's common means to keep ungodly men from the love of godliness, and so from repentance and salvation. And backbiting professors of religion encourage men to this; for with what measure they mete, it shall be measured to them again. And they that are themselves evil spoken of, will think that they are warranted to requite the backbiters with the like.

11. It is a sin which commonly excludeth true, profitable reproof and exhortation. They that speak most behind men's backs, do usually say least to the sinner's face, in any way which tendeth to his salvation. They will not go lovingly to him in private, and set home his sin upon his conscience, and exhort him to repentance; but any thing shall serve as a sufficient excuse against this duty; that they may make the sin of backbiting serve instead of it: and all is out of carnal self-saving; they fear men will be offended if they speak to their faces, and therefore they will whisper against them behind their backs.

12. It is at the least, but idle talk and a misspending of your time: what the better are the hearers for hearing of other men's misdoings? And you know that it no whit profiteth the person of whom you speak. A skilful, friendly admonition might do him good! But to neglect this, and talk of his faults unprofitably, behind his back, is but to aggravate the sin of your uncharitableness, as being not contented to refuse your help to a man in sin, but you must also injure him and do him hurt.

CHAPTER XXIV.

CASES AND DIRECTIONS AGAINST CENSORIOUSNESS AND UNWARRANTABLE JUDGING.

Tit. 1. Cases of Conscience about Judging of Others.

Quest. I. Am I not bound to judge truly of every one as he is?

Answ. 1. There are many that you are not bound to meddle with, and to pass any judgment at all upon. 2. There are many whose faults are secret, and their virtues open; and of such you cannot judge as they are, because you have no proof or evidence to enable you: you cannot see that which is latent in the heart, or done in darkness. 3. You neither ought on pretence of charity, nor can believe an evident known untruth of any man.

Quest. Doth not charity bind me to judge men better than they are?

Answ. Charity bindeth you, 1. Rather to observe the best in them, than the worst. 2. And, as I said, to judge of no man's faults uncalled. 3. Nor to judge of that which is not evident, but out of sight; and thus consequently it bindeth you to judge some men to be better than they are; but not directly.

Object. Then a man is bound to err and believe an untruth.

Answ. No: you are not bound to believe that it is certainly true, that such a man is better than he is; because you have no evidence of its certain truth. But you are bound to believe it a thing probable or verisimile, likely to be true, by an opinion or fallible human faith; and this is not a falsehood; for that is likely and probable to you, which hath the more probable evidence, and more for it than against it: so that the thing which you are to believe immediately is this proposition, There is more evidence to me to prove it likely that this man is sincere than contrary: and consequently you believe this, and believe not the contrary, because the contrary hath no evidence. But you are not to take it as a certain thing, that the contrary hath no latent reality.

Quest. II. How far may I judge ill of one by outward appearances, as by the countenance, gestures, and other uncertain but suspicious signs?

Answ. There are some signs which are not so much as probable, but a little suspicious, and which men are very ordinarily mistaken by: as those that will judge of a man at the first look by his face; and those that will judge a studious, serious person (a lawyer, a judge, or a divine) to be morose or proud, because they are not complimental, but of few words; or because they have not patience to waste precious hours in hearing an empty vessel sound, an ignorant, self-conceited person talk foolishly. Such censures are but the effects of injudiciousness, [862]unrighteousness, and rash haste. There are other signs which make it probable to a wise and charitable person, that the man is bad (e. g. proud, or covetous, or a hypocrite). If with these, there are as great sins to make the contrary probable, we must rather incline to the better than the worse. But if not, we may fear the worst of that person, but not conclude it as a certainty; and therefore we may not in public censures, proceed upon such uncertainties, nor venture to divulge them; but only use them to help us for due caution, and pity, and prayer, and endeavour for such a one's recovery and help.

Quest. III. How far may I censure upon the report of others?

Answ. According to the degree of the credibility of the persons, and evidence of the narrative; not simply in themselves, but as compared with all that is to be heard on the contrary part; else you are partial and unjust.

Quest. IV. Doth not the fifth command oblige me in honour to parents and princes, to judge them to be better than their lives declare them to be?

Answ. You are gradually to honour them more than others, and therefore to be more afraid of dishonouring them, and must not sit in judgment on them, to believe any harm of them, which evidence doth not compel you to believe. But you are not to judge any sin the less, because it is theirs; nor to judge contrary to evidence, nor to call evil good, nor to be wilfully blind, nor to flatter any in their sin.

Quest. V. Whom must we judge for sincere and sanctified christians?

Answ. 1. All those that profess to be such, whom you cannot disprove. 2. But as there are several degrees of evidence and probability, so must there be several degrees of your good opinion of others. Of some who give you the highest probability, you may have the strongest confidence short of certainty: of others you may have less; and of some you may have much more fear than hope. 3. And yet in matters of church rights and public communion, your fears will not allow you to use them as no christians; for their profession of faith and repentance is certain; and as long as your fears of their hypocrisy or unsoundness are but uncertain, it must not (on that account) prevail to deprive another of his right.

Quest. VI. But is not my error my sin, if I prove mistaken, and take that man for a sincere christian who is none?

Answ. If you judged it to be certain, your judgment and error was your sin; but if you only judged him a professor of christianity, and one that on that account you were bound to have church communion with as if he were sincere, because you cannot prove the contrary, this was no error; or if you erred for want of sufficient evidence to know the truth, this error is not in itself a sin.

Quest. VII. Whom must I judge a visible member of the church, with whom I am thus bound to hold communion?

Answ. 1. If you are the pastor of the church who are made the judge, at his admission by baptism, or afterwards, you must so judge of every one who maketh a credible profession of true christianity, that is, of his present consent to the sacramental covenant: and that profession is credible, which is, 1. Understood by him that maketh it. 2. Deliberate. 3. Voluntary. 4. Seemingly serious. 5. And is not disproved by valid evidence of the contrary. These are the true measures of church communion; for every man, next God, is the judge of his own heart; and God would have every man the chooser or refuser of his own mercies.

2. But if you are but a private member of the church, you are to judge that person a visible member of the church, whom the pastor hath taken in by baptism, and not cast out again by excommunication; except the contrary be notorious: and even then you are oft obliged for order sake to carry yourself towards him as a visible member, till he be regularly cast out.

Quest. VIII. Whom must I judge a true worshipper of God, and whom not?

Answ. Him that professeth true christianity, and joineth in true worship with a christian church, or privately (when hindered) acknowledgeth the true God in all his essential attributes, and heareth his word, and prayeth to him for all things necessary to salvation, and praiseth him accordingly, not giving the worship proper to God unto any creature; and doth all this as a sinner redeemed by Jesus Christ, trusting in his merits, sacrifice, and intercession, and giveth not his office to any other. And he is a false worshipper who denieth any essential attribute of God, or essential part of the office of Christ, or giveth these to any other; or refuseth his word, or excludeth in his prayers any thing essential to christianity, or absolutely necessary to salvation. But *secundum quid*, in lesser parts, or in circumstances, or measures, every man on earth is a false worshipper, that is, he offereth God a worship some way faulty and imperfect, and hath some sin in his worshipping of God; and sin is a thing that God requireth not, but forbiddeth even in the smallest measures.

Quest. IX. Which must I judge a true church of Christ, and which a false church?

Answ. The universal church is but one, and is the whole society of christians as united to Christ their only Head; and this cannot be a false church. But if any other set up a usurper as the universal head, and so make another policy and church, this is a false church formally, or in its policy; but yet the members of this false church or policy may some of them as christians be also members of the true church of Christ: and thus the Roman church as papal is a false catholic church, having the policy of a usurper; but as christians they may be members of the true catholic church of Christ. But for a particular church which is but part of the universal, that is a true church considered merely as an ungoverned community, which is a true part of the catholic, prepared for a pastor, but yet being without one: but that only is a true political church, which consisteth of professed christians conjoined under a true pastor, for communion in the profession of true christianity, and for the true worshipping of God, and orderly walking for their mutual assistance and salvation.

Quest. X. Whom must we judge true prophets and pastors of the church.

Answ. He is a true prophet who is sent by God, and speaketh truth by immediate supernatural revelation or inspiration. And he is a false prophet who either falsely saith that he hath divine revelations or inspiration, or prophesieth falsehood as from God. And he is a true pastor at the bar of God, who is, 1. Competently qualified with abilities for the office. 2. Competently disposed to it, with willingness and desire of success; and hath right ends in undertaking and discharging it. 3. Who hath a just admission, by true ordination of pastors, and consent of the flock; and he is to be accounted a true pastor *in foro ecclesia,* in the church's judgment, whom the church judgeth to have all these qualifications, and thereupon admitteth him into possession of the place, till his incapacity be notoriously or publicly and sufficiently proved, or he be removed or made uncapable.[863]

Tit. 2. Directions for the Cure of Sinful Censoriousness.

Direct. I. Meddle not at all in judging of others without a call. Know first whether it be any of your work; if not, be afraid of those words of your Judge, Matt. vii. 1-5, "Judge not, that ye be not judged; for with what judgment ye judge, you shall be judged," &c. And Rom. xiv. 4, "Who art thou that judgest another man's servant? To his own master he standeth or falleth." And verses 10, and 13, "But why dost thou judge thy brother? or why dost thou set at nought thy brother? We shall all stand before the judgment-seat of Christ.—Every one of us shall give account of himself to God. Let us not therefore judge one another any more." 1 Cor. iv. 3-5, "But with me it is a very small thing that I should be judged of you, or of man's judgment—Therefore judge nothing before the time till the Lord come, who both will bring to light the hidden things of darkness, and will make manifest the counsels of the hearts—." Col. ii. 16, "Let no man judge you in meat or in drink, or in respect of any holy day, or of the new moon, or sabbath."

Quest. But when have I a call to judge another?

Answ. You may take the answer to this from the answer to quest. x. chap. xxiii. tit. 1. 1. If your office and place require it as a magistrate, pastor, parent, master, tutor, &c. 2. If the safety of the church or your neighbour do require it. 3. If the good of the sinner require it that you may seek his repentance and reformation. 4. If your own preservation or welfare (or any other duty) require it.

Direct. II. Keep up a humble sense of your own faults, and that will make you compassionate to others. He that is truly vile in his own eyes, is least inclined to vilify others: and he that judgeth himself with the greatest penitent severity, is the least inclined to be censorious to his brother. Pride is the common cause of censoriousness: he that saith with the Pharisee, "I fast twice a week, and pay tithes of all that I have, I am no adulterer," &c. will also say, "I am not as other men, nor as this publican:" when the true penitent findeth so much of his own to be condemned, that he smiteth on his own breast and saith, "God be merciful to me a sinner." The prouder, self-conceited sort of christians are ever the most censorious of their neighbours.

Direct. III. Be much therefore at home in searching, and watching, and amending your own hearts: and then you will find so much to do about yourselves, that you will have no mind or leisure to be censuring others; whereas the superficial hypocrite, whose religion is in externals, and is unacquainted with his heart and heaven, is so little employed in the true work of a christian, that he hath leisure for the work of a censorious Pharisee.

Direct. IV. Labour for a deep experimental insight into the nature of religion, and of every duty. For no men are so censorious as the ignorant who know not what they say; whilst experienced persons know those difficulties and other reasons which calm their minds. As in common business, no man will sooner find fault with a workman in his work, than idle praters who least understand it. So is it commonly in matters of religion: women and young men that never saw into the great mysteries of divinity, but have been lately changed from a vicious life, and have neither acquaintance with the hard points of religion, nor with their own ignorance of them, are the common, proud censurers of their brethren much wiser than themselves, and of all men that are more moderate and peaceable than themselves, and are more addicted to unity, and more averse to sects and separations than they. Study harder, and wait till you grow up to the experience of the aged, and you will be less censorious and more peaceable.

Direct. V. Think not yourselves fit judges of that which you understand not: and think not proudly that you are more like to understand the difficulties in religion, with your short and lazy studies, than those that in reading, meditation, and prayer have spent their lives in searching after them. Let not pride make you abuse the Holy Ghost, by pretending that he hath given you more wisdom in a little time, and with little means and diligence, than your betters have by the holy industry of their lives: say not, God can give more to you in a year than to others in twenty; for it is a poor argument to prove that God hath done it, because he can do it. He can make you an angel, but that will not prove you one. Prove your wisdom before you pretend to it, and overvalue it not: Heb. v. 11, 12, showeth that it is God's ordinary way to give men wisdom according to their time and means, unless their own negligence deprive them of his blessing.

Direct. VI. Study to keep up christian love, and to keep it lively. For love is not censorious, but is inclined to judge the best, till evidence constrain you to the contrary. Censoriousness is a vermin which crawleth in the carcass of christian love, when the life of it is gone.

Direct. VII. Value all God's graces in his servants; and then you will see something to love them for, when hypocrites can see nothing: make not too light of small degrees of grace, and then your censure will not overlook them.

Direct. VIII. Remember the tenderness of Christ, who condemneth not the weak, nor casteth infants out of his family, nor the diseased out of his hospital; but dealeth with them in such a gracious gentleness, as beseemeth a tender-hearted Saviour: he will not break the bruised reed: he carrieth his lambs in his arms, and gently driveth those with young! He taketh up the wounded man, when the priest and Levite pass him by. And have you not need of the tenderness of Christ yourselves as well as others? Are you not afraid lest he should find greater faults with you than you find in others; and condemn you as you condemn them?

Direct. IX. Let the sense of the common corruption of the world, and imperfection of the godly, moderate your particular censures. As Seneca saith, To censure a man for that which is common to all men, is in a sort to censure him for being a man, which beseemeth not him that is a man himself. Do you not know the frailty of the best, and the common pravity of human nature? How few are there that must not have great allowance, or else they will not pass for current in the balance! Elias was a man subject to passions: Jonah to peevishness: Job had his impatience: Paul saith even of the teachers of the primitive church, "They all (that were with him) seek their own, and not the things of Jesus Christ." What blots are charged on almost all the churches, and almost all the holy persons, mentioned throughout all the Scriptures! Learn then of Paul a better lesson than censoriousness: Gal. vi. 1, "Brethren, if a man be overtaken in a fault, ye which are spiritual restore such an one in the spirit of meekness; considering thyself, lest thou also be tempted. Bear ye one another's burdens, and so fulfil the law of Christ. Let every man prove his own work, and then he shall have rejoicing in himself alone," &c.

Direct. X. Remember that judgment is God's prerogative (further than as we are called to it for the performance of some duty, either of office, or of [864]private charity, or self-preservation): and that the Judge is at the door! and that judging unmercifully maketh us liable to judgment without mercy. The foresight of that near universal judgment, which will pass the doom on us and all men, will do much to cure us of our rash censoriousness.

Direct. XI. Peruse and observe all the directions in the last chapter against evil-speaking and backbiting, that I may not need to repeat them: especially avoid, 1. The snare of selfishness and interest. For most men judge of others principally by their own interest. He is the good man that is good to them, or is on their side; that loveth and honoureth them, and answereth their desires: this is the common false judgment of the corrupted, selfish world; who vilify and hate the best, because they seem unsuitable to them and their carnal interest. Therefore take heed of their judgment about any man that you have a falling out with: for it is two to one but you will wrong him through this selfishness. 2. Avoid passion; which blindeth the judgment. 3. Avoid faction; which maketh you judge of all men as they agree or disagree with your opinions, or your side and party. 4. Avoid too hasty belief of censures, and rebuke them. 5. Hear every man speak for himself before you censure him, if it be possible, and the case be not notorious.

Direct. XII. Keep still upon your mind a just and deep apprehension of the malignity of this sin of rash censuring. It is of greatest consequence to the mortifying of any sin, what apprehensions of it are upon the mind. If religious persons apprehended the odiousness of this as much as they do of swearing, drunkenness, fornication, &c. they would as carefully avoid it. Therefore I shall show you the malignity of this sin.

Tit. 3. The Evil of the Sin of Censoriousness.

1. It is a usurpation of God's prerogative, who is the Judge of all the world: it is a stepping up into his judgment-seat, and undertaking his work; as if you said, I will be God as to this action. And if he be called the antichrist, who usurpeth the office of Christ, to be the universal monarch and head of the church, you may imagine what he doth, who (though but in one point) doth set up himself in the place of God.

2. They that usurp not God's part in judging, yet ordinarily usurp the part of the magistrate or pastors of the church. As when mistaken, censorious christians refuse to come to the sacrament of communion, because many persons are there whom they judge to be ungodly, what do they but usurp the office of the pastors of the church, to whom the keys are committed for admission and exclusion, and so are the appointed judges of that case? The duty of private members is but to admonish the offender first secretly, and then before witnesses, and to tell the church if he repent not, and humbly to tell the pastors of their duty, if they neglect it: and when this is done, they have discharged their part, and must no more excommunicate men themselves, than they must hang thieves when the magistrate doth neglect to hang them.

3. Censoriousness signifieth the absence or decay of love: which inclineth men to think evil, and judge the worst, and aggravate infirmities, and overlook or extenuate any good that is in others. And there is least grace where there is least love.

4. It showeth also much want of self-acquaintance, and such heart employment as the sincerest christians are taken up with. And it showeth much want of christian humility and sense of your own infirmities and badness; and much prevalency of pride and self-conceitedness. If you knew how ignorant you are, you would not be so peremptory in judging: and if you knew how bad you are, you would not be so forward to condemn your neighbours. So that here is together the effect of much self-estrangedness, hypocrisy, and pride. Did you ever well consider the mind of Christ, when he bid them that accused the adulterous woman, John viii. 7, "He that is without sin among you, let him first cast a stone at her?" Certainly adultery was a heinous crime, and to be punished with death, and Christ was no patron of uncleanness; but he knew that it was a hypocritical sort of persons whom he spake to, who were busy in judging others rather than themselves. Have you studied his words against rash censurers, Matt. vii. 3, 4; "And why beholdest thou the mote in thy brother's eye, but considerest not the beam that is in thine own eye? Or how wilt thou say to thy brother, Let me pull out the mote out of thine eye; and behold a beam is in thine own eye? Thou hypocrite! first cast out the beam out of thine own eye, and then shalt thou see clearly to cast out the mote which is in thy brother's eye." I know well that impenitent sinners do use to pervert all these words of Christ, against any that would bring them to repentance for their sin; and account all men rash censurers, who would

make them acquainted with their unsanctified hearts and lives. But it is not their abuse of Scripture, which will justify our overpassing it with neglect. Christ spake it not for nothing; and it must be studied by his disciples.

5. Censoriousness is injustice, in that the censurers would not be so censured themselves. You will say, Yes, if we were as bad, and did deserve it. But though you have not that same fault, have you no other? And are you willing to have it aggravated, and be thus rashly judged? You do not as you would be done by: yea, commonly censurers are guilty of false judging; and whilst they take things hastily upon trust, and stay not to hear men speak for themselves, or to inquire thoroughly into the cause, they commonly condemn the innocent; and call good evil, and put light for darkness; and take away the righteousness of the righteous from him, when God hath cursed such with a woe.

6. And false censuring is the proper work of the devil, the accuser of the brethren, Rev. xii. 10, "who accuseth them before God, day and night;" And christians should not bear his image, nor do his work.

7. Censoriousness is contrary to the nature and office of Jesus Christ: he came to pardon sin, and cover the infirmities of his servants, and to cast them behind his back, and into the depth of the sea, and to bury them in his grave; and it is the censurer's work to rake them up, and to make them seem more and greater than they are, and to bring them into the open light.

8. Censoriousness causeth uncharitableness and sinful separations in the censurers: when they have conceited their brethren to be worse than they are, they must then reproach them, or have no communion with them, and avoid them as too bad for the company of such as they: or when they have usurped the pastor's work in judging, they begin the execution by sinful separation.

9. Censoriousness is an infectious sin, which easily taketh with the younger and prouder sort of christians, and so setteth them on vilifying others: and at this little gap there entereth all uncharitableness, backbitings, revilings, church divisions, and sects, yea, and too often rebellious and bloody wars at last.

10. Censoriousness is a sore temptation to them [865]that are censured, either to contemn such as censure them, and go on the other hand too far from them; or else to comply with the errors and sinful humours of the censurers, and to strain their consciences to keep pace with the censorious.

And here I must leave it on record to posterity for their warning, that the great and lamentable actions, changes, and calamities of this age have arisen (next to gross impiety) from this sin of censoriousness producing these two contrary effects, and thereby dividing men into two contrary parties: the younger sort of religious people, and the more ignorant, and many women, having more zeal than judgment, placed too much of their religion in a sharp opposition to all ceremonies, formalities, and opinions which they thought unlawful; and were much inclined to schism and unjust separations upon that account; and therefore censured such things as antichristian, and those that used them as superstitious and temporizers; and no man's learning, piety, wisdom, or laboriousness in the ministry could save him from these sharp, reproachful censures. Hereupon one party had not humility and patience enough to endure to be so judged of; nor love and tenderness enough for such peevish christians, to bear with them in pity, as parents do with froward infants; but because these professed holiness and zeal, even holiness and zeal were brought under suspicion for their sakes; and they were taken to be persons intolerable, as unfit to lie in any building, and unmeet to submit to christian government; and therefore meet to be used accordingly. Another sort were so wearied with the profaneness and ungodliness of the vulgar rabble, and saw so few that were judiciously religious, that they thought it their duty to love and cherish the zeal and piety of their censorious weak ones, and to bear patiently with their frowardness, till ripeness and experience cured them (and so far they were right). And because they thought that they could do them no good, if they once lost their interest in them, (and were also themselves too impatient of their censure,) some of them seemed (to please them) to be more of their opinion than they were; and more of them forbore to reprove their petulance, but silently suffered them to go on; especially when they fell into the sects of antinomians, anabaptists, and separatists, they durst not reprove them as they deserved, lest they should drive them out of the hive, to some of these late swarms. And thus censoriousness in the ignorant and self-conceited drove away one part to take them as their enemies; and silenced or drew on another party to follow them that led the van in some irregular, violent actions; and the wise and sober moderators were disregarded, and in the noise of these tumults and contentions could not be heard, till the smart of either party in their suffering forced them to honour such, whom in their exaltation again they despised or abused. This is the true sum of all the tragedies in Britain of this age.

Tit. 4. Directions for those that are rashly censured.

Direct. I. Remember when you are injured by censures, that God is now trying your humility, charity, and patience; and therefore be most studious to exercise and preserve these three. 1. Take heed lest pride make you disdainful to the censurer; a humble man can bear contempt; hard censures hurt men so far as they are proud. 2. Take heed lest imbecility add to your impatience, and concur with pride: cannot you bear greater things than these? Impatience will disclose that badness in yourselves, which will make you censured much more; and it will show you as weak in one respect as the censurers are in another. 3. Take heed lest their fault do not draw you to overlook or undervalue that serious godliness which is in many of the censorious; and that you do not presently judge them hypocrites or schismatics, and abate your charity to them, or incline to handle them more roughly than the tenderness of Christ alloweth you. Remember that in all ages it hath been thus: the church hath had peevish children within, as well as persecuting enemies without; insomuch as Paul, Rom. xiv. giveth you the copy of these times, and giveth them this counsel, which from him I am giving you. The weak in knowledge were censorious, and judged the strong; the strong in knowledge were weak in charity, and contemned the weak: just as now one party saith, These are superstitious persons, and antichristian; the other saith, What giddy schismatics are these! but Paul chideth them both; one sort for censuring, and the other for despising them.

Direct. II. Take heed lest whilst you are impatient under their censures, you fall into the same sin yourselves. Do they censure you for differing in some forms or ceremonies from them? Take heed lest you over-censure them for their censoriousness: if you censure them as hypocrites who censure you as superstitious, you condemn yourselves while you are condemning them. For why will not censuring too far, prove you hypocrites also, if it prove them such?

Direct. III. Remember that Christ beareth with their weakness, who is wronged by it more than you, and is more against it. He doth not quit his title to them for their frowardness, nor cease his love, nor turn every infant out of his family that will cry and wrangle, nor every patient out of his hospital that doth complain and groan; and we must imitate our Lord, and love where he loveth, and pity where he pitieth, and be merciful as our heavenly Father is merciful.

Direct. IV. Remember how amiable a thing the least degree of grace is, even when it is clouded and blotted with infirmities. It is the divine nature, and the image of God, and the seed of glory; and therefore as an infant hath the noble nature of a man, and in all his weakness is much more honourable than the best of brutes (so that it is death to kill an infant, but not a beast): so is the most infirm and froward true christian more honourable and amiable than the most splendid infidel. Bear with them in love and honour to the image and interest of Christ.

Direct. V. Remember that you were once weak in grace yourselves; and if happy education under peaceable guides did not prevent it, it is two to one but you were yourselves censorious. Bear therefore with others as you bear with crying children, because you were once a child yourself. Not that the sin is ever the better, but you should be the more compassionate.

216

Direct. VI. Remember that your own strength and judgment is so great a mercy, that you should the easilier bear with a censorious tongue. The rich and noble can bear with the envious, remembering that it is happy to have that worth or felicity which men do envy. You suffer fools gladly, seeing you yourselves are wise. If you are in the right let losers talk.

Direct. VII. Remember that we shall be shortly together in heaven, where they will recant their censures, and you will easily forgive them, and perfectly love them. And will not the foresight of such a meeting cause you to bear with them, and forgive and love them now?

Direct. VIII. Remember how inconsiderable a thing it is as to your own interest, to be judged of man; and that you stand or fall to the judgment of [866]the Lord, 1 Cor. iv. 3, 4. What are you the better or the worse for the thoughts or words of a man; when your salvation or damnation lieth upon God's judgment. It is too much hypocrisy, to be too much desirous of man's esteem and approbation, and too much troubled at his disesteem and censure, and not to be satisfied with the approbation of God. Read what is written against man-pleasing, part i.

Direct. IX. Make some advantage of other men's censures, for your own proficiency. If good men censure you, be not too quick in concluding that you are innocent, and justifying yourselves; but be suspicious of yourselves, lest they should prove the right, and examine yourselves with double diligence. If you find that you are clear in the point that you are censured for, suspect and examine lest some other sin hath provoked God to try you by these censures; and if you find not any other notable fault, let it make you the more watchful by way of prevention, seeing the eyes of God and men are on you; and it may be God's warning, to bid you take heed for the time to come. If you are thus brought to repentance, or to the more careful life, by occasion of men's censures, they will prove so great a benefit to you, that you may bear them the more easily.

CHAPTER XXV.

CASES AND DIRECTIONS ABOUT TRUSTS AND SECRETS.
Tit. 1. Cases of Conscience about Trusts and Secrets.

Quest. I. How are we forbidden to put our trust in man? And how may it be done?

Answ. 1. You must not trust man for more than his proportion, and what belongs to man to do: you must not expect that from him which God alone can do. 2. You must not trust a bad, unfaithful man to do that which is proper to a good and faithful man to do. 3. You must not trust the best man, being imperfect and fallible, as fully as if you supposed him perfect and infallible: but having to do with a corrupted world, we must live in it with some measure of distrust to all men (for all that Cicero thought this contrary to the laws of friendship). But especially ignorant, dishonest, and fraudulent men must be most distrusted. As Bucholtzer said to his friend that was going to be a courtier, *Commendo tibi fidem diabolorum, crede et contremisce:* he that converseth with diabolical men, must believe them no further than is due to the children of the father of lies. But we must trust men as men, according to the principles of veracity that are left in corrupted nature; and we must trust men so far as reason showeth us cause, from their skill, fidelity, honesty, or interest: so a surgeon, a physician, a pilot may be trusted with our lives: and the skilfuller and faithfuller any man is, the more he is to be trusted.

Quest. II. Whom should a man choose for a matter of trust?

Answ. As the matter is: one that hath wisdom, skill, and fidelity, through conscience, honesty, friendship, or his own apparent interest.

Quest. III. In what cases may I commit a secret to another?

Answ. When there is a necessity of his knowing it, or a greater probability of good than hurt by it, in the evidence which a prudent man may see.

Quest. IV. What if another commit a thing to me with charge of secrecy, and I say nothing to him, and so promise it not; am I bound to secrecy in that case?

Answ. If you have cause to believe that he took your silence for consent, and would not else have committed it to you, you are obliged in point of fidelity, as well as friendship: except it be with robbers, or such as we are not bound to deal openly with, and on terms of equality.

Quest. V. What if it be a secret, but I am under no command or promise at all about it?

Answ. You must then proceed according to the laws of charity and friendship; and not reveal that which is to the injury of another, without a greater cause.

Quest. VI. What if it be against the king, or state, or common good?

Answ. You are bound to reveal it, so far as the safety of the king, or state, or common good requireth it; yea, though you swear the contrary.

Quest. VII. What if it be only against the good of some third ordinary person.

Answ. You must endeavour to prevent his wrong, either by revealing the thing, or dissuading from it, or by such means as prudence shall tell you are the meetest, by exercising your love to one, without doing wrong to the other.

Quest. VIII. What if a man secretly intrust his estate to me, for himself or children, when he is in debt, to defraud his creditors?

Answ. You ought not to take such a trust: and if you have done it, you ought not to hold it, but resign it to him that did intrust you. Yea, and to disclose the fraud, for the righting of the creditors, except it be in such a case as that the creditor is some such vicious or oppressing person, as you are not obliged to exercise that act of charity for; or when the consequents of revealing it will be a greater hurt, than the righting of him will compensate; especially when it is against the public good.

Quest. IX. What if a delinquent intrust me with his estate or person to secure it from penalty?

Answ. If it be one that is prosecuted by a due course of justice, *cujus pœna debetur reipublicæ,* whose punishment the common good requireth, the case must be decided as the former: you must not take nor keep such a trust. But if it be one whose repentance giveth you reason to believe, that his impunity will be more to the common good than his punishment, and that if the magistrate knew it, he ought to spare or pardon him, in this case you may conceal his person or estate; so be it you do it not by a lie, or any other sinful means, or such as will do more hurt than good.

Quest. X. What if a friend intrust me with his estate to secure it from some great taxes or tributes to the king? May I keep such a trust or not?

Answ. No: if they be just and legal taxes, for the maintenance of the magistrate or preservation of the commonwealth: but if it be done by a usurper that hath no authority, (or done without or beyond authority, the oppressing of the subject,) you may conceal his estate or your own by lawful means.

Quest. XI. What if a man that suffereth for religion, commit his person or estate to my trust?

Answ. You must be faithful to your trust, 1. If it be true religion and a good cause for which he suffereth. 2. Or if he be falsely accused of abuses in religion. 3. Or if he be faulty, but the penalty intended, from which you secure him, is incomparably beyond his fault and unjust. Supposing still that you save him only by lawful means, and that it be not like to tend to do more hurt than good, to the cause of religion or the commonwealth.

[867]*Quest.* XII. What if a papist or other erroneous person intrust me (being of the same mind) to educate his children in that way, when he is dead, and afterward I come to see the error, must I perform that trust or not?

Answ. No: 1. Because no trust can oblige you to do hurt. 2. Because it is contrary to the primary intent of your friend; which was his children's good. And you may well suppose that had he seen his error, he would have intrusted you to do

218

accordingly: you are bound therefore to answer his primary intention, and truly to endeavour his children's good.

Quest. XIII. But what if a man to whom another hath intrusted his children, turn papist or heretic, and so thinketh error to be truth? what must he do?

Answ. He is bound to turn back again to the truth, and do accordingly.

Object. But one saith this is the truth and another that; and he thinketh he is right.

Answ. There is but one of the contraries true. Men's thinking themselves to be in the right doth not make it so. And God will not change his laws, because they misunderstand or break them: therefore still that which God bindeth them to is to return unto the truth. And if they think that to be truth which is not, they are bound to think otherwise. If you say, They cannot; it is either not true, or it is long of themselves that they cannot: and they that cannot immediately, yet mediately can do it, in the due use of means.

Quest. XIV. What if I foresee that the taking a trust may hazard my estate, or otherwise hurt me, and yet my dying (or living) friend desireth it?

Answ. How far the law of christianity or friendship oblige you to hurt yourself for his good, must be discerned by a prudent considering, what your obligations are to the person, and whether the good of your granting his desires, or the hurt to yourself, is like to be the greater, and of more public consequence: and whether you injure not your own children or others by gratifying him. And upon such comparison, prudence must determine the case.

Quest. XV. But what if afterward the trust prove more to my hurt than I foresaw?

Answ. If it was your own fault that you foresaw it not, you must suffer proportionably for that fault; but otherwise you must compare your own hurt with the orphans', in case you do not perform the trust: and consider whether they may not be relieved another way; and whether you have reason to think that if the parent were alive and knew the danger, he would expect you should perform your trust, or would discharge you of it. If it be some great and unexpected dangers, which you think upon good grounds the parent would acquit you from if he were living, you fulfil your trust if you avoid them, and do that which would have been his will if he had known it. Otherwise you must perform your promise though it be to your loss and suffering.

Quest. XVI. But what if it was only a trust imposed by his desire and will, without my acceptance or promise to perform it?

Answ. You must do as you would be done by, and as the common good, and the laws of love and friendship, do require. Therefore the quality of the person, and your obligations to him, and especially the comparing of the consequent good and evil together, must decide the case.

Quest. XVII. What if the surviving kindred of the orphan be nearer to him than I am, and they censure me and calumniate me as injurious to the orphan, may I not ease myself of the trust, and cast it upon them?

Answ. In this case also, the measure of your suffering must first be compared with the measure of the orphan's good; and then your conscience must tell you whether you verily think the parent who intrusted you, would discharge you if he were alive and knew the case. If he would, though you promised, it is to be supposed that it was not the meaning of his desire or your promise, to incur such suffering: and if you would not believe that he would not discharge you if he were alive, then if you promised you must perform; but if you promised not, you must go no further than the law of love requireth.

Quest. XVIII. What is a minister of Christ to do, if a penitent person confess secretly some heinous or capital crime to him (as adultery, theft, robbery, murder); must it be concealed or not?

Answ. 1. If a purpose of sinning be antecedently confessed, it is unlawful to further the crime, or give opportunity to it by a concealment: but it must be so far opened as is necessary for the prevention of another's wrong, or the person's sin; especially if it be treason against the king or kingdom, or any thing against the common good.

2. When the punishment of the offender is apparently necessary to the good of others, especially to right the king or country, and to preserve them from danger by the offender or any other, it is a duty to open a past fault that is confessed, and to bring the offender to punishment, rather than injure the innocent by their impunity.

3. When restitution is necessary to a person injured, you may not by concealment hinder such restitution; but must procure it to your power where it may be had.

4. It is unlawful to promise universal secrecy absolutely to any penitent. But you must tell him before he confesseth, If your crime be such, as that opening it is necessary to the preservation or righting of king, or country, or your neighbour, or to my own safety, I shall not conceal it. That so men may know how far to trust you.

5. Yet in some rare cases, (as the preservation of our parents, king, or country,) it may be a duty to promise and perform concealment, when there is no hurt like to follow but the loss or hazard of our own lives, or liberties, or estates; and consequently if no hurt be like to follow but some private loss of another, which I cannot prevent without a greater hurt.

6. If a man ignorant of the law, and of his own danger, have rashly made a promise of secrecy, and yet be in doubt, he should open the case *in hypothesi* only, to some honest, able lawyer, inquiring if such a case should be, what the law requireth of the pastor, or what danger he is in if he conceal it; that he may be able further to judge of the case.

7. He that made no promise of secrecy, virtual or actual, may, *cæteris paribus*, bring the offender to shame or punishment rather than to fall into the like himself for the concealment.

8. He that rashly promised universal secrecy, must compare the penitent's danger and his own, and consider whose suffering is like to be more to the public detriment, all things considered, and that must be first avoided.

9. He that findeth it his duty to reveal the crime to save himself, must yet let the penitent have notice of it, that he may fly and escape; unless as aforesaid, when the interest of the king, or country, or others, doth more require his punishment.

10. But when there is no such necessity of the offender's punishment, for the prevention of the hurt or wrong of others, nor any great danger by concealment to the minister himself, I think that the [868]crime, though it were capital, should be concealed. My reasons are,

(1.) Because though every man be bound to do his best to prevent sin, yet every man is not bound to bring offenders to punishment. He that is no magistrate, nor hath a special call so to do, may be in many cases not obliged to it.

(2.) It is commonly concluded that (in most cases) a capital offender is not bound to bring himself to punishment: and that which you could not know but by his free confession, is confessed to you only on your promise of concealment, seemeth to me to put you under no other obligation to bring him to punishment than he is under himself.

(3.) Christ's words and practice, in dismissing the woman taken in adultery, showeth that it is not always a duty for one that is no magistrate to prosecute a capital offender, but that sometimes his repentance and life may be preferred.

(4.) And magistrates' pardons show the same.

(5.) Otherwise no sinner would have the benefit of a counsellor to open his troubled conscience to: for if it be a duty to detect a great crime in order to a great punishment, why not a less also in order to a less punishment. And who would confess when it is to bring themselves to punishment?

11. In those countries where the laws allow pastors to conceal all crimes that penitents freely confess, it is left to the pastor's judgment to conceal all that he

discerneth may be concealed without the greater injury of others, or of the king or commonwealth.

12. There is a knowledge of the faults of others, by common fame, especially many years after the committing, which doth not oblige the hearers to prosecute the offender. And yet a crime publicly known is more to be punished (lest impunity imbolden others to the like) than an unknown crime, revealed in confession.

Tit. 2. Directions about Trusts and Secrets.

Direct. I. Be not rash in receiving secrets or any other trusts: but first consider what you are thereby obliged to, and what difficulties may arise in the performance; and foresee all the consequents as far as is possible, before you undertake the trust; that you cast not yourselves into snares by mere inconsiderateness, and prepare not for perplexities and repentance.

Direct. II. Be very careful what persons you commit either trusts or secrets to; and be sure they be trusty by their wisdom, ability, and fidelity.

Direct. III. Be not too forward in revealing your own secrets to another's trust: for, 1. You cannot be certain of any one's secrecy, where you are most confident. 2. You oblige yourself too much to please that person, who by revealing your secrets may do you hurt; and are in fear lest carelessness, or unfaithfulness, or any accident should disclose it. 3. You burden your friend with the charge and care of secrecy.[168]

Direct. IV. Be faithful to your friend that doth intrust you; remembering that perfidiousness or falseness to a friend, is a crime against humanity, and all society, as well as against christianity; and stigmatizeth the guilty in the eyes of all men, with the brand of an odious, unsociable person.

Direct. V. Be not intimate with too many, nor confident in too many; for he that hath too many intimates, will be opening the secrets of one to another.

Direct. VI. Abhor covetousness and ambition; or else a bribe or the promise of preferment, will tempt you to perfidiousness. There is no trusting a selfish, worldly man.

Direct. VII. Remember that God is the avenger of perfidiousness, who will do it severely: and that even they that are pleased and served by it, do yet secretly disdain and detest the person that doth it; because they would not be so used themselves.

Direct. VIII. Yet take not friendship or fidelity to be an obligation to perfidiousness to God, or the king, or commonwealth, or to another, or to any sin whatsoever.

[168] Quod tacitum esse velis nemini dixeris. Si tibi non imperasti, quomodo ab alio silentium speras? Martin. Dumiens, de morib.

CHAPTER XXVI.

DIRECTIONS AGAINST SELFISHNESS AS IT IS CONTRARY TO THE LOVE OF OUR NEIGHBOUR.

THE two tables of the law are summed up by our Saviour in two comprehensive precepts: "Thou shalt love the Lord thy God with all thy heart, and soul, and might:" and, "Thou shalt love thy neighbour as thyself." In the decalogue the first of these is the true meaning of the first commandment, put first because it is the principle of all obedience: and the second is the true meaning of the tenth commandment, which is therefore put last, because it is the comprehensive sum of other duties to our neighbour or injuries against him, which any other particular instances may contain; and also the principle of the duty to, or sin against, our neighbour. The meaning of the tenth commandment is variously conjectured at by expositors: some say that it speaketh against inward concupiscence and the sinful thoughts of the heart; but so do all the rest, in the true meaning of them, and must not be supposed to forbid the outward action only, nor to be any way defective: some say that it forbiddeth coveting and commandeth contentment with our state; so doth the eighth commandment; yet there is some part of the truth in both these. And the plain truth is, (as far as I can understand it,) that the sin forbidden is selfishness as opposite to the love of others, and the duty commanded is to love our neighbours; and that it is as is said, the sum of the second table, "Thou shalt love thy neighbour as thyself:" as the captain leadeth the van, and the lieutenant bringeth up the rear; so, "Thou shalt love God above all," is the first commandment, and "Thou shalt love thy neighbour as thyself," is the last, for the aforesaid reason. I shall therefore in these following directions speak to the two parts of the tenth commandment.

Direct. I. The first help against selfishness is to understand well the nature and malignity of the sin. For want of this it commonly prevaileth, with little suspicion, lamentation, and opposition. Let me briefly therefore anatomize it.

1. It is the radical, positive sin of the soul, comprehending seminally or causally all the rest. The corruption of man's nature, or his radical sin, hath two parts, the positive part, and the privative part: the positive part is selfishness, or the inordinate love of carnal self; the privative part is ungodliness or want of the love of God. Man's fall was his turning from God to himself; and his regeneration consisteth in the turning of him from himself to God; or the generating of the love of God (as comprehending [869]faith and obedience) and the mortifying of self-love. Selfishness therefore is all positive sin in one, as want of the love of God is all privative sin in one. And self-denial and the love of God are all duties virtually; for the true love of man is comprehended in the love of God. Understand this, and you will understand what original and actual sin is, and what grace and duty are.

2. Therefore selfishness is the cause of all sin in the world, both positive and privative, and is virtually the breach of every one of God's commandments. For even the want of the love of God is caused by the inordinate love of self; as the consuming of other parts is caused by the dropsy, which tumefieth the belly. It is only selfishness which breaketh the fifth commandment, by causing rulers to oppress and persecute their subjects, and causeth subjects to be seditious and rebellious; and causeth all the bitterness, and quarrellings, and uncomfortableness, which ariseth among all relations. It is only selfishness which causeth the cursed wars of the earth, and desolation of countries, by plundering and burning; the murders which cry for revenge to heaven (whether civil, military, or religious): which causeth all the railings, fightings, envyings, malice; the schisms, and proud overvaluings of men's own understandings and opinions; and the contending of pastors, who shall be the greatest, and who shall have his will in proud usurpations and tyrannical impositions and domination: it is selfishness which hath set up and maintaineth the papacy, and causeth all the divisions between the western and the eastern churches; and all the cruelties, lies, and treachery exercised upon that account. It is selfishness which troubleth families and corporations, churches and kingdoms; which violateth vows, and bonds of friendship, and causeth all the tumults, and strifes, and troubles in the world. It is selfishness which causeth all covetousness, all pride and ambition, all luxury and voluptuousness, all surfeiting and drunkenness, chambering and wantonness, time-wasting and heart-corrupting sports, and all the riots and revelling of the sensual; all the contending for honours and preferments, and all the deceit in buying and selling, the stealing and robbing, the bribery and simony, the law-suits which are unjust, the perjuries, false witnessing, unrighteous judging, the oppressions, the revenge, and in one word, all the uncharitable and unjust actions in the world. This is the true nature of carnal selfishness, and it is no better.

3. Selfishness is the corruption of all the faculties of the soul. It is the sin of the mind, by self-conceitedness and pride; it is the sin of the will and affections, by self-love, and all the selfish passions which attend it; selfish desires, angers, sorrows, discontents, jealousies, fears, audacities, &c. It is the corruption of all the inferior faculties, and the whole conversation by self-seeking, and all the forementioned evils.

4. Selfishness is the commonest sin in the world. Every man is now born with it, and hath it more or less; and therefore every man should fear it.

5. Selfishness is the hardest sin in the world to overcome. In all the unregenerate it is predominant; for nothing but the sanctifying Spirit of God can overcome it. And in many thousands that seem very zealous in religion, and very mortified in all other respects, yet in some way or other selfishness doth so lamentably appear, yea, and is so strong in many that are sincere, that it is the greatest dishonour to the church of Christ, and hath tempted many to infidelity, or to doubt whether there be any such thing as true sanctification in the world. The persons that seemed the most mortified saints, if you do but cross them in their self-interest, or opinion, or will, or seem to slight them, or have a low esteem of them, what swellings, what heart-burnings, what bitter censurings, what proud impatience, if not schisms and separations, will it cause? God hath better servants; but too many which seem to themselves and others to be the best, are no better. How then should every christian abhor and watch against this universal evil!

Direct. II. Consider oft how amiable a creature man would be, and what a blessed condition the world and all societies would be in, if selfishness were but overcome. There would then be no pride, no covetousness, no sensuality, no tyranny or oppressing of the poor, no malice, cruelty, or persecution; no church divisions, no scandals, nothing to dishonour religion, or to hinder the saving progress of the gospel; no fraud or treacheries, no over-reaching or abusing others; no lying nor deceit, no neglect of our duty to others; in a word, no injustice or uncharitableness in the world.

Direct. III. Judge of good and evil by sober reason, and not by brutish sense. And then oft consider, whether really there be not a more excellent end than your selfish interest? even the public good of many, and the pleasing and glorifying of God. And whether all mediate good or evil should not be judged of principally by those highest ends? Sense leadeth men to selfishness or privateness of design; but true reason leadeth men to prefer the public, or any thing that is better than our self-interest.

Direct. IV. Nothing but returning by converting grace to the true love of God, and of man for his sake, will conquer selfishness. Make out therefore by earnest prayer for the Spirit of sanctification; and be sure that you have a true apprehension of the state of grace; that is, that it is indeed the love of God and man. Love is the fulfilling of the law; therefore love is the holiness of the soul: set your whole study upon the exercise and increase of love, and selfishness will die as love reviveth.

Direct. V. Study much the self-denying example and precepts of your Saviour. His life and doctrine are the liveliest representation of self-denial that ever was given to the world. Learn Christ, and you will learn self-denial. He had not sinful selfishness to mortify, yet natural self was so wonderfully denied by him, for his Father's will and our salvation, that no other book or teacher in the world will teach us this lesson so perfectly as he. Follow him from the manger, or rather from the womb, to the cross and grave; behold him in his poverty and contempt; enduring the contradiction and ingratitude of sinners, and making himself of no reputation; behold him apprehended, accused, condemned, crowned with thorns, clothed in purple, with a reed in his hand, scourged, and led away to execution, bearing his cross, and hanged up among thieves; forsaken by his own disciples, and all the world, and in part by him who is more than all the world; and consider why all this was done; for whom he did it, and what lesson he purposed hereby to teach us. Consider why he made it one half the condition of our salvation, and so great a part of the christian religion, to deny ourselves, and take up our cross and follow him; and will have no other to be his disciples, Luke xiv. 26, 31, 33. Were a crucified Christ more of our daily study, and did we make it our religion to learn and follow his holy example, self-denial would be better known and practised, and christianity would appear as it is, and not as it is misunderstood, adulterated and abused in the world. But because I have long ago written a "Treatise of Self-denial," I shall add no more.

[870]

CASES AND DIRECTIONS FOR LOVING OUR NEIGHBOUR AS OURSELVES.

Tit. 1. Cases of Conscience about loving our Neighbour.

Quest. I. In what sense is it that I must love my neighbour as myself? Whether in the kind, of love, or in the degree, or only in the reality.

Answ. The true meaning of the text is, you must love him according to his true worth, without the diversion and hinderance of selfishness and partiality. As you must love yourself according to that degree of goodness which is in you, and no more; so must you as impartially love your neighbour according to that degree of goodness which is in him. So that it truly extendeth to the reality, the kind and the degree of love, supposing it in both proportioned to the goodness of the object. But before this can be understood, the true nature of love must be well understood.

Quest. II. What is the true nature of love, both as to myself and neighbour?

Answ. Love is nothing but the prime motion of the will to its proper object; which is called complacence: the object of it is simple goodness, or good as such: it ariseth from suitableness between the object and the will, as appetite doth from the suitableness of the appetent fancy and food. This good, as it is variously modified, or any way differeth, doth accordingly cause or require a difference in our love; therefore that love which in its prime act and nature is but one, is diversely denominated, as its objects are diversified. To an object as simply good, in itself, it followeth the understanding's estimation, and is called, as I said, mere complacence or adhesion: to an object as not yet attained, but absent, or distant, and attainable, it is called desire or desiring love: and as expected, hope, or hoping love (which is a conjunction of desire and expectation): to an object nearest and attained, it is called fruition, or delight, or delighting love: to an object which by means must be attained, it is called seeking love, as it exciteth to the use of those means: and to an object missed it is, by accident, mourning love. But still love itself in its essential act is one and the same. As it respecteth an object which wanteth something to make it perfect, and desireth the supply of that want, it is called love of benevolence; denominated from this occasion, as it desireth to do good to him that is loved. And it is a love of the same nature which we exercise towards God, who needeth nothing, as we rejoice in that perfection and happiness which he hath; though it be not to be called properly by the same name. Goodness being the true object of love, is the true measure of it; and therefore God is infinitely and primitively good, is the prime and only simple object of our absolute, total love. And therefore those who understand no goodness in any being, but as profitable to them, or to some other creature, do know no God, nor love God as God, nor have any love but selfish and idolatrous. By this you may perceive the nature of love.

Quest. III. But may none be loved above the measure of his goodness? How then did God love us when we were not, or were his enemies? And how must we love the wicked? And how must an ungodly person love himself?

Answ. If only good, as such, be the object of love, then certainly none should be loved but in proportion to his goodness. But you must distinguish between mere natural and sensitive love or appetite, and rational love; and between love, and the effects of love; and between natural goodness in the object, and moral goodness. And so I further answer, 1. There is in every man a natural and sensitive love of himself and his own pleasure and felicity, and an averseness to death and pain and sorrow, as there is in every brute: and this God hath planted there for the preservation of the creature. This falleth not under commands or prohibitions directly, because it is not free but necessary; as no man is commanded or forbidden to be hungry, or thirsty, or weary, or the like: it is not this love which is meant when we are commanded to love our neighbour as ourselves. For I am not commanded to feel hunger, and thirst, nor to desire meat and drink by the sensitive appetite for my neighbour: nor sensitively to feel his pain or pleasure, nor to have that natural aversation from death and pain, nor sensitive desire of life and pleasure, for him as for myself. But the love here spoken of, is that volition with the due affection conjunct, which is our rational love, as being the act of our highest faculty, and falling under God's command. As to the sensitive love, it proceedeth not upon the sense or estimate of goodness in the person who loveth himself or any other (as beasts love their young ones without respect to their excellency). But it is rational love which is proportioned to the estimated goodness of the thing beloved. 2. Physical goodness may be in an object which hath no moral goodness; and this may contain a capacity of moral goodness: and each of them is amiable according to its nature and degree. 3. Beneficence is sometimes an effect of love, and sometimes an effect of wisdom only as to the object, and of love to something else; but it is never love itself. Usually benevolence is an act of love, and beneficence an effect, but not always. I may do good to another without any love to him, for some ends of my own, or for the sake of another. And a man may be obliged to greater beneficence, where he is not obliged to greater love.

And now to the instances, I further answer, 1. When we had no being, God did not properly love us *in esse reali* (unless you will go to our co-existence in eternity; for we were not *in esse reali*); but only as we were *in esse cognito*; which is but to love the idea in himself: but he purposed to make us, and to make us lovely, and to do us good, and so he had that which is called *amor benevolentiæ* to us: which properly was not love to us, but a love to himself, and the idea in his own eternal mind, which is called a loving us *in esse cognito*, and a purpose to make us good and lovely. That which is not lovely is not an object of love: man was not lovely indeed, when he was not; therefore he was not an object of love (but *in esse cognito*.) The same we say of God's loving us when we were enemies: he really loved us with complacency so far as our physical goodness made us lovely; and as morally lovely he did not love us, otherwise than *in esse cognito*. But he purposed to make us morally lovely, and gave us his mercies to that end; and so loved us with a love of benevolence, as it is called; which signifieth no more than out of a complacence (or love) to himself, and to us, as physically good, to purpose to make us morally good and happy. As to the incident difficulty of love beginning *de novo* in God, I have fully resolved it elsewhere.[169]

2. So also we must love a wicked man with a love of benevolence: which properly is but to love him in his physical worth, and his capacity of moral [871]goodness and happiness, and thereupon (but especially through the love of God) to desire his happiness.

3. And as to the loving of ourselves, (besides the sensitive love before mentioned which respecteth self as self, and not as good,) a wicked man may rationally love himself according to his physical goodness as a man, which containeth his capacity of moral goodness, and so of being holy and serviceable to God and to good men, and happy in the fruition of God. But beyond all such goodness (which only is amiableness) no man may rationally love himself or any other, with the true formal act of love, which is complacence; though he may wish good to himself or another beyond the present goodness which is in them; nay, he wisheth them good, not because they are good, but because they want good.

And though some define loving to be *bene velle alicui ut illi bene sit*, to desire another's welfare, yet indeed this may be without any true formal love at all. As I may desire the welfare of my horse, without any proper love to him, even for myself and use. When God from eternity willeth to make Paul, and to convert and save him, *ut illi bene sit*, it is called love of benevolence; but properly it is only to be called, a will to make Paul good and lovely;[170] it being only God himself who is the original and ultimate end of that will and purpose; and himself only which he then loveth, there being nothing but himself to love; till in that instant that Paul is existent, and so really lovely. For Paul *in esse cognito* is not Paul; yet no reality doth *oriri de novo* in God; but a new respect and denomination, and in the creature new effects. (Of which elsewhere.)

Quest. IV. Must I love every one as much as myself in degree, or only some?

225

Answ. You must love every one impartially as yourself, according to his goodness; and you must wish as well to every one as to yourself; but you must love no man complacentially so much as yourself, who is not or seemeth not to have as much loveliness, that is, as much goodness, or as much of God, as yourself.

Quest. V. Must I love any one more than myself?

Answ. Yes, every one that is and appeareth better than yourself. Your sensitive love to another cannot be as much as to yourself; and your beneficence (ordinarily) must be most to yourself, because God in nature and his laws hath so appointed it; and your benevolence to yourself and to others must be alike; but your rational estimation, and love or complacence, (with the honour and praise attending it,) must be more to every one that is better than yourself; for that which is best is most amiable, and that which hath most of God.

Quest. VI. Will it not then follow, that I must love another man's wife and children better than mine own, when they are really better?

Answ. Yes, no doubt; but it is only with that rational, estimative love. But there is besides a love to wife and children, which is in some measure sensitive, which you are not obliged to give to others; and rationally they are more amiable to you, in their peculiar relations and respects, though others are more amiable in other respects; and besides, though you value and rationally love another more, yet the expressions must not be the same; for those must follow the relation according to God's command. You may not cohabit or embrace, nor maintain and provide for others as your own, even when you rationally love them more; the common good requires this order in the expressive part, as well as God's command.

Quest. VII. Who is my neighbour that I must love as myself?

Answ. Not devils or damned souls, who are under justice and from under mercy, and are none of our society: but, 1. Every natural man *in via*, being a member of God's kingdom in the same world, is to be loved as my natural self; and every spiritual man as a member of the same kingdom of Christ, must be loved as my spiritual self; and every spiritual man as such, above my natural self as such; and no natural man as such, so much as my spiritual self as such: so that no man on earth is excluded from your love, which must be impartial to all as to yourself, but proportioned to their goodness.

Quest. VIII. Are not antichrist and those that sin against the Holy Ghost excepted out of this our love, and out of our prayers and endeavours of their good?

Answ. Those that (with Zanchy) think Mahomet to be antichrist, may so conclude, because he is dead and out of our communion. Those that take the papacy to be antichrist (as most protestants do) cannot so conclude; because, as there is but one antichrist, that is, one papacy, though a hundred popes be in that seat, so every one of those popes is *in via*, and under mercy, and recoverable out of that condition; and therefore is to be loved and prayed for accordingly. And as for those that blaspheme the Holy Ghost, it is a sin that one man cannot certainly know in another, ordinarily at least; and therefore cannot characterize a person unfit for our love, and prayers, and endeavours.

Quest. IX. May we not hate the enemies of God? How then must we love them as ourselves?

Answ. We may and must hate sin in every one; and where it is predominant, as God is said to hate the sinner for his sin, so must we; and yet still love him as ourselves: for you must hate sin in yourselves as much or more than in any other; and if you are wicked you must hate yourselves as such; yea, if you are godly, you must *secundum quid*, or in that measure as you are sinful, abhor, and loathe, and hate yourselves as such; and yet you must love yourselves according to the measure of all that natural and moral goodness which is in you; and you must desire and endeavour all the good to yourselves that you can. Just so must you hate and love another; love them and hate them impartially as you must do yourselves.

Quest. X. May I not wish hurt sometimes to another, more than to myself?

Answ. You may wish a mediate hurt which tendeth to his good, or to the good of others; but you must never wish any final hurt and misery to him. You may wish your friend a vomit or bloodletting for his cure; and you may wish him some affliction, when it is needful and apt to humble him and do him good, or to restrain him from doing hurt to others; and on the same accounts, and for the public good, you may desire penal justice to be done upon him, yea, sometimes unto death; but still with a desire of the saving of his soul. And such hurt you may also wish yourself as is necessary to your good; but you are not to wish the same penalties to yourself, 1. Because you have somewhat else first to wish and do, even to repent and prevent it. 2. Because you are not bound ordinarily to do execution upon yourself. It is more in your power to repent yourself, and make repentance less necessary by humble confession and amendment, than to bring another to repentance. Yet I may add also, that hypothetically you may wish that destruction to the [872]enemies of God in this life, which absolutely you may not wish; that is, you must desire first that they may repent, and secondly, that they may be restrained from hurting others; but if neither of these may be attained, that they may be cut off.

Tit. 2. Directions for Loving our Neighbour as Ourselves.

Direct. I. Take heed of selfishness and covetousness, the two great enemies of love. Of which I have spoken more at large before.

Direct. II. Fall out with no man; or if you do, be speedily reconciled; for passions and dissensions are the extinguishers of love.

Direct. III. Love God truly, and you will easily love your neighbour; for you will see God's image on him, or interest in him, and feel all his precepts and mercies obliging you hereunto. As 1 John iii. 11, 23; and iv. 7, 12, 20, 21.

Direct. IV. To this end let Christ be your continual study. He is the full revelation of the love of God; the lively pattern of love, and the best teacher of it that ever was in the world: his incarnation, life, and sufferings, his gospel and covenant, his intercession and preparations for our heavenly felicity, all are the great demonstrations of condescending, matchless love. Mark both God's love to us in him, and his love to man, and you will have the best directive and incentive of your love.

Direct. V. Observe all the good which is in every man. Consider of the good of humanity in his nature, and the goodness of all that truth which he confesseth, and of all that moral good which appeareth in his heart and life; and let not oversight or partiality cause you to overlook it, or make light of it. For it is goodness which is the only attractive of love; and if you overlook men's goodness, you cannot love them.

Direct. VI. Abhor and beware of a censorious disposition, which magnifieth men's faults, and vilifieth their virtues, and maketh men seem worse than indeed they are. For as this cometh from the want of love, so doth it destroy that little which is left.

Direct. VII. Beware of superstition and an erring judgment, which maketh men place religion where God never placed it. For when this hath taught you to make duties and sins of your own humour and invention, it will quickly teach you to love or hate men accordingly as they fit or cross your opinion and humour: thus many a papist loveth not those that are not subjects of the Roman monarch, and that follow not all his irrational fopperies. Many an anabaptist loveth not those that are against his opinion of re-baptizing: one loveth not those who are for liturgies, forms of worship, and church music; and many love not those who are against them; and so of other things (of which more anon).

Direct. VIII. Avoid the company of censorious backbiters and proud contemners of their brethren: hearken not to them that are causelessly vilifying others, aggravating their faults and extenuating their virtues. For such proud, supercilious persons (religious or profane) are but the messengers of Satan, by whom he entreateth you to hate your neighbour, or abate your love to him. And to hear them speak evil of others, is but to go hear a sermon against charity, which may take with such hearts as ours before we are aware.

227

Direct. IX. Keep still the motives and incentives of love upon your minds. Which I shall here next set before you.

Tit. 3. The Reasons or Motives of Love to our Neighbour.

Motive I. Consider well of the image and interest of God in man. The worst man is his creature, and hath his natural image, though not his moral image; and you should love the work for the workman's sake. There is something of God upon all human nature above the brutes; it is intelligent, and capable of knowing him, of loving him, and of serving him; and possibly may be brought to do all this better than you can do it. Undervalue not the noble nature of man, nor overlook that of God which is upon them, nor the interest which he hath in them.

Motive II. Consider well of God's own love to man. He hateth their sins more than any of us; and yet he loveth his workmanship upon them: "And maketh his sun to shine and his rain to fall on the evil and on the good, on the just and on the unjust," Matt. v. 45. And what should more stir us up to love, than to be like to God?

Motive III. And think oft of the love of Christ unto mankind; yea, even unto his enemies. Can you have a better example, a livelier incentive, or a surer guide?

Motive IV. Consider of our unity of nature with all men: suitableness breedeth and maintaineth love. Even birds and beasts do love their kind; and man should much more have a love to man, as being of the same specific form.

Motive V. Love is the principle of doing good to others. It inclineth men to beneficence: and all men call him good who is inclined to do good.

Motive VI. Love is the bond of societies; of families, cities, kingdoms, and churches: without love, they will be but enemies conjunct; who are so much the more hurtful and pernicious to each other, by how much they are nearer to each other. The soul of societies is gone when love is gone.

Motive VII. Consider why it is that you love yourselves, (rationally,) and why it is that you would be beloved of others. And you will see that the same reasons will be of equal force to call for love to others from you.

Motive VIII. What abundance of duty is summarily performed in love! And what abundance of sin is avoided and prevented by it! If it be the fulfilling of the law, it avoideth all the violations of the law (proportionably). So far as you have love, you will neither dishonour superiors, nor oppress inferiors, nor injure equals: you will neither covet that which is your neighbour's, nor envy, nor malice them, nor defame, nor backbite, nor censure them unjustly; nor will you rob them or defraud them, nor withhold any duty or kindness to them.

Motive IX. Consider how much love pleaseth God; and why it is made so great a part of all your duty; and why the gospel doth so highly commend it, and so strictly command it, and so terribly condemn the want of it! And also how suitable a duty it is for you, who are obliged by so much love of God! These things well studied will not be without effect.

Motive X. Consider also that it is your own interest, as well as your great duty. 1. It is the soundness and honesty of your hearts. 2. It is pleasing to that God on whom only you depend. 3. It is a condition of your receiving the saving benefits of his love. 4. It is an amiable virtue, and maketh you lovely to all sober men: all men love a loving nature, and hate those that hate and hurt their neighbours. Love commandeth love, and hurtfulness is hatefulness. 5. It is a sweet, delightful duty: all love is essentiated with some complacence and delight. 6. It tendeth to the ease and quietness of your lives. What contentions and troubles will love avoid! What peace and pleasure doth it cause in families, neighbourhoods, and all societies! And what brawling vexations come where it is wanting! It will make all your neighbours and relations to be a [873]comfort and delight to you, which would be a burden and trouble, if love were absent. 7. It maketh all other men's felicity and comforts to be yours. If you love them as yourselves, their riches, their health, their honours, their lordships, their kingdoms, yea, more, their knowledge, and learning, and grace, and happiness, are partly to you as your own: as the comforts of wife and children, and your dearest friends, are; and as our love to Christ, and the blessed angels and saints in heaven, do make their joys to be partly ours. How excellent, and easy, and honest a way is this, of making all the world your own, and receiving that benefit and pleasure from all things both in heaven and earth, which no distance, no malice of enemies can deny you! If those whom you truly love have it, you have it. Why then do you complain that you have no more health, or wealth, or honour, or that others are preferred before you? Love your neighbour as yourselves, and then you will be comforted in his health, his wealth, and his preferment, and say, Those have it whom I love as myself, and therefore it is to me as mine own. When you see your neighbour's houses, pastures, corn, and cattle, love will make it as good and pleasant to you as if it were your own. Why else do you rejoice in the portions and estates of your children as if it were your own? The covetous man saith, Oh how glad should I be if this house, this land, this corn were mine: but love will make you say, It is all to me as mine own. What a sure and cheap way is this of making all the world your own! Oh what a mercy doth God bestow on his servants' souls, in the day that he sanctifieth them with unfeigned love! How much doth he give us in that one grace! And oh what a world of blessing and comforts do the ungodly, the malicious, the selfish, and the censorious cast away, when they cast away or quench the love of their neighbours; and what abundance of calamity do they bring upon themselves! In this one summary instance we may see, how much religion and obedience to God doth tend to our own felicity and delight; and how easy a work it would be, if a wicked heart did not make it difficult! and how great a plague sin is unto the sinner; and how sore a punishment of itself! And by this you may see, what it is that all fallings-out, divisions, and contentions tend to; and all temptations to the abatement of our love; and who it is that is the greater loser by it, when love to our neighbour is lost; and that backbiters and censurers who speak ill of others, come to us as the greatest enemies and thieves, to rob us of our chiefest jewel and greatest comfort in this world; and accordingly should they be entertained.

[169]   Apology against Dr. Kendal.

[170]   But if any be resolved to call mere benevolence by the name of love, I will not contend about a name.

CHAPTER XXVIII.

SPECIAL CASES AND DIRECTIONS FOR LOVE TO GODLY PERSONS AS SUCH.

Tit. 1. Cases of Conscience about Love to the Godly.

WHOM we must take for godly I answered before, chap. xxiv. tit. 1. quest. v.

Quest. I. How can we love the godly when no man can certainly know who is sincerely godly?

Answ. Our love is not the love of God, which is guided by infallibility; but the love of man, which is guided by the dark and fallible discerning of a man. The fruits of piety and charity we infallibly see in their lives; but the saving truth of that grace which is or ought to be the root, we must judge of according to the probability which those signs discover, and love men accordingly.

Quest. II. Must we love those as godly, who can give no sensible account of their conversion, for the time, or manner, or evidence of it?

Answ. We must take none for godly, who show no credible evidence of true conversion, that is, of true faith and repentance: but there is many a one truly godly, who through natural defect of understanding or utterance, are not able in good sense to tell you what conversion is, nor to describe the manner in which it was wrought upon them, much less to define exactly the time or sermon when it was first wrought, which few of the best christians are able to do; especially of them who had pious education, and were wrought on in their childhood. But if the covenant of grace be wisely opened to them according to their capacity, and they deliberately, and soberly, and voluntarily profess their present assent and consent thereto, they do thereby give you the credible evidence of a true conversion, till you have sufficient contrary evidence to disprove it. For none but a converted man can truly repent and believe in God the Creator, Redeemer, and Sanctifier, according to the baptismal covenant.

Quest. III. But what if he be so ignorant that he cannot tell what faith, or repentance, or redemption, or sanctification, or the covenant of grace is?

Answ. If you have sufficient evidence that indeed he doth not at all understand the essentials of the sacramental covenant, you may conclude that he is not truly godly; because he cannot consent to what he knoweth not: *ignorantis non est consensus*, and if you have no evidence of such knowledge, you have no evidence of his godliness, but must suspend your judgment. But yet many a one understandeth the essentials of the covenant, who cannot tell another what they are; therefore his mind (in case of great disability of utterance) must be fished out by questions, to which his yea or no will discover what he understandeth or consenteth to: you would not refuse to do so by one of another language, or a dumb man, who understood you, but could answer you but by broken words or signs: and very ill education may make a great many of the phrases of Scripture, and religious language, as strange to some men, though spoken in their native tongue, as if it were Greek or Latin to them, who yet may possibly understand the matter. A wise teacher by well composed questions may (without fraud or formality) discern what a man understandeth, though he say but yea or no; when an indiscreet, unskilful man, will make his own unskilfulness and uncharitableness the occasion of contemptuous trampling upon some that are as honest as himself. If a man's desires and endeavours are to that which is good, and he be willing to be taught, and use the means, it must be very gross ignorance indeed, and well proved, that must disprove his profession of faith. If he competently understand what it is to believe in God the Father, Son, and Holy Ghost, the Creator, Redeemer, and Sanctifier, he understandeth all that is absolutely necessary to salvation. And his yea or no may sometimes signify his understanding it.

Quest. IV. Must I take the visible members of the church, because such, for truly godly?

Answ. Yes, except when you have particular sufficient proof of their hypocrisy. Certainly no man doth sincerely enter into the baptismal covenant, but he that is sincerely a penitent believer (if at age). For that covenant giveth actual pardon and adoption to those that sincerely enter into it: the [874]very consenting to it (which is repentance and faith) being the very condition of the present reception of these benefits.[171] And therefore it is that the ancient writers still affirmed that all the baptized were regenerated, justified, and adopted. Whether an adult person be truly fit for baptism, or not, the pastor that baptizeth is to judge; and he must see the credible signs of true faith and repentance before he baptize him; which are no other than his understanding, voluntary, sober profession of consent to the baptismal covenant: but when he is baptized, and professeth to stand to that covenant once made, he is to be judged a godly person by all the church members, who have not sufficient proof of the contrary: because if he be sincere in what he did and still professeth, he is certainly godly; and whether he be sincere or not, he himself is the best and regular judge or discerner, so far as to put in his claim to baptism, which the pastor is obliged not to deny him, without disproving him: and the pastor is judge as to his actual admittance; and therefore the people have nothing necessarily to do, but know whether he be baptized and stand to his baptism; for which they are to take him as sincere, unless by his notorious discovery of the contrary they can disprove him. These are not only the true terms of church communion, but of love to the godly; and though this goeth hardly down with some good men, who observe how few of the baptized seem to be seriously religious, and therefore they think that a visible church member as such, is not at all to be accounted sincere, that is, to be believed in his profession, and that we owe him not the special love which is due to the godly, but only a common love due only to professors without respect to their sincerity; yet this opinion will not hold true; nor is a profession required without respect to the truth or falsehood of it; the credibility of it being the very reason that it is requisite. Nor is it any other faith or consent to the covenant below that which is sincere and saving, which must be professed by all that will be taken for church members. And though those that are of the contrary opinion are afraid lest this will occasion too much strictness in the pastors in judging whose profession is credible, and consequently will countenance separation in the people, yet God hath provided a sufficient remedy against that fear, by making every man the opener of his own heart, and tying us by the law of nature and of Scripture, to take every man's profession for credible, which is sober, understanding, and voluntary, unless they can disprove it, or prove him a liar, and perfidious, and incredible. And whereas it is a latitude of charity which bringeth them to the contrary opinion, for fear lest the incredible professors of christianity should be all excluded from the visible church, yet indeed it is but the image of charity, to bring catechumens into the church, (as to set the boys of the lowest form among them that are in their Greek,) and to deny all special christian love to all visible members of the church as such; and to think that we are not bound to take any of them (as such) to be sincere, or in the favour of God, or justified, for fear of excluding those that are not. But of this I have largely written in a treatise of this subject.[172]

Quest. V. Must we take all visible church members alike to be godly, and love them equally?

Answ. No: there are as many various degrees of credit due to their profession, as there are various degrees of credibility in it: some manifest their sincerity by such full and excellent evidences in a holy life, that we are next to certain that they are sincere; and some make a profession so ignorantly, so coldly, and blot it by so many false opinions and vices, that our fear of them may be greater than our hope; of whom we can only say, that we are not altogether hopeless of their sincerity, and therefore must use them as godly men, because we cannot prove the contrary; but yet admonish them of their danger, as having much cause to fear the worst: and there may be many notorious wicked men in some churches, through the pastors' fault, for want of discipline; and these for order sake we must assemble with, but not dissemble with them and our own consciences, so as to take them for godly men, when the contrary is notorious; nor yet to admit them to our familiarity. The pastor hath the keys of the church, but we have the keys of our own houses and hearts.

Quest. VI. Must we love all equally that seem truly godly, the strong and the weak?

Answ. No: he that loveth men for their holiness, will love them according to the degrees of their holiness, as far as he can discern it.

Quest. VII. Must we love him more who hath much grace (or holiness) and is little useful for want of gifts, or him that hath less grace and eminent useful gifts?

Answ. They must both be loved according to the diversity of their goodness. He that hath most grace is best, and therefore most to be loved in himself; but as a means to the conversion of souls and the honour of God in the good of others, the man that hath the most eminent gifts, must be most loved. The first is more loved in and for his own goodness: the second is more lovely *propter aliud*, as a means to that which is more loved than either of them.

Quest. VIII. Must we love him as a godly man, who liveth in any great or mortal sin?

Answ. Every man must be loved as he is: if by a mortal sin, be meant a sin inconsistent with the love of God, and a state of grace, then the question is no question; it being a contradiction which is in question. But if by a great and mortal sin, be meant only this or that act of sinning, and the question be, Whether that act be mortal, that is, inconsistent with true grace or not? then the particular act, with the circumstances, must be considered, before that question can be answered. Murder is one of the most heinous sins; and one man may be guilty of it, out of deliberate, habituate malice; and another through a sudden passion; and another through mere inadvertency, carelessness, and negligence. Stealing may be done by one man presumptuously, and by another merely to save the life of himself or his children: these will not equally prove a man in a state of death, and without true grace. And which is a mortal sin inconsistent with the life of grace, and which not, is before spoken to, and belongeth not to this place. Only I shall say, that the sin (be it great or small as to the outward act or matter) which certainly excludeth the habitual devotedness of the soul to God, by resignation, obedience, and love, is mortal, or a mark of spiritual death; and so is all sin, which consisteth not with habitual repentance, and a predominant hatred of sin as sin, and of a disobedient, unholy heart and life; and therefore all sin, which is not repented of as soon as it is known, and the sinner hath time and opportunity of deliberation; because in such a case, the habit of repentance will produce the act.

Quest. IX. Must an excommunicate person be loved as godly or not?

[875]*Answ.* You must distinguish, 1. Of excommunication. 2. Of the person that is to judge. 1. There is an excommunication which censureth not the state of the sinner, but only suspendeth him from church communion as at the present actually unfit for it: and there is an excommunication which habituately or statedly excludeth the sinner from his church relation, as an habituate, impenitent, obstinate person. 2. Some persons have no opportunity to try the cause themselves, being strangers, or not called to it; but must take it upon the pastor's judgment: and some have no opportunity to know the person and the cause, whether he be justly excommunicated or not. Now, 1. Those that know by notoriety or proof that the person is justly excommunicated with the second sort of excommunication, must not, nor cannot love him as a godly man. 2. Those that know by notoriety or proof that the person is unjustly excommunicated, are not therefore to deny him the estimation and love which is due to a godly man: though for order sake they may sometimes be obliged to avoid external church communion with him. 3. Those that know nothing of the cause themselves, must judge as the pastor judgeth, who is the legal judge; yet so, as to take it to be but a human, fallible, and no final judgment.

Quest. X. Can an unsanctified hypocrite unfeignedly love a godly man?

Answ. There is no doubt but he may materially love him, on some other consideration; as because he is a kinsman, friend, benefactor, or is witty, learned, fair, &c.

Quest. XI. But can he love a godly man because he is godly?

Answ. He may love a godly man (at least) as he may love God. An unholy person cannot love God in all his perfections respectively to himself, as a God who is most holy and just in his government, forbidding all sin, and condemning the ungodly; for the love of his sins is inconsistent with this love. But he may love him as he is most great, and wise, and good in the general, and as he is the Maker and Benefactor of the world and of the sinner; yea, and in general as his Governor; and so he may verily think that he loveth God as God, because he loveth him for his essentialities; but indeed he doth not, (speaking strictly,) because he leaveth out some one or more of these essentialities; even as he that loveth man as rational, but not as a voluntary free agent, loveth not man as man: and as a heretic is no christian, because he denieth some one essential part of christianity; even so as to the love of godly men, an ungodly man may believe that they are better than others, and therefore love them; but not as godliness is the consent to that holiness and justice of God, which would restrain him from his beloved sins, and condemn him for them. So far as they are simply godly to themselves, without respect to him and his sins, he may love them.

Quest. XII. May he love a godly man as he would make him godly, and convert him?

Answ. He may love him as a better man than others, and in general he may wish himself as good, and may love him because he wisheth him well; but as he cannot be (or rather is not) willing himself to leave his sins and live in holiness, so another is not grateful to him, who urgently persuadeth him to this.

232

Quest. XIII. Doth any ungodly person love the godly comparatively more than others?

Answ. So far as he doth love them as godly, so far he may love them more than those that are not such; many a bad father loveth a religious child better than the rest; because they think that wisdom and godliness are good; and they are glad to see their children do well, as long as they do not grate upon them with troublesome censures: for another man's godliness costeth a bad man little or nothing; he may behold it without the parting with his sins.

Quest. XIV. Doth every sincere christian love all the godly with a special love? even those that oppose their opinions, or that they think do greatly wrong them?

Answ. 1. Every true christian loveth a godly man as such, and therefore loveth all such, if he take them to be such. 2. No godly man doth habitually and impenitently live in such malice or enmity, as will not suffer him to see the godliness of a dissenter or adversary, when it hath sufficient evidence. 3. But ill education and company, and want of opportunity, may keep a true christian from discerning the godliness of another, and so from loving him as a godly man. 4. And error, and faction, and passion may in a temptation so far prevail as at present to pervert his judgment, and make him misjudge a godly man to be ungodly, though when he hath opportunity to deliberate and come to himself, he will repent of it.

Quest. XV. What is that love to the godly which proveth a man's sincerity, and which no hypocrite or unregenerate person doth attain to?

Answ. It hath in it these essential parts: 1. He loveth God best, and his servants for his sake. 2. He loveth godliness, and the person as godly, and therefore would fain be such himself; or loveth it for himself as well as in others. 3. He loveth not one only, but all the essential parts of godliness (our absolute resignation to God our Owner, our absolute obedience to God our Ruler, and our highest gratitude and love to God our Benefactor and our End). 4. He loveth godliness and godly men, above his carnal, worldly interest, his honour, wealth, or pleasure; and therefore will part with these in works of charity, when he can understand that God requireth it. These four set together make up that love which will prove your sincerity, and which no hypocrite doth perform. Hypocrites either love the godly only as their benefactors with a self-love; or they love them as godly to themselves, but would not be like them, and love not godliness itself to make them godly; or they love them for some parts of godliness, and not for all; or they love them but in subjection to their worldly love; with such a dry and barren love as James rejecteth, James ii. as will not be at any great cost upon them, to feed, or clothe, or visit, or relieve them.

Tit. 2. Directions for Loving the Children of God.

Direct. I. Once get the love of God, and you cannot choose but love his children. Therefore first set your hearts to that, and study the directions for it, part i. God must be first loved as God, before the godly can be loved as such; though perhaps this effect may sometimes be more manifest than the cause: fortify the cause and the effect will follow.

Direct. II. Get Christ to dwell in your hearts by faith, Eph. iii. 17; and then you will love his members for his sake. The study of the love of God in Christ, and the belief of all the benefits of his love and sufferings, will be the bellows continually to kindle your love to your Redeemer, and to all those that are like him and beloved by him.

Direct. III. Cherish the motions of God's Spirit in yourselves. For he is a Spirit of love; and it is the same Spirit which is in all the saints; therefore the more you have of the Spirit, the more unity and the [876]more love will you have to all that are truly spiritual. The decays of your own holiness, containeth a decay of your love to the holy.

Direct. IV. Observe their graces more than their infirmities. You cannot love them unless you take notice of that goodness which is their loveliness. Overlooking and extenuating the good that is in others, doth show your want of love to goodness, and then no wonder if you want love to those that are good.

233

Direct. V. Be not tempters and provokers of them to any sin. For that is but to stir up the worser part which is in them, and to make it more apparent; and so to hide their amiableness, and hinder your own love. They that will be abusing them, and stirring up their passions, or oppressing wise men to try if they can make them mad, or increasing their burdens and persecutions to see whether there be any impatience left in them, are but like the horseman who was still spurring his horse, and then sold him because he was skittish and unquiet; or like the gentleman that must needs come as a suitor to a beautiful lady, just when she had taken a vomit and purge, and then disdained her as being unsavoury and loathsome.

Direct. VI. Stir up their graces, and converse much with them in the exercises of grace. If Aristotle or Socrates, Demosthenes or Cicero, stood silent by you among other persons, you will perceive no difference between them and a fool or a vulgar wit: but when once they open their lips and pour out the streams of wisdom and eloquence, you will quickly perceive how far they excel the common world, and will admire, love, and honour them. So when you converse with godly men about matters of trading or common employments only, you will see no more but their blamelessness and justice; but if you will join with them in holy conference or prayer, or observe them in good works, you will see that the Spirit of Christ is in them. When you hear the longings of their souls after God, and their heavenly desires and hopes and joys, and their love to piety, charity, and justice, express themselves in their holy discourse and prayers, and see the fruits of them in their lives, you will see that they are more than common men.

Direct. VII. Foresee the perfection of their graces in their beginnings. No man will love a seed or stock of those plants or trees which bear the most beautiful flowers and fruits, unless in the seed he foresee the fruit or flower which it tendeth to. No man loveth the egg aright, who doth not foreknow what a bird it will bring forth. Aristotle or Cicero were no more amiable in their infancy than others, except to him that could foretell what men they were like to prove. Think oft of heaven, and what a thing a saint will be in glory, when he shall shine as the stars, and be equal to the angels; and then you will quickly see cause to love them.

Direct. VIII. Frequently think of the everlasting union and sweet agreement which you must have with them in heaven for ever. How perfectly you will love each other in the love of God! How joyfully you will consent in the love and praises of your Creator and Redeemer! The more believingly you foresee that state, and the more you contemplate thereon, and the more your conversation is in heaven, the more will you love your fellow-soldiers and travellers, with whom you must live in blessedness for ever.

Tit. 3. Motives or Meditative Helps to the Godly.

Motive I. Consider what relation all the regenerate have to God. They are not only his creatures, but his adopted children: and are they not honourable and amiable who are so near to God?

Motive II. Think of their near relation to Jesus Christ: they are his members, and his brethren, and the purchase of his sufferings, and co-heirs of everlasting life, Rom. viii. 16, 17; Eph. v. 26, 27.

Motive III. Think of the excellency of that spirit and holy nature which is in them. Regeneration hath made them partakers of the divine nature, and hath endued them with the Spirit of Christ, and hath by the incorruptible seed made them new creatures, of a holy and heavenly mind and life; and hath renewed them after the image of God! And what besides God himself can be so amiable as his image?

Motive IV. Think of the precious price which was paid for their redemption: if you will estimate things by their price, (if the purchaser be wise,) how highly must you value them!

Motive V. Remember how dearly they are beloved of God, their Creator and Redeemer. Read and observe God's tender language towards them, and his tender dealings with them. He calleth them his children, his beloved, yea, dearly beloved, his jewels, the apple of his eye, Deut. xxxiii. 12; Psal. lx. 5; cxxvii. 2; Col. iii. 12; Jer. xii. 7; Mal. iii. 17; Zech. ii. 8; Deut. xxxii. 10. Christ calleth the least of them his brethren, Matt. xxv. Judge of his love to them by his incarnation, life, and sufferings! Judge of it by that one heart-melting message after his resurrection, John xx. 17, "Go to my brethren and say unto them, I ascend to my Father and your Father, to my God and your God." And should we not love them dearly who are so dearly beloved of God?

Motive VI. They are our brethren, begotten by the same Father and Spirit, of the same holy seed, the word of God; and have the same nature and disposition: and this unity of nature and nearness of relation, is such a suitableness as must needs cause love.

Motive VII. They are our companions in labour and tribulation, in our duty and sufferings: they are our fellow-soldiers and travellers, with whom only we can have sweet and holy converse, and a heavenly conversation; when the carnal savour not the things of God.

Motive VIII. Consider how serviceable their graces render them, for the pleasing of God and the good of men. They are the work of God, created to good works, Eph. ii. 10. They are fitted by grace to love and praise their Maker and Redeemer, and to obey his laws, and to honour him in their works, as shining lights in a dark generation. They are the blessings of the place where God hath planted them; they pray for sinners, and exhort them, and give them good examples, and call them from their sins, and lovingly draw them on to conversion and salvation. For their sakes God useth others the better where they live. Ten righteous persons might have saved Sodom. They are lovely therefore for the service which they do.

Motive IX. All their graces will be shortly perfected, and all their infirmities done away. They are already pardoned and justified by Christ; and every remaining spot and wrinkle will be shortly taken away, Eph. v. 26, 27, and they shall be presented perfect unto God. And they that shall be so perfect then, are amiable now.

Motive X. They shall see the glory of God, and live for ever in his presence: they shall be employed in his perfect love and praise, and we shall be their companions therein: and those that must sing hallelujahs to God in perfect amity and concord, such an harmonious, blessed choir, should live in great endearedness in the way.

[877]

Tit. 4. The Hinderances and Enemies of Christian Love.

Enemy I. The first enemy of christian love, is the inward unregeneracy and carnality of the mind: "for the carnal mind is enmity to God, and neither is nor can be subject to his law," Rom. vi. 7; and therefore it is at enmity with holiness, and with those that are seriously holy. The excellency of a christian is seen only by faith, believing what God speaketh of them, and by spiritual discerning of their spiritual worth: but the "natural man discerneth not the things of the Spirit, but they are as foolishness to him, because they must be spiritually discerned," 1 Cor. ii. 14. There must be a suitableness of nature before there can be true love; and he that will love them as holy, must first love holiness himself.

Enemy II. Another enemy to christian love is selfishness, or inordinate self-love; for this will make men love no one heartily, but as they serve, or love, or honour them, and according to the measures of their selfish interest: if a godly man will not flatter such persons, and serve their proud or covetous humours, they cannot love him. A selfish person maketh so great a matter of every infirmity which crosseth his interest, or every mistake which crosseth his opinion, or every little injury that is done him, that he crieth out presently, Oh what wicked and unconscionable people are these! What hypocrites are they! Is this their religion? Is this justice or charity? All virtues and vices are estimated by them according to their own ends and interest chiefly; they can think better of a common whoremonger, or swearer, or atheist, or infidel that loveth, and honoureth, and serveth them, than of the most holy and upright servant of God, who thinketh meanly or hardly of them, and standeth in their way, and seemeth to be against their interest; it is no commendation to him in this man's account, that he loveth God, and all that are godly, if he seem to injure or cross a selfish man. A carnal self-lover can love none but himself and for himself; and maketh all faults which are against himself to be the characters of an odious person, rather than those which are committed against God.

Enemy III. Christian love is often diminished and marred by degenerating into a carnal sort of love, through the prevalency of some carnal vice. Thus they that loved a man for godliness, turn it into a selfish love, for some honour, or favour, or benefits to themselves. And young persons of different sexes begin to love each other for piety, and by undiscreet, and unwary, and sinful familiarities, are drawn before they are aware, to carnal, fond, and sinful love; and these persons think that their holy love is stronger than before; whenas it is stifled, consumed, and languishing, as natural heat by a burning fever, and is overcome and turned into another thing.

Enemy IV. Passion and impatiency is a great enemy to christian love. It is stirring up displeasing words and carriage, and then cannot bear them; it meeteth every where with matter of displeasure and offence, and is still casting water on this sacred fire, and feigning or finding faults in all.

Enemy V. Self-ignorance and partiality is a great enemy to love; when it maketh men overlook their own corruptions, and extenuate all those faults in themselves, which in others they take for heinous crimes; and so they want that compassion to others which would bear with infirmities, because they know not how bad they are themselves, and what need they have of the forbearance of others.

Enemy VI. Censoriousness is an enemy to brotherly love (as is aforesaid): a censorious person will tell you how dearly he loveth all the godly; but he can allow so few the acknowledgment of their godliness, that few are beholden to him for his love. His sinful humour blindeth his mind, that he cannot see another's godliness; he will love them for their sincerity when he can see it, but that will not be till he hath better eyes. Timon was a great lover of wisdom, but a hater of all men, because he took no man to be wise.

Enemy VII. Faction and parties, or siding in religion, is one of the greatest enemies of christian love. For this causeth censoriousness, and maketh men so overvalue the opinions which they have chosen, and the interest of their party, that they hardly see goodness in any that are not of their mind, and quickly find faults (or devise them) in those that are against them.

Enemy VIII. Conversing with malicious, wicked, or censorious persons, is a great hinderance of the love of godly men; for he that heareth them daily slandered, and represented as brain-sick, seditious, self-conceited, humorous, hypocritical people, will easily take them as odious, but hardly as amiable, unless he come nearer them, and know them better than by a liar's words.

Enemy IX. Too high expectations are great enemies to love. When men either look that saints on earth should be like saints in heaven, who have no infirmity; or look for greater parts of nature or art, ingenuity or excellency of speech, than is in other persons, or when selfishness and covetousness or pride doth make men look for great respect, and observance, and esteem, or gifts, or commodity from others; when sin and error raiseth these unreasonable expectations, and the imperfect graces of christians do not answer them, such persons think contemptibly of good men, and call them hypocrites, and as bad as others, because they are not such as they expected.

Enemy X. The placing of men's goodness in lesser matters in which it doth not consist, is also a common enemy of love. When a man is himself so carnal as not to know what spiritual excellency is, but prefers some common gifts before it, such a one can never be satisfied in the ordinary sort of upright men. Thus some make a great matter of compliment, and courtship, and handsome deportment, when some holy persons are so taken up with the great matters of God and their salvation, and so retired from the company of complimenters, that they have neither time, nor mind, nor skill, nor will for such impertinencies. Some place so much in some particular opinions, or ceremonies, or forms of church government and worship, that they can think well of no man that is against them; whereas good men on earth are so imperfect, that they are, and will be, of several opinions about such things; and so these persons oblige themselves by their own opinionativeness, to be always against one part of the sincerest servants of Christ. One man can think well of none that is not for his church party, or way of government and worship; and another can think well of none that is not for his way. One can think well of none that prayeth not by his book, and doth not turn, and bend, and look just in the same manner, garb, and posture with himself, and that useth not all the ceremonies which he affecteth; or at least, if his weakness make him guilty of any unhandsome tone or gesture, or of any incompt and unapt expressions, or needless repetitions, or unpleasing style (all which we wish that all good men were free from). Another can think well of no man, that is for pomp and force in church government, or for ceremonies, forms, and books in prayer, and for prescribed words in worshipping [878]God. And thus placing religion where they should not, causeth too many to take up with a mistaken religion for themselves, and to dislike all that are not of their mind, and certainly destroyeth christian love in one part of christians towards the other.

Enemy XI. Pride also is a pestilent extinguisher of love. For a proud man is so much overwise in his own eyes, that he can without remorse stigmatize all that dissent from him with the names of ignorant or erroneous, schismatical, heretical, or what other name the humour or advantage of the times shall offer him: and he is so good in his own eyes, that he measureth men's goodness and godliness by their agreement with him, or compliance with his will. And he is so great in his own eyes, that he thinketh himself and his complices only fit to make laws for others, and to rule them in their opinions, and in the worship of God; and no man fit to say any thing publicly to God, but what he putteth into their mouths. He can think well of none that will not obey him: like the pope of Rome, that saith, No man on earth hath church communion with him that is not subject to him. A humble christian thinketh that himself and the gospel have great and unusual prosperity in the world, when they have but liberty; but proud men think that religion is ruinated, and they are persecuted, when they have not their will upon their brethren, and when their brethren will be but brethren, and deny them obedience. Subjects they can think well of and command, but brethren they cannot love nor tolerate.

Enemy XII. Lastly, The counterfeits of christian love deceive abundance, and keep them from that which is love indeed. They might be brought to it, if they had not thought that they had it already, when they have it not.

Tit. 5. The Counterfeits of Christian Love.

Count. I. It is but counterfeit love to christians, when they are loved only for being of the common religion of the country, and the same that you say you are of yourselves: as one Mahometan loveth another.

Count. II. Or to love one only sect or party of christians, which you espouse as the only party or church; and not to love a christian as a christian, and so to love all true christians whom you can discern to be such.

Count. III. To love only those christians who are your kindred or relations, or those that have been some way benefactors to you.

Count. IV. To love christians only for their familiarity, or kind and loving conversation, and civil, obliging deportment among men.

Count. V. To love them only because they are learned, or have better wits or abilities of speech, in preaching, prayer, or conference than others.

Count. VI. To love them only upon the praise which common commendations may sometimes give them, and for being magnified by fame, and well spoken of by all men. Thus many wicked men do love the saints departed, when they hate those that are alive among them.

Count. VII. To love them only for being godly in themselves at a distance, so they will not trouble them with their godliness; while they love not those that reprove them, and would draw them to be as godly.

Count. VIII. To love them only for suffering with them in the same cause. Thus a profane person taken by the Turks may love his fellow-captives who refuse to renounce Christ. And thus a sufferer for an ill cause, or an erroneous sect, may love those that suffer with him above others.

Count. IX. To love them only for holding strict and right opinions, while they will not endure to live accordingly. Thus many love the light, that cannot bear the heat and motion; many love an orthodox person, of a sound judgment, that is against looseness and profaneness in his opinion, and do not like the folly of the licentious; who yet like licentious practice best.

Count. X. To love them for some parts of godliness only; while some other essential part will not be endured (of which before).

Count. XI. To love them in a kind fit only, as Saul with tears professed to do his son David; but to have no habitual, constant love.

Count. XII. Lastly, To love godly men a little, and the world and fleshly interest more; to love them only so as will cost them nothing; to wish them fed, but not to feed them; and to wish them clothed, but not to clothe them; and to wish them out of prison, but not to dare to visit them for fear of suffering themselves. He that hath this world's goods, and seeth his brother have need, and shutteth up the bowels of his compassion from him, how dwelleth the love of God in him? 1 John iii. 17. Surely if the love of his brother were in him, the love of God had been in him. But he hath no true love to his brother, that will only love him on terms that cost him little, and cannot give and suffer for his love. All these are deceiving counterfeits of love to the children of God.

Tit. 6. Cases and Directions for intimate, special Friends.

Quest. I. Is it lawful to have an earnest desire to be loved by others? especially by some one person above all other?

Answ. There is a desire of others' love which is lawful, and there is a desire which is unlawful.

I. It is lawful, 1. When we desire it as it is their duty, which God himself obligeth them to perform, and so is part of their integrity, and is their own good, and pleaseth God. So parents must desire their children to love them, and one another, because it is their duty, and else they are unnatural and bad. And husband and wife may desire that each other discharge that duty of love which God requireth, and so may all others. 2. It is lawful also to desire for our own sakes to be loved by others; so be it it be, 1. With a calm and sober desire, which is not eager, peremptory, or importunate, nor overvalueth the love of man. 2. According to the proportion of our own worth; not desiring to be thought greater, wiser, or better than indeed we are, nor to be loved erroneously by an overvaluing love. 3. When we desire it for the benefits to which it tendeth, more than to be valued and loved for ourselves: as, 1. That we may receive that edification and good from a friend which love disposeth them to communicate. 2. That we may do that good to our friends, which love disposeth them to receive. 3. That we may honour and please God, who delighteth in the true love and concord of his children.

II. But the unlawful desire of others' love to us, is much more common, and is a sin of a deeper malignity than is commonly observed. This desire of love is sinful, when it is contrary to that before described; as, 1. When we desire it over-eagerly. 2. When we desire it selfishly and proudly, to be set up in the good opinion of others; and not to make a benefit of it to ourselves or them; but our own honour is more desired in it, than the honour of God. 3. When we desire to be thought greater, [879]wiser, or better than we are, and to be loved with such an overvaluing love; and have no desire that the bounds of truth and usefulness should restrain and limit that love to us which we affect. 4. When it is an erroneous, fanciful, carnal, or lustful esteem of some one person, which maketh us desire his love more than others. As because he is higher, richer, fairer, &c.

238

This eager desire to be overloved by others, hath in it all these aggravations. 1. It is the very sin of pride, which God hath declared so great a detestation of. For pride is an overvaluing ourselves, for greatness, wisdom, or goodness, and a desire to be so overvalued of others. And he that would be overloved, would be overvalued.

2. It is self-idolizing: when we would be loved as better than we are, we rob God of that love which men should render to him, who can never be overloved, and we would fain seem a kind of petty deities to the world, and draw men's eyes and hearts unto ourselves. When we should be jealous of God's interest and honour, lest we or any creature should have his due, this proud disposition maketh people set up themselves in the estimation of others, and they scarce care how good or wise they are esteemed, nor how much they are lifted up in the hearts of others.

3. It is an injurious insnaring the minds of others, and tempting them to erroneous opinions of us, and affections to us; which will be their sin, and may bring them into many inconveniences. It is an ordinary thing to do greater hurt to a friend whom we value, by insnaring him in an inordinate love, than ever we did or can do to an enemy by hating him.

Quest. II. Is it lawful, meet, or desirable to entertain that extraordinary affection to any one, which is called special friendship; or to have an endeared, intimate friend, whom we love far above all others?

Answ. Intimate, special friendship is a thing that hath been so much pleaded for by all sorts of men, and so much of the felicity of man's life hath been placed in it, that it beseemeth not me to speak against it. But yet I think it meet to tell you with what cautions and limits it must be received, and how far it is good, and how far sinful (for there are perils here to be avoided, which neither Cicero, nor his Scipio and Lælius, were acquainted with).

I. 1. It is lawful to choose some one well qualified person, who is fittest for that use, and to make him the chief companion of our lives, our chiefest counsellor and comforter, and to confine our intimacy and converse to him in a special manner above all others. 2. And it is lawful to love him not only according to his personal worth, but according to his special suitableness to us, and to desire his felicity accordingly, and to exercise our love to him more frequently and sensibly (because of his nearness and presence) than towards some better men that are further off.

The reasons of such an intimate friendship are these: 1. No man is sufficient for himself, and therefore nature teacheth them to desire a helper. And there is so wonderful a diversity of temperaments and conditions, and so great a disparity and incongruity among good and wise men towards each other, that one that is more suitable and congruous to us than all the rest, may on that account be much preferred.

2. It is not many that can be so near us as to be ordinary helpers to us; and a wiser man at a distance, or out of reach, may be less useful to us, than one of inferior worth at hand.

3. The very exercise of friendly love and kindness to another is pleasant: and so it is to have one to whom we may confidently reveal our secrets, to bear part of our burden, and to confirm us in our right apprehensions, and to cure us of wrong ones.

4. And it is no small benefit of a present bosom friend, to be instead of all the world to us; that is, of common, unprofitable company: for man is a sociable creature, and abhorreth utter solitude. And among the common sort, we shall meet with so much evil, and so little that is truly wise or good, as will tempt a man to think that he is best when he is least conversant with mankind. But a selected friend is to us for usefulness instead of many, without these common encumbrances and snares.

5. And it is a great part of the commodity of a faithful friend, to be assisted in the true knowledge of ourselves: to have one that will watch over us, and faithfully tell us of the sin, and danger, and duty, which we cannot easily see without help, and which other men will not faithfully acquaint us with.

II. But yet it is rare to choose and use this friendship rightly; and there are many evils here to be carefully avoided. The instances shall be mentioned anon in the directions, and therefore now passed by.

Quest. III. Is it meet to have more such bosom friends than one?

Answ. 1. Usually one only is meetest: 1. Because love diffused is oft weak, and contracted is more strong. 2. Because secrets are seldom safe in the hands of many. 3. Because suitable persons are rare. 4. And though two or three may be suitable to you, yet perhaps they may be unsuitable among themselves. And the calamities of their own disparities will redound to you; and their fallings-out may turn to the bewraying of your secrets, or to some other greater wrong.

2. But yet sometimes two or three such friends may be better than one alone. 1. In case they be all near and of an approved suitableness and fidelity. 2. In case they be all suitable and endeared to one another. 3. If a man live *per vices* in several places, and his friends cannot remove with him, he may have one friend in one place, and another in another, and so many will be but as one that is constant. 4. And in case that many may add to our help, our counsel and comfort, more than to our danger, hurt, or trouble. In all these cases many are better than one.

Quest. IV. Is it fit for him to take another bosom friend who hath a pious wife? And is any other so fit to be a friend, as he and she that are as one flesh?

Answ. When a wife hath the understanding, and virtue, and fidelity fit for this sort of friendship, then no one else is so fit, because of nearness and united interests. The same I say of a husband to a wife. But because that it seldom falls out that there is such a fitness for this office, especially in the wife, in that case it is lawful and meet to choose a friend that is fit indeed, and to commit those secrets to him which we commit not to a wife: for secrets are not to be committed to the untrusty, nor wise counsel to be expected from the unwise, how near soever. And the great writers about this special friendship, do think that no woman is fit for it, but men only; but that conclusion is too injurious to that sex.

Quest. V. Is it agreeable to the nature of true friendship to love our friend not only for himself, but for our own commodity? And whether must he or I be the chief end of my love and friendship?

Answ. 1. Indeed in our love to God, he that is the object is also our chief and ultimate end, and we must love him more for himself than for ourselves. And yet here it is lawful subordinately to intend ourselves.

2. And our love to the commonwealth should be [880]greater than our love to ourselves, and therefore we may not love it chiefly for ourselves.

3. And if our bosom friend be notoriously better than we are, and more serviceable to God and to the common good, we should love him also above ourselves, and therefore not chiefly for ourselves.

4. But in case of an equality of goodness and usefulness, we are not bound to love our most intimate friend more than ourselves; and therefore may at least equally love him for ourselves as for himself. And if we are really and notoriously better and more useful, we may love him chiefly for ourselves, and ourselves above him. But still we must love God and the public good, above both ourselves and him, and must love both ourselves and him in order to God, who is the beginning and end of all.

Quest. VI. Is it contrary to the nature of true friendship to keep any secret from such a bosom friend, or to retain any suspicion of him, or to suppose that he may possibly prove unfaithful to us and forsake us?

Answ. Cicero and the old doctors say of friendship, that all this is inconsistent with true friendship; and it is true that it is contrary to perfect friendship: but it is as true, that perfect friendship cannot be and must not be among imperfect men: and that the nature of mankind is so much depraved, that the best are unmeet for perfect friendship: and certainly few men, if any in the world, are fit for every secret of our hearts. Besides that we are so bad, that if all our secret thoughts were known to one another, it might do much to abate our friendship and love to each other. And it is certain that man is so corrupt a creature, and good men so imperfectly cured of their corruption, that there is selfishness, uncertainty, and mutability in the best. And therefore it is not a duty to judge falsely of men, but contrarily to judge of them as they are; and therefore to suppose that it is possible the closest friend may reveal our secrets, one time or other, and that the stedfastest friend may possibly become our enemy. To think that possible which is possible, (and more,) is injurious to none.

Quest. VII. Is it lawful to change a bosom friend, and to prefer a new one whom we perceive to be more worthy before an old one?

Answ. An old friend, *cæteris paribus*, is to be preferred before a new one, and is not to be cast off without desert and necessity. But for all that, 1. If an old friend prove false, or notably unfit, 2. Or if we meet with another that is far more able, fit, and worthy, no doubt but we may prefer the latter; and may value, love, and use men as they are for goodness, worth, and usefulness.

Quest. VIII. What love is due to a minister that hath been the means of our conversion? And can such a one be loved too much?

Answ. 1. There is a special love due to such a one, as the hand by which God did reach out to us his invaluable mercies; and ingratitude, and sectarian, proud contempt of such as have been our fathers in Christ, is no small sin.

2. But yet another that never did us good, who is much wiser, and better, and more serviceable to the church, must be better loved, than he by whom we were converted. Because we are to love men more for the sake of God and his image and service, than for ourselves.

3. And it is a very common thing, for passionate women and young people, when they are newly converted, to think that they can never too much value, and honour, and love those that converted them; and to think that all such love is holy and from God; whereas the same love may be of God as to the principle, motives, and ends, in the main, and yet may have great mixtures of passionate weakness, and sinful excess, which may tend to their great affliction in the end. Some that have been converted by the writings of a minister a hundred or a thousand miles off, must needs go see the author: some must needs remove from their lawful dwellings and callings, to live under the ministry of such a one; yea, if it may be, in the house with him: some have affections so violent, as proveth a torment to them when they cannot live with those whom they so affect: some by that affection are ready to follow those that they so value into any error. And all this is a sinful love by this mixture of passionate weakness, though pious in the main.

Quest. IX. Why should we restrain our love to a bosom friend (contrary to Cicero's doctrine)? And what sin or danger is in loving him too much?

Answ. All these following: 1. It is an error of judgment and of will, to suppose any one better than he is, (yea, perhaps than any creature on earth is,) and so to love him.

2. It is an irrational act, and therefore not fit for a rational creature, to love any one further than reason will allow us, and beyond the true causes of regular love.

3. It is usually a fruit of sinful selfishness: for this excess of love doth come from a selfish cause, either some strong conceit that the person greatly loveth us, or for some great kindness which he hath showed us, or for some need we have of him, and fitness appearing in him to be useful to us, &c. Otherwise it would be purely for amiable worth, and then it would be proportioned to the nature and measure of that worth.

4. It very often taketh up men's minds, so as to hinder their love to God, and their desires and delights in holy things: while Satan (perhaps upon religious pretences) turneth our affections too violently to some person, it diverteth them from higher and better things: for the weak mind of man can hardly think earnestly of one thing, without being alienated in his thoughts from others; nor can hardly love two things or persons fervently at once, that stand not in pure subordination one to the other: and

we seldom love any fervently in a pure subordination to God; for then we should love God still more fervently.

5. It oft maketh men ill members of the church and commonwealth. For it contracteth that love to one overvalued person, which should be diffused abroad among many; and the common good, which should be loved above any single person, is by this means neglected (as God himself): which maketh wives, and children, and bosom friends become those gulfs that swallow up the estates of most rich men; so that they do little good with them to the public state, which should be preferred.

6. Over-much friendship engageth us in more duty than we are well able to perform, without neglecting our duty to God, the commonwealth, and our own souls. There is some special duty followeth all special acquaintance; but a bosom friend will expect a great deal. You must allow him much of your time in conference, upon all occasions; and he looketh that you should be many ways friendly and useful to him, as he is or would be to you. When, alas, frail man can do but little: our time is short; our strength is small; our estates and faculties are narrow and low. And that time which you must spend with your bosom friend; where friendship is not moderated and wisely managed, is perhaps taken from God and the public good, to which you first owed it. Especially if you are magistrates, ministers, physicians, schoolmasters, or such other as are [881]of public usefulness. Indeed if you have a sober, prudent friend, that will look but for your vacant hours, and rather help you in your public service, you are happy in such a friend. But that is not the excess of love that I am reprehending.

7. This inordinate friendship prepareth for disappointments, yea, and for excess of sorrows. Usually experience will tell you that your best friends are but uncertain and imperfect men, and will not answer your expectation; and perhaps some of them may so grossly fail you, as to set light by you, and prove your adversaries. I have seen the bonds of extraordinary dearness many ways dissolved: one hath been overcome by the flesh, and turned drunkard and sensual, and so proved unfit for intimate friendship (who yet sometime seemed of extraordinary uprightness and zeal). Another hath taken up some singular conceits in religion, and joined to some sect where his bosom friend could not follow him. And so it hath seemed his duty to look with strangeness, contempt, or pity on his ancient friend, as one that is dark and low, if not supposed an adversary to the truth, because he espouseth not all his misconceits. Another is suddenly lifted up with some preferment, dignity, and success, and so is taken with higher things and higher converse, and thinks it is very fair, to give an embrace to his ancient friend, for what he once was to him, instead of continuing such endearedness. Another had changed his place and company, and so by degrees grown very indifferent to his ancient friend, when he is out of sight, and converse ceaseth. Another hath himself chosen his friend amiss, in his unexperienced youth, or in a penury of wise and good men, supposing him much better than he was; and afterwards hath had experience of many persons of far greater wisdom, piety, and fidelity, whom therefore reason commanded him to prefer. All these are ordinary dissolvers of these bonds of intimate and special friendship.

And if your love continue as hot as ever, its excess is like to be your excessive sorrow. For, 1. You will be the more grieved at every suffering of your friend, as sicknesses, losses, crosses, &c. whereof so many attend mankind, as is like to make your burden great. 2. Upon every removal, his absence will be the more troublesome to you. 3. All incongruities and fallings-out will be the more painful to you, especially his jealousies, discontents, and passions, which you cannot command. 4. His death, if he die before you, will be the more grievous, and your own the more unwelcome, because you must part with him. These and abundance of sore afflictions are the ordinary fruits of too strong affections; and it is no rare thing for the best of God's servants to profess, that their sufferings from their friends who have overloved them, have been ten times greater than from all the enemies that ever they had in the world.

And to those that are wavering about this case, Whether only a common friendship with all men according to their various worth, or a bosom intimacy with

242

some one man, be more desirable? I shall premise a free confession of my own case, whatever censures for it I incur. When I was first awakened to the regard of things spiritual and eternal, I was exceedingly inclined to a vehement love to those that I thought the most serious saints, and especially to that intimacy with some one, which is called friendship; by which I found extraordinary benefit, and it became a special mercy to my soul. But it was by more than one or two of the aforementioned ways, that the strict bond of extraordinary friendship hath been relaxed, and my own excessive esteem of my most intimate friends confuted. And since then I have learned to love all men according to their real worth, and to let out my love more extensively and without respect of persons, acknowledging all that is good in all; but with a double love and honour to the excellently wise and good; and to value men more for their public usefulness, than for their private suitableness to me; and yet to value the ordinary converse of one or a few suitable friends, before a more public and tumultuary life, except when God is publicly worshipped, or when public service inviteth me to deny the quiet of a private life: and though I more difference between man and man than ever, I do it not upon so slight and insufficient grounds as in the time of my unexperienced credulity; nor do I expect to find any without the defects, and blots, and failings of infirm, imperfect, mutable man.

Quest. X. What qualifications should direct us in the choice of a special bosom friend?

Answ. 1. He must be one that is sincere and single-hearted, and not given to affectation, or any thing that is much forced in his deportment; plain, and open-hearted to you, and not addicted to a hiding, fraudulent, or reserved carriage.

2. He must be one that is of a suitable temper and disposition; I mean not guilty of all your own infirmities, but not guilty of a crossness or contrariety of disposition. As if one be in love with plainness of apparel, and frugality in diet and course of life, and the other be guilty of curiosity, and ostentation, and prodigality; if one be for few words, and the other for many; if one be for labour, and the other for idleness, and frequent interruptions; if one be for serving the humours of men, and the other for a contempt of human censure, in the way of certain duty; these disparities make them unfit for this sort of bosom friendship.

3. He must not be a slave to any vice; for that which maketh him false to God, and to betray his own soul, may make him false to man, and to betray his friend.

4. He must not be a selfish person; that is, corruptly and partially for himself, and for his own carnal ends and interest. For such a one hath no true love to others, but when you seem cross to his own interest, his pleasure, wealth, or honour he will forsake you; for so he doth by God himself.

5. He must be humble, and not notably proud. For pride will make him quarrelsome, disdainful, impatient, and quite unsuitable to a humble person.

6. He must be one that is thoroughly and resolvedly godly: for you will hardly well centre any where but in God; nor will he be useful to all the ends of friendship, if he be not one that loveth God, and holy things, and is of a pious conversation: nor can you expect that he that is false to God, and will sell his part in him for the pleasure or gain of sin, should long prove truly faithful unto you.

7. He must be one that is judicious in religion; that is, not of an erroneous, heretical wit; nor ignorant of those great and excellent truths, which you should oft confer about; but rather one that excelleth you in solid understanding, and true judgment, and a discerning head, that can teach you somewhat which you know not; and is not addicted to corrupt you with false opinions of his own.

8. He must be one that is not schismatical and embodied in any dividing sect; for else he will be no longer true to you, than the interest of his party will allow him; and if you will not follow him in his conceits and singularities, he will withdraw his love, and despise you; and if he do not, yet he may endanger your stedfastness, by the temptation of his love.

243

9. He must be one that hath no other very intimate [882]friend, unless his friend be also as intimate with you as with him; because else he will be no further secret and trusty to you, than the interest or will of his other friend will allow him.

10. He must be one that is prudent in the management of business, and especially those which your converse is concerned in; else his indiscretion in words or practice, will not suffer your friendship to be long entire.

11. He must be one that is not addicted to loquacity, but can keep your secrets; otherwise he will be so untrusty as to be uncapable of doing the true office of a friend.

12. He must have a zeal and activity in religion and in all well-doing; otherwise he will be unfit to warm your affections, and to provoke you to love and good works, and to do the principal works of friendship, but will rather cool and hinder you in your way.

13. He must be one that is not addicted to levity, unconstancy, and change; or else you can expect no stability in his friendship.

14. He must not much differ from you in riches, or in poverty, or in quality in the world. For if he be much richer, he will be carried away with higher company and converse than yours, and will think you fitter to be his servant than his friend. And if he be much poorer than you, he will be apt to value your friendship for his own commodity, and you will be still in doubt whether he be sincere.

15. He must be one that is like to live with you or near you, that you may have the frequent benefit of his converse, counsel, example, and other acts of friendship.

16. He must be one that is not very covetous, or a lover of riches or preferment; for such a one will no longer be true to you, than his mammon will allow him.

17. He must be one that is not peevish, passionate, and impatient; but that can both bear with your infirmities, and also bear much from others for your sake, in the exercise of his friendship.

18. He must be one that hath so good an esteem of your person, and so true and strong a love to you, as will suffice to move him, and hold him to all this.

19. He must be yet of a public spirit, and a lover of good works, that he may put you on to well-doing, and not countenance you in an idle self-pleasing and unprofitable life. And he ought to be one that is skilful in the business of your calling, that he may be fit to censure your work, and amend it, and direct you in it, and confer about it; and it is best for you if he be one that excelleth you herein, that he may add something to you (but then you will not be such to him, and so the friendship will be unequal.)

20. Lastly, There must be some suitableness in age and sex. The young want experience to make them meet for the bosom friendship of the aged (though yet they may take delight in instructing them, and doing them good). And the young are hardly reconcilable to all the gravity of the aged. And it must not be a person of a different sex, unless in case of marriage. Not but that they may be helpful to each other as christians, and in a state of distant friendship; but this bosom intimacy they are utterly unfit for, because of unsuitableness, temptation, and scandal.

Directions for the Right Use of Special Bosom Friendship.

Direct. I. Engage not yourself to any one as a bosom friend, without great evidence and proof of his fitness in all the foregoing qualifications. By which you may see that this is not an ordinary way of duty or benefit, but a very unusual case. For it is a hard thing to meet with one among many thousands, that hath all these qualifications; and when that is done, if you have not all the same qualifications to him, you will be unmeet for his friendship, whatever he be for yours. And where in an age will there be two that are suited in all those respects? Therefore our ordinary way of duty is, to love all according to their various worth, and to make the best use we can of every one's grace and gifts, and of those most that are nearest us; but without the partiality of such extraordinary affection to any one above all the rest. For young persons usually make their choice rashly, of one that afterwards proveth utterly unmeet for the office of such a friend, or at least, no better than many other persons; nay, ten to one, but after-experience will acquaint them with many that are much wiser, and better, and fitter for their love. And hasty affections are guilty of blind partiality, and run men into sin and sorrow, and often end in unpleasant ruptures. Therefore be not too forward in this friendship.

Direct. II. When you do choose a friend, though he must be one that you have no cause to be suspicious of, yet reckon that it is possible that he may be estranged from you, yea, and turn your enemy. Causeless jealousies are contrary to friendship on your part; and if there be cause, it is inconsistent with friendship on his part. But yet no friendship should make you blind, and not to know that man is a corrupt and mutable creature; especially in such an age as this, wherein we have seen, how personal changes, state changes, and changes in religion, have alienated many seeming friends. Therefore love them, and use them, and trust them, but as men, that may possibly fail all your expectations, and open all your secrets, and betray you, yea, and turn your enemies. Suspect it not, but judge it possible.

Direct. III. Be open with your approved friend, and commit all your secrets to him, still excepting those, the knowledge of which may be hurtful to himself, or the revealing of them hereafter may be intolerably injurious to yourself, to the honour of religion, to the public good, or to any other. If you be needlessly close, you are neither friendly, nor can you improve your friend enough to your own advantage. But yet if you open all without exception, you may many ways be injurious to your friend and to yourself; and the day may come which you did not look for, in which his weakness, passion, interest, or alienation, may trouble you by making all public to the world.

Direct. IV. Use as little affectation or ceremony with your friend as may be; but let all your converse with him be with openness of heart, that he may see that you both trust him, and deal with him in plain sincerity. If dissimulation and forced affectation be but once discovered, it tendeth to breed a constant diffidence and suspicion. And if it be an infirmity of your own which you think needeth such a cover, the cloak will be of worse effect, than the knowledge of your infirmity.

Direct. V. Be ever faithful to your friend, for the cure of all his faults; and never turn friendship into flattery: yet still let all be done in love, though in a friendly freedom, and closeness of admonition. It is not the least benefit of intimate friendship, that what an enemy speaketh behind our backs, a friend will open plainly to our faces. To watch over one another daily, and be as a glass to show our faces or faults to one another, is the very great benefit of true friendship. Eccles. iv. 9-11, "Two are better than one, because they have a good reward for their labour. For if they fall, the one will lift up his fellow: but woe to him that is alone when he falleth, for he hath not another to help him up." It is a [883]flatterer and not a friend, that will please you by concealing or extenuating your sin.

Direct. VI. Abhor selfishness as most contrary to real friendship. Let your friend be as yourself, and his interest as your own. If we must love our neighbour as ourselves, much more our dearest bosom friends.

Direct. VII. Understand what is most excellent and useful in your friend, and that improve. Much good is lost by a dead-hearted companion, that will neither broach the vessel and draw that out which is ready for their use; nor yet feed any good discourse, by due questions or answers, but stifle all by barren silence. And a dull, silent hearer, will weary and silence the speaker at the last.

Direct. VIII. Resolve to bear with each other's infirmities: be not too high in your expectations from each other; look not for exactness and innocence, but for human infirmities, that when they fall out, you may not find yourselves disappointed. Patience is necessary in all human converse.

Direct. IX. Yet do not suffer friendship to blind you, to own or extenuate the faults of your dearest friend. For that will be sinful partiality, and will be greatly injurious to God, and treachery against the soul and safety of your friend.

245

Direct. X. And watch lest the love, estimation, or reverence of your friend, should draw you to entertain his errors, or to imitate him in any sinful way. It is no part of true friendship to prefer men before the truth of Christ, nor to take any heretical, dividing, or sensual infection from our friend, and so to die and perish with him; nor is it friendly to desire it.

Direct. XI. Never speak against your friend to a third person; nor open his dishonourable weakness to another. As no man can serve two masters, so no man can well please two contrary friends: and if you whisper to one the failings of another, it tendeth directly to the dissolution of your friendship.

Direct. XII. Think not that love will warrant your partial, erroneous estimation of your friend. You may judge him fittest for your intimacy; but you must not judge him better than all other men, unless you have special evidence of it, as the reason of such a judgment.

Direct. XIII. Let not the love of your friend draw you to love all, or any others, the less, and below their worth. Let not friendship make you narrow-hearted, and confine your charity to one: but give all their due, in your valuation and your conversation, and exercise as large a charity and benignity as possibly you can; especially to societies, churches, and commonwealth, and to all the world. It is a sinful friendship, which robbeth others of your charity; especially those to whom much more is due than to your friend.

Direct. XIV. Exercise your friendship in holiness and well-doing: kindle in each other the love of God and goodness, and provoke each other to a heavenly conversation. The more of God and heaven is in your friendship, the more holy, safe, and sweet, and durable it will prove. It will not wither, when an everlasting subject is the fuel that maintaineth it. If it will not help you the better to holiness and to heaven, it is worth nothing. Eccles. iv. 11, "If two lie together, then they have heat; but how can one be warm alone." See that your friendship degenerate not into common carnal love, and evaporate not in a barren converse, instead of prayer and heavenly discourse, and faithful watchfulness and reproof.

Direct. XV. Prepare each other for suffering and death, and dwell together in the house of mourning, where you may remember your nearer everlasting friendship; and not only in the house of mirth, as if it were your work to make each other forget your latter end.

[171] Lege quam plurima veterum testimonia in D. Gatakero contra Davenantium de Baptismo.

[172] "Disputations of Right to Sacraments."

CHAPTER XXIX.

CASES AND DIRECTIONS FOR LOVING AND DOING GOOD TO ENEMIES.

MOST which belongeth to this subject is said before, chap. ix. about forgiving enemies, and therefore thither I refer the reader.

Tit. 1. Cases about Loving and Doing Good to Enemies.

Quest. I. Whom must I account an enemy, and love under that name?

Answ. 1. Not every one that is angry with you, or that giveth you foul words, or that undervalueth you, or that speaketh against you, or that doth you wrong; but he that hateth you, and seeketh or desireth your destruction or your hurt as such designedly. 2. And no man must be taken for such, that doth not manifest it, or by whom you cannot prove it. 3. But if you have reasonable suspicion you may carry yourself the more warily for your own preservation, lest he should prove your enemy, and his designs should take you unprovided.

Quest. II. With what kind of love must an enemy be loved, and on what accounts?

Answ. Primarily with a love of complacence, for all the good which is in him, natural or moral: he must be loved as man for the goodness of his nature; and his understanding and virtues must be acknowledged as freely, and loved as fully, as if he were no enemy of ours: enmity must not blind and pervert our judgment of him, and hinder us from discerning all that is amiable in him; nor must it corrupt our affections, and hinder us from loving it and him. 2. Secondarily we must love him with a love of benevolence, desiring him all that happiness which we desire to ourselves, and endeavouring it according to our opportunities.

Quest. III. Must I desire that God will pardon and save him, while he repenteth not of the wrong he doth me; and being impenitent, is uncapable of pardon?

Answ. 1. You must desire at once that God will give him repentance and forgiveness. 2. If he be impenitent in a state and life of ungodliness, or in a known and wilful sin, he is indeed uncapable of God's pardon and salvation in that case: but if you know him not to be ungodly, and if mistake or passion only, or some personal offence or falling out, have made him your enemy, and you are not sure that the enmity is so predominant as to exclude all true charity; or if he think you to be a bad person, and be your enemy on that account, you must pray for his pardon and salvation, though he should not particularly repent.

Quest. IV. What if he be my enemy upon the account of religion, and so an enemy to God?

Answ. 1. There are too many who have too much enmity to each other, upon the account of different opinions and parties in religion, in an erroneous zeal for godliness, who are not to be taken for enemies to God. What acts of hostility have in this age been used by several sects of zealous christians against each other! 2. If you know them to be enemies of God and godliness, you must hate their sin, and love their humanity and all that is good [884]in them, and wish their repentance, welfare, and salvation.

Quest. V. What must I do for an enemy's good, when my benefits are but like to imbolden, encourage, and enable him to do hurt to me or others?

Answ. 1. Usually kindness tendeth to convince and melt an enemy, and to hinder him from doing hurt. 2. Such ways of kindness must be chosen, as do most engage an enemy to returns of kindness, without giving him ability or opportunity to do mischief in case he prove implacable. You may show him kindness, without putting a sword into his hand. Prudence will determine of the way of benefits, upon consideration of circumstances.

Quest. VI. May I not defend myself against an enemy, and hurt him in my own defence? And may I not wish him as much hurt as I may do him?

Answ. When you can save yourself by fair words, or flight, or some tolerable loss, without resisting him to his hurt, you should rather choose it, and "resist not evil," Matt. v. 39. When you cannot do so, you must defend yourself with as little hurt to your enemy as you can. And if you cannot save yourself from a lesser hurt, without doing him a greater, you must rather suffer it.

Object. But if I hurt him in my own defence, it is his own fault.

Answ. So it may, and yet be yours too: you are bound to charity to your enemy, and not to justice only.

Object. But if I run away from him, or resist him not, it will be my dishonour; and I may defend my honour as well as my life.

Answ. Such objections and reasonings (which the Jesuits use against Jesus) were fitter for the mouth of an atheist than of a christian. It is pride which setteth so much by the esteem of men, yea, of bad and foolish men, as to plead honour for uncharitableness: and the voice of pride is the voice of the devil, contrary to him "who made himself of no reputation," Phil. ii. 7, 8, and submitted to be arrayed in a garb of mockery, and led out with scorn like a fool, and bowed to, and buffeted, and spit upon, and crucified; who calleth to us to learn of him to be meek and lowly, and to deny ourselves, and take up the cross, (which is shameful suffering,) if we will be his disciples, Matt. xi. 28, 29; Luke xiv. 30-33. To every christian it is the greatest honour to be like Jesus Christ, and to excel in charity. It is a greater dishonour to want love to an enemy, than to fly from him, or not resist him. He that teacheth otherwise, and maketh sin honourable, and the imitation and obedience of Christ to be more dishonourable, doth preach up pride, and preach down charity, and doth preach for the devil against Jesus Christ; and therefore should neither call himself a Jesuit nor a christian.

Yea more, if the person that would hurt or kill you, be one that is of more worth and usefulness as to the public good, you should rather suffer by him, or be slain by him, than you should equally hurt him or kill him in your own defence. As if the king of another kingdom that hath no authority over you, (for of your own there is no question,) should assault you; or any one whose death would be a greater loss than yours. For the public good is better than your own.

And it will not always hold, that you may wish another as much hurt as you may do him: for in defending yourself, you may sometimes blamelessly do more hurt than you were willing to do. And you must never wish your enemies hurt as such, but only as a necessary means of good, as of preservation of himself, or you, or others.

Quest. VII. Must kings and states love their enemies? How then can war be lawful?

Answ. Kings and states are bound to it as much as private men; and therefore must observe the foresaid law of love as well as others. Therefore they must raise no war unnecessarily, nor for any cause be it never so just in itself, when the benefits of the war are not like to be a greater good, than the war will bring hurt both to friends and foes set together. A lawful offensive war is almost like a true general council: on certain suppositions such a thing may be; but whether ever the world saw such a thing, or whether ever such suppositions will come to existence, is the question.

Tit. 2. Motives to Love and do Good to Enemies.

Motive I. God loveth his enemies, and doth them good; and he is our best exemplar. Matt. v. 44, 45, "But I say unto you, Love your enemies, bless them that curse you, do good to them that hate you, and pray for them which despitefully use you, and persecute you; that ye may be the children of your Father which is in heaven: for he maketh his sun to rise on the evil and on the good, and sendeth rain on the just and on the unjust."

Motive II. Jesus Christ was incarnate to set us a pattern, especially of this virtue: he sought the salvation of his enemies; he went up and down doing good among them. He died for his enemies: he prayeth for them even in his sufferings on the cross: he wept over them when he foresaw their ruin. When he was reviled, he reviled not again. This is the pattern which we must imitate.

Motive III. God loved even us ourselves when we were his enemies; or else what had become of us? And Christ died even for us, as enemies, to reconcile us by his death to God, Rom. v. 9, 10. Therefore we are specially obliged to this duty.

Motive IV. To be God's enemies is to be wicked and unlovely; so that in such God could see nothing amiable, but our nature and those poor remainders of virtue in it, and our capacity of being made better by his grace; and yet he then loved us: but to be an enemy to you or me, is not to be ungodly or wicked as such; it is an enmity but against a vile, unworthy worm, and therefore is a smaller fault.

Motive V. We do more against ourselves than any enemy or devils, and yet we love ourselves; why then should we not love another who doth less against us.

Motive VI. All that is of God and is good must be loved; but there may be much of God, and much natural and moral good, in some enemies of ours.

Motive VII. To love an enemy signifieth a mind that is impartial, and loveth purely on God's account, and for goodness' sake; but the contrary showeth a selfish mind, that loveth only on his own account.

Motive VIII. If you love only those that love you, you do no more than the worst man in the world may do; but christians must do more than others, Matt. v. 47; or else they must expect no more than others.

Motive IX. Loving and doing good to enemies is the way to win them and to save them. If there be any spark of true humanity left in them, they will love you when they perceive indeed that you love them. A man can hardly continue long to hate him whom he perceiveth unfeignedly to love him. And this will draw him to love religion for your sake, when he discerneth the fruits of it.

Motive X. If he be implacable, it will put you into a condition fit for God to own you in, and to judge you according to your innocency. These two together [885]contain the sense of "heaping coals of fire on his head:" that is, q. d. If he be not implacable, you will melt and win him; and if he be implacable, you will engage God in your cause, who best knoweth when and how to revenge.

Tit. 3. Directions for Loving and doing Good to Enemies.

Direct. I. Make no man your enemy, so far as you can avoid it: for though you may pretend to love him when he is your enemy, you have done contrary to love in making him your enemy; for thereby he is deprived of his own love to you. And if his charity be his best commodity, then he that robbeth him (though he be never so culpable himself) hath done that which belongeth to the worst of enemies; it is a thousand times greater hurt and loss to him, to lose his own love to others, than to lose another's love to him: and therefore to make him hate you, is more injurious or hurtful to him, than to hate him.

Direct. II. Take not those for your enemies that are not, and believe not any one to be your enemy, till cogent evidence constrain you. Take heed therefore of ill, suspicious, and ungrounded censures; except defensively so far only as to secure yourselves or others from a possible hurt.

Direct. III. Be not desirous or inquisitive to know what men think or say of you (unless in some special case where your duty or safety requireth it). For if they say well of you, it is a temptation to pride; and if they say ill of you, it may abate your love and tend to enmity. "Also take no heed to all words that are spoken, lest thou hear thy servant curse thee: for ofttimes also thy own heart knoweth, that thou thyself likewise hast cursed (or spoken evil of) others," Eccles. vii. 21. It is strange to see how the folly of men is pleased with their own temptations.

Direct. IV. Frown away those flatterers and whisperers who would aggravate other men's enmity to you or injuries against you, and think to please you by telling you needlessly of other men's wrongs. While they seem to show themselves enemies to your enemies, indeed they show themselves enemies consequently to yourselves; for it is your destruction that they endeavour in the destruction of your love. "If a whisperer separate chief friends," Prov. xvi. 28, much more may he abate your love to enemies: let him therefore be entertained as he deserveth.

Direct. V. Study, and search, and hearken after all the good which is in your enemies. For nothing will he the object of your love, but some discerned good. Hearken not to them that would extenuate and hide the good that is in them.

Direct. VI. Consider much how capable your enemy (and God's enemy) is of being better. And for aught you know God may make him much better than yourselves! Remember Paul's case. And when such a one is converted, forethink how penitent and humble, how thankful and holy, how useful and serviceable he may be; and love him as he is capable of becoming so lovely to God and man.

Direct. VII. Hide not your love to your enemies, and let not your minds be satisfied that you are conscious that you love them; but manifest it to them by all just and prudent means; for else you are so uncharitable as to leave them in their enmity, and not to do your part to cure it. If you could help them against hunger and nakedness, and will not, how can you truly say you love them? And if you could help them against malice and uncharitableness, and will not, how can you think but this is worse? If they knew that you love them unfeignedly, as you say you do, it is two to one but they would abate their enmity.

Direct. VIII. Be not unnecessarily strange to your enemies, but be as familiar with them as well as you can. For distance and strangeness cherish suspicious and false reports, and enmity; and converse in kind familiarity, hath a wonderful power to reconcile.

Direct. IX. Abhor above all enemies that pride of heart, which scorneth to stoop to others for love and peace. It is a devilish language to say, Shall I stoop or crouch to such a fellow? I scorn to be so base. Humility must teach you to give place to the pride and wrath of others, and to confess it when you have wronged them, and ask them forgiveness: and if they have done the wrong to you, yet must you not refuse to be the first movers and seekers for reconciliation. Though I know that this rule hath some exceptions; as when the enemies of religion or us are so malicious and implacable, that they will but make a scorn of our submission, and in other cases, when it is like to do more harm than good, it is then lawful to retire ourselves from malice.

Direct. X. However, let the enmity be in them alone: watch your own hearts with a double carefulness, as knowing what your temptation is; and see that you love them, whether they will love you or not.

Direct. XI. Do all the good for them that lawfully you can; for benefits melt and reconcile: and hold on though ingratitude discourage you.

Direct. XII. Do them good first in those things that they are most capable of valuing and relishing; that is (ordinarily) in corporal commodities: or if it be not in your power to do it yourselves, provoke others to do it (if there be need). And then they will be prepared for greater benefits.

Direct. XIII. But stop not in your enemy's corporal good, and in his reconciliation to yourself; for then it will appear to be all but a selfish design which you are about. But labour to reconcile him to God, and save his soul, and then it will appear to be the love of God, and him that moved you.

Direct. XIV. But still remember that you are not bound to love an enemy as a friend, but as a man so qualified as he is; nor to love a wicked man, who is an enemy to godliness, as if he were a godly man; but only as one that is capable of being godly. This precept of loving enemies was never intended for the levelling all men in our love.

CHAPTER XXX.

CASES AND DIRECTIONS ABOUT WORKS OF CHARITY.
Tit. 1. Cases of Conscience about Works of Charity.

Quest. I. What are the grounds, and reasons, and motives to charitable works?

Answ. 1. That doing good doth make us likest to God. He is the universal Father and Benefactor to the world. All good is in him or from him, and he that is best and doth most good is likest him.

2. It is an honourable employment therefore: it is more honourable to be the best man in the land, than to be the greatest: greatness is therefore honourable, because it is an ability to do good; and wisdom is honourable because it is the skill of doing good: so that goodness is that end which maketh them honourable, and without respect to which they [886]were as nothing. A power or skill to do mischief is no commendation.

3. Doing good maketh us pleasing and amiable to God, because it maketh us like him, and because it is the fulfilling of his will. God can love nothing but himself, and his own excellencies or image appearing in his works; or his works so far as his attributes appear and are glorified in them.

4. Good works are profitable to men, Tit. iii. 8. Our brethren are the better for them: the bodies of the poor are relieved, and men's souls are saved by them.

5. In doing good to others we do good to ourselves; because we are living members of Christ's body, and by love and communion feel their joys, as well as pains. As the hand doth maintain itself by maintaining and comforting the stomach; so doth a loving christian by good works.

6. There is in every good nature a singular delight in doing good: it is the pleasantest life in all the world. A magistrate, a preacher, a schoolmaster, a tutor, a physician, a judge, a lawyer, hath so much true pleasure as his life and labours are successful in doing good. I know that the conscience of honest endeavours may afford solid comfort to a willing though unsuccessful man; and well-doing may be pleasant though it prove not a doing good to others; but it is a double, yea, a multiplied comfort to be successful. It is much if an honest, unsuccessful man (a preacher, a physician, &c.) can keep up so much peace, as to support him under the grief of his unsuccessfulness; but to see our honest labours prosper, and many to be the better for them, is the pleasantest life that man can here hope for.

7. Good works are a comfortable evidence that faith is sincere, and that the heart dissembleth not with God: whenas a faith that will not prevail for works of charity, is dead and uneffectual, and the image or carcass of faith indeed, and such as God will not accept, James ii.

8. We have received so much ourselves from God, as doubleth our obligation to do good to others: obedience and gratitude do both require it.

9. We are not sufficient for ourselves, but need others as well as they need us: and therefore as we expect to receive from others, we must accordingly do to them. If the eye will not see for the body, nor the hand work for the body, nor the feet go for it, the body will not afford them nutriment, and they shall receive as they do.

10. Good works are much to the honour of religion, and consequently of God; and much tend to men's conviction, conversion, and salvation. Most men will judge of the doctrine by the fruits. Matt. v. 16, "Let your light so shine before men, that they may see your good works, and glorify your Father which is in heaven."

11. Consider how abundantly they are commanded and commended in the word of God. Christ himself hath given us the pattern of his own life, which from his first moral actions to his last, was nothing but doing good and bearing evil. He made love the fulfilling of the law, and the works of love the genuine fruits of christianity, and an acceptable sacrifice to God. Gal. vi. 10, "As we have opportunity let us do good to all men, especially to them of the household of faith." Heb. xiii. 10, "To do good and communicate forget not; for with such sacrifices God is well pleased." Tit. iii. 8, "This is a faithful saying, and these things I will that thou constantly affirm, that they which have believed in God might be careful to maintain good works: these things are good and profitable to men." Eph. ii. 10, "For we are his workmanship, created in Christ Jesus to good works, which God hath before ordained that we should walk in them." Tit. ii. 14, "To purify to himself a peculiar people, zealous of good works." Acts xx. 35, "That so labouring ye ought to support the weak, and to remember the words of the Lord Jesus, how he said, It is more blessed to give than to receive." Eph. iv. 28, "Let him that stole steal no more, but rather let him labour, working with his hands the thing that is good, that he may have to give to him that needeth." You see poor labourers are not excepted from the command of helping others: insomuch that the first church sold all their possessions, and had all things common; not to teach levelling and condemn propriety, but to show all after them that christian love should use all to relieve their brethren as themselves.

12. Consider that God will in a special manner judge us at the last day according to our works, and especially our works of charity: as in Matt. xxv. Christ hath purposely and plainly showed; and so doth many another text of Scripture. These are the motives to works of love.

Quest. II. What is a good work, even such as God hath promised to reward?

Answ. 1. The matter must be lawful, and not a sin. 2. It must tend to a good effect, for the benefit of man, and the honour of God. 3. It must have a good end;

even the pleasing and glory of God, and the good of ourselves and others. 4. It must come from a right principle, even from the love of God, and of man for his sake. 5. It must be pure and unmixed: if any sin be mixed with it, it is sinful so as to need a pardon: and if sin be predominant in it, it is so far sinful as to be unacceptable to God, in respect to the person, and is turned into sin itself. 6. It must be in season; or else it may sometimes be mixed with sin, and sometimes be evil itself and no good work. 7. It must be comparatively good as well as simply. It must not be a lesser good instead of a greater, or to put off a greater; as to be praying when we should be quenching a fire, or saving a man's life. 8. It must be good in a convenient degree. Some degrees are necessary to the moral being of a good work, and some to the well-being. God must be loved and worshipped as God, and heaven sought as heaven, and men's souls and lives must be highly prized and seriously preserved: some sluggish doing of good is but undoing it. 9. It must be done in confidence of the merits of Christ, and presented to God as by his hands, who is our Mediator and Intercessor with the Father.

Quest. III. What works of charity should one choose in these times, who would improve his Master's talents to his most comfortable account?

Answ. The diversity of men's abilities and opportunities, make that to be best for one man which is impossible to another.[173] But I shall name some that are in themselves most beneficial to mankind, that every man may choose the best which he can reach to.

1. The most eminent work of charity, is the promoting of the conversion of the heathen and infidel parts of the world: to this princes and men of power and wealth might contribute much if they were willing; especially in those countries in which they have commerce and send ambassadors: they might procure the choicest scholars, to go over with their ambassadors and learn the languages, and set themselves to this service according to opportunity; or they might erect a college for the training up of students purposely for that work, in which they might maintain some natives procured from the several infidel countries, (as two or three Persians, [887]as many Indians of Indostan, as many Tartarians, Chinese, Siamites, &c.) which might possibly be obtained; and these should teach students their country languages. But till the christian world be so happy as to have such princes, something may be done by volunteers of lower place and power; as Mr. Wheelock did in translating the New Testament, and Mr. Pococke by the honourable Mr. Robert Boyle's procurement and charge, in translating "Grotius de Verit. Christ. Relig." into Arabic, and sending it to Indostan and Persia. And what excellent labour hath good Mr. John Elliot (with some few assistants) bestowed these twenty years and more in New England; where now he hath translated and printed the whole Scriptures in their American tongue, (with a Catechism and Call to the Unconverted,) by the help of a press maintained from hence.

2. The attempt of restoring the christian churches to their primitive purity and unity, according to men's several opportunities, is a most excellent and desirable work; which though the ignorance and wickedness of many, and the implacableness and bloodiness of the carnal, proud, domineering part, and the too great alienation of some others from them, do make it so difficult as to be next to desperate, at the present, yet is not to be cast off as desperate indeed; for great things have been done by wise and valiant attempts. Princes might do very much to this, if they were both wise and willing. And who knoweth but an age may come that may be so happy? The means and method I would willingly describe, but that this is no fit place or time.

3. The planting of a learned, able, holy, concordant ministry in a particular kingdom, and settling the primitive discipline thereby, is a work also which those princes may very much promote, whose hearts are set upon it, and who set up no contrary interest against it; but because these lines are never like to be known to princes, (unless by way of accusation,) it is private men's works which we must speak to.

252

4. It is a very good work to procure and maintain a worthy minister in any of the most ignorant parishes in these kingdoms, (of which, alas, how many are there!) where the skilful preaching of the gospel is now wanting; or to maintain an assistant in populous parishes, where one is not able to do the work; or by other just means to promote this service.

5. It is a very good work to set up free-schools in populous and in ignorant places, especially in Wales; that all may be taught to read, and some may be prepared for the universities.

6. It is an excellent work to cull out some of the choicest wits, among the poorer sort in the country schools, who otherwise would wither for want of culture; and to maintain them for learning in order to the ministry, with some able, godly tutor in the university, or some country minister who is fit and vacant enough thereunto.

7. It is an excellent work to give among poor ignorant people, Bibles and catechisms, and some plain and godly books which are most fitted to their use. But it were more excellent to leave a settled revenue for this use, (naming the books, and choosing meet trustees,) that so the rent might every year furnish a several parish, which would in a short time be a very extensive benefit, and go through many countries.

8. It is a very good work to set poor men's children apprentices to honest, religious masters, where they may at once get the blessing to their souls of a godly education, and to their bodies, of an honest way of maintenance.

9. It will not be unacceptable to God, to relieve some of the persons, or poor children, of those very many hundred faithful ministers of Christ, who are now silenced and destitute of maintenance, many having nothing at all, but what charity sendeth them, to maintain themselves and desolate families, who were wont to exercise charity to the bodies and souls of others. Read Matt. xxv.; Gal. vi. 5-8.

10. It is a good work of them who give stocks of money, or yearly rents, to be lent for five, or six, or seven years to young tradesmen, at their setting up, upon good security, choosing good trustees, who may choose the fittest persons; and if it be a rent, it will still increase the stock, and if any should break, the loss of it may be borne.

11. It would be a very good work for landlords to improve their interest with their tenants, to further at once their bodily comfort and salvation, to hire them by some abatement at their rent days, to learn catechisms, and read the Scripture and good books in their families, and give the pastor an account of their proficience. Whether the law will enable them to bind them to any such thing in their leases, I cannot tell.

12. And the present work of charity for every one, is to relieve the most needy which are next at hand. To know what poor families are in greatest want, and to help them as we are able; and to provoke the rich to do that which we cannot do ourselves, and to beg for others; and still to make use of bodily relief, to further the good of their souls, by seconding all with spiritual advice and help.

Quest. IV. In what order are works of charity to be done? And whom must we prefer when we are unable to accommodate all?

Answ. 1. The most public works must be preferred before private. 2. Works for the soul, *cæteris paribus*, before works for the body; and yet bodily benefits in order of time, must oft go first as preparations to the other. 3. Greatest necessities, *cæteris paribus*, must be supplied before lesser: the saving of another's life must be preferred before your own less necessary comforts. 4. Your own and families' wants must, *cæteris paribus*, be supplied before strangers; even before some that you must love better; because God hath in point of provision and maintenance, given you a nearer charge of yourselves and families than of others. 5. Nature also obligeth you to prefer your kindred before strangers, if there be a parity as to other reasons. 6. And, *cæteris paribus*, a good man must be preferred before a bad. 7. And yet that charity which is like to tend to the good of the soul as well as of the body is to be preferred; and in that case ofttimes a bad man is to be preferred, when a greater good is like to be the effect. 8. A

253

friend, *cæteris paribus*, is to be preferred before an enemy; but not when the good is like to be greater which will follow the relieving of an enemy. Many other rules might be given, but they are laid down already, part i. chap. where I treat of good works; whither I refer you.

Quest. V. Should I give in my lifetime, or at my death?

Answ. According as it is like to do most good; but none should needlessly delay: both are best.

Quest. VI. Should one devote or set by a certain part of daily incomes?

Quest. VII. What proportion is a man bound to give to the poor?

Answ. These two questions having answered in a letter to Mr. Thomas Gouge, now printed, and the book being not in many hands, I will here recite that letter as it is published.

[888]Most dear, and very much honoured brother,

Even the philosopher hath taught me so to esteem you, who said, that "He is likest to God, who needeth fewest things for himself, and doth most good to others." And Christ telleth us, that universal charity (extending even to them that hate and persecute us) doth make us, as his children, like our heavenly Father, Matt. v. 44-46, 48. As hating and hurting their neighbours is the mark of the children of the devil, (John viii. 44,) so loving and doing good is the mark of the children of God. And it is observable, that no one treateth so copiously and pathetically of love (both of Christ's love to us, and ours to him) as the blessed disciple, whom Jesus is said to have eminently loved (as John xiii. 14-17, and 1 John, show).

It hath often pleased me to hear how dearly you were beloved, by that exceeding great and populous parish, where lately you were preacher, for your eminent charity to their souls and bodies; and to see that still you take it for your work and calling, to be a provoker of others to love and to good works, Heb. x. 24; whilst many that are taken for good christians, do deal in such works as rarities or recreations, only a little now and then upon the by, and whilst Satan's ministers are provoking others to hatred and to hurtfulness.

Your labour is so amiable to me, that it would contribute to my comforts, if I were able to contribute any thing to your assistance.

You desire me to give you my judgment of the *quota pars*, What proportion it is meet for most men to devote to charitable uses; whether the tenth part of their increase be not ordinarily a fit proportion?

The reason why I use not to answer such questions without much distinguishing (when lazy, impatient readers would have them answered in a word) is, because the real difference of particular cases is so great, as maketh it necessary; unless we will deceive men, or leave the matter as dark and unresolved as we found it.

I. Before I answer your question, I shall premise, that I much approve of the way which you insist upon, of setting so much constantly apart as is fit for us to give, that it may be taken by us to be a devoted or consecrated thing. And methinks that there is much of a divine direction for the time in 1 Cor. xvi. 1, 2, together with the ancient church, "That upon the first day of the week, every one lay by him in store, as God had prospered him." And it will do much to cure pharisaical sabbatizing, when the Lord's day is statedly used in this, with holy works; and will teach hypocrites to know what this meaneth, "I will have mercy and not sacrifice," Matt. ix. 13; xii. 7. And that works of charity are an odour, a sweet smell, a sacrifice acceptable and well pleasing to God, who of the riches of his glory in Christ, will supply all the need of such, as bring forth such fruit to abound unto their account, Phil. iv. 17-19. So it be done without any insnaring vows, or rash engagements to unnecessary things; this constant setting apart a certain proportion for pious and charitable uses, will have these advantages:

1. Our distribution will be made deliberately and prudently, when beforehand we study a due proportion, and determine accordingly; whereas they that give only occasionally as some object suddenly inviteth them, will do it at random, without due

respect to their own accounts, whether the proportion given be answerable to their own estate and duty.

2. This stated way will make men's charity much more extensive: when objects of charity are not in their sight, they will inquire after them, and they will seek for the needy, if the needy seek not unto them; because they have so much by them to dispose of, which is devoted to God. But those who give but as occasional objects draw it from them, will give to none but those that crave, or will pass by many as needy, whom they see not, while they relieve only these few that they hap to see.

3. And it will make men's charity also to be more constant, and done obediently as a christian's daily work and duty; when occasional charity will be more rarely and unconstantly exercised. In a word, as the observation of the Lord's day, which is a stated proportion of time, secureth the holy improvement of our time, much better than if God be served but occasionally, without a stated time; and as a constant stated course of preaching excelleth mere occasional exhortation; even so a constant course of giving, wisely, will find out objects, and overcome temptations, and discharge our duty with much more integrity and success. And if we can easily perceive that occasional praying will not so well discharge the duty of prayer, as a constant stated course will do; why should we not think the same of occasional giving, if men did but perceive that giving according to our ability, is as sure and great a duty as praying? Now to your question of the proportion of our gifts.

II. We must distinguish,

1. Between them that have no more than will supply their own and their families' true necessities, and those that have more.

2. Between them that have a stock of money which yieldeth them no increase, and those that have more increase by their labour, but little stock.

3. Between them whose increase is like to be constant, and theirs that is uncertain, sometimes more and sometimes less.

4. Between them that have many children, or near kindred, that nature casteth upon them for relief; and those that have few or no children, or have a competent provision for them, and have few needy kindred that they are especially obliged to relieve.

5. Between those that live in times and places where the necessities of the poor are very great, or some great works of piety are in hand; and those that live where the poor are in no great necessity, and no considerable opportunity for any great work of piety or charity doth appear. These distinctions premised, I answer as followeth:

1. It is certain that every true sanctified christian hath devoted himself and all that he hath to God, to be used in obedience to his will, and for his glory, 1 Cor. vi. 19, 20; x. 31; Luke xviii. 33. The question therefore is not, Whether the tenth part of our estate should be devoted to and employed in the service of God, one way or other, as he directeth us; for it is out of question that all is his, and we are but his stewards; and must give account of our stewardship, and of all our receivings, Matt. xxv. But the question is only what proportion is best pleasing to God in our giving to others.

2. A christian being unfeignedly thus resolved in the general, to lay out that he hath or shall have as God would have him, and to his glory (as near as he can); his next inquiry must be, (for finding out the will of God,) to know in the ordinary course of his distribution, where God hath gone before him by any particular prescript, and tied him to one certain way of giving; and where God hath only given him some general direction, and left him to discern his duty in particulars, by that general rule, and the [889]further direction of objects and providence. And in this inquiry he will find,

1. That God hath first prescribed to him in nature, the necessary sustentation of his own life. And,

2. The necessary maintenance of his children and family.

3. The necessary maintenance of the preachers of the gospel, for the worship of God, and the salvation of men, 1 Cor. ix.; Phil. iv. 10, 11, 14, 17, 18; Luke x. 7; 1 Tim. v. 17, 18.

4. The necessary maintenance of the commonwealth, and paying tribute to the higher powers, who are the ministers of God to us for good; attending continually upon this very thing, Rom. xiii. 4, 6.

5. The saving of the lives of those that are in apparent danger of famine or perishing, within our sight or reach, 1 John iii. 17; Luke x. 33. Thus far God hath prescribed to us, how he would have us use our estates in an ordinary way. In many other things he hath left us to more general directions.

3. To know among good works, which is to be preferred, it principally concerneth us next to know, what works do most contribute to our chiefest ends; which God is most honoured by; which tend to the greatest good: and here we shall find that, *cæteris paribus,*

1. The souls of men are to be preferred before their bodies, in estimation and intention; but in time, the body is oft to be preferred before the soul, because if the body be suffered to perish, the helping of the soul will be past our power.

2. And so the church is finally and estimatively to be preferred before the commonwealth; but the commonwealth must be first served in time, when it is necessary to the church's support and welfare; for the church will else perish with the commonwealth.

3. The good of many is to be preferred before the good of few, and public good to be valued above private, Rom. ix. 3.

4. A continued good is greater than a short and transitory good. And so necessary is it to have chief respect in all our works to our chiefest end, (the greatest good,) that even when God seemeth to have prescribed to us the way of our expenses, yet that is but as to our ordinary course: for if in an extraordinary case it fall out, that another way is more to God's glory and the common good, it must be then preferred; for all means are to be judged of by the end, and chosen and used for it. For example, if the good of church and commonwealth, or of the souls of many, do stand up against our corporal provision of our children or families, it is to be preferred; which is easily proved *a fortiore,* because it is to be preferred before our own good, even the saving of our lives. A good subject will lose his life to save the life of his king; and a good soldier will die to save his general or the army; and a useless member of the church should be content to die, if it be necessary, to save the life of a pastor that is greatly useful. If a poor, ordinary christian then had been so put to it, that either Paul or he must famish, no doubt but his ultimate end would have commanded him to prefer the apostle before himself: so that in extraordinary cases, the end and greatest good must be our guide.

4. Though I may ordinarily prefer my own life before another's, yet I must not prefer my mere delight or health before another's life: and though men must provide for the lives of their children before the lives of others, yet the life of a poor neighbour (*cæteris paribus*) must be preferred and provided for, before the portions of your own children, and before the supply of their tolerable wants: so that as long as there are poor about you, that are in necessity of food to save their lives, the portions or comeliest clothing of your children must rather be neglected, than the poor be suffered to perish. How else do I love my neighbour as myself, if I make so great a difference between myself and him?

5. Even the food and raiment, and other necessaries, which a christian useth himself, he must use for God, and not for his carnal self at all; not taking it as his own, which he may use at and for his own pleasure, but as part of his Master's goods, which are all to be used only for his service. As a steward, that when he giveth every servant his part, and taketh his own part, it is not as if it were primarily his own, but as a servant on the same account with the rest: so when I devote all that I have to God, I am so far from excepting my own part, even my food and raiment, that I do more

confidently intend the serving of God with that, than with the rest, because it is more in my power, and there is in it more of my duty. The same I may say of that which is given to our children and other relations.

6. Therefore when more of the service and interest of God, lieth upon your own or your children's using of his talents, than upon other men's, you are bound (for God, and not for yourselves) to retain so much the more to yourselves and children. It is a fond conceit that a man is bound to give all to others, rather than to himself or children, when it is most probable, that those others would do God less service with it, than himself or his children would do: as suppose such a man as Mr. Elliot in New England (that devoteth himself to the conversion of the Indians) had riches, when some neighbour ministers were poor, that are engaged in no such work. He that knoweth that God hath given him a heart and an opportunity to do him more service with it than another would do, is not bound to put it out of his own hands into another's, that is less like to be a faithful improver of it. If you have a son of your own that is a preacher of the gospel, and is more able and serviceable than other ministers in equal want, no doubt you have then a double obligation to relieve your own son before another; as he is your son, and as he is more serviceable to God. If other men are bound to supply your want for the work and interest of the gospel, you are not bound to give away your own supplies, to the disabling you from your work, unless when you see a greater work, or the present absolute necessity of others, doth require it.

7. It is imprudent and unsafe, and therefore unlawful, ordinarily, to tie yourself unchangeably for continuance, to any one particular way of using your estates for God; as to vow that you will give it to ministers, or to the poor, or to schools, &c.; because the changes may be such which God will make, as shall make that way to be one year necessary, which before was not, and so change your duty. We cannot prescribe to God what way he shall appoint us for the future, to use his talents in. His word bids us prefer the greatest good; but which is the greatest his providence must tell us.

8. He that hath no more than is necessary to the very preservation of his own life and his family's, is not bound to give to others (unless in some extraordinary case, which calleth him to prefer a greater and more public good): and he that hath no more than is needful to the comfortable support of himself and family, is not bound to relieve those that have no greater wants than himself. And his own necessity is not to be measured merely by what he hath, but by the use he hath for it: for a magistrate, or[890]one that is engaged in public works, may have need of as many hundreds a year, as a private man of pounds.

9. Those that have many children to provide for, or poor kindred that nature casteth on them, cannot give so much (proportionably) to other poor, as those are bound to do that have few or none; for these are bound to give all, except their personal necessaries, to public, pious, or charitable works, because God calleth not for it any other way.

10. To pamper the flesh, is a sin as well in the rich as in the poor: the rich therefore are bound not only to give all that the flesh can spare, when its own inordinate desires are satisfied, but deny themselves, and mortify the flesh, and be good husbands for God, and studious to retrench all unnecessary expenses, and to live laboriously and thriftily, that they may have the more to do good with. It is a great extenuation of the largest gifts, as to God's esteem, when they are but the leavings of the flesh, and are given out of men's abundance, and when we offer that to God that costeth us nothing: as Christ doth purposely determine the case; comparing the rich man's gifts with the widow's two mites, he said, "Of a truth I say unto you, that this poor widow hath cast in more than they all: for all these have of their abundance cast in unto the offerings of God; but she of her penury hath cast in all the living that she had," Luke xxi. 1-4; that is, all the stock she had beforehand, though she had need of it herself. It is a very considerable thing in our charity, how much mortification and self-

denial is expressed in it, and how much it costeth our own flesh to give to others. And therefore they that think they are excused from doing good to others, as long as they have any need of it themselves, and will give nothing but what they have no need of, (it being not of absolute necessity to their lives,) do offer a sacrifice of no great value in the eyes of God. What then shall we say of them, that will not give even out of their abundance, and that which without any suffering they may spare?

11. The first and principal thing to be done by one that would give as God would have him, is, to get a truly charitable heart, which containeth all these parts:

1. That we see God in his needy creatures, and in his cause or work that needs our help.

2. That we be sensible of his abundant love in Christ to us, in giving pardon and eternal life, and that from the sense of this our thankful hearts are moved to do good to others.

3. That therefore we do it ultimately as to Christ himself; who taketh that which is done for his cause and servants, as done to him, Matt. xxv. 40.

4. That we conquer the cursed sin of selfishness, which makes men little regard any but themselves.

5. That we love our neighbours as ourselves, and love most where there is most of God and goodness, and not according to self-interest: and that as members of the same body, we take our brethren's wants and sufferings as our own; and then we should be as ready to help them as ourselves.

6. That we know the vanity of worldly riches, and be not earthly-minded, but regard the interest of God and our souls above all the treasures of the world.

7. That we unfeignedly believe the promises of God, who hath engaged himself to provide for us, and everlastingly to reward us in glory with himself. If these seven qualifications be wrought upon the heart, good works will plentifully follow. Make but the tree good, and the fruit will be good. But when the heart is void of the root and life which should produce them, the judgment will not be persuaded that so much is necessary, and required of us; and the will itself will still hang back, and be delaying to do good, and doing all pinchingly and hypocritically, with unwillingness and distrust.

No wonder if good works are so rare, when it is evident that to do them sincerely and heartily as our trade and business, it is necessary that the whole soul be thus renewed by faith, and love, and self-denial, and mortification, and by a heavenly hope and mind. They are the fruits and works of the new creature (which is, alas, too rare in the world): "For we are his workmanship, created in Christ Jesus unto good works, which God hath before ordained that we should walk in them," Eph. ii. 10. Therefore our first and chiefest labour should be to be sure that we are furnished with such hearts, and then if we have wherewith to do good, such hearts will be sure to do it: such hearts will best discern the time and measure, as a healthful man's appetite will in eating; for they will take it for a mercy and happiness to do good, and know, that it is they that give that are the great receivers. It is but a little money or alms that the poor receive of us, but it is God's acceptance, and favour, and reward that we receive, which is in "this life a hundred-fold, (in value,) and in the world to come eternal life," Matt. xix. 29. But if we have little or nothing to give, such a heart is accepted, as if we had given as much as we desire to give; so that if you have a heart that would give thousands if you had it, God will set down upon your account, so many thousands given (in desire). Your two mites shall be valued above all the superfluities of sensual worldlings: "For if there be first a willing mind, it is accepted according to that a man hath, and not according to that he hath not," 2 Cor. viii. 12. But God taketh not that for a willing mind, which only saith, I would give if I should suffer nothing by it myself, or were I sure I should not want; but that which saith, I will serve God as well as I can with my estate while I have it, and deny my flesh, that I may have to do good with, and trust God for my provision and reward; for if there be a readiness to will, there will be a performance also out of that which you have, 2 Cor. viii. 11.

258

12. Such a holy, self-denying, charitable heart, with the help of prudence, is the best judge of the due proportion which we should give: for this willing readiness being supposed, prudence will discern the fittest objects, and the fittest time, and the fittest measure, and will suit the means unto the end: when once a man's heart is set upon doing good, it will not be very hard to perceive how much ourselves, our families, the poor, and religious uses should have; for if such a person be prudent himself, he hath always with him a constant counsellor, with a general rule, and directing providence; if he want prudence sufficient to be his own director, he will take direction from the prudence of others.

13. Such a truly willing mind will not be much wanting in the general of doing good, but one way or other will serve God with his estate; and then if in any particulars he should come short, it will comparatively be a very small sin, when it is not for want of willingness, but of skill. The will is the chief seat of all moral good and evil; there is no more virtue than there is will, nor any more sin or vice than there is will. He that knoweth not how much he should give, because he is not willing to give it, and therefore not willing to know it, is indeed the miser and sinfully ignorant; but if it be not for want of a willing mind that we mistake the proportion, it will be a very pardonable mistake.

[891]14. Your proportion of the tenth part is too much for some, and much too little for others, but for the most, I think it as likely a proportion as it is fit for another to prescribe in particular, with these following explications.

1. He that hath a full stock of money, and no increase by it, must give proportionably out of his stock; when he that hath little or no stock, but the fruits of his daily industry and labour, may possibly be bound to give less than the other.

2. It is not the tenth of our increase, deducting first all our families' provision, that you mean when you direct to give the tenth (for it is far more, if not all, that after such provision must be given); but it is the tenth without deduction that you mean; therefore when family necessaries cannot spare the tenth, it may be too much (else even the receivers must all be givers): but when family necessities can spare much more than the tenth, then the tenth is not enough.

3. In those places where church, and state, and poor are all to be maintained by free gift, there the tenth of our increase is far too little, for those that have any thing considerable to spare, to give to all these uses.

This is apparent in that the tenths alone were not thought enough even in the time of the law, to give towards the public worship of God: for besides the tenths, there were the first-fruits, and oblations, and many sorts of sacrifices; and yet at the same time, the poor were to be maintained by liberal gifts besides the tenths: and though we read not of much given to the maintenance of their rulers and magistrates, before they chose to have a king, yet afterwards we read of much; and before, the charges of wars and public works lay upon all.

In most places with us, the public ministry is maintained by glebe and tithes, which are none of the people's gifts at all, for he that sold or leased them their lands, did suppose that tithes were to be paid out of it, and therefore they paid a tenth part less for it, in purchase, fines, or rents, than otherwise they should have done; so that I reckon, that most of them give little or nothing to the minister at all. Therefore they may the better give so much the more to the needy, and to other charitable uses. But where minister, and poor, and all are maintained by the people's contribution, there the tenths are too little for the whole work; but yet to most, or very many, the tenths to the poor alone, besides the maintenance of the ministry and state, may possibly be more than they are able to give. The tenths even among the heathens, were given in many places to their sacrifices, priests, and to religious, public, civil works, besides all their private charity to the poor.

I find in Diog. Laertius, lib. i. (mihi) 32. that Pisistratus the Athenian tyrant, proving to Solon (in his epistle to him) that he had nothing against God or man to blame him for, but for taking the crown; telling him, that he caused them to keep the same laws which Solon gave them, and that better than the popular government could have done, doth instance thus: *Atheniensium singuli decimas frugum suarum separant, non in usus nostros consumendas, verum sacrificiis publicis, commodisque communibus, et si quando bellum contra nos ingruerit, in sumptus deputandas.* that is, Every one of the Athenians do separate the tithes of their fruits, not to be consumed to our uses, but to defray the charge in public sacrifices, and in the common profits, and if war at any time invade us. And Plautus saith, *Ut decimam solveret Herculi.* Indeed as among the heathens the tithes were conjunctly given for religious and civil uses, so it seems that at first the christian emperors settled them on the bishops for the use of the poor, as well as for the ministers, and church service, and utensils. For to all these they were to be divided, and the bishop was as the guardian of the poor: and the glebe or farms that were given to the church, were all employed to the same uses; and the canons required that the tithes should be thus disposed of by the clergy; *non tanquam propriæ, sed domino oblatæ.* and the emperor Justinian commanded the bishops, *Ne ea quæ ecclesiis relicta sunt sibi adscribant sed in necessarios ecclesiæ usus impendant,* lib. xliii. cap. de Episc. et Cler. vid. Albert. Ranzt. Metrop. lib. i. cap. 2. et sax. lib. vi. cap. 52. And Hierom (ad Damasc.) saith, *Quoniam quicquid habent clerici pauperum est; et domus illorum omnibus debent esse communes; susceptioni peregrinarum et hospitum invigilare debent; maxime curandum est illis, ut de decimis et oblationibus, cænobiis et Xenodochiis qualem voluerint et potuerint sustentationem impendant.*

Yet then the paying of tithes did not excuse the people from all other charity to the poor: Austin saith, *Qui sibi aut præmium comparat, aut peccatorum desiderat indulgentiam promereri, reddat decimam, etiam de novem partibus studeat eleemosynam dare pauperibus.* And in our times there is less reason that tithes should excuse the people from their works of charity, both because the tithes are now more appropriate to the maintenance of the clergy, and because (as is aforesaid) the people give them not out of their own. I confess, if we consider how decimation was used before the law by Abraham and Jacob, and established by the law unto the Jews, and how commonly it was used among the gentiles, and last of all by the church of Christ, it will make a considerate man imagine, that as there is still a divine direction for one day in seven, as a necessary proportion of time to be ordinarily consecrated to God, besides what we can spare from our other days; so that there is something of a divine canon, or direction, for the tenth of our revenues or increase to be ordinarily consecrated to God, besides what may be spared from the rest. And whether those tithes, that are none of your own, and cost you nothing, be now to be reckoned to private men, as any of their tenths, which they themselves should give, I leave to your consideration. Amongst Augustine's works we find an opinion that the devils were the tenth part of the angels, and that man is now to be the tenth order among the angels, the saints filling up the place that the devils fell from, and there being nine orders of angels to be above us, and that in this there is some ground of our paying tenths; and therefore he saith, that *Hæc est Domini justissima consuetudo; ut si tu illi decimam non dederis, tu ad decimam revocaberis, id est, dæmonibus, qui sunt decima pars angelorum, associaberis.* Though I know not whence he had this opinion, it seemeth that the devoting of a tenth part ordinarily to God, is a matter that we have more than a human direction for.

15. In times of extraordinary necessities of the church, or state, or poor, there must be extraordinary bounty in our contributions: as if an enemy be ready to invade the land, or if some extraordinary work of God (as the conversion of some heathen nations) do require it, or some extraordinary persecution and distress befall the pastors, or in a year of famine, plague, or war, when the necessities of the poor are extraordinary; the tenths in such cases will not suffice, from those that have more to give: therefore in such a time, the primitive christians sold their possessions, and laid down the price at the feet of the apostles.

In one word, an honest, charitable heart being presupposed as the root or fountain, and prudence [892]being the discerner of our duty, the apostle's general rule may much satisfy a christian for the proportion, 1 Cor. xvi. 2, "Let every one of you lay by him in store, as God hath prospered him;" and 2 Cor. viii. 12, "according to that a man hath:" though there be many intimations, that ordinarily a tenth part at least is requisite.

III. Having thus resolved the question of the *quota pars* or proportion to be given, I shall say a little to the question, Whether a man should give most in his lifetime, or at his death?

Answ. 1. It is certain that the best work is that which is like to do most good.

2. But to make it best to us, it is necessary that we do it with the most self-denying, holy, charitable mind.

3. That, *cæteris paribus*, all things else being equal, the present doing of a good work, is better than to defer it.

4. That to do good only when you die, because then you can keep your wealth no longer, and because then it costeth you nothing to part with it, and because then you hope that this shall serve instead of true repentance and godliness; this is but to deceive yourselves, and will do nothing to save your souls, though it do never so much good to others.

5. That he that sinfully neglecteth in his lifetime to do good, if he do it at his death, from true repentance and conversion, it is then accepted of God; though the sin of his delay must be lamented.

6. That he that delayeth it till death, not out of any selfishness, backwardness, or unwillingness, but that the work may be better, and do more good, doth better than if he hastened a lesser good. As if a man have a desire to set up a free-school for perpetuity, and the money which he hath is not sufficient; if he stay till his death, that so the improvement of the money may increase it, and make it enough for his intended work, that is to do a greater good with greater self-denial: for,

(1.) He receiveth none of the increase of the money for himself.

(2.) And he receiveth in his lifetime none of the praise or thanks of the work. So also, if a man that hath no children, have so much land only as will maintain him, and desireth to give it all to charitable uses when he dieth, this delay is not at all to be blamed, because he could not sooner give it; and if it be not in vain-glory, but in love to God and to good works that he leaveth it, it is truly acceptable at last. So that all good works that are done at death, are not therefore to be undervalued, nor are they rejected of God; but sometimes it falleth out that they are so much the greater and better works, though he that can do the same in his lifetime, ought to do it.

IV. But though I have spent all these words in answering these questions, I am fully satisfied that it is very few that are kept from doing good by any such doubt or difficulty, in the case which stalls their judgments; but by the power of sin and want of grace, which leave an unwillingness and backwardness on their hearts. Could we tell how to remove the impediments in men's wills, it would do more than the clearest resolving all the cases of conscience, which their judgments seem to be unsatisfied in. I will tell you what are the impediments in your way, that are harder to be removed than all these difficulties, and yet must be overcome before you can bring men to be like true christians, "rich in good works."

1. Most men are so sensual and selfish, that their own flesh is an insatiable gulf that devoureth all, and they have little or nothing to spare from it to good uses. It is better cheaply maintaining a family of temperate, sober persons, than one fleshly person that hath a whole litter of vices and lusts to be maintained: so much a year seemeth necessary to maintain their pride in needless curiosity and bravery, and so much a year to maintain their sensual sports and pleasures; and so much to please their throats or appetites, and to lay in provision for fevers, and dropsies, and coughs, and consumptions, and a hundred such diseases, which are the natural progeny of gluttony, drunkenness, and excess; and so much a year to maintain their idleness, and so of many other vices. But if one of these persons have the pride, and idleness, and gluttony, and sportfulness of wife, and children, and family also to maintain, as well as their own, many thousand pounds a year perhaps may be too little. Many a conquering

261

army hath been maintained at as cheap a rate, as such an army of lusts (or garrison at least) as keep possession of some such families, when all their luxury goeth for the honour of their family, and they glory in wearing the livery of the devil, the world, and the flesh (which they once renounced, and pretended to glory in nothing but the cross of Christ); and when they take care in the education of their children, that this entailed honour be not cut off from their families: no wonder if God's part be little from these men, when the flesh must have so much, and when God must stand to the courtesy of his enemies, and have but their leavings. I hope the nobility and gentry of England that are innocent herein, will not be offended with me, if I tell them that are guilty, that when I foresee their accounts, I think them to be the miserablest persons upon earth, that rob God, and rob the king of that which should defray the charges of government, and rob the church, and rob the poor, and rob their souls of all the benefits of good works, and all to please the devouring flesh. It is a dreadful thing to foresee with what horror they will give up their reckoning, when instead of so much in feeding and clothing the poor, and promoting the gospel, and the saving of men's souls, there will be found upon their account, so much in vain curiosities and pride, and so much in costly sports and pleasures, and so much in flesh-pleasing luxury and excess. The trick that they have got of late, to free themselves from the fears of this account, by believing that there will be no such day, will prove a short and lamentable remedy: and when that day shall come upon them unawares, their unbelief and pleasures will die together, and deliver them up to never-dying horror and despair. I have heard it often mentioned as the dishonour of France, that the third part of the revenues of so rich a kingdom should be devoted and paid to the maintaining of superstition: but if there be not many (and most) kingdoms in the world, where one half of their wealth is devoted to the flesh, and so to the devil, I should be glad to find myself herein mistaken: and judge you which is more disgraceful, to have half your estates given in sensuality to the devil, or a third part too ignorantly devoted to God! If men laid out no more than needs upon the flesh, they might have the more for the service of God and of their souls. You cannot live under so much a year, as would maintain twice as many frugal, temperate, industrious persons, because your flesh must needs be pleased, and you are strangers to christian mortification and self-denial. Laertius tells us that Crates Thebanus put all the money into the banker's or usurer's hands, with this direction, That if his sons proved idiots it should all be paid to them, but if they proved philosophers it should be given to the poor; because philosophers can live upon a little, and therefore [893]need little. So if we could make men mortified christians, they would need so little for themselves, that they would have the more to give to others, and to do good with.

2. Men do not seriously believe God's promises; that he will recompense them in this life (with better things) an hundred-fold, and in the world to come with life eternal!" Matt. xix. 29. And that "by receiving a prophet, or righteous man, they may have a prophet's or righteous man's reward," Matt. x. 41. And that "a cup of cold water (when you have no better) given to one of Christ's little ones in the name of a disciple, shall not be unrewarded," Matt. x. 42. They believe not that heaven will pay for all, and that there is a life to come in which God will see that they be no losers. They think there is nothing certain but what they have in hand, and therefore they lay up a treasure upon earth, and rather trust to their estates than God; whereas if they verily believed that there is another life, and that judgment will pass on them on the terms described, Matt. xxv. they would more industriously lay up a treasure in heaven, Matt. vi. 20, and "make themselves friends of the mammon of unrighteousness," and study how to be rich in good works, and send their wealth to heaven before them, and "lay up a good foundation against the time to come, that they may lay hold upon eternal life," and then they would be "ready to distribute, and willing to communicate," 1 Tim. vi. 17-19; Luke xvi. 9. They would then know how much they are beholden to God, that will not only honour them to be his stewards, but reward them for distributing his maintenance to his children, as if they had given so much of their own;

they would then see that it is they that are the receivers, and that giving is the surest way to be rich, when for transitory things (sincerely given) they may receive the everlasting riches. Then they would see that he that saveth his riches loseth them, and he that loseth them for Christ doth save them, and lay them up in heaven; and that it is more blessed to give than to receive; and that we should ourselves be laborious that we may have wherewith to support the weak, and to give unto the needy. Read Acts xx. 35; Eph. iv. 28; Prov. xxxi. 20, &c. Then they would not be weary of well-doing, if they believed that, "in due season, they shall reap if they faint not; but as they have opportunity, would do good to all men; but especially to them that are of the household of faith," Gal. vi. 9, 10. They would not "forget to do good, and communicate, as knowing that with such sacrifices God is well pleased, Heb. xiii. 16. A true belief of the reward, would make men strive who should do most.

3. Another great hinderance is the want of love to God and our neighbours, to Christ and his disciples. If men loved Christ, they would not deal so niggardly with his disciples, when he has told them that he taketh all that they do to the least of them, (whom he calleth his brethren,) as done to himself, Matt. xxv.; x. 39, 40.

If men loved their neighbours as themselves, I leave you to judge in what proportion and manner they would relieve them! Whether they would find money to lay out on dice and cards, and gluttonous feastings, on plays, and games, and pomp, and pride, while so many round about them are in pinching want.

The destruction of charity or christian love is the cause that works of charity are destroyed. Who can look that the seed of the serpent, that hath an enmity against the holy seed, should liberally relieve them? or that the fleshly mind, which is enmity against God, should be ready to do good to the spiritual and holy servants of God? Gen. xv.; Rom. viii. 6-8; or that a selfish man should much care for any body but himself and his own? When love is turned into the hatred of each other, upon the account of our partial interests and opinions; and when we are like men in war, that think he is the bravest, most deserving man that hath killed most; when men have bitter, hateful thoughts of one another, and set themselves to make each other odious, and to ruin them, that they may stand the faster, and think that destroying them is good service to God; who can look for the fruits of love from damnable uncharitableness and hatred; or that the devil's tree should bring forth holy fruit to God?

4. And then (when love is well spoken of by all, even its deadly enemies) lest men should see their wickedness and misery, (and is it not admirable that they see it not?) the devil hath taught them to play the hypocrite, and make themselves a religion which costs them nothing, without true christian love and good works, that they may have something to quiet and cheat their consciences with. One man drops now and then an inconsiderable gift, and another oppresseth, and hateth, and destroyeth (and slandereth and censureth, that he may not be thought to hate and ruin without cause); and when they have done, they wipe their mouths with a few hypocritical prayers or good words, and think they are good christians, and God will not be avenged on them. One thinks that God will save him because he is of this church, and another because he is of another church. One thinks to be saved because he is of this opinion and party in religion, and another because he is of that. One thinks he is religious because he saith his prayers this way, and another because he prayeth another way. And thus dead hypocrites, whose hearts were never quickened with the powerful love of God, to love his servants, their neighbours, and enemies, do persuade themselves that God will save them for mocking and flattering him with the service of their deceitful lips; while they want the love of God, which is the root of all good, and are possessed with the love of money, which is the root of all evil, 1 Tim. vi. 10, and are "lovers of pleasures more than of God," 2 Tim. iii. 4.

They will join themselves forwardly to the cheap and outside actions of religion; but when they hear much less than "One thing thou yet wantest: sell all that thou hast and distribute to the poor, and thou shalt have a treasure in heaven:—they

263

are very sorrowful, because they are very rich," Luke xviii. 22, 23. Such a fruitless love as they had to others, James ii. such a fruitless religion they have as to themselves. For "pure religion and undefiled before God, is to visit the fatherless and widows in their adversity, and to keep yourselves unspotted from the world," James i. 27. See 1 John ii. 15; iii. 17, "Whoso hath this world's goods, and seeth his brother have need, and shutteth up his bowels of compassion from him, how dwelleth the love of God in him?" There are three texts that describe the case of sensual, uncharitable gentlemen.

1. Luke xvi. "A rich man clothed in purple and silk, (for so, as Dr. Hammond noteth, it should rather be translated,) and fared sumptuously every day," you know the end of him.

2. Ezek. xvi. 49. "Sodom's sin was pride, fulness of bread, and abundance of idleness, neither did she strengthen the hand of the poor and needy."

3. James v. 1-7. "Go to now, ye rich men, weep and howl for the miseries that shall come upon you.—Ye have lived in pleasure on earth, and been [894]wanton; ye have nourished your hearts, as in (or for) the day of slaughter.—Ye have condemned and killed the just, and he doth not resist you—." And remember Prov. xxi. 13, "Whoso stoppeth his ears at the cry of the poor, he also shall cry himself and shall not be heard." And James ii. 13, "He shall have judgment without mercy that showed no mercy, and mercy rejoiceth against judgment." Yea, in this life it is oft observable that, Prov. xi. 24, "There is that scattereth, and yet increaseth, and there is that withholdeth more than is meet, but it tendeth to poverty."

Tit. 2. Directions for Works of Charity.

Direct. I. Love God, and be renewed to his image; and then it will be natural to you to do good; and his love will be in you a fountain of good works.

Direct. II. Love your neighbours, and it will be easy to you to do them all the good you can; as it is to do good to yourselves, or children, or dearest friends.

Direct. III. Learn self-denial, that selfishness may not cause you to be all for yourselves, and be Satan's law of nature in you, forbidding you to do good to others.

Direct. IV. Mortify the flesh, and the vices of sensuality: pride and curiosity, gluttony and drunkenness, are insatiable gulfs, and will devour all, and leave but little for the poor: though there be never so many poor families which want bread and clothing, the proud person must first have the other silk gown, or the other ornaments which may set them out with the forwardest in the mode and fashion; and this house must first be handsomer built, and these rooms must first be neatlier furnished; and these children must first have finer clothes: let Lazarus lie never so miserable at the door, the sensualist must be clothed in purple and silk, and fare deliciously and sumptuously daily, Luke xvi. The glutton must have the dish and cup which pleaseth his appetite, and must keep a full table for the entertainment of his companions that have no need. These insatiable vices are like swine and dogs, that devour all the children's bread. Even vain recreations and gaming shall have more bestowed on them, than church or poor (as to any voluntary gift). Kill your greedy vices once, and then a little will serve your turns, and you may have wherewith to relieve the needy, and do that which will be better to you at your reckoning day.

Direct. V. Let not selfishness make your children the inordinate objects of your charity and provision, to take up that which should be otherwise employed. Carnal and worldly persons would perpetuate their vice, and when they can live no longer themselves, they seem to be half alive in their posterity, and what they can no longer keep themselves, they think is best laid up for their children to feed them as full, and make them as sensual and unhappy as themselves. So that just and moderate provisions will not satisfy them; but their children's portions must be as much as they can get, and almost all their estates are *sibi et suis*, for themselves and theirs: and this pernicious vice is as destructive to good works, as almost any in the world. That God who hath said that he is worse than an infidel who provideth not for his own family, will judge many thousands to be worse than christians, and than any that will be saved must be, who make their families the devourers of all which should be expended upon other works of charity.

Direct. VI. Take it as the chiefest extrinsical part of your religion to do good; and make it the trade or business of your lives, and not as a matter to be done on the by. James i. 27, "Pure religion and undefiled before God and the Father is this, to visit the fatherless and widows in their affliction, and to keep himself unspotted from the world." "If we are created for good works," Eph. ii. 10; "and redeemed and purified to be zealous of good works," Tit. ii. 14; and must be judged according to such works, Matt. xxv.; then certainly it should be our chiefest daily care and diligence, to do them with all our hearts and abilities. And as we keep a daily account of our own and our servants' business in our particular callings, so should we much more of our employment of our Master's talents in his service; and if a heathen prince could say with lamentation, Alas, I have lost a day! if a day had passed in which he had done no one good, how much more should a christian, who is better instructed to know the comforts and rewards of doing good!

Direct. VII. Give not only out of your superfluities, when the flesh is glutted with as much as it desireth; but labour hard in your callings, and be thrifty and saving from all unnecessary expenses, and deny the desires of ease and fulness, and pride and curiosity, that you may have the more to do good with. Thriftiness for works of charity is a great and necessary duty, though covetous thriftiness for the love of riches be a great sin. He that wasteth one half of his master's goods through slothfulness or excesses, and then is charitable with the other half, will make but a bad account of his stewardship. Much more he that glutteth his own and his family's and retainers' fleshly desires first, and then giveth to the poor only the leavings of luxury, and so much as their fleshly lusts can spare. It is a dearer, a laborious and a thrifty charity, that God doth expect of faithful stewards.

Direct. VIII. Delay not any good work which you have present ability and opportunity to perform. Delay signifieth unwillingness or negligence. Love and zeal are active and expeditious; and delay doth frequently frustrate good intentions. The persons may die that you intend to do good to; or you may die, or your ability and opportunities may cease; that may be done to-day which cannot be done to-morrow. The devil is not ignorant of your good intentions, and he will do all that possibly he can to make them of no effect; and the more time you give him, the more you enable him to hinder you. You little foresee what abundance of impediments he may cast before you; and so make that impossible which once you might have done with ease. Prov. iii. 28, "Say not to thy neighbour, Go and come again, and to-morrow I will give, when thou hast it by thee." Prov. xxvii. 1, "Boast not thyself of to-morrow, for thou knowest not what a day may bring forth."

Direct. IX. Distrust not God's providence for thy own provision. An unbelieving man will needs be a God to himself, and trust himself only for his provisions, because indeed he cannot trust God. But you will find that your labour and care are vain, or worse than vain, without God's blessing. Say not distrustfully, What shall I have myself when I am old? Though I am not persuading you to make no provision, or to give away all; yet I must tell you, that it is exceeding folly to put off any present duty, upon distrust of God, or expectation of living to be old. He that over-night said, "I have enough laid up for many years," did quickly hear, "Thou fool, this night shall thy soul be required of thee; and whose then shall the things be which thou hast provided?" Luke xii. 20. Rather obey that, Eccles. ix. 10, "Whatsoever thy hand findeth to do, do it with thy might: for there is no work, nor device, nor [895]knowledge, nor wisdom in the grave whither thou goest." Do you think there is not a hundred thousand whose estates are now consumed in the flames of London, who could wish that all that had been given to pious or charitable uses? Do but believe from the bottom of your hearts, that "he that hath pity on the poor, lendeth to the Lord, and that which he layeth out he will pay him again," Prov. xix. 17. And that, Matt. x. 40-42, "He that receiveth you, receiveth me, and he that receiveth me,

265

receiveth him that sent me: he that receiveth a prophet in the name of a prophet, shall receive a prophet's reward; and he that receiveth a righteous man, in the name of a righteous man, shall receive a righteous man's reward: and whosoever shall give to drink to one of these little ones, a cup of cold water only (i. e. when he hath no better) in the name of a disciple, verily I say unto you, he shall in no wise lose his reward." I say, believe this, and you will make haste to give while you may, lest your opportunity should overslip you.

Direct. X. What you cannot do yourselves, provoke others to do who are more able: "Provoke one another to love and to good works." Modesty doth not so much forbid you to beg for others as for yourselves. Some want but information to draw them to good works: and some that are unwilling, may be urged to it, to avoid the shame of uncharitableness: and though such giving do little good to themselves, it may do good to others. Thus you may have the reward when the cost is another's as long as the charity is yours.

Direct. XI. Hearken to no doctrine which is an enemy to charity or good works; nor yet which teacheth you to trust in them for more than their proper part. He that ascribeth to any of his own works, that which is proper to Christ, doth turn them into heinous sin. And he that ascribeth not to them all that which Christ ascribeth to them, is a sinner also. And whatever ignorant men may prate, the time is coming, when neither Christ without our charity, nor our charity without Christ, (but in subordination to him,) will either comfort or save our souls.

[173] See the Preface to my book, called, "The Crucifying of the World."

CHAPTER XXXI.

CASES AND DIRECTIONS ABOUT CONFESSING SINS AND INJURIES TO OTHERS.

Tit. 1. Cases about Confessing Sins and Injuries to others.

Quest. I. In what cases is it a duty to confess wrongs to those that we have wronged?

Answ. 1. When in real injuries you are unable to make any restitution, and therefore must desire forgiveness, you cannot well do it without confession. 2. When you have wronged a man by a lie, or by false witness, or that he cannot be righted till you confess the truth. 3. When you have wronged a man in his honour or fame, where the natural remedy is to speak the contrary, and confess the wrong. 4. When it is necessary to cure the revengeful inclination of him whom you have wronged, or to keep up his charity, and so to enable him to love you, and forgive you. 5. Therefore all known wrongs to another must be confessed, except when impossibility, or some ill effect which is greater than the good, be like to follow. Because all men are apt to abate their love to those that injure them, and therefore all have need of this remedy. And we must do our part to be forgiven by all whom we have wronged.

Quest. II. What causes will excuse us from confessing wrongs to others?

Answ. 1. When full recompence may be made without it, and no forgiveness of the wrong is necessary from the injured, nor any of the aforesaid causes require it. 2. When the wrong is secret and not known to the injured party, and the confessing of it would but trouble his mind, and do him more harm than good. 3. When the injured party is so implacable and inhumane that he would make use of the confession to the ruin of the penitent, or to bring upon him greater penalty than he deserveth. 4. When it would injure a third person who is interested in the business, or bring them under oppression and undeserved misery. 5. When it tendeth to the dishonour of religion, and to make it scorned because of the fault of the penitent confessor. 6. When it tendeth to set people together by the ears, and breed dissension, or otherwise injure the commonwealth or government. 7. In general, it is no duty to confess our sin to him that we have wronged, when, all things considered, it is like in the judgment of the truly wise, to do more hurt than good: for it is appointed as a means to good, and not to do evil.

Quest. III. If I have had a secret thought or purpose to wrong another, am I bound to confess it, when it was never executed?

Answ. 1. You are not bound to confess it to the party whom you intended to wrong, as any act of justice to make him reparation; nor to procure his forgiveness to yourself: because it was no wrong to him indeed, nor do thoughts and things secret come under his judgment, and therefore need not his pardon. 2. But it is a sin against God, and to him you must confess it. 3. And by accident, *finis gratia*, you must confess it to men, in case it be necessary to be a warning to others, or to the increase of their hatred of sin, or their watchfulness, or to exercise your own humiliation, or prevent a relapse, or to quiet your conscience, or in a word, when it is like to do more good than hurt.

Quest. IV. To whom, and in what cases, must I confess to men my sins against God, and when not?

Answ. The cases about that confession which belongeth to church discipline, belongeth to the second part; and therefore shall here be passed by. But briefly and in general, I may answer the question thus: There are conveniences and inconveniences to be compared together, and you must make your choice accordingly. The reasons which may move you to confess your sins to another are these: 1. When another hath sinned with you, or persuaded or drawn you to it, and must be brought to repentance with you. 2. When your conscience hath in vain tried all other fit means for peace or comfort, and cannot obtain it, and there is any probability of such advice from others as may procure it. 3. When you have need of advice to resolve your conscience, whether it be sin or not, or of what degree, or what you are obliged to in order to forgiveness. 4. When you have need of counsel to prevent the sin for the time to come, and mortify the habit of it.

The inconveniences which may attend it, are such as these: 1. You are not certain of another's secrecy; his mind may change, or his understanding fail, or he may fall out with you, or some great necessity may befall him to drive him to open what you told him. 2. Then whether your shame or loss will not make you repent it, should be foreseen. 3. And how far others may suffer in it. 4. And how far it [896]will reflect dishonour on religion. All things being considered on both sides, the preponderating reasons must prevail.

Tit. 2. Directions about Confessing Sin to others.

Direct. I. Do nothing which you are not willing to confess, or which may trouble you much, if your confession should be opened. Prevention is the easiest way: and foresight of the consequents should make a wise man still take heed.

Direct. II. When you have sinned or wronged any, weigh well the consequents on both sides before you make your confession: that you may neither do that which you may wish undone again, nor causelessly refuse your duty: and that inconveniences foreseen may be the better undergone when they cannot be avoided.

Direct. III. When a well-informed conscience telleth you that confession is your duty, let not self-respects detain you from it, but do it whatever it may cost you. Be true to conscience, and do not wilfully put off your duty. To live in the neglect of a known duty, is to live in a known sin: which will give you cause to question your sincerity, and cause more terrible effects in your souls, than the inconveniences of confession could ever have been.

Direct. IV. Look to your repentance that it be deep and absolute, and free from hypocritical exceptions and reserves. For half and hollow repentance will not carry you through hard and costly duties. But that which is sincere, will break over all: it will make you so angry with yourselves and sins, that you will be as inclined to take shame to yourselves in an honest revenge, as an angry man is to bring shame upon his adversary. We are seldom over-tender of a man's reputation whom we fall out with: and repentance is a falling out with ourselves. We can bear sharp remedies, when we feel the pain, and perceive the mortal danger of the disease: and repentance is such a perception of our pain and danger. We will not tenderly hide a mortal enemy, but bring him to the most open shame: and repentance causeth us to hate sin as our mortal enemy. It is want of repentance that maketh men so unwilling to make a just confession.

Direct. V. Take heed of pride, which maketh men so tender of their reputation, that they will venture their souls to save their honour: men call it bashfulness, and say they cannot confess for shame; but it is pride that maketh them so much ashamed to be known by men to be offenders, while they less fear the eye and judgment of the Almighty. Impudence is a mark of a profligate sinner; but he that pretendeth shame against his duty, is foolishly proud; and should be more ashamed to neglect his duty, and continue impenitent in his sin. A humble person can perform a self-abasing, humbling duty.

Direct. VI. Know the true uses of confession of sin, and use it accordingly. Do it with a hatred of sin, to express yourselves implacable enemies to it: do it to repair the wrong which you have done to others, and the dishonour you have done to the christian religion, and to warn the hearers to take heed of sin and temptation by your fall; it is worth all your shame, if you save one sinner by it from his sin: do it to lay the greater obligation upon yourselves for the future, to avoid the sin and live more carefully; for it is a double shame to sin after such humbling confessions.

CHAPTER XXXII.

CASES AND DIRECTIONS ABOUT SATISFACTION AND RESTITUTION.
Tit. 1. Cases of Conscience about Satisfaction and Restitution.

Quest. I. When is it that proper restitution must be made, and when satisfaction? and what is it?

Answ. Restitution properly is *ejusdem*, of the same thing, which was detained or taken away. Satisfaction is *solutio æquivalentis, vel tantidem*, alias *indebiti*, that which is for compensation or reparation of loss, damage, or injury; being something of equal value or use to the receiver. Primarily *res ipsa debetur*, restitution is first due, where it is possible; but when that is unavoidably hindered or forbidden by some effectual restraint, satisfaction is due. Whilst restitution of the same may be made, we cannot put off the creditor or owner with that which is equivalent without his own consent; but by his consent we may at any time. And to the question, What is due satisfaction? I answer, that when restitution may be made, and he that should restore doth rather desire the owner to accept some other thing in compensation, there that proportion is due satisfaction which both parties agree upon. For if it be above the value it was yet voluntarily given, and the payer might have chosen: and if it be under the value, it was yet voluntarily accepted, and the receiver might have chosen. But if restitution cannot be made, or not without some greater hurt to the payer than the value of the thing, there due satisfaction is that which is of equal value and use to the receiver; and if he will not be satisfied with it, he is unjust, and it is *quoad valorem rei et debitum solventis*, full satisfaction, and he is not (unless by some other accident) bound to give any more; because it is not another's unrighteous will that he is obliged to fulfil, but a debt which is to be discharged. But here you must distinguish betwixt satisfaction in commutative justice, for a debt or injury, and satisfaction in distributive, governing justice, for a fault or crime. The measure of the former satisfaction, is so much as may compensate the owner's loss; not only so much as the thing was worth to another, but what it was worth to him: but the measure of the latter satisfaction, is so much as may serve the ends of government instead of actual obedience; or so much as will suffice to the ends of government, to repair the hurts which the crime hath done, or avoid what it would do.

Why did they restore fourfold?

And here you may see the answer to that question, Why a thief was commanded to restore fourfold, by the law of Moses; for in that restitution there was a conjunction of both these sorts of satisfaction, both in point of commutative and distributive justice: so much as repaired the owner's loss was satisfaction to the owner for the injury: the rest was all satisfaction to God and the commonwealth for the public injury that came by the crime or violation of the law. Other answers are given by some, but this is the plain and certain truth.

Quest. II. How far is restitution or satisfaction necessary?

Answ. As far as acts of obedience to God and justice to man are necessary: that is, 1. As a man that repenteth truly of sin against God, may be saved without external obedience, if you suppose him cut off by death immediately upon his repenting, before [897]he hath any opportunity to obey; so that the *animus obediendi* is absolutely necessary, and the *actus obediendi* if there be opportunity: so is it here, the *animus restituendi*, or true resolution or willingness to restore, is ever necessary to the sincerity of justice and repentance in the person, as well as necessary *necessitate præcepti*; and the act of restitution primarily, and of satisfaction secondarily, is necessary, if; there be time and power: I say necessary always as a duty, *necessitate præcepti*; and necessary *necessitate medii*, as a condition of pardon and salvation, so far as they are necessary acts of true repentance and obedience, as other duties are: that is, as a true penitent may in a temptation omit prayer or church communion, but yet hath always such an habitual inclination to it, as will bring him to it when he hath opportunity by deliberation to come to himself; and as in the same manner a true penitent may omit a work of charity or mercy, but not give over such works; even so is it in this case of restitution and satisfaction.

Quest. III. Who are they that are bound to make restitution or satisfaction?

Answ. 1. Every one that possesseth and retaineth that which is indeed another man's, and hath acquired no just title to it himself, must make restitution. Yet so, that if he came lawfully by it (as by finding, buying, or the like) he is answerable for it only upon the terms in those titles before expressed. But if he came unlawfully by it, he must restore it with all damages. The cases of borrowers and finders are before resolved. He that keepeth a borrowed thing longer than his day, must return it with the damage. He that loseth a thing which he borrowed, must make satisfaction, unless in cases where the contract, or common usage, or the quality of the thing, excuseth him. 2. He that either by force, or fraud, or negligence, or any injustice, doth wrong to another, is bound to make him a just compensation, according to the proportion of the guilt and the loss compared together; for neither of them is to be considered alone. If a servant neglect his master's business, and it fall out that no loss followeth it, he is bound to confess his fault, but not to pay for a loss which might have been, but was not. And if a servant by some such small and ordinary negligence, which the best servants are guilty of, should bring an exceeding great damage upon his master, (as by dropping asleep to burn his house, or by an hour's delay which seemed not very dangerous, to frustrate some great business) he is obliged to reparation as well as to confession; but not to make good all that is lost, but according to the proportion of his fault. But he that by oppression or robbery taketh that which is another's, or bringeth any damage to him, or by slander, false-witness, or any such unrighteous means, is bound to make a fuller satisfaction; and those that concur in the injury, being accessories, are bound to satisfy. As, 1. Those that teach or command another to do it. 2. Those who send a commission, or authorize another to do it. 3. Those who counsel, exhort, or persuade another to do it. 4. Those who by consenting are the causes of it. 5. Those who co-operate and assist in the injury knowingly and voluntarily. 6. Those who hinder it not when they could and were obliged to do it. 7. Those who make the act their own, by owning it, or consenting afterward. 8. Those who will not reveal it afterward, that the injured party may recover his own, when they are obliged to reveal it. But a secret consent which no way furthered the injury, obligeth none to restitution, but only to repentance; because it did no wrong to another, but it was a sin against God.

Quest. IV. To whom must restitution or satisfaction be made?

Answ. 1. To the true owner, if he be living and to be found, and it can be done. 2. If that cannot be, then to his heirs, who are the possessors of that which was his. 3. If that cannot be, then to God himself, that is, to the poor, or unto pious uses; for the possessor is no true owner of it; and therefore where no other owner is found, he must discharge himself so of it, to the use of the highest and principal Owner, as may be most agreeable to his will and interest.[174]

Quest. V. What restitution should he make who hath dishonoured his governors or parents?

Answ. He is bound to do all that he can to repair their honour, by suitable means; and to confess his fault, and crave their pardon.

Quest. VI. How must satisfaction be made for slanders, lies, and defaming of others?

Answ. By confessing the sin, and unsaying what was said, not only as openly as it was spoken, but as far as it is since carried on by others, and as far as the reparation of your neighbour's good name requireth, if you are able.

Quest. VII. What reparation must they make who have tempted others to sin, and hurt their souls?

Answ. 1. They must do all that is in their power to recover them from sin, and to do good to their souls. They must go to them, and confess and lament the sin, and tell them the evil and danger of it, and incessantly strive to bring them to repentance. 2. They must make reparation to the Lord of souls, by doing all the good they can to others, that they may help more than they have hurt.

Quest. VIII. What reparation can or must be made for murder or manslaughter?

Answ. By murder there is a manifold damage inferred: 1. God is deprived of the life of his servant. 2. The person is deprived of his life. 3. The king is deprived of a subject. 4. The commonwealth is deprived of a member. 5. The friends and kindred of the dead are deprived of a friend. 6. And perhaps also damnified in their estates. All these damages cannot be fully repaired by the offender; but all must be done that can be done. 1. Of God he can only beg pardon, upon the account of the satisfactory sacrifice of Christ; expressing true repentance as followeth. 2. To the person murdered no reparation can be made. 3. To the king and commonwealth, he must patiently yield up his life, if they sentence him to death, and without repining, and think it not too dear to become a warning to others, that they sin not as he did. 4. To disconsolate friends no reparation can be made; but pardon must be asked. 5. The damage of heirs, kindred, and creditor, must be repaired by the offender's estate, as far as he is able.

Quest. IX. Is a murderer bound to offer himself to death, before he is apprehended?

Answ. Yes, in some cases: as, 1. When it is necessary to save another who is falsely accused of the crime. 2. Or when the interest of the commonwealth requireth it. But otherwise not; because an offender may lawfully accept of mercy, and nature teacheth him to desire his own preservation: but if the question be, When doth the interest of the commonwealth require it? I think much oftener than it is done: as the common interest requireth that murderers be put to death, when apprehended; so it requireth that they may not frequently and easily be hid, or escape by secrecy or flight; for then it would imbolden others to murder: whereas when few escape, it will [898]more effectually deter men. If therefore any murderer's conscience shall constrain him in true repentance, voluntarily to come forth and confess his sin, and yield up himself to justice, and exhort others to take heed of sinning as he did, I cannot say that he did any more than his duty in so doing; and indeed I think that it is ordinarily a duty, and that ordinarily the interest of the commonwealth requireth it; though in some cases it may be otherwise. The execution of the laws against murder, is so necessary to preserve men's lives, that I do not think that self-preservation alone will allow men to defeat the commonwealth of so necessary a means of preserving the lives of many, to save the life of one, who hath no right to his own life, as having forfeited it. If to shift away other murderers from the hand of justice be a sin, I cannot see but that it is so ordinarily to do it for oneself: only I think that if a true penitent person have just cause to think that he may do the commonwealth more service by his life than by his death, that then he may conceal his crime or fly; but otherwise not.

Quest. X. Is a murderer bound to do execution on himself, if the magistrate upon his confession do not?

Answ. No: because it is the magistrate who is the appointed judge of the public interest, and what is necessary to its reparation, and hath power in certain cases to pardon: and though a murderer may not ordinarily strive to defeat God's laws and the commonwealth, yet he may accept of mercy when it is offered him.

Quest. XI. What satisfaction is to be made by a fornicator or adulterer?

Answ. Chastity cannot be restored, nor corrupted honour repaired. But, 1. If it was a sin by mutual consent, the party that you sinned with must by all importunity be solicited to repentance; and the sin must be confessed, and pardon craved for tempting them to sin. 2. Where it can be done without a greater evil than the benefit will amount to, the fornicators ought to join in marriage, Exod. xxii. 16. 3. Where that cannot be, the man is to put the woman into as good a case for outward livelihood, as she would have been in if she had not been corrupted by him; by allowing her a proportionable dowry, Exod. xxii. 17; and the parents' injury to be recompensed, Deut. xxii. 28, 29. 4. The child's maintenance also is to be provided for by the fornicator. That is, 1. If the man by fraud or solicitation induced the woman to the sin, he is obliged to all as aforesaid. 2. If they sinned by mutual forwardness and consent, then they must jointly bear the burden; yet so that the man must bear the greater part, because he is supposed to be the stronger and wiser to have resisted the temptation. 3. If the woman importuned the man, she must bear the more: but yet he is responsible to parents and others for their damages, and in part to the woman herself, because he was the stronger vessel, and should have been more constant: and *volenti non fit injuria*, is a rule that hath some exceptions.

Quest. XII. In what case is a man excused from restitution and satisfaction?

Answ. 1. He that is utterly disabled cannot restore or satisfy. 2. He that is equally damnified by the person to whom he should restore, is excused in point of real equity and conscience, so be it that the reasons of external order and policy oblige him not. For though it may be his sin (of which he is to repent) that he hath equally injured the other, yet it requireth confession, rather than restitution or satisfaction, unless he may also expect satisfaction from the other. Therefore if you owe a man an hundred pounds, and he owe you as much and will not pay you, you are not bound to pay him, unless for external order sake, and the law of the land. 3. If the debt or injury be forgiven, the person is discharged. 4. If nature or common custom do warrant a man to believe that no restitution or satisfaction is expected, or that the injury is forgiven, though it be not mentioned, it will excuse him from restitution or satisfaction: as if children or friends have taken some trifle, which they may presume the kindness of a parent or friend will pass over, though it be not justifiable.

Quest. XIII. What if the restitution will cost the restorer far more than the thing is worth?

Answ. He is obliged to make satisfaction, instead of restitution.

Quest. XIV. What if the confessing of the fault may engage him that I must restore to, so that he will turn it to my infamy or ruin?

Answ. You may then conceal the person, and send him satisfaction by another hand; or you may also conceal the wrong itself, and cause satisfaction to be made him, as by gift, or other way of payment.

Tit. 2. Directions about Restitution and Satisfaction.

Direct. I. Foresee the trouble of restitution, and prevent it. Take heed of covetousness, which would draw you into such a snare. What a perplexed case are some men in, who have injured others so far as that all they have will scarce make them due satisfaction! Especially public oppressors, who injure whole nations, countries, or communities: and unjust judges, who have done more wrong perhaps in one day or week than all their estates are worth: and unjust lawyers, who plead against a righteous cause: and false witnesses, who contribute to the wrong: and unjust juries, or any such like: also oppressing landlords; and soldiers that take men's goods by violence; and deceitful tradesmen, who live by injuries. In how sad a case are all these men!

Direct. II. Do nothing which is doubtful, if you can avoid it, lest it should put you upon the trouble of restitution. As in case of any doubtful way of usury or other gain, consider, that if it should hereafter appear to you to be unlawful, and so you be obliged to restitution, (though you thought it lawful at the taking of it,) what a snare then would you be in, when all that use must be repaid! And so in other cases.

Direct. III. When really you are bound to restitution or satisfaction, stick not at the cost or suffering, be it never so great, but be sure to deal faithfully with God and conscience. Else you will keep a thorn in your hearts, which will smart and fester till it be out: and the ease of your consciences will bear the charge of your costliest restitution.

Direct. IV. If you be not able in your lifetime to make restitution, leave it in your wills as a debt upon your estates; but never take it for your own.

Direct. V. If you are otherwise unable to satisfy, offer your labour as a servant to him to whom you are indebted; if at least by your service you can make him a compensation.

Direct. VI. If you are that way unable also, beg of your friends to help you, that charity may enable you to pay the debt.

Direct. VII. But if you have no means at all of satisfying, confess the injury and crave forgiveness, and cast yourself on the mercy of him whom you have injured.

[174] Heb. v. 23; 1 Sam xii. 3; Neh. v. 11; Numb. v. 8; Luke xix. 8.
[899]

CHAPTER XXXIII.

CASES AND DIRECTIONS ABOUT OUR OBTAINING PARDON FROM GOD.

Tit. 1. Cases of Conscience about Obtaining Pardon of Sin from God.

Quest. I. Is there pardon to be had for all sin without exception, or not?

Answ. 1. There is no pardon procured or offered, for the final non-performance of the conditions of pardon; that is, for final impenitency, unbelief, and ungodliness. 2. There is no pardon for any sin, without the conditions of pardon, that is, without true faith and repentance, which is our conversion from sin to God. 3. And if there be any sin which certainly excludeth true repentance to the last, it excludeth pardon also; which is commonly taken to be the case of blasphemy against the Holy Ghost; of which I have written at large in my "Treatise against Infidelity."

But, 1. All sin, except the final non-performance of the conditions of pardon, is already conditionally pardoned in the gospel; that is, if the sinner will repent and believe. No sin is excepted from pardon to penitent believers.

2. And all sin is actually pardoned to a true penitent believer.

Quest. II. What if a man do frequently commit the same heinous sin; may he be pardoned?

Answ. Whilst he frequently committeth it (being a mortal sin) he doth not truly repent of it; and whilst he is impenitent he is unpardoned: but if he be truly penitent, his heart being habitually and actually turned from the sin, it will be forgiven him; but not till he thus forsake it.

Quest. III. Is the day of grace and pardon ever past in this life?

Answ. The day of grace and pardon to the penitent is never past in this life;[175]there is no day or hour in which a true penitent person is not pardoned; or in which the impenitent is not conditionally pardoned, that is, if he will truly repent and believe in Christ: and as for the day of true penitence, it is not past to the impenitent; for it never yet came, that is, they never truly repented. But there is a time, with some provoking, forsaken sinners, when God who was wont to call them to repentance by outward preaching and inward motions, will call and move them so no more, but leave them more quietly in the blindness and hardness of their hearts.

Quest. IV. May we be certain of pardon of sin in this life?

Answ. Yes, every man that understandeth the covenant of grace, may be certain of pardon, so far as he is certain of the sincerity of his faith and repentance, and no further; and if a man could not be sure of that, the consolatory promises of pardon would be in a sort in vain; and we could not tell how to believe and repent, if we cannot tell when we truly do it.

Quest. V. Can any man pardon sins against God? and how far?

Answ. Pardon is the remitting of a punishment. So far as man is to punish sinners against God, so far they may pardon, that is, remit that punishment. (Whether they do well in so doing, is another question.) Magistrates are to execute corporal penalties upon subjects for many sins against God, and they may pardon accordingly. The pastors of the church, who are its guides as to public church communion, may remove offenders from the said communion, and they may absolve them when they are penitent, and they may (rightfully or wrongfully) remit the penalty which they may inflict. 2. The pastors of the church may, as God's officers, declare the conditional general pardon, which is contained in the covenant of grace; and that with particular application to the sinner, for the comforting of his mind: q. d. Having examined your repentance, I declare to you as the minister of Christ, that if it be as you express it, without dissembling or mistake, your repentance is sincere, and your sin is pardoned. 3. On the same terms a pastor may as the minister or messenger of Christ, deliver this same conditional pardon contained in the covenant of grace, as sealed by the sacraments of baptism and the Lord's supper; which is an act of investiture: q. d. I do as the minister of Christ, hereby seal and deliver to you in his name, the pardon of all your sins through his blood; supposing your professed faith and repentance be sincere; otherwise it is void and of no such effect. But this is, 1. But a conditional pardon, though with particular application. 2. And it is but a ministerial act of delivery or investiture, and not the act of the donor by himself; nor the gift of the first title: so that it is no whit proper to say, that the minister pardoneth you; but that the minister bringeth and delivereth you the pardon, and sealeth it in his Master's name; or that Christ doth pardon you, and send it you by his minister. As it is utterly improper to say, that the king's messenger pardoneth a traitor, because he bringeth him a pardon from the king. And though (if we agree of this sense) the controversy remaining will be but *de nomine*, yet it is not of small moment, when abused words do tend to abuse the people's understandings: he that saith, I forgive your sins, doth teach the people to take him for a god, whatever he meaneth in himself; and blasphemous words will not be sufficiently excused, by saying that you have not a blaspheming sense. So that a pastor may, 1. Declare Christ's pardon. 2. And seal and deliver it conditionally in Christ's name. But he cannot pardon the internal punishments in this life, nor the eternal punishments of the next. 3. But the punishments of excommunication he may pardon, who must execute them.

Quest. VI. Doth God forgive sin before it be committed (or justify the sinner from it)?

Answ. No, no: for it is a contradiction to forgive that which is not, or to remit a penalty which is not due; but he will indeed justify the person, not by Christ's righteousness, but by his own innocency *in tantum*, so far as he is no sinner. He that hath not committed a sin, needeth no pardon of it, nor any righteousness but his innocency, to justify him against the false accusation of doing that which he never did.

God doth prepare the sacrifice and remedy before upon the foresight of the sin: and he hath made a universal act of pardon beforehand, which shall become an actual pardon to him who penitently accepteth it; and he is purposed in himself to pardon all whom he will pardon; so that he hath the decretive *nolle punire* before. But none of this is proper pardon, or the justification of a sinner, in the gospel sense, as shall be further showed.

Quest. VII. Is an elect person pardoned and justified, before faith and repentance?

Answ. (Laying aside the case of infants, which dependeth on the faith of others) the former answer will serve for this question.

[900]*Quest.* VIII. Is pardon or justification perfect before death?

Answ. 1. *De re.* 1. The pardon which you have this year extendeth not to the sins which you commit the next year, or hour; but there must be a renewed act of pardon for renewed sins; though not a new gospel, or covenant, or act of oblivion to do it; but the same gospel covenant doth morally perform a new act of pardon, according to the Redeemer's mind and will. 2. The pardon which we have now, is but constitutive and *in jure*, and but virtual as to sentential justification; but the sentence of the judge is a more perfective act: or if any think that God doth now sentence us just before the angels in any celestial court, yet that at judgment will be a more full perfective act. 3. The executive pardon which we have now, which is opposite to actual punishing, is not perfect till the day of judgment; because all the punishment is not removed till the last enemy, death, be overcome, and the body be raised from the earth. 2. And now the controversy *de nomine*, whether it be proper to call our present justification or pardon perfect, is easily decided from what is said *de re.*

Quest. IX. Is our pardon perfect as to all the sins that are past?

Answ. 1. As to the number of sins pardoned, it is; for all are pardoned. 2. As to the species of the act, and the plenary effect, it is not. For, 1. All the punishment is not removed. 2. The final absolving sentence is to come. 3. The pardon which we have is, as to its continuance, but conditional; and the tenor of the covenant would cease the pardon even of all sins past, if the sinner's faith and repentance should cease; I speak not *de eventu*, whether ever any do fall away, but of the tenor of the covenant; which may prevent falling away. Now a pardon which hath much yet to be done, as the condition of its continuance, is not so perfect, as it will be when all those things are performed.

Quest. X. May pardon or justification be reversed or lost?

Answ. Whether God will eventually permit his true servants, to fall so far as to be unjustified, is a controversy which I have written of in a fitter place. 2. But *quoad robur peccatoris*, it is, alas, too easy to fall away, and be unjustified. 3. And as to the tenor of the covenant, it continueth the promise and threatening conditionally, and supposing the sinner defectible, doth threaten damnation to them that are now justified, if they should not persevere, but apostatize, Col. i. 33; Rom. xi. 22; John xv. 9.

Quest. XI. Is the pardon of my own sins to be believed *fide divina?* And is it the meaning of that article of the creed, I believe the pardon of my sins?

Answ. 1. I am to believe *fide divina*, that Christ hath purchased and enacted a conditional pardon, which is universal, and therefore extendeth to my sins as well as to other men's; and that he commandeth his ministers to offer me this, and therein to offer me the actual pardon of all my sins, to be mine if I truly repent and believe: and that if I do so, my sins are actually pardoned. And I am obliged accordingly to believe in Christ, and take him for my Saviour, for the pardon of my sins. But this is all the meaning of the creed, and Scripture, and all that is of divine belief. 2. But that I am actually pardoned, is not of divine faith, but only on supposition that I first believe; which Scripture telleth not, whether I do or not. In strict sense, I must first believe in Christ for pardon: and next, in a larger sense, I must believe that I am pardoned; that

274

is, I must so conclude by an act of reason, one of the premises being *de fide*, and the other of internal self-knowledge.

Quest. XII. May a man trust in his own faith or repentance for his pardon and justification, in any kind?

Answ. Words must be used with respect to the understanding of the hearers; and perilous expressions must be avoided lest they deceive men. But *de re*, 1. You must not trust to your faith or repentance, to do that which is proper to God, or to Christ, or to the gospel, or for any more than their own part, which Christ hath assigned them. 2. You must trust to your faith and repentance for that which is truly their own part. And should you not trust them at all, you must needs despair, or trust presumptuously to you know not what: for Christ will not be instead of faith or repentance to you.

Quest. XIII. What are the several causes and conditions of pardon?

Answ. 1. God the Father is the principal efficient, giving us Christ, and pardon with and through him. 2. Christ's person by his sacrifice and merits is the meritorious cause. 3. The gospel covenant or promise is the instrumental cause, or God's pardoning act or grant. 4. Repentance is the condition *sine qua non*, directly *gratia finis*, in respect to God, to whom we must turn. 5. Faith in Christ is the condition *sine qua non*, directly *gratia medii principalis*, in respect to the Mediator, who is thereby received. 6. The Holy Ghost worketh us to these conditions.

Tit. 2. Directions for Obtaining Pardon from God.

Direct. I. Understand well the office of Jesus Christ as our Redeemer, and what it is that he hath done for sinners, and what he undertaketh further to do. For if you know not Christ's office and undertaking, you will either be ignorant of your true remedy, or will deceive yourselves by a presumptuous trust, that he will do that which is contrary to his office and will.

Direct. II. Understand well the tenor of the covenant of grace; for there it is that you must know what Christ will give, and to whom, and on what terms.

Direct. III. Understand well the nature of true faith and repentance; or else you can neither tell how to obtain pardon, nor to judge of it.

Direct. IV. Absolutely give up yourselves to Christ, in all the offices of a Mediator, Priest, Prophet, and King. And think not to be justified by one act or part of christianity, by alone believing in Christ as a sacrifice for sin. To be a true believer and to be a true christian is all one; and is the faith in Christ which is the condition of justification and salvation. Study the baptismal covenant; for the believing in God the Father, Son, and Holy Ghost there meant, is the true faith, which is the condition of our pardon.

Direct. V. Be sure that your repentance contain in it a desire to be perfectly holy and free from all sin, and a resolution against all known and wilful sinning, and particularly that you would not commit the same sins if you had again the same temptations (supposing that we speak not of such infirmities as good men live in; which yet you must heartily desire to forsake).

Direct. VI. Pray earnestly and believingly for pardon through Christ; even for the continuance of your former pardon, and for renewed pardon for renewed sins; for prayer is God's appointed means, and included in faith and repentance, which are the summary conditions.

Direct. VII. Set all right between you and your neighbours, by forgiving others, and being reconciled |901|to them, and confessing your injuries against them, and making them restitution and satisfaction; for this also is included in your repentance, and expressly made the condition of your pardon.

Direct. VIII. Despise not the sacramental delivery of pardon, by the ministers of Christ; for this belongeth to the full investiture and possession of the benefit: nor yet the spiritual consolation of a skilful, faithful pastor, nor public absolution upon public repentance, if you should fall under the need of such a remedy.

Direct. IX. Sin no more. I mean, resolvedly break off all that wilful sin of which you do repent: for repentings, and purposes, and promises of a new and holy life, which are uneffectual, will never prove the pardon of your sins; but show your repentance to be deceitful.

Direct. X. Set yourselves faithfully to the use of all those holy means, which God hath appointed for the overcoming of your sins; and to that life of holiness, righteousness, love, and sobriety, which is contrary to them. Otherwise your repentance is fraudulent and insufficient: these means, and no less than all these, must be used by him, that will make sure of the pardon of his sins from God: and he that thinketh all these too much, must look for pardon some other way, than from the mercy of God, or the grace of Christ; for God's pardon is not to be had upon any other terms, than those of God's appointment. He that will make new conditions of his own, must pardon himself if he can, on those conditions; for God will not be tied to the laws of sinners.

[175] Some speak too ignorantly and dangerously about the day of grace being past in this life.

CHAPTER XXXIV.

CASES AND DIRECTIONS ABOUT SELF-JUDGING.
Tit. 1. Cases of Conscience about Self-judging.

BECAUSE I have said so much of this subject in the third part of my "Saints' Rest," and in a "Treatise of Self-acquaintance," and in my "Directions for Peace of Conscience," and before in this book, I shall be here the briefer in it.

Quest. I. What are the uses and reasons of self-judging, which should move us to it?

Answ. In the three foresaid treatises I have opened them at large. In a word, without it we shall be strangers to ourselves; we can have no well-grounded comfort, no true repentance and humiliation, no just estimation of Christ and grace, no just observance of the motions of God's Spirit, no true application of the promises or threatenings of the Scripture, yea, we shall pervert them all to our own destruction; no true understanding of the providence of God, in prosperity or adversity; no just acquaintance with our duty: a man that knoweth not himself, can know neither God, nor any thing aright, nor do any thing aright; he can neither live reasonably, honestly, safely, nor comfortably, nor suffer or die with solid peace.

Quest. II. What should ignorant persons do, whose natural capacity will not reach to so high a work, as to try and judge themselves in matters so sublime?

Answ. 1. There is no one who hath reason and arts sufficient to love God, and hate sin, and live a holy life, and believe in Christ, but he hath reason and parts sufficient to know (by the use of just means) whether he do these things indeed or not. 2. He that cannot reach assurance, must take up with the lower degrees of comfort, of which I shall speak in the directions.

Quest. III. How far may a weak christian take the judgment of others, whether his pastor, or judicious acquaintance, about his justification and sincerity?

Answ. 1. No man's judgment must be taken as infallible about the sincerity of another; nor must it be so far rested on, as to neglect your fullest search yourself; and for the matter of fact, what you have done, or what is in you, no man can be so well acquainted with it as yourselves. 2. But in judging whether those acts of grace which you describe, be such as God hath promised salvation to, and in directing you in your self-judging, and in conjecturing at your sincerity by your expressions and your lives, a faithful friend or pastor may do that, which may much support you, and relieve you against inordinate doubts and fears, and show you that your sincerity is very probable. Especially if you are assured that you tell him nothing but the truth yourselves; and if he be one that is acquainted with you and your life, and hath known you in temptations, and one that is skilful in the matters of God and conscience, and one that is truly judicious, experienced, and faithful, and is not biassed by interest or affection; and especially when he is not singular in his judgment, but the generality of judicious persons who know you are of the same mind; in this case you may take much comfort in his judgment of your justification, though it cannot give you any proper certainty, nor is to be absolutely rested in.

Tit. 2. Directions for Self-judging as to our Actions.

Direct. I. Let watchfulness over your hearts and lives be your continual work. Never grow careless or neglectful of yourselves: keep your hearts with all diligence. As an unfaithful servant may deceive you, if you look after him but now and then; so may a deceitful heart. Let it be continually under your eye.

Object. Then I must neglect my calling, and do nothing else.

Answ. It need not be any hinderance to you at all. As every man that followeth his trade and labour, doth still take heed that he do all things right, and every traveller taketh heed of falling, and he that eateth taketh heed of poisoning or choking himself, without any hinderance, but to the furtherance of that which he is about; so is it with a christian about his heart: vigilant heedfulness must never be laid by, whatever you are doing.

Direct. II. Live in the light as much as is possible. I mean under a judicious, faithful pastor, and amongst understanding, exemplary christians; for they will be still acquainting you with what you should be and do; and your errors will be easily detected, and in the light you are not so like to be deceived.

Direct. III. Discourage not those that would admonish or reprove you, nor neglect their opinion of you. No, not the railings of an enemy; for they may tell you that in anger (much more in fidelity) which it may concern you much to hear, and think of, and may give you some light in judging of yourselves.

Direct. IV. If you have so happy an opportunity, engage some faithful bosom friend to watch over you, and tell you plainly of all that they see amiss in you. But deal not so hypocritically as to do this in the general, and then be angry when he performeth his trust, and discourage him by your pride and impatience.

[902]*Direct.* V. Put yourselves in another's case, and be impartial. When you cannot easily see the faults of others, inquire then whether your own be not as visible, if you were as ready to observe and aggravate them. And surely none more concern you than your own, nor should be so odious and grievous to you; nor are so, if you are truly penitent.

Direct. VI. Understand your natural temper and inclination, and suspect those sins which you are naturally most inclined to, and there keep up the strictest watch.

Direct. VII. Understand what temptations your place, and calling, and relations, and company do most subject you to; and there be most suspicious of yourselves.

Direct. VIII. Mark yourselves well in the hour of temptation: for then it is that the vices will appear, which before lay covered and unknown.

Direct. IX. Suspect yourselves most heedfully of the most common and most dangerous sins. Especially unbelief and want of love to God, and a secret preferring of earthly hopes before the hopes of the life to come; and selfishness, and pride, and sensual pleasing of the fleshly appetite and fancy: these are the most common, radical, and most mortal, damning sins.

Direct. X. Take certain times to call yourselves to a special strict account. As, 1. At your preparation for the Lord's day at the end of every week. 2. In your preparation for the sacrament of Christ's body and blood. 3. And before a day of humiliation. 4. In a time of sickness or other affliction. 5. Yea, every night review the actions of the foregoing day. He that useth to call his conscience seriously to account, is likest to keep his accounts in order, and to be ready to give them up to Christ.

Direct. XI. Make not light of any sin which you discover in your self-examination. But humble yourselves for it before the Lord, and be affected according to its importance, both in its guilt and evil signification.

277

Direct. XII. And let the end of all be the renewed exercise of faith and thankfulness, and resolutions for better obedience hereafter. That you may see more of the need and use of a Saviour, and may thankfully magnify that grace which doth abound where sin abounded; and may walk the more watchfully and holily for the time to come.

Tit. 3. Directions for Self-judging as to our Estates, to know whether we are in a Regenerate and Justified State, or not.

Direct. I. If you would so judge of the state of your souls, as not to be deceived, come not to the trial with an over-confident prejudice or conceit of your own condition, either as good or bad. He that is already so prepossessed as to resolve what to judge before he trieth, doth make his trial but a means to confirm him in his conceit.

Direct. II. Let not self-love, partiality, or pride, on the one side, or fear on the other side, pervert your judgment in the trial, and hinder you from the discerning of the truth. Some men cannot see the clearest evidences of their unsanctified hearts, because self-love will give them leave to believe nothing of themselves which is bad or sad. They will believe that which is good and pleasant, be it never so evidently false. As if a thief could be saved from the gallows, by a strong conceit that he is a true man; or the conceit that one is learned, would make him learned. Others through timorousness can believe nothing that is good or comfortable of themselves: like a man on the top of a steeple, who though he know that he standeth fast and safe, yet trembleth when he looketh down, and can scarce believe his own understanding. Silence all the objections of an over-timorous mind, and it will doubt and tremble still.

Direct. III. Surprise not yourselves on the sudden and unprepared, with the question, whether you are justified or not; but set about it as the most serious business of your life. A great and difficult question must have a well-studied answer, and not be answered hastily and rashly. If one should meet you in the street, and demand some great and long account of you, you would desire him to stay till you review your memorials, or have time to cast it up. Take some appointed time to do this, when you have no intruding thoughts to hinder you; and think not that it must be resolved easily or quickly upon the first inquiry, but by the most sober and judicious consideration, and patient attendance till it be done.

Direct. IV. Understand the tenor of the covenant of grace, which is the law that you must judge of your estates by: for if you mistake that, you will err in the conclusion. He is an unfit judge, who is ignorant of the law.

Direct. V. Mistake not the nature of true faith in Christ. Those that think it is a believing that they are actually pardoned, and shall be saved, do some of them presume or believe it when it is false, and some of them despair, because they cannot believe it. And those that think that faith is such a recumbency on Christ as always quieteth the mind, do think they have no faith when they have no such quietness. And those that think it is only the resting on the blood of Christ for pardon, do take up with that which is no true faith. But he that knoweth that faith in Christ, is nothing else but christianity, or consenting to the christian covenant, may know that he consenteth, even when he findeth much timorousness and trouble, and taketh not up with a deceitful faith.

Direct. VI. Remember in your self-judging, that the will is the man, and what you truly would be, that you are, in the sense of the covenant of grace.

Direct. VII. But remember also that your endeavours must prove the truth of your desires, and that idle wishes are not the denominating acts of the will.

Direct. VIII. Also your successes must be the proof of the sincerity of your endeavours: for such striving against sin as endeth in yielding to it, and not in victory, is no proof of the uprightness of your hearts.

Direct. IX. Mark what you are in the day of trial; for at other times it is more easy to be deceived: and record what you then discover in yourself: what a man is in trial, that he is indeed.

Direct. X. Especially try yourselves in the great point of forsaking all for Christ, and for the hopes of the fruition of God in glory. Know once whether God or the creature can do more with you, and whether heaven or earth be dearer to you, and most esteemed, and practically preferred, and then you may judge infallibly of your state.

Direct. XI. Remember that in melancholy and weakness of understanding, you are not fit for the casting up of so great accounts; but must take up with the remembrance of former discoveries, and with the judgment of the judicious, and be patient till a fitter season, before you can expect to see in yourselves the clear evidence of your state.

Direct. XII. Neither forget what former discoveries you have made, nor yet wholly rest in them, without renewing your self-examination. They that have found their sincerity, and think that the next time they are in doubt, they should fetch no comfort from what is past, do deprive themselves of much of |903|the means of their peace. And those that trust all to the former discoveries of their good estate, do proceed upon unsafe and negligent principles; and will find that such slothful and venturous courses will not serve turn.

Direct. XIII. Judge not of yourselves by that which is unusual and extraordinary with you, but by the tenor and drift of your hearts and lives. A bad man may seem good in some good mood; and a good man may seem bad in some extraordinary fall. To judge of a bad man by his best hours, and of a good man by his worst, is the way to be deceived in them both.

Direct. XIV. Look not unequally at the good or evil that is in you; but consider them both impartially as they are. If you observe all the good only that is in you, and overlook the bad; or search after nothing but your faults, and overlook your graces; neither of these ways will bring you to true acquaintance with yourselves.

Direct. XV. Look not so much either at what you should be, or at what others are, as to forget what you are yourselves. Some look so much at the glory of that full perfection which they want, as that their present grace seemeth nothing to them; like a candle to one that hath been gazing on the sun. And some look so much at the debauchery of the worst, that they think their lesser wickedness to be holiness.

Direct. XVI. Suffer not your minds to wander in confusion, when you set yourselves to so great a work: but keep it close to the matter in hand, and drive it on till it have come to some satisfaction and conclusion.

Direct. XVII. If you are not able by meditation to do it of yourselves, get the help of some able friend or pastor, and do it in a way of conference with him: for conference will hold your own thoughts to their task; and your pastor may guide them, and tell you in what order to proceed, and confute your mistakes, besides confirming you by his judgment of your case.

Direct. XVIII. If you cannot have such help at hand, write down the signs by which you judge either well or ill of yourself; and send them to some judicious divine for his judgment and counsel thereupon.

Direct. XIX. Expect not that your assurance should be perfect in this life; for till all grace be perfect, that cannot be perfect. Unjust expectations disappointed are the cause of much disquietment.

Direct. XX. Distinguish between the knowledge of your justification, and the comfort of it. Many a one may see and be convinced that he is sincere, and yet have little comfort in it, through a sad or distempered state of mind or body, and unpreparedness for joy; or through some expectations of enthusiastic comforts.

Direct. XXI. Exercise grace whenever you would see it: idle habits are not perceived. Believe and repent till you feel that you do believe and repent, and love God till you feel that you love him.

Direct. XXII. Labour to increase your grace if you would be sure of it. For a little grace is hardly perceived; when strong and great degrees do easily manifest themselves.

Direct. XXIII. Record what sure discoveries you have made of your estate upon the best inquiry, that it may stand you in stead at a time of further need; for though it will not warrant you to search no more, it will be very useful to you in your after-doubtings.

Direct. XXIV. What you can do at one time, follow on again and again till you have finished. A business of that consequence is not to be laid down through weariness or discouragement. Happy is he that in all his life hath got assurance of life everlasting.

Direct. XXV. Let all your discoveries lead you up to further duty. If you find any cause of doubt, let it quicken you to diligence in removing it. If you find sincerity, turn it into joyful thanks to your Regenerator; and stop not in the bare discovery of your present state, as if you had no more to do.

Direct. XXVI. Conclude not worse of the effects of a discovery of your bad condition, than there is cause. Remember that if you should find that you are unjustified, it followeth not that you must continue so: you search not after your disease or misery as uncurable, but as one that hath a sufficient remedy at hand, even brought to your doors, and cometh a begging for your acceptance, and is freely offered and urged on you; and therefore if you find that you are unregenerate, thank God that hath showed you your case; for if you had not seen it, you had perished in it: and presently give up yourselves to God in Jesus Christ, and then you may boldly judge better of yourselves: it is not for despair, but for recovery, that you are called to try and judge. Nay, if you do but find it too hard a question for you, whether you have all this while been sincere or not, turn from it, and resolvedly give up yourselves to God by Christ, and place your hopes in the life to come, and turn from this deceitful world and flesh, and then the case will be plain for the time to come. If you doubt of your former repentance, repent now, and put it out of doubt from this time forward,

Direct. XXVII. When you cannot at the present reach assurance, undervalue not a true probability or hope of your sincerity: and still adhere to universal grace, which is the foundation of your special grace and comfort. I mean, 1. The infinite goodness of God, and his mercifulness to man. 2. The sufficiency of Jesus Christ our Mediator. 3. The universal gift of pardon and salvation, which is conditionally made to all men, in the gospel. Remember that the gospel is glad tidings even to those that are unconverted. Rejoice in this universal mercy which is offered you, and that you are not as the devils, shut up in despair; and much more rejoice if you have any probability that you are truly penitent and justified by faith: let this support you till you can see more.

Direct. XXVIII. Spend much more time in doing your duty, than in trying your estate. Be not so much in asking, How shall I know that I shall be saved? as in asking, What shall I do to be saved? Study the duty of this day of your visitation, and set yourselves to it with all your might. Seek first the things that are above, and mortify your fleshly lusts; give up yourselves to a holy, heavenly life, and do all the good that you are able in the world: seek after God as revealed in and by our Redeemer: and in thus doing, 1. Grace will become more notable and discernible. 2. Conscience will be less accusing and condemning, and will easilier believe the reconciledness of God. 3. You may be sure that such labour shall never be lost; and in well-doing you may trust your souls with God. 4. Thus those that are not able in an argumentative way to try their state to any full satisfaction, may get that comfort by feeling and experience, which others get by ratiocination. For the very exercise of love to God and man, and of a heavenly mind and holy life, hath a sensible pleasure in itself, and delighteth the person who is so employed: as if a man were to take the comfort of his learning or wisdom, one way is by the discerning his learning and wisdom, and thence inferring his own felicity; but another way is by exercising that learning and wisdom which he [904]hath, in reading and meditating on some excellent books, and making discoveries of some mysterious excellencies in arts and sciences, which delight him more by the very acting, than a bare conclusion of his own learning in the general would do. What delight had the inventors of the sea-chart and magnetic attraction, and of printing, and of guns, in their inventions! What pleasure had Galileo in his telescopes, in finding out the inequalities and shady parts of the moon, the Medicean planets, the adjuncts of Saturn, the changes of Venus, the stars of the *via lactea*, &c.! Even so a serious, holy person, hath more sensible pleasures in the right exercise of faith, and love, and holiness, in prayer, and meditation, and converse with God, and with the heavenly hosts, than the bare discerning of sincerity can afford. Therefore though it be a great, important duty to examine ourselves, and judge ourselves before God judge us, and keep close aquaintance with our own hearts and affairs, yet is it the addition of the daily practice of a heavenly life, which must be our chiefest business and delight. And he that is faithful in them both, shall know by experience the excellences of christianity and holiness, and in his way on earth, have both a prospect of heaven, and a foretaste of the everlasting rest and pleasures.

[905]

A

MORAL PROGNOSTICATION.
FIRST,

WHAT SHALL BEFALL THE CHURCHES ON EARTH, TILL THEIR CONCORD,
BY THE RESTITUTION OF THEIR PRIMITIVE PURITY, SIMPLICITY, AND CHARITY:

SECONDLY,

HOW THAT RESTITUTION IS LIKELY TO BE MADE, (IF EVER,) AND WHAT SHALL BEFALL
THEM THENCEFORTH UNTO THE END, IN THAT GOLDEN AGE OF LOVE.

WRITTEN BY

RICHARD BAXTER;

WHEN BY THE KING'S COMMISSION, WE (IN VAIN) TREATED FOR CONCORD, 1661.

AND NOW PUBLISHED, NOT TO INSTRUCT THE PROUD THAT SCORN TO LEARN; NOR TO MAKE THEM WISE,
WHO WILL NOT BE MADE WISE: BUT TO INSTRUCT THE SONS OF LOVE AND PEACE, IN THEIR DUTIES AND EXPECTATIONS.

TO TELL POSTERITY, THAT

THE THINGS WHICH BEFALL THEM WERE FORETOLD;

AND THAT THE EVIL MIGHT HAVE BEEN PREVENTED, AND BLESSED PEACE ON EARTH ATTAINED,
IF MEN HAD BEEN BUT WILLING; AND HAD NOT SHUT THEIR EYES AND HARDENED THEIR HEARTS
AGAINST THE BEAMS OF LIGHT AND LOVE.

281

TO THE READER.

READER,

IT is many years since this Prognostication was written (1661, except the thirteen last lines); but it was cast by, lest it should offend the guilty. But the author now thinketh, that the monitory usefulness may overweigh the inconveniences of men's displeasure; at least, to posterity, if not for the present age; of which he is taking his farewell. His suppositions are such as cannot be denied: viz.

1. Eccles. i. 9, "The thing that hath been, is that which shall be; and that which is done is that which shall be done: and there is no new thing under the sun."

2. The same causes, with the same circumstances, will have the same effects on recipients, equally disposed.

3. *Operari sequitur esse:* as natures are, so they act; except where overpowered.

4. The appetite, sensitive and rational, is the principle of motion; and what any love they will desire and seek.

5. Therefore, interest will turn the affairs of the world; and he that can best understand all interests, will be the best moral prognosticator; so far men are causes of the events.

6. The pleasing of God, and the happiness of their own and others' souls, being the interest of true believers; and temporal life, pleasure, and prosperity, being the seeming and esteemed interest of unbelievers' cross interests, will carry them contrary ways.

7. Contraries, when near and militant, will be troublesome to each other, and seek each other's destruction or debilitation.

[906]8. The senses and experience of all men, in all ages, are to be believed about their proper objects.

9. Men of activity, power, and great numbers, will have advantage for observance and success, above those that are modest, obscure, and few.

10. Yet men will still be men; and the rational nature will yield some friendly aspect towards the truth.

11. Those that are ignorant, and misled by passion, and carried down the stream, by men of malignity or faction, may come to themselves, when affliction, experience, and considerateness have had time to work; and may repent, and undo somewhat that they have done.

12. As sense will be sense, when faith hath done its best; so faith will be faith, when flesh or sense hath done its worst.

13. Men that fix on a heavenly, everlasting interest, will not be temporizers, and changed by the worldly men's wills or cruelties.

14. When all men have tired themselves with their contrivances and stirs, moderation and peace must be the quiet state.

15. When all worldly wisdom hath done its utmost, and men's endeavours are winged with the greatest expectations, God will be God, and blast what he nilleth; and will overrule all things, to the accomplishment of his most blessed will. Amen.

On these suppositions it is, that the following Prognostications are founded; which I must admonish the reader, not to mistake for historical narratives: but I exhort him to know *what hath been*, and *what is*, if he would know *what will be*; and to make sure of everlasting rest with Christ, when he must leave a sinful, restless world.

A

MORAL PROGNOSTICATION

OF WHAT MUST BE EXPECTED

IN THE CHURCHES OF CHRISTENDOM,

TILL THE
GOLDEN AGE RETURNS, OR TILL THE TIME OF TRUE REFORMATION AND UNITY.

1. MANKIND will be born in a state of infancy and nescience, that is, without actual knowledge.

2. Yea, with a nature that hath the innate dispositions to sloth, and to diverting pleasures and business; and more than so, to an averseness from those principles which are needful to sanctification and heavenly wisdom. The carnal mind will have an enmity against God, and will not mind the things of the Spirit, nor be subject to God's law, Rom. viii. 5-8.

3. Sound learning, or wisdom, in things of so high a nature as are the matters of salvation, will not be attained without hard study, earnest prayer, and humble submission to instructions; and all this a long time patiently endured, or rather willingly and delightfully performed.

4. And if the seeds of wisdom be not born with us, in a capacious disposition of understanding; but contrarily a natural unapprehensiveness blocks up the way; even time and labour will never (without a miracle) bring any to any great eminency of understanding.

5. And they that have both capacity, and an industrious disposition, must have also sound, and able, and diligent teachers; or at least escape the hands of seducers, and of partial, factious guides.

6. There are few born with good natural capacities, much less with a special dispositive acuteness; and few that will be at the pains and patience, which the getting of wisdom doth require; and few that will have the happiness of sound and diligent teachers; but fewest of all that will have a concurrence of all these three.

7. Therefore there will be but few very wise men in the world; ignorance will be common, wisdom will be rare.

8. Therefore error or false opinions will be common. For unless men never think of the things of which they are ignorant, or judge nothing of them one way or other, they are sure to err, so far as they judge in ignorance. But when things of greatest moment are represented as true or false, to be believed or rejected, the most ignorant mind is naturally inclined to pass its judgment or opinion of them one way or other; and to apprehend them according to the light he standeth in, and to think of them as he is disposed. So that ignorance and error will concur.

9. He that erreth, doth think that he is in the right, and erreth not: for to err, and to know that he erreth in judgment, is a contradiction, and impossible. (However in words and deeds a man may err, and know that he erreth.)

10. He that knoweth not, and that erreth, perceiveth not that evidence of truth which should make him receive it, and which maketh other men receive it; and therefore knoweth not that indeed another is in the right, or seeth any more than he.

11. Especially when every man is a stranger to another's mind and soul, as to any immediate inspection; and therefore knoweth not another's knowledge, nor the convincing reasons of his judgment.

12. As no man is moved against his own errors, by the reasons which he knoweth not; so pride, self-love, and partiality thence arising, incline all men naturally to be overvaluers of their own understandings, and so over-confident of all their own conceptions, and over-stiff in defending all their errors. [907]As pride and selfishness are the firstborn of Satan, and the root of all positive evil in man's soul; so a man is more naturally proud of that which is the honour of a man, which is his understanding and goodness, than of that which is common to a beast, as strength, beauty, ornaments, &c. Therefore pride of understanding and goodness oft live, when sordid apparel telleth you that childish pride of ornaments is dead. And this pride maketh it very difficult, to the most ignorant and erroneous, to know their ignorance and error, or so much as to suspect their own understandings.

13. He that seeth but few things, seeth not much to make him doubt, and seeth not the difficulties which should check his confidence and stiffness in his way.

14. He that seeth many things, and that clearly knoweth much; especially, if he see them in their order, and respects to one another, and leaveth out no one substantial part which is needful to open the signification of the rest.

15. He that seeth many things disorderly and confusedly, and not in due method, and leaveth out some substantial parts, and hath not a digested knowledge, doth know much, and err much, and may make a bustle in the world of ignorants, as if he were an excellent, learned man; but hath little of the inward delight, or of the power and benefits of knowledge.

16. He that seeth many things but darkly, confusedly, and not in the true place and method, cannot reconcile truths among themselves; but is like a boy with a pair of tarrying irons, or like one that hath his clock or watch all in pieces, and knoweth not how to set them together. And therefore is inclined to be a sceptic.

17. This sort of sceptics differ much from humble christians; and have oft as high thoughts of their understandings as any others: for they lay the cause upon the difficulties in the objects, rather than on themselves: unless when they incline to brutishness or Sadducism, and take man's understanding to be incapable of true knowledge, and so lay the blame on human nature as such, that is, on the Creator.

18. Few hope so much as to see the difficulty of things, and make them doubt, or sceptical. But far fewer know, so much as to resolve their doubts and difficulties: therefore, though (as Bishop Jewel saith of faithful pastors) I say not that there will be few cardinals, few bishops, few doctors, few deans, few Jesuits, few friars, (there will be enow of these,) yet there will be few wise, judicious divines and pastors, even in the best and happiest countries.

19. Seeing he that knoweth not, or that erreth, knoweth not that another knoweth, or is in the right, when he is in the wrong; therefore he knoweth not whose judgment to honour and submit to, if he should suspect or be driven from his own: and therefore is not so happy, as to be able to choose the fittest teacher for himself.

20. In this darkness therefore he either carnally casteth himself on the highest and most honoured in the world, where he hath the most advantages for worldly ends; or he followeth the fame of the time and country where he is, or he falleth in with the major vote of that party, whatsoever it be, which his understanding doth most esteem and honour; or else with some person that hath most advantage on him.

21. If any of these happen to be in the right, he will be also in the right materially, and may seem an orthodox, peaceable, and praiseworthy man; but where they are in the wrong, he is contented with the *reputation* of being in the right, and of the good opinion of those whom he concurreth with; who flatter and applaud each other in the dark.

22. When wise men are but few, they can be but in few places; and therefore will be absent from most of the people, high or low, that need instruction. Besides, that their studiousness inclineth them, like Jerome, to be more retired than others, that know less.

23. This confidence in an erring mind, is not only the case of the teachers, as well as of the flocks; but is usually more fortified in them than in others: for they think that the honour of learning and wisdom is due to their place, and calling, and name, and standing in the universities; how empty soever they be themselves. And they take it for a double dishonour (as it is) for a teacher to be accounted ignorant; and an injury to their work and office, and to the people's souls, that must by their honour be prepared to profit by them; and therefore they smart more impatiently under any detection of their ignorance, than the common people do.

24. It is not mere honesty and godliness, that will suffice to save ministers or people from this ignorance, injudiciousness, and error; there having ever been among the very godly ministers, a few judicious men, that are fit to investigate a difficult truth,

or to defend it against a subtle adversary, or to see the system of theological verities in their proper method, harmony, and beauty.

25. Morality hath innumerable difficulties, as well as school divinity; because that moral good and evil are ordinarily such by preponderating accidents (actions as actions, being neither; but only of physical consideration). And the work of a true casuist is to compare so many accidents, and to discern in the comparison which preponderateth, that it requireth both an acute and a large, capacious, farseeing wit, to make a man a true resolver of cases of conscience. And consequently to be a judicious pastor, that shall not lead the people into errors.

26. As few teachers have natural capacity for exactness, and a willingness and patience for long, laborious studies; so many by their pastoral oversight of souls, and many by the wants of their families, (especially in times of persecution, when all their public maintenance is gone, and they must live, with their families, on the charity of people, perhaps poor and persecuted as well as they,) are hindered from those studies, which else they would undergo.

27. It is few that grow to much exactness of judgment without much *writing* (for themselves or others); for study which is to be exactly ordered and expressed by the pen, is usually (at last) the exactest study: as the Lord Bacon saith, "Much reading maketh a man full; much conference maketh a man ready; and much writing maketh a man exact." There are few Cameros, men of clear judgment, and abhorring to write. And there are few divines comparatively that have opportunity to write much.

28. They that err in divinity, do think *their falsehoods* to be *God's truth*; and so will honour that which he hates, with the pretence of his authority and name.

29. Therefore they will call up their own and other men's zeal, to defend those falsehoods as for God, and think that in so doing they do God service.

30. And the interest of their own place, and honour, and ends, will secretly insinuate when they discern it not, and will increase their zeal against opposers.

31. Therefore, seeing they are usually many, and wise men but few, they will expect that number should give the precedency to their opinions, and will call those proud, or heretical, that gainsay them, and labour to defame them, as self-conceited, opinionative men.

[908]32. Therefore too many godly ministers will be great opposers of many of those truths of God, which they know not, and which they err about, and will help on the service of Satan in the world; and will be the authors of factions and contentions in the churches; whilst too many are "proud, knowing nothing," (in those matters when they think they are most orthodox,) "but doting about questions and strifes of words, whereof cometh envy, strife, railing, evil surmisings, perverse disputings of men of corrupt minds, (in this,) and destitute of the truth," 1 Tim. vi. 4, 5.

33. And if many good men will erroneously stand up against that truth which any man wiser than themselves maketh known, the worldly and malicious, that have a manifold enmity against it, will be ready to strengthen them by their concurrence, and to join in the opposition.

34. Not they that are wisest at a distance, but they that are nearest the people, and are always with them, are most likely to prevail to make disciples of them, and bring them to their mind: so great an advantage it is, to talk daily and confidently to ignorant souls, when there is none to talk against them, and to make their folly known.

35. Especially if the same men can get interest in their esteem as well as nearness, and make themselves esteemed the best or wisest men.

36. Therefore Jesuitical, worldly clergymen, will always get about great men, and insinuate into nobles, and will still defame them that are wise and good, that they may seem odious, and themselves seem excellent, and so may carry it by deceitful shows.

37. And they will do their best, to procure all wise and good men, that are against their interest, to be banished from the palaces of princes and nobles, where they are; lest their presence should confute their slanderers, and they should be as

"burning and shining lights," that carry their witness with them where they come: and also to bring them under public stigmatizing censures and sufferings; that their names may be infamous and odious in the world.

38. And heretical pastors will play a lower game, and creep into the houses of silly people, prepared by ignorance and soul-disturbers to receive their heresies.

39. Between these two sorts of naughty pastors, (the WORLDLY and the HERETICAL,) and also the multitude of weak, erroneous, honest teachers, the soundest and worthiest will be so few, that far most of the people (high and low) are like to live under the influences and advantages of erring men; and, therefore, themselves to be an erring people.

40. In that measure that men are carnal, their own carnal interest will rule them. And both the WORLDLY and HERETICAL clergy, are ruled by carnal interests, though not the same materially. And the more honest, erring ministers, are swayed by their interests too much; insomuch, that on this account, it was no overvaluing of Timothy, or wrong to the other pastors, that it should plainly be said by Paul, "For I have no man like-minded, who will naturally care for your state. For all seek their own, not the things which are Jesus Christ's," Phil. ii. 20, 21. "Of your ownselves shall men arise, and speak perverse things, to draw away disciples after them," Acts xx. 30. Besides the grievous wolves which would not spare the flocks.

41. The interest then of the WORLDLY clergy, will consist in pleasing the great ones of the world; for lordships, and worldly wealth, and honour, and to be made the rulers of their brethren, and to have their wills: and the interest of heretics will be to have many to be of their own opinion to admire them: and the interest of upright ministers will be to please God, and propagate the gospel, increase the church, and save men's souls; yet so that they have a subordinate interest, for food and raiment, and families, and necessary reputation, which they are too apt to overvalue.

42. Therefore, it will be the great trade of the WORLDLY clergy, to please and flatter the rulers of the world, and by all artificial insinuations, and by their friends, to work themselves into their favour, and by scorns and calumnies to work out all other that are against their interest.

43. And it will be the trade of heretics, to insinuate into the more ductile people, especially as ministers of truth and righteousness, that have somewhat more excellent in knowledge or holiness, than the faithful ministers of Christ.

44. And it will be the work of faithful ministers, to save men's souls. But with such various degrees of self-denial or selfishness, as they have various degrees of wisdom and holiness.

45. Many great and piously disposed princes, like Constantine, will think that to honour and advance the clergy, into worldly power and wealth, is to honour God and the christian religion; and great munificence is fit for their own greatness.

46. And because such honour and wealth cannot possibly be bestowed on all, it must make a great disparity, and set some as lords over the rest.

47. And the unavoidable weakness, passions, and divisions of the clergy, will make rulers think, that there is a necessity; that besides the civil government, there should, be some of their own office, to rule the rest, and to keep them in order, obedience, and peace.

48. Ambition and covetousness will abuse this munificence of princes: and whilst that any church preferments are so great (beyond the degree of a mere encouraging subsistence) as to be a strong bait to tempt the desires of a proud and worldly mind, the most proud and worldly that are within the reach of hope, will be the seekers, by themselves, and by their friends.

49. Mortified, humble, heavenly men, will either never seek them, or with no great eagerness; their appetite being less, and their restraints much greater.

50. Therefore they that have the keenest appetites to church grandeur and preferments, and are the eager seekers, are most likely to find.

51. Therefore the lovers of wealth and honour, are more likely still to be the lords among the clergy; except in such marvellous happy times, when wise and pious princes call the more worthy that seek it not, and reject these thirsty seekers.

52. The greatest lovers of worldly wealth and honour, are the worst men, 1 John ii. 15; James iv. 4, &c.

53. Therefore, except in such times as aforesaid, the worst men will be still the rich and powerful in the clergy, for the most part, or at least, the worldly that are very bad.

54. These carnal minds are enmity to God, and cannot be subject to his law. And the friendship of the world is enmity to God. And the honour and wealth of these worldly men, will be taken by them for their interest; and they will set themselves to defend it, against all that would endanger it.

55. The doctrine and practice of humility, mortification, contempt of the world, forsaking all, taking up the cross, &c. is so much of the christian religion, that however the worldly clergy may formally preach it, their minds and interests are at enmity to it.

[909]56. Such men will make church canons according to their interests and minds.

57. And they will judge of ministers and people according to their interest and mind; who is sound, and who is erroneous; who is honest, and who is bad; who is worthy of favour, and who is worthy of all the reproaches that can be devised against him.

58. The humble, mortified ministers and people, that are seriously the servants of a crucified Christ, and place their hopes and portion in another world, have a holy disposition, contrary to this worldly, carnal mind; and their manner of preaching will be of a different relish, and the tenor of their lives of a contrary course.

59. The generality of the best people in the christian churches will perceive the difference between the worldly and the heavenly manner of preaching and of living, and will love and honour the latter far above the former; because their new nature suiteth with things spiritual, and fitteth them to relish them.

60. The worst of vicious and worldly men will disrelish the spiritual manner of preaching and living, and will join with the worldly clergy against it.

61. The worldly clergy being hypocrites, as to christianity and godliness, (like Judas that loved the bag better than Christ,) they will make themselves a religion, consisting of the mere corpse and dead image of the true religion; of set words, and actions, and formalities, and orders, which in themselves are (many, at least, if not all) good; but the life they will not endure.

62. This image of true religion, or corpse of godliness, they will dress up with many additional flowers out of their own gardens, some tolerable, and some corrupting: that so they may have something which both their own consciences and the world may take to be honourable religion; lest known ungodliness should terrify conscience within, and shame them in the world without.

63. This image of religion, so dressed up, will suit their carnal auditors and people too, to the same ends; and therefore will become their uniting interest.

64. That which is but a weed among these flowers, the more heavenly ministers and people will dislike, and much more dislike the loathsome face of death (or lifelessness) in their religion.

65. These differences of mind and practice, will engage both parties in some kind of opposition to each other. The worldly clergy, or hypocrites, will have heart-risings against the ministers and people that think meanly of them, and will take it for their interest to bring them down: for enmity is hardly restrained from exercise. And Cain will be wroth that Abel's sacrifice is better accepted than his own.

66. The better ministers will be apt, through passion, to speak too dishonourably of the other; and the rash and younger sort, and the heretical hypocrites that fall in with them, will take it for part of a godly zeal to speak against them to the people, in such words as Christ used of the scribes and Pharisees.

67. Hereupon the exasperations of each party will be increased more and more; and the powerful, worldly clergy will think it their interest to devise some new impositions, which they know the other cannot yield to, to work them out.

68. Whether they be *oaths, subscriptions, words,* or *actions,* which they believe to be against God's word, the spiritual and upright part of the clergy and people will not perform them; resolving to obey God rather than man.

69. Hereupon the worldly part will take the advantage, and call them disobedient, stubborn, proud, schismatical, self-opinionated, disturbers of the public peace and order, "pestilent fellows, and movers of sedition among the people," that will let nothing be quiet, but "turn the world upside down," Acts xxiv. 5, 6; and will endeavour to bring them to such sufferings, as men really guilty of such crimes deserve.

70. And because the suffering and dissenting party of ministers, when silenced, will leave many vacancies in the churches, they will be fain to fill them with men, how empty and unworthy soever, that are of their own spirit, and will be true to their interests.

71. The exasperation of their sufferings will make many, otherwise sober ministers, too impatient, and to give their tongues leave to take down the honour of the clergy whom they suffer by, more than beseemeth men of humility, charity, and patience.

72. When the people, that most esteem their faithful ministers, are deprived of their labours, by the prohibitions of the rest, and themselves also afflicted with them; it will stir up in them an inordinate, unwarrantable, passionate zeal; which will corrupt their very prayers, and make them speak unseemly things, and pray for the downfal of that clergy, which they take to be the enemies of God, and godliness. And they will think that to speak easily or charitably of such men, as dare forbid Christ's ministers to preach his gospel, and by notorious sacrilege alienate the persons and gifts that were consecrated solemnly to God, is but to be lukewarm, and indifferent between God and the devil.

73. And when they take them as enemies to religion, and to themselves, the younger and rasher sort of ministers, but much more the people, will grow into a suspicion of all that they see their afflicters stand for: they will dislike not only their faults, but many harmless things, yea, many laudable customs, which they use; and will grow into some superstition in opposition to them, making new sins in the manner of worship, which God never forbad or made to be sins; and taking up new duties, which God never made duties; yea, ready to forsake some old and wholesome doctrines, because their afflicters own them; and to take up some new, unsound doctrines, and expositions of God's word, because they are inclined by opinion and passion conjoined, to go as far as may be from such men, whom they think so bad of.

74. And the vulgar people that have but little sense of religion, (that are not by the aforesaid interest united to the afflicting clergy,) having a reverence to the worth of those that are afflicted, and an experience of the rawness and differing lives of many that possess their rooms, will grow to compassionate the afflicted, and to think that they are injured themselves, and so to think hardly of the causers of all this.

75. Hereupon the powerful clergy will increase their accusations against the party that is against them, and declare to the world in print and from the pulpits, their ignorance, unpeaceableness, unruliness, giddiness, false opinions and conceits about the manner of worship, and how unsufferable a sort of men they are.

76. By this time the devil will have done the radical part of his work; which is to destroy much of christian love to one another, and make them take each other for unlovely, odious persons: the one part, for persecuting enemies of godliness, and hypocrites, and Pharisees; the other for peevish, seditious, turbulent, unruly sectaries. And on these suppositions, all their after characters, affections, and practices towards each other will proceed.

288

[910]77. By this enmity and opposition against each other, both parties will increase in wrath, and somewhat in numbers. The worldly, afflicting clergy will multiply not only such as are disaffected to them, but downright fanatics, and sectaries that will run as far from them as they can, into contrary extremes. For when they are once brought into a distaste of the old hive, the bees will hardly gather into one new one; but will divide into several swarms and hives. As every man's zeal is more against the afflicting party, so he will go further from them; some to be separatists, some anabaptists, some antinomians, some seekers, some quakers, and some to they know not what themselves.

78. For the women, and apprentices, and novices in christianity, that have more passion than judgment, will abundance of them quite overrun, even their own afflicted teachers, and will forsake them, if they will not overrun their own judgments, in forsaking those that do afflict them.

79. And many hypocrites that have no sound religion; but ignorance, pride, and uncharitableness, will thrust in among them, in these discontents; or spring up in the nurseries of these briers of passion, and will bring in new doctrines, and new ways of worship, and make themselves preachers, and the heads of sects; by reason of whom, the way of truth shall be evil spoken of.

80. And many unstable persons seeing this, will dread and loathe so giddy a sort of men, and will turn papists, upon the persuasions of them that tell them that there is no true unity nor consistency but at Rome; and that all must thus turn giddy at last, that are not fixed in the papal head. And thus they that fly too far from the Common Prayer Book, will drive men to the mass; and the afflicters will make sectaries, and the sectaries will make papists.

81. When the violent clergy, instead of a fatherly government of the flocks, have driven the people into passions, distempers, and uncharitable disaffections to themselves, and have also been the great cause of multiplied heresies and sects by the same means, instead of being humbled and penitent for their sin, they will be hardened, and justify all their violences, by the giddiness and miscarriages of those sectaries, which they themselves have made.

82. And when they publish the faults of such, for the justification of their own violence, they will draw thousands into an approbation of their courses, (to think that such a turbulent people can never be too hardly called or used,) and consequently into a participation of their guilt.

83. By all this, the dissenters will be still more alienated from them; and many will aggravate the crime of the ministers that conform to their impositions, and obey them: and for the sake of a few that afflict them, they will condemn many laudable conforming ministers, that never consented to it, but could heartily wish that it were otherwise.

84. And the younger, and more indiscreet, passionate sort, will frequently reproach such, as unconscionable temporizers, that will do any thing for worldly ends, and that as hypocrites for a fleshly interest, concur with the corrupters and afflicters of the godly.

85. These censures and reproaches will provoke those conforming ministers, who are not masters of their passions, nor conquerors of their pride, to think as badly of the censurers as their afflicters do, and to join with them in the displaying of all enormities, and promoting their further sufferings, and publishing the folly and turbulency of their spirits, with spleen and partiality.

86. By these kind of speeches, preachings, and writings, multitudes of the debauched will be hardened in their sin against all religion: for when they observe that it is the same party of men, who are thus reproached, that are the strictest reprovers of their lewdness, their fornications, tippling, gaming, luxuries, and ungodliness; they will think it is no great matter what such a defamed, giddy sort of people say, and that really they are worse themselves.

87. Each party of these adversaries will characterize the adverse party as hypocrites: the passionate sufferers will call the afflicters hypocrites and Pharisees, that have no religion, but a formal show of outside ceremonies and words, and that tithe mint and cummin, and wash the outside, while within they are full of persecuting cruelty, and are wolves in sheep's clothing, loving the uppermost seats, and great titles, and ceremonious phylacteries, whilst they are enemies to the preaching of the gospel of Christ, and get revenues to themselves, and devour not only the houses, but the peace and lives of others, under pretence of long liturgies; and that devour the living saints, while they keep holy days and build monuments for the dead ones, whom their fathers murdered, &c. And the powerful clergy will call the others hypocrites, and labour to show that the Pharisees' character belongeth to them, and that their pretences of strictness in religion, and their long praying and preaching, is but a cloak to cover their disobedience, and covetousness, and secret sins; and that their hearts and inside are as bad as others, and that their fervency in devotion is but a hypocritical, affected whining and canting; and that they are worse than the lesser religious sort of people, because they are more unpeaceable, and disobedient, and add hypocrisy to their sin.

88. The ignorant, worldlings, drunkards, and ungodly despisers of holiness and heaven, being in all countries most contradicted in their way, by this stricter sort of men, and hearing them in pulpit and press so branded for hypocrites, will joyfully unite themselves with the censurers; and so they will make up as one party, in crying down the precise hypocrites; and usually make some name to call them by, as their brand of common ignominy: and they will live the more quietly in all their sins, and think they shall be saved as soon as the precisest, that make more show, but have no more sincerity, but more hypocrisy, than themselves.

89. The suffering party, seeing the ungodly and the conforming afflicters of them thus united, and made one party in opposition to them, will increase their hard thoughts of the adverse clergy, and take them for downright profane, and the leading enemies of godliness in the world, that will be captains in the devil's army, and lead on all the most ungodly against serious godliness, for their worldly ends.

90. And the young and indifferent sort of people, in all countries, that were engaged in neither part, being but strangers to religion, and to the differences, will be ready to judge of the cause by the persons: and seeing so many of the dignified, advanced clergy, and the more sensual sort of the people, on one side, and so many men of *strict lives* on the other, that suffer also for their religion, and hearing too that it is some name of *preciseness* that they are reproached by, will think them to be the *better side*; and so the title of the godly will grow by degrees to be almost appropriated to their party, and the title of *profane* and *persecutors* to the other.

91. All this while the nonconforming ministers will be somewhat differently affected, according to the different degrees of their judiciousness, experience, and self-denial.

[911]Some of them will think these passions of the people needful, to check the fierceness of the afflicters (which doth but exasperate it); and therefore will let them alone, though they will not encourage them.

Some of the younger or more injudicious, hot-brained sort will put them on, and make them believe, that all communion with any conforming ministers or their parish churches is unlawful, and their forms of worship are sinful and antichristian; and that they are all temporizers and betrayers of truth and purity, that communicate or assemble with them.

The judicious, and experienced, and most patient and self-denying sort, will themselves abstain from all that is sin; and as far as it is in their choice and power, will join with the churches that worship God most agreeably to his word and will; but so, as that they will not be loud in their complaints, nor busy to draw men to their opinions in controvertible points; nor will unchurch and condemn all the churches that have something which they dislike as sinful; nor will renounce communion of all faulty churches, lest they renounce the communion of all in the world, and teach all others to renounce theirs: but they will sometimes communicate with the more faulty churches, to show that they unchurch them not (so they be not forced in it to any sin); though usually they will prefer the purest: yea, ordinarily they will join with the more faulty, when they can have no better, or when the public good requireth it. They will never prefer the interest of their nonconforming party, before the interest of christianity, or the public good. They will so defend lesser truths, as not to neglect or disadvantage the greater, which all are agreed in. They will so preserve their own innocency, as not to stir up other men's passions, nor to make factions or divisions by their difference. They will so dislike the pride and worldliness of others, and their injuries against God and godliness, as not to speak evil of dignities, nor to cherish in the people's minds any dishonourable, injurious thoughts of their kings, or any in authority over them. They will labour to allay the passions of the people, and to rebuke their censorious and too sharp language, and to keep up all due charity to those by whom they suffer; but especially *loyalty* to their kings and rulers, and peaceableness as to their countries. They will teach them to distinguish between the cruel that are masters of the game, and all the rest that have no hand in it; and at least not to separate from all the rest for the sake of a few. If they will go as far as Martin (in Sulpitius Severus) to avoid all communion with Ithacius and Idacius, and the councils of bishops, that prosecuted the Priscillianists, to the scandal of godliness itself; yet not for their sakes to avoid all others, that never consented to it: nor with Gildas, to say of all the bad ministers, that he was not *eximius christianus*, that would call them ministers, or pastors, rather than traitors. They will persuade the people to discern between good and evil, and not to run into extremes, nor to dislike all that their afflicters hold or use; nor to call things lawful, by the name of sin, and anti-christianity; nor to suffer their passions to blind their judgments, to make superstitiously *new sin* and *duties*, in opposition to their adversaries; nor to disgrace their understandings and the truth, by errors, factions, revilings, or miscarriages; nor to run into sects; nor to divide Christ's house and kingdom, while they pretend to be his zealous servants. They will persuade the people to patience, and moderation, and peace, and to "speak evil of no man," nor by word or deed to revenge themselves; much less to resist the authority that is set over them by God; but to imitate their Saviour, and quietly suffer, and being reviled not to revile again, but to love their enemies, and bless their cursers.

92. The more sober sort of the people will be ruled by these counsels, and will do much to quiet the rest. But the heretical part, with their own passions, will exasperate many novices and injudicious persons, to account this course and counsel aforesaid, to be but the effect of *lukewarmness* and *carnal compliance* with sin, and a halting between two opinions, and a participation in the sin of persecutors and malignant enemies of godliness: and they will believe that whoever joineth with the parish churches, in their way, is guilty of encouraging them in sin, and of false worship.

93. Hereupon they will defame the nonconforming ministers last described, as men of no zeal, neither flesh nor fish; and perhaps as men that would save their skin, and shift themselves out of sufferings, and betray the truth. And when such ministers acquaint them with their unsound principles and passions, they will say of them that they speak bitterly of the godly, and join with the persecutors in reproaching them.

94. And they will carry about among themselves many false reports and slanders against them; partly because passion taketh off charity and tenderness of conscience; and partly because an opinionative model, and siding religiousness, hath ever more followers, and a quicker zeal, than true holiness; and partly because they will think that human converse obligeth them to believe the reports which those that are accounted good men utter; and partly because that they will think, that the upholding of their cause (which they think is God's) doth need the suppression of these men's credit and reputation that are against it.

95. But the greater part of the honest nonconformist ministers will dislike the headiness and rashness of the novices and the sectaries, and will approve of the aforesaid moderate ways. But their opportunities and dispositions of expressing it will be various. Some of them will do it freely, whatever be thought of it; and some of them that have impatient auditors, will think that it is no duty to attempt that which will not be endured, and that it is better to do what good they can, than none. And some will think, that seeing the worldly clergy forbid them to preach the gospel of salvation, they are not bound to keep up any of their reputation or interest, as long as they have themselves no hand in the extremes and passions of the people. And some that have wives and children, and nothing but the people's charity to find them food and raiment, being turned out of all public maintenance by their afflicters, and prosecuted still with continued violence, will think that it is not their duty to beg their bread from door to door; nor to turn their families to be kept on the alms of the parish, by losing the affection of those people, whose charity only they can expect relief from: and therefore, they will think that necessity, and preservation of their families' lives and health, will better excuse their silence, when they defend not those that would destroy them, against the over-much opposition of the people; than the command of their afflicters will excuse their silence, if they neglect to preach the christian faith. And some will think, that finding themselves hated and hunted by one party, if they lose the affection of the other also, they shall have none to do their office with, nor to do any good to; and that they shall but leave the people whom they displease, to follow those passionate leaders, that will tempt them |912|to more dangerous extremities, against the peace of christian societies.

But the most judicious and resolved ministers, that live not on the favour or maintenance of the people, or are quite above all worldly interest, will behave themselves wisely, moderately, and yet resolvedly; and will do nothing that shall distaste sober and wise men, nor yet despise the souls of the most impotent or indiscreet: but by solid principles, endeavour to build them upon solid grounds; and to use them with the tenderness, as nurses should do their crying children. But yet they will not cherish their sin, under the pretence of profiting their souls; nor, by silence, be guilty of their blood; nor so much as connive at those dangerous extremes, that seem to serve some present exigence and job; but threaten future ruin to the churches, and dishonour to the christian cause. And therefore they resolve not to neglect the duties of charity to the bitterest of their persecutors; and the rather, because it will prove in the end a charity to the church, and to the souls of the passionate, whose charity they labour to keep alive. And silence at sin is contrary to their trust and office: and they will not be guilty of that carnal wisdom, which would do evil that good may come by it; or that dare not seek to cure the principles of uncharitableness, divisions, or extremities in the people, for fear of losing advantages of doing them good; or that dare not disown unlawful schisms and separations, for fear of encouraging those malignants that call lawful practices by that name. They will do God's work (though with prudence, and not destructive rashness, yet) with fidelity and self-denial. And they will lay at Christ's feet, not only their interest in the favour of superiors; and their peace, and safety, and liberty, and estates, and lives, which are exposed to malignant cruelty, among the Cainites of the world; but also all the good thoughts, and words, and favour of the religious sort of people, yea, and pastors too. And they will look more to the interest of the whole church, than of a narrow party; and of posterity, than of the present time; as knowing, that at long running, it is only truth that will stand uppermost, when malignant violence, and sectarian passions, are both run out of breath. And therefore, in simplicity, and godly sincerity, they will have their conversations in the world; and not in fleshly wisdom, or selfish blinding passions or factions. Let all men use them how they will, or judge or call them what they will; they will not therefore be false to God and to their consciences. And seeing it is their office to govern and teach the people, they will not be governed by the favour of the most censorious, ignorant, or proud; but will guide them as faithful teachers, till they are deserted by them, and disabled. But the sober, ancient, wise, and experienced, will always cleave to them, and forsake the giddy and sectarian way.

96. In the heat of these extremities, the most peaceable and sober part, both of the conformists and nonconformists, will be in best esteem with the grave and sober people; but in the greatest strait, with both the extremes.

97. The godly and peaceable conformists, will get the love of the sober, by their holy doctrine and lives: but they will be despised by the sectaries, because they conform; and they will be suspected by the proud and persecuting clergy, as leaning to the dissenters, and strengthening them by their favour; because these ministers will, in all their parishes, more love and honour the godly nonconformists, than the irreligious, ignorant, worldly, dead-hearted multitude, or the malignant enemies of godliness.

98. Hereupon these conformists being taken for the chief upholders of the nonconformists, will be under continual jealousies and rebukes. And perhaps new points of conformity shall be devised, to be imposed on them, which it is known their consciences are against; that so they may be forced also to be nonconformists, because secret enemies are more dangerous than open foes.

99. These conformists being thus troubled, will feel also the stirring of passion in themselves; and by the injury, will be tempted to think more hardly of their afflicters than before. And so will part of them turn downright nonconformists; and the other part will live in displeasure, till they see an opportunity to show it. And these are the likeliest to cross and weaken the worldly, persecuting clergy, of any men.

100. And as for the moderate nonconformists, that understand what they do, and why, and seek the reconciling of all dissenters; they will also be loved and honoured by the sober, grave, and experienced christians: but both extremes will be against them. The sectaries will say, as before, that they are lukewarm, and carnal, selfish, complying men. The proud, imposing clergy will say, that it is they that have drawn the people into these extremes; and then complain of them that they cannot rule them. And they will tell them, that till they conform themselves, their moderation doth but strengthen the nonconformists, and keep up the reputation of sobriety among them. And the nearer they come to conformity, the more dangerous they are, as being more able to supplant it. And thus the moderate and reconcilers, will be as the wedge that is pressed by both sides, in the cleft of church divisions; and no side liketh them, because they are not given up to the factious passions or interest of either.

101. Only those will, in all these extremities and divisions, keep their integrity; who are, 1. Humble and self-denying. 3. Charitable, and principled with a spirit of love. 4. And do take the favour of God and heaven alone for their hope and portion, whatever becometh of them in the world. But the WORLDLY persecuting, and the SECTARIAN party, will be both constituted by these contrary principles: 1. Ignorance and error. 2. Pride of their own understandings; every one thinking that all are intolerable that are not of their mind and way. 3. Uncharitableness, malice, or want of love to others as to themselves. 4. And overvaluing their worldly accommodations, honours, and estates.

102. Hereupon the instruments of a foolish shepherd, will still be used to the greater scattering of the flocks. And because none are so able to dispute against them as the moderate, therefore they will be taken for their most dangerous adversaries. And when they are greatly inclined to the healing of these wounds, the violent and lordly will not suffer them; but will pour oil upon the flames, which moderate men would quench. And, as if they were blindfolding and scourging Christ again, they will follow the people with afflicting wounds; and then charge the moderate ministers with their discontents; and charge them to reduce them to peace and conformity. And if they cannot get them to love and honour those that are still scourging them with scorpions, the scourgers will lay the blame on these ministers, and say, it is all long of them that the people love not those that wound them. And they that cry out most for peace will not endure it, nor give the peace-makers leave to do any thing that will accomplish it; nor will keep the spur out of the people's sides, whilst they look that

others (spurred more sharply) should hold the reins; which yet at the same time [913]they take out of their hands, and forbid them to hold, by forbidding them to preach the gospel. So that it will be the sum of their expectations, Perform not the office of pastors, nor preach the gospel of peace and piety to the people any more: but yet, without preaching to them, see that you teach them all to love and honour us, while we silence you, and afflict them; or else we will account you intolerable, seditious schismatics, and use you as such.

103. In some kingdoms or countries, it will be thought, that the people will be brought to no obedience to the *lordly pastors,* till their most *able* or *moderate ministers* are kept from them, by banishment, imprisonment, or confinement; which will accordingly be done.

104. When the ministers are banished or removed, that restrained the people's passions, the people will make preachers of themselves; even such as are suited to their minds.

105. Where papists or heretics are shut out by laws, they will secretly contribute the utmost of their endeavours, to make the sufferings of *dissenting protestants* as grievous as possibly they can; that in despite of them, their own necessities may compel them to cry out for liberty, till they procure a common toleration for all, and open the door for *papists* and *heretics,* as well as for *themselves.*

106. "Surely oppression will make wise men mad," Eccl. vii. 7.

107. Madmen will speak madly, and do madly.

108. They that speak and do madly, will be thought meetest for Bedlam, and for chains.

109. When the ministers are banished or removed, and the people left to their passions, and their own-made guides and teachers; passionate women and boys, and unsettled novices, will run into unwarrantable words and deeds; and will think those means lawful, which seem to promise them deliverance, though they be such as God forbiddeth.

110. The seditions and miscarriages of some few will be imputed to the innocent.

111. For the sake of such miscarriages, in some kingdoms, the sword will be drawn against them, and the blood of many will be shed.

112. Hereupon the misguided, passionate youth, being by the proud clergy deprived of the presence of that ministry that should moderate them, are likely enough to think rebellion and resisting of authority, a lawful means for their own preservation; and will plead the law of nature and necessity for their justification.

113. If any of the sober, wise, experienced pastors be left among them, that would restrain them from unlawful ways, and persuade them to patient suffering; they will be taken for complying betrayers of religion, and of the people's lives; that would have them tamely surrender their throats to butchery.

As in a parenthesis, I will give them some instances for this prognostic.

(1.) The great Lord Du Plessis (one of the most excellent noblemen that ever the earth bore, that is known to us by any history) being against the holding of an assembly of the French churches, against the king's prohibition, was rejected by the assembly, as complying with the courtiers (because they said, the king had before promised or granted them that assembly); but the refusing of his counsel cost the blood of many thousand protestants, and the loss of all their garrisons and powers, and that lowness of the protestant interest there that we see at this day.

(2.) The great divine, Peter De Moulin, was also against the Rochellers' proceedings against the king's prohibitions (and so were some chief protestant nobles); but he was rejected by his own party, who paid for it, by the blood of thousands, and their ruin.

(3.) I lately read of a king of France, that hearing that the protestants made verses and pasquels against the mass and processions of the papists, made a severe law to prohibit it. When they durst not break that law, their indiscreet zeal carried them to make certain ridiculous pictures of the mass priests and the processions; which moderate ministers would have dissuaded them from, but were accounted temporizers and lukewarm: by which the king being exasperated, shut up the protestant churches, took away their liberties, and it cost many thousand men their lives. And the question was, Whether God had commanded such jeers, and scorns, and pictures, to be made at so dear a rate, as the rooting out of the churches, and religion, and the people's lives?

(4.) Great Camero (one of the most judicious divines in the world) was in Montabon, when it stood out in arms against the king (accounted formerly impregnable). He was against their resistance, and persuaded them to submit. The people of his own religion reviled him as a traitor: one of the soldiers threatened to run him through. In a Scottish passion he unbuttoned his doublet, and cried, *Feri, miser*, Strike, varlet, or do thy worst; and in the heat, striving to get his own goods out of the city, fell into a fever and died. The city was taken, and the rest of the holds through the kingdom after it, to the great fall of all the protestants, and the loss of many thousand lives.

114. Where the devil can bring differences to extremities of violence, the issues are not hard to be conjecturally foreseen; but are such as my prognostics shall no further meddle with, than to foretell you, that both sides are preparing for the increase of their fury and extremities, and at last for repentance, or ruinous calamities, if they do as I have described.

115. Carnal and discontented statesmen and politicians, will set in on both sides, to blow the coals, and draw on feuds for their own ends, and head the discontented people to their ruin.

116. But in those countries, where the difference never cometh to such disorders, there will be a war bred, and kept up in the people's hearts; and neighbours will be against neighbours, as Guelphs and Gibellines.

117. When kingdoms are thus weakened by intestine discontents, it will increase the hopes and plots of foreign enemies, and make them think that one party (that suffer) will be backward to their own defence, as thinking they can be no worse (which is the hopes of the Turks in Hungary).

118. It will be a great injury, and grief, and danger to christian kings and states, to have their kingdoms and commonwealths thus weakened, and the cordial love and assistance of their subjects made so loose and so uncertain.

119. And it will be a continual vexation to wise and peaceable princes, to govern such divided, discontented people; but to rule a united, loving, concordant, peaceable people, will be their delight and joy.

120. A WORLDLY, covetous, proud, domineering, malignant, lazy clergy, will, in most christian nations, be the great plague of the world, and troublers of princes, and dividers of churches; who, for the interest of their grandeur, and their wills, will not give the sober, and peaceable, and godly ministers, or people, leave to serve God quietly, and live in peace. And the impatient, self-conceited, sectarian spirit, which, like gunpowder, takes fire upon such injuries, is the secondary divider of the churches, and hinderer [914]of christian love and peace; and by their mutual enmity and abuses, they will drive each other so far into the extremity of aversion and opposition, that they will but make each other mad; and then, like madmen, run and quarrel, while sober men stand by and pity them; but can help neither the one party nor the other, nor preserve their own or the public peace.

121. The grand endeavour of the worldly clergy, will be (in most kingdoms of the world) to engage princes on their side, and to borrow their sword, to do their work with, against gainsayers: for they have no confidence in the power of the keys; but will despise them secretly in their hearts, as leaden, uneffectual weapons, while they make it the glory of their order, that the power of the keys is theirs.

122. If princes suppress disorders by the sword, the said clergy will ascribe the honour of it to themselves; and say it was *their order*, that kept up so much order in the

churches. And when they have put princes to that trouble, will assume to themselves the praise.

123. The devil will set in, and do his utmost, to make both rulers and people believe, that all this confusion is long of the christian religion, and the strict principles of the sacred Scriptures; and so to make men cast off all religion, and take christianity to be contrary to their natural and civil interests.

124. And the papists will every where persuade high and low, that all this cometh by meddling so much with the Scriptures, and busying the common people with religion; and leaving every man to be a discerning judge of truth and duty, instead of trusting implicitly in the judgment of their church. And so they would tempt princes tamely to surrender half their government (that is, in all matters of religion) to the pope; and persuade the people to resign their reason or humanity to him; (that he who is so far off may rule it all over the world, by his missionaries and agents, who must live upon the prey;) and then he knoweth that he shall have both swords, and be the universal king.

125. To this end, they will strive to make some rulers as bad as they would have them, to do their work, and to make the rest thought worse of than they are, that they may have a fair pretence for their treasons and usurpations; which was the case of all the writers, that plead for Pope Gregory the Seventh, against the German emperors; who took that advantage, to settle the cardinals' power of elections; and, in a council at Rome, to declare the pope to be above the emperor, and to have power to depose him: and as bad was done in the general council, at Lateran, under Innocent the Third. Can. 2, 3.

126. Concerning princes, I shall give you no prognostics but Christ's; that it will "be as hard for a rich man to enter into heaven, as for a camel to go through a needle's eye." And therefore, you may know what men the rich will be, in most countries of the world.

127. And the rich will be the rulers of the world; and it is meet it should be so: not that men should rule because they are rich, but they that rule should be rich; and not exposed to contempt, by a vulgar garb and state.

128. But some wise and good princes and magistrates God will raise up, to keep the interest of truth and justice from sinking in barbarousness, and diabolical wickedness.

129. And where princes and magistrates are bad, they will seldom do so much hurt as good, or prove very cruel, where the worldly and corrupt clergy do not animate and instigate them; their reason, their interest, and their experience will lead them, by man-like usage, to seek the people's love and quietness, and their kingdom's unity and strength. But bloody persecutions (such as that of the Waldenses, Piedmont lately, France, Ireland, Queen Mary's, &c.) are ordinarily the effects of clergy interest and zeal.

130. The grand design of the devil, through the world, will be to corrupt the two great ordinances of God, *magistracy* and *ministry*; and turn them both against Christ, who giveth them their power. The instances of his success, are most notorious in the Turkish empire, and the papal kingdom, called by them the catholic church; which Campanella, de Regno Dei, doth labour to prove, by all the prophecies cited by the millenarians, or fifth-monarchy men, to be the true universal kingdom of Christ; in which, by his vicar the pope, he shall reign over all the kings and kingdoms of the earth.

A

PROGNOSTICATION

OF THE

TIME OF TRUE REFORMATION AND UNITY.

1. BECAUSE it is made part of our prayers, "Thy will be done on earth, as it is in heaven;" and, "we look for a new heaven, and a new earth, wherein dwelleth righteousness." I hope their opinion is not true, who think that the earth shall still grow more and more like to hell, till the general conflagration turn it into hell, and make it the proper seat of the damned. Yet, lest this should prove true, I will place my chief hopes in heaven; remembering who said, "Sell all, and follow me, and thou shalt have treasure in heaven" (and not on earth). But supposing that ever the world will come to full reformation and concord, (of which I am uncertain, but do not despair of,) I proceed to my prognostics of the way.

2. God will stir up some happy king, or governor, [915]in some country of christendom, endowed with wisdom and consideration; who shall discern the true nature of godliness and christianity, and the necessity and excellency of serious religion; and shall see what is the corruption and hinderance of it in the world; and shall place his honour and felicity in pleasing God, and doing good, and attaining everlasting happiness; and shall subject all worldly respects unto these high and glorious ends. And shall know, that wisdom, and godliness, and justice leave the most precious name on earth, and prepare for the most glorious reward in heaven: in comparison of which, all fleshly pomp and pleasure is dross and dung, and worthy of nothing but contempt.

3. This prince shall have a discerning mind, to know wise men from foolish, good from bad; and among the ministers of Christ, to discern the judicious, spiritual, heavenly, sober, charitable, and peaceable sort, from self-seeking, worldly men; that make but a trade of the ministry, and strive not so much for heaven, and the people's salvation, as they do for worldly honours, power, and wealth. And he shall discern how such do trouble the churches and the world, and cause divisions, and stir up violence, for their own worldly interests and ends.

4. He will take the counsel neither of worldlings, nor true fanatics, and dividing persons; but of the learned, godly, self-denying, sober, peaceable divines; with his grave and reverend senators, judges, and counsellors; that know what is reason and justice, and what belongeth to the public good, as well as to the true interest of the church, and of men's souls.

5. He will know those men, whom he is concerned to use, and to judge of, as far as may be, by personal acquaintance and observation; and not by the partial reports of adversaries, behind their backs: and so he will neither be deceived in his instruments, nor disappointed by them.

6. He will call together the wise, peace-making persons; and with the strictest charge, commit to them the endeavours of reconciling and uniting the several parties; by drawing their differences into the narrowest compass, and stating them more correctly than passionate men do; and by persuading them to love and peace, and to all such abatements and forbearances, as are necessary. And his own prudent oversight and authority (like Constantine's at Nice) will facilitate the success.

7. He and his people will inquire, what terms of concord are meet, not only for some one corner or country, but for all the christian world; that when he hath found it out, he and his kingdom may be a pattern to all christendom, and the spring and leaven of a universal concord of all christians.

8. Therefore, he will inquire of Vincent. Lirinensis, Catholic Terms of *Quod*, 1. *Ab omnibus.* 2. *Ubique.* 3. *Semper, receptum est.*

(1.) What all christians are agreed in, as christians, in the essentials of their religion.

(2.) What all christians did agree on, in the apostles' time, which was the time of greatest light, love, and purity.

(3.) What all christians, in all kingdoms of the world, since then, to this day, in the midst of all their other differences, have been and still are agreed in, as their religion.

For he will see, that there is no hope of agreeing the disagreeing world (at least, in many an age) by changing men's judgments from what they are, and bringing them all in controverted things to the mind of some party; nor to agree them on any terms, in which they do not really agree. But that their concord must be founded in that, which they are indeed all agreed in; leaving the superfluities or additions of each party, out of the agreement.

9. The peace-makers will then find, that the christian religion is contained in three forms.

(1.) In the sacramental covenant with God the Father, Son, and Holy Ghost, as the briefest formula.

(2.) In the creed, Lord's prayer, and decalogue; as the summaries of the *credenda,appetenda*, and *agenda*, matters of faith, will, (or desire,) and practice, as the larger form.

(3.) In that canon of Scripture, which all the churches receive, as the largest form or continent.

And that he who is understandingly a sacramental covenanter with God the Father, Son, and Holy Ghost, was ever taken for a visible christian. And therefore baptism was called our christening; and the baptized taken for christians, before they knew the controversies of *this* church, or *that*: and that the competent, explicit understanding of the creed, the Lord's prayer, and decalogue, was ever taken for a competent understanding of the sacramental covenant, and more. And that he that implicitly receiveth the commonly received canonical Scripture, as God's word, (though he understand no more than as followeth,) and that explicitly understandeth the creed, Lord's prayer, and decalogue, and receiveth them, and consenteth to the sacramental covenant, always was accounted, and is still to be accounted, a christian. On these terms, therefore, the peace-makers will resolve to endeavour the union of the churches.

10. Therefore they will pare off, and cast away, (as the greatest enemy to unity,) all those unnecessary controversies, or things doubtful, which christians (yea, or divines) were never agreed in, and which never were the happy and successful means or terms of any extensive concord; and which have long been tried to be the great occasions of all the scruples, and contentions, and divisions, and woeful consequents in the churches. And they will once more say, "IT SEEMETH GOOD TO THE HOLY GHOST, AND TO US, TO LAY UPON YOU NO GREATER BURDEN THAN THESE NECESSARY THINGS," Acts xv. 28. All christians shall, in general, receive the canonical Scripture as God's word; and more particularly, the creed, Lord's prayer, and decalogue, as the summary of necessaries; and shall profess, with competent understanding of it, their consent to the sacramental covenant; and vow and devote themselves therein to God. And this shall be all the title, which they shall be forced to show, for their visible church communion. And though a higher measure of the understanding of the same principles and rules, shall be required in teachers, than in the flock; and accordingly, the ordainers shall try their understandings, together with their utterance and ministerial readiness of parts; yet shall the teachers themselves be (ordinarily) forced to no other subscriptions, professions, or oaths, (besides their civil allegiance,) than to assent and consent to all aforesaid; and to promise ministerial fidelity in their places. All councils, called general or provincial, canons, decretals, articles, formulas, rubrics, &c. shall be reserved to their proper use; but be no more used for insnaring and dividing subscriptions, professions, or oaths; or made the engines to tear the churches.

11. When all those superfluities, and foot-balls of contention, are cast out of the way, the power of the keys, or pastoral government, shall come to be better known

and exercised, and the primitive discipline set up; which took place before Cyril of Alexandria took up the sword, and pride swelled the bishops into a secular state, and way of rule. Then it shall be church government, to see that the people [916]be duly taken into the sacramental covenant, and learn the creed, Lord's prayer, and decalogue; and be instructed in the word of God, and live together in sobriety, righteousness, and godliness. And the pastors shall leave secular matters to the magistrates; and be no more troubled nor corrupted by their use of any forcing power: their government shall be a paternal, authoritative exercise of instruction, and of love, and no more; like that of a tutor to his pupils, a physician in his hospital, a philosopher in his school (supposing a divine commission and rule). The church itself shall be all their courts, (supposing the magistrates,) and the people the witnesses; and the present incumbent pastors be the judges, without excommunicating and absolving lay-chancellors, surrogates, commissaries, or officials. And all the materials of contention being now gone, they shall have nothing to do in these courts, but to try whether the people have learned and understand their catechisms, and consent to God's covenant, and communicate in his worship with the church; and when any are accused of wicked living, contrary to sobriety, righteousness, and godliness, to try whether these accusations be well proved: and if so, to persuade the offenders to repent; and by plain Scripture arguments, to convince them of the sin; and with tears, or fatherly tenderness and love, to melt them into remorse, and bring them to confess and forsake the sin. And if this cannot be done at once, to try again and again, and pray for their repentance. And, when there is no other remedy, to declare such a one openly incapable of church communion; and to require the church to avoid communion with him, and him to forbear intruding into their communion: and to bind him over by a ministerial denunciation of God's displeasure, (as against the impenitent,) to answer it at the bar of God himself; as one that is under his wrath, till he do repent. And this is the utmost of the pastoral power that shall then be used (supposing private admonitions): and this only in that church or congregation wherein the sinner had before his communion; and not at a distance, nor in other churches, or parts of the world, where the pastor hath no charge. Yea, this much shall not be exercised irregularly, and at random, to the injury of the flock; but under the rules and remedies afterward here expressed.

12. The primitive church form shall be restored: and as (where there are christians enough) no churches shall be too small, so none shall be greater for number or distance, than to be one true particular church; that is, a society of christians united as pastor and people, for personal communion and assistance in God's public worship, and holy living: that is, so many as may have this personal communion, if not all at once, yet *per vices*, as oft as is fit for them to meet with the church (which all in a family cannot usually do at once). So that Ignatius's church mark shall be restored, To every church there is one altar, and one bishop, with his fellow-presbyters and deacons. And there shall no more be a hundred, or six hundred, or a thousand altars to one bishop, *primi gradus*, and in one church of the first form, called a particular church. Nor shall all the particular churches be unchurched for want of true bishops; nor all their pastors degraded into a new order of teaching ministers, that have no power of pastoral government; nor the true discipline of the churches be made a mere impossible thing, whilst it is to be exercised by one bishop only over many hundred congregations, which do every one of them afford full work for a present bishop. Nor shall the bishop's office be thought so little holy, any more than preaching, and sacramental administrations, as to be performable by a lay-delegate, or any one that is not really a bishop. But the people shall know them that are "over them in the Lord, which labour among them, and admonish them; and shall esteem them very highly in love for their work's sake; and shall be at peace among themselves," 1 Thess. v. 12, 13. Such bishops as Dr. Hammond in his "Annotations" describeth; that had but one church, and preached, baptized, catechised, visited the sick, took care of the poor, administered the Lord's supper, guided every congregation as at present in public

worship, and privately instructed and watched over all the flocks; shall be in every church that can obtain such.

13. Where the churches are so great as to need, (as most will do,) and so happy as to obtain, many faithful presbyters or pastors, whether they shall live together in a single college life, or married, and at a distance; and whether one as the chief, or bishop, shall be president, and have a negative voice, or all be equal in a concordant guidance of the flocks; shall be left to the choice and liberty of the several churches, by mutual consent of pastors, and people, and magistrates, to do and vary, as their several states and exigences shall require: and shall neither be called antichristian or odious tyranny on the one side, nor made of necessity to the church's communion or peace on the other, as long as the true pastoral or episcopal office is exercised in every particular church.

14. Neither magistrates nor other bishops shall make the bishop's or pastor's sermons and prayers for him; but leave it as the work of the speaker's office, to word his own sermons and prayers; and to choose a set form or no set form, the same or various, as the case requireth: yet so as to be responsible (as after) for all abuses and mal-administrations, and not suffered to deprave God's worship, by confusion or hurtful errors, or passionate and perverse expressions; but to be assisted and directed to use his office in the most edifying ways, by such kind of helps as his personal weaknesses shall require. And where set forms are used, none shall quarrel with them as unlawful.

15. None of the people shall have the high privileges of church communion and sacraments bestowed on them, against their wills; no more than a man impenitent and unwilling, shall be ministerially absolved from the guilt of sin. For every sacramental administration, whether of baptism, or of the body and blood of Christ, is as full an act of ministerial absolution as any pastor can perform: and what he doth to particular persons upon their penitence after a lapse, that the pastor doth to the whole church at the Lord's supper. And as consent is made by Christ the condition of pardon and covenant benefits, which no non-consenter hath a title to; so therefore professed consent is necessary to the sacramental collation or investiture: and those that are but constrained by the apparent danger of a fine or gaols, are not to be accounted voluntary consenters by the church; when the Lord of the church will account none for consenters, that will not forsake all, and endure fines and gaols, rather than to be deprived of the benefits of mystical and visible church communion. The magistrate therefore will wisely, and moderately, bring all the people to hear that which is necessary to their good; but will not by penalties force the unwilling to receive either absolutions or communion with the church, in its special privileges. But if the baptized refuse church communion afterwards, they lamentably punish themselves; and if it be found meet to declare them excommunicate, it will be a terrible penalty, sufficient to its proper use.

[917]16. The magistrate will not imprison, harm, confiscate, banish, or otherwise punish any of his subjects, *eo nomine*, because they are excommunicate; for that is to punish his body because his soul is punished. Nor will he hearken to those unbelieving clergymen, that cry up the power of the keys as their office; and when they have done, scorn it as an ineffectual shadow of power, which will do nothing without the magistrate's force. But he will himself hear and judge before he punish, and not be debased to be the clergy's executioner, to punish before he have tried the cause; because clergymen's pride and passions may else engage him to be the instrument of their vices and revenge. Yea, as he that seeth a man punished in one court, will be the more dilatory to bring him to punishment in another, for the same crime; so the magistrate that seeth a man excommunicated for his fault, will rather delay his civil force against that man, to see what effect his excommunication will have: because the conjunction of the sword against the excommunicate as such, doth corrupt Christ's ordinance, and make the fruit of it utterly undiscernible, so that no one can see whether ever it did any thing at all, or whether all was done by the fear of the sword.

And verily, a faithful minister, that seeth a sinner come to confession of his fault, but when he must else lie in gaol and be undone, will be loth to take that man for a true penitent. And to force pastors to absolve or give the sacrament to every one that had rather take it than lie in gaol and be undone, is to set up such new terms of church communion, which Christ will give men little thanks for. Church communion is only a privilege due to volunteers and penitents. But yet the magistrate may punish men with fines or other penalties for the same faults for which they are excommunicated, having tried and judged them in his own court; but not "*quarterus*" excommunicate, but according to the nature of the crime.

17. The schools of learning, and academies, shall not educate youth either in idleness, luxury, or hypocritical formality; but under learned, pious tutors, in learning sobriety and piety; from whence they shall not over-hastily leap into the pastoral office.

18. None under thirty years of age (at what time Christ himself entered on his public works) shall take a pastoral charge, except in case of mere necessity of the church, no, not on pretence of extraordinary fitness; but till then shall employ themselves as learners, catechists, schoolmasters, or probationers. Nor shall they meddle in the pulpits with matters of such controversies as the church is in danger to be troubled with.

19. Ministers shall all be commanded by the magistrate, and advised by the neighbour pastors, to forbear all unnecessary controversies in the pulpits; and to teach the people the foresaid substantials, the covenant of grace, the creed, Lord's prayer, and decalogue, the duties of faith, love, repentance, and obedience; and shall reserve their subtle and curious speculations for schools and theological writings: and so the christian people shall be bred up in the primitive, plain simplicity of doctrine and religion; and their brains shall not be heated and racked with those new-coined phrases and subtleties, which will but distemper them into a proud, contentious, wrangling disease; but will not be truly understood by them, when all is done. And so, when it is the people's work to hear only (usually) the doctrine of the catechism, and simple old christianity, and to talk of no other; 1. Their time will be employed in promoting faith, repentance, love, and obedience, which was wont to be spent in vain janglings and strife of words. And, 2. Religion will be an easier thing; and, consequently, will be more common (as cheap food and raiment is every one's pennyworth): and ministers may hope to bring the generality of their people to be savingly and practically religious: whereas the fine-spun religion of novelists, and wranglers, that pretend new light and increase of knowledge, doth not only dwindle into a cobweb of no use, or life, or power; but must be confined to a few, that can have leisure to learn to talk in new phrases, and will but become the matter of ignorant men's pride and ostentation; and make them think, that they only are the religious people; and all that cannot talk as they, are profane, and not to be admitted to their communion. Whenas the apostolic, primitive, plain religion, without the laces, and whimsies, that dreamers have since introduced, would make men humble, holy, heavenly, obedient, meek, and patient; and spare men the loss of a great deal of time.

20. The maintenance of the ministry shall neither be so poor, as to discourage men from devoting their children to the office, or disable them from a total addictedness to their proper work, by any distracting wants or cares; nor yet wholly disable them from works of charity: nor yet so great, as may be a strong bait to proud, covetous, worldly-minded men, to intrude into the ministry for fleshly ends. It shall be so much, as that the burden of their calling may not be increased by want; but yet not so much, but that self-denial shall be exercised by all that undertake the ministry; and of the two, the burden of the ministerial labours, with its proper sufferings, shall to flesh and blood seem to preponderate the worldly advantage. So greatly needful is it to the church, that all ministers be self-denying men; that valuing things spiritually can practise humility, mortification, and contempt of the world, as well as preach it.

21. There shall be a treble lock upon the door of the ministry:—

(1.) Whether they are fit to be ministers in general, the ordainers shall judge.

(2.) Whether they are fit to be the pastors of this or that particular church, the members of the church shall so far judge, as that none shall become their pastors without their own consent.

(3.) Whether they be fit for the magistrate's countenance, maintenance, and protection, the magistrate himself shall judge.

And therefore, all three shall severally try and approve each pastor: yet so, that the two first only be taken as necessary to the office itself; and the third only to the maintenance and encouragement or defence of the officer. And though sometimes this may occasion disagreements and delays for a time; yet, ordinarily, the securing of a faithful ministry, and other good effects, will countervail many such inconveniences.

22. No one church shall have the government of another church; and the secular differences of metropolitans, patriarchs, &c. which was set up in one empire, upon secular accounts, and from secular reasons, shall all cease. And no differences shall be made necessary among them, which Christ hath not made necessary. But christian princes shall take warning by the Greek and Latin churches, and by all the calamities and ruins which have been caused in the christian world, by bishops striving who should be the greatest, when Christ decided the controversy long ago, Luke xxii.

23. As christians hold personal, christian communion, in their several particular churches; so churches hold a communion of churches, by necessary correspondencies and associations: not making a major vote of bishops in synods, to have a proper government [918]over the minor part; but that by counsel and concord, that may help and strengthen one another, and secure the common interest of christianity. And that he that is a member of one church, may be received of the rest; and he that is cast out of one, may not be received by the rest, unless he be wronged. So that it shall not be one politic church, but a communion of churches.

24. The means of this communion shall be,

(1.) By messengers.

(2.) By letters and certificates communicatory.

(3.) By synods.

25. These synods shall, as to a few neighbour churches, be ordinary and stated; and the meetings of ministers in them shall be improved,

(1.) To the directing and counselling of one another, in matters doubtful; especially of discipline.

(2.) To edify each other by conference, prayer, and disputations.

(3.) That the younger may be educated under the grave advice and counsels of the elder.

(4.) That the concord of themselves, and the churches under them, may be preserved.

But if they would grow imperious, tyrannical, heretical, or contentious, the magistrate shall hinder their stated, ordinary meetings; that it be not accounted a thing simply necessary, nor used to the disturbance of the church or state. And all provincial, national, and larger councils, shall be held by the magistrate's consent.

26. He that taketh himself to be wrongfully excommunicated in one church, shall have a treble remedy:

(1.) To have his cause heard by the associated pastors of the neighbour churches; though not as rulers of the bishop or pastor of that particular church, yet as counsellors, and such whose judgment bindeth to concord in lawful things.

(2.) To be admitted by another church, if it appear that he is wronged. And,

(3.) To appeal to the magistrate, as the preserver of justice and order in all societies.

27. The magistrate shall appoint some of the most grave, and wise, and godly, and moderate of the ministers, to have a general inspection over many churches; and to see that they be well taught and ordered, and that pastors and people do their duty: who shall therefore oft visit them, and shall instruct and exhort the younger ministers;

and with the countenance of the magistrate, and their own seniority and ability, shall rebuke the slothful and faulty ministers; and persuade them to diligence and fidelity: but shall exercise no outward force by the sword; nor any excommunication by themselves alone, or otherwise than in the aforesaid regular way.

28. All ordinations shall be performed, (except in case of necessity,) either in the assembly of the associated pastors, with their president; or in the vacant church, by some of them, appointed by the rest; or by the general visitor, last mentioned, with a competent number of assistants. But still, an ordination to the ministry in general, shall not be taken to be formally the same as the affixing him to this or that church in particular; nor more than the licensing of a physician is the same with the affixing him to a particular hospital.

29. A catalogue shall be drawn up of some of the greatest verities, which are not expressly found in the creed, Lord's prayer, or decalogue; which, as the articles of confession of the associated churches of the nation, shall serve for these three uses:—

(1.) To satisfy all foreign churches, against any accusation, that they are orthodox.

(2.) To examine the knowledge of such as are admitted to the ministry by (but not to be subscribed, unless only as to a general acknowledgment of the soundness of their doctrine; without saying that, There is nothing faulty in them).

(3.) To be a rule of restraint to ministers, in their preaching; that none be allowed publicly, after admonition, to preach against any doctrine contained in them.

30. The usurped ecclesiastical power of bishops, and presbyteries, and councils, (which were coercive, or imitated secular courts, or bound the magistrate to execute their decrees,) being cast out, and all pastors restrained from playing the bishops in other churches, out of their own charge, the magistrate shall exercise all coercive church government himself; and no more trust the sword directly, or indirectly, in the hands of the clergy, who have long used it so unhappily, to the disturbance of the christian world, and the shedding of so much innocent blood. Where it may be had, there shall be a church justice, or magistrate, in every considerable parish; who, being present, shall himself hear how ministers preach, and behave themselves among their people. And all ministers and churches shall be responsible to the magistrate, for all abuses, and mal-administration. If any minister preach or pray seditiously, abusively, factiously, railingly, against tolerable dissenters, to the destroying of christian love and unity; or heretically, to the danger of the people's souls; or shall exercise tyranny over the people, or live a vicious life; or be negligent in his office of teaching, worship, or discipline, or otherwise grossly misbehave himself; he shall be responsible both (as aforesaid) to the associated pastors and visitor, (or archbishop,) and also to the magistrate; who shall rebuke and correct him, according to the measure of his offence. And it shall appear, that the magistrate is sufficient for all coercive church government, without all the clergy's usurpations; which uphold the Roman and other tyrannical societies.

31. The question, Who shall be judge of heresy, schism, or church sins? shall be thus decided.

(1.) The bishops or pastors of the particular churches shall be the judges, who is to be denied communion in their churches as heretics, schismatics, &c.

(2.) The associated churches shall be judges, (in their synods, or by other correspondence,) who is to be commonly denied communion in all their churches; and what pastors and churches shall have the *dextram communionis*, and who not.

(3.) The magistrate shall be the only judge, who is to be punished for heresy or schism, &c. with fines, or any outward, corporal penalty. And no one shall usurp the other's right.

32. The magistrate shall silence all preachers that, after due admonition, so grossly misbehave themselves in doctrine, worship, or conversation, as to be the plagues of the churches, and to do apparently more hurt than good. But as to all worthy and able ministers, if they commit any fault, they shall be punished as other

subjects, only with such penalties as shall not, by silencing or restraint, be a punishment to the innocent people's souls, nor hinder the preaching of the gospel of salvation: even as if the common bakers, brewers, butchers, carpenters, perform their work perniciously, (poisoning their beer, bread, and meat,) they shall be forbid the trade; but for other faults, they shall be so punished, that the people be not left without bread, beer, meat, houses, for their faults.

33. If any heretics (as Arians, Socinians, &c.) [919]would creep into the ministry, there shall not be new forms of subscription made to keep them out; (which it is likely, with their vicious consciences, would be ineffectual, and would open a gap to the old church tyrannies and divisions;) nor an uncertain evil be ineffectually resisted by a certain greater mischief. But while he keepeth his error to himself, he is no heretic as to the church (*non apparere* being equal to *non esse*): and when he venteth his heresy, he is responsible all the ways aforesaid, and may be by the magistrate punished for his crime, and by the churches be branded as none of their communion; which is the regular way of reforming crimes, viz. By judgment and execution, and not by making new rules and laws, as fast as men break the old; as though laws could be made which no man can break.

34. The magistrate shall countenance or tolerate no sin or error, so far as he can cure it by just remedies, which will not do more harm than good: but he shall unwillingly tolerate many tolerable errors and faults; because it is not in his power to remedy them, but by such means. But,

(1.) The sound and concordant ministry only shall have his countenance and maintenance.

(2.) Smaller errors and disorder shall be best cured by gentle rebukes, and discountenance, and denial of maintenance; together with the disgrace that will be cast upon them, by the judgment and dissent of all the united, concordant ministers and churches (which together will do more and better, than exasperating cruelties will do).

(3.) The publishing of pernicious principles shall be restrained more severely.

But though men may be restrained from venting pernicious falsehoods, they cannot be constrained to believe the truth; (we are not so happy;) nor shall they be constrained to lie, and say that they believe it when they do not.

35. All matters of quarrels, division, and cruel usage of each other, being thus cut off and gone, bitterness and revengeful thoughts will cease, and love will revive in all men's breasts, and unity and peace will follow of its own accord. And if any heretical or contentious sect arise, the hearts of all united people will so rise against them, that desertion and shame will quickly kill them.

36. Then will the hearts of the people cleave to their pastors: and they will be no more put on the great difficulties of loving the bishops that hurt them, or of loving them in gaols; but it will be as easy to love them, when they feel the love to their souls in the labours and kindness of their pastors, as to love their dearest and nearest friends. And then love will open the people's ears to the teacher's doctrine, and it will do them good: and then the labours and lives of faithful ministers will be sweet and easy, when the love, and the unity, and faithfulness of the people, is their daily encouragement. Oh how good, and how happy, will it be for pastors and people thus to live in love and unity! It will not only remind us of Aaron's perfume, but of the Spirit of love that dwelt in our Redeemer, and which he promised should be his seal and mark upon all his true disciples; yea, and of the celestial society, and life of perfect love.

37. Then shall neighbours exercise their charity, for the help of the ignorant about them, without the suspicions of venting heresies, or sedition, or encroaching on the pastor's office. And neighbours, when they come together, shall not take praying together, or holy conference, or singing God's praise, or reading good books, or repeating their teachers' sermons, or counselling each other, to be a bad or dangerous work: but the ignorant, that cannot spend the Lord's day in holy exercises at home, (because they cannot read or remember much,) shall join with the families of their

more understanding neighbours, who can help them; (as they met, Acts xii. 12, for prayer; and as neighbour families were to join in eating the passover with the family that had not enough to eat it;) for love and unity shall end these jealousies. And all shall be done under the guidance and oversight of their pastors; and not in enmity of opposition to them, or to the concordant church assemblies. And oh what helps and comfort will this be to all faithful pastors, when all the work lieth not on them alone; but every one sets his hand to build, in his proper place; and when they that converse together all the week, are seconding that which he more seldom teacheth them in public!

38. The younger sort of ministers, that are now bred up in Vulcan's forge, shall be then trained up under grave and peaceable men; where uniting and peace-making principles shall be the rudiments of their literature.

39. And the younger sort of the people shall be no more tempted into envious heats against their afflicters; nor into contentious sects, because of controversies; but shall be fed with the milk of peaceable principles, and be educated in the love of love itself. And the names of sects, and church divisions, and proud pretendings, shall, by use, be made as disgraceful, as now the names of swearing, drunkenness, and whoredom are.

40. And oh how dear, how amiable, how honourable will their governors be, to such a people (especially that blessed prince, that shall first perform this work)! How heartily will they pray for them, plead for them, and fight for them! and how freely will they contribute any thing in their power to their aid! and how impatient will they be against every word that would dishonour them! How blessed will the people be under such a prince! and how sweet and easy will the life of that prince be, that is to govern such a people!

GRANT, O LORD, THAT THIS GREAT HONOUR AND COMFORT MAY FALL INTO THE HANDS OF THE KING OF ENGLAND, BEFORE ALL OTHERS IN THE WORLD. Kings will then see, that it is their interest, their honour, and their greatest happiness on earth, to be the wise, pious, righteous governors, of a wise, pious, just, united people; that love them so much, that still they would fain serve them better than they are able.

41. The ignorant, vulgar, and ruder sort, observing this amiable concord, and all the blessed fruits thereof, will admire religion, and fall in love with it: and multitudes that shall be saved, will be daily added to the seriously religious, and the house of Christ will be filled with guests.

42. Hereupon the scandalous and flagitious lives of common protestants will be much cured; for the number of the flagitious will grow small, and crimes will be under common disgrace. Besides that, they will be punished by the magistrate; so that gross sin will be a marvel.

43. The books of plain doctrine and holy living, with the pacificatory treatises of reconcilers, will then be most in esteem and use; which now are so disrelished by turbulent, discontented, siding persons. And abundance of controversial writings, about church government, liturgies, ceremonies, and many other matters, will be forgotten and cast aside as useless things; for the swords shall be made into plough-shares and pruning-hooks.

44. The happy example of that happy prince and country, that shall begin and first accomplish this [920]work, will be famous through all the protestant churches; and will inflame such desires of imitation in them all, and be such a ready direction in the way, that it will greatly expedite their answerable reformation. And the famous felicity of that prince, in the reformation and concord of his subjects, will kindle in the hearts of other protestant princes and states an earnest desire of the same felicity. And so, as upon the invention of printing, and of guns, the world was presently possessed of guns and of printed books, that never before attained any such thing; so here, they that see the happiness of one kingdom brought about, and see how it was done, will

have matter enough before their eyes, both to excite their desires and guide their endeavours in the means to bring all this to pass.

45. The protestant kingdoms and states, being thus reformed and united in themselves, will be inflamed with an earnest desire of the good of all other churches, and of all the world: and therefore, as divines have held something called general councils for the union of all those churches; so these princes will by their agents hold assemblies for maintaining correspondence, to the carrying on of the common good of the world, by the advantage of their united counsels and strength; and then no enemy can stand long before them. For they that love and serve them zealously at home, will venture their lives for them zealously abroad, if there be cause.

46. The excellent and successful use of the magistrate's government of the churches in their dominions, will quite shame all the usurping claims of the pope and general councils, and their mongrel ecclesiastic courts, and all the train of artifices and offices, by which their government of the world is managed. And the world, and especially princes, will plainly see how much they were abused by their usurpations, and that there is no need of pope or cardinal, nor any of those officers or acts at all; but that these are the mere contrivances of carnal policy, to keep up an earthly kingdom under the name of the catholic church. And also the purity and unity of the reformed churches, where the vulgar have more religion and union than their monasteries, will dazzle the eyes of the popish princes, states, and people; and when they see better, and especially the happiness of the princes, they will forsake the usurper that had captivated them by fraud, and will assume their freedom and felicity; and so the Roman church kingdom will fall.

47. The deluded Mahometans seeing the unity and glory of christendom, as they were before kept from Christ by the wicked lives and the divisions of christians (thinking that we are far worse than they); so now they will be brought to admire and honour the christian name, and fear the power of the christian princes. And one part of them will turn christians; and the rest, even the Turkish power, the christian's force, by the power of God, will easily break. And so the Eastern churches will be delivered and reformed, and the Mahometans come into the faith of Christ.

48. The poor scattered Jews also, when they see the glory and concord of christians, will be convinced that Christ is indeed the true Messias: and being converted, perhaps, shall by the christian powers be some of them re-established in their own land; but not to their ancient peculiarity, or policy and law.

49. And then the christian zeal will work to the conversion of the poor idolatrous, heathen world; and part of them will yield to reason and faith, and the rest by just victories be subdued. And so the kingdoms of the world will become the kingdoms of the Lord and his Christ; and the gospel shall be preached in all the world.

50. And when the kingdom of grace is perfected, and hath had its time, the kingdom of glory shall appear, upon the glorious appearing of Christ our King; and the dead shall arise, and they that have overcome, shall reign with Christ, and sit with him upon the throne, even as he overcame, and is set down with the Father on his throne. Amen. Even so, come, Lord Jesus.

"Neither pray I for these alone, but for them also, which shall believe on me through their word; that they all may be one, as thou, Father, art in me, and I in thee; that they also may be one in us, that the world may believe that thou hast sent me. And the glory which thou gavest me, I have given them, that they may be one, even as we are one. I in them, and thou in me; that they may be made perfect in one; and that the world may know that thou hast sent me, and hast loved them, as thou hast loved me. Father, I will that they also whom thou hast given me, be with me where I am, that they may behold my glory which thou hast given me," John xvii. 20-24.

Object. But if this world should ever become so happy, it would be more amiable, and so be a greater snare to our affections, and make us willing to stay from heaven.

306

Answ. No amiableness or pleasantness stealeth the heart from God, or keepeth it from heaven, but that which hideth the glory and goodness of God and heaven from our minds, or corrupteth and diverteth the will and affections by some inconsistency or contrariety; but the spiritual excellency of the reformed concordant church on earth, will so much more clearly represent heaven to our conceptions, and give our hearts so pleasant a foretaste of it, that above all things it will excite our desires of that fuller glory, and call us most powerfully to a heavenly mind and life: as the first-fruits and earnest do make us desire the harvest, and the full possession; and as now those that live in the most heavenly society, and under the most excellent helps and means, have usually more heavenly minds and lives, than they that in more tempting and distracting company never enjoy such heavenly beams.

CONSECTARY.

ALL the Romish dreams of church union arise from ignorance of the true state and interest of the church, and the true and necessary terms of union.

And all the plots also of the moderating papists, that talk of a political church catholic having a visible constitutive or governing head; whether monarchical, (the pope,) or aristocratical, or democratical (the patriarchs, or a general council): and that talk of universal laws of this church, made by such a universal head, besides the universal laws of Christ; and falsely feign the councils called general, in a particular empire, called or ruled by one emperor only, in his own dominions, to have been universal, as to all the catholic churches on earth; and that feign these councils to have been infallible, which so often erred, and crossed each other; and that set the world upon the undeterminable controversy, Which were true general councils; and, How many we must receive and conform to: whether only four, or six, or eight; and till what age. [921]And that would persuade the christian world, that whatever diversity of canons, customs, or church laws, or ceremonies, are allowed among them, it must all be done or held by this same authority of the pope or council, or both: to which (though foreign) kings and bishops must all be subject; and from which they must receive their christianity; and by which all their reformations must be tried: and that none must be taken as catholics, nor any churches tolerated, that hold not such a factious union, under such a usurping head, personal or collective: but as Tertullian speaketh, rather than endure such wiser and better societies, *Solitudinem facerent, et vocarent pacem*: and as a WORLDLY CLERGY, whose church and kingdom is only of and in this world, would banish from it all (save a lifeless image) which hath any kin to heaven; and suffers none to live in this world among them but themselves.

I say, all this is, 1. From ignorance of the true nature of the christian religion, church state, and terms of unity and concord; which I have lately opened in a book, entitled, "The True and only Terms of the Concord of all the Churches."

2. And from contention about ambiguous words, and self-conceitedness in their controversies, ignorantly thence raised; which I have sought to end in a book, called, "Catholic Theology."

3. And from vicious passions and partiality; which I have sought to heal in a book, called, "The Cure of Church Divisions."

All written long since the writing of this foregoing Prognostication.
[922]

THE

REFORMED LITURGY.

ON THE

LORD'S DAY.

The Congregation being reverently composed, let the Minister first crave God's assistance and acceptance of the Worship, to be performed in these or the like words.

ETERNAL, incomprehensible, and invisible God, infinite in power, wisdom, and goodness, dwelling in the light which no man can approach, where thousand thousands minister unto thee, and ten thousand times ten thousand stand before thee, yet dwelling with the humble and contrite, and taking pleasure in thy people: Thou hast consecrated for us a new and living way, that with boldness we may enter into the holiest, by the blood of Jesus, and hast bid us seek thee while thou mayst be found: We come to thee at thy call, and worship at thy footstool. Behold us in thy tender mercies. Despise us not, though unworthy. Thou art greatly to be feared in the assembly of the saints, and to be had in reverence of all that are about thee. Put thy fear into our hearts, that with reverence we may serve thee; sanctify us, that thou mayst be sanctified of us, when we draw nigh thee. Give us the Spirit of grace and supplication to help our infirmities, that our prayers may be faithful, fervent, and effectual. Let the desire of our souls be to thee: let us draw near thee with our hearts, and not only with our lips, and worship thee, who art a Spirit, in spirit and truth. Let thy word be spoken and heard by us as the word of God. Give us attentive, hearing ears, and opened, believing, understanding hearts, that we may no more refuse thy calls, nor disregard thy merciful, outstretched hand, nor slight thy counsels and reproofs; but be more ready to hear, than to give the sacrifice of fools. Put thy laws into our hearts, and write them in our minds, and let us be all taught of God. Let thy word be unto us quick and powerful; a discerner of the thoughts and intents of the heart; mighty to pull down strong-holds, casting down imaginations and reasonings, and every high thing that advanceth itself against the knowledge of God; and bringing into captivity every thought to the obedience of Christ. Let us magnify thee with thanksgiving, and triumph in thy praise. Let us rejoice in thy salvation, and glory in thy holy name. Open thou our lips, O Lord, and let our mouths show forth thy praise. And let the words of our mouths, and the meditation of our hearts, be acceptable in thy sight, through Jesus Christ our Lord and only Saviour.[176] Amen.

Or thus, when brevity is necessary.

O ETERNAL, almighty, and most gracious God, heaven is thy throne, and earth is thy footstool, holy and reverend is thy name; thou art praised by the heavenly hosts, and in the congregation of thy saints on earth, and wilt be sanctified in all that come nigh unto thee. We are sinful and unworthy dust, but being invited by thee, are bold, through our blessed Mediator, to present ourselves and our supplications before thee. Receive us graciously, help us by thy Spirit; let thy fear be upon us; let thy word come unto us in power, and be received in love, with attentive, reverent, and obedient minds. Make it to us the savour of life unto life. Cause us to be fervent in prayer, and joyful in thy praises, and to serve thee this day without distraction, that we may find that a day in thy courts is better than a thousand, and that it is good for us to draw near to God; through Jesus Christ our Lord and Saviour.[177] Amen.

Next, let one of the Creeds be read by the Minister, saying,

In the profession of this christian faith we are here assembled.

I believe in God the Father, &c.

I believe in one God, &c.

And sometimes Athanasius' Creed.

[923]

The Ten Commandments.

God spake these words, and said, &c.

For the right informing and affecting the People, and moving them to a penitent, believing Confession, some of these Sentences may be read.

God created man in his image.[178]

By one man sin entered into the world, and death by sin; and so death passed upon all men, for that all have sinned.[179]

For all have sinned, and come short of the glory of God.[180]

God so loved the world, that he gave his only begotten Son, that whosoever believeth in him should not perish, but have everlasting life.[181]

He that believeth on him shall not be condemned: but he that believeth not is condemned already, because he hath not believed in the name of the only begotten Son of God.[182]

And this is the condemnation, that light is come into the world, and men loved darkness rather than light, because their deeds were evil.[183]

For every one that doth evil hateth the light, neither cometh to the light, lest his deeds should be reproved.[184]

Christ hath redeemed us from the curse of the law, being made a curse for us.[185]

Except a man be born of water and of the Spirit, he cannot enter into the kingdom of God.[186]

That which is born of the flesh is flesh; and that which is born of the Spirit is spirit.[187]

Verily I say unto you, Except ye be converted, and become as little children, ye shall not enter into the kingdom of heaven.[188]

Say unto them, As I live, saith the Lord God, I have no pleasure in the death of the wicked; but that the wicked turn from his way and live: turn ye, turn ye from your evil ways; for why will ye die, O house of Israel?[189]

I say unto you, there is joy in the presence of the angels of God over a sinner that repenteth.[190]

I will arise and go to my father, and say unto him, Father, I have sinned against heaven, and before thee, and am no more worthy to be called thy son.[191]

The Confession of Sin, and Prayer for Pardon and Sanctification.

O MOST holy, righteous, and gracious God, who hatest all the workers of iniquity, and hast appointed death to be the wages of sin, but yet for the glory of thy mercy hast sent thy Son to be the Saviour of the world, and hast promised forgiveness of sin through his blood, to all that believe in him, and by true repentance turn unto thee, and that whosoever confesseth and forsaketh his sin, shall have mercy; we confess that we are vile and miserable sinners, being conceived in sin; by nature children of wrath, and transgressors from the womb. All we like sheep have gone astray, and turned every one to his own way. Thou madest us, and not we ourselves. Thou boughtest us with a price, and we are not our own; therefore we should have wholly given up ourselves unto thee, and have glorified thee with our souls and bodies as being thine. Whatever we did should have been done to thy glory, and to please thee, in the obeying of thy will. But we have displeased and dishonoured thee, and turned from thee, exalting, seeking, and pleasing ourselves. Thou art the King of all the world, and thy laws are holy, just, and good. But we have denied thee our due subjection and obedience, being unruly and self-willed, minding the things of the flesh, and making provision for its lusts. We have staggered at thy word through unbelief, and have not fully placed our trust and hope in thee. We have rather feared man that is dust, and can but kill the body, than thee, that canst destroy both soul and body in hell. Thou art infinitely good, and love itself, yet have we not fully taken thee for our portion, nor loved thee with all our heart, and soul, and might, nor made thee our full desire and delight. But we have inordinately loved ourselves, and the world, and the things of the world, and lived by sense when we should have lived by faith, and cared and laboured for the food that perisheth, when we should have laboured for the one thing needful, and that which endureth to everlasting life. We have been slothful servants, yielding to temptations, ashamed of our duty, losing our precious time, when we should have been fervent in spirit, serving the Lord, cleaving to thee with full resolution, redeeming the time, and with diligence making sure our calling and election. We have not with due holiness and reverence drawn near thee, and used thy holy name, thy worship, and thy day. We have dishonoured and disobeyed our superiors, and neglected our inferiors. We have been guilty of not loving our neighbours as ourselves, and not doing to others as we would they should do to us; but have sought our own against their welfare, not forbearing and forgiving, not loving our enemies as we ought, not following peace, nor studying to do good to all according to our power. We have sinned secretly and openly, in thought, word, and deed, ignorantly and presumptuously, in passion and upon deliberation, against thy precepts, promises, and threats; against thy mercies and thy judgments, under thy patience and in thy sight; against our consciences, our purposes, and our covenants. When we were hastening to death and judgment, for which through all our lives we should have prepared, thou hast commended thy wonderful love towards us in giving thy Son to die for sinners, to reconcile us to thee, while we were enemies; and all things being made ready, thou hast sent thy messengers to invite us to come in, preaching to us the glad tidings of salvation, and freely offering us pardon and life in Jesus Christ; but we have made light of it, and [924]neglected this great salvation, and made excuses or too long delays; undervaluing our Redeemer, his blood and merits, his offered grace and endless glory, rejecting his holy doctrine and example, resisting his Spirit, ministers, and word. We have sinned, O Lord, against thee, and against our own souls, and are not worthy to be called thy children. We have deserved everlasting wrath; to us belongeth confusion, but mercy and forgiveness to thee. Have mercy upon us, O God, according to the multitude of thy mercies. Heal our souls that have sinned against thee, and enter not into judgment with thy servants. Hide thy face from our sins, and blot out all our iniquities. Cast us not away from thy presence, and avenge not upon us the quarrel of thy covenant. Wash us in the blood of the Lamb of God, who taketh away the sin of the world. Accept us in thy beloved Son, who was made a curse for us, and was wounded for our transgressions, that we might be healed by his stripes. Turn us, O God of our salvation, and cause thy face to shine upon us. Give us repentance unto life: cause us to loathe ourselves for all the evils that we have committed. Give us that broken, contrite spirit which thou wilt not despise. Create in us a clean heart, O God, and renew a right spirit within us. Take out of us the old and stony heart, and give us a new and tender heart. Give us the Spirit of thy Son, and be our God, and let us be thy people. Enlighten our understandings to know the wonderful things of thy law, the dimensions of thy love in Christ, the mysteries of thy kingdom, and the riches of the glory of thy inheritance in the saints, and that we may approve the things that are excellent, and may escape the snares of the devil, and may hate every false way. Shed abroad thy love in our hearts by thy Holy Spirit, and cause us so to love thee, that nothing may separate us from thy love. Put thy fear into our hearts, that we may never depart from thee. Cause us to seek first thy kingdom, and its righteousness, and (as those that are risen with Christ) to seek the things that are above, and to lay up a treasure in heaven, and let our hearts and conversations be there. Mortify our earthly inclinations and desires. Crucify the world to us, and us unto the world by the cross of Christ. Cause us to live by faith, and look at the things that are unseen; and use the world as not over-using it, seeing the fashion of it passeth away; striving to enter in at the strait gate, and running so as to obtain. Let us no longer live the rest of our time to the lust of men, but the will of God, studying in all things to please thee, and to be accepted of thee. Let us not seek our own wills, but the will of him that called us; yea, let us delight to do thy will, O God; let our delight be in thy law, and let us meditate therein day and night. Cause us to deny ungodliness and worldly lusts, and to live soberly, and righteously, and godly in this present world, as obedient children, not fashioning ourselves to the former lusts of our ignorance; but as he that hath called us is holy, let us be holy in all manner of conversation. Cause us to love one another with a pure heart, forbearing and forgiving one another, if any have a quarrel against another, even as Christ forgave us. Give us the wisdom which is first pure, and then peaceable. In our eyes let a vile person be contemned, but let us honour them that fear the Lord. Cause us to walk circumspectly without offence, and to be zealous of good works; to love our enemies, and not to give place to wrath; and in patience to possess our souls. Help us to deny ourselves, and take up our cross, and follow Christ; esteeming his reproach to be greater riches than the treasures of the world; that having suffered with him, we may also be glorified with him. Though we must be tempted, help us to overcome, and be faithful unto the death; and then let us receive that crown of life, through the merits and intercession of Christ Jesus our Lord and only Saviour; in whose comprehensive words we sum up our requests, saying as he hath taught us, Our Father which art in heaven, hallowed be thy name. Thy kingdom come, &c.[192]

Or thus, when brevity is necessary.

O MOST great, most just, and gracious God, thou art of purer eyes than to behold iniquity, thou condemnest the ungodly, impenitent, and unbelievers; but hast promised mercy through Jesus Christ to all that repent and believe in him. We confess that we were conceived in sin, and are by nature children of wrath; and have all sinned and come short of the glory of God. In our baptism thou tookest us into the bond of the holy covenant, but we remembered not our Creator in the days of our youth, with the fear, and love, and obedience which we owed thee: not pleasing and glorifying thee in all things, nor walking with thee by faith in a heavenly conversation, nor serving thee fervently with all our might; but fulfilled the desires of the flesh, and of the carnal mind. We have neglected and abused thy holy worship, thy holy name, and thy holy day. We have dishonoured our superiors, and neglected our inferiors. We have dealt unjustly and uncharitably with our neighbours, not loving them as ourselves, nor doing to others as we would they should do to us. We have not sought first thy kingdom and righteousness, and been contented with our daily bread, but have been careful and troubled about many things, neglecting the one thing necessary. Thou hast revealed thy wonderful love to us in Christ, and offered us pardon and salvation in him; but we made light of it, and neglected so great salvation, and resisted thy Spirit, word, and ministers, and turned not at thy reproof. We have run into temptations; and the sin which we should have hated, we have committed in thy sight, both secretly and openly, ignorantly and carelessly, rashly and presumptuously, against thy precepts, thy promises, and threats, thy mercies and thy judgments. Our transgressions are multiplied before thee, and our sins testify against us. If thou deal with us as we deserve, thou wilt cast us away from thy presence into hell, where the worm never dieth, and the fire is not quenched. But in thy mercy, thy Son, and thy promise, is our hope. Have mercy upon us, most merciful Father. Be reconciled to us, and let the blood of Jesus Christ cleanse us from all our sins. Take us for thy children, and give us the Spirit of thy Son. Sanctify us wholly, shed abroad thy love in our hearts, and cause us to love thee with all our hearts. O make thy face to shine upon thy servants; save us from our sins, and from the wrath to come; make us a peculiar people to thee, zealous of good works, that we may please thee, and show forth thy praise. Help us to redeem the time, and give all diligence to make our calling and election sure. Give us things necessary for thy service, and keep us from sinful discontent and cares. And seeing all these things must be dissolved, let us consider [925]what manner of persons we ought to be, in all holy conversation and godliness. Help us to watch against temptations, and resist and overcome the flesh, the devil, and the world; and being delivered out of the hand of all our enemies, let us serve thee without fear, in holiness and righteousness before thee all the days of our life. Guide us by thy counsel, and after receive us into thy glory, through Jesus Christ our only Saviour.[193] Amen.

[Here use the Lord's Prayer as before.]

For the strengthening of Faith, and raising the Penitent, some of these Sentences of the Gospel may be here read.

311

Hear what the Lord saith to the absolution and comfort of penitent believers.

The Lord your God is gracious and merciful, and will not turn away his face from you, if ye return unto him.[194]

If any man sin, we have an advocate with the Father, Jesus Christ the righteous: and he is the propitiation for our sins: and not for ours only, but also for the sins of the whole world.[195]

Be it known unto you, men and brethren, that through this man is preached to you the forgiveness of sins: and by him all that believe are justified from all things, from which they could not be justified by the law of Moses.[196]

Where sin abounded, grace did much more abound: that as sin reigned unto death, even so might grace reign through righteousness unto eternal life, through Jesus Christ our Lord.[197]

If we walk in the light, as he is in the light, we have fellowship one with another, and the blood of Jesus Christ his Son cleanseth us from all sin. If we say that we have no sin, we deceive ourselves, and the truth is not in us. If we confess our sin, he is faithful and just to forgive us our sin, and to cleanse us from all unrighteousness.[198]

Come unto me, all ye that labour and are heavy laden, and I will give you rest. Take my yoke upon you, and learn of me; for I am meek and lowly in heart: and ye shall find rest unto your souls. For my yoke is easy, and my burden is light.[199]

Whosoever will, let him take of the water of life freely.[200]

All that the Father hath given me shall come to me; and him that cometh to me I will in nowise cast out.[201]

I will be merciful to their unrighteousness, and their sins and iniquities I will remember no more.[202]

Hear also what you must be and do for the time to come, if you would be saved.

Now if any man have not the Spirit of Christ, he is none of his.[203]

If any man be in Christ, he is a new creature: old things are passed away; behold, all things are become new.[204]

There is no condemnation to them that are in Christ Jesus, who walk not after the flesh, but after the Spirit. For they that are after the flesh do mind the things of the flesh; but they that are after the Spirit the things of the Spirit.[205]

For to be carnally-minded is death, but to be spiritually-minded is life and peace.[206]

For the carnal mind is enmity against God: for it is not subject to the law of God, neither indeed can be.[207]

So then they that are in the flesh cannot please God.[208]

For if ye live after the flesh, ye shall die: but if through the Spirit ye mortify the deeds of the body, ye shall live.[209]

Now the works of the flesh are manifest, which are these; Adultery, fornication, uncleanness, lasciviousness, idolatry, witchcraft, hatred, variance, emulations, wrath, strife, seditions, heresies, envyings, murders, drunkenness, revellings, and such like: of the which I tell you before, as I have told you in time past, that they which do such things shall not inherit the kingdom of God.[210]

But the fruit of the Spirit is love, joy, peace, long-suffering, gentleness, goodness, faith, meekness, temperance: against such there is no law. And they that are Christ's have crucified the flesh with the affections and lusts.[211]

Let us walk honestly, as in the day; not in rioting and drunkenness, not in chambering and wantonness, not in strife and envying. But put ye on the Lord Jesus Christ, and make no provision for the flesh, to fulfil the lusts thereof.[212]

Love not the world, neither the things that are in the world. If any man love the world, the love of the Father is not in him. For all that is in the world, the lust of the flesh, the lust of the eye, and the pride of life, is not of the Father, but is of the world.[213]

Enter ye in at the strait gate: for wide is the gate, and broad is the way, that leadeth to destruction, and many there be that go in thereat: because strait is the gate, and narrow is the path, that leadeth unto life, and few there be that find it.[214]

For the grace of God that bringeth salvation hath appeared unto all men, teaching us that, denying ungodliness and worldly lusts, we should live soberly, and righteously, and godly, in this present world; looking for the blessed hope, and the glorious appearing of the great God and our Saviour Jesus Christ; who gave himself for us, that he might redeem us from all iniquity, and purify to himself a peculiar people, zealous of good works.[215]

Blessed is the man that walketh not in the counsel of the ungodly, nor standeth in the way of sinners, nor sitteth in the seat of the scornful. But his delight is in the law of the Lord; and in his law doth he meditate day and night.[216]

The ungodly shall not stand in the judgment, nor sinners in the congregation of the righteous.[217]

Wherefore we receiving a kingdom which cannot be moved, let us have grace, whereby we may serve God acceptably with reverence and godly fear: for our God is a consuming fire.[218]

Seeing then that these things shall be dissolved, what manner of persons ought ye to be, in all holy conversation and godliness, looking for and hasting to the coming of the day of God?[219]

Therefore, my beloved brethren, be ye stedfast, unmoveable, always abounding [926]in the work of the Lord, for as much as ye know that your labour is not in vain in the Lord.[220]

Then may be said the ninety-fifth or the hundredth Psalm, or the eighty-fourth.

And next the Psalms in order for the day; and next shall be read a chapter of the Old Testament, such as the Minister findeth most seasonable; or with the liberty expressed in the admonition before the second book of Homilies.[221]

After which may be sung a Psalm, or the Te Deum said; then shall be read a chapter of the New Testament, and then the Prayer for the King and Magistrates. And after that, the sixty-seventh, or ninety-eighth, or some other Psalm, may be sung or said, or the Benedictus, or Magnificat. And the same order to be observed at the Evening Worship, if time allow it.[222]

Next after the psalm the minister shall (in the pulpit) first reverently, prudently, and fervently pray, according to the state and necessities of the church, and those especially that are present, and according to the subject that he is to preach on. And after prayer, he shall preach upon some text of holy Scripture, suiting his matter to the necessities of the hearers, and the manner of delivery to their quality and benefit. Always speaking from faith and holy experience in himself, with plainness and perspicuity, with reverence and gravity, with convincing evidence and authority, with prudence, caution, faithfulness, and impartiality, with tender love and melting compassion, with fervent zeal and persuading importunity, and with frequency and unwearied patience, waiting on God for the success. After sermon he shall pray for a blessing on the word of instruction and exhortation, which was delivered; and in his prayers (before or after sermon) ordinarily he shall pray for the conversion of heathens, Jews, and other infidels; the subversion of idolatry, infidelity, Mahometanism, heresy, papal tyranny and superstition, schism and profaneness, and for the free progress of the gospel, and the increase of faith and godliness, the honouring of God's name, the enlargement of the kingdom of Christ, and the obedience of his saints through the nations of the earth. And in special for these nations; for the king's Majesty, and the rest of the royal family; for the lords of his Majesty's council, the judges, and other magistrates of the land; for the pastors of the church, and all congregations committed to their care and government. Always taking heed that no mixtures of imprudent, disorderly expressions, of private discontent and passion, of unreverent, disobedient, seditious, or factious intimations, tending to corrupt, and not to edify, the people's minds, do turn either prayer or preaching into sin. And ordinarily in church communion, especially on the Lord's day, (which is purposely separated for the joyful commemoration of the blessed work of man's redemption,) a considerable proportion of the public worship must consist of thanksgiving and praises to God, especially for Jesus Christ, and his benefits; still leaving it to the minister's discretion to abbreviate some parts of worship, when he seeth it needful to be longer on some other.[223]

313

The Sermon and Prayer being ended, let the Minister dismiss the Congregation with a benediction, in these or the like words.

Blessed are they that hear the word of God, and keep it.[224]

The Lord bless you, and keep you: the Lord make his face to shine upon you, and be gracious unto you: the Lord lift up his countenance upon you, and give you peace.[225]

The grace of our Lord Jesus Christ, and the love of God the Father, and the communion of the Holy Ghost, be with you all.[226] Amen.

Except there be a Communion in the Sacrament of the Lord's Supper to be celebrated, or any further Worship to be performed, and then the Minister may delay the Benediction till the End.

And because, when there is leisure, the Prayers of the Church should be as full as the Rule and our Necessities require; let the following General Prayer be used, when the Minister findeth it convenient, instead of the Litany and Collects.

Here are also adjoined a Thanksgiving for Christ and his benefits, and a Hymn to be used at the discretion of the minister, either after sermon, or at the communion, or on other days.

A Prayer for the King, the Royal Family, and Magistrates.

ALMIGHTY God, by whom kings reign, and princes decree justice, who rulest in all the kingdoms of men, and givest them to whomsoever thou wilt, who by thy special providence hast set over us thy servant, Charles, our king; crown him with thy blessings, and satisfy him with thy goodness. Save him by thy right hand, and defend him against such as rise up against him; prolong his life in peace and righteousness; grant him the spirit of wisdom and counsel, the spirit of holiness, and the fear of the Lord, that he may know how to go in and out before this great people over whom thou hast set him. Let not thy law depart out of his mind, or mouth, but let him meditate in it day and night. Make him as an angel of God to discern between good and evil, that in his eyes a vile person may be contemned, but he may honour them that fear the Lord; that his eyes may be upon the faithful of the land, that they may dwell with him, and they that are perfect in the way serve him. Remove the wicked from before him, that his throne may be established in righteousness; and grant that under him we may lead a quiet and peaceable life in all godliness and honesty. And when he hath finished his course on earth, let him inherit a crown of righteousness, and reign with Christ for ever. Bless the queen mother, the illustrious prince, James, duke of York, and the rest of the royal family; endue them with thy Holy Spirit, enrich them with thy heavenly grace, and make them blessings in their generation. Endue the lords of his Majesty's council, and all the nobility, the judges, and all the magistrates of the land, with wisdom from above, that they may rule as in thy fear, and judge righteous judgment, and may take heed what they do, as judging not for man, but for the Lord, that justice may run down as water, [927]and righteousness as a mighty stream. Let all his Majesty's subjects duly submit to him and obey him, not only for wrath, but for conscience' sake. Let all his kingdoms be the kingdoms of the Lord, and of his Son Christ, that God may dwell amongst us, and that it may be said of them, The Lord bless thee, O habitation of Justice, and mountain of Holiness: for thine, O Father, with the Son and Holy Ghost, is the kingdom, and power, and glory for ever.[227] Amen.

The General Prayer.

O MOST holy, blessed, and glorious Trinity, Father, Son, and Holy Ghost, Three Persons and One God, our Creator, Redeemer, and Sanctifier, our Lord, our Governor and Father, hear us, and have mercy upon us, miserable sinners.

O Lord our Saviour, God and man! who, having assumed our nature, by thy sufferings, and death, and burial, wast made a ransom to take away the sins of the world; who being raised from the dead, ascended and glorified, art made head over all things to the church, which thou gatherest, justifiest, sanctifiest, rulest, and preservest, and which at thy coming thou wilt raise and judge to endless glory; we beseech thee to hear us, miserable sinners: make sure to us our calling and election, our unfeigned faith and repentance; that being justified, and made the sons of God, we may have peace with him, as our reconciled God and Father.[228]

Let thy Holy spirit sanctify us, and dwell in us, and cause us to deny ourselves, and to give up ourselves entirely to thee, as being not our own, but thine.

As the world was created for thy glory, let thy name be glorified throughout the world; let self-love, and pride, and vain-glory be destroyed; cause us to love thee, fear thee, and trust in thee with all our hearts, and to live to thee.[229]

Let all the earth subject themselves to thee, their King. Let the kingdoms of the world become the kingdoms of the Lord, and of his Christ. Let the atheists, idolaters, Mahometans, Jews, and other infidels, and ungodly people, be converted. Send forth meet labourers into the harvest, and let the gospel be preached throughout all the world. Preserve and bless them in thy work. Sustain in patience, and seasonably deliver, the churches that are oppressed by idolaters, infidels, Mahometans, or other enemies, or by the Roman papal usurpations.[230]

Unite all christians in Jesus Christ, the true and only universal Head, in the true christian and catholic faith and love; cast out heresies and corruptions, heal divisions, let the strong receive the weak, and bear their infirmities; restrain the spirit of pride and cruelty, and let nothing be done in strife or vain-glory.[231]

Keep us from atheism, idolatry, and rebellion against thee; from infidelity, ungodliness, and sensuality; from security, presumption, and despair. Let us delight to please thee, and let thy word be the rule of our faith and lives; let us love it, and understand it, and meditate in it day and night.[232]

Let us not corrupt or neglect thy worship; nor take thy holy name in vain. Keep us from blasphemy, perjury, profane swearing, lying, contempt of thy ordinances, and from false, unworthy, and unreverent thoughts and speeches of God, or holy things; and from the neglect and profanation of thy holy day.[233]

Put it into the hearts of the kings and rulers of the world to submit to Christ, and rule for him as nursing-fathers to his church: and save them from the temptations that would drown them in sensuality; or would break them upon Christ as a rock of offence, by engaging them against his holy doctrine, ways, and servants.[234]

Have mercy on thy servant Charles, our king, protect his person, illuminate and sanctify him by thy Spirit, that above all things he may seek thine honour, the increase of faith, and holy obedience to thy laws; and may govern us as thy minister, appointed by thee for the terror of evil-doers, and the praise of them that do well, that under him we may live a quiet and peaceable life, in all godliness and honesty.[235]

Have mercy upon all the royal family, upon the lords of the council, and all the nobility, the judges, and other magistrates of these lands. Let them fear thee, and be ensamples of piety and temperance, haters of injustice, covetousness, and pride, and defenders of the innocent: in their eyes let a vile person be contemned, but let them honour them that fear the Lord.[236]

Let every soul be subject to the higher powers, and not resist; let them obey the king, and all in authority, not only for wrath, but for conscience' sake.[237]

Give all the churches able, holy, faithful pastors, that may soundly and diligently preach thy word, and guide the flocks in ways of holiness and peace; overseeing and ruling them not by constraint, but willingly, not for filthy lucre, but of a ready mind; not as being lords over thy heritage, but the servants of all, and ensamples to the flock; that when the chief Pastor shall appear, they may receive the crown of glory.[238]

Let the people know those that are over them in the Lord, and labour among them, preaching to them the word of God; let them highly esteem them in love for their work's sake, account them worthy of double honour, and obey them in the Lord.[239]

Let parents bring up their children in holy nurture, that they may remember their Creator in the days of their youth; and let children love, honour, and obey them. Let husbands love their wives, and guide them in knowledge and holiness; and let wives love and obey their husbands. Let masters rule their servants in thy fear, and servants obey their masters in the Lord.[240]

Keep us from murders and violence, and injurious passionate words and actions.[241]

Keep us from fornication and all uncleanness, from chambering and wantonness, from lustful thoughts and filthy communications, and all unchaste behaviour.[242]

Keep us from stealing or wronging our neighbour in his property, from perverting justice, from false witnessing [928]and deceit, from slandering, backbiting, uncharitable censuring or other wrong to the reputation of our neighbours.[243]

Keep us from coveting any thing that is our neighbour's. Let us love our neighbours as ourselves, and do to others as we would they should do to us.[244]

Cause us to love Christ in his members with a pure and fervent love, and to love our enemies, and do good to all, as we are able; but especially to the household of faith.[245]

Give us our necessary sustentation and provision for thy service and contentedness therewith. Bless our labours, and the fruits of the earth in their season, and give us such temperate weather as tendeth hereunto. Deliver us and all thy servants from such sickness, wants, and other distresses, as may unseasonably take us off thy service. Keep us from gluttony and drunkenness, slothfulness, unlawful gain, and from making provision for the flesh to satisfy its lusts.[246]

When we sin, restore us by true repentance and faith in Christ. Let us loathe ourselves for our transgressions; forgive them all, and accept us in thy well-beloved Son; save us from the curse and punishment which they deserve, and teach us heartily to forgive others. Convert our enemies, persecutors, and slanderers, and forgive them.[247]

Cause us to watch against temptations, to resist and overcome the flesh, the devil, and the world; and by no allurements of pleasure, profit, or honour, to be drawn from thee to sin. Let us patiently suffer with Christ that we may reign with him.[248]

Deliver us and all thy people from the enmity and rage of Satan, and all his wicked instruments; and preserve us to thy heavenly kingdom.[249]

For thou only art the universal King; all power is thine in heaven and earth: of thee, and through thee, and to thee are all things, and the glory shall be thine for ever.[250]Amen.

Concerning the Psalms for public use.

We desire that instead of the imperfect version of the Psalms in metre now in use, Mr. William Barton's Version, and that perused and approved by the Church of Scotland there in use, (being the best that we have seen,) may be received and corrected by some skilful men, and both allowed (for grateful variety) to be printed together on several columns or pages, and publicly used; at least until a better than either of them shall be made.

A Thanksgiving for Christ, and his gracious Benefits.

MOST glorious God, accept, through thy beloved Son, though from the hands of sinners, of thanksgiving, which thy unspeakable love and mercies, as well as thy command, do bind us to offer up unto thee. Thou art the Father of mercies, and the God of all consolation, full of compassion, gracious, long-suffering, plenteous in goodness and truth, keeping mercy for thousands, forgiving iniquity, transgression, and sin. For thy glory thou didst create us after thine image; thou madest us a little lower than the angels, and crownedst us with glory and honour, giving us dominion over the works of thy hands, and putting all these things under our feet. And when we forsook thee, and broke thy covenant, and rebelled against thee, and corrupted ourselves, and turned our glory into shame thou didst not leave us in the hands of death, nor cast us out into utter desperation; but thou didst so love the sinful world, as to give thy Son to be our Saviour. He took not upon him the nature of angels, but of man; the Word was made flesh and dwelt among us. This is the unsearchable mystery of love which the angels desire to pry into: he was tempted, that he might succour them that are tempted, and conquered the tempter, that had conquered us. He became poor that was Lord of all, to make us rich. He did not sin, but fulfilled all righteousness, to save us from our unrighteousness. He made himself of no reputation, but was reviled, scorned, and spit upon, enduring the cross, and despising the shame to cover our shame, and to bring us unto glory; thou laidst upon him the iniquity of us all. He was bruised and wounded for our transgressions, that we might be healed by his stripes. He gave himself a ransom for us, and died for our sins, and rose again for our justification. We thank thee for his death that saveth us from death, and that he bore the curse to redeem us from the curse, and for his life which opened to us the way to life. Thou hast given him to be Head over all things to the church, and hast given the heathen to be his inheritance, and given him a name above every name, and given all power and judgment unto him. We thank thee for the new and better covenant, for thy great and precious promises; that thou hast given us eternal life in Christ. That we have the clear and sure revelation of thy will in the holy Scriptures. That thou foundest thy church upon apostles and prophets, Jesus Christ himself being the head corner-stone. And hast committed to thy ministers the word of reconciliation, that as ambassadors speaking in the stead of Christ, they might beseech us to be reconciled unto thee. We thank thee that by them thou hast opened our eyes, and turned us from darkness unto light, and from the power of Satan unto God. We were sometimes foolish, disobedient, deceived, serving divers lusts and pleasures, taken captive by Satan at his will; but thy mercy saved us by the washing of regeneration, and renewing of the Holy Ghost. Thou mightest justly have left us to the blindness of our minds, and to the hardness of our hearts, to seared consciences, to be past feeling, to our own hearts' lusts, to walk in our own counsels, and to work uncleanness with greediness, when we so oft refused to come to Christ that we might have life, and would not have him to reign over us. But thy patience waited on us in our sin; and all the day long didst thou stretch forth thy hand to a disobedient and gainsaying people. When we turned from thee, thou calledst after us, to turn and live. Thou drewest us to thy Son, and openedst our hearts to attend to thy call. Thou lovedst us first, and was found of them that sought thee not. Thou hast pardoned our great and manifold transgressions, and justified us by faith in Christ, and [929]given us repentance unto life. Thou hast adopted us to be thy sons, and joint heirs with Christ; and made us his members, and given us his Spirit: we are no more strangers, but fellow-citizens with the saints, and of thy household. Blessed be the God and Father of our Lord Jesus Christ, who of his abundant mercy hath begotten us again unto a lively hope, by the resurrection of Jesus Christ from the dead, to an inheritance incorruptible, undefiled, that fadeth not away, reserved in heaven for us. Thou keepest us by thy mighty power through faith unto salvation: ready at last to be revealed, though (when they are needful) we must for a season be in heaviness under tribulations. Thou hast promised, that all things shall work together for our good; in all our straits thou grantest us access to the throne of grace, bidding us call upon thee in the time of trouble, and promising to deliver us, that we may glorify thee: every where we have leave to lift up unto thee holy hands, especially in the house of prayer, and the assembly of the saints. Thou hast heard the voice of our supplications when we have cried unto thee; great is thy mercy towards us. O Lord, thou hast delivered our souls from the lowest hell; thou hast sent forth from heaven thy mercy and truth; and saved us from the reproach of him that would swallow us up. Thou art our hiding-place: in the secrets of thy presence thou preservest us from trouble, from the pride of men, and from the strife of tongues. Thou dost compass us about with songs of deliverance. O love the Lord, all ye his saints! for the Lord preserveth the faithful, and plentifully rewardeth the proud doer. He dealeth not with us after our sins; his anger is but for a moment, but in his favour is life. In his wrath he remembereth mercy: all thy paths, O Lord, are mercy and truth to such as keep thy covenant. We come into thy house in the multitude of thy mercies; O give thanks unto the Lord, for he is good, for his mercy endureth for ever. Glory ye in his holy name; let the hearts of them rejoice that seek him. Blessed are the people that know the joyful sound; they shall walk, O Lord, in the light of thy countenance. In thy name they shall rejoice all the day, and in thy righteousness and favour shall they be exalted. Blessed are they that dwell in thy house, they will be still praising thee. O satisfy us early with thy mercy, that we may rejoice and be glad in thee all our days. Guide us by thy counsel, and afterwards receive us unto thy glory; where with all the blessed host of heaven, we may behold, admire, and perfectly and joyfully praise thee, our most glorious Creator, Redeemer, and Sanctifier, for ever and for ever.[251] Amen.

The Hymn.

The First Part.

BLESS the Lord, O my soul: and all that is within me, bless his holy name. Bless the Lord, O my soul, and forget not all his benefits: who forgiveth all thine iniquities, and healeth all thy diseases; who redeemed thy life from destruction, and crowneth thee with loving-kindness and tender mercies. As far as the east is from the west, so far hath he removed our transgressions from us. Behold, what love the Father hath bestowed on us, that we should be called the sons of God. Because thy loving-kindness is better than life, my lips shall praise thee. Thus will I bless thee while I live; I will lift up my hands in thy name. My soul shall be satisfied as with marrow and fatness, and my mouth shall praise thee with joyful lips. Whom have I in heaven but thee? and there is none on earth that I desire besides thee. My flesh and my heart faileth, but God is the strength of my heart, and my portion for ever. For, lo, all that are far from thee shall perish; but it is good for me to draw near to God. I am continually with thee: thou hast holden me by my right hand. In the multitude of my thoughts within me, thy comforts delight my soul. Thou shalt guide me with thy counsel, and afterward receive me to glory.[252]

The Second Part.

HOW excellent is thy loving-kindness, O God! therefore do the sons of men put their trust under the shadow of thy wings. They shall be abundantly satisfied with the fatness of thy house; and thou shalt make them drink of the rivers of thy pleasures: for with thee is the fountain of life. In thy light we shall see light. Therefore my heart is glad, and my glory rejoiceth. My flesh also shall rest in hope. Thou wilt show me the path of life. In thy presence is fulness of joy, and at thy right hand are pleasures for evermore. Surely goodness and mercy shall follow me all the days of my life; and I shall dwell in the house of the Lord for ever. O continue thy loving-kindness to them that know thee, and thy righteousness to the upright in heart. To the end that my glory may sing praise unto thee, and not be silent. O Lord my God, I give thanks to thee for ever.[253]

The Third Part.

GLORY to God in the highest: on earth peace, good will towards men. Praise ye the Lord: sing to the Lord a new song; his praise is in the congregation of saints. For the Lord taketh pleasure in his people; he will beautify the meek with salvation. Let the saints be joyful in glory. Let the high praises of God be in their mouths. All thy works praise thee, O Lord, and thy saints shall bless thee. They shall speak of the glory of thy kingdom, and talk of thy power; to make known to the sons of men thy mighty acts, and the glorious majesty of thy kingdom. Thy kingdom is an everlasting kingdom, and thy dominion is through all generations. The elders and saints about thy throne, rest not day nor night, saying, Holy, holy, holy, Lord God Almighty, which was, and is, and is to come. Thou art worthy, O Lord, to receive glory, and honour, and power; for thou hast created all things, and for thy pleasure they are and were created. They sing unto thee the song of Moses, and of the Lamb, saying, Great and marvellous are thy works, Lord God Almighty; just and true are thy ways, thou King of saints. Who shall not fear thee, O Lord, and glorify thy name; for thou only art holy: for all nations shall come and worship before thee, for thy judgments are made manifest. Worthy is the Lamb that was slain, to receive power, and riches, and wisdom, and strength, and honour, and glory. For thou hast redeemed us to God by thy blood, and made us kings and priests to God.[254]

[930]

The Fourth Part.

OH that men would praise the Lord for his goodness, and for his wonderful works to the children of men! Let them sacrifice the sacrifices of thanksgiving, and declare his works with rejoicing. Sing unto the Lord, bless his name; show forth his salvation from day to day. Worship the Lord in the beauty of holiness: fear before him, all the earth. Let the heavens rejoice, and the earth be glad before the Lord; for he cometh, for he cometh to judge the earth. With righteousness shall he judge the world, and the people with equity. Bless the Lord, ye his angels, that excel in strength, that do his commandments, hearkening to the voice of his word. Bless ye the Lord, all ye his hosts, ye ministers of his that do his pleasure. Bless the Lord, all his works in all places of his dominions. Bless the Lord, O my soul. My mouth shall speak the praises of the Lord; and let all flesh bless his holy name for ever and ever. Let every thing that hath breath praise the Lord. Praise ye the Lord.[255]

THE ORDER OF CELEBRATING THE SACRAMENT OF THE BODY AND BLOOD OF CHRIST.

This, or the like Explication of the Nature, Use, and Benefits of this Sacrament, may be used at the Discretion of the Minister, when he seeth it needful to the Instruction of the Communicants.

THAT you may discern the Lord's body, and understand the nature, use, and benefits of this sacrament; you must know that God created man in his own image, to know, and love, and serve his Maker; that man fell under the guilt of sin and condemnation, and left his holy fitness for the work for which he was created. That hereupon the wonderful love and wisdom of God provided us a remedy in our Redeemer, to the end he might not lose the glory of his creation, that he might pardon and save us upon terms; securing the honour of his justice, and attaining the ends of his law and government, and recover us to his love and service, by appearing to the world, in the greatest demonstrations of goodness, love, and mercy. By the greatest miracle of condescension, he first promised, and then gave his only Son, the Eternal Word, to take man's nature into personal union with his Godhead; that being God and man, he might be a fit Mediator between God and man, to restore us, and reconcile us to himself. Thus Jesus Christ, conceived by the Holy Ghost, and born of the Virgin Mary, became the Second Adam, the Physician and Saviour of undone sinners, the Captain of our salvation, to be the glorious King and Head of all that are sanctified and saved. He revealed the holiness, the goodness, and the love of God, by the perfect holiness, goodness, and love of his blessed person, doctrine, and conversation, and by suffering for us all the afflictions of this life, and at last the cursed death of the cross, as a sacrifice and ransom for us. That all this might be effectual to our recovery, he made for us a new and better covenant, and preached it himself, undertaking the pardon, justification, and sanctification of all that by unfeigned faith do take him for their Saviour, repenting of their sins, and consenting to be sanctified by his word and Spirit (by which also he inviteth and draweth men to himself, and giveth them to believe): into this blessed, pardoning, saving covenant, we are first solemnly entered by baptism. And when Christ was ready to leave the world, and to give up himself a sacrifice for us, and intercede and exercise the fulness of his kingly power, and the church's Head; and by his grace to draw men to himself, and prepare them for his glory; he did himself institute this sacrament of his body and blood at his last supper, to be a continued representation and remembrance of his death, and therein of his own and his Father's love, until his coming; appointing his ministers, by the preaching of the gospel, and administration of these sacraments, to be his agents without, and his Spirit within, effectually to communicate his grace.

319

[The Lord's supper, then, is a holy sacrament instituted by Christ, wherein bread and wine being first by consecration made sacramentally, or representatively, the body and blood of Christ, are used by breaking and pouring out to represent, and commemorate, the sacrifice of Christ's body and blood, upon the cross once offered up to God for sin; and are given in the name of Christ unto the church, to signify and solemnize the renewal of his holy covenant with them, and giving of himself unto them, to expiate their sins by his sacrifice, and sanctify them further by his Spirit, and confirm their right to everlasting life: and they are received, eaten, and drunk by the church, to profess that they willingly receive Christ himself to the ends aforesaid, (their justification, sanctification, and glorification,) and to signify and solemnize the renewal of their covenant with him, and their holy communion with him, and with one another.]

It being the renewing of a mutual covenant that is here solemnized, as we commemorate Christ's sacrifice, and receive him and his saving benefits, so we offer and deliver to him ourselves, as his redeemed, sanctified people, to be a living acceptable sacrifice, thankfully and obediently to live unto his praise.

Before the receiving of his holy sacrament, we must examine ourselves, and come preparedly; in the receiving of it, we must exercise holy affections suited to the work; and after the receiving of it, we must, by consideration of it, endeavour to revive the same affections, and perform our covenant there renewed.

The holy qualifications to be before provided, and in receiving exercised, and after receiving, are these. 1. A true belief of the articles of the christian faith concerning Father, Son, and Holy Ghost; the person, offices, works, sufferings, and benefits of Christ. 2. The sense of our sinful and undone condition, as in ourselves, and of our need of Christ: so as humbly to loathe ourselves for our transgressions, with the sense of our present weaknesses to be strengthened, and sins to be forgiven. 3. A true desire after Christ for pardon, and spiritual nourishment and salvation. 4. A thankful sense of the wonderful love of God, declared in our redemption, and in the present offers of Christ, and life. 5. The exercise of holy love and joy in the sense of this unspeakable love. (If these two be not felt before we come, yet in and after the sacrament we must strive to exercise them.) 6. A love to one another, and forgiving wrongs to one another, with a desire after the communion of saints. 7. The giving up ourselves in covenant to God, with resolution for renewed obedience. 8. A patient hope for the coming of Christ himself, and of the everlasting kingdom, where we shall be perfectly united in him, and glorified with him.

[931]Those only are to be invited to the Lord's table, and to come, that truly repent and believe, and unfeignedly consent to the terms of the covenant (though all are not to be invited thus to believe and repent, and so to come). But those are to be admitted, by the pastors, if they come, who, having the use of reason to understand what they do, and examine themselves, have made a personal profession of faith, repentance, and obedience; and are members of the church, and not justly for heresy or scandalous sin, removed from its present communion.

The benefit of the sacrament is not to be judged of only by present experience and feeling, but by faith. God having appointed us to use it, and promised his blessing, we may and must believe, that he will make good his promise; and whatever we feel at present, that we sincerely wait not on him in vain.

The Exhortation.

YOU are invited hither, dear brethren, to be guests at this holy table, by the Lord's command, to receive the greatest mercy, and to perform the greatest duty. On Christ's part, all things are made ready. The feast is prepared for you, even for you that by sin have deserved to be cast out of the presence of the Lord; for you that have so oft neglected and abused mercy. A feast of the body and blood of Christ, free to you, but dear to him. You were lost, and in the way to be lost for ever, when by the greatest miracle of condescending love, he sought and saved you. You were dead in sin, condemned by the law, the slaves of Satan; there wanted nothing but the executing stroke of justice to have sent you into endless misery; when our dear Redeemer pitied you in your blood, and shed his own to wash and heal you. He suffered that was offended, that the offender might not suffer. He cried out on the cross, "My God, my God, why hast thou forsaken me?" that we who had deserved it, might not be everlastingly forsaken. He died that we might live. Oh how would the mercy of redemption have affected you, if you had first lain one year, or month, or day in hell! Had you but seen your dying Lord, or seen the damned in their misery, how do you think you should have valued the salvation that is now revealed and tendered to you? See here Christ dying in this holy representation. Behold the sacrificed Lamb of God, that taketh away the sins of the world. It is his will to be thus frequently crucified before your eyes. Oh how should we be covered with shame, and loathe ourselves, that have both procured the death of Christ by sin, and sinned against it! And how should we all be filled with joy, that have such mysteries of mercy opened, and so great salvation freely offered to us! O hate sin, O love this Saviour: see that you come not hither without a desire to be more holy, nor with a purpose to go on in wilful sin. Be not deceived, God is not mocked; but if you heartily repent, and consent to the covenant, come and welcome; we have commission from Christ to tell you, that you are welcome. Let no trembling, contrite soul draw back, that is willing to be Christ's upon his covenant terms, but believe that Christ is much more willing to be yours. He was first willing, and therefore died for you, and made the covenant of grace, and sent to invite and importune you to consent, and stayed for you so long, and gave you your repentance, your willingness, and desire. Question not then his willingness, if you are willing. It is Satan and unbelief that would have you question it, to the injury both of Christ and you. Come near, observe, believe, and wonder at the riches of his love and grace; for he hath himself invited you to see and taste, that you may wonder. You are sinners, but he inviteth you to receive a renewed, sealed pardon of your sins, and to give you more of his Spirit to overcome them. See here his broken body and his blood, the testimonies of his willingness. Thus hath he sealed the covenant, which pardoneth all your sins, and secureth you of your reconciliation with God, and your adoption, and your right to everlasting blessedness. Deny not your consent, but heartily give up yourselves to Christ, and then doubt not but your scarlet, crimson sins shall be made as white as wool or snow. Object not the number or greatness of them against his grace. There is none too great for him to pardon to penitent believers. Great sins shall bring great glory to his blood and grace. But strive you then for great loathing of your sins, and greater love to such a God, and greater thanks to such a Saviour. Unfeignedly say, I am willing, Lord, to be wholly thine, and then believingly take Christ, and pardon, and life, as given you by his own appointment in the sealed covenant. And remember that he is coming. He is coming with thousands of his mighty angels, to execute judgment on the ungodly, but to be glorified in his saints, and admired in all that do believe. And then we shall have greater things than these. Then shall you see all the promises fulfilled, which now are sealed to you, on which he causeth you to trust. Revive now your love to one another, and forgive those that have wronged you, and delight in the communion of the saints; and then you shall be admitted into the church triumphant, where with perfect saints you shall perfectly rejoice, and love and praise the Lord for ever. Receive now a crucified Christ here represented, and be contented to take up your cross, and follow him. And then you shall reign with a glorified Christ, in the blessed vision and fruition of that God, to whom by Christ you are now reconciled. Let faith and love be working upon these things, while you are at this holy table.

Then shall the Minister use this or the like Prayer.

MOST holy God, we are as stubble before thee, the consuming fire. How shall we stand before thy holiness, for we are a sinful people, laden with iniquity, that have gone backward and provoked the Holy One of Israel. When we were lost, thy Son did seek and save us; when we were dead in sin, thou madest us alive. Thou sawest us polluted in our blood, and saidst unto us, Live. In that time of love thou coveredst our nakedness, and enteredst into a covenant with us, and we became thine own. Thou didst deliver us from the power of darkness, and translate us into the kingdom of thy dear Son; and gavest us remission of sin, through his blood. But we are grievous revolters, we have forgotten the covenant of the Lord our God. We were engaged to love thee with all our hearts, and to hate iniquity, and serve thee diligently, and thankfully to set forth thy praise. But we have departed from thee, and corrupted ourselves by self-love, and by loving the world, and the things that are in the world, and have fulfilled the desires of the flesh, which we should have crucified. We have neglected our duty to thee, and to our neighbour, and the [932]necessary care of our own salvation. We have been unprofitable servants, and have hid thy talents, and have dishonoured thee, whom in all things we should have pleased and glorified. We have been negligent in hearing and reading thy holy word, and in meditating and conferring of it, in public and private prayer, and thanksgiving, and in our preparation to this holy sacrament, in the examining of ourselves, and repenting of our sins, and stirring up our hearts to a believing and thankful receiving of thy grace, and to love and joyfulness, in our communion with thee and with one another. We have not duly discerned the Lord's body, but have profaned thy holy name and ordinance, as if the table of the Lord had been contemptible. And when thou hast spoken peace to us, we returned again to folly. We have deserved, O Lord, to be cast out of thy presence, and to be forsaken, as we have forsaken thee, and to hear our confusion, Depart from me, I know you not, ye workers of iniquity. Thou mayst justly tell us, thou hast no pleasure in us, nor wilt receive an offering at our hand. But with thee there is abundant mercy. And our advocate Jesus Christ the righteous, is the propitiation for our sins; who bare them in his body on the cross, and made himself an offering for them, that he might put them away by the sacrifice of himself: have mercy upon us, and wash us in his blood, clothe us with his righteousness, take away our iniquities, and let them not be our ruin; forgive them and remember them no more. O thou that delightest not in the death of sinners, heal our backslidings, love us freely, and say unto our souls, that thou art our salvation. Thou wilt in nowise cast out them that come unto thee; receive us graciously to the feast thou hast prepared for us; cause us to hunger and thirst after Christ and his righteousness, that we may be satisfied. Let his flesh and blood be to us meat and drink indeed; and his Spirit be in us a well of living water, springing up to everlasting life. Give us to know thy love in Christ, which passeth knowledge. Though we have not seen him, let us love him; and though now we see him not, yet believing let us rejoice with joy unspeakable, and full of glory. Though we are unworthy of the crumbs that fall from thy table, yet feed us with the bread of life, and speak and seal up peace to our sinful, wounded souls. Soften our hearts that are hardened by the deceitfulness of sin: mortify the flesh, and strengthen us with might in the inner man; that we may live and glorify thy grace, though Jesus Christ our only Saviour.[256] Amen.

Here let the Bread be brought to the Minister, and received by him, and set upon the Table, and then the Wine in like manner, (or if they be set there before,) however, let him bless them, praying in these or the like words.

ALMIGHTY God, thou art the Creator and the Lord of all things. Thou art the Sovereign Majesty whom we have offended; thou art our most loving and merciful Father, who hast given thy Son to reconcile us to thyself, who hath ratified the new testament and the covenant of grace with his most precious blood; and hath instituted this holy sacrament to be celebrated in remembrance of him till his coming. Sanctify these thy creatures of bread and wine, which according to thy institution and command, we set apart to this holy use, that they may be sacramentally the body and blood of thy Son Jesus Christ.[257] Amen.

Then (or immediately before this Prayer) let the Minister read the words of the Institution, saying,

HEAR what the apostle Paul saith: "For I have received of the Lord, that which also I deliver unto you, That the Lord Jesus, the same night in which he was betrayed, took bread; and when he had given thanks, he brake it, and said, Take, eat, this is my body which is broken for you: this do in remembrance of me. After the same manner also he took the cup, when he had supped, saying, This cup is the new testament in my blood: this do ye, as oft as ye drink it, in remembrance of me; for as often as ye eat this bread, and drink this cup, ye do show the Lord's death till he come."|258|

Then let the Minister say,

THIS bread and wine being set apart, and consecrated to this holy use by God's appointment, are now no common bread and wine, but sacramentally the body and blood of Christ.

Then let him thus pray:

MOST merciful Saviour, as thou hast loved us to the death, and suffered for our sins, the just for the unjust, and hast instituted this holy sacrament to be used in remembrance of thee till thy coming; we beseech thee, by thine intercession with the Father, through the sacrifice of thy body and blood, give us the pardon of our sins, and thy quickening Spirit, without which the flesh will profit us nothing. Reconcile us to the Father; nourish us as thy members to everlasting life.[259] Amen.

Then let the Minister take the Bread, and break it in the sight of the people, saying,

THE body of Christ was broken for us, and offered once for all to sanctify us. Behold the sacrificed Lamb of God, that taketh away the sins of the world.

In like manner let him take the Cup, and pour out the Wine in the sight of the Congregation, saying,

WE were redeemed with the precious blood of Christ, as of a Lamb without blemish, and without spot.

Then let him thus pray:

MOST Holy Spirit, proceeding from the Father and the Son, by whom Christ was conceived, by whom the prophets and apostles were inspired, and the ministers of Christ are qualified and called, that dwellest and workest in all the members of Christ, whom thou sanctifiest to the image and for the service of their Head, and comfortest them that they may show forth his praise; illuminate us, that by faith we may see him that is here represented to us. Soften our hearts, and humble us for our sins. Sanctify and quicken us, that we may relish the spiritual food, and feed on it to our nourishment and growth in grace. Shed abroad the love of God upon our hearts, and draw |933|them out in love to him. Fill us with thankfulness and holy joy, and with love to one another: comfort us by witnessing that we are the children of God. Confirm us for new obedience. Be the earnest of our inheritance, and seal us up to everlasting life.[260] Amen.

Then let the Minister deliver the Bread thus consecrated and broken to the Communicants, first taking and eating it himself as one of them, when he hath said,

TAKE ye, eat ye; This is the body of Christ which is broken for you; do this in remembrance of him.[261]

In like manner he shall deliver them the Cup, first drinking of it himself, when he hath said,

THIS cup is the new testament in Christ's blood, |or Christ's blood of the new testament,| which is shed for you for the remission of sins; drink ye all of it in remembrance of him.[262]

Let it be left to the Minister's choice, whether he will consecrate the bread and wine together, and break the bread and pour out the wine immediately; or whether he will consecrate and pour out the wine, when the Communicants have eaten the bread. If he do the latter, he must use the foregoing Prayers and expressions twice accordingly. And let it be left to his discretion, whether he will use any words at the breaking of the bread, and pouring out the wine, or not; and if the Minister choose to pray but once, at the consecration, commemoration, and delivery; let him pray as followeth, or to this sense:

ALMIGHTY God, thou art the Creator and the Lord of all. Thou art the Sovereign Majesty whom we have offended. Thou art our merciful Father, who hast given us thy Son to reconcile us to thyself; who hath ratified the new testament and covenant of grace with his most precious blood, and hath instituted this holy sacrament to be celebrated in memorial of him, till his coming. Sanctify these thy creatures of bread and wine, which, according to thy will, we set apart to this holy use, that they may be sacramentally the body and blood of thy Son Jesus Christ. And through his sacrifice and intercession, give us the pardon of all our sins, and be reconciled to us, and nourish us by the body and blood of Christ to everlasting life. And to that end, give us thy quickening Spirit to show Christ to our believing souls, that is here represented to our senses. Let him soften our hearts, and humble us for our sins, and cause us to feed on Christ by faith. Let him shed abroad thy love upon our hearts, and draw them on in love to thee, and fill us with holy joy and thankfulness, and fervent love to one another. Let him comfort us by witnessing that we are thy children, and confirm us for new obedience, and be the earnest of our inheritance, and seal us up to life everlasting; through Jesus Christ, our Lord and Saviour. Amen.

Let it be left to the Minister's discretion, whether to deliver the bread and wine to the people (at the table) only in general, each one taking it, and applying it to themselves; or to deliver it in general to so many as are in each particular form; or to put it into every person's hand: as also at what season to take the contribution for the poor. And let none of the people be forced to sit, stand, or kneel, in the act of receiving, whose judgment is against it.

The Participation being ended, let the Minister pray thus, or to this sense.

MOST glorious God, how wonderful is thy power and wisdom, thy holiness and justice, thy love and mercy in this work of our redemption, by the incarnation, life, death, resurrection, intercession, and dominion of thy Son! No power or wisdom in heaven or earth could have delivered us but thine. The angels desire to pry into this mystery, the heavenly host do celebrate it with praises, saying, Glory be to God in the highest; on earth peace, good-will towards men. The whole creation shall proclaim thy praises. Blessing, honour, glory, and power be unto him that sitteth upon the throne, and unto the Lamb for ever and ever. Worthy is the Lamb that was slain, to receive power, and honour, and glory; for he hath redeemed us to God by his blood, and made us kings and priests unto our God. Where sin abounded, grace hath abounded much more. And hast thou indeed forgiven us so great a debt, by so precious a ransom? Wilt thou indeed give us to reign with Christ in glory, and see my race, and love thee, and be beloved of thee for ever? Yea, Lord, thou hast forgiven us, and thou wilt glorify us, for thou art faithful that hast promised. With the blood of thy Son, with the sacrament, and with thy Spirit, thou hast sealed up to us these precious promises. And shall we not love thee, that hast thus loved us? Shall we not love thy servants, and forgive our neighbours their little debt? After all this shall we again forsake thee, and deal falsely in thy covenant? God forbid! O set our affections on the things above, where Christ sitteth at thy right hand. Let us no more mind earthly things, but let our conversation be in heaven, from whence we expect our Saviour to come and change us into the likeness of his glory. Teach us to do thy will, O God, and to follow him, who is the author of eternal salvation to all them that do obey him. Order our steps by thy word, and let not any iniquity have dominion over us. Let us not henceforth live unto ourselves, but unto him who died for us and rose again. Let us have no fellowship with the unfruitful works of darkness, but reprove them. And let our light so shine before men, that they may glorify thee. In simplicity, and godly sincerity, and not in fleshly wisdom, let us have our conversation in the world. Oh that our ways were so directed that we might keep thy statutes! Though Satan will be desirous again to sift us, and seek as a roaring lion to devour, strengthen us to stand against his wiles, and shortly bruise him under our feet. Accept us, O Lord, who resign ourselves unto thee, as thine own; and with our thanks and praise, present ourselves a living sacrifice to be acceptable through Christ, useful for thine honour: being made free from sin, and become thy servants, let us have our fruit unto holiness, and the end everlasting life, through Jesus Christ our Lord and Saviour.[263]Amen.

Next add this, or some such Exhortation, if there be time.

DEAR brethren, we have been here feasted with the Son of God at his table, upon his flesh and blood, in preparation for the feast of endless glory. You [934]have seen here represented, what sin deserveth, what Christ suffered, what wonderful love the God of infinite goodness hath expressed to us. You have had communion with the saints; you have renewed your covenant of faith, and thankful obedience unto Christ; you have received his renewed covenant of pardon, grace, and glory unto you. O carry hence the lively sense of these great and excellent things upon your hearts: you came not only to receive the mercy of an hour, but that which may spring up to endless joy: you came not only to do the duty of an hour, but to promise that which you must perform while you live on earth. Remember daily, especially when temptations to unbelief and sinful heaviness assault you, what pledges of love you here received; remember daily, especially when the flesh, the devil, or the world, would draw your hearts again from God, and temptations to sin are laid before you, what bonds God and your own consent have laid upon you. If you are penitent believers, you are now forgiven, and washed in the blood of Christ. O go your way, and sin no more: no more through wilfulness; and strive against your sins of weakness. Wallow no more in the mire, and return not to your vomit. Let the exceeding love of Christ constrain you, having such promises, to cleanse yourselves from all filthiness of flesh and spirit, perfecting holiness in the fear of God; and as a chosen generation, a royal priesthood, a holy nation, a peculiar people, to be zealous of good works, and show forth the praises of him that hath called you.

Next sing part of the Hymn in metre, or some other fit Psalm of praise (as the Twenty-third, One Hundred and Sixteenth, One Hundred and Third, or One Hundredth, &c.) And conclude with this or the like Blessing:

NOW the God of peace, which brought again from the dead our Lord Jesus Christ, that great Shepherd of the sheep, through the blood of the everlasting covenant, make you perfect in every good work, to do his will, working in you that which is well-pleasing in his sight, through Jesus Christ, to whom be glory for ever and ever. Amen.

THE CELEBRATION OF THE SACRAMENT OF BAPTISM.

LET no minister, that is therein unsatisfied, be forced against his judgment, to baptize the child of open atheists, idolaters, or infidels, or that are unbaptized themselves, or of such as do not competently understand the essentials of christianity, (what it is to be a christian,) and the essentials of baptism; nor of such as never, since they were baptized, did personally own their baptismal covenant, by a credible profession of faith and obedience, received and approved by some pastor of the church, as before confirmation is required, and in his Majesty's Declaration. Nor yet the child of parents justly excommunicate, or that live in any notorious, scandalous sin, or have lately committed such a sin, (as if the child be gotten in adultery or fornication,) and being justly convicted of it, refuseth penitently to confess it, and promise reformation. But if either of the parents be duly qualified, and present the child to be baptized, (or another for them in case they cannot be present,) the child is to be received unto baptism.

And if both the natural parents are infidels, excommunicate, or otherwise unqualified, yet if any become the pro-parents and owners of the child, and undertake to educate it in the faith of Christ, and fear of God, and so present it to be baptized, let it be done by a minister whose judgment doth approve it, but let no minister be forced to it against his judgment. Let the parents or owners come to the minister at some convenient time the week before, and acquaint him when they intend to offer their child to baptism, and give an account of their foresaid capacity, and receive his further ministerial assistance for the fuller understanding of the use and benefits of the sacrament, and their own duty. The font is to be placed to the greatest conveniency of the minister and people. The child or children being there presented, the minister may begin with this or the like speech directed to the parent or parents that present it.

THAT you may perform this service to God with understanding, you must know, that God having made man in his own image, to love and serve him, our first parents wilfully corrupted themselves by sin, and became the children of death, and the captives of Satan, who had overcome them by his temptation. And as by one man sin entered into the world, and death by sin, so death passed upon all, for that all have sinned, and come short of the glory of God. We are conceived in sin, and are by nature children of wrath; for who can bring a clean thing out of an unclean? By the offence of one, judgment came upon all men to condemnation. But the infinite wisdom and love of the Father hath sent his Son to be the Saviour of the world. The Word was made flesh, and dwelt on earth, and overcame the devil and the world; fulfilled all righteousness, and suffered for our sins upon the cross, and rose again, and reigneth in glory, and will come again, and judge the world in righteousness. In him God hath made and offered to the world a covenant of grace, and in it the pardon of sin to all true penitent believers, and power to be the sons of God and heirs of heaven. This covenant is extended to the seed also of the faithful, to give them the benefits suitable to their age, the parents dedicating them unto God, and entering them into the covenant, and so God in Christ will be their God, and number them with his people.

This covenant is to be solemnly entered into by baptism, which is a holy sacrament instituted by Christ, in which a person professing the christian faith (or the infant of such) is baptized in water into the name of the Father, Son, and Holy Ghost, in signification and solemnization of the holy covenant; in which, as a penitent believer, (or the seed of such,) he giveth up himself (or is by the parent given up) to God the Father, Son, and Holy Ghost, from henceforth (or from the time of natural capacity) to believe in, love, and fear this blessed Trinity, against the flesh, the devil, and the world; and this especially on the account of redemption; and is solemnly entered a visible member of Christ and his church, a child of God, and an heir of heaven. How great now is the mercy, and how great the duty that is before you! Is it a small mercy for this child to be accepted into the covenant of God, and washed from its original sin in the blood of Christ, which is signified and sealed by this sacramental washing in water, to be accepted as a member of Christ and of his church, where he vouchsafeth his protection and provision, and the means and Spirit of grace, and the renewed pardon of sin upon repentance, and for you to see this happiness of your child? The duty on [935]your part is, first to see that you are stedfast in the faith and covenant of Christ, that you perish not yourself, and that your child is indeed the child of a believer; and then you are believingly and thankfully to dedicate your child to God, and to enter it into the covenant in which you stand. And you must know, that your faith, and consent, and dedication will suffice for your children no longer than till they come to age themselves; and then they must own their baptismal covenant, and personally renew it, and consent, and give up themselves to God, or else they will not be owned by Christ. You must therefore acquaint them with the doctrine of the gospel, as they grow up, and with the covenant now made, and bring them up in the fear of the Lord. And when they are actually penitent believers, they must present themselves to the pastors of the church, to be approved and received into the communion of the adult believers.

If the persons be before well instructed in the nature of Baptism, and time require brevity, the Minister may omit the first part of this Speech, and begin at the description of Baptism, or after it. If there be need of satisfying the people of the duty of baptizing infants, the Minister may here do it; otherwise let the questions here immediately follow.

The Minister shall here say to the Parent, and the Parent answer as followeth.

IT being the faithful and their seed to whom the promises are made; and no man will sincerely dedicate his child to that God that he believeth not in himself; I therefore require you to make profession of your own faith.

Quest. Do you believe in God the Father Almighty, &c.?

Answ. All this I do unfeignedly believe.

Quest. Do you repent of your sins, and renounce the flesh, the devil, and the world, and consent to the covenant of grace, giving up yourself to God the Father,

Son, and Holy Ghost, as your Creator and reconciled Father, your Redeemer and your Sanctifier?

Answ. I do.

[Or thus rather, if the parent be fit to utter his own faith.]

Quest. Do you remain stedfast in the covenant which you made in baptism yourself?

Answ. Repenting of my sins, I do renounce the flesh, the devil, and the world, and I give up myself to God the Father, Son, and Holy Ghost, my Creator and reconciled Father, my Redeemer and my Sanctifier.

Quest. Do you present and dedicate this child unto God, to be baptized into this faith, and solemnly engaged in this covenant unto God the Father, Son, and Holy Ghost, against the flesh, the devil, and the world?

Answ. It is my desire, (or,) I do present and dedicate him for this end.

Quest. Do you here solemnly promise, that if God continue it with you till it be capable of instructions, you will faithfully endeavour to acquaint this child with the covenant in which he was here by you engaged, and to instruct and exhort him to perform this covenant, as ever he looks for the blessings of it, or to escape the curses and wrath of God; that is, that he renounce the flesh, the world, and the devil; and live not after them: and that he believe in this one God, in three Persons, the Father, Son, and Holy Ghost, his Creator, Redeemer, and Sanctifier. That he resign himself to him as his absolute Owner, and obey him as his supreme Governor, and love him as his most gracious Father, hoping to enjoy him as his felicity in endless glory?

Answ. I will faithfully endeavour it.

Quest. Will you to this end faithfully endeavour to cause him to learn the articles of the christian faith, the Lord's prayer, and the ten commandments, and to read or hear the holy Scriptures, and to attend on the public preaching of God's word? Will you endeavour, by your own teaching, and example, and restraint, to keep him from wickedness, and train him up in a holy life?

Answ. I will faithfully endeavour it by the help of God.

Then let the Minister pray thus, or to this sense:

O MOST merciful Father, by the first Adam sin entered into the world, and death by sin, and we are all by nature children of wrath; but thou hast given thy only Son, to be the Seed or the woman, the Saviour of the world, the Captain of our salvation, to put away sin by the sacrifice of himself, and to wash us in his blood, and reconcile us unto thee, and to renew us by the Holy Ghost, and to bruise Satan under our feet. In him thou hast established the covenant of grace, and hast appointed this holy sacrament of baptism for our solemn entrance into the bonds of the covenant, and stating us in the blessings of it, which thou extendest to the faithful and their seed. We dedicate and offer this child to thee, to be received into thy covenant and church. We beseech thee to accept him as a member of thy Son, and wash him in his blood from the guilt of sin, as the flesh is washed by this water. Be reconciled to him, and take him for thy child, renew him to the image of thy Son, make him a fellow-citizen with the saints, and one of thy household. Protect him and provide for him as thy own, and finally preserve him to thy heavenly kingdom, through Jesus Christ our Lord and Saviour.[264] Amen.

Then the Minister shall ask of the Parent the name of the child to be baptized, and naming him, shall either dip him under the water, or else pour the water upon his face, if he cannot be safely or conveniently dipt, and shall use these words without alteration.

I Baptize thee in the name of the Father, and of the Son, and of the Holy Ghost.

And he shall thus declare:

THIS child is now received by Christ's appointment into his church, and solemnly entered into the holy covenant, and engaged, if he lives to the use of reason, to rise with Christ to newness of life, as being buried with him by baptism, and to bear his cross, and confess Christ crucified, and faithfully to fight under his banner against the flesh, the devil, and the world, and to continue his faithful soldier and servant to the death, that he may receive the crown of life.

Then he shall give thanks and pray.

WE thank thee, most merciful Father, that when we had broken the law, and were condemned by it, thou hadst given us a Saviour, and life in him, and hast extended thy covenant of grace to believers, [936]and to their seed, and hast now received this child into thy covenant and church, as a member of Christ by this sacrament of regeneration. We beseech thee, let him grow up in holiness; and when he comes to years of discretion, let thy Spirit reveal unto him the mysteries of the gospel, and the riches of thy love in Jesus Christ; and cause him to renew and perform the covenant that he hath now made, and to resign himself, and all that he hath, entirely unto thee his Lord, to be subject and obedient to thee his Governor, and to love thee his Father with all his heart, and soul, and might; and adhere unto thee, and delight in thee as the portion of his soul, desiring and hoping to enjoy thee in everlasting glory. Save him from the lusts and allurements of the flesh, the temptations of the devil, and the baits of pleasure, profit, and honour of the world, and from all the corruptions of his own heart, and all the hurtful violence of his enemies. Keep him in communion with the saints, in the love and use of thy word and worship. Let him deny himself, and take up his cross and follow Christ the Captain of his salvation, and be faithful unto the death, and then receive the crown of life, through Jesus Christ our Saviour.[265]

Then use this Exhortation or the like to the Parents.

YOU that have devoted this child to God, and engaged it in covenant to him, must be thankful for so great a mercy to the child, and must be faithful in performing what you have promised on your parts, in instructing and educating this child in the faith and fear of God, that he may own and perform the covenant now made, and receive all the blessings which God hath promised. Hear what God hath made your duty, "Fathers, provoke not your children to wrath; but bring them up in the nurture and admonition of the Lord." "Train up a child in the way he should go, and when he is old he will not depart from it." "The rod and reproof give wisdom; but a child left to himself bringeth his mother to shame." "Thou shalt love the Lord thy God with all thy heart, and with all thy soul, and with all thy might: and these words which I command thee this day, shall be in thy heart; and thou shalt teach them diligently unto thy children, and thou shalt talk of them when thou sittest in the house, and when thou walkest by the way, and when thou liest down, and when thou risest up." Joshua saith, "As for me and my house, we will serve the Lord." And Paul saith of Timothy, "From a child thou hast known the holy Scriptures, which are able to make thee wise unto salvation, through faith which is in Christ Jesus."[266]

Then say to the People thus, or to this sense.

YOU have heard, beloved, how great a dignity we were advanced to in our baptism, to how great duty we are all engaged. O search and try, whether you have kept or broken the covenant which you made, and have lived according to the dignity of your calling. And if any of you be atheists, unbelievers, or ungodly, and love not God above all, and neglect Christ and his salvation, and are yet unsanctified, and live after the flesh, the devil, and the world, which you here renounced; as you love your souls, bewail your perfidious covenant-breaking with God. Trust not the water of baptism alone: if you are not "born again of the Spirit also, you cannot enter into the kingdom of God." Baptism will not save you, if you have not the answer of a good conscience unto God. "If any man have not the Spirit of Christ, the same is none of his." Much less those wretches that hate sanctification, and despise and scorn a holy life, when they were by baptism engaged to the Holy Ghost the Sanctifier. Can you think to be saved by the covenant which you keep not? O no! Your perfidiousness aggravateth your sin and misery. "When thou vowest a vow to God, defer not to pay it, for he hath no pleasure in fools: pay that which thou hast vowed: better it is that thou shouldest not vow, than that thou shouldest vow and not pay." O bless the Lord, that it is a covenant of such grace which is tendered to you. That upon true repentance and conversion, even your covenant-breaking shall be forgiven; and therefore penitently cast down yourselves before the Lord, and believingly cast yourselves on Christ, and yield to the teachings and sanctifying operations of the Holy Ghost. Yet know the day of your visitation, and forsake the flesh, the devil, and the world, and turn to God with all your hearts, and give up yourselves entirely to your Creator, Redeemer, and Sanctifier, and he will have mercy upon you, and will abundantly pardon you. But if you still live after the flesh, you shall die: and if you continue to neglect this great salvation, there remaineth no more sacrifice for sin, but a certain fearful looking for of judgment, and fire, which shall devour the adversaries.[267]

Let no children be privately baptized, nor any Minister forced to baptize them any where, besides in the public assembly, unless upon some special weighty cause. If there be occasion for baptizing the adult, let the minister accordingly suit his expressions.

OF CATECHISING, AND THE APPROBATION OF THOSE THAT ARE TO BE ADMITTED TO THE LORD'S SUPPER.

Seeing none can be saved at years of discretion, that do not actually believe, and personally give up themselves in covenant to God the Father, Son, and Holy Ghost; therefore as parents must do their parts, so ministers must catechise the ignorant, and diligently labour to cause them both to learn the form of wholesome words, (even the Lord's prayer and the ten commandments, and some brief, yet full and sound catechism,) and to understand the meaning of them, and to engage their hearts into the love of God, and a holy obedience to his laws.

To this end, let the minister, either every Lord's day, before the evening prayers, or at some convenient hour, or on some other day of the week, as oft as he can, examine publicly such as are not admitted to the Lord's supper, and take an account of their learning, and understanding the creed, the ten commandments, the Lord's prayer, and the catechism. And let him by questioning and explication, help them to understand them. And let such of the several families of the parish come in their turns, when they are called by the minister to be thus catechised. Also let the minister either go to their houses, or rather appoint the persons aforesaid in their courses at a certain hour and place, (in the church or any other [937]fit place,) to come to him for personal instructions, where he may confer with those that are unmeet to be catechised publicly, or unwilling to submit to it; and there with humble, prudent, serious instruction and exhortation, let him endeavour to acquaint them with the substance of christian faith and duty, and to help them to make sure their calling and election, and to prepare for death and judgment, and exhort them to love and to good works, and warn them lest they be hardened through the deceitfulness of sin. But let him not in public or private meddle with impertinencies, or spend the time about smaller matters, or singular opinions, nor sift people to know things unfit or unnecessary to be disclosed, nor meddle with matters that do not concern him as a minister to inquire after; but help them to learn, and understand, and practise the christian religion expressed in the catechism.

The Catechism.

See the Rubric for Catechism and Confirmation in the Common Prayer, and also his Majesty's Declaration concerning ecclesiastical affairs.

Let none be admitted by the minister to the sacrament of the Lord's supper, till they have at years of discretion understood the meaning of their baptismal covenant, and with their own mouths, and their own consent openly before the church, ratified and confirmed, and also promised, that by the grace of God, they will evermore endeavour themselves faithfully to observe and keep such things as by their mouth and confession they have assented to; and so being instructed in the christian religion, do openly make a credible profession of their own faith, and promise to be obedient to the will of God.

A profession is credible, when it is made understandingly, seriously, voluntarily, deliberately, and not nullified by contradiction in word or deed. And that profession is incredible, that is made ignorantly, ludicrously, forcedly, rashly, or that is nullified by verbal or practical contradiction. And it must be practice first, that must make words credible, when the person by perfidiousness hath forfeited his credit. It is not private persons only, but the pastors of the church that must approve of this profession. Therefore, before any are admitted to the Lord's supper, they shall give a good account of their knowledge, faith, and christian conversation conformable thereunto, unto the pastors of their respective congregations, or else shall produce a certificate, that they have been approved or admitted to the Lord's supper in another congregation, of which they were members, and that by an allowed minister, upon such approved profession as aforesaid.

If the person be able and willing, let him before the congregation give the aforesaid account at large, of his knowledge, faith, and obedience; but if through backwardness, or disability for public speech, he shall refuse it, let him make the same profession privately to the minister, and own it in the assembly, when the minister shall declare it, and ask him whether he owns it. But unless it be in case of some extraordinary natural imperfection, and disability of utterance, let him at least openly recite the creed, and profess his consent to the covenant with God the Father, Son, and Holy Ghost.

Let the minister of every parish keep a double register: one of the names of all that are there baptized; another of the names of all that are approved upon their foresaid credible profession, and so admitted into the number of communicants, or that have a certificate of such approbation, regularly elsewhere performed.

And if confirmation be continued, let his Majesty's Declaration be observed, requiring, That confirmation be rightly and solemnly performed, by the information, and with the consent, of the minister of the place.

Let no minister be enforced to admit any himself to the Lord's supper, who hath been clancularly and irregularly approved.

Those that after this approbation prove scandalous offenders, shall not by the minister be suffered to partake of the Lord's table, until they have openly declared themselves to have truly repented, and amended their former naughty lives.

OF THE CELEBRATION OF MATRIMONY.

BEFORE the solemnizing of marriage between any persons, their purpose of marriage shall be published by the minister, three several Lord's days in the congregation, at the place or places of their most usual abode respectively. And of this publication, the minister who is to join them in marriage shall have sufficient testimony, before he proceed to solemnize the marriage; the parents' consent being first sufficiently made known.

At the celebration, the minister shall either by a sermon, or other exhortation, open to them the institution, ends, and use of marriage, with the conjugal duties which they are faithfully to perform to each other. And then shall demand of them whether it be their desire and purpose to be joined together in the bond of the marriage covenant; and if they answer affirmatively, he shall say to them,

I REQUIRE and charge you, as you will answer at the dreadful day of judgment, (when the secrets of all hearts shall be disclosed,) that if either of you do know any impediment by pre-contract or otherwise, why you may not lawfully be joined together in marriage, you discover it, and proceed not.

If no impediment be discovered by them or others, he shall proceed to pray.

MOST merciful Father, who hast ordained marriage for mutual help, and for the increase of mankind with a legitimate issue, and of the church with a holy seed, and for prevention of uncleanness; bless thy own ordinance to these persons, that entering this state of marriage in thy fear, they may there entirely devote themselves unto thee, and be faithful in all conjugal affections and duties unto each other; If they be young, it may be said, Bless them with children, and let them be devoted, &c. [and if thou bless them with children,] let them be devoted unto thee, and accepted as thine own, and blessed with thy grace, and educated in thy fear. Subdue those corruptions that would make their lives unholy or uncomfortable, and deliver them from temptations to impiety, worldliness, unquietness, discontent, or disaffection to each other, or to any unfaithfulness to thee or to each other. Make them meet helps to each other in thy fear, and in the lawful management of the affairs of this world. Let them not hinder, but provoke one another to love and to good works; and foreseeing the day of their separation by death, let them spend their days in a holy preparation, and live here together as the heirs [938]of life that must rejoice at the great marriage day of the Lamb, and live for ever with Christ and all the holy angels and saints in the presence of thy glory.[268] Amen.

330

The woman if she be under Parents or Governors, being by one of them, or some deputed by them, given to be married, the man with his right hand shall take the woman by the right hand, and shall say,

I A. do take thee B. to be my married wife, and do promise and covenant in the presence of God, and before this congregation, to be a loving and faithful husband to thee, till God shall separate us by death.

Then the woman shall take the man by the right hand with her right hand, and say,

I B. do take thee A. to be my married husband, and I do promise and covenant in the presence of God, and before this congregation, to be a loving, obedient, and faithful wife unto thee, till God shall separate us by death.

Then let the Minister say,

These two persons, A. and B. being lawfully married according to God's ordinance, I do pronounce them husband and wife. And those whom God hath conjoined, let no man put asunder.

Next he may read the duty of Husbands and Wives out of Eph. v. 2; Col. iv. 2; 1 Pet. iii.; and Psalm cxxviii. or some other pertinent Psalm, may be said or sung: and let the minister exhort them to their several duties, and then pray:

MOST merciful Father, let thy blessings rest upon these persons now joined in lawful marriage; sanctify them and their conversations, their family, estates, and affairs, unto thy glory. Furnish them with love to thee and to each other, with meekness, patience, and contentedness. Let them not live unto the flesh, but unto the Spirit, that of the Spirit they may reap everlasting life, through Jesus Christ our Lord and Saviour.[269]Amen.

Then let him conclude with a Benediction.

GOD Almighty, the Creator, Redeemer, and Sanctifier, bless you in your souls and bodies, families and affairs, and preserve you to his heavenly kingdom. Amen.

THE VISITATION OF THE SICK, AND THEIR COMMUNION.

THE visitation of the sick being a private duty, and no part of the public Liturgy of the church, and the case of the sick being so exceeding various, as to soul and body; and it being requisite that ministers be able to suit their exhortations and prayers to the condition of the sick, but the words of such exhortations and prayers be left to their prudence.

So urgent is the necessity of the sick, and so seasonable and advantageous the opportunity, that ministers may not negligently overpass them, but in love and tenderness instruct them according to their several conditions; endeavouring the conversion of the ungodly, the strengthening of the weak, and comforting such as need consolation; directing them how to improve their afflictions, and helping them to be sensible of the evil of sin, the negligences and miscarriages of their lives, the vanity of the world, their necessity of a Saviour, the sufficiency of Christ, the certainty and excellency of the everlasting glory; exhorting them to repentance and to faith in Christ, and to set their affections on the things above; and (if they are penitent believers) comfortably to hope for the kingdom which God hath promised to them that love him, committing their souls to their Redeemer, and quietly resting in the will, and love, and promises of God; resolving if God shall recover them to health, to redeem the time, and live the rest of their lives unto his glory; and being willing, if it be their appointed time, to depart and be with Christ. And they must be exhorted to forgive such as have wronged them, and to be reconciled to those with whom they have been at variance, and to make a pious, just, and charitable disposal of their worldly estates.

THE ORDER OF SOLEMNIZING THE BURIAL OF THE DEAD.

IT is agreeable to nature and religion, that the burial of christians be solemnly and decently performed. As to the cases, Whether the corpse shall be carried first into the church, that is to be buried in the church-yard; and whether it shall be buried before the sermon, reading, or prayer, or after, or in the midst of the reading, or whether any prayer shall be made at the grave, for the living; let no christians uncharitably judge one another about these things. Let no people keep up groundless usages, that being suspicious grieve their minister and offend their brethren. Let no minister that scrupleth the satisfying of people's ungrounded desires in such things, be forced to do it against his conscience; and let ministers that do use any of these customs or ceremonies, have liberty, when they suspect that the people desire them upon some error, to profess against that error, and teach the people better.

Whether the minister come with the company that brings the corpse from the house, or whether he meet them, or receive them at the burial-place, is to be left to his own discretion. But while he is with them, let him gravely discourse of man's mortality, and the useful truths and duties thence to be inferred: and either at the grave, or in the reading place, or pulpit, by way of sermon, according to his discretion, let him (at least if it be desired) instruct and exhort the people concerning death, and the life to come, and their necessary preparation; seeing the spectacle of mortality, and the season of mourning, do tend to prepare men for a sober, considerate entertainment of such instructions: and he may read such scriptures as may mind them of death, resurrection, and eternal life, as 1 Cor. xv. or from verse 10 to the end, and Job i. 21; xix. 25, 26, 27; John xi. 25, 26; v. 28, 29. And his prayer shall be suited to the occasion.

Whenever the rain, snow, or coldness of the season, make it unhealthful to the minister or people to stand out of doors, at least then let the reading, exhortation, and prayers, be used within the church.

[939]

OF EXTRAORDINARY DAYS OF HUMILIATION AND THANKSGIVING, AND ANNIVERSARY FESTIVALS.

WHEN great afflictions lie upon the church, or any special part or members of it, or when any great sins have been committed among them, it is meet that in public, by fasting and prayer, we humble ourselves before the Lord, for the averting of his displeasure; and on such occasions it is the pastor's duty to confess his own and the people's sins, with penitence, and tenderness of heart, and by his doctrine and exhortation, to endeavour effectually to bring the people to the sight and sense of their sin, and the deserts of it, and to a firm resolution of better obedience for the time to come, being importunate with God in prayer for pardon and renewed grace.

Upon the receipt of great and extraordinary mercies, the church (having opportunity) is to assemble for public thanksgiving unto God, and the minister to stir up the people to a lively sense of the greatness of those mercies, and joyfully to celebrate the praises of God, the author of them. And it is not unmeet on these days to express our joy in feasting and outward signs of mirth, provided they be used moderately, spiritually, and inoffensively, and not to gratify our sensual desires, and that we relieve the poor in their necessities (which also on days of humiliation and other seasons we must not forget). The occasions of such days of humiliation and thanksgiving being so various, as cannot be well suited by any standing forms, the minister is to apply himself to the respective duties, suitable to the particular occasions.

Though it be not unlawful or unmeet to keep anniversary commemoration by festivals, of some great and notable mercies to the church or state, the memory whereof should be transmitted to posterity; nor to give any persons their due honour who have been the instruments thereof: yet because the festivals of the church's institution now observed, are much abused, and many sober, godly persons, ministers, and others, are unsatisfied of the lawfulness of the celebrating them as holidays, let the abuse be restrained; and let not the religious observation of those days by public worship, be forced upon any that are thus unsatisfied, provided they forbear all offensive behaviour thereupon.

OF PRAYER AND THANKSGIVING FOR PARTICULAR MEMBERS OF THE CHURCH.

BESIDES the petitions that are put up for all in such distresses, in the general prayer, it is meet that persons in dangerous sickness, or other great affliction of body or mind, and women that are near the time of child-bearing, when they desire it, shall be particularly recommended to God in the public prayers of the church. Because all the members constitute one body, and must have the same care one for another, as suffering all with one that suffereth, and rejoicing all with one that is honoured. And the effectual fervent prayer of the righteous, especially of the whole congregation, availeth much with God. But because diseases, distresses, and grief of mind, are so various that no forms that are particular can suit them all; and because every minister should be able to suit his prayers to such various necessities of the people; we desire that it may be left to his discretion to pray for such according *to their several cases, before or after sermon. But we desire that except in case of sudden necessity, they may send in their bills of request to him the night before, that he may consider of their cases, and may publish only such, and in such expressions, as in prudence he shall judge meet for the ears of the assembly.*

In the more ordinary cases of persons in sickness, danger, and distress, and that are delivered from them; these following prayers may be used, or such like.

A Prayer for the Sick, that is in hopes of Recovery.

MOST merciful Father, though our sin doth find us out, and we are justly afflicted for our transgressions, yet are we not consumed in thy wrath; but thou punishest us less than our iniquities do deserve: though thou causest grief, yet wilt thou have compassion according to the multitude of thy mercies, for thou dost not willingly afflict and grieve the children of men. Thou revivest the spirit of the humble, and the heart of the contrite ones, for thou wilt not contend for ever, neither wilt thou be always wroth, for the spirit would fail before thee, and the soul which thou hast made. Look down in tender mercy on the affliction of this thy servant. O Lord, rebuke him not in thy wrath; neither chasten him in thy hot displeasure. All his desire is before thee, and his groaning is not hid from thee; have mercy upon him, O Lord, for he is weak. O Lord, heal him, whose bones and soul is vexed. In death there is no remembrance of thee: in the grave who shall give thee thanks? Remember that we are but flesh; a wind that passeth away and cometh not again. Wilt thou break a leaf driven to and fro? and wilt thou pursue the dry stubble? Remember not the iniquities of his youth, or his transgressions: look upon his affliction, and his pain, and forgive all his sins. Though the sorrows of death do compass him about, yet if it be for thy glory and his good, recover him, and let him live and praise thy name. Rebuke his sickness; direct unto such means as thou wilt bless. In the time of his trouble we call upon thee, do thou deliver him, and let him glorify thee: however, show him the sin that doth offend thee; let him search and try his ways, and confess and turn from his iniquity, and let it be good for him that he was afflicted. Let this be the fruit of it, to purge and take away his sin, that being chastened of the Lord, he may not be condemned with the world. And though chastisement for the present seemeth not to be joyous, but grievous, yet afterwards let it yield the peaceable fruit of righteousness to this thy servant, that is exercised therein. In the mean time, O Lord, be thou his portion, who art good to the soul that seeketh thee, and waiteth for thee. Let him patiently and silently bear thy yoke; let him hope and quietly wait for thy salvation: considering that thou wilt not cast off for ever; that thy anger is but for a moment, but in thy favour is life. Weeping may endure for a night, but joy cometh in the morning: and that whom thou lovest, thou chastenest, and scourgest every son whom thou receivest; and that if he endure chastening, thou dealest with him as a son. If he [940]be recovered, let him devote himself entirely to they glory: that when thou hast put off his sackcloth and mourning, and girded him with gladness, he may speak thy praise, and give thee thanks. If he receive the sentence of death in himself, let it cause him to trust in thee that raisest the dead, knowing that as thou didst raise up the Lord Jesus, thou wilt raise him up also by Jesus: therefore suffer not his hope to faint; but though his outward man perish, yet let his inner man be renewed from day to day; and let him live by faith, and look at the things which are not seen, ever at the exceeding eternal weight of glory. Let him be found in Christ, not having his own righteousness, but that which is of God by faith. Restrain the tempter, and deliver thy servant from the sinful fears of death, by Christ, who, through death destroyed the devil that had the power of death; that he may find that death hath lost its sting, and triumph over it by faith in him, through whom we are made more than conquerors. That, by faith and love, his soul may now ascend unto his Father and our Father, and to his God and our God; and is gone to prepare a place for us; and hath promised, that where he is, there his servants shall be also, that they may behold the glory which thou hast given him. Magnify thyself in his body, whether by life or death, and safely bring him into thy glorious

333

presence, where is fulness of joy, and everlasting pleasures, through Jesus Christ our Life and Righteousness.[270] Amen.

A Prayer for Women drawing near the time of Child-bearing.

MOST merciful Father, who hast justly sentenced woman, that was first in the transgression, to great and multiplied sorrows, and particularly in sorrow to bring forth children; yet grantest preservation and relief, for the propagation of mankind. Be merciful to this thy servant; be near her with thy present help, in the needful time of trouble; and though in travail she hath sorrow, give her strength to bring forth. Being delivered, let her remember no more the anguish, for joy that a child is born into the world. Bless her in the fruit of her body; and being safely delivered, let her return thee hearty thanks, and devote it and the rest of her life to thy service, through Jesus Christ our Saviour.[271] Amen.

A Thanksgiving for those that are restored from Dangerous Sickness.

WE thank thee, O most gracious God, that thou hast heard us when we cried unto thee, for thy servant in his weakness and distress; that thou hast not turned away our prayer nor thy mercy from him. We cried to thee, and thou hast delivered and healed him, thou hast brought him from the grave, thou hast kept him alive, that he should not go down into the pit, thou hast forgiven his iniquity, and healed his diseases, thou hast redeemed his life from destruction, and hast crowned him with loving-kindness and tender mercies, thou hast not deprived him of the residue of his years, thou hast repented thee of the evil. His age is not departed; thou hast renewed his youth, and given him to see man, with the inhabitants of the world; and to see the goodness of the Lord in the land of the living. Day and night thy hand was heavy upon him, but thou hast turned away thy wrath, and hast forgiven the iniquity of his sin: for this every one that is godly shall pray unto thee in a time of trouble. Thou art a hiding-place, thou preservest us from trouble: when our flesh and our heart faileth us, thou art the strength of our heart, and our portion for ever; indeed, Lord, thou art good unto thine Israel; even to such as are clean of heart. Many are the afflictions of the righteous, but thou deliverest them out of all: though all the day long they be afflicted, and chastened every morning, yet are they continually with thee; thou holdest them by thy right hand; thou art a present help in trouble, when all the help of man is vain. Let thy servant love thee, because thou hast heard his voice and supplication. Let him offer unto thee the sacrifice of thanksgiving; and pay his vows to the Most High; and take the cup of salvation, and call upon thee all his days. Let him be wholly devoted to thy praise, and glorify thee in soul and body, as being thine, and seasonably depart in peace unto thy glory; through Jesus Christ, our Life and Righteousness.[272] Amen.

A Thanksgiving for the Deliverance of Women in Child-bearing.

WE return thee thanks, most gracious God, that thou hast heard our prayers for this thy handmaid; and hast been her help in the time of her necessity, and delivered her from her fears and sorrows. Death and life are in thy power; thou killest, and thou makest alive; thou bringest down to the grave, and thou bringest up; thou makest the barren to keep house, and to be a joyful mother of children. We thank thee, that thou hast given thy servant to see the fruit of her womb, and that thou hast brought her again to thy holy assembly, to go with the multitude to thy house, and worship thee with the voice of joy and praise, that she may enter into thy gates with thanksgiving, and into thy courts with praise, and we may all be thankful to thee on her behalf, and speak good of thy name. Thou art good, O Lord, to all, and thy tender mercies are over all thy works; thou preservest them that love thee; thou raisest up them that are bowed down; thou fulfillest the desire of them that fear thee; thou also dost hear their cry, and save them. Command thy blessing yet upon thy servant and her offspring; let her not forget thee and thy mercies, but let her devote the life which thou hast given her to thy service, and educate her offspring, as a holy seed, in the nurture and admonition of the Lord. And as thou hast said, that thy curse is in the house of the wicked, but thou blessest the habitation of the just; let her and her house serve thee, and let holiness to the Lord be written upon all wherewith thou blessest her: let her make thee her refuge and habitation. Give her the ornament of a meek and quiet spirit, which in thy sight is of great price. Let her not love the world, nor mind earthly things, but use the world as not abusing of it; seeing the time is short, and the fashion of this world passeth away. Restore her soul, and lead her in the paths of righteousness: though she must walk through the valley of the shadow of death, let her fear no evil. Let thy goodness and [941]mercy follow her all the days of her life, and let her dwell for ever in thy glorious presence, through Jesus Christ, our Lord and Saviour.[273] Amen.

If the Child be dead, those passages which imply its living must be omitted; and if the Woman be such as the Church hath cause to judge ungodly, the Thanksgiving must be in words more agreeable to her condition, if any be used.

OF PASTORAL DISCIPLINE, PUBLIC CONFESSION, ABSOLUTION, AND EXCLUSION FROM THE HOLY COMMUNION OF THE CHURCH.

THE recital of the curses are said in the book of Common Prayer, to be instead of the godly discipline of the primitive church, till it can be restored again, which is much to be wished, which is the putting of notorious sinners to open penitence. His Majesty's Declaration concerning ecclesiastical affairs, determineth that all public diligence be used for the instruction and reformation of scandalous offenders, whom the minister shall not suffer to partake of the Lord's table, until they have openly declared themselves to have truly repented and amended their former naughty lives, provided there be place for due appeals to superior powers.

And the law of Christ commandeth, that if thy brother trespass against thee, go and tell him his faults between him and thee alone: if he shall hear thee, thou hast gained thy brother, but if he will not hear thee, then take with thee one or two more, that in the mouth of two or three witnesses, every word may be established; and if he shall neglect to hear them, tell it unto the church; but if he shall neglect to hear the church, let him be unto thee as a heathen man, or as a publican. And it is the office of the pastors of the several congregations, not only to teach the people in general, and guide them in the celebration of the public worship, but also to oversee them, and watch over each member of their flock particularly; to preserve them from errors, heresies, divisions, and other sins, defending the truth, confuting gainsayers and seducers, instructing the ignorant, exciting the negligent, encouraging the despondent, comforting the afflicted, confirming the weak, rebuking and admonishing the disorderly and scandalous, and directing all according to their needs in the matters of their salvation; and the people in such needs should have ordinary recourse to them, as the officers of Christ, for guidance, and resolution of their doubts; and for assistance in making their salvation sure; and in proving, maintaining, or restoring the peace of their consciences, and spiritual comfort.[274]

If therefore any member of the church be a scandalous sinner, and the crime be either notorious or fully proved, let the pastor admonish him, and set before him the particular command of God which he transgresseth, the supreme authority of God which he despiseth, the promises and mercies which he treadeth under foot, and the curse and dreadful condemnation which he draweth upon himself. Let this be done with great compassion and tender love to the offender's soul, and with gravity, reverent and serious importunity, as beseemeth men employed on the behalf of God, for the saving of a soul; and yet with judgment, and cautelous prudence, not taking that for sin which is no sin, nor that for a gross and scandalous sin, which is but an ordinary human frailty; not dealing as unreverently with a superior as with an inferior; not making that public which should be concealed; nor reproving before others when it should be done more secretly; nor unreasonably speaking to those who through drink or passion are incapable of the benefit; nor yet offending by bashfulness, or the fear of man, or lukewarmness, negligence, or slighting over great offences, on the other extreme.

Prudence also requireth them to be cautelous of over-meddling, where the magistrate's honour or concernment, or the church's unity or peace, or the reputation of others, or the interest of their ministry, requireth them to forbear.

These cautions observed, if the scandalous offender continue impenitent, or unreformed, after due admonitions and patience, let the pastor in the congregation, when he is present, rebuke him before all, that the church may sufficiently disown the crime, and others may see the odiousness and danger of the sin. But let this also be with the love and prudence before mentioned.

If the offender in obstinacy will not be there, the pastor may open the crime before the congregation: and present or absent, (in case he remain impenitent,) if the case will bear so long a delay, it is convenient, that the pastor publicly pray for his conviction and repentance, that he may be saved.

And this he may do one, or two, or three, or more days, as the nature of the case and prudence shall direct him.

If during these means for his recovery (after the proof of the crime) there be a communion of the church in the Lord's supper, let the pastor require him to forbear, and not suffer him to partake of the Lord's table.

If yet the offender remain impenitent, let the pastor openly declare him unmeet for the communion of the church, and require him to abstain from it, and require the church to avoid communion with him. And let him bind him by the denunciations of the threatenings of God against the impenitent.

But before this is done, let no necessary consultation with other pastors, or concurrence of the church, be neglected: and after let there be place for due appeals, and let ministers consent to give account when they are accused of mal-administration.

But if, after private admonition, (while the offence is such as requireth not public confession,) the sinner be penitent, let the minister privately apply to his consolation the promises of the gospel, with such cautelous prudence, as is most suitable to his condition.

And if he repent not till after public admonition, or that the scandal be so great and notorious, as that a public confession is necessary, let him, at a seasonable time appointed by the pastor, with remorse of conscience, and true contrition, confess his sin before the congregation, and heartily lament it, and clear the honour of his christian profession which he had stained, and crave the prayers of the church to God for pardon and reconciliation through Christ, and also crave the ministerial absolution and restoration to the communion of the church, and profess his resolution to do so no more; but to live in new obedience to God, desiring also their prayers for corroborating and preserving grace.

It is only a credible profession of repentance, that is to be accepted by the church.

The foregoing cautions must be carefully observed in such confessions, that they be not made to the injuring of the magistrate, or of the church, or of the reputation of others, or of the life, estate, or liberty of the offender, or to any other shame than [942]is necessary to the manifesting of his repentance, and the clearing of his profession, and the righting of any that he hath wronged, and the honour and preservation of the church.

When he hath made a credible profession of repentance, it is the pastor's duty, ministerially to declare him pardoned by Christ, but in conditional terms. [If his repentance be sincere.] And to absolve him from the censure of non-communion with the church, if he was under such a censure before his penitence, and to declare him meet for their communion, and to encourage him to come, and require the church to entertain him into their communion with gladness, and not upbraid him with his fall, but rejoice in his recovery, and endeavour his confirmation and preservation for the time to come: and it is his duty accordingly to admit him to communion, and theirs to have loving communion with him: all which the penitent person must believingly, lovingly, and joyfully receive. But if any by notorious perfidiousness, or frequent covenant-breaking, have forfeited the credit of their words, or have long continued in the sin which they do confess, so that their forsaking it hath no proof; the church then must have testimony of the actual reformation of such as these, before they may take their professions and promises as credible: yet here the difference of persons and offences is so great, that this is to be much left to the prudence of pastors that are present, and acquainted with the persons and circumstances of the case. In the transacting of all this, these following forms, to be varied as the variety of cases do require, may be made use of.

A Form of Public Admonition to the Impenitent.

The sin may be named and aggravated when it is convenient.

A. B. you are convict of a gross and scandalous sin; you have been admonished and entreated to repent. The promises of mercies to the penitent, and the threatenings of God against the impenitent, have not been concealed from you. We have waited in hope of your repentance, as having compassion on your soul, and desiring your salvation; but we must say with grief, you have hitherto disappointed us. We are certain from the word of God, that you must be penitent, if ever you will be pardoned, and that except you repent, you shall everlastingly perish. To acquaint you publicly with this, and yet here to offer you mercy from the Lord, is the next duty laid upon us for your recovery. Oh! blame us not, if, knowing the terrors of the Lord, we thus persuade you, and are loth to leave you in the power of Satan, and loth to see you cast out into perdition, and that your blood should be required at our hands, as not having discharged our duty to prevent it.[275]

Be it known unto you therefore, that it is the God of heaven and earth, the great, the jealous, and the terrible God, whose laws you have broken, and whose authority you despise. You refuse his government, and is coming with ten thousands of his saints, to execute judgment upon all, and to convince all that are ungodly of their ungodly deeds and speeches; who hath told us that "evil shall not dwell with him." "The foolish shall not stand in his sight." "He hateth all workers of iniquity." "The ungodly shall not stand in judgment, nor sinners in the congregation of the righteous." God hath not his laws in vain. "Though the wicked contemn God, and say in their hearts he will not require it;" "yet their damnation slumbereth not, they are reserved to the day of judgment, to be punished." "And he seeth that their day is coming." If men cut off the lives of those that break their laws, will God be outfaced by the pride and stubbornness of sinners? He will not; you shall know he will not; he threateneth not in jest. "Who hath hardened himself against him, and hath prospered?" "Are you not as chaff and stubble? and is not our God a consuming fire?" "If briers and thorns be set against him in battle, will he not go through them, and burn them up together?" "Can your heart endure, or your hands be strong, in the day when God shall deal with you? It is the Lord that hath spoken it, and he will do it." What will you do, when you must bear with the pains of hell from God, that now can scarce endure to be thus openly and plainly warned of it? If we to please you should be silent and betray you, do you think the God of heaven will fear or flatter you to please a worm? "Do you provoke the Lord to jealousy? are you stronger than he?" O man! for your soul's sake, let not Satan abuse your understanding, and sin befool you. Must you not die? And doth not judgment follow, when all secrets shall be opened, and God will no more entreat you to confess. "Behold, the Judge standeth at the door." Will sin go then with you for as light a matter as it doth now? Will you then deny it, or will you stand to all the reasonings, or excuses, by which you would now extenuate or cover it? Will you defend it as your friend; and be angry with ministers and reprovers as your enemies? Or will you not mourn at last, (with weeping and gnashing of teeth,) and say, "How have I hated instruction, and my heart despised reproof; and have not obeyed the voice of my teachers, nor inclined mine ear to them that instructed me!" "Oh that you were wise, that you understood this, and that you would consider your latter end!" Believe God's wrath before you feel it: be convinced by the word and servants of the Lord, before you are confounded by the dreadfulness of his majesty. Yet there is hope; but shortly there will be none, if you neglect it. Yet "if you confess and forsake your sins, you shall have mercy; but if you cover them, you shall not prosper. And if, being oft reproved, you harden your neck, you shall suddenly be destroyed, and that without remedy." "Be not deceived, God is not mocked. Whatsoever you sow, that shall you also reap." O man! you know not what it is to deal with an offended and revenging God. Nor what it is to hear Christ say, "Depart from me, ye workers of iniquity; I never knew you: depart from me, ye wicked, into everlasting fire." You know not what it is to be shut out of heaven, and concluded under utter desperation; and in hell to look back upon this obstinate impenitence, and rejecting of the mercy that would have saved you; and there to have conscience telling you for ever, what it is that you have done. Did you know what this is, could you, think a penitent confessing and forsaking your sin to be a condition too hard for the preventing of such a doleful state? O no! You know not what a case you are casting your immortal soul into. The Lord give you repentance, that you may never know it by experience. To prevent this, is our business with you: we delight not to displease or shame you. But God hath told us, "That if any do err from the truth, and one convert him, let him know, that he which converteth a sinner from the error of his way, shall save [943]a soul from death, and shall hide a multitude of sins." I do therefore by the command, and in the name of Jesus Christ, require and beseech you, that you do, without any more delay, confess your sins and heartily bewail them; and beg pardon of them, and resolve and promise by the help of God to do so no more. And bless God that you have an advocate with the Father, Jesus Christ the righteous, whose blood will cleanse you from your sins, if you penitently confess them; and that mercy may be yet had on so easy terms. If you had any sense of your sin and misery, or any sense of the dishonour done to God, or of the wrong that you have done to others, and of the usefulness of your penitent confession, and amendment, to the reparation of all these, you would cast yourself in the dust, in shame and grief before the Lord, and before the church. "To-day, therefore, if you will hear his voice, harden not your heart, lest God forsake you, and give you over unto your own heart's lust, to walk in your own counsels, and resolve in his wrath, you shall never enter into his rest." And then God and this congregation will be witnesses that you were warned; and your blood will be upon your own head. But if, in penitent confession, you fly to Christ, and loathe yourself for your iniquities, and heartily forsake them, I have authority to promise you free forgiveness, and that your iniquity shall not be your ruin.[276]

A Form of Confession, to be made before the Congregation.

* Here the sin must be named and aggravated, when by the pastor it is judged requisite.

I DO confess before God and this congregation, that I have greatly sinned. * I have offended and dishonoured God, wronged the church, and the souls of others. I have deserved to be forsaken of the Lord, and cast out of his presence and communion of saints, into desperation, and remediless misery in hell. I am no more worthy to be called thy son, or to have a name or place among thy servants. I do here declare mine iniquity, and am sorry for my sins; they are gone over my head as a heavy burden, they are too heavy for me, they take hold upon me. I am ashamed, as unworthy to look up towards heaven, but my hope is in the blood and grace of Christ, who made his life a sacrifice for sin, and came to seek and save that which was lost; whose grace aboundeth where sin hath abounded. The Lord be merciful to me a sinner. I humbly beg of the congregation that they will earnestly pray, that God will wash me thoroughly from mine iniquity, and cleanse me from my sins; that he will forgive them, and blot them out, and hide his face from them, and remember them no more; that he will not cast me away from his presence, nor forsake me as I have forsaken him, nor deal with me according to my deserts: but that he will create in me a clean heart, and renew a right spirit in me, and grant me the joy of his salvation. And I beg pardon of the church, and all that I have wronged; and resolve by the grace of God to do so no more; but to walk more watchfully as before the Lord. And I desire all that are ungodly, that they think never the worse of the laws, or ways, or servants of the Lord for my misdoings; for if I had been ruled by God, and by his servants, I had never done as I have done. There is nothing in religion that befriendeth sin; there is nothing so contrary to it, as God and his holy laws, which I should have obeyed. Rather let all take warning by me, and avoid temptations, and live not carelessly, and hearken not to the inclinations or reasonings of the flesh, nor trust their weak and sinful hearts; but live in godly fear and watchfulness, and keep under the flesh, and keep close to God, and hearken to the faithful counsel of his servants. And I entreat your prayers to God, that I may be strengthened by his grace, that I may sin thus no more, lest worse befall me.[277]

A form of Prayer for a Sinner impenitent, after Public Admonition.

MOST gracious God, according to thy command we have warned this sinner, and told him of thy threatenings, and foretold him of thy certain terrible judgments, that he might flee from the wrath to come; but alas, we perceive not that he repenteth or relenteth, but hardeneth his heart against reproof; as if he were able to contend with

338

thee, and overcome thy power. O let us prevail with thee for grace, that we may prevail with him for penitent confession and reformation. O pity a miserable sinner! so miserable, as that he layeth not to heart his misery, nor pitieth himself. O save him from the gall of bitterness, and from the bonds of his iniquity. Give him repentance unto life, that he may recover himself out of the snare of the devil, who is taken captive by him at his will. Give him not up to a blind mind, to a seared conscience, a heart that is past feeling, nor to walk in his own counsels, and after his own lusts. Let him no longer despise the riches of thy goodness, and forbearance, and long-suffering, nor with a hardened, impenitent heart, treasure up wrath against the day of wrath and revelation of thy righteous judgment; who wilt render to every man according to his deeds, even to them that are contentious and obey not the truth, but obey unrighteousness, indignation and wrath, tribulation and anguish, upon every soul of man that doeth evil. Let him be sure that the judgment of God is according to truth against them that commit such things; and let him not think in his impenitency to escape thy judgment. O suffer him not, when he heareth the threatenings of thy word, to bless himself in his heart, and say, I shall have peace, though I walk in the imaginations of my heart, and add sin to sin; lest thy anger and jealousy smoke against him, and thou wilt not spare him, but blot out his name from under heaven, and all thy curses lie upon him, and thou separate him to evil, even to the worm that dieth not, and to the fire that is not quenched. O save him from his sins, from his impenitency, and the pride and stubbornness of his heart. O save him from the everlasting flames, and from thy wrath, which he is the more in danger of, because he feeleth not, and feareth not his danger. Let him know how hard it is for him to kick against the pricks, and how woeful to strive against his Maker. Lay him at thy footstool in sackcloth and ashes, in tears and lamentation, crying out, Woe unto me that I have sinned; and humbling his soul in true contrition, and loathing himself, and begging thy pardoning and healing grace, and begging the prayers and communion [944]of thy church, and resolving to sin wilfully no more, but to live before thee in uprightness and obedience all his days. O let us prevail with thee for the conversion of this impenitent sinner, and so for the saving of his soul from death, and the hiding and pardoning of his sins; that he that is lost may be found, and he that is dead may be alive, and the angels of heaven, and we thy unworthy servants here on earth, may rejoice at his repenting. Let us see him restored by thy grace, that we may joyfully receive him into our communion, and thou mayst receive him at last into thy heavenly kingdom, and Satan may be disappointed of his prey; for thy mercy' sake, through Jesus Christ our Lord and only Saviour.[278] Amen.

A Form of Rejection from the Communion of the Church.

JESUS Christ, the King and Lawgiver of the church, hath commanded, that, If a brother trespass against us, we go and tell him his fault between him and us alone; and if he will not hear us, we shall then take with us one or two more, that in the mouth of two or three witnesses every word may be established; and if he shall neglect to hear them, that he tell it to the church; and if he neglect to hear the church, that he be to us as a heathen man, and a publican. And that we keep no company, if any that is called a brother, be a fornicator, or covetous, or an idolater, or a railer, or a drunkard, or an extortioner, with such a one, no, not to eat. And that we withdraw ourselves from every brother that walketh disorderly, and note him, and have no company with him, that he may be ashamed. According to these laws of Christ, we have admonished this offending brother, who hath greatly sinned against God, and grieved and injured the church; we have earnestly prayed and patiently waited for his repentance, but we have not prevailed. But after all, he continueth impenitent, and will not be persuaded to confess and forsake his sin: we do therefore, according to these laws of Christ, declare him unmeet for the communion of the church, and reject him from it; requiring him to forbear it, and requiring you to avoid him; and we leave him bound to the judgment of the Lord, unless his true repentance shall prevent it.[279]

A Form of Absolution, and Reception of the Penitent.

THOUGH you have greatly sinned against the Lord, and against his church, and your own soul, yet seeing you humble yourself before him, and penitently fly to Christ for mercy, resolving to do so no more; hear now the glad tidings of salvation, which I am commanded to declare unto you. If any man sin, we have an advocate with the Father, Jesus Christ the righteous, and he is the propitiation for our sins. If we confess our sins, he is faithful to forgive us our sins, and to cleanse us from all unrighteousness. Seek the Lord while he may be found; call upon him while he is near. Let the wicked forsake his way, and the unrighteous man his thoughts, and let him return unto the Lord, and he will have mercy upon him, and to our God, for he will abundantly pardon. He that covereth his sins shall not prosper; but whoso confesseth and forsaketh them shall have mercy. Brethren, if a man be overtaken in a fault, restore such a one in the spirit of meekness, considering thyself lest thou also be tempted. According to this word of grace, * This must be omitted if the person was not first rejected. [* I do loose the bonds here laid upon you, and receive you again into the communion of the church,] requiring to receive you, and not upbraid you with your sin, but rejoice in your recovery. And I do declare to you the pardon of all your sins in the blood of Christ, if your repentance be sincere. And I exhort and charge you, that you believingly and thankfully accept this great, unspeakable mercy, and that you watch more carefully for the time to come, and avoid temptations, and subdue the flesh, and accept reproofs, and see that you return not to your vomit, or to wallow again in the mire, when you are washed; but obey the Spirit, and keep close to God in the means of your preservation.[280]

A Form of Thanksgiving, or Prayer, for the Restored Penitent.

O MOST merciful Father, we thank thee that thou hast brought as under so gracious a covenant, as not only to pardon the sins of our unregenerate state; but also upon our penitent confession, and return, to cleanse us from all our unrighteousness, and pardon our falls by the blood of Christ, and to restore our souls, and lead us again in the paths of righteousness, and command thy servants to receive us. We thank thee that thou hast thus restored this thy servant, giving him repentance and remission of sin, * Leave out this if he was not rejected. [* and returning him to the communion of thy church.] We beseech thee, comfort him with the believing apprehensions of thy forgiveness and reconciliation through Jesus Christ. Restore unto him the joy of thy salvation, and uphold him by thy free Spirit; stablish, strengthen, settle him, that with full purpose of heart he may cleave unto thee; and now thou hast spoken peace to him he may not return again to folly. As he nameth the name of Christ, let him depart from iniquity, and never more dishonour thee, thy church or truth, nor his holy profession, but save him from temptation. Let him watch and stand fast, and sin no more, lest worse befall him. Let him not receive this grace in vain, nor turn it into wantonness, nor continue in sin, that grace may abound. But let his old man be crucified with Christ, and the body of sin be destroyed; that henceforth he may no more serve sin, remembering what fruit he had in those things whereof he is now ashamed, and that the end and wages of sin is death: and let us all take warning by the falls of others, and be not high-minded, but fear; and let him that thinketh he standeth take heed lest he fall. Let us watch and pray that we enter not into temptation, remembering that the flesh is weak; and our adversary the devil walketh about seeking whom he may devour. And let none of us hate our brother in our hearts, but in any wise rebuke our neighbour, and not suffer sin upon him: and confirm us unto the end, that we may be blameless in the day of our Lord Jesus Christ; to whom with thee, O Father, and thy Holy Spirit, be kingdom, and power, and glory for ever.[281] Amen.

[945]

APPENDIX.

340

A LARGER LITANY, OR GENERAL PRAYER, TO BE USED AT DISCRETION.

O MOST holy, blessed, and glorious Trinity, Father, Son and Holy Ghost, three Persons and one God, infinite in power, wisdom, and goodness, our Creator, Redeemer, and Sanctifier; our Owner, Governor, and Father; hear our prayers, and have mercy upon us, miserable sinners.

O Lord our Saviour, whose incarnation, nativity, subjection, fasting, temptation, poverty, reproaches, agony and bloody sweat, scourging, desertion, crucifying, death, and burial, were all undergone to take away the sins of the world; who being risen, ascended, and glorified, art the great Priest, and Prophet, and King of thy universal church, for which thou makest intercession, which thou dost gather, teach, and guide by thy Spirit, word, and ministers, which thou dost justify and wilt glorify with thyself, who wilt come again, and raise the dead, and judge the world in righteousness; we beseech thee hear us, miserable sinners. Cast us not out that come unto thee. Make sure to us our calling and election, our unfeigned faith and repentance, that being justified, and made the sons of God, we may have peace with him as our reconciled God and Father.[282]

Let our hearts be right with thee our God, and stedfast in thy covenant. Cause us to deny ourselves, and give up ourselves entirely unto thee, our Creator, Redeemer, and Sanctifier, as being not our own, but thine.[283]

Let thy Holy Spirit dwell in us, and sanctify us throughout, that we may be new creatures, and holy as thou art holy; let it be in us the Spirit of adoption and supplication, and the seal and earnest of our glorious inheritance; and let us know that we are thine, and thou abidest in us, by the Spirit which thou hast given us.[284]

As thy name, O Lord, is holy, and thy glory covereth the heavens, so let the earth be filled with thy praises. Let our souls ever magnify thee, O Lord, and our tongues extol thee. Let us speak of the glorious honour of thy majesty, of thy greatness, thy power, thy glorious kingdom, thy wisdom, holiness, truth, and righteousness, thy goodness, thy mercy, and thy wondrous works. Let all flesh bless thy holy name.[285]

Let the desire of our souls be to thy name: cause us to love thee with all our hearts, to fear thee, trust in thee, and to delight in thee, and be satisfied in thee as our portion, and whatever we do to do it to thy glory.[286]

Keep us from inordinate self-love; from pride, and vain-glory, and self-seeking; and from dishonouring thee, thy word, or service in the world.[287]

Let the world acknowledge thee, the universal King. Give thy Son the heathen for his inheritance, and the uttermost parts of the earth for his possession. Let the kingdoms of the world become his kingdoms. Convert the atheistical, idolatrous, infidel, Mahometan, and ungodly nations of the earth, that every knee may bow to Christ, and every tongue confess him the King of kings, and Lord of lords, to the glory of God the Father.[288]

Let the word of thy kingdom and salvation be preached to all the world; let it have free course and be glorified: and by the power of thy Spirit convert many unto Christ; and let him be thy salvation to the ends of the earth. Send forth more labourers into the harvest, which is great, and fit them for so great a work; and deliver them from unreasonable and wicked men, that (to fill up their sins) forbid them to speak to the people, that they might be saved.[289]

Deliver the churches that are oppressed by idolaters, Mahometans, or other infidels and enemies. Give all thy servants prudence, patience, and innocency, that, suffering as christians, and not as evil-doers, they may not be ashamed, but may glorify thee, and wait for thy salvation, committing the keeping of their souls unto thee, in hope of a reward in heaven.[290]

Deliver the church from the Roman papal usurpations and corruptions. Dispel the deceits of heresies, and false worship, by the light of thy prevailing truth. Unite all christians in Christ Jesus, the true and only universal Head; that by the true christian, catholic faith and love, they may grow up in him, and may keep the unity of the Spirit in the bond of peace; the strong receiving and bearing the infirmities of the weak. Heal the divisions that are among believers. Let nothing be done through strife or vain-glory, but in lowliness of mind let each esteem other better than himself; and let all men know that we are Christ's disciples, by our fervent love to one another.[291]

Let us be heartily and entirely thy subjects, believing that thou art just, and the rewarder of them that diligently seek thee. Keep us from atheism, idolatry, and disobedience; from infidelity, ungodliness, and sensuality; from security, presumption, and despair.[292]

Let us study to please thee in all things. Let thy law be written in our hearts; and let us delight to do thy will. [946]Let our faith and lives be ruled by thy word, which is able to make us wise unto salvation; let us love it, search it, and understand it, and meditate in it day and night.[293]

Let us not please ourselves or other men against thee, nor be led by the wisdom or desires of the world and flesh, nor regard lying vanities, nor through carelessness, rashness, or presumption, offend thee.[294]

As all nations must be judged by thee, let them be ruled by thy laws, and not make them void by men's traditions, nor worship thee in vain, teaching for doctrine the commandments of men. But whatever thou commandest, let them take heed to do; let them add nothing thereto, nor take aught therefrom.[295]

Let us not take thy holy name in vain, but use it in truth and reverence. Keep us from all blasphemy, perjury, profane swearing; from lying before the God of truth; and from contempt and forgetfulness of thy presence; from false, unworthy, unreverent thoughts or speeches of God, and holy things; and from neglecting or abusing thy holy word and worship.[296]

Help us to keep holy thy day, in remembrance of the blessed work of our redemption, and reverently to attend thee in public worship; and obediently to receive thy word; and fervently to call upon thy name; and to delight ourselves in thanksgiving and joyful praises to thy holiness in the communion of thy saints: and let us carefully see that our households, and all within our gates, do serve thee, and not abuse thy holy day.[297]

Have mercy on the kings and rulers of the earth, that they may escape the temptations of worldly greatness, honours, and prosperity, which would captivate them to the flesh, and draw their hearts from thee, thy laws, and ways, and would engage them against thee and thy servants. And as they are thy ministers, and magistracy is thine ordinance, sanctify and dispose them to be nursing fathers to thy church, to own thy interest, and rule for thee.[298]

Especially have mercy on thy servant Charles, our king: illuminate and sanctify him by thy Holy Spirit, that above all things he may seek thy glory, the increase of faith and obedience to thy laws, and may rule us as being thy minister for good, not to be a terror to good works, but to evil; that under him we may lead a quiet and peaceable life in all godliness and honesty.[299]

Have mercy upon all the royal family, the lords of the council, and all the nobility, the judges, and magistrates of these lands. Cause them to fear thee, and to be eminent in sobriety, righteousness, and godliness, to protect the innocent, and be a terror to the wicked, hating injustice, covetousness, and pride.[300]

Let every soul be subject to the higher powers, and not resist. Let them obey the king, and all that are in authority under him, not only for wrath, but for conscience' sake, as knowing that they rule by thee, and for thee.[301]

Give all the churches able, holy, faithful pastors; and cause them laboriously to preach, and rightly to divide the word of truth, to feed thy people with knowledge, and lead them in the way of faith and love, of holiness and peace, and to watch for their souls as those that must give account; overseeing and ruling them, not by constraint, but willingly, not for filthy lucre, but of a ready mind, not as being lords over thy heritage, but as the servants of all, and ensamples to the flock; that when the chief Pastor shall appear, they may receive a crown of glory.[302]

Let the congregations know those that have the ruling of them, and are over them in the Lord, that labour among them, preaching to them the word of God. Let them submissively and obediently hear, and esteem them very highly in love for their work's sake, and account them worthy of double honour.[303]

Let parents bring up their children in the nurture and admonition of the Lord, diligently teaching them thy word, talking of it when they are in their house, and when they walk by the way, when they lie down, and when they rise up, that they may know their Creator, Redeemer, and Sanctifier, in the days of their youth: and cause children to hear, love, honour, and obey their parents, that they may have the blessing of thine especial promise unto such.[304]

Let husbands love their wives, and prudently guide them in knowledge and holiness; and let wives love, honour, and obey their husbands, as meet helpers to them.[305]

Let masters rule their servants in holiness and mercy, remembering they have a Master in heaven; and let servants reverently, singly, and willingly be obedient, and do service to their masters as to the Lord, from him expecting their reward.[306]

Keep us from murder, violence, and all injury to our neighbour's life or health; from malice, cursing, reviling, and unadvised anger. Let us not resist evil with evil, but forbear one another, and not give place to wrath.[307]

Keep us from adultery, fornication, and all uncleanness, and the occasions and appearances thereof. Let us take care as becometh saints, that they be not immodestly named among us, and that no corrupt communication proceed out of our mouths. Keep us from chambering and wantonness, from lustful thoughts, and all immodest attire, behaviour, looks, and actions.[308]

Keep us from theft and oppression, and any way wronging our neighbour in his property and estate.[309]

Keep us from false witness-bearing, lying, and deceiving; from slandering, backbiting, unjust, uncharitable censuring or reproaching; from all perverting of justice, and wronging the reputation of our neighbour; and from all consent or desire of such wrongs.[310]

Keep us from envy, and from coveting any thing that is our neighbour's, to his wrong, and from seeking our own, or drawing to ourselves, to the injury of his welfare; but let us love our neighbours as ourselves, and do to others as we would they should do to us.[311]

Teach us to love Christ and his holy image in his members, with a dear and special love, and to love our enemies, and pray for them that hate and persecute us, and to do good to all as we are able, but especially to them of the household of faith.[312]

[947]Cause us with patience to submit to all the disposals of thy will, and wait thy end, and to love the demonstrations of thy holiness and justice, though grievous to the flesh; and keep us from impatient murmurings, and discontent, and arrogant reasoning against thy will.[313]

Give us our daily bread, our necessary sustentation and provision for thy service; and let us use it for thee, and not to satisfy the flesh. Let us depend on thee, and trust thee for it in the lawful use of the means. And bless thou our labours, and give us the fruits of the earth in season, and such temperate weather as tendeth thereunto.[314]

Deliver us and all thy servants from such wants, distresses, griefs, and sickness, as will unseasonably take us off thy service, and from untimely death; and teach us to value and redeem our time, and work while it is day.[315]

Keep us from gluttony, drunkenness, and all intemperance; from sloth and idleness; from inordinate desires of pleasures or abundance; but having food and raiment, let us be therewith contented.[316]

Of thy abundant mercy, through the sacrifice and merits of thy Son according to thy promise, forgive us all our sins, and save us from thy deserved wrath and condemnation. Remember not, O Lord, our offences, nor the offences of our forefathers; but though our iniquities testify against us, spare us and save us for thy mercy's sake. O let not our sin deprive us of thy Spirit, or of access unto thee, or communion with thee, or of thy favour or comfort, or the light of thy countenance, or of everlasting life.[317]

Cause us to forgive from our hearts, the injuries done against us, as we expect to be forgiven by thee the greatest debt. Keep us from all revengeful desires and attempts. And do thou convert and pardon our enemies, slanderers, oppressors, persecutors, and others that have done us wrong.[318]

Keep us from running upon temptations: suffer not the tempter by subtlety or importunity to corrupt our judgments, wills, affections, or conversations. Cause us to maintain a diligent and constant watch over our thoughts and hearts, our senses and appetites, our words and actions; and as faithful soldiers, by the conduct and strength of the Captain of our salvation, with the whole armour of God, to resist and overcome the world, the devil, and the flesh unto the end.[319]

Save us from the temptations of prosperity and adversity. Let us not be drawn from thee to sin by the pleasures, profits, or honours of the world. Strengthen us for sufferings. Let us not forsake thee, or fall in time of trial. Help us to deny ourselves, and take up our cross and follow Christ, accounting the sufferings of this present time unworthy to be compared with the glory to be revealed.[320]

Deliver us from the enmity and rage of Satan and his instruments; and give not up thy servants, their souls or bodies, their peace or liberties, estates or names, to their malicious wills; but save us and preserve us to thy heavenly kingdom.[321]

We ask all this of thee, O Lord; for thou art the universal King, holy and just, to whom it belongeth in righteousness to judge the world, and save thy people. All power is thine to execute wrath upon thine enemies, and to deliver and glorify thy flock; and none is able to resist thee. Of thee, and through thee, and to thee, are all things, and the glory shall be thine, for ever.[322] Amen.

THE CHURCH'S PRAISE FOR OUR REDEMPTION, TO BE USED AT DISCRETION.

OUR souls do magnify thee, O Lord; our spirits rejoice in God our Saviour, who remembered us in our low and lost estates, for his mercy endureth for ever. By one man sin entered into the world, and death by sin. We kept not the covenant of God, and refused to walk in his law; for all have sinned and come short of the glory of God, and judgment came upon all men to condemnation. But blessed be the Lord God of Israel, that hath visited and redeemed his people, and hath raised up a mighty salvation for us in the house of his servant David: as he spake by the mouth of his holy prophets, which have been since the world began. A virgin hath conceived and brought forth: the Holy Ghost did come upon her; the power of the Highest did overshadow her; therefore the Holy One that is born of her, is called the Son of God: his name is called Jesus, for he saveth his people from their sins. To us is born a Saviour, which is Christ the Lord: he is the image of the invisible God, the firstborn of every creature; for by him all things were created that are in heaven and in earth, visible and invisible, whether thrones or dominions, or principalities or powers, all things were created by him and for him, and he is before all things, and by him all things do consist. He is the power of God and the wisdom of God; the true Light that lighteth every man that cometh into the world. The Word was made flesh and dwelt among us, and men beheld his glory as the glory of the only begotten of the Father, full of grace and truth; for it pleased the Father that in him should all fulness dwell. When the fulness of time was come, God sent his Son, made of a woman, made under the law, to redeem them that are under the law. This is the beloved Son in whom the Father is well pleased. For such a High Priest became us, who is holy, harmless, undefiled, separate from sinners. He did no sin, neither was there any guile found in his mouth; when he was reviled, he reviled not again, leaving us an example: who his own self bare our sins in his own body on the tree; for God laid on him the iniquity of us all, and by his stripes we are healed. When we were without strength, in due time Christ died for the ungodly, the just for the unjust: in this was manifest the love of God towards us, that God sent his only begotten Son into the world, that we might live by him. Forasmuch as the children were partakers of flesh and blood, he himself likewise took part with them, that he might destroy through death him that had the power of death, that is, the devil; and might deliver them, who through fear of |948|death, were all their lifetime subject to bondage. Having spoiled principalities and powers, he made a show of them openly, triumphing over them in his cross. He was buried, and rose again the third day according to the Scriptures; for God raised him, having loosed the pains of death, because it was not possible that he should be holden of it. He hath abolished death, and brought life and immortality to light by the gospel. O death! where is thy sting? O grave! where is thy victory?|323|

All power is given him in heaven and earth. When he ascended up on high, he led captivity captive, and gave gifts to men. And he gave some apostles, and some prophets, and some evangelists, and some pastors, and some teachers, for the perfection of the saints, for the work of the ministry, for the edifying of the body of Christ, till we all come in the unity of the faith, and of the knowledge of the Son of God, to a perfect man. He is set at God's right hand in the celestials, far above all principalities, and powers, and might, and dominion, and every name that is named, not only in this world, but in that to come. God hath put all things under his feet, and gave him to be Head over all things to the church, which is his body, the fulness of him that filleth all in all.|324|

Without controversy great is the mystery of godliness: God manifested in the flesh, justified in the spirit, seen of angels, preached to the Gentiles, believed on in the world, received up into glory. This is the record, that God hath given us eternal life, and this life is in his Son. He that hath the Son hath life, and he that hath not the Son hath not life. He was in the world, and the world was made by him, and the world knew him not. He came to his own, and his own received him not. This is the condemnation, that light is come into the world, and men loved darkness rather than light, because their deeds are evil. But as many as receive him, to them gives he power to become the sons of God, even to them that believe in his name. There is therefore now no condemnation to them which are in Christ Jesus, who walk not after the flesh, but after the Spirit. He forgiveth our iniquities, and will remember our sins no more. Who shall lay any thing to the charge of God's elect? It is God that justifieth: who is he that condemneth? It is Christ that died; yea rather, that is risen again, who is even at the right hand of God, who also maketh intercession for us. Who gave himself for us, that he might redeem us from all iniquity, and purify to himself a peculiar people, zealous of good works. If any man have not the Spirit of Christ, the same is none of his. He that nameth the name of Christ must depart from iniquity. If we regard iniquity in our hearts, God will not hear our prayers. But we are washed, we are sanctified, we are justified in the name of the Lord Jesus, and by the Spirit of our God. Not by works of righteousness which we have done, but according to his mercy he saved us, by the washing of regeneration, and renewing of the Holy Ghost. And being justified by faith, we have peace with God through our Lord Jesus Christ: by whom also we have access by faith into this grace wherein we stand, and rejoice in hope of the glory of God; and hope maketh not ashamed, because the love of God is shed abroad in our hearts by the Holy Ghost which is given us. For if when we were enemies we were reconciled to God by the death of his Son, much more being reconciled, we shall be saved by his life. He that spared not his own Son, but gave him up for us all, how shall he not with him also freely give us all things? He that is gone to prepare a place for us, will come again and receive us to himself, that where he is, there we may be also. It is his will that they that the Father hath given him be with him where he is, that they may behold the glory that is given him. Because he liveth we shall live also; for we are dead, and our life is hid with Christ in God. When Christ who is our life shall appear, then shall we also appear with him in glory; when he shall come to be glorified in his saints, and to be admired in all them that do believe. Then shall men discern between the righteous and the wicked, between those that serve God, and those that serve him not. Then shall the righteous shine forth as the sun in the kingdom of their Father. He that overcometh shall inherit all things. He shall enter into the joy of his Lord. He shall be a pillar in the temple of God, and shall go out no more. Christ will grant him to sit with him in his throne, even as he overcame and is set down with his Father in his throne. He will rejoice over us with joy, he will rest in his love, then, in the holy city, the new Jerusalem, prepared as a bride adorned for her husband, where the tabernacle of God will be with men, and he will dwell with them, and they shall be his people, and God himself shall be with them, their God, and shall wipe away all tears from their eyes, and there shall be no more death, nor sorrow, no crying, nor pain, for the former things are passed away. And the city needeth not the sun, or the moon to shine in it, for the glory of God doth lighten it, and the Lamb is the light thereof. The throne of God and of the Lamb shall be in it, and his servants shall serve him, and shall see his face, who is the blessed and only Potentate, the King of kings, and Lord of lords. Of him, through him, and to him, are all things; to whom be glory for ever.[325] Amen.

[176]   1 Tim. 1. 15; Psal. 147. 5; Matt. 19. 17; 1 Tim. 6. 16; Dan. 7. 10; Isa. 57. 15; Psal. 149. 4; Heb. 10. 19, 20; Isa. 55. 6; Psal 95. 6; 12. 2; 99. 5; 51. 1, 17; 89. 7; Jer. 32. 40; Heb. 12. 28; 1 Thess. 5. 23; Lev. 10. 3; Zech. 12. 10; Rom. 8. 26; James 5. 16; 1. 6; Isa. 26. 8; Matt. 15. 18; John 4. 23, 24; 1 Thess. 2. 13; Acts 16. 14; Mark 4. 12; Phil. 1. 29; Prov. 1. 24, 25; Eccles. 5. 1; John 6. 45; Heb. 4. 22, 13; 2 Cor. 10. 4, 6; Psal. 69. 30; 106. 46; 9. 14; 105. 3; 51. 15; 19. 14; Heb. 13. 21.

[177]   Isa. 66. 1; Psal. 111. 9; Luke 2. 13; Psal. 103. 20; Heb. 1. 6; Psal. 149. 1; Lev. 10. 3; Gen. 18. 27; 2 Tim. 2. 5; Dan. 9. 18; Hos. 14. 2; Rom. 8. 26; Heb. 12. 28; 2 Thess. 2. 10; Luke 19. 48; Isa. 1. 19; 2 Cor. 2. 16; James 5. 16; Psal. 63. 5; 1 Cor. 7. 35; Psal. 84. 10; 73. 28.

[178]   Gen. 1. 27.

[179]   Rom. 5. 12.

[180]   Rom. 3. 23.

[181]   John 3. 16.

[182]   Ver. 18.

[183]   Ver. 19.

[184]   Ver. 20.

[185]   Gal. 3. 13.

[186]   John 3. 5.

[187]   Ver. 6.

[188]   Matt. 18. 3.

[189]   Ezek. 33. 11.

[190]   Luke 15. 10.

[191]   Ver. 18, 19.

[192]   Psal. 5. 5; Rom. 6. 23; Eph. 1. 6, 12; John 4. 42; Rom. 3. 25; Eph. 1. 5; Luke 24. 47; Acts 5. 37; Prov. 28. 13; Rev. 3. 17; Psal. 51. 5; Eph. 2. 3; Isa. 48. 8; 53.6; Psal. 100. 3; 1 Cor. 6. 20; 2 Cor. 8. 5; 1 Cor. 10. 31; 7. 32; 1 Thess. 4. 1; 1 John 3. 22; Rom. 2. 23; 1 Chron. 21. 7; Phil. 2. 21; Luke 18. 14; Rom. 15. 1; Psal. 47. 7; Rom. 7. 12; Dan. 9. 9, 10; Tit. 1. 7, 10; Rom. 8. 5; 13. 14; 4. 20; Psal. 78. 7, 22; Isa. 51. 7, 8; Luke 12. 4, 5; Psal. 100. 5; 1 John 4. 16; Psal. 16. 5; Matt. 22. 7, 3; Psal. 37. 4; 1 John 2. 15; 2 Tim. 5. 7; John 6. 27; Luke 10. 21, 22; Matt. 25. 26; Rom. 12. 11; Eph. 6. 11, 13, 14; Mark 8. 38; 2 Tim. 1. 8; Eph. 5. 15; Rom. 12. 1, 19; Acts 11. 23; 2 Pet. 1. 10; Luke 1. 71; Heb. 12. 28; Psal. 111. 9; 2 Tim. 2. 19; Phil. 3. 3; Psal. 29. 2; Rev. 1. 10; Rom. 13. 7; Tit. 3. 1; Eph. 6; Matt. 29. 39; 7. 12; 1 Cor. 10. 24; Eph. 4. 2, 32; Matt. 5. 44; Heb. 12. 14; Gal. 6. 10; Psal. 19. 12, 13; Rom. 2. 4; Psal. 51. 4; Rom. 2. 15; Psal. 78. 32, 37, 42; Luke 12. 35, 36, 40; Rom. 5. 6, 8, 10; Luke 14. 17; 8. 1; Acts 13. 26; Rev. 22.

17; 1 John 5. 11, 12; Matt. 22. 5; Heb. 2. 3; Psal. 119. 60; John 12. 40; Heb. 12. 25; Acts 7. 51; 2 Tim. 3. 8; Luke 15. 18; Numb. 16. 38; Rom. 1. 18; Eph. 5. 6; Dan. 9. 7, 8; Psal. 51. 1; 41. 1; 143. 2; 51. 9, 11; Lev. 26. 25; Rev. 1. 5; John 1. 29; Eph. 1. 6; Matt. 12. 18; Gal. 3. 13; Isa. 53. 5; Psal. 85. 4; 67. 1; Acts 11. 18; Ezek. 20. 43; Psal. 51. 17; Ezek. 36. 26; Gal. 4. 6, 2; 2 Cor. 6. 16; Jer. 13. 13; Ezek. 11. 20; Psal. 119. 18; Eph. 3. 18; Matt. 13. 11; Eph. 1. 18; Rom. 2. 18; 2 Tim. 2. 26; Psal. 119. 104; Rom. 5. 5; 8. 35, 39; Jer. 32. 40; Mar. 6. 3; Col. 3. 1; Matt. 6. 20, 21; Phil. 3. 20; Col. 3. 5; Gal. 6. 14; Rom. 1. 17; Heb. 11. 1; 1 Cor. 4; 1 Pet. 3. 11; Luke 13. 14; 1 Cor. 9. 24; 1 Pet. 4. 2; Col. 1. 10; 2 Cor. 5. 9; John 6. 38; Psal. 40. 8; 1. 2; Tit. 2. 12; 1 Pet. 1. 14, 15; 1. 22; Eph. 4. 2, 32; James 5. 17; Psal. 15. 4; Eph. 5. 15; Phil. 1. 10; Titus 2. 14; Matt. 5. 44; Rom. 12. 19; Luke 21. 19; Mark 8. 34; Heb. 11. 26; Rom. 8. 17; Rev. 2. 10, 11.

[193] Hab. 1. 13; Jude 15. Luke 13. 3; Mark 16. 16; Psal. 51. 5; Eph. 2. 3; Rom. 3. 22; Ezek. 20. 37; Matt. 28. 19; Eccl. 12. 1; Deut. 11. 1; Col. 1. 10; 1 Cor. 10. 31; Gen. 5. 22; 2 Cor. 5. 7; Phil. 3. 20; Rom. 12. 11; Deut. 6. 5; Eph. 2. 3; Rom. 8. 7; Exod. 20. 4, 7, 8, 11, 12, &c.; 2 Pet. 2. 9; Rom. 13. 8, 9; Mat. 7. 12; Mark 6. 33. 1 Tim. 6. 8; Luke 10. 41, 42; Rom. 5. 8; Luke 24. 47; Rom. 3. 25; Matt. 22. 4, 5; Heb. 2. 3; Acts 7. 51; Prov. 1. 23; Jam. 4. 7; 1 Pet. 5. 9; Psal. 51. 4; Psal. 19. 12, 13; Isa. 59. 12; Psal. 103. 110; 50. 11; Mark 9. 44; Psal. 52. 8; Eph. 1. 12, 13; Psal. 71. 5; 78. 7; 119. 81; 51. 1; 2 Cor. 5. 18; 1. 19; John 1. 7; Gal. 4. 6; 1 Thess. 5. 23; Rom. 5. 5; Deut. 30. 6; Psal. 31. 16; Matt. 1. 21; 1 Thess. 1. 10; Tit. 2. 14; Col. 1. 10; 1 Pet. 2. 3; Ephes. 5. 16; 2 Pet. 1. 10; Matt. 6. 11; 1 Tim. 6. 4; Heb. 13. 5; Matt. 6. 25; 2 Pet. 3. 11; Matt. 26. 41; James 4. 6; Gal. 5. 17; 1 John 5: 4, 5; Rev. 2. 17; 2 Pet. 2. 10; Luke 1. 17; Psal. 73. 24.

[194] 2 Chron. 30. 9.

[195] 1 John 2. 1, 2.

[196] Acts. 13. 38, 39.

[197] Rom. 5. 20, 21.

[198] 1 John 1. 7, 8, 9.

[199] Matt. 11. 28-30.

[200] Rev. 22. 17.

[201] John 6. 37.

[202] Heb. 8. 12.

[203] Rom. 8. 9.

[204] 2 Cor. 5. 17.

[205] Rom. 8. 1, 5.

[206] Ver. 6.

[207] Ver. 7.

[208] Ver. 8.

[209] Ver. 13.

[210] Gal. 5. 19-21.

[211] Ver. 22-24.

[212] Rom. 13. 13, 14.

[213] 1 John 2. 15, 16.

[214] Matt. 7. 13, 14.

[215] Tit. 2. 11-14.

[216] Psal. 1. 1, 2.

[217] Ver. 5.

[218] Heb. 12. 28, 29.

[219] 2 Pet. 3. 11, 12.

[220] 1 Cor. 15. 56.

[221] Luke 4. 16-18.

[222] Acts 13. 27; 1. 2.

[223] Neh. 8. 4, 6; 9. 2-6, 10, 38; Acts 12. 12; 1 Tim. 4. 5; Acts 1. 14; 16. 13, 16; 1 Tim. 2. 8; 1 Cor. 14, 15, 16; Luke 4. 16, 18; Neh. 8. 8; Acts 20. 7, 9; 2 Tim. 4. 1, 2; Acts 4. 20; 2 Cor. 4. 13; John 16. 20; 1 Cor. 2. 7, 13; Matt. 7. 29. Tit. 2. 15; Matt. 21. 45; Mark 12. 12, 13, 17; Eph. 6. 19, 20; Jude 22, 23; Acts 18. 25; 2 Tim. 2. 24, 25;

1 Tim. 5. 17; Acts 20. 36; Psal. 2; Rev. 11. 15; 1 Tim. 2. 1-3; 2 Thess. 2. 1, 2; 2. 8; 1 Thess. 2. 16; Rev. 18. 19; Matt. 6. 9; 9. 37, 38; 1 Tim. 2. 3; Eph. 6. 19; 1 Thess. 5; 2 John 17, 20; 1 Sam. 12. 23; 2 Cor. 4. 5; Phil. 1. 15, 16; James 3. 1, 15-17; Luke 9. 55; 1 Cor. 14. 26; 2 Cor. 10. 8; Psal. 92. 1; Rev. 1. 10; Acts 20. 7; Col. 3. 16, 17; Psal. 118; 1 Cor. 4. 1, 2; 1 Tim. 3. 5; 3. 15; 2 Tim. 2. 2, 15; Acts 20. 7, 9.

[224] Luke 11. 28.

[225] Num. 6. 24-26.

[226] 2 Cor. 13. 14.

[227] Prov. 8. 15; Dan. 4. 32; Heb. 2. 9; Psal. 65. 11; 93. 14; 65. 4; 60. 5; 80. 13; 59. 1; 61. 6; Isa. 45. 13; Matt. 3. 3; Isa. 59. 8; 11. 2; 1 Kings 1. 3, 7, 9; Josh. 1. 8; Zech. 12. 8; 2 Sam. 14. 17; Psal. 15. 4; 101. 6. Prov. 25. 5; 1 Tim. 2. 2; 2 Tim. 4. 7, 8; Rev. 21. 5; Zech. 8. 13; Isa. 60. 15; James 3. 17; 2 Sam. 23. 3; John 7. 27; 2 Chron. 19. 6; Amos 5. 24; Rom. 13. 1-3; Rev. 11. 16; Psal. 68. 28; Jer. 31. 23; Matt. 6. 13.

[228] Matt. 28. 19; John 5. 7; 1 Cor. 8. 4, 6; 1 Tim. 1. 17; Mal. 2. 10; Heb. 1. 2, 3, 5, 8; 1 Pet. 2. 8; Psal. 22. 28; 1 Cor. 12. 4-6; Psal. 103. 19; Acts 7. 59; Heb. 2. 14, 9; 1 Cor. 15. 4; 1 Tim. 3. 6; John 1. 29; Eph. 1. 20, 22; Rom. 8. 30, 33, 24; Eph. 5. 1; 1 Thess. 4. 16, 17; 2 Pet. 1. 10; 2 Tim. 1. 5; Rom. 5. 1, 2, 10; 2 Cor. 6. 18; Gal. 4. 6.

[229] 1 Pet. 1. 2; Rom. 8. 11; Matt. 8. 34, 35; 2 Cor. 8. 5; 1 Cor. 6. 19, 20; Rev. 4. 11; John 12. 28; Matt. 5. 16; Psal. 22. 23, 27, 28; 2 Tim. 3. 2; Matt. 7. 22; Gal. 5. 26; 2. 19.

[230] Psal. 2.; 47. 7; Rev. 11. 15; 2 Tim. 2. 26; Acts 26. 18; Rom. 11. 25; Matt. 9. 38; 24. 14; 2 Thess. 3. 1, 2; Rev. 2. 3, 19; 3. 10; Luke 18. 7; Rev. 18.; 19.

[231] Eph. 4. 3, 5, 13, 15, 16; Tit. 3. 10; 2 Cor. 2. 17; 1 Cor. 1. 10; Rom. 14. 1; 15. 1; 3 John 9; Rom. 1. 31; Luke 9. 55; Psal. 77. 10; Phil. 2. 3.

[232] Psal. 14.; Eph. 2. 3, 12; 2 Tim. 3. 2-4; 1 Cor. 6. 9; 2 Thess. 2. 10; Rom. 8. 24; Psal. 40. 8; 1. 2; Isa. 8. 20; Psal. 119. 97, 27.

[233] Matt. 15. 9; Exod. 20. 4, 7, 8; Mark 7. 21, 22; Jam. 5. 12; Eccl. 5. 1, 6; Ezek. 2. 26; Neh. 13. 17; Rev. 1. 10.

[234] Prov. 21. 1; Psal. 2. 10-12; Isa. 49. 23; 2 Chron. 19. 6; Rom. 1. 11; 1 Tim. 6. 9; Matt. 21. 44; John 11. 48; Psal. 2. 2-4.

[235] 1 Tim. 2. 2; Psal. 59. 1; 2 Chron. 1. 10; 29. 3; 15. 12, 13; Rom. 13. 3, 4; 1 Pet. 2. 14; 1 Tim. 2. 2.

[236] Psal. 72. 1; Prov. 8. 16; Exod. 18. 21. Job 29; Isa. 1. 17, 23; Psal. 15. 4.

[237] Rom. 13. 1, 2, 5; 1 Tim. 2. 2; 1 Pet. 2. 13.

[238] 2 Cor. 3. 6; Jer. 3. 15; 2 Tim. 4. 2; Eph. 4. 11, 13; James 3. 17; Ezek. 34.; 1 Pet. 5. 1-4; Matt. 20. 25, 26, 27.

[239] Heb. 13. 7, 17; 1 Thess. 5. 12, 13; 1 Tim. 5. 17.

[240] Eph. 6. 1; Eccl. 12. 1; Exod. 20. 12; Eph. 6. 1, 2; 5. 25, 22; 1 Pet. 3. 7; Col. 4. 1; 3. 22-24.

[241] 1 John 3. 15; Luke 3. 14; 2 Cor. 7. 2; Prov. 29. 22; Matt. 5. 22.

[242] Matt. 5. 27, 28; 1 Cor. 6. 9; Rom. 13. 13; Eph. 5. 3, 4, 12.

[243] Eph. 4. 28; 1 Thess. 4. 6; Psal. 82. 2; Prov. 19. 5; 10. 18; Psal. 15. 3; Matt. 7. 12.

[244] Exod. 20. 17; Matt. 22. 39; 7. 12; 25. 40.

[245] 1 Pet. 1. 22.

[246] Matt. 5. 44; Gal. 6. 10; Luke 11. 3; 1 Tim. 6. 8; Deut. 28. 3, 4; Psal. 112.; 128.; Deut. 11. 14; Phil. 2. 27; Rom. 13. 13, 14; 12. 11; Mark 8. 36.

[247] 1 John 2. 1, 2; Gal. 6. 1; Jam. 5. 19, 20; Ezek. 6. 9; Eph. 1. 6, 7; Heb. 7. 25; Matt. 6. 12, 14, 15; 5. 44; Luke 23. 34; Matt. 26. 41.

[248] Jam. 4. 7; 1 John 2. 13; 5. 4; Rom. 8. 13; Gal. 5. 17; 1 John 2. 16, 17; 2 Tim. 2. 18; Rom. 8. 17.

[249] 1 Pet. 5. 8; Psal. 140. 1-3; 2 Tim. 4. 18.

[250] 1 Tim. 1. 17; Matt. 6. 13; Rom. 11. 36.

[251] Psal. 119. 108; Eph. 1. 6; Psal. 116. 17; 2. Cor. 9. 15; Psal. 107. 22; 2 Cor. 1. 3; Psal. 86. 15; Exod. 33. 6, 7; Isa. 43. 7; Rev. 4. 11; Gen. 1. 27; Psal. 8. 5, 6; Deut.

348

31. 16; 32. 5; Hos. 4. 7; Psal. 6. 10; Hos. 13. 4; Gen. 4. 4; John 3. 16; Heb. 2. 16; John 1. 14; Eph. 3. 8; 1 Tim. 3. 16; 1 Pet. 1. 12; Heb. 2. 18; Matt. 4. 10; 2 Cor. 8. 9; 1 Pet. 2. 22; Matt. 4. 10; 1 John 1. 9; Phil. 2. 7; Heb. 12. 2; Rev. 3. 18; Psal. 32. 1; 1 Pet. 2. 23; Heb. 2. 10; Isa. 53. 5, 6; 1 Tim. 1. 6; 1 Cor. 15. 3; Heb. 2. 14; Gal. 3. 13; Matt. 11. 28; Rev. 22. 14; Eph. 1. 22; Psa. 2. 8; Phil. 2. 9; Matt. 28. 19; John 5. 22; Heb. 8. 6; 2 Pet. 1. 4; 1 John 5. 11; 2 Pet. 1. 19; Psal. 119. 130; Eph. 2. 20; 2 Cor. 5. 19, 20; Acts 26. 17, 18; Tit. 3. 3-6; 2 Tim. 2. 25; Eph. 4. 18; John 12. 40; 1 Tim. 4. 2; Psal. 81. 11, 12; John 5. 4; Luke 19. 27; 1 Pet. 3. 20; Rom. 10. 21; Heb. 12. 25; Ezek. 33. 11; Prov. 1. 22, 23; John 6. 44; Acts 16. 14; 1 John 4. 19; Rom. 10. 20; Amos 5. 12; Rom. 5. 1; Acts 11. 18; Rom. 8. 14-17; Eph. 5. 30; Gal. 4. 6; Eph. 2. 19; 1 Pet. 1. 3-6; Rom. 8. 28; Eph. 3. 12; Heb. 4. 16; Psal. 50. 15; 1 Tim. 2. 8; Matt. 11. 13; Psal. 89. 7; 28. 6; 31. 22; 86. 13; Psal. 57. 3; 31. 20; 32. 7; 31. 33; 103. 10; 30. 5; Hab. 3. 2; Psal. 32. 6; 25. 10; 5. 7; 107. 1; 105. 3; 89. 15, 16; Psal. 84. 4; 90. 14; 73. 24; John 17. 24; Rev. 22. 4.

[252] Psal. 103. 1-4, 12; 1 John 3. 1; Psal. 63. 3, 4; Psal. 73. 25-27, 23; 94. 19; 73. 24.

[253] Psal. 36. 7-9; 16. 9, 11; 23. 6; 36. 10; 30. 12.

[254] Luke 2. 14; Psal. 149. 1, 4-6; 145. 10-13; Rev. 4. 8, 11; 15. 3, 4; 5. 12; 13. 9, 10.

[255] Psal. 107. 8, 21, 22; 96. 2; 29. 2; 96. 9, 11, 13; 103. 20-22; 145. 21; 150. 6.

[256] Mal. 4. 1; Heb. 12. 29; 1 Sam. 6. 20; Mal. 3. 2; Isa. 1. 4; Luke 19. 10; Eph. 2. 5; Luke 15. 32; Ezek. 16. 6, 8, 9; Col. 1. 13; Jer. 6. 28; Deut. 4. 23; 6. 5, 6; 11. 22; Psal. 100. 3, 4; Heb. 12. 25; Deut. 9. 12; 32. 5; 2 Tim. 3. 2; 1 John 2. 15; Eph. 2. 2; Gal. 5. 24; Matt. 22. 37, 40; Luke 10. 42; Matt. 25. 30; Rom. 2. 23; 1 Cor. 10. 31; 1 Thess. 4. 1; Luke 8. 18; Matt. 24. 15; Psal. 1. 2; Deut. 6. 6; Phil. 4. 6; 1 Cor. 11. 27, 28; Isa. 64. 7; Col. 2. 7; Acts 2. 42, 45-47; 1 Cor. 11. 29; Mal. 1. 7, 10, 12; 2. 10, 11; Psal. 85. 8; Gen. 4. 16; Psal. 51. 11; 2 Chron. 15. 2; Matt. 22. 12; 7. 23; Mal. 1. 10; 1 Pet. 2. 24; Isa. 53. 10; Psal. 51. 1; Rev. 1. 5; Hos. 14. 2; Ezek. 18. 38; Heb. 8. 12; Ezek. 33. 11; Hos. 14. 4; Psal. 35. 3; John 6. 37; Hos. 14. 2; Matt. 22. 4; 5. 6; John 6. 55; 4. 14; Eph. 3. 18, 19; 1 Pet. 1. 8; Matt. 15. 27; John 6. 35, 51; Psal. 85. 8; Eph. 4. 30; Heb. 3. 13; Col. 3. 5; Eph. 3. 16; Psal. 119. 175.

[257] Psal. 100. 3; Rev. 4. 11; 1 Tim. 1. 17; Psal. 51. 4; Deut. 32. 6; 1 John 3. 1; John 3. 16; Luke 22. 20; Heb. 9. 17; Luke 22. 19.

[258] 1 Cor. 11. 23-26.

[259] Acts 7. 59, 60; Rev. 1. 5; 1 Pet. 3. 18; Luke 22. 2, 19, 20; 1 Cor. 11. 26; Heb. 7. 25, 27; 9. 26; John 4. 10; 6. 63; Rom. 8. 9, 11; Heb. 2. 17; Col. 2. 19; John 6. 27; Matt. 26. 26; Heb. 10. 12; John 1. 29.

[260] Matt. 28. 19; John 15. 26; Matt. 1. 20; 2 Pet. 1. 21; Acts 20. 23; Rom. 8. 9; 1 Cor. 12. 11; 1 Pet. 1. 15; 2. 9; John 14. 16; Eph. 1. 17, 18; Luke 24. 31; Ezek. 36. 26; Zech. 12. 10; Rom. 8. 5; John 6. 53-57; Rom. 5. 5; Cant. 1. 4; Eph. 5. 18, 20; Rom. 14. 17; 1 Thess. 4. 9; Rom. 8. 16; 1 Cor. 1. 8; Eph. 1. 13, 14.

[261] 1 Cor. 11. 24.

[262] Matt. 26. 27. 28; 1 Cor. 11. 25.

[263] Rom. 1. 4. 1 Cor. 1. 24. Eph. 3. 10. Rom. 3. 22, 26; Tit. 3. 4; Rom. 5. 6; Acts 4. 12; 1 Pet. 1. 12; Luke. 2. 13, 14; Rev. 5. 12, 13; 9. 10; Rom. 5. 20; 1 Pet. 1. 19; Matt. 18. 32, 33; Rev. 3. 21; 22. 4; Rom. 8. 38, 39; Heb. 10. 23; 2 Pet. 1. 4; Heb. 9. 15; Eph. 4. 30; Luke 7. 47; Matt. 18. 33; 1 John 4. 11; Ezek. 9. 13, 14; Psal. 44. 17; Rom. 6. 1, 2; Col. 3. 2; Phil. 3. 18-21; Psal. 143. 10; Heb. 5. 9; Psal. 119. 133; 2 Cor. 5. 15; Eph. 1. 11; Matt. 5. 16; 2 Cor. 1. 12; Psal. 119. 5; Luke 22. 31; 1 Pet. 5. 8, 10; Eph. 6. 11; Rom. 16. 20; 1 Cor. 6. 20; Rom. 12. 1; 2 Tim. 2. 21; Rom. 6. 22.

[264] Rom. 5. 12; Eph. 2. 3; John 3. 16; Gen. 3. 15; John 4. 42; Heb. 9. 26; Rev. 1. 5; Rom. 5. 10; Tit. 3. 5; Rom. 16. 10; Heb. 8. 6; Matt. 28. 19, 20; Gen. 17. 10, 11; Ezek. 20. 37; Rom. 6. 3, 4; Tit. 3. 5; 1 Cor. 12. 12; Gen. 17.; Rom. 9. 8; Acts 2. 39; Matt. 23. 37; Deut. 30. 10-12; Matt. 10. 13, 14; 1 Cor. 12. 12, 13; Rev. 1. 5; Eph. 5. 26; Job 11. 52; Heb. 2. 13; Eph. 2. 19; 3. 15; Zech. 9. 11, 15, 16; 1 Pet. 5. 7; 2 Tim. 4. 18.

[265] Rom. 5. 12, 18; Gal. 3. 13; 1 John 5. 11; Acts 2. 39; 1 Cor. 12. 12, 13; Psal. 44. 3, 4; 2 Cor. 8. 5; Psal. 119. 94; Eph. 5. 24; Matt. 22. 37; Deut. 10. 20, 21; 11. 22-30; Psal. 16. 5; 27. 4; Tit. 1. 2; 2. 13; 3. 7; 1 John 2. 5, 6, 17; Gal. 5. 14; Matt. 6. 13; Psal. 81. 12; James 1. 14; Luke 1. 71; 1 Cor. 10. 16; 1 John 1. 7; 2 Cor. 6. 14; 1 Pet. 1. 2; John 9. 31; Luke 9. 23; Heb. 2. 10; Rev. 2. 10.

[266] Eph. 6. 4; Prov. 22. 6; 29. 15; Deut. 6. 5-7; Josh. 24. 15; 2 Tim. 3. 15.

[267] John 3. 5, 6; 1 Pet. 3. 21; Rom. 8. 9; Eccl. 5. 4, 5.

[268] Gen. 2. 18, 1. 28; Mal. 2. 15; 2 Cor. 7. 14, 9; Heb. 13. 4; Luke 1. 6; Eph. 5. 22, &c.; Mal. 2. 15, 16; Psal. 127. 3; Matt. 19. 13, 14; Deut. 29. 11, 12; Ezek. 16. 8; Prov. 20. 7; Eph. 6. 4; 1 Pet. 3. 1, 7; 1 Tim. 3. 11; 5. 13, 14; 1 Cor. 7. 5, 29; Gen. 2. 18; Prov. 5. 18; Heb. 10. 26; 1 Cor. 7. 29; Luke 12. 40; 1 Pet. 3. 7; Rev. 19. 7; John 17. 24.

[269] Gen. 28. 3; Tit. 1. 15; 1 Tim. 4. 5; 1 Cor. 10. 31; 1 Thess. 3. 12; Eph. 5. 25; Gal. 5. 22; Rom. 8. 1, 13; Gal. 6. 8.

[270] Luke 23. 41; Lam. 3. 22; Ezra 9. 13; Lam. 3. 32, 33; Isa. 57. 15-17; Psal. 25. 18; 6. 1; 38. 9; 6. 2, 3, 5; 78. 39; Job 13. 25; Psal. 25. 7, 18; 116. 3; Isa. 38. 16, 19; Psal. 119. 175; Luke. 4. 39; Isa. 38. 21; Psal. 50. 15; Job. 10. 2; Psal. 139. 13; Lam. 3. 40; Psal. 119. 71, 67; Isa. 27. 9; 1 Cor. 11. 32; Heb. 12. 11; Lam. 3. 24-27, 31; Psal. 30. 5; Heb. 12. 6, 7; Isa. 38. 19, 20; Psal. 116.9, 12, &c.; 30. 11, 12; 2 Cor. 1. 9; 4. 16; 5. 8; Heb. 10. 38; 2 Cor. 4. 18, 17; Phil. 3. 9; 1 Cor. 10. 13; Heb. 2.14; 1 Cor. 15. 55; Rom. 8. 37; Col. 3. 1; John 20. 17; 14. 23; 17. 26; 17. 24; Phil. 1. 2; Psal. 16. 11.

[271] 1 Tim. 2. 14; Gen. 3. 16; 1 Tim. 2. 15; Psal. 46. 1; Isa. 37. 3; John 16. 12; Deut. 28. 4; 2 Cor. 1. 10, 11; 1 Sam. 2; 1. 28.

[272] Psal. 30. 2; 3. 4; 66. 20; 30. 3; 103. 3, 4; Isa. 38. 10, 12; Jer. 26. 3, 13; Psal. 103. 5; Isa. 38. 11; Psal. 27. 13; 32. 4, 5; 106. 23; 32. 6, 7; 73. 26; 73. 1; 34. 19; 73. 19, 23; 60. 11; 46. 1; 116. 1, 12, 18, 13, 14; Isa. 38. 20; 1 Cor. 6. 20; Luke 2. 29; 1 Cor. 1. 30.

[273] Psal. 34. 3, 4; Rev. 1. 18; 1 Sam. 2. 6; Psal. 113. 9; 127. 3; 42. 4; 110. 4; 145. 9, 20, 14; 19.; Deut. 28. 8; Psal. 13. 3 Isa. 44. 3; Deut. 8. 11, 14; Psal. 116.; Isa. 83. 10; Mal. 2. 15; 1 Cor. 7. 14; Eph. 6. 4; Deut. 6. 6; Prov. 6. 33; Josh. 24. 15; Zech. 14. 20, 21; Psal. 91. 4; 1 John 2. 15; Phil. 3. 1, 18; 1 Cor. 7. 31, 29, 30; Psal. 23. 3, 4, 6; Jude 24.

[274] Matt. 18. 15-17.

[275] Luke 13. 3, 5; Acts 5. 31; Luke 12. 47.

[276] Jude 14. 15; Psal. 5. 4, 5; 1. 5, 6; Psal. 10. 13; 2 Pet. 2. 3, 9; Psal. 37. 13; Job 9. 4; Psal. 1. 4; Isa. 5. 24; Heb. 12. 29; Isa. 27. 4; Ezek. 22. 14; 1 Cor. 10. 22; Matt. 10. 26; James 5. 9; Matt. 13. 42, 50; Prov. 5. 11-13; Deut. 32. 29; Prov. 28. 13; 29. 1; Gal. 6. 7; Matt. 7. 23; 25. 41; James 5. 19, 20; 1 John 1. 7, 9; 2. 1, 2; Psal. 95. 8, 12; 81. 11, 12; Luke 24. 4, 7; Ezek. 18. 30-32.

[277] Josh. 7. 19; Prov. 28. 13; Psal. 32. 5; Exod. 10. 16; Gal. 1. 13; 2 Chron. 15. 2; Gen. 4. 16; Psal. 51. 11; Matt. 27. 5; Luke 15. 21; Mark 12. 8; Psal. 38. 18, 4; 40. 12; Luke 13. 13; 1 Tim. 1. 1; Heb. 9. 26; Luke 19. 10; Rom. 5. 10; James 5. 16; Psal. 51. 2, 1, 9; Heb. 8. 12; Psal. 51. 11, 27; 9.; 103. 10; 51. 10, 12; 2 Cor. 2. 7, 10; John 8. 11; Mark 13. 37; Psal. 73. 1, 15; Eccles. 8. 12; 2 Chron. 20. 20; James 1. 13, 14; Psal. 5. 5; 1 John 3. 4; Gal. 6. 1; 1 Cor. 10. 11, 12; 2 Sam. 11. 2; Gen. 3. 6; Matt. 26. 41, 75; Heb. 12. 28; 1 Cor. 9. 25-27; 2 Chron. 25. 16; Eph. 3. 16; John 5. 14.

[278] 2 Cor. 5. 11; Matt. 3. 7; Prov. 29. 1; 1 Cor. 10. 22; Acts 8. 22, 23; 11. 18; 2 Tim. 2. 25, 26; 1 Tim. 4. 2; Eph. 4. 19; Psal. 81. 12; Rom. 2. 4-6, 8, 9; Deut. 29. 19-21; Mark 9. 24; Matt. 1. 21; Deut. 9. 17; 2 Cor. 6. 2; Luke 19. 41, 42; Prov. 28. 14; Acts 9. 5; Isa. 45. 9; Joel 2. 1-3; Lam. 5. 16; Psal. 51.; James 5. 20; Gal. 6. 1; Luke 15. 27; Ezek. 33. 14, 16; 2 Tim. 2. 26.

[279] Luke 19. 27; Micah 4. 2; Matt. 18. 15, 16; 1 Cor. 5. 11; Tit. 3. 10; Matt. 18. 15-17; 2 Thess. 3. 6, 14, 15; 1 Cor. 11. 5; 2 Sam. 12. 14; 2 Thess. 3. 6, 14; Acts 8. 24; 2 Tim. 2. 25, 26; 1 Cor. 5. 13; Matt. 18. 18.

[280] 2 Sam. 12. 13; 2 Chron. 33. 12, 13; Rom. 10. 15; 1 John 2. 1, 2; 1 John 1. 9; Isa. 55. 6, 7; Prov. 28. 13; Gal. 6. 1; Matt. 18. 8; Luke 15.; 2 Cor. 2. 7. 10; Acts 13.

38; 8. 8; Luke 15. 25, 27; Matt. 26. 41; Psal. 85. 8; 1 Cor. 9. 25-27; Psal. 141. 5; 2 Pet. 2. 22.

[281]   Rom. 3. 25; 1 John 1. 9; 2. 1, 2; Psal. 23; 103. 3; Matt. 9. 2; Rom. 5. 1-3; Psal. 51. 12; 1 Pet. 5. 10; Acts 11. 23; Psal. 85. 8; 2 Tim. 2. 19; John 5. 14; 2 Cor. 6. 1; Rom. 6. 1; Matt. 6. 13; 1 Cor. 16. 13; Jude 24.

[282]   Matt. 28. 19; 1 John 5. 7; 1 Cor. 8. 4, 6; 1 Tim. 1. 17; Psal. 139. 7-9; 14. 7, 4; Isa. 40. 17; Neh. 9.; Rev. 4. 8; 15.; Ezek. 18. 4; Psal. 47. 7; 119. 68; 147. 9; Mal. 2. 10; Deut. 32. 6; Luke 11. 2; Acts 7. 59, 60; Heb. 2. 11; Phil. 2. 7-9; Luke 2. 51; Matt. 4. 1, 2; 2 Cor. 8. 9; Matt. 12. 24; Luke 22. 24; Matt. 27. 26, 28, 30. Mark 14. 50; 15. 34; 1 Cor. 15. 3, 4; John 1. 29; Heb. 1. 3; 2. 9; 3. 1; 4. 14; Acts 3. 22, 23; Heb. 7. 25; John 12. 32; Matt. 28. 19, 20; 1 Cor. 12.; Eph. 4.; 5. 26, 27; John 17. 4; 1 Thess. 4. 14-16; John 5. 22; Acts 17. 31; John 6. 37; 2 Peter 1. 10; 1 Tim. 1. 5; Acts 5. 31; John 1. 12; Rom. 5. 10; 2 Cor. 16. 18.

[283]   Psal. 78. 37; Matt. 8. 34; 1 Cor. 8. 6; 6. 19, 20.

[284]   Rom. 8. 9; 1 Thess. 5. 23; 1 Cor. 5. 17; 1 Pet. 1. 16; Rom. 8. 15; Zech. 12. 10; Eph. 1. 13, 14; 1 John 3. 24.

[285]   Luke 1. 49; Hab. 3. 3; Luke 1. 46; Psal. 66. 17; 145. 5-8, 11, 12, &c., 21.

[286]   Isa. 26. 8; Deut. 11. 22; 10. 12, 20, 21; Psal. 4. 5; 63. 5; 1 Cor. 10. 31.

[287]   2 Tim. 3. 2, 4; Phil. 2. 3, 21; Rom. 2. 23, 24; Matt. 5. 16.

[288]   Psal. 47. 2, 7; 2. 8, 12; Rev. 11. 15; 1 Tim. 2. 1, 4; John 11. 52; 12. 32; Phil. 2. 10, 11.

[289]   Matt. 24. 14; 2 Thess. 3. 1; Dan. 12. 3; Isa. 49. 6; Matt. 9. 38; Eph. 6. 19; 2 Thess. 3. 2; 1 Thess. 2. 16.

[290]   Luke 18. 7; Matt. 10. 16; Luke 21. 19; 1 Pet 2. 15; 3. 14, 17; 4. 15, 16, 19; Micah 7. 7; Matt. 5. 11, 12.

[291]   Psal. 119. 134; Matt. 15. 9, 13; Rev. 12; 19. 3; John 9. 10; Luke 22. 25, 26; 2 Pet. 2; Jude; 2 Tim. 3. 9; Eph. 4. 15, 16; 3. 5; Rom. 14. 1; 15. 1; Jer. 32. 39; 1 Cor. 1. 10; Phil. 2. 3; John 13. 35; Eph. 5. 2.

[292]   Rom. 3. 26; Heb. 11. 6; Eph. 2. 2, 3; 2 Thess. 2. 12; Rom. 8. 13; Psal. 19. 13; Rom. 8. 24.

[293]   Col. 1. 10; Heb. 8. 10; Psal. 40. 8; Isa. 8. 20; Acts 28. 32; 2 Tim. 3. 15; 2 Thess. 2. 10; John 5. 39; Luke 24. 45; Psal. 1. 2.

[294]   Rom. 15. 1, 2; Gal. 1. 10; 1 Cor. 3. 19; 2 Cor. 1. 12; Rom. 8. 13; John 2. 8; Psal. 19. 11-13.

[295]   Rom. 2. 16; Micah 4. 2; Matt. 15. 3, 6, 9, 11; Deut. 31.

[296]   Exod. 20. 7; Psal. 89. 7; Jer. 4. 2; Matt. 15. 19; James 5. 12; Rev. 22. 12; Jer. 5. 22; Acts 5. 3; 8. 20; Mal. 1. 6, 7, 12; 2. 2, 7-9.

[297]   Rev. 1. 10; Acts 20. 7; 1 Cor. 16. 2; Isa. 58. 13; Heb. 10. 25; 1 Cor. 14; Acts 3. 42, 46; Psal. 98. &c.; 119. 1. Josh. 24. 15; Exod. 20. 10.

[298]   1 Tim. 2. 2; Psal. 2. Jer. 5; 5, 6. Luke 18. 21, 25; 1 Cor. 1. 26; Luke 21. 12; John 7. 48; Ezra 4. 12, &c.; Rom. 13. 2, 4; Isa. 49. 23; 2 Chron. 19. 6.

[299]   Lam. 4. 20; 1 Kings 3. 19, 11; Psal. 51. 10; 1 Sam. 10. 9; 2 Kings 18. 3, 4, 6; Rom. 13. 4, 5; 1 Tim. 2. 2.

[300]   Psal. 72. 1; Prov. 8. 16; Exod. 18. 17; Job 29.; Isa. 17. 23; Luke 1. 51-53.

[301]   Rom. 13. 1, 6; 1 Pet. 2. 13; 1 Tim. 2. 2.

[302]   2 Cor. 3. 6; 1 Tim. 5. 17; 2 Tim. 2. 15; Jer. 3. 15; 2 Tim. 4. 2; 2. 22; 1. 13; Heb. 13. 17; 1 Pet. 5. 1-4.

[303]   1 Thess. 5. 11; Heb. 13. 17; 1 Tim. 5. 17.

[304]   Eph. 6. 4; Deut. 6. 6, 7; Eccles. 12. 1; Eph. 6. 1-3.

[305]   Eph. 5. 25, 22; 1 Pet. 3. 1, 7; Gen. 2. 22.

[306]   Eph. 6. 9, 5.

[307]   1 John 3. 15; Luke 3. 14; 2 Cor. 7. 2; Matt. 5. 22, 39; Rom. 12. 17.

[308]   Eph. 4. 2; Rom. 12. 19; Matt. 5. 27, 28; 1 Cor. 6. 9; Rom. 13. 13; 1 Thess. 5. 22; Eph. 5. 3; 4. 29; 1 Pet. 3. 2, 3; Job 31. 1.

[309]   Eph. 4. 28; Psal. 62. 10; 73. 8; 1 Thess. 4. 6.

351

[310]   Prov. 19. 5; 12. 17; 10. 10; Matt. 7. 1, 2; Psal. 15. 3; 82. 2; Lev. 19. 17; Prov. 23.

[311]   Gal. 5. 21, 26; Exod. 20. 17; Phil. 2. 21; Matt. 22. 39; 7. 12.

[312]   Matt. 15. 40; 1 Pet. 1. 22; Matt. 5. 44-46; Gal. 6. 10.

[313]   Psal. 39. 9; Matt. 26. 30; Acts 21. 14; Jam. 5. 7, 8, 11; 2 Kings 20. 19; Mal. 3. 13, 14.

[314]   Luke 11. 13; Deut. 28. 45; Rom. 13. 14; Luke 12. 20; Eph. 5. 16; John 9. 4.

[315]   Deut. 28. 6, 8, &c.; Phil. 2. 27; Psal. 102. 24; Luke 12. 20; Eph. 5. 16; John 9. 4.

[316]   Rom. 13. 13; 1 Cor. 9. 25; 1 Tim. 5. 6, 13; Eph. 4. 28; Prov. 21. 17; 23. 4; 1 Tim. 6. 8, 9.

[317]   Psal. 51. 1; 1 John 1. 2; Heb. 8. 12; Dan. 9. 6, 16; Jer. 14. 7; Psal. 31. 16; 51. 11, 12, 19; Rom. 8. 1.

[318]   Matt. 6. 2, 14, 15; Rom. 12. 19; Luke 6. 27-29; Acts 7. 60.

[319]   Matt. 26. 41; James 4. 7; Prov. 4. 23; Job 31. 1; Matt. 12. 36; Heb. 2. 10; 2 Tim. 2. 3; 1 John 2. 13; 5. 4; Rom. 8. 13; 2 Tim. 2. 8.

[320]   Prov. 30. 8, 9; 1 John 2. 15, 16; Rom. 8. 17; Matt. 13. 21, 22; 8. 24; Rom. 8. 18.

[321]   Matt. 6. 13; Rom. 16. 20; Psal. 140. 1-3; 31. 8; 17. 2, 12; 1 Tim. 4. 18.

[322]   1 Tim. 1. 17; Psal. 145. 17; Acts 17. 31; Psal. 72. 4, 13; Jude 14, 15; 2 Thess. 1. 10; Psal. 62. 1; 147. 5; Job 9. 4; Rom. 11. 36.

[323]   Luke 1. 46; Psal. 136. 23; Rom. 5. 12; Psal. 78. 10; Rom. 3. 23; 5. 18; Luke 1. 68-70; Isa. 7. 14; Luke 1. 35; Matt. 1. 21; Luke 2. 17; Col. 1. 15-17; 1 Cor. 1. 24; John 1. 9, 14; Col. 1. 19; Gal. 4. 4; Matt. 17. 5; Heb. 7. 26; 1 Pet. 2. 22, 23, 24; Isa. 53. 5, 6; 1 Pet. 3. 18; 1 John 4. 4; Heb. 2. 14, 15; Col. 2. 15; 1 Cor. 15. 4; Acts 2. 24; 2 Tim. 1. 10; 1 Cor. 15. 55.

[324]   Matt. 28. 18; Eph. 4. 8-13; Eph. 1. 20-23.

[325]   1 Tim. 3. 16; 1 John 5. 11; John 1. 10, 11; 3. 19; 1. 12; Rom. 8. 1; Psal. 103. 3; Heb. 8. 12; Rom. 8. 33, 34; Tit. 2. 14; Rom. 8. 9; 2 Tim. 2. 19; Psal. 66. 18; 1 Cor. 6. 11; Tit. 3. 5; Rom. 5. 1, 2, 5, 10; 8. 32; John 14. 2, 3; 17. 24; 14. 19; Col. 3. 4; 2 Thess. 1. 10; Mal. 3. 18; Matt. 13. 34; Rev. 21. 7; Matt. 25. 21; Rev. 3. 12, 21; Zeph. 3. 17; Rev. 21. 2-4, 23; 22. 3, 4; 1 Tim. 6. 15; Rom. 11. 36.

END OF VOL. I.

Made in the USA
Las Vegas, NV
30 September 2022

56239963R00197